Composing a
Life's Work

Composing a Life's Work

WRITING, CITIZENSHIP, AND YOUR OCCUPATION

DOMINIC DELLI CARPINI

York College of Pennsylvania

PEARSON
Longman

New York   San Francisco   Boston
London   Toronto   Sydney   Tokyo   Singapore   Madrid
Mexico City   Munich   Paris   Cape Town   Hong Kong   Montreal

Senior Vice President and Publisher: Joseph Opiela
Vice President and Publisher: Eben W. Ludlow
Development Manager: Janet Lanphier
Development Editor: Michael Greer
Marketing Manager: Deborah Murphy
Senior Supplements Editor: Donna Campion
Media Supplements Editor: Nancy Garcia
Production Manager: Doug Bell
Project Coordination, Text Design, and Electronic Page Makeup:
   Electronic Publishing Services Inc., NYC
Cover Design Manager/Designer: Nancy Danahy
Cover Photo: Copyright © Photographer's Choice/Getty Images, Inc.
Senior Manufacturing Buyer: Alfred C. Dorsey
Printer and Binder: Courier Corporation, Westford
Cover Printer: Coral Graphics Services, Inc.

For permission to use copyrighted material, grateful acknowledgment is made to the copyright holders on pp. 581–586, which are hereby made part of this copyright page.

Library of Congress Cataloging-in-Publication Data
Delli Carpini, Dominic.
  Composing a life's work : writing, citizenship, and your occupation / Dominic Delli Carpini.
     p. cm.
  Includes bibliographical references (p.) and index.
  ISBN 0-321-10528-1
     1. English language—Rhetoric. 2. Rhetoric—Political aspects. 3. Rhetoric—Social aspects.
  4. Vocational guidance. 5. Report writing. 6. Citizenship. I. Title.

PE1408.D438 2005
808'.042—dc22

                    2004004706

Please visit us at http://www.ablongman.com/dellicarpini

ISBN 0-321-10528-1

1 2 3 4 5 6 7 8 9 10—CRW—07 06 05 04

For Rebecca:
Without her,
perhaps a life's work;
With her,
a life.

Brief Contents

Detailed Contents

PART II   Reading and Writing in Academic and Professional Communities   185

PART IV Casebooks for Further Reading and Research 493

Readings on the World of Work: Contents by Theme

Thinking and reading about the work done by professionals in various occupations can help prepare you for the work you will do in college and beyond. It can also give you lots to write about in your present occupation as a student.

In *Composing a Life's Work*, you'll have the opportunity to examine questions like the ones below as you read works written by students, creative writers, scholars, and professionals in many fields:

Preface

What do you want to be?

This familiar question at once intrigues and plagues young people from their earliest memories through their college years. In a culture that values work as highly as ours does, it isn't difficult to see that what we "do" plays a pivotal role in what we will "be." It should come as no surprise, then, when statistics tell us that the desire for a satisfying and lucrative career is by far the primary motivating factor for attending college.

What, then, of the broader aims of a liberal arts education? Is education nothing more than training for a job?

Composing a Life's Work suggests that polemical questions like these are counterproductive, drawing us away from what might be a more productive question: What relationship might exist between the motives students bring with them to college and the wider goals of education? This text seeks to recreate and reinforce the link between the desire to find a satisfying line of work and the process of active, rhetorical inquiry that drives a liberal education.

This book also attempts to restore the natural connections between work and civic responsibilities. As streamlined educational programs promise job preparation without the fuss of general education courses, more and more students are *trained* to do a job without developing the critical and rhetorical skills to examine the implications of that work on the wider community. Yet traditional academic institutions often *seem* unresponsive to the primary goals of college students, forcing them to choose between occupational motives and the motives of a liberal education. Faced with such a choice, students have chosen work—often at the expense of the larger goals of a broad education, an education that fosters civic responsibility.

Composing a Life's Work responds to the exigencies of the current educational climate. It approaches composition as a site where the goals of a rhetorical, liberal education and the occupational motives of students can be brought together. It insists, following John Dewey, that one's occupation ought not be defined merely as one's career (in the narrow sense), but as the totality of one's work as it relates to one's community—as a "life's work."

Composing a Life's Work has two theoretical bases. Following Dewey's definition of an "occupation" as a life's work, it encourages students to use reading and writing as ways to examine their educational and career goals with a good deal of care—and always with an eye to the democratic community that houses their occupational selves. And, drawing on lessons from the rhetorical tradition, it provides a model of inquiry for investigating these goals. As such, this book provides both the occasion and the mechanisms for learning through writing, centering on three major and interrelated goals:

- It gives students a basic introduction to various processes of invention and composing suggested by the rhetorical canons;

- It provides students with guided practice in rhetorical reading and analysis; and

- It uses the composing process and rhetorical reading as tools of inquiry through which students might explore the discourses of various academic disciplines and occupational fields. These inquiries will also help students to situate themselves within the larger community.

Though many textbooks provide a "disciplinary" approach to writing, few help students to see the connections between academic disciplines and the set of motives they bring with them to class. This textbook makes that search the primary motivating force for student writing. *Composing a Life's Work* differs from composition texts in other significant ways as well:

- *It makes students' educational motives its primary focus.* In short, it speaks to students about issues that matter to them.

- *It tells stories*—stories of other students, of workers, of citizens, and of how they view the work that they do. It also invites students to construct their own stories. This initial narrative focus allows students to understand motives for writing that go beyond the purely academic.

- *It uses the logic of the composing process* to move students from occupational self-discovery to a wider inquiry into the discourse communities of various occupations and community positions.

- *It helps students to understand how rhetoric can provide a framework for inquiry*, allowing them to hone their critical thinking and analytical skills while giving them experience with the types of writing that exist within and beyond the academy. In the process, students will also learn a good deal about the field of rhetoric itself.

- *It breaches the boundaries between career motives and service to community*, instead insisting on the vital relationship that exists between the two. Rather than treating "service" as isolated acts of volunteerism, it instead helps students to see the consistent effects of their work on, and the value of their occupational skills to, the wider community.

- *It illustrates the defining nature of writing.* "Writing to learn" comes to mean a number of things: that writing is a process of discovery and synthesis through which one can construct and demonstrate disciplinary knowledge;

that writing is both self-presentation and self-construction; and that one's understanding of how writing works can also be a heuristic for knowing how various occupations work within discourse communities.

ORGANIZATION AND FEATURES

Composing a Life's Work is organized to help students to learn about academic fields and related professions through writing. The structure first encourages students to consider their own goals and talents through reflective writing, and then it asks them to use rhetorical skills as a mode of inquiry into various disciplines and occupational fields. More specifically, the text is divided into four parts: Part 1 asks students to reflect on their own occupational goals and educational experiences, challenging them to consider not only the work they hope to do but *why* they hope to do it and *what it means* to do it—both to themselves and to the wider community. It also helps them to develop the facility with language that can encourage such inventive thinking, providing them with a wide variety of writing prompts and exercises. Part 2 then extends this reflective inquiry, providing students with strategies for critical reading drawn from the rhetorical tradition. Students are asked to apply these reading techniques to writing from various academic fields and professions. This reading can enrich their understanding of both the techniques themselves and various occupational and disciplinary fields. Part 3 then provides students with the tools for active and motivated research, moving them from the early processes of defining a topic and developing search terms to the final delivery of a researched essay. Finally, Part 4 is a storehouse of readings and topics surrounding the central theme of work. This part is divided into a series of casebooks that suggest areas for further inquiry.

Throughout all of these sections, *Composing a Life's Work* stays focused on the student writer and his or her motives. This focus on student writing as a means to discover "a life's work" is kept central through several recurring features:

1. *Testimony from workers and students:* Students will read a number of stories: firsthand accounts by workers discussing their occupation and the rhetorical situations and writing processes that they face, interviews with workers about their place in a wider community, and the writings of students like themselves as they struggle to find their own niche as workers.

2. *Writing to Explore prompts:* These frequent informal writing prompts help students to learn the rhetorical principles of reading and writing through their hands-on applications.

3. *Writer's notebook/Commonplace book:* Students are asked to collect, organize, and draw on their exploratory writings through the development of a writer's notebook (in either a paper or electronic format) and to use that notebook as a record of their reading and responses to it.

4. *Reading and Writing Applications:* In the six Reading and Writing Applications sections, students are provided with readings and writing prompts that help them to put into practice the rhetorical skills that are presented in the chapters preceding them.

5. *Readings and rhetorical analyses:* Students are provided with examples of writing taken from a wide range of academic disciplines and occupational fields. They are asked to analyze the ways in which various fields and professions define themselves through the writing they do, and how these defining moments create a relationship with a wider community.

6. *Interaction with other courses:* Students are encouraged to find points of connection with other coursework they are doing. Writing prompts allow students to consider the discursive methods used in other fields of study within their curriculum.

7. *Web bibliographies:* Students are directed to profession-based websites that can help them to understand how various occupations construct their values in writing and present themselves to the public.

SUPPLEMENTS

Composing a Life's Work is supplemented with the following resources for teachers and students:

Instructor's Manual: Each of the chapters of this text, and the Reading and Writing Applications sections, includes writing prompts of varying complexity that can help students to integrate rhetorical concepts into writing practices; more detailed explications of those concepts and further ideas for writing assignments are provided in the accompanying Instructor's Manual. The Instructor's Manual also includes suggestions for several course designs that might be appropriate to the use of the textbook as well as background information on the rhetorical principles that inform the text.

Companion Website: This book's Companion Website (http://www.ablongman.com/dellicarpini) forms an integral part of the student's experience of this text, providing hyperlinks to examples of occupational and civic-based writing, with accompanying heuristic prompts. It encourages the building of a student community through interactive electronic discussions—discussions that will, it is hoped, extend to students at other institutions as well. It also encourages students to use technology to break the bounds of the classroom and interact with actual workers in various occupations and civic organizations.

ACKNOWLEDGMENTS

A number of reviewers have provided substantial commentary that has been vital to the development of this book. I'd like to thank the following for their valuable contributions: Rosa A. Eberly, Penn State University; Judith Gardner, University of Texas–San Antonio; Susanmarie Harrington, Indiana University–Purdue University, Indianapolis; Paul Heilker, Virginia Tech; Van E. Hillard, Duke University; Dennis A. Lynch, Michigan Technological University; Miles McCrimmon, J. Sargent Reynolds Community College; and Mary M. Salibrici, Hobart and William Smith Colleges. I am also deeply indebted to Eben Ludlow, who consistently encouraged me, prodded me, and challenged me to write to students in ways that matter to them. Without his faith and support for this project, it simply would not have been possible. I am also in the debt of my book team at Longman, including Doug Bell, Liliana Kim, Nancy Garcia, Stacy Dorgan, and Teresa Ward as well as Jim Hill and the team at Electronic Publishing Services.

Like any writer, I am a compilation of the many voices whose echoes I hear in every word I write—too many to acknowledge here. I hear the voices of my colleagues in the conference on College Composition and Communication (CCCC) and the Council of Writing Program Administrators (WPA), whose dedication and scholarship have educated me in the fields of rhetoric and composition. I hear the voices of my teachers and fellow graduate students at The Pennsylvania State University, especially Edward (Ted) Armstrong, Ann George, Rosa Eberly, Jeff Walker, Marie Secor, and Janet Zepernick (who I am now pleased to have as a colleague at York College). I hear the voices of the many dedicated writing teachers with whom I have worked at York College of Pennsylvania and elsewhere—Paul Puccio, Mike Zerbe, Deborah Vause, Julie Amberg, David Walters, and Owen Rogal—and the many others who have committed themselves to the rigorous work of teaching First-year writing, including our underappreciated adjunct faculty members.

Among the voices present in this text, there are those who stand out. The work of Michael Greer, who worked closely with me in the numerous revisions of this text, is everywhere present. On any given page, his words are so merged with my own that the term *collaborative writing* takes on new meaning.

Jack Selzer, my friend and mentor, deserves my special thanks. It was Jack who first showed me the joys of teaching first-year writing when I was a teaching assistant at Penn State, and it has been Jack who has helped me at every stage of my development as a teacher and as an author. Jack introduced me to the joys of writing for an audience of students and has been present at every step of this process with advice and encouragement.

I hear the voices of my students as well. Though each of my students has influenced my approach to writing pedagogy, I am especially in the debt of those whose work is included in this text: Emylee McFarland, Christina Jaffe, James Bowman, Kristin Lease, Sarah Threnhauser, Audra Shearer, Matthew V. Robinson, Jerry Hamsher, Amanda Stafford, and Stacy Crist. Their hard work as writers, represented here through their words and images, is a model for those who will use this text. I would especially like to acknowledge Tracy Hanegraaf. The many pieces of writing that she has contributed to this text have greatly enriched it—so much so that one reviewer called her the "chimerical Tracy Hanegraaf," asking whether such a student could really exist. She does, and I can happily report that she will be a teacher herself very soon. I would also like to thank my wife, Rebecca Delli Carpini, for enriching this book with her writing and artworks.

This book also features the words of workers whose dedication to their life's work and the larger community was an inspiration to me—and which I hope will be an inspiration to others. The reflections on work by Robert Colleluori, Eric Engle, Jane Whittaker, Jodi Heller, and Maureen Bradley all enrich this text and have helped me to understand the deeply satisfying nature of commitment to work as an act of civic engagement.

Finally, there are those with whom I share my life's work everyday. My brother, Michael Delli Carpini, has always been for me a model of successful scholarship, which he undertakes with a special humility and grace despite his very successful career. My parents, Domenick and Frances Delli Carpini, helped me to understand the satisfaction that comes from a job well done; as my father put it, "It doesn't matter what job you do, as long as you do it well." And there are many others whose words are always with me: our matriarch, Nannie Rose, who always reminds me that "You have to fight for another day"; Uncle Tut, who has inspired hard work in students and athletes for many, many years; and Cousin Craig, whose work is always a function of his role as a husband and father. The list could go on endlessly.

But in the end, it is my wife, Rebecca, and my children, Danielle, Derek, Ariel, and Tess, who have made for me the *life* that drive's a *life's work*. Without them, no work could satisfy. With them, all my work is important. Theirs are the voices that I hear in every word I speak or write.

Dominic Delli Carpini

Composing a
Life's Work

Introduction

ROBERT AND JEN HAVE JUST announced the birth of their new baby boy. Relatives and friends flock to their house, bearing good wishes and gifts. Grandpa brings the boy a savings bond—for his college education. Aunt Rebecca brings little Robert Louis a package of crayons (washable, of course) to set his creativity in motion. Uncle Nick brings the boy his first book—*Pat the Bunny*—so he can experience right from the start the all-important love of reading. Uncle Vic brings along some educational toys, designed to stimulate the baby's curiosity (which all good scientists need). Amidst all the love and good wishes, baby Robert's family is already imagining what the boy will become. Once he learns to talk, he will become familiar with a key question of his childhood: What do you want to be when you grow up?

It is a loving question, a question fraught with imagination and good wishes, with dreams and hopes. And for many, the path to those dreams now runs right through the college or university. It wasn't always that way, of course. If you had graduated from high school in 1900 and were going on to college, you'd have been part of only 3–4 percent of the population doing so (and if you were a woman or nonwhite, you would have been even less likely to attend college). As recently as the 1950s, only about 20 percent of high school graduates went on to college.

Now, according to a recent study at Stanford University, about 88 percent of graduating seniors go on to some form of postsecondary education, and over 70 percent go to college within two years of graduation—and more than 50 percent of college students are women. The number of nontraditional or returning adult students has grown enormously as people seek ways to learn more and to advance in their careers. So whatever your reasons for attending college, and whether college seems to you a great privilege or just what everyone does, one thing is clear: College has become closely linked to what a great many of you will be.

There's that concept again. What will you *be*? Not what you will *do*—what you will *be*. How is it that *doing* can be so closely tied to *being*? Have we as a society, perhaps, put too much emphasis on our career goals? Do we put too much

1

pressure on ourselves, focusing so much energy on the work we plan to do? Perhaps. But perhaps there are more positive ways to look at the situation as well.

If you are like most students entering college, you are in the midst of figuring out the work that seems right for you—and that's an important thing to be doing. But you have probably been told that education has other purposes as well, purposes suggesting that education is about more than simply choosing a career (as if there's anything simple about that!). Some people may have suggested to you that a college education should make you a more well-rounded person, or that it should enable you to explore a range of new ideas and perspectives. The tradition of the liberal arts, for example, asks you to value education in its own right rather than as a means to an end. Then again, the liberal arts tradition is rooted in times when college was a privilege largely afforded only to the wealthy, to future clergy members, or to men. And that's just not the way things are now—thankfully so, many people would say.

However, that doesn't mean that the ideals of a liberal arts education don't remain important; it suggests, rather, that those ideals must be adapted to the times in which we live and to the practical motives and goals of twenty-first-century students like yourselves. That's what this book is about: helping you to use reading and writing to find—or to develop—an occupation, a life's work.

But let's be clear from the start. When this book talks about occupations, it means something larger than just training yourself to be a lawyer, a doctor, an economist, or a teacher. That approach suggests that you are nothing more than a role and that your education is about nothing more than learning to do a job. And you're bigger than that. Simply choosing a field because it is hot (because it offers many openings and much room for advancement), because it pays well, or because someone has told you to do so neglects the fact that our education and our lives cannot be wholly defined by our work. Conversely, ignoring the centrality of the work we do to the lives we lead is equally shortsighted. Can we find a balance?

This book suggests that there *are* ways to develop that balance and that rhetoric (the arts of reading, writing, and speaking) can play a central role in bringing together our interests, our education, and our role within a wider community. As we urge throughout this book, an understanding of rhetoric can make you sensitive to the ways that language is used by thinkers, writers, and speakers in varied academic fields and professions. As such, a rhetorical education is a practical form of liberal education. It can help you to make the most of the learning that you do in college—since that learning is contained in language.

A rhetorical education is also a conscious education, an active education that demands that you question that which you read. It is an education that demands critical thinking as you engage with the words of others and a strong voice as you create and express ideas through words of your own. In this way, a rhetorical education can make you more active, engaged workers and citizens, helping you to occupy fully the roles you play in your professional and civic communities through a deep understanding of the way such communities communicate. (It is no accident that *communities* and *communicate* come from the same Latin root, *communis*, meaning "common." We find common ground in the use of language.)

Reading, writing, and speaking, of course, are forms of communication. But, as we'll learn in the first part of the book, they can also be valuable methods of learning about yourself. For this reason, Part 1 asks you to be reflective. You'll learn ways to use your reading and writing to discover your own interests and talents and to imagine a future within which those interests and talents can be put to good use. As such, you'll use reading and writing as ways to uncover as much as you can about your occupational interests and then to discover as much as you can about fields of work that you may be considering for your future. Thought of in this way, the search for an occupation can be approached with a hunger to learn all you can about work, how it fits your own special talents, and how it can contribute to the communities in which you live.

But let's be honest. Imagining and planning for the future is not the same as getting there. So you must be careful not to neglect the important work you are doing in the present. Though each of you has unique goals for the future, in the present you all share an occupation: You are all students. And being a student means more than learning about yourself; being a student means learning as much as you can about others.

One of the best ways to learn about the occupational lives of others—and so to find communities within which you can do your best work—is to become more active readers. Part 2 of this book helps you to begin a process that will continue throughout your college education and the life's work that it prepares you for: the process of becoming informed and literate members of a community. Those two goals—becoming informed and becoming literate—are related. To become literate—that is, able to speak and write within a particular field or community—you need to be informed. However, in order to become informed, you need to be literate—that is, able to read and write within a given field. In this part of the book, you learn strategies for doing both. We discuss methods of active and engaged reading, ways to get at the crux of an argument and better understand it. We also discuss ways to better understand how practitioners within particular academic disciplines (and related occupational fields) tend to think and reason, allowing you to become better readers of complex texts.

One of the key goals of the active reading addressed in Part 2 is to allow you to respond intelligently and thoughtfully to what you read—not just to read other people's arguments but also to construct informed, literate arguments of your own. In Part 3 of this book, we will discuss methods for using those active reading techniques to do independent research. You'll learn to ask good questions, to use research tools to investigate those questions, to reflect on and evaluate what you learn through your research, and to construct informed arguments of your own. You'll also develop techniques of revision, editing, and document design that can help you can make those arguments, both written and oral, as polished, credible, and attractive as possible.

Finally, Part 4 of the book provides resources through which you can put your reading and writing skills into practice. This research sourcebook introduces a number of current issues from the world of work, provides readings on those issues, and challenges you to develop your own informed, literate statements on the issues or on related topics. The cases included in this section give you the opportunity to engage with current research questions that face you as students, as future professionals, and as citizens.

This book challenges you to take your education seriously and treat it as the search for an occupation—for a life's work, not just a job—by learning about your own goals and interests and then learning how those interests can be applied to academic and professional work. To make the most of these challenges, you'll need to throw yourself into your education in ways that go beyond merely asking "What will I do someday?" Instead, this book asks you to consider what you might do *right now* to compose your life's work.

Writing to Inquire

PART 1 OF THIS BOOK helps you to use writing to develop your ideas. It provides you with techniques and activities that can help you to discover your own thoughts and to enrich those thoughts through writing activities. You will learn techniques for moving from reflective writing (writing you do to discover your own thoughts and reactions) to public writing (writing you do with an audience in mind).

More specifically, you'll have the opportunity to use reading and writing to inquire into—and to reflect upon—various academic and occupational fields. You'll investigate websites and print information that can help you to understand what professionals in various fields do, what they believe, what they stand for. You'll meet many writers, workers, and citizens—people who have used similar processes to find their own life's work. You'll read personal narratives of people engaged in the process of finding a life's work—work that spans many occupations. You'll hear how a Nobel Prize–winning physicist found his life's work by observing nature and how students like you found their way to fields of study that they love. Most of all, you'll learn that social workers, teachers, artists, scientists, and businesspeople share a common trait: They are all writers. And you'll learn that you are a writer as well.

You'll meet people who can teach you a great deal about the value of work. You'll be introduced to Maureen Bradley, a poet who has dedicated herself to a life of social work; you'll meet Jane Whitaker, who worked as a senior systems architect for a major financial firm and who takes great satisfaction in "working with various incompatible groups of people and getting them to work together." You'll meet Jodi Heller, a high school English teacher who takes great pleasure in the stories her students tell and in the "excitement in their eyes" when they find that learning can be a fulfilling experience. You'll hear from Eric Engle, a geologist who must balance his love for the environment with the needs of builders and developers. "The fact that I care about the existing water users and the environment motivates me," says Engle, "to go the extra mile to ensure, to the best of my ability, that the new guys will not harm the existing residents." And you'll meet Robert Colleluori, an artist, actor, entrepreneur—and the father of little Robert Louis of our opening scenario. Colleluori has used his talents and his liberal arts education to found and run a successful advertising and marketing firm. But he didn't stop there. Colleluori, like the others, has used his life's work to make his community a better place. He is on the board of directors of a small theater, he is a persistent and committed fundraiser for the fight against leukemia, and he is an active advocate for the arts in his community. "The busier I am," he quips, "the more motivated I am." And he is both.

If you approach the activities in this part of the book with energy and care, you too can begin to find what motivates you. You'll also find that exploring those motives is crucial to taking your education seriously as a pathway to a satisfying life's work.

And you'll find that writing is an important way to discover that path.

CHAPTER ONE

Discovering and Presenting Yourself in Writing

For our friends Robert and Jen, the birth of a new son brought relatives and friends bearing gifts—gifts that imagined a successful future and a variety of occupations for the baby's future. From the start, the boy was asked to consider what he would make of himself—what he would *be*. Such concerns follow us into adulthood as well. At a recent party, I met a new neighbor, and one of his first questions was "What do you do?" I could have answered, "I play golf (badly)," or "I raise my four children." Instead, I said, "I teach writing at the college." And I knew that's what his question meant, partly because I was wondering about his occupation as well. Like the familiar college question "What's your major?" the common social inquiry "What do you do?" suggests that, in our culture, the work we do helps to define who we are.

WRITING TO EXPLORE 1.1

List some people you know who are identified by the work that they do—Joan the engineer, for example, or Nick the plumber, Marvin the schoolteacher, or Tamara the actor. What expectations or impressions do their occupations create in you? Write freely, listing and describing as many examples as you can to illustrate the ways that your impressions of people are informed by their work.

ETHOS AND RHETORICAL SITUATION

The above exercise gave you the chance to consider not only the ways that our culture defines us by our jobs but also how such jobs create a particular role to be occupied by its workers. As we consider how the work we do (or are preparing to do) helps to define us, we might also pause to consider the many perspectives from which our character might be defined. Is the self you present to your teacher the same one that you present to your parents, coworkers, or friends? Is there a single, unified self that guides how we act in any situation, or is it the actions themselves that define us?

Asking questions like that, of course, is a tough business. In fact, questions of identity and personality have long been topics for consideration by philosophers and psychologists. In this book, however, we examine the question of identity from *rhetorical* and *occupational* perspectives—asking how our communication and our work helps to define us.

The field of rhetoric has a word for the concept of self or character: *ethos*. *Ethos* refers to the *character that we project to others* as we communicate. *Ethos* is largely about credibility: Is the character that we project as a writer or speaker one that our audience is likely to trust? That trust can be established in many ways—by showing our credentials, by showing we've read the work of others with credentials, by developing an open and honest relationship with our audience, by showing that we are willing to listen to contrary views, or by demonstrating our experience in a particular field. While *ethos* generally means "character," it refers more specifically to those parts of our character that we choose to project *on any given occasion* in order to establish the trust of our *audience*. That's why the concept of *ethos* is so important as we develop as writers: It reminds us that though we remain the same person, we are not always writing with the same voice and personality, from the same pool of knowledge, or to the same readers—that is, our *ethos* must be adapted to various rhetorical situations.

A *rhetorical situation* can be defined as the set of circumstances involved in a speaking or writing occasion: Who is the audience? What is the purpose? What are the surrounding circumstances? Why is the topic pressing or important at the present time? Each day we move from one rhetorical situation to another, since the circumstances we face are constantly shifting. Each situation prompts us to bring a different self into the foreground—the good student or the sympathetic listener, for example. While this might seem like we are being disingenuous, I would suggest that such shifts in the way we behave are in fact quite genuine. We become that which, in our judgment, the situation calls for. The judgments we make in each case help to define us—both in our own minds and in the minds of others. They also help us to construct writing that will be effective for that specific occasion.

As we continue to behave in certain ways, our reputation can begin to define us as well. A student who perpetually does her homework, responds well to questions, and hands in assignments on time will be seen as having a bad day if she performs poorly on a quiz. A colleague who becomes known as a good listener at work will gain the confidence of her peers and may find herself included in important conversations and projects as a result.

In the academic world, certain people become associated with what they do best. When these people speak or write, they begin from a position of established authority (or, in the negative, an authority that has already been undermined). They establish what rhetoricians such as Sharon Crowley call "situated" or "community" *ethos*.

WRITING TO EXPLORE 1.2

Think about the ways in which your own ethos is situated within a particular community. What role have you come to occupy within your family—the peacemaker, the "smart one," the athlete, the dependable son? Think about work situations: For what tasks or responsibilities did a boss come to depend on you? What jobs did you inherit by showing a special talent or willingness? Consider your role among your friends: Are you the trustworthy one, the goal-oriented student, the one to lighten up a situation? Write informally about some of the roles you have come to occupy over the past few years.

ETHOS AND COMMUNITY

Though our character or *ethos* is a fluid notion, continually redefined by the situations we encounter and to which we respond, we also tend to become specialists as we regularly take on specific roles. These roles not only help us to define ourselves but also help others to define us. This role-playing also helps to define our place in wider occupational communities. As a person becomes associated with worthwhile responses to specific types of situations, he or she takes on an expert voice. When we hear the name Carl Sagan, we think of science. Shakespeare is defined by his special skill in poetry and drama. Bill Gates has come to represent the technological revolution, while Mother Theresa of Calcutta's name has become synonymous with works of charity.

There are also people whose names have become associated with specific types of work within smaller, more specialized communities. For those interested in the environmental movement, the name Rachel Carson represents a foundational source to whom they look for wisdom on the topic. Those interested in media and politics recognize the name of Kathleen Hall Jamieson, who writes frequently on the topic and who has become an important analyst of political elections. The name of Nobel laureate Richard Feynman resonates with physicists, as does the name Jack Welch, the former CEO of General Electric, with those in business-related fields.

Once such an *ethos* is developed within a particular community, large or small, the person's voice as a speaker or writer carries with it a special authority—an authority that can carry the weight of proof based almost solely on reputation. Each time Federal Reserve chairman Alan Greenspan speaks on the state of the economy, for example, his opinions immediately reverberate throughout the U.S. business community and stock market. This effect occurs quickly—so quickly that it is surely based on his situated *ethos* rather than on careful consideration of what he says on a given occasion. People tend to simply accept his words as authoritative due to his prior reputation. Here's another example—this one from the world of science:

> The idea that humans might someday be cloned—created from a single somatic cell without sexual reproduction—moved further away from science fiction and closer to a genuine scientific possibility on February 23, 1997. On that date, *The Observer* broke the news that Ian Wilmut, a Scottish scientist, and his colleagues at the Roslin Institute were about to announce the successful cloning of a sheep by a new technique which had never before been fully successful in mammals. The technique involved transplanting the genetic material of an adult sheep, apparently obtained from a differentiated somatic cell, into an egg from which the nucleus had been removed. The resulting birth of the sheep, named Dolly, on July 5, 1996, was different from prior attempts to create identical offspring since Dolly contained the genetic material of only one parent, and was, therefore, a "delayed" genetic twin of a single adult sheep. (National Bioethics Advisory Commission 217)

In this passage, the mention of the name Ian Wilmut provides a certain authority for the writer's point, based not only in the words of the expert voice but also in Wilmut's previous reputation as a credible, reliable person on this topic. (The name of Dolly the sheep has taken on a certain celebrity status as well.) Since this piece was not written for other biologists, however, the name is first accompanied by the phrase "a Scottish scientist, and his colleagues at the Roslin Institute." Had this been written for an expert audience, this description of Wilmut and his previous work would have been unnecessary—the name itself would have resonated with that audience due to its situated *ethos*. But even here, once that description is provided, the article can rely upon this expert voice. The authors note that "in this report we refer to the technique, first described by

Wilmut, of nuclear transplantation using nuclei derived from somatic cells other than those of an embryo or fetus as 'somatic cell nuclear transfer'"—and so use the authority of Wilmut's scientific breakthrough to increase the credibility of their own writing. Developing such a position within a community, of course, is a process that can span a good deal of one's career, though it sometimes also appears as a sudden leap into that community's public eye (as was the case with Ian Wilmut's cloning of Dolly). In either case, the name of the speaker comes to carry with it a good deal of credibility.

As a student writer, of course, creating *ethos* can be more difficult. Consider the academic situations in which you've been asked to write over your years in school. A ninth-grader is asked to deliver an essay on the following topic:

> *Write a report on the ways in which Abraham Lincoln tried to reunify the country after the Civil War.*

This student is faced with a difficult challenge, but one that is probably quite familiar. She must provide information to a teacher who she knows is *already an expert* on the topic. She is in no position to question "facts" that are in the encyclopedia or textbooks that she uses as her sources; the writing situation, instead, becomes an attempt to prove that she knows things that her audience (her teacher) already accepts as true. In this case, the writer is attempting to establish the *ethos* of the "good student"—one who can read, digest, and structure received information in acceptable academic style.

For students, then, establishing *ethos* is often accomplished by inventing a speaking or writing voice that *participates in the knowledge* of a certain community—a voice that (1) speaks the language of that academic community, and (2) draws on the base of evidence that the audience will find reliable.

ESTABLISHING *ETHOS* AND AUTHORITY

The above example of the ninth-grader writing on Lincoln to a teacher who is a history expert might suggest that such exercises are worthless, at least insofar as they allow writers to develop their own *ethos*. However, we might look at the situation in another way. What can the act of writing about Abraham Lincoln's actions to reconstruct the country do for a student learning about history as a discipline? Let's say that the writer creates an essay that starts like this:

Well, I think that Abraham Lincoln's role was important. He was important because he tried to make things better. He tried to fix the country by helping the South back onto its feet and by deciding not to punish the South for quitting the country. I think that this was pretty smart. Because if he had punished the South, then I think they might have held a grudge and just got madder and madder until they decided to quit again. Look at Germany. The Germans were punished too strongly for their role in World War I, and then they decided to start World War II because they were so poor that they had nothing to lose. So the same thing would have happened if Lincoln had not let the South get back on its feet.

We might say many things about this opening to the essay. First, we might note the informality of the piece. The writer begins by saying "Well, I think," much like an oral answer to a question discussed among friends. He uses words like "grudge" and "madder" and "quit" to describe the potential actions of the South (and by association, the actions of the German nation). He also claims at the end of the paragraph that "the same thing would have happened" to the United States as to post–World War I Europe had Lincoln not allowed for reconstruction. So, is the writer thinking like a historian?

Tough question. Though on the surface the speculations sound highly informal and so not very "academic," the underlying argument reveals a good deal of historical thinking. The writer uses (or "occupies") some of the methods of historical thought by considering the implications of political decisions, by creating analogies with other historical moments, and by interpreting history through its differing consequences. But the *ethos* established is so offhand, and in some cases so generalized, that it lacks the credible tone expected of an historian. Compare the previous passage to the one below:

In the aftermath of the Civil War, Abraham Lincoln mandated a series of efforts at Reconstruction that were carried out in the period 1865–1877. The main problem that Lincoln faced was Constitutional, since the existing Constitution made no provision for this situation. Further, Lincoln was faced with a series of other issues, such as the readmission of the Southern States to the United States, how to reprimand those soldiers who had attacked the United States, the integration of freed slaves into our country, and the relationship between the federal and state governments. The reconstruction of the South was essential to assure that the freed slaves would have a place, and so that the country as a whole would not be dragged down economically.

Clearly, the second passage has the tone of a more conventional piece of historical writing. It uses terminology that is readily recognizable to historians and cites dates, key historical and political issues, and generally accepted information about the Reconstruction period of history. These are all good ways to establish the *ethos* of the writer within that particular rhetorical situation—by "speaking the language" of historians. But unlike the first passage, this one merely reports information that is common knowledge among historians and that can be found in most encyclopedias and textbooks. Which passage, then, establishes the *ethos* of its writer more effectively?

There is no easy way to answer that question. The informal, breezy tone of the first passage undermines the credibility of its author, yet the content certainly represents some intriguing thinking. The second passage has the tone expected of credible historians, but it lacks any real contribution to the ongoing discussion of the Reconstruction period. Each of these passages, however, illustrates something about *ethos*.

Establishing or "inventing" *ethos* involves both one's unique ideas and thought processes and one's willingness to use the established practices and writing styles of that field. As you work your way through college, one of your goals as a student and a future professional in some field should be to learn the way people in various fields communicate with one another. Doing so requires you to consider another aspect of *ethos*, and the one that forms the basis of this book's explorations of the writing processes: occupational *ethos*.

WRITING TO EXPLORE 1.3

One of the most difficult things to learn about writing is that the definition of "good writing" changes from one situation to another. Writing well in science might be very different from writing well in an English class. From your experience, what aspects or features of your writing are most valued by teachers? Do those expectations change depending on the course or subject area? Do you write the same way for an English class as for a history or a science class? Are there any features of your academic writing that seem to be valued in all the subject areas (or disciplines)?

Make a list of ten features of successful academic writing that are true of all fields. Then make a list of features of successful writing as they apply to specific subject areas: marketing, engineering, or literary studies, for example.

Keep these lists for your writer's notebook (discussed in Chapter 2), adding to them as you discover throughout this course new things about communication in various fields or disciplines. We return to this key question frequently, since becoming an effective college writer (and, more generally, a successful college student) requires that we understand how "good writing" is defined differently in different fields and situations.

OCCUPATIONAL *ETHOS*

Now that we've established some fundamental ideas associated with *ethos*, let's return one last time to the opening scenario. Recall that Robert and Jen's baby boy has been inundated with gifts that represent the hopes of family and friends for the child's "successful" future. Each gift suggests aspects of character or *ethos* that are valued by those friends and family—education, curiosity, creativity, love of reading, among others. As little Robert Louis grows, he will face difficult decisions about his future—decisions that will suddenly become quite pressing as he graduates from high school and goes on to college. What will he study? What will he become?

If he is like most incoming college students, his choice of a major will represent his hopes for a future career, but it will change several times as he continues his studies (as well as during the first years of his entry into the workforce). And though part of him will always be determined by factors unassociated by the work he chooses to do, we cannot underestimate the ways in which he will be defined by his occupational choices—not only by his work itself but also by the place in society that that work creates for him.

One useful way to explore occupations is to see how different careers and organizations present themselves and to consider how their vision of a successful person in a particular career might fit your own goals and personality. CE Technologies offers, via a website, a software program for helping people find suitable fields of work:

> Our MatchMe technology allows visitors to quickly and easily chart a successful, complete, and comprehensive personal attribute profile based on their own education, skills, passions, values, and other personal qualities.

Whether such technologies work or not, we can certainly acknowledge that analyzing one's skills and passions seems like a reasonable way to begin an investigation of the types of work that might be of interest. While we may begin by considering who we are now, we generally then move on to the things we must be able to do—and want to do—within a particular career field.

Consider the way another website, *insurance.ce.com,* presents itself.

> *Insurance.ce.com* recommends the following courses and conferences for individuals who are seeking success in the Customer Service & Support sector.

Course Outline:
This course will cover the following topics:

- Developing a Managerial Attitude
- Weaving Four Irreplaceable Fundamentals into Your Style
- Dealing with Special Problems

Upon completion of this course the student will be able to:

- Remain positive under stress
- Take time to teach employees what they know
- Build and maintain mutually rewarding relationships with their employees
- Set reasonable and consistent authority lines
- Delegate for results

- Establish standards of high quality and set good examples
- Counsel and coach employees effectively
- Build team effort to achieve high productivity
- Overcome obstacles and problems related with new supervision

If we read carefully, the list suggests a specific *ethos* associated with this particular career field—the positions one will be able to better occupy after successful completion of the course. It imagines that a successful worker in this field will need skills like "delegating for results" or "developing a managerial attitude." In a sense, this course of studies envisions a successful insurance executive.

Likewise, an employer-specific site, that of The Hartford, provides intriguing descriptions of a career model:

> Career Development: Growth at The Hartford is a two way street. As the company grows and meets new business challenges, so too can your career. In order for us to meet our ever-changing business challenges, it is very important to our success that you continue to build your skills, knowledge and abilities.
>
> The Hartford is committed to career development and continuous learning in order to help our employees grow both professionally and personally. Our career development program allows employees to develop, maintain and enhance skills and competencies, in alignment with strategic business plans, in order to provide for both the individual's and the company's success.

This description envisions a career and specifies the types of skills and continuing education that might be attractive to potential employees. At the same time, it considers how the professional *ethos* of its employees might be enhanced. By featuring courses in "communication skills" and "leadership" as well as by offering tuition reimbursement and information on colleges and universities, it suggests that its ideal employee is a continuous learner.

That's the corporate perspective. As an individual with many occupational options, it's your job to relate the information provided by such employers or placement firms to your own search for an occupation. Doing so need not be in conflict with the strictly professional *ethos* portrayed by potential employers—in fact, quite the contrary. Since a good part of your life will be spent in the work you do, it makes sense to imagine your life's work as involving (though not being dominated by) career choices.

However, accepting this key challenge of college—finding a future life's work—should not cause you to look past your current activities as a student. Through that present occupation—college student—you can find connections among your talents, your aspirations, and the education that your college has planned for you through its carefully planned curriculum. If you think of your education and your occupation in wider terms—not merely as a career, but as a life's work—you might question whether there is more to an education than a streamlined training for a specific job. In fact, considering how frequently people change careers (seven to ten times), what employers look for in employees, and the personal satisfaction people take in their work, constructing your education toward a fulfilling life's work can be complex. Employers often acknowledge a commitment to "career development and continuous learning" and offer tuition reimbursement for college coursework for a good reason: because lifelong learners are generally the happiest and most productive employees as well.

As you claim an education, the energy you bring to learning activities can influence the inventiveness you bring to your later occupations as well. If you think of yourself as more than a passive recipient of information, your program of studies can gain a stronger coherence. Rather than think "What knowledge does this course or this teacher need me to know?" you might think "What can *I* take from a course like this?" If you start to seek the connections among the various things you are learning, you might find more coherence than you expect. This book is largely about that type of pragmatic education and how to achieve it through the mechanisms of reading, writing, and rhetorical studies.

WRITING TO EXPLORE 1.4

List the classes you are currently taking and try to find points of connection among them as well as to the major that you have chosen (or are considering). How can each class contribute to your overall educational goals? To what occupational goals can each contribute, directly or indirectly? Try to be positive, looking at the potential usefulness of each course rather than those features that don't seem to fit directly into your career plans, narrowly defined. In order to do this in an informed way, you might examine your syllabi, course descriptions in your college catalog, or the table of contents of your textbooks. Then look back to your earlier freewriting to see how what you are learning may connect with your own talents, plans, or interests.

WRITING TO EXPLORE 1.5

Construct a list of the personal attributes, skills, and abilities that seem to inform a profession you are considering. Then, visit your college catalog or website, noting the course requirements for the major field of study that you have declared or one that you are considering. Read over the course descriptions for each course in the major and the suggested sequence of courses. Try to imagine the ways in which that course of studies can prepare you for the work of that profession. Write a clear description of potential relationships among the courses.

The two exercises above ask you to widen your focus a bit and to consider how the various parts of your curriculum fit together. Though your work is instrumental in forming who you are, you need not let that process happen *to you*—instead, you can guide the course of your life and work in a way that doesn't segment one from the other. As you go through this process of learning, it is important for you to continually question, inquire into, and test the ideas that you encounter. One of the best ways to do so is to write frequently in response to the reading you do, the ideas you discover, and the people with whom you work in this academic environment. Using writing in this way can help you to approach your college education inventively.

A RHETORICAL APPROACH TO WRITING

Rhetoric is more than "the art of persuasion"—the most common definition of the term. In this book, you are asked to use language not only to *express* ideas but also to *generate* them. The complementary acts of reading and writing can help to make you conscious of those things you believe but haven't fully expressed. And sometimes they can help you to realize that there's more to investigate before you can reach even a *working* conclusion.

A rhetorical approach to education begins with a simple yet important idea: The first person who must be convinced by your ideas on a topic is *you*! Writing should not be perceived narrowly, as a way of convincing others of what you already think (or think you know). Nor is writing a process of simply assembling and accepting what others have written or said about a topic. Instead, reading and writing rhetorically means delving deeply into a topic in order to develop your own insights and to consider those of others. Through this mental scrutiny, you can discover new ideas about a topic. In this way, rhetoric is as much about writing to learn as it is about learning to write.

To enrich your approach to the writing process, you can benefit from the advice of the rhetorical tradition. Much as understanding the concept of *ethos* allows you to think about the self or character you project as a rhetorical act— as a way of developing your own credible voice—so too can other concepts from classical rhetoric help you to better understand the full benefits of treating writing as a dynamic process of discovery. Classical rhetoric identifies five *canons*, or rhetorical activities involved with composing:

- invention (gathering and assessing ideas and information, both from your own mind and from other sources)
- arrangement (organizing and finding connections among those ideas)
- style (finding appropriate modes of language to contain and express those ideas)
- memory (techniques and methods for retaining and synthesizing those ideas for later use)
- delivery (techniques and methods for expressing your ideas to a specific audience)

Though these canons can be treated as a sequence, proceeding from invention (getting ideas) to delivery (expressing those ideas), that's not the only way to look at them. Educating yourself on any topic is too complex to be reduced to a linear sequence with a successful piece of writing or speaking as its goal; in the rhetorical approach to education, the canons share a single purpose: they are *heuristics*.

A heuristic is a tool for discovery, for generating new knowledge. It's easy to see, as we discuss in the next chapter, how the first of the canons, invention, is heuristically based. After all, invention is about gathering and evaluating ideas and information. However, if you continue to treat writing as an opportunity for learning, you will find that the other canons have similar heuristic capabilities.

The second canon, arrangement, involves the ordering and structuring of the various things you have to say on a given topic. But it's more than outlining. Arrangement involves many thought processes and heuristic questions: How can I order my argument in a way suitable for the topic, the audience, and the surrounding circumstances? Which information should I lead with? At what point should I present my most impressive evidence or striking observations? Arrangement questions like these necessarily ask you also to consider the nature of the topic. Arranging ideas requires a deeper understanding of a topic; it asks you to consider not only what you know but also how to best articulate what you know within a specific rhetorical situation.

Likewise, the third canon, style, is more than just learning to dress up ideas in words. That would suggest that words and ideas are wholly separate—that words express ideas. It's not quite that simple. Words do contain ideas; but it is also true that ideas are contained and defined by the words that you choose. Developing your style is a process of inventing and reinventing ideas in language—of learning what you know and what you believe by putting it into words. Many of the stylistic techniques we discuss, then, are as much about learning about a topic and discovering its intricacies as about expressing those ideas. Style, too, is heuristic.

Memory, the fourth canon, is perhaps the most complex of all for writers today. Originally, memory was considered one of the canons because of the necessity of speakers to not only remember ideas but also to remember specific words and phrases within which those ideas are contained—and to have those key words and phrases available for use on any given speaking occasion. In an age of technology (including the first of those technologies, writing and print), memory may seem to have lost its importance. But I suggest that memory has, rather, been transformed to encompass those technologies. As we discuss later, computer-based information systems have become storehouses of public memory. The process of searching for, and working with, the glut of information has changed the role of memory significantly. However, the human mind is still the most effective synthesizing mechanism for complex thoughts. Despite the great amount of available information, the individual memory is still the place where that information can be boiled down to new discoveries and perspectives. Memory, then, is another heuristic.

Finally, the act of delivery—of expressing your thought-laden words to an audience—brings together the processes leading up to this moment. Though the canons are not wholly linear, delivery is clearly the endgame (or at least *an* endgame), since it represents a moment of going public with what you've learned and what you think. But we still ought not view writing and speaking as monologic, as a one-way form of communication. Rather, finding what Aristotle called the "available means of persuasion" for a specific rhetorical situation requires you to continue your process of invention and discovery even as you deliver your speech or present your writing.

So why, then, does considering your present and future occupations make a sensible paradigm for your writing activities? Because if you consider your occupations in the widest sense, as a way of composing a life's work, the education you are pursuing can be given a context and a new value. You can use your writing to help make sense of not only the future you are planning but also of your present occupation as a student. Those are the processes that this book encourages you to use as you pursue your education, and through that education, your life's work.

CHAPTER TWO

Strategies for Discovering and Developing Your Ideas

Like the process of finding a life's work, writing is a creative act, an exercise in imagination. Imagination and creative thinking are valued in college and in the workplace as well, because they can breed ideas that are truly new—ideas that, until an individual thought them, had yet to be considered. College writing is designed to provide you with opportunities for that type of innovative thinking—the type of thinking that involves you in your studies in active, rather than passive, ways.

Rhetoric—which we defined in the previous chapter as the arts devoted to writing and speaking well—has a word for the generation of new ideas and new approaches: *invention*. In everyday usage, *inventing* something means developing an idea or product that solves a theoretical or practical problem. A new product might be touted as providing cleaner windows, brighter teeth, or longer life. A newly invented scientific theory may provide a more satisfactory explication of a natural phenomenon or ecological problem. Invention is an essential element of writing as well, a process that allows you to discover new ideas through your writing.

In order to take full advantage of writing as a process of discovery, you need to write regularly, not just when you have a formal assignment or when you plan to make that writing public. Writing informally, as a way of working out ideas or figuring out how to respond to the ideas of others, is an indispensable step in becoming a better student and a better writer. One good way to develop the habits of constant inquiry and frequent writing is to have a place where you can write inventively—without restrictions and in ways that will help you to work out ideas. One such place will be your writer's notebook.

DEVELOPING A WRITER'S NOTEBOOK

We must therefore write as much as possible and with utmost care. For as deep ploughing makes the soil more fertile for production and support of crops, so, if we improve our minds by something more than superficial study, we shall produce a richer growth of knowledge and shall retain it with greater accuracy.
— *Quintilian*, The Institutes of Oratory

As Roman rhetorician Quintilian suggests, regular writing creates a fertile environment for the growth of new ideas. Effective writers use their private writings to try out ideas by putting them in words. Considering your own thoughts and words in light of those you hear, read, or remember can be a powerful way to spur invention. This process of recording your thoughts and the thoughts of others occurs over time, and the writing you do in a writer's notebook does not need to be polished—just thoughtful and inventive and as voluminous as possible. It is this need to develop habits of regular and inventive writing that makes the writer's notebook a useful tool.

A writer's notebook, as we use the term here, is a specific type of journal. It is *not* a private diary (though keeping a diary can also be a wonderful use of writing). It is a record of your learning, a place where you can collect ideas you find elsewhere, a verbal attic where you store those things that you're sure you'll need some day or that at least give you some pleasure to have now. But unlike an attic, where you might just leave things for decades, a writer's notebook should be active and recursive—a place to return to frequently to add new items and to rethink what's already there.

You will be asked to use your writer's notebook in a number of ways—as a place to work out ideas, as a site to record the ideas and words of others, and as a laboratory to develop stylistic techniques. You have already begun this process if you've been working with the Writing to Explore exercises. Below, we discuss ways to organize those pieces of informal writing, and ones that you will invent throughout the course, into a writer's notebook.

SETTING UP A WRITER'S NOTEBOOK

A successful writer's notebook is balanced between being a place of freedom, where there are few restrictions (an inventive place) and an *accessible* storehouse of information (an organized place). I'll make suggestions that I think can help you to find that balance. These suggestions can help you to learn a little bit about organizing ideas and can provide a physical space for them. Let's first think about the purpose and process of a writer's notebook. What are its key characteristics?

- It should be a place where you can go whenever you have a brainstorm or run across an idea worth saving.

- It should be easy to use, since you want to be able to get that idea that came to you into writing quickly, not spend time following procedures.

- It should be with you all the time, since you never know when you'll come across a great idea, read something that captures your fancy, or hear something that makes you angry—all things that you might wish to record or respond to.

- It should allow you to access those ideas with less difficulty than finding an old baseball mitt in the attic.

FIGURE 2.1 The use of a three-ring binder or similar system allows you to create a writer's notebook that is flexible, that can be continuously reorganized, and which allows you to add new pieces of writing or other artifacts that you find. It is an important way for you to collect inventive thoughts—both your own and others'—to which you might respond more formally in later writings.

How can you do all that? Though you obviously can't create a perfect tool for the job, there are models for creating a writer's notebook that fulfills many of these needs. First, it is especially difficult to create a truly useful tool from a notebook whose pages are fixed or bound. With that type of notebook, the organization can only be chronological (in the order in which you wrote them) or in fixed categories— and you're probably not sure what categories you'll need right from the start. In short, this type of tool fails because it places too many restrictions on your processes.

If you use something like a three-ring binder, you have a much more versatile tool. You can add to it, rearrange pages, even change the method of organization in response to your changing thoughts and goals. You also can add pocket folders if you decide to include "artifacts"—bumper stickers or advertisements that capture an idea in a particularly interesting way, clippings from newspapers or magazines, scraps of ideas you've jotted down and will transcribe and organize later, images that capture an idea visually. When you add the newly captured pieces to the old, the whole dynamic of the book can change.

You might also create an electronic binder. I can imagine, for example, creating disk files that can be organized, reorganized, copied, and cross-referenced to create conversations among the ideas. You could download or scan images that you find, add links to Web resources and react to them, or share parts of the

FIGURE 2.2 An electronic writer's notebook allows you to draw upon various webs of information—the World Wide Web as well as your own thoughts and writing. The bits and pieces of inventional thought can be then be organized into files and folders through word-processing programs. Creating an e-notebook allows you to later import the words and images you've collected into more polished writings, and to continuously build upon and reorganize what you collect there.

notebook via e-mail or a website. Such an electronic notebook might require more maintenance and would necessitate your keying in any ideas you had while you didn't have access to a computer. However, once created, it would be a powerful tool for your writing. You could easily import some of the materials you generate there into formal papers, should you later choose to do so.

WRITING TO EXPLORE 2.1

I've offered some ideas for what would make for a successful organization of a writer's notebook; now it's your turn to do some inventing. What are some ways that you think you could create a successful writer's notebook? What categories might you begin with? After you've brainstormed some successful models, share your ideas with others in your class (via e-mail or class discussion) to see if you can create an initial model that works. Be sure to remain flexible; the organization might change many times as you keep adding new writing and notes.

GETTING STARTED ON YOUR WRITER'S NOTEBOOK

One of the major goals of your writer's notebook is to identify areas for further investigation and more formal writing—to discover the topics that most interest you as you continue to learn through your present occupation as a student. You can use the writer's notebook as a place where some of your rough ideas or offhand thoughts gestate into something more—lines of thought for further inquiry.

FIGURE 2.3 As time goes on, your notebook—paper or electronic—can be enriched with various inventional writing and other artifacts. It becomes a storehouse of ideas for future writing as well as a place to work out your ideas.

CULTIVATING INVENTIVE THINKING

Making ideas come to you when you need them is never an easy affair—they seem to have a life (and a schedule) of their own. But there *are* ways to induce the mind toward productive thought. One such way is known as *brainstorming*. As indicated by its somewhat violent name, brainstorming suggests that you can experience an uncontrollable rush of ideas. People experience brainstorms all the time, usually when they least expect them. Like dreams, brainstorms often lack coherent or logical form, and they throw aside (at least for the moment) the restraints of practicality in favor of something hopeful and visionary.

One of the brainstorms most people experience involves their future. You may see yourself within a world that doesn't yet exist. You may imagine a fulfilled dream, a completed journey, an achieved success. Sometimes those visions involve financial success; sometimes they involve some great humanitarian action; sometimes they cause you to picture yourself dressed in the traditional trappings of a career field (a doctor's scrubs, a lawyer's suit, a field researcher's khakis). And sometimes they place you within a moment of great honor—winning a key ball-game, solving an important scientific problem, writing an Academy Award–caliber screenplay. Though you might shrug off these experiences as daydreams or childish hopes, there may be more in them than you think. In fact, brainstorms can grab hold of you with such force that it's hard to deny their effect.

WRITING TO EXPLORE 2.2

Take a moment to recall moments in which you imagined your future. Using brainstorming, list and describe some of the occupations you envisioned for yourself over the years. Be as descriptive as you can in remembering those moments, trying to recall not only the dream itself but also the details—what about that future especially drew you in, and how it felt to be in that imagined position. You might, if you'd like, share some of those memories with others.

So what do these whimsical moments have to do with cultivating good writing habits? Certainly, you can't count on visionary ideas every time you're asked to write something—people who wait for moments of inspiration usually get very little done. Still, you can train your mind to be receptive to the many ideas that you have at any given moment, can stimulate the growth of those ideas, and can give credence to what at the time might seem like fancy. Writing them down and seeing where they lead can be a good start.

The arts of rhetoric provide many strategies for such mental gymnastics. By acknowledging the potential value of your brainstorms, you can create the habits of mind that encourage rather than resist invention. You can also establish habits of thinking and writing that can be applied to the academic tasks you face. In order to nurture the mental processes through which you can encourage brain-storms, you might start with three key concepts:

1. Ideas develop over time and so cannot be forced into coherence immediately.

2. Thoughts rarely occur in a vacuum but instead generally appear in response to some lived or mental stimulus—usually one that comes to you in the form of a challenge or a problem that is important to you and that you discover through reading, listening, or considering the activities of daily life.

3. Writing is a powerful way of developing these ideas in inventive ways.

If you acknowledge these three basic concepts, you might also see that com-posing involves a series of processes that alternate between the world outside (lived experience as well as reading) and your own thoughtful reactions to those stimuli—reactions that can be teased out by inventional writing.

To examine some of the ways that invention works, I'd like you to imagine something that you might not normally think much about as you read a text-book—that someone needed to conceive of its ideas, develop those ideas into a coherent sequence, and write and revise those thoughts in the most accessible and useful ways possible. Not only that, the author had to consider ways to per-suade you, a student of writing, that what he has to say has enough value to war-rant your attention.

The author, a teacher of writing, is sitting on a porch on an early spring day. He is wondering what he might say to students that can help them through the difficult processes of writing. He is also considering how to interest that audi-ence. He is searching for ideas.

As I sat on that porch, considering what would make for a sensible program of studies for student writers, several ideas occurred to me. I first wondered why it was that such a natural process—the process of developing and communicating ideas—becomes so difficult when people are asked to write essays and papers in an academic environment. Why do so many students struggle to generate ideas and to create a logical, coherent organization for those ideas? How can I, as a teacher, help students to better understand those processes? Notice that I began with a set of questions and challenges directly related to the work I do.

As I considered these questions, the comments of my students started com-ing to me—like a brainstorm. Comments over the years consistently praised assignments that gave students freedom to write about issues that truly mattered to them; conversely, I recalled, students expressed dissatisfaction with those assignments that seemed to lack any real relevance to their own lives and goals. Those thoughts, in turn, made me think about my contact with younger chil-dren, including my own.

The worst indictment of an activity that a child can think of is "It's boring." Boredom is the emotion that young children most avoid (that's why a bored child is usually a mischievous one). But even as children grow older, I remem-bered, boredom can be an awful feeling—and certainly not one that is likely to inspire inventive thinking. So what was it that students care about that can also be the impetus to a solid education?

That question took me back into the many years that I had spent teaching in high schools. There, I recalled, the most pressing question was "When will I ever use this information that you are giving me?" Though direct applicability to life isn't the whole point of education, the question always struck me as having a certain wisdom. People do learn better when they can see a point to their education, when they have a place to put those things they are learning—a context for it all. Yes, I remembered, that question was a good one. So what could that tell me about this book I am writing?

That, in turn, reminded me of the works of John Dewey that I had been reading. I recalled one statement that he had made that seemed to apply to my own task:

> From the standpoint of a child, the great waste in school comes from his inability to utilize the experiences he gets outside school in any complete and free way within the school itself; while on the other hand, he is unable to apply in daily life what he is learning at school. That is the isolation of the school—its isolation from life.

Dewey, who had spent lots of time visiting high schools, saw just the same problem that I recalled from my experience. His solution was to argue for a set of educational experiences that worked from the "genuine motives" of students. That might help me, I thought, to conceive a writing curriculum that engaged students in writing that they truly care about.

My brainstorming, my original thoughts and questions, led me to lots of other thoughts: back into lived experience, into reading I had been doing, into the words of my past students. Even my decision to read John Dewey's works, which had come quite a while before my decision to write a textbook, came from lived experience. After hearing several references to Dewey's ideas from friends and colleagues, I decided to check out his work myself. As we discuss later, this habit of following up on ideas and finding out more about them is crucial, since a good writer needs to become informed on an array of ideas that exist around her—by listening well and by reading whatever she can get her hands on.

Being receptive to ideas being discussed around me helped me to bring my own ideas together. What truly helped the ideas for this book click in my mind was a demographic report that I stumbled across. This report stated that the percentage of students who said that they were attending college in order to improve their chances for a lucrative and satisfying career had skyrocketed since the 1960s, just as colleges opened their doors to a wider range of students—a wider range economically, racially, in terms of gender, and in academic preparation. This report confirmed to me what I could see through my experience as a teacher—the purposes for attending college had changed significantly over the past four decades. Had teaching methods changed to accommodate this new mission? When I allowed myself to conjecture (or imagine) that they had *not* changed—at least not *enough*—suddenly, things started to come into focus for my project.

This example is not unlike what *any* writing task asks of you. Brainstorming is really a process through which you can make incremental moves toward a clearer vision of that task. Of course, you don't always have much time to think through and produce a document. But even when you don't, there is *always* time to ask good questions, examine what you already know—and to acknowledge that which you don't know but might need to. Taking the time to ask questions early in your writing processes not only increases the likelihood of a brainstorm hitting you; it can also can help you to make productive use of those brainstorms.

The process of collecting and judging the value of ideas—your own and others'—is a key facet of what learning in college is about. In college, you are bombarded with ideas from many fields of study, ideas that can be timber for your own inventive thoughts. Writing down those ideas can help you to see how they fit together and to develop them into a more cohesive knowledge set; this informal writing can help you to find new ideas that contribute to the conversation on many topics. And being involved in such conversations can help you to find your own life's work, just as the questions and challenges that led to the idea of this textbook came from the work I had been doing for many years, my role as a parent, my reading of materials related to these topics, and my own occupational goals as a teacher.

Though you may or may not have years of work behind you yet, you do have many areas of interest and many potential occupational goals. And you no doubt can envision a future—though that future might sometimes seem quite distant, quite changeable, and rather unclear. Just the act of seeking an education suggests that you are envisioning a richer life for yourself—however you define *rich*. What follows are more specific suggestions for how you might approach the processes of invention as a way to investigate topics and ideas that truly interest you and that can have an impact on your future course.

WRITING TO EXPLORE 2.3

Some of the processes that led to the writing of this textbook are detailed above. Take a minute to write a profile about yourself as a writer. What kind of writing comes most easily to you? What is most difficult? What are some of the things that you do, or places that you go, to get ideas? What seems to stand in the way of having brainstorms? Thinking about these things might help you to develop a disciplined attitude toward your writing that is also sensitive to your own unique needs and strengths.

FREEWRITING

The act of writing itself can help you to see new ideas and to develop those ideas through inventive language. Even if you're not sure what you want to express, how you feel, or what you know about a particular topic, the act of writing about it can help you to discover just those things. Spilling your thoughts onto paper (or a computer screen) can help you to generate one of those brainstorms we've been discussing.

Freewriting, a concept popularized by writing expert Peter Elbow, is one type of writing to learn. It's really very simple (though it gives rise to some pretty complicated mental processes). You write nonstop on a topic for a fixed period, perhaps fifteen or twenty minutes, seeing where the words lead you. That might not sound like a very long time, but if you really write nonstop, it can be a productive (and tiring) experience. The writing that you completed in the Writing to Explore exercise above was really a version of freewriting—writing designed to get your thoughts (and words) flowing.

That's the basic idea. But think about all there is to overcome to make this freewriting experience as productive as possible. First, you need to free yourself of obstacles that can get in the way of your brainstorm. As you follow a particularly convoluted thought, you might hear your seventh-grade teacher in the back of your head labeling that thought a run-on sentence or asking you to produce a thesis. You might wonder where the comma goes or whether you are switching tenses. And how do you spell committ, comit, commit . . . ? Such thoughts interrupt the flow of your ideas and keep you from reaching your most innovative thoughts.

At the heart of these obstacles is the fact that writing has many purposes. In some situations you are trying to communicate ideas, and to do so in a particularly structured way. In that case, run-on sentences and misspellings can really be a problem, since they interfere with smooth communication and can undermine your credibility as a writer. But when you are freewriting, communicating with others isn't really the point. If you treat freewriting as even a *rough* draft of an essay, you may already put too many restrictions on the thought processes that it is meant to activate. You might do better to call it a "zero draft" or "throwaway draft"—the stuff of a writer's notebook.

To succeed in your freewriting, it is important that you find a place to work with as few interruptions as possible, since good ideas tend to flee when you need to stop in the middle of a thought. It may take some time—even a few sessions—before something of value starts to show itself. There are many ways to get started:

- Write questions about your topic.
- List all the things you know about a topic—or the things you don't know.
- Recall a story that seems to apply, retell it, and then apply it to your topic.
- Explore your reasons for wanting to know more about this topic.

Let's say that your teacher has asked you to write about a past educational experience and how it benefited you—or failed to benefit you. Rather than try to figure the whole thing out from the start, just start putting words down on the page, even if it's just nonsense or repetitions:

O.K., I'm supposed to write something about my educational experiences. But that's the last thing I want to write about because I'm right in the middle of a very long and difficult academic career and for goodness sake, I'm not all that thrilled by education right now. I really hate this topic. I hate this topic. This topic I hate. Education Education Education. We don't need no education, we don't need no thought control. what's the deal with education and why do educators always want to talk about education??? (although I guess guitarists always want to talk about guitars too and I like talking about tennis because I'm A WHOLE LOT BETTER AT TENNIS THAN I AM AT WRITING!!) Maybe I should write about tennis. This topic is typical though, typical of what teachers ask us to do, asking us to write about topics that matter to them all the time—like education. Well of course education is a topic they're interested in since that's their job and do they ever stop to think that maybe the reason students get sick of school is because they don't get to talk about things that really matter to them all that much. Hey, maybe there's something to that. Maybe I might write about how writing assignments or education generally doesn't have enough connection to the things that matter to us. Maybe I can. . . . "

As you can see from this example, part of the point is to have fun, and by having fun, to see what new ideas you can generate. It's coloring outside the lines. This playfulness allows for the inventive thinking that is crucial at the early stages of the writing process. And though little, if any, of the above freewriting is usable in the conventional sense, you can see at the end how an idea finally clicks in.

WRITING TO EXPLORE 2.4

Using the methods discussed above, freewrite in your writer's notebook for fifteen to twenty minutes on each of at least two of the following topics:

a. Think back as far as you can into your childhood and consider the ways that you most liked spending your time. Then, consider if any of those activities somehow relate to your present major or career goals.

b. Do people regularly call on you for help in specific tasks? Are you a good listener? Do you have artistic skills? Do others ask your advice in writing? Are you able to negotiate conflicts or offer solace to those in pain? Using freewriting, describe the capabilities that others most seem to value in you.

c. What jobs have you have held? Which were most satisfying to you—and why? Which did you find particularly challenging or trying?

   Using freewriting, describe some of the work experiences that stick in your mind. After listing those jobs, explore what each of your experiences might suggest about potential career fields.

d. Pick a career you might consider pursuing. Then freewrite on the role of that profession within the larger community. Why is it important that people do this job? What does this occupation add to our culture?

e. What subjects have always come easiest to you? Which subjects most intrigue you or make you think most deeply? What might those subjects have in common with your other interests? By thinking about the subjects that most intrigue you (and those that don't), can you draw any conclusions about your talents and interests? Do those talents and interests seem to point you toward particular occupational fields?

EXPLORING IMPLICATIONS

As valuable as they are, brainstorming and freewriting are not ends in themselves. Though these techniques allow you to free yourself from restraints, invention does not end with scattered words and thoughts; it also involves considered judgments. You must develop, extend, and, eventually, test those ideas. That is, it is also important to examine the implications of your initial ideas, looking at them in greater depth and considering them in light of the world around you. Here's where the invention process might go in a number of directions—all of which are designed to tease out the implications of your brainstorms and raise questions for further examination.

So what becomes of what you write during a brainstorming or freewriting session? First, you ought to return frequently to earlier writings, searching what you wrote for ideas worth pursuing. You can sort through the thoughts that have spilled out, pulling from your freewriting any special moments of clarity. You can look for phrasings that capture what you think in innovative or especially striking ways.

You might call the process of finding the most inventive ideas to emerge from your freewriting *gleaning*. In technical usage, gleaning is a process of gathering the grain left behind reapers, but it also has come to mean "to collect (knowledge or information, for example), bit by bit." Consider the way that those two images play against one another: You've gone through the process of planting and growing ideas through the early composing processes of freewriting and brainstorming. Now you can return to what you've written and glean from it what may be of value—that which can be refined into something useful. But, as with any such process, you can't expect what you find there to be in its finished or polished form—after all, gleaning yields bits of grain, not loaves of bread. Invention in general, and freewriting in particular, is really about generating raw material for future use. Then you can follow those ideas to see where they lead you.

WRITING TO EXPLORE 2.5

Go back to your freewriting (Writing to Explore 2.4) and see if you can glean the ideas there that seem most worth pursuing. If you find nothing that intrigues you, feel free to try again: Do some freewriting, let it sit, and then come back to it. Begin by choosing a line that you find particularly compelling, and then try to develop it further, searching for topics that bear further investigation.

THREE INVENTION STRATEGIES

Though there are many ways that you can put to use the words that you glean from your early writing, I suggest three possibilities here. These three methods of thinking through your ideas represent very different approaches to invention, and so you might try them out and see how each works for you. By doing so, you'll not only be able to continue composing a vision of your life's work but also will begin to gather strategies that work best for you as a writer.

Imagining an Uninformed Audience

One way to tease out the implications of your ideas is to consider how you would explain them to someone who hasn't thought about the topic as much as you have. Let's say you begin with a thought like this: "I've always imagined being a scientist, because I love understanding how nature works." Next, imagine someone who finds science baffling, boring, or much too technical to interest him. What could you possibly say to this person in order to help him understand why you are considering devoting a portion of your life to its pursuit?

Imagining such a situation requires that you examine your own motivations as well as what you already know about the topic. It can also help you to gather your best reasoning—ideas and wordings and phrasings that seem to capture your thoughts and emotions. As you go through this process, you will likely discover many facets of the topic that you had not yet consciously considered.

An uninformed or uninterested audience presents you with a situation that requires clarity. As you attempt to explain an idea that is close to you, you are forced to step back and think about that idea in more specific and detailed ways. If I am asked to explain my love of teaching (or someone else is asked to explain a desire to be a scientist), I am challenged to assemble a series of ideas to illustrate my reply. At the inventional stage, of course, you are not yet ready to go public with your ideas, but imagining what you would say if asked to do so can be useful.

WRITING TO EXPLORE 2.6

Thinking back to some of the entries in your writer's notebook and to the useful ideas that you have gleaned from it, list as many good reasons as you can why someone ought to share your interest in a particular topic, consider the value of a particular occupation, or see the value in a particular talent that you have. Remember that your uninformed audience needs as much detail as you can provide; your descriptions need not yet be polished, but they should be as specific and descriptive as possible.

Using Patterns of Development

The above exercise asked you to develop your early ideas in more detail. You have likely been asked to do just that on many writing occasions before; just think of all the times a teacher or employer has asked you to "be more specific" or "provide more details" in order to explain your ideas or make them more convincing. But developing your ideas can be difficult without knowing specific strategies for teasing out the fine points of the topic. Fortunately, the rhetorical tradition provides patterns of development to enrich your ideas. Though these patterns can be used later in the writing process to structure and arrange your writing, they can also help you to invent ideas by looking at the topics from a number of perspectives.

The patterns of development discussed below are meant as inventional tools—tools that can enrich your writing with details. But details take many forms, some more appropriate to a specific rhetorical situation than others. That's why a writer needs *many* tools. Sometimes you can develop your ideas by providing a more detailed **definition** of key terms or ideas. Sometimes the occasion calls for vivid **description,** using graphic and sensory language to help readers imagine what something looks like, tastes like, sounds like, feels like, or smells like. On some occasions, providing specific **examples** of a general idea or principle is the best way to invent things to say about the topic. Sometimes an illustrative story or **narrative** can help you and your readers to see how an idea plays out in the context of action and characters. In other cases, the best approach is through **analysis**—helping the reader see logical connections among a series of ideas or things. Similarly, you might better understand a topic by breaking it into parts and considering the ways that those parts function as part of a system (**division and classification**); sometimes analysis can be enriched by noting how things or concepts are similar or different from one another (**comparison and contrast**); and in still other cases, you can gain new insights by considering how events or ideas interact with and influence one another (**cause and effect**). All these patterns of development are useful methods of invention because they can provide specific and detailed language with which to think about, and eventually to express, your initial ideas.

Definitions are formed by showing the distinguishing characteristics of something—the defining characteristics that separate the thing from all others. In order to use definition as a way of exploring an idea, begin with the most general features of the concept or thing, and then add the details that distinguish this specific concept from other similar concepts. For example, if you were defining a chair, you might begin by calling it a piece of furniture, but to distinguish it from other pieces of furniture, you'd have to add "on which people sit"—and then probably go on to distinguish it from a couch, a stool, etc. It is this process of continually revising and refining that can help you to generate new ideas.

Let's consider a more specific use of definition. If you were asked to provide specific reasons for your interest in becoming a businessperson, you might invent ideas by attempting to define the field of business. This definition need not be the kind you find in a dictionary but rather might describe the most important features of the profession and show how that profession is unique. So, to define the business field, you might begin with the general class of occupation, and then consider all the features you can that define that particular type of work—details that make it unique. Business is a field concerned primarily with finances, with maximizing profits, with successfully managing people and money, etc. As this example suggests, this inventional tool asks you to consider increasingly specific features of the thing or concept that you are defining.

WRITING TO EXPLORE 2.7

Define the work done in an occupation that interests you. If you are interested in being a scientist, define *scientist* for an audience of college students who are less interested than you in that field. If you are considering being a teacher, or a doctor, or a lawyer, try to clearly define the most important attributes of a person who works in that profession. Provide as many details as you can that distinguish this profession from others (and keep track of questions that arise as well, things you don't already know about the profession that you might investigate later). Try to go beyond the conventional definitions to discover important but little thought-of facets of the job. And remember that this is not yet meant to be polished writing, so feel free to keep revising your thoughts as you go, adding new ideas as they come to you.

Sometimes you can find out more about an object or topic by considering how it affects your senses. **Description** requires language that is vivid and specific enough to help others to experience the object through sensory details that bring it to life. Description is largely about diction (word choice), since the words you use carry mental and sensory images. This pattern of development asks you to search your mind for words and phrases that capture not only the general meaning but also the more specific feelings and connotations associated with an idea.

For example, if you are interested in becoming a surgeon, you might describe the various sense impressions (the sights, smells, sounds, and tactile sensations) you imagine in an operating room: the purplish-red blood, the pungent scent of powerful disinfectants, the blinding brightness of the scorching hot lights reflected in the gleaming stainless-steel implements. You might also describe the life-or-death intensity in the faces—and hands—of the surgeon, or the restrained terror as a patient's pulse threatens to slip away. Finding just the right phrasings to bring those sensory details to life is crucial. But as you play with possible phrasings to describe something, you are not just finding words; you are imagining the many facets of the topic that are contained in those words.

WRITING TO EXPLORE 2.8

Describe a moment or a scene involved in the work of a particular occupation (one in which you have worked or are working, or just one that interests you), focusing on the specific sense details of that moment. Take care to use as many descriptive details as possible to bring the scene to life for your readers. In order to learn as much as you can about the topic, try as many possible phrasings and multiple word choices as you can think of.

Sometimes topics cannot be made clear in the abstract, or even through vivid and descriptive word choices. In those cases, **examples** can often make abstract ideas more tangible and understandable to your readers. You might have noticed that each time I attempt to explain a rhetorical concept, I usually provide an example to illustrate it (recall the example of the surgeon I used above).

Good examples are both typical (people can accept that they are based on a likely occurrence, not an anomaly) and illustrative (they illustrate a general principle through a specific case). Though examples are not usually in and of themselves a sufficient form of proof (unless you have lots of them, and other variables are controlled), they can be very helpful in inventing ideas. Each new example can add a new perspective on your topic and so enrich your understanding of it.

So, if you were considering ways to illustrate the work of a marketing specialist, you might gather (either from your own knowledge and experience or from other sources) specific examples of the work done in marketing. You might provide an example of a successful advertising campaign (or plan for that campaign), an example of a failed strategy, or an example of a particularly successful marketer's thought processes (perhaps through a published personal interview). In each case, your goal would be to show how details about the typical work of and the products created by a marketer can help everyone understand the field more generally.

WRITING TO EXPLORE 2.9

Try to illustrate the work done in a particular occupation by providing a specific example of that work. For example, if you want to explain why using statistical analysis is so important in the social sciences, you might provide an example of how a sociologist prepared and interpreted a survey in a city to determine attitudes toward race relations there. Your goals in this exercise are to seek examples that are typical of this type of work and to describe the ways in which each example illustrates key facets of the occupation.

Another way to invent ideas is to create a **narrative** or story. Because narratives are slices of life, they can illustrate in vivid detail key aspects of any subject you investigate—and so can help you to generate ideas. As an inventional technique, narrative combines methods from the previous two types: It functions as a type of *example,* as a specific case that helps you to explore a more general idea, and it uses *description* to make that case vivid and real. Of course, no single story or example can capture all the complexity of a topic, but that's not the point here. The point is for you to either imagine or recall a story that helps you to explore the subtleties of a topic in action, narrating a specific incident that illustrates a more general principle or point. Again, as you think through the ways you would capture that moment, you will necessarily be helping yourself to think through specific facets of that topic—facets that can be expanded on later.

WRITING TO EXPLORE 2.10

Tell the story of a single incident involving someone working in a profession that interests you. Through the characterizations and actions of the story, illustrate why the work of this occupation is intriguing, important, useful, etc. You might draw the story from a real incident in which you were involved, you might write about an incident that you read or heard about, or you might create a fictional account, imagining the work of that occupation. In any case, your goal is to generate as many illustrative details on the work done in that field as you can by showing that work in action.

The patterns of development discussed above all function to help you to invent a specific set of details that flesh out a particular topic. But sometimes, rather than widening your understanding of a topic, you might want to *deepen* it by breaking the topic into its constituent parts through various types of analysis. Breaking a topic into parts gives you an engineer's view of how it works—how the parts fit together, and why. This technique works not only for machines and other physical objects; by breaking down any subject, you can gain a richer insight into it.

One way to analyze a topic is through **division and classification.** This pattern of developing ideas really involves two related activities. First, you *divide* a large topic into parts; then you *classify* those parts, showing some of the ways that they can be organized within the overall topic. Though the two activities seem like polar opposites—one taking something apart, the other putting it together—they are really two facets of the same activity. Imagine how much a mechanic learns about an engine by taking it apart and reassembling it.

To use this pattern, then, you need to first find some reasonable ways to break a topic into constituent parts—and, of course, there are, in any given case, many ways to do so. But once you have decided on a method of division, you have also begun the process of classification, since you need to know the ways things fit together in order to divide them into reasonable subsections.

In the case of occupations, you might illustrate the work in a particular field by showing its sub-areas and how they are organized. For example, if you are investigating the sciences, you might divide them into social sciences, natural sciences, and physical sciences. You might then divide them further into biology, chemistry, physics, etc. Then you could show how organizing the sciences in a particular way reveals something about each of its sub-areas—and about the whole. Why are psychology, sociology, and criminal justice all considered social sciences? What do philosophy, music, and visual arts have in common as subsets of the humanities? What do marketing, accounting, and economics share?

WRITING TO EXPLORE 2.11

Divide a general career field into some of the professions that exist within it. Try to show how each area has its own unique characteristics as well as how it fits into the larger occupational field. For example, what specific areas fall into the category of business? art? social sciences? criminal justice? In order to invent within this topic, you might read descriptions of the various fields in your course catalog or other sources, or speak with professionals in the field.

Sometimes the best way to analyze a thing or topic is to consider its similarities to, and differences from, related ideas using the pattern of development called **comparison and contrast.** Using this line of thinking can help you to invent more precise understandings of each of the topics being compared, raising ideas that may not have been apparent when either topic was viewed in isolation.

For example, in the case of your investigation of a particular occupation, you might compare how professionals in that field approach problems to how professionals in other fields do. If you are describing the work of a psychologist treating a patient, you might differentiate it from—and show similarities to—the work of a medical doctor treating that same patient. If you are describing the work of an art teacher, you might compare it to and differentiate it from the work of an artist who works for an advertising company. You might show how a scientist approaches questions about human life differently than a minister or priest does.

WRITING TO EXPLORE 2.12

As in the previous examples, describe the work of a particular occupation (as you imagine it) by showing how it is similar to and different than another field with which it shares specific concerns. Invent as many details about each profession as you can, using freewriting and brainstorming as well as other techniques that work well for you. Your goal is to help the subtleties of one occupation's work emerge as you compare it to similar types of work.

Another way to analyze a topic is to show the relationship between an action or idea and the results of that action or idea, highlighting a pattern of reasoning known as **cause and effect**. Used as a form of invention, this technique can help you to better understand a topic by investigating its sphere of influence or consequence—what it does, how it changes things, etc. The idea here is to generate details about something by showing how it spurs specific results and, in some cases, other actions.

Considering the chain of cause and effect is a particularly useful form of invention because it requires you to consider relationships among ideas and actions. More specifically, as a form of analysis, cause and effect can breed new ideas because it asks a set of questions related specifically to consequences. Rather than collecting ideas about what something *is* (as with definition) or what it looks, feels, or tastes like (as with description), you are asking about what it *does*—what effects it has on its environs. By doing so, you ask questions that analyze (and in some cases judge) the thing or action.

As a mode of invention, considering causes and effects can open many areas for further investigation. You, of course, must be careful about what conclusions you draw about the relationship between cause and effect; just because two things happen one after another doesn't mean the first caused the second. For that reason, it is often best to consider potential areas of cause and effect rather than to draw conclusions too quickly.

WRITING TO EXPLORE 2.13

All occupations involve many actions, and most of those actions are designed to bring about specific effects or cause other desirable actions. Advertising is an attempt to spur the purchase of goods and services. Teaching attempts to stimulate the thought processes of students. Choose a common action performed in an occupation that interests you and demonstrate the link between that action and its effects. In the process, you should also help your readers to see the value in that occupation's work.

Collaborative Invention

The inventional strategies discussed above each place you in the position of assumed expertise. But, as you invent, you also learn what you *don't* know about a topic. That's a good thing too, since it helps you to generate a list of questions that can enrich your writing. Still, you are unlikely to discover as many gaps in your understanding as you probably should. No matter how you challenge yourself to be as thorough and detailed as possible, other perspectives are crucial to widening your view of a topic. That gathering of the insights of others is often termed *research*—a detailed process that we discuss in later chapters. But even at the early stages of invention, developing your thoughts need not be a wholly private process.

For example, say you are attempting to define the work done by a marketer. You draw on your life experience, things you've read, and course descriptions. Based on the information that you have, you imagine the work of this field. But in order to be reasonably sure that you are investigating as many facets of the profession as you can, you would benefit by welcoming questions and calls for clarification about your topic. Doing so can help you to incorporate the ideas and insights of others into your processes of invention.

WRITING TO EXPLORE 2.14

Prepare a brief description of a profession that you may be interested in pursuing (if you completed some of the exercises above, you might draw on them for ideas). Then, either in a small group discussion or by e-mail, invite two people to ask you questions about the profession that were not addressed in your description. Do your best to prompt rich replies and challenging questions, not just cursory responses. Collect these questions and classify them as questions you could answer on your own and those that would require you to learn more about the topic through some form of research.

The processes involved in collaborative invention help you remember that even at the earliest stages, writing is not a wholly private matter. Although there is certainly lots of room for personal reflection and individual thought in writing, much of the writing you do (especially in your academic and professional careers) is ultimately social—it takes into consideration the previous ideas and future reactions of others.

The series of readings and writing prompts that follow in the first of our Reading and Writing Applications will help you to do further inventing. By using the inventional strategies discussed so far and by reading the thoughts and words of others who have considered their own life's work and the role of work in making lives, you will do some deep thinking and sustained writing.

Finding Meaningful Work

Case 1 VIOLENCE OR JOY? WHAT DOES WORK MAKE OF US?

When you think about the lifetime of work that lies ahead of you, what do you imagine? Are you excited and intrigued by the prospects of becoming a professional, an expert, a positive contributor to some field or occupation? Or do you worry about your work consuming you? Studs Terkel opens his best-selling book *Working* this way: "This book, being about work, is, by its very nature, about violence—to the spirit as well as to the body." Richard Reeves, conversely, asks us to "call a halt to the rhetorical carpet-bombing of work" and to admit that "work is good."

Questions about the love-hate relationship Americans have with their jobs, the declining amount of leisure and family time, and the balance between *earning a living* and *just living* have long been subjects of interest—and subjects for study and writing. What follows are two essays that address such issues. As you read, consider how the choices people make about work affect both their personal lives and the health of the culture more generally. After reading these essays, you'll have the opportunity to consider your own place within the world of work (considering your own character or *ethos,* as discussed in Chapter 1), to respond to what you've read (using some of the inventional techniques from Chapter 2), and to consider ways in which you might further investigate the issues raised by each of these authors.

Introduction to Working

Studs Terkel

Studs Terkel, born in 1912, is best known for his oral histories of the American working class. From working-class roots himself, Terkel received a law degree in 1934 and went on to become a successful radio personality, hosting "The Studs Terkel Program." He is Distinguished Scholar-in-Residence at the Chicago Historical Society and continues to interview people about their work. The excerpt below is from the introduction to his best-selling 1980 book, *Working,* which recounts the thoughts of workers in a variety of career fields.

Work is, by its very nature, about violence—to the spirit as well as to the body. It is about ulcers as well as accidents, about shouting matches as well as fistfights, about nervous breakdowns as well as kicking the dog around. It is, above all (or beneath all), about daily humiliations. To survive the day is triumph enough for the walking wounded among the great many of us.

The scars, psychic as well as physical, brought home to the supper table and the TV set, may have touched, malignantly, the soul of our society. More or less. ("More or less," that most ambiguous of phrases, pervades many of the conversations that comprise this book, reflecting, perhaps, an ambiguity of attitude toward The Job. Something more—than Orwellian[1] acceptance, something less than Luddite[2] sabotage. Often the two impulses are fused in the same person.)

It is about a search, too, for daily meaning as well as daily bread, for recognition as well as cash, for astonishment rather than torpor; in short, for a sort of life rather than a Monday through Friday sort of dying. Perhaps immortality, too, is part of the quest. To be remembered was the wish, spoken and unspoken, of the heroes and heroines of this book.

There are, of course, the happy few who find a savor in their daily job: the Indiana stonemason, who looks upon his work and sees that it is good; the Chicago piano tuner, who seeks and finds the sound that delights; the book-binder, who saves a piece of history; the Brooklyn fireman, who saves a piece of life . . . But don't these satisfactions, like Jude's[3] hunger for knowledge, tell us more about the person than about his task? Perhaps. Nonetheless, there is a common attribute here: a meaning to their work well over and beyond the reward of the paycheck.

For the many, there is a hardly concealed discontent. The blue-collar blues is no more bitterly sung than the white-collar moan. "I'm a machine," says the spot-welder, "I'm caged," says the bank teller, and echoes the hotel clerk. "I'm a mule," says the steelworker. "A monkey can do what I do," says the receptionist. "I'm less than a farm implement," says the migrant worker. "I'm an object," says the high-fashion model. Blue collar and white call upon the identical phrase: "I'm a robot." *There is nothing to talk about,* the young accountant despairingly enunciates. It was some time ago that John Henry sang, "A man ain't nothin' but a man." The hard, unromantic fact is: he died with his hammer in his hand, while the machine pumped on. Nonetheless, he found immortality. He is remembered.

As the automated pace of our daily jobs wipes out name and face—and, in many instances, feeling—there is a sacrilegeous [*sic*] question being asked these days. To earn one's bread by the sweat of one's brow has always been the lot of mankind. At least, ever since Eden's slothful couple was served with an eviction notice. The scriptural precept was never doubted, not out loud. No matter how demeaning the task, no matter how it dulls the senses and breaks the spirit, one *must* work. Or else.

Lately there has been a questioning of this "work ethic," especially by the young. Strangely enough, it has touched off profound grievances in others, hitherto devout, silent, and anonymous. Unexpected precincts are being heard from in a show of discontent. Communiqués from the assembly line are frequent and alarming: absenteeism. On the evening bus, the tense, pinched faces of young file clerks and elderly secretaries tell us more than we care to know. On the expressways, middle management men pose without grace behind their wheels as they flee city and job.

There are other means of showing it, too. Inchoately, sullenly, it appears in slovenly work, in the put-down of craftsmanship. A farm equipment worker in Moline complains that the careless worker who turns out more that is bad is better regarded than the careful craftsman who turns out less that is good. The first is an ally of the Gross National Product. The other is a threat to it, a kook—and the sooner he is penalized the better. Why, in these circumstances, should a man work with care? Pride does indeed precede the fall.

Others, more articulate—at times, visionary—murmur of a hunger for "beauty," "a meaning," "a sense of pride." A veteran car hiker sings out, "I could drive any car like a baby, like a woman changes her baby's diaper. Lots of customers say, 'How you do this?' I'd say, 'Just the way you bake a cake, miss.' When I was younger, I could swing with that car. They called me Lovin' Al the Wizard."

Dolores Dante graphically describes the trials of a waitress in a fashionable restaurant. They are compounded by her refusal to be demeaned. Yet pride in her skills helps her make it through the night. "When I put the plate down, you don't hear a sound. When I pick up a glass, I want it to be just right. When someone says, 'How come you're just a waitress?' I say, 'Don't you think you deserve being served by me?'"

Peggy Terry has her own sense of grace and beauty. Her jobs have varied with geography, climate, and the ever-felt pinch of circumstance. "What I hated worst was being a waitress. The way you're treated. One guy said, 'You don't have to smile; I'm gonna give you a tip anyway.' I said, 'Keep it. I wasn't smiling for a tip.' Tipping should be done away with. It's like throwing a dog a bone. It makes you feel small.''

In all instances, there is felt more than a slight ache. In all instances, there dangles the impertinent question: Ought not there be an increment, earned though not yet received, from one's daily work—an acknowledgement [*sic*] of man's *being*?

An American President is fortunate—or, perhaps, unfortunate—that, offering his Labor Day homily, he didn't encounter Maggie Holmes, the domestic, or Phil Stallings, the spot-welder, or Louis Hayward, the washroom attendant. Or especially, Grace Clements, the felter at the luggage factory, whose daily chore reveals to us in a terrible light that Charles Dickens's London is not so far away nor long ago.

Obtuseness in "respectable" quarters is not a new phenomenon. In 1850 Henry Mayhew, digging deep into London's laboring lives and evoking from the invisible people themselves the wretched truth of their lot, astonished and horrified readers of the *Morning Chronicle*. His letters ran six full columns and averaged 10,500 words. It is inconceivable that Thomas Carlyle[4] was unaware of Mayhew's findings. Yet, in his usual acerbic—and, in this instance, unusually mindless—manner, he blimped, "No needlewoman, distressed or other, can be procured in London by any housewife to give, for fair wages, fair help in sewing. Ask any thrifty housemother. No *real* needlewoman, 'distressed' or other, has been found attainable in any of the houses I frequent. Imaginary needlewomen, who demand considerable wages, and have a deepish appetite for beer and viands, I hear of everywhere. . . .'"* A familiar ring?

Smug respectability, like the poor, we've had with us always. Today, however, and what few decades remain of the twentieth century, such obtuseness is an indulgence we can no longer afford. The computer, nuclear energy for better or worse, and sudden, simultaneous influences flashed upon everybody's TV screen have raised the ante and the risk considerably. Possibilities of another way, discerned by only a few before, are thought of—if only for a brief moment, in the haze of idle conjecture—by many today.

The drones are no longer invisible nor mute. Nor are they exclusively of one class. Markham's Man with the Hoe may be Ma Bell's girl with the headset. (And can it be safely said, she is "dead to rapture and despair"? Is she really "a thing that grieves not and that never hopes"?) They're in the office as well as the warehouse; at the manager's desk as well as the assembly line; at some estranged company's computer as well as some estranged woman's kitchen floor.

Bob Cratchit[5] may still be hanging on (though his time is fast running out, as did his feather pen long ago), but Scrooge has been replaced by the conglomerate.

Hardly a chance for Christmas spirit here. Who knows Bob's name in this outfit—let alone his lame child's? ("The last place I worked for, I was let go," recalls the bank teller. "One of my friends stopped by and asked where I was at. They said, 'She's no longer with us.' That's all. I vanished.") It's nothing personal, really. Dickens's people[6] have been replaced by Beckett's.[7]

*E. P. Thompson and Eileen Yeo, *The Unknown Mayhew* (New York: Pantheon Books, 1971).

Endnotes

1. George Orwell is the pen name of English novelist, essayist, and political satirist Eric Blair (1902–1950). He is perhaps most famous for his depiction of a dangerous future, filled with surveillance and oppression, in his novel *Nineteen Eighty-Four*. What Terkel calls an "Orwellian acceptance" by workers refers to the willingness of citizens to give up their freedoms willingly, as most do in this novel.
2. In contrast to the "Orwellian acceptance," the "Luddite sabotage" refers to British workers who revolted against mechanization of textile factories, fearing the loss of their jobs. The word *Luddite* refers to Neal Lud, an eighteenth-century worker who destroyed such machinery.
3. "Jude's hunger for knowledge" refers to the title character in Thomas Hardy's *Jude the Obscure*, a poor young man who dreams of someday attaining a college education.
4. Thomas Carlyle (1795–1881) was an English essayist and historian. Terkel refers to him here as an example of a conservative voice (which he became later in his career) that denies the reality of work's oppressive nature.
5. Bob Cratchit is the poor but kindly hero of Charles Dickens's *A Christmas Carol*, and here serves as an example of the oppressed but diligent worker.
6. Charles Dickens (1812–1870) was an English novelist famous for (among other things) his depictions of difficult working conditions during the Industrial Revolution. Terkel refers to "Dickens's people," including the likes of Bob Cratchit (see previous note), as examples of noble though oppressed workers.
7. Terkel here refers to the characters of Irish playwright Samuel Beckett (1906–1989). More specifically, Terkel seems to refer to the bank teller in this paragraph who left her job only to be remembered with the phase "She's no longer with us" as reminiscent of Beckett's characters, who illustrated the emptiness and loneliness of the human experience.

The Joy of Work

Richard Reeves

Richard Reeves is a syndicated columnist, recipient of the 1998 Lifetime Achievement Award from the National Society of Newspaper Columnists, and has worked as a visiting assistant professor at the Annenberg School for Communication at the University of California. Reeves has also made a number of award-winning documentary films. His most recent publication, *Happy Mondays: Putting the Pleasure Back into Work* (2002) explores, like the article below, the "joy of work."

How was your day? Don't give one of the approved answers: "OK, I guess" or "Well, it's just a job, isn't it?" Be honest. You probably had a great day, engaged in interesting tasks with agreeable people. You like your job more than you dare admit. Maybe you don't have hobbies, because your work is more fascinating than any evening class. Maybe you like being at work more than being at home. You may feel more valued at work than elsewhere. Perhaps you have made most of your friends through work. Even your love life may revolve around the office. Maybe it doesn't really feel like work at all. Don't worry. You are not alone.

Working hard at a job you love does not make you a social pariah. Work is becoming more central to all our lives. It is a provider of friends, gossip, networks, fun, creativity, purpose, comfort, belonging, identity—and even love. Work is where life is. And where the heart is. It is OK to derive more satisfaction, pleasure and pride from your labour than from your leisure. There is nothing wrong with preferring to complete a work project rather than slump in front of mindless TV soaps. Lots of us do. If you love your job, come out. Declare your affection.

If, on the other hand, you are stuck in a job that is, in American writer Studs Terkel's phrase, "too small for the human spirit," don't accept it as your fate. Ignore the voices telling you that it's just the way life is and you have to learn to lump it. That is not the way life is. And no-one has to lump it. Would you stay with a partner who made you miserable? No. You expect better. Do the same at work. Demand more, and the chances are you'll get it.

Our attitudes to work need a radical overhaul. The popular myth is that work is wicked—that it saps our energy, steals our time and erodes our spirit. Two of the most depressing mantras of modern times capture the anti-work ethos. The worst is "I work to live, I don't live to work." The truth is that people who work to live have no kind of life. Work takes up more waking hours than any other activity. Most of us would work whether we needed the money or not. The idea that we should willingly endure dull or demeaning work for the sake of a few hours off is a crime against humanity. We are now more interested in living life than simply making a living. And a full life means fulfilling work.

Depressing phrase number two is "Nobody ever says on their deathbed they wish they'd spent more time in the office." First, there are plenty who would if they were being more honest. Lots of us get more out of our work than other aspects of our lives. It is just not socially acceptable to say so. And there are many more people who would like to say they had found work that was interesting enough for them to want to spend more time in the office. When asked: "What do you most regret in your life?" four out of five retired people picked the response "Staying in a job I did not like." Our old-age regrets are not about the lovers that got away, much as we like to think so. They are about the jobs that got away.

Wicked Work is not a new myth, of course. Work has been bashed for centuries—as divine curse, punishment, wage slavery, as a price to be paid for our leisure. Bertrand Russell declared 70 years ago that "a great deal of harm is being done in the modern world by belief in the virtuousness of work, and the road to happiness and prosperity lies in an organised diminution of work."

Today, work is diagnosed as the disease behind some of the worst symptoms of modern life—stress, divorce, heart disease, juvenile delinquency, suicide, sleeplessness, cancer, depression, lack of sex. Even the haven of the toilet has allegedly been invaded, with stress at work linked to irritable bowel syndrome. Pick up any newspaper on any day of the week and there's a good chance of finding a story that links work to one or other of society's ills: "Working mothers damage children's education." "Stress at work on the rise." "Workplace blues." "The death of career." "Workaholism—the new killer." "Overwork drives up divorce rate." And so on.

The only disease that is genuinely spreading is whingitis—a tendency to moan consistently in the face of the most wonderful developments. We are like an adolescent schoolgirl meeting a naked Robbie Williams in a candlelit boudoir and complaining that the thermostat is a bit high. Some facts: average earnings have increased by more than half in the past decade. The proportion of firms offering maternity leave in excess of the statutory minimum has quintupled. A third of firms now offer sabbaticals: two-thirds allow their staff to work from home some of the time. Four out of 10 British workers declare themselves "very satisfied" with their jobs—more than in than France, Germany, Italy or Spain. Most of us are satisfied with our working lives. A third of us say that work is the "most important thing in our lives." We feel at least as appreciated at work as at home. Work is how we identify ourselves, where we learn and make friends. Work is our community.

It is time to call a halt to the rhetorical carpet-bombing of work. Work is good. And by insisting it is bad we limit the opportunities to make it even better. People in soul-destroying jobs accept them because they are continually told that work is not supposed to be enjoyable. At the same time, the real impact of downsizing is downplayed: companies kid themselves (and sometimes us) they fire somebody or push them into early retirement they are liberating them from work. They are "letting them go."

We get the politicians we deserve, and so it is with work. If we expect it to be unfulfilling, the chances are it will be. The Greek philosopher Epictetus said: "It is not things in themselves that trouble us but our opinion of things." In this case, the problem is not bad work, it is our bad attitude towards work. We need a new and better conversation, one that better reflects the reality. Governments, companies and trade unions remain stuck, by and large, in an anti-work rut. So it is up to us, as individuals, to shape a new, positive consensus. We have to break the impasse. A few have already started. . . .

David loves his work. He is a young assistant vicar in North London. "I love being a priest. I love the contact with a wide range of people. I love being able to give people support, often at very difficult times in their lives. I get to share people's stories, and I feel enormously privileged for that. Of course there are days when I wake up and wish I earned a bit more. But I simply cannot imagine doing anything else with my life."

Marsha loves her work. A former special assistant to Donna Shalala, the US Health and Human Resources Secretary, she says: "My work is an expression of who I essentially am. The values by which I live my life are the same ones I apply to my work. My jobs have allowed me to do the work that I love. I have never seen work as limiting. I get blown away by it. Positively. It's a riot."

Ramesh loves his work. An assistant accountant for Dixons, the electronics retailer, he says: "In the past 14 years I have not had a single day off work with illness. There are some people who have a cold or sore throat and can't be bothered to go to work. The English whine all the time about two things—weather and work. I understand about the weather: I'm from Sri Lanka. But I have never understood why about work. I love it. I love numbers. I'm very proud of what I produce—and I'm very proud of myself."

Charlene loves her work. A senior vice-president at Fleishman-Hillard, one of the world's biggest PR agencies, she is young and ambitious. "If people were to ask me what I do with my time, it would be work. I can't say I have a really strong hobby that uses up my time. I worry about that. . . . Actually, I don't—I think I ought to worry about it. The truth is that my work has given me the most amazing opportunities. My work is my hobby. My work is my life."

Sue loves her work. Running the bakery in a Safeway supermarket, she has just been promoted from the checkouts. "I love my job now, even though it has more responsibility. And I loved the checkouts too. Some people want to be a nuclear physicist or a brain surgeon; I wanted to work in Safeway. On the checkouts you get your regulars. I wear big earrings, and some of them started bringing me pairs in. They stop me on the street and say hello. The other girls ask why talk to the customers, but I think a job is what you make it. You get out what you put in. I'm proud of my work."

David, Marsha, Ramesh, Charlene and Sue are honest about their relationship with their work. They are pioneers. As such, they can be subject to fierce attacks. "There's something really creepy about people who 'love' their work," says journalist Julie Burchill. "And really class-traitorous, too." Which class is Burchill talking about? And how is someone who loves their work a traitor?

Burchill's view, apparently, is that progressive people are obliged to spend their working hours engaged in hateful and demeaning tasks. She perfectly expresses the lazy, reactionary view of work that has condemned so many to suffer so much for so little, There is nothing admirable about sticking at a soulless task, nothing liberating about working to live, nothing cool about hating your job and doing nothing about it.

Nowadays it is pretty much OK to openly love anybody or anything. It is OK for people to say they love their spouse, to say they love their same-sex partner, to say they love their dog. The one thing they cannot say without fear of stigma is that they love their job. Love of work is now the only love that dare not speak its name.

But not only is it OK to love our work, it is necessary for us to have the kind of lives we want. Money is important, but in a post-materialist society we need much more. Research shows that happiness rises with income, but only up to a point. And the vast majority of people in the West are past that point. So the fact that we are getting collectively wealthier does not mean we are getting collectively happier—a source of consternation to many politicians and social commentators. People doing work they enjoy are happy—not only at work but generally in the other areas of their lives too.

If we want happiness, the solution lies not in GOP growth or nuclear families. It lies in meaningful work for us all. Terkel says work is now "about a search . . . for daily meaning as well as daily bread, for recognition as well as cash, for astonishment rather than torpor: in short, for a sort of life rather than a Monday through Friday sort of dying."

Once we see work in this light, entrenched debates—in particular over working hours, the work/life divide and family breakdown—take on a different flavour. Work stands accused, for example, of sucking all the hours out of our days, for taking over our lives. And it is true that some people are working longer hours. But the idea that it is being forced on us doesn't stack up. Take the people working the longest hours, more than 80 a week. Official figures show that they are the ones with most control over their time and the ones who say they like their jobs the most. Who'd have thought it? That people who like something might do more of it than people who do not? Shocking! It never seems to occur to the critics of working hours that people might actually, er, like their jobs.

People who put in more hours than is strictly required don't have a problem—they are simply made to feel as if they have one because of the "work is bad for you" consensus. There is a wonderful cartoon of an artist snarling at his wife late at night: "I'm not a workaholic! Lawyers and accountants are workaholics. Artists are driven." The truth, of course, is that lawyers and accountants can be just as driven. And there's nothing wrong with that.

In any case, the line between "work" and "life" is rapidly being rubbed out. Few people want to put their work in a box labelled "nine to five." Knowledge work can't be corseted into a standard workday. More people are working from home some of the time. And people are finding that work provides community, friendship, gossip and romance—all of the things that home has traditionally supplied. We are working at home, but also "homing at work."

There remains the argument that long hours, even if freely chosen, are wrecking families. Two-thirds of working women say they are too tired for sex, and that their relationships suffer because of a lack of time. Commenting on these findings, *Guardian* writer Madeleine Bunting asks: "How obvious does the connection between Britain's longest working hours and highest divorce rates in Europe have to get before we start doing something about it?" There may be a connection between long working hours and divorce, but there is no evidence that the former causes the latter. Indeed, it is more likely to be the other way around. People who get divorced take their work more seriously than those in relationships, perhaps because they now have to fend financially for themselves. That may make them inclined to work longer hours. It is simply nonsense to blame work for the break-up of marriages. Relationships end. When people—especially women—are economically independent their relationships end more often. But work is not to blame: it is simply a handy scapegoat for an emotionally dishonest society.

On all counts charged, work is Not Guilty. It has simply become the scapegoat of choice for the chattering classes. Work is one of the activities that defines our humanity. Through our work we discover who we are and what we might become. Albert Camus believed that "without work, all life goes rotten." His words have never been more true than today. It is time to give work a break, to stop carping about it and start celebrating it. Kahlil Gibran said work was "love made visible." Let's have a bit of that spirit back.

Writing to Respond

After reading the previous essays, freewrite in your writer's notebook to articulate your responses to each essay.

1. The brief excerpt from Studs Terkel's *Working* includes these words: "No matter how demeaning the task, no matter how it dulls the senses and breaks the spirit, one *must* work. Or else." Freewrite in response to this statement, drawing on examples from your own experience, the experiences of others you know, and Reeves's essay.

2. In what ways does Reeves respond to negative characterizations of work like Terkel's? Does Reeves offer a reasonable rebuttal to those who blame work for "most of our ills"?

3. Studs Terkel wrote, in the first line of his book *Working*, "This book, being about work, is, by its very nature, about violence—to the spirit as well as to the body. It is about ulcers as well as accidents, about shouting matches as well as fistfights, about nervous breakdowns as well as kicking the dog around. It is, above all (or beneath all), about daily humiliations. To survive the day is triumph enough for the walking wounded among the great many of us." Henry David Thoreau wrote, "It is not necessary to earn your bread by the sweat of your brow, unless you sweat easier than me," advocating a simpler life that requires less time spent at work. Considering these two quotations, and after reading the essays above, freewrite on your own priorities for your future. Do you anticipate work to be a great drain on your energies, or one that will provide joy?

4. What effect has work (or lack thereof) had on people that you know—friends, family, acquaintances? What values would you most value for your own future or present life? Do you hear your parents or others complain about work?

5. How do you imagine the relationship between your work and your leisure time? Will what you do at work influence what matters to you at home or in the community—or do you envision "leaving your work at the office"? Do people you know (and respect) seem to be identified by the work they do?

6. As an English teacher, I am often called upon by family and friends to help with writing tasks—helping children with homework, editing letters to the editor or complaining about consumer problems, etc. Consider ways that family or friends have used their occupational or educational skills to enrich their communities. Have any of their educational or occupational skills created a special *ethos* for them?

7. Considering your own talents (some of which you might have written about in the earlier freewriting exercises) and your possible fields of study, what could you do to contribute to your community? How could the expertise you will bring to your home and neighborhood enrich those communities?

8. Consider your career goals in light of the essays you've read. Do the essays in any way cause you to pause and reconsider those goals? How do you envision a successful life? Are you concerned about finding a balance between work and other important facets of your life?

Writing Applications

1. Talk with at least three people that you know about their work—why they work, what motivates them, how they found their way to their profession. Then, based on what you find in these informal interviews, write an essay that discusses the effect of work on the lives of these individuals. You might also include ideas or excerpts from the above essays, comparing the conclusions drawn by those essays with the ideas you collect from the people with whom you speak.

2. Read about an individual whom you consider successful in a line of work that interests you—an artist whose work you love, an engineer who solved a key problem in her field, a businessperson who built a successful organization, etc. Then, write an essay that highlights keys to this person's success and draws conclusions about the central elements of this line of work. As you prepare to write your essay, you might consider some of the issues regarding work that have been raised in the essays above. You might also consider the ways in which being inventive helped the individual toward his or her specific successes.

Case 2 WHAT IS A CAREER? REAL PEOPLE AT WORK

The path leading from school to work is rarely as simple as choosing a major and following that major to a career. The narratives below introduce you to a few people whose experiences are at the same time typical and unique. They are typical in that finding a life's work is always a search without a clear end—a quest whose goal keeps changing as people grow and learn. But each story is unique, as is each individual who attempts to compose a life's work—as individual as you are.

All of these pieces of writing are informal musings—workers speaking or writing about what they do, why they do it, how they got there, and where they might go next. As such, they tell us a good deal about finding a life's work. We hear more from these folks throughout this book, but what the stories below begin to tell us is that the path to a career is not a straight one. At the same time, they tell us how exciting and full of surprises that path can be, and how large a role that the education you are currently pursuing can play in that journey.

Inventional Exercises

As you read, list in your writer's notebook the discoveries about the world of work that each of these people has made. Pay special attention to the ways in which their jobs have helped them to (1) redefine what having a career means, (2) better understand the connection between school and work, and (3) draw on and develop their talents, skills, and character (or *ethos*).

Writer/Social Worker

Maureen Bradley

The other day I told a friend that I have a "very unfocused resume." While this is the case, I know that the running themes of my life are very clear. I have two passions that are forever intertwined: literature/writing/language and working with children. I entered college figuring on using these two passions as an English teacher. What better fit? Over the next four years, I bounced back and forth between the two. After an intense summer job with children at Trail Blazers, I decided to forgo my education major and focus on my writing. I was obsessed with working with the kind of children I met during my summer: economically disadvantaged, emotionally and behaviorally challenged youth. I didn't feel that a traditional classroom was the best venue, so I figured that my easiest way through college would be to do what I loved and what I knew I could do: write. What I didn't know was that writing would help to determine every step I took from there on out.

Writing classes in my Junior and Senior years found me writing often-cynical pieces about social issues. I wanted to make the world a better place for the kids, but didn't know how; so I wrote. I started keeping a journal, and I started using writing workshops to figure out my role in my community. I was acknowledged by peers and professors, who encouraged me to continue writing and to perform my pieces. And so I did.

Looking back, I guess I had two educations in college. (1) The classroom, where I learned that writing is a way of life. As an English major, I discovered that writing is not just for enjoyment, and it's not just for punishment. It was a way to find out who I was, and what my views were. (2) An outdoor experiential education program called Trail Blazers, where I worked with economically disadvantaged, emotionally and behaviorally challenged youth.

As a poet, I write largely about social issues. I write about things I see that affect children, that negate the positive work that I've done with a few youths. Once I stopped working for Trail Blazers, I found that I was less inspired to write. I met my goal of having more time, but realized that there was little point to writing about issues that I did nothing to change. I'm constantly asked what I do "for a living." I finally came up with the best answer I know: I'm a writer by training and a social worker by heart. Once I was able to identify myself, I realized that there must be a million careers that somehow place the two together. I've learned this through writing; keeping track of my passions has allowed me to see the patterns that I have formed. It enabled me to realize who I am, and what I want out of life. My ideals of social justice lead me toward a career of service. My skills as a writer allow me creativity as needed with children.

High School Teacher

Jodi Heller

What follows is an informal letter I received from Jodi Heller soon after she took her first teaching position, a letter that showed how her education, and specifically our conversations in an Advanced Composition course, came back to her when she needed it on the job.

Dominic,

I just wanted to let you know about something amazing that happened! This week I saw an episode of *Boston Public* (a show I started watching due to the fact that the school has similarities to where I am teaching . . . and the same name, "Winslow High"). Well, on Thursday a huge fight broke out in our cafeteria during my lunch break. It included about 5 black kids against 5 white kids. My job was to drag all the students off the tables that they were standing on to get a better look at the action. Some of my male coworkers went right into the fire and were slammed against walls before they could finally subdue these kids. It was a scary experience to walk into such a mob scene . . . knowing that it is your responsibility to take care of these kids.

Anyway, I went into my eighth period still a bit shaken and they all wanted to tell me about the situation . . . So I thought . . . ok, teachable moment. So we spent the entire period talking about racism and discrimination and it was one of the most productive conversations that I have ever had with any of my students. My class is about 60–70 percent black and the rest white with one mixed student and one Spanish student. They range in age from 15–19. Well, many black students said that they felt that when they are walking down the hall that teachers will stop them first to ask for a pass or will flock to them in a fight, or give them harsher sentences for what they do. Some white students said that they were scared, because they were always being called "White Boy" or being pushed around—that sometimes black kids would steal their chairs at lunch and they couldn't do anything about it. One student brought up the *Boston Public* episode and the word "Nigger." In turn we all talked about the fear and anger that that word evokes, and how some people feel that when African-Americans use the word it gives them the power over something that has been used against them.

It was strange to see my students trying desperately to use their language so not to offend anyone or be seen as a racist. At one point an African-American student kept saying "Caucasians this, and Caucasians that." And a girl responded, "It's o.k. dude, we're white. You can say white." And some students actually got agitated when one white student kept saying "African-Americans"; they said that they would rather him say "Black."

It reminded me so much of one of our Advanced Composition classes we had about language and the word "nigger" and how our society has made us scared to use our words and language. And I will tell you, to see even my most economically disadvantaged kids speaking clearly and rationally and listening intently to everyone else in the room was a powerful moment. People who could care less about school had their eyes and ears fixed on the situation. And you know what? They carried that conversation into the halls and on the bus and even into the next day. And they made sure to let me know that even though there might be injustice in this school, that I was one of the good guys, someone who never sees their color but instead "the content of their character."

Senior Systems Architect

Jane Whittaker

Asked about her work, Jane Whittaker supplied what she called "some random thoughts on work, communication, and community."

Lots of people—I'm one of them—don't have and never have had jobs with one-word titles, such as "teacher," "lawyer," "scientist," "dancer." My jobs always required a few minutes of explanation. I suspect many, many jobs are like this. Yet, as with most everything, if it doesn't have a name, it's invisible, off the radar screen.

I worked on Wall Street for Merrill Lynch for almost 20 years. Every employee had to have a job description on file. Nice idea; never really worked. All the job descriptions were very general, and each one was shared by many, sometimes hundreds, of people. But this never meant that all those people did the same job—far from it. I was a Senior Systems Architect for several years—on paper.

What this system did was allow the person who hired you to assign you a grade level, a title, and a starting salary. Your boss had a pretty good idea of what you'd be doing, and you might actually do whatever that was for a few weeks or months. But eventually things changed: you, your boss, the organization, the world. And what happened over and over and over again was that employees reinvented themselves based on the changing scene. One could, if one were observant, see what was needed and create a position for oneself. The whole scene was surprisingly fluid. I say "surprisingly," because I had had a notion of life in a corporation that was very different: rigid, static. Rather like a parking lot—all the spaces are defined and laid out and you parked in one for a while, then pulled out and moved into another one as you progressed through the organization. Neat, clean, well-thought out. Not so. My experience was far different. I found the organization (and I use that word loosely) to be more like children playing on the beach. Some are busy, some are not. There are fights and tears. There is competition. Some groups are organized and build nice sand castles; some kid is digging a big hole alone. Other kids wander around and help or destroy as the fancy strikes. Coalitions form and then dissolve. Waves come through and cause some damage. Parents pay some attention and kept them from drowning or killing one another, but there's not a lot of guidance. Plans change on the fly, and within all this, any one child's role changes, depending on opportunity, talent, peer pressure, personal desire, parental intervention—you name it.

Although I was hired as a Technical Writer, writing actually became *more* important as my career progressed. Because I could write clearly, organize ideas, build arguments, and explain complex ideas to people new to them, I was valued. For much of my work life I worked in an extremely technical environment (with computer and telecommunications engineers and systems architects), and although I had no technical training myself, my liberal arts background gave me a solid grounding in language (vocabulary), sensitivity and respect for other people and their ideas, and analytical skills, in addition to the ability to write. My job required that I listen to and understand what the technical guys needed and wanted to do and how much it would cost (usually millions of dollars), what was essential and what would be "cool," what the business absolutely required, what would give us an edge or merely allow us to keep up. Then I would have to explain this to non-technical people, like senior management, lawyers, and accountants, each of whom had their own concerns. I got great satisfaction from writing business plans or justifications for spending such enormous sums of money that conveyed to many audiences the technical and business conditions driving the request, and getting them approved!

One thing about communication skills: a natural offshoot for me is enhanced respect for people. Where I worked, if I wanted to be effective, I really had to understand conceptually, if not in detail, what the technical people were doing, what they needed, what their roadblocks were, and so on. So I really had to listen. I had to care. I paid attention. I asked questions. I respected these guys for what they knew and what they did. And I was respected in return.

Owner, Marketing and Advertising Agency

Robert Colleluori

I asked Robert Colleluori to talk a bit about the many types of work he does in his position as a company owner and as an active citizen. Here are some of his thoughts:

It's a life in progress. It will never be finished, never stop until the day we die—and then is life really over when we die? The question I always ask myself, "Is life complete for me?" I'm always searching for something else, something more. I know it's out there, but where and when will I find it? Don't get me wrong, if I died this minute, I would not be feeling like I didn't do anything or get anywhere. I just don't feel like I'm finished contributing to my life's work.

Many don't ever venture into owning their own business and taking the risk. Is it the right business for me? Well, it feels right. It gives me a venue to do the artistic things I like to do. It helps others who can't do what we do to get the service they need. It's different all the time. It provides flexibility and the ability to make decisions that are right for my family and me. I'm very committed and responsible, but I have flexibility when I need it. And, if I can be providing a valuable service at the same time, it works. Is it the be-all and end-all? Not for me. I'm not sure what that is yet. Maybe it's the artist in me. Or maybe I just get bored too easily.

I don't really remember my parents specifically saying "what do you want to become when you grow up?" I do remember at one point thinking about becoming a dentist. How that faded away, I don't remember. I do remember that I could be punished and sent to my room and it didn't faze me. I would find something of interest to occupy the time, even building a sculpture out of the bed sheets. You see they weren't only sheets for a bed to lie down on and cover yourself with. They could be used for a million things. I would think about all of the possibilities to use those sheets. A tent, a lifesaving rope or tourniquet, add glue and make a harder form of some kind, a protective cover, etc. etc. etc. There are so many possibilities for all things; you just have to imagine them and explore them.

My life is very full. I think it always was, from the time I was a child. I was always involved in church activities, school projects, shows, household projects; I always had something going. Loved to watch things unfold and become something else. Marveled over a pile of building supplies and what they could become—and being a part of making them become something other than the piece of wood or glue or nail. If you explore enough, research enough, are open enough to accept change, new and different ways, you will know what is right and what is a true part of your soul. To do so, you need to be open-minded. Open to hearing and listening. And, open to doing something about it. Open to RISK.

I guess that's how my community involvement started. Had backyard carnivals as kids in Wildwood to raise money for Cancer, sat on a float in a Trenton Parade, dropped off donation envelopes door to door and collected them. The point is it felt right for me to serve others. That's continued in my business and in my work outside of my business.

Geologist

Eric Engle

In the many conversations about the professions that I've been having, I had the opportunity to speak with Eric Engle, a man who revels in the joys of science. Eric is a geologist with a company that evaluates land before it is developed. He too changed majors many times, beginning college with the goal of becoming an aeronautical engineer ("I just loved planes and rockets, and my dream job was with Lockheed"), a civil engineer, a geographer, and finally, a geologist. Eric found his way to geology through a general education course that introduced him to the subject area. Before that, though always intrigued by rocks and other aspects of the physical world ("I was a science geek"), Eric "didn't see it as a career."

Eric is intrigued by many facets of his work, and always has been. "I always loved tracking things, reading field guides, keeping charts, and evaluating data. I just seemed to be good at taking notes and using the information to draw conclusions—which is just what I do in my present job." Eric attributes many of these characteristics to his father, "who was a technically-oriented thinker too," and his Uncle Bill, who is now a professor of physical sciences. Eric remembers learning from these two influences ways to read instruments and maps and finding the practical applications of mathematics. He also remembers other teachers, like his seventh-grade teacher, Mr. Coltrane, who helped nurture Eric's love of astronomy—a love that continues today. In fact, on any given night, you're likely to find Eric out in his yard with his telescope or waiting for satellites to appear in the night sky.

All of those early influences have served Eric in a job that he couldn't imagine specifically at the time—mostly because he didn't know it existed. As an environmental geologist, Eric spends a good deal of his time just where you would have expected this child to end up—out in nature. On the other hand, Eric's not just playing scientist any longer. He performs studies of land and water to help developers to make judgments about whether a lot is suitable to its proposed use. In that position, Eric needs not only his ability to collect data but also his skill in making subjective (but informed) decisions from that data. In all these ways, Eric has found a way to use those skills and interests that were originally just the impulses of a young boy toward finding a satisfying life's work.

Writing Application

As the previous examples suggest, the relationship between education and work is not as simple as being trained for a particular job. In what ways can education prepare you for a career? In what ways must you adapt and restructure what you learn to particular work situations? What seem to be the most important things that workers have taken from their education? In what ways have they been surprised by what it means to have a career?

Drawing on the thoughts of the discussed workers, and perhaps using interviews with other people you know that have established a career path, write an essay that redefines what it *really* means to have a career or a life's work, and how college can help you to prepare for that life's work. Write this essay for your fellow college students in order to help them to think more broadly about their career plans as well as what they might seek to gain from their education. You might structure your essay like this: "We might think that we go to college just to gather information for the work we will do, but real workers help us to understand that it is much more complicated than that in the following ways."

Case 3 REFLECTING ON INTERESTS AND TALENTS

Though considering your life's work is very much about your future, it sometimes involves looking into the past as well to trace the ways in which your particular talents, skills, and interests were developed. In this casebook, you'll have the chance to read the stories of others doing just that—considering how they found the set of interests that engaged them in their present occupations or fields of study.

Writing to Respond

Read over these essays, and then freewrite on the following topics:

- Do the individuals in these essays seem to share any characteristics?
- What motivates them?
- What types of activities or decisions seem to have stimulated them toward finding their own talents and skills, or using them most effectively?
- How do personal talents, skills, and interests seem to show themselves?

The Amateur Scientist

Richard Feynman

Richard Feynman (1918–1988), a Nobel Prize–winning physicist, was well known for his ability to communicate with a wide audience through his accessible and personal writing style, which made him a celebrity as well as a brilliant scientist. He also attained a great deal of attention due to his contributions to the investigation of the Challenger space shuttle disaster. He obtained his B.Sc. from Massachusetts Institute of Technology and Ph.D. from Princeton University. He taught physics at Princeton, Cornell University, and the California Institute of Technology. His popular publications include *The Pleasure of Finding Things Out* and *Surely You're Joking, Mr. Feynman,* from which the following essay is taken.

When I was a kid I had a "lab." It wasn't a laboratory in the sense that I would measure, or do important experiments. Instead, I would play: I'd make a motor, I'd make a gadget that would go off when something passed a photocell. I'd play around with selenium: I was piddling around all the time. I did calculate a little bit for the lamp bank, a series of switches and bulbs I used as resistors to control voltages. But all that was for application. I never did any laboratory kind of experiments.

I also had a microscope and *loved* to watch things under the microscope. It took patience: I would get something under the microscope and I would watch it interminably. I saw many interesting things, like everybody sees—a diatom slowly making its way across the slide, and so on.

One day I was watching a paramecium and I saw something that was not described in the books I got in school—in college, even. These books always simplify things so the world will be more like *they* want it to be: When they're talking about the behavior of animals, they always start out with, "The paramecium is extremely simple: it has a simple behavior. It turns as its slipper shape moves through the water until it hits something, at which time it recoils, turns through an angle, and then starts out again."

It isn't really right. First of all, as everybody knows, the paramecia, from time to time, conjugate with each other—they meet and exchange nuclei. How do they decide when it's time to do that? (Never mind; that's not my observation.)

I watched these paramecia hit something, recoil, turn through an angle, and go again. The idea that it's mechanical, like a computer program—it doesn't look that way. They go different distances, they recoil different distances, they turn through angles that are different in various cases; they don't always turn to the right; they're very irregular. It looks random, because you don't know what they're hitting; you don't know all the chemicals they're smelling, or what.

One of the things I wanted to watch was what happens to the paramecium when the water that it's in dries up. It was claimed that the paramecium can dry up into a sort of hardened seed. I had a drop of water on the slide under my microscope, and in the drop of water was a paramecium and some "grass"—at the scale of the paramecium, it looked like a network of jackstraws. As the drop of water evaporated, over a time of fifteen or twenty minutes, the paramecium got into a tighter and tighter situation: there was more and more of this back-and-forth until it could hardly move. It was stuck between these "sticks," almost jammed.

Then I saw something I had never seen or heard of: the paramecium lost its shape. It could flex itself, like an amoeba. It began to push itself against one of the sticks, and began dividing into two prongs until the division was about halfway up the paramecium, at which time it decided *that* wasn't a very good idea, and backed away.

So my impression of these animals is that their behavior is much too simplified in the books. It is not so utterly mechanical or one-dimensional as they say. They should describe the behavior of these simple animals correctly. Until we see how many dimensions of behavior even a one-celled animal has, we won't be able to fully understand the behavior of more complicated animals.

I also enjoyed watching bugs. I had an insect book when I was about thirteen. It said that dragonflies are not harmful; they don't sting. In our neighborhood it was well known that "darning needles," as we called them, were very dangerous when they'd sting. So if we were outside somewhere playing baseball, or something, and one of these things would fly around, everybody would run for cover, waving their arms, yelling, "A darning needle! A darning needle!"

So one day I was on the beach, and I'd just read this book that said dragonflies don't sting. A darning needle came along, and everybody was screaming and running around, and I just sat there. "Don't worry!" I said. "Darning needles don't sting!"

The thing landed on my foot. Everybody was yelling and it was a big mess, because this darning needle was sitting on my foot. And there I was, this scientific wonder, saying it wasn't going to sting me.

You're *sure* this is a story that's going to come out that it stings me—but it didn't. The book was right. But I did sweat a bit.

I also had a little hand microscope. It was a toy microscope, and I pulled the magnification piece out of it, and would hold it in my hand like a magnifying glass, even though it was a microscope of forty or fifty power. With care you could hold the focus. So I could go around and look at things right out in the street.

When I was in graduate school at Princeton, I once took it out of my pocket to look at some ants that were crawling around on some ivy. I had to exclaim out loud, I was so excited. What I saw was an ant and an aphid, which ants take care of—they carry them from plant to plant if the plant they're on is dying. In return the ants get partially digested aphid juice, called "honeydew." I knew that; my father had told me about it, but I had never seen it.

So here was this aphid and sure enough, an ant came along, and patted it with its feet—all around the aphid, pat, pat, pat, pat, pat. This was terribly exciting! Then the juice came out of the back of the aphid. And because it was magnified, it looked like a big, beautiful, glistening ball, like a balloon, because of the surface tension. Because the microscope wasn't very good, the drop was colored a little bit from chromatic aberration in the lens—it was a gorgeous thing!

The ant took this ball in its two front feet, lifted it off the aphid, and *held* it. The world is so different at that scale that you can pick up water and hold it! The ants probably have a fatty or greasy material on their legs that doesn't break the surface tension of the water when they hold it up. Then the ant broke the surface of the drop with its mouth, and the surface tension collapsed the drop right into his gut. It was *very* interesting to see this whole thing happen!

In my room at Princeton I had a bay window with a U-shaped windowsill. One day some ants came out on the windowsill and wandered around a little bit. I got curious as to how they found things. I wondered, how do they know where to go? Can they tell each other where food is, like bees can? Do they have any sense of geometry?

This is all amateurish; everybody knows the answer, but *I* didn't know the answer, so the first thing I did was to stretch some string across the U of the bay window and hang a piece of folded cardboard with sugar on it from the string. The idea of this was to isolate the sugar from the ants, so they wouldn't find it accidentally. I wanted to have everything under control.

Next I made a lot of little strips of paper and put a fold in them, so I could pick up ants and ferry them from one place to another. I put the folded strips of paper in two places: Some were by the sugar (hanging from the string), and the others were near the ants in a particular location. I sat there all afternoon, reading and watching, until an ant happened to walk onto one of my little paper ferries. Then I took him over to the sugar. After a few ants had been ferried over to the sugar, one of them accidentally walked onto one of the ferries nearby, and I carried him back.

I wanted to see how long it would take the other ants to get the message to go to the "ferry terminal." It started slowly, but rapidly increased until I was going mad ferrying the ants back and forth.

But suddenly, when everything was going strong, I began to deliver the ants from the sugar to a *different* spot. The question now was, does the ant learn to go back to where it just came from, or does it go where it went the time before?

After a while there were practically no ants going to the first place (which would take them to the sugar), whereas there were many ants at the second place, milling around, trying to find the sugar. So I figured out so far that they went where they just came from.

In another experiment. I laid out a lot of glass microscope slides and got the ants to walk on them, back and forth, to some sugar I put on the windowsill. Then, by replacing an old slide with a new one, or by rearranging the slides, I could demonstrate that the ants had no sense of geometry: they couldn't figure out where something was. If they went to the sugar one way, and there was a shorter way back, they would never figure out the short way.

It was also pretty clear from rearranging the glass slides that the ants left some sort of trail. So then came a lot of easy experiments to find out how long it takes a trail to dry up, whether it can be easily wiped off, and so on. I also found out the trail wasn't directional. If I'd pick up an ant on a piece of paper, turn him around and around, and then put him back onto the trail, he wouldn't know that he was going the wrong way until he met another ant. (Later, in Brazil, I noticed some leaf-cutting ants and tried the same experiment on them. They *could* tell, within a few steps, whether they were going toward the food or away from it—presumably from the trail, which might be a series of smells in a pattern: A, B, space, A, B, space, and so on.)

I tried at one point to make the ants go around in a circle, but I didn't have enough patience to set it up. I could see no reason, other than lack of patience, why it couldn't be done.

One thing that made experimenting difficult was that breathing on the ants made them scurry. It must be an instinctive thing against some animal that eats them or disturbs them. I don't know if it was the warmth, the moisture, or the smell of my breath that bothered them, but I always had to hold my breath and kind of look to one side so as not to confuse the experiment while I was ferrying the ants.

One question that I wondered about was why the ant trails look so straight and nice. The ants look as if they know what they're doing, as if they have a good sense of geometry. Yet the experiments that I did to try to demonstrate their sense of geometry didn't work.

Many years later, when I was at Caltech and lived in a little house on Alameda Street, some ants came out around the bathtub. I thought, "This is a great opportunity," I put some sugar on the other end of the bathtub, and sat there the whole afternoon until an ant finally found the sugar. It's only a question of patience.

The moment the ant found the sugar, I picked up a colored pencil that I had ready (I had previously done experiments indicating that the ants don't give a damn about pencil marks—they walk right over them—so I knew I wasn't disturbing anything), and behind where the ant went I drew a line so I could tell where his trail was. The ant wandered a little bit wrong to get back to the hole, so the line was quite wiggly, unlike a typical ant trail.

When the next ant to find the sugar began to go back, I marked his trail with another color. (By the way, he followed the first ant's return trail back, rather than his own incoming trail. My theory is that when an ant has found some food, he leaves a much stronger trail than when he's just wandering around.)

This second ant was in a great hurry and followed, pretty much, the original trail. But because he was going so fast he would go straight out, as if he were coasting, when the trail was wiggly. Often, as the ant was "coasting," he would find the trail again. Already it was apparent that the second ant's return was slightly straighter. With successive ants the same "improvement" of the trail by hurriedly and carelessly "following" it occurred.

I followed eight or ten ants with my pencil until their trails became a neat line right along the bathtub. It's something like sketching: You draw a lousy line at first; then you go over it a few times and it makes a nice line after a while.

I remember that when I was a kid my father would tell me how wonderful ants are, and how they cooperate. I would watch very carefully three or four ants carrying a little piece of chocolate back to their nest. At first glance it looks like efficient, marvelous, brilliant cooperation. But if you look at it carefully, you'll see that it's nothing of the kind: They're all behaving as if the chocolate is held up by something else. They pull at it one way or the other way. An ant may crawl over it while it's being pulled at by the others. It wobbles, it wiggles, the directions are all confused. The chocolate doesn't move in a nice way toward the nest.

The Brazilian leaf-cutting ants, which are otherwise so marvelous, have a very interesting stupidity associated with them that I'm surprised hasn't evolved out. It takes considerable work for the ant to cut the circular arc in order to get a piece of leaf. When the cutting is done, there's a fifty-fifty chance that the ant will pull on the wrong side, letting the piece he just cut fall to the ground. Half the time, the ant will yank and pull and yank and pull on the wrong part of the leaf, until it gives up and starts to cut another piece. There is no attempt to pick up a piece that it, or any other ant, has already cut. So it's quite obvious, if you watch very carefully, that it's not a brilliant business of cutting leaves and carrying them away; they go to a leaf, cut an arc, and pick the wrong side half the time while the right piece falls down.

In Princeton the ants found my larder, where I had jelly and bread and stuff, which was quite a distance from the window. A long line of ants marched along the floor across the living room. It was during the time I was doing these experiments on the ants, so I thought to myself, "What can I do to stop them from coming to my larder without killing any ants? No poison; you gotta be humane to the ants!"

What I did was this: In preparation, I put a bit of sugar about six or eight inches from their entry point into the room, that they didn't know about. Then I made those ferry things again, and whenever an ant returning with food walked onto my little ferry, I'd carry him over and put him on the sugar. Any ant coming toward the larder that walked onto a ferry I also carried over to the sugar. Eventually the ants found their way from the sugar to their hole, so this new trail was being doubly reinforced, while the old trail was being used less and less. I knew that after half an hour or so the old trail would dry up, and in an hour they were out of my larder. I didn't wash the floor; I didn't do anything but ferry ants.

Science: Choosing a Life of Reasoning

Emylee McFarland

When Emylee McFarland wrote the following essay, she was a junior biology major with a minor in English. Her studies bridge the gap between the sciences and humanities, and have allowed her to hone her dual interests in the arts (including the art of writing) and biology. This essay, which recounts her decision to "choose a life of reasoning," was written for a class in interdisciplinary writing.

Science has been a consistent presence in life. My parents were both in science, but I've no recollection of them pushing me in that direction. However, I gained a general respect for the discipline and a mental picture of myself as a scientist. Instinctively I reasoned as a scientist would. This influenced how I played sports and approached my concentration, dance and music, in high school. All these disciplines require patience and repetitive practice.

As a child I visited my Dad's lab. Complicated-looking glassware cluttered the lab benches, all with mysterious purposes. This quiet lab also included a wall of windows over looking a wooded park. Here, problems were solved and for a break you could take a hike. They seemed to go together very nicely.

As a young child I developed a deep respect for nature and wanted to learn more about it. In Girl Scouts I was always the one that wanted to get my hands dirty. I was excited when we got to dissect a cow's eye during a science center camp-in. Driven by curiosity, I loved poking and prying. Mostly I think I enjoyed finding out how to do something, doing it, and reasoning how to do it better. Elementary school gave me a first chance to do this as an Odyssey of the Mind team member. As a team we reasoned and then put our ideas into action to complete the long-term problem. Spontaneous brainstorming of answers was the other part of these competitions, and coming up with creative answers is still one of my favorite things to do.

The moment that I really knew I would do what it took to be in science came during my senior year of high school. I had arrived at the goal to be a veterinarian because I enjoyed animals and solving problems. So I became a veterinary technician at a teaching emergency animal hospital. A hit-by-car cat came in and I was the assisting tech for the vet. I watched as the doctor used reasoning to assess the injuries suffered and the overall state of health of the cat. Without verbal exchange she watched and carefully checked the cat. I can't even tell you what happened to the cat. I simply remember vividly watching the silent connection and care, and it was beautiful. I reasoned that if I could reason and solve problems while helping an animal I could be happy.

The decision to study science has and is very difficult. I was good at dancing, writing, making music, and teaching. However, science has always been a struggle. Family, friends, and teachers reasoned with me to teach or go into the arts. Not just because I would have been less stressed but because those are the disciplines that I could make contributions to. I've faced learning disabilities that, although recognized five years ago, are still not conquered. I failed tests and studied harder for years before I would be treated for depression. Ironically, I only kept going because I left reasoning behind and rationalized that I would be happiest in a biological profession. I can't seem to convince myself that I would be better off with my hobbies as my job.

Science also excites me. I know that I could never be bored as a scientist because there is more information available than I could ever hope to know. The deeper I delve into the discipline, the more magnificent it seems. One cell is the starting point that grows and changes into life, and thousands of chemical reactions are constantly taking place in our bodies. This always sounded magnificent, but understanding how it happens takes it to a new level for me.

As a scientist I constantly reason each side of a situation. Valid or not, every possibility is researched. The ability to be rational and not subjective becomes a part of your character. When solving a problem I feel like I can escape into the discipline. My shortcomings become insignificant when compared to the world of animals. Judgment takes a back seat to answers whose statistics are accepted. Science also makes things clear and simple. Questions as to what should or shouldn't be done don't have to be tackled. We just try to understand how things work. The relationship between all life does not have to be labeled good or bad because we just want to understand it.

Although they are few and far between, I have experienced moments of success. When a problem is solved correctly and your comprehension of something is verified, it is very inspiring. You are that much closer to seeing the big picture, and you have another piece of information that will help you reason your next answer. Recently my study of organic chemistry has reinforced all the reasoning that got me here. I am seeing myself learning to think more critically and abstractly, using each piece of learned material to solve or clarify things. It takes me a long time to learn things but is incredibly satisfying to watch oneself learn and build. I also have two cats that inspire me. When I see them, I long to understand the details of the relationships that bring me joy.

Science includes so many details that must be reasoned with. Discovery of these details will keep me happy forever. Through reasoning about my discipline I have learned invaluable things about myself. My future in science is still unknown. I want to complete graduate studies, work outdoors, build relationships with animals, and never stop learning. Eventually I would like to write about science. I would love to write in a way that would make everyone appreciate science. Science has given me a profession as well as a way to understand others and myself through constant reasoning.

Beyond the Wardrobe and above the Bar

Christina Jaffe

Christina Jaffe is an elementary school teacher with a strong interest in social and political issues. She has presented her work on the importance of civic writing at a statewide English conference, and is interested in the work of Paolo Freire, Bob Dylan, and other liberatory thinkers. She was a college senior when she wrote this essay, and she used it to reflect on the ways that her education led her to the pleasures of reading, learning, and thinking—what she calls her "adventures in literacy."

Somewhere between one book and another a child's passive acceptance had slipped away from me also. I could no longer see the world's array as a backdrop to my private play, a dull,

*neutral backdrop about which I had learned all I needed to
know. I had been chipping away at the world idly and had by
accident uncovered vast and labyrinthine further worlds within
it. I peered in one day, stepped in the next and soon wandered
in deep over my head. Month after month, year after year, the
true and brilliant light, and the complex and multifaceted col-
oration, of this actual, historical, waking world invigorated me.*
—Annie Dillard, *An American Childhood*

Madonna is not yet a pop princess, Evita, or a mother, but the Material Girl.
Time is a concept made fathomable by measuring it in increments of *The Cosby
Show.* My brother Rod sings me "The Gambler," which is the only song he
knows, but it does nicely for a lullaby. My brother Matt approaches adolescence
by oddly coming to resemble his heroes, MacGyver and Michael J. Fox. It is the
1980s. My parents are probably arguing downstairs, because that is what they
do. But I listen beyond them to outside, where next door I hear the sounds of
an Italian restaurant/bar. Within live Angie and Lisa Butera, and their small children. There is Mr. Butera senior who calls my father Lorenzo, which annoys my
father, but amuses me. It is loud out there each night, beyond my bedroom window, but they are shouts of jubilation: baseball scores, promises of rematches,
good-nights to departing friends, laughter, car doors, and crickets. These were
my own Italian arias. It was pasta. It was pizzelles. It was poetry.

I think that listening to the activity of our neighbors provided endless "scope
to my imagination," as dear Anne of Green Gables preferred to call it. In
remembering the merry souls and patrons of The Graterford Hotel, I wonder if
perhaps that is where *the story* begins. Lying in bed I went to sleep each night
working on a novel in my head, picturing the lives of characters employed at a
NYC diner: Katherine the shy waitress, the crotchety Cook, the matronly waitress Maddy, and the mysterious busboy Cary. Inseparable from my own storytelling was the literate, rich environment provided by my parents. Together
these experiences led to my perception of myself as a writer.

The setting of much of my childhood was an assortment of libraries. My father
worked as a junior high librarian while teaching library science first at Villanova and
then the University of Delaware. Visits to his school after hours meant my sister
and I could take home the new bookmarks or check out selections from the book
fair. On Sundays my mother helped out as the librarian at our church, where each
week she signed the card to help me check out *Dorcas Sews for Others.* The
Schwenksville library was closest to our house; I believe it was there in basement
dance class that I first discovered my inherent lack of rhythm. The Norristown
library meant locking our car doors and browsing the children's section to the

sound of sirens. There the librarians kindly found me the "Shoe" books by Noel Streatfield that I wanted. Cupcake resided at my elementary school library. A kind puppet canine, she came out of her box to warn us of the perils of not washing our hands before we opened the volumes we clung too. I read about a pink sea monster called Serendipity, and the morals of a bear clan of the name Berenstain. I adopted the incantation from the heroine of the "Alice in Bible-Land" series: "Reading is the magic key that takes you where you want to be."

Amongst the books at Villanova flitted these fascinating creatures in blue, white, and black habits. They presided over holiday parties where my sister and I had the indescribable experience of competing with *the sisters* in party games such as musical chairs and the egg-on-the-spoon relay. From then on, when I spotted a similarly dressed woman in public, I would exclaim "Look, a librarian!" My father brought home *Newsweek* and *Time* for us to read. My mother read to us before we went to bed, and then when we were older, the scenario reversed itself. Those minutes before sleep were reserved for passages of the Bible or tales of the noble Aslan and the land of winter beyond the wardrobe in *The Chronicles of Narnia*.

I emerged from those biblio-ravages in my coming of age years and I was a writer. I'm not sure it is possible to fully describe how it happened, but I do know that my parents' preference for library cards over credit cards made an indelible impression.

Somewhere along the way I think my sister and I perceived that it was more socially acceptable to be journalists than writers, in the fiction-writing, living in a NYC garret, poor as a church-mouse sense of the word. I made that my career aspiration, but with the secret wish of writing fiction. The occasional seething editorial aside, I learned soon that journalism for all its intriguing aspects was not what I scribbled in the margins of my notes and across page after page of journals. I can still remember the time my dad introduced us to his boss as future journalists. The poor man remarked that we could be the next Anne and Abby Landers, which was probably a nod to our being twins. My sister and I thought his remark sexist and politely shot him withering looks of scorn when he had rounded the corner. Besides reading with us and surrounding us with books, my parents often welcomed us into their conversations with other grown-ups. Teacher gathering after teacher gathering, my sister and I—the crown princesses of precocity— would find our way into the fascinating twists and turns of adult discussion. Language in any form proved addictive, and we satisfied our cravings by reading *Huckleberry Finn* as we faced backwards in the blue station wagon or trying to contribute to a grown-up conversation on Dan Quayle or the Exxon oil spill.

Madonna is still around and still re-inventing herself, but the new torch-bearers are only slightly past adolescence, and seem to be mass produced and assembled from some factory for the purposes of consuming hair care products and selling Pepsi.

I now continue to watch public television after "this show was brought to you by...."

My brother sings "The Gambler" to his son, but he now knows lots of lullabies, and even how to make up his own. Welcome to the 21st century. It is years later and my sister and I have acquired new nicknames from our beloved 12th grade English teacher: the Bronte sisters. We glow. I still sometimes feel like a child lingering over the ice bucket to hear the grown-ups discuss politics. I know that when I can't help but chime in that it won't seem as strange and wonderful as it used to when boldness found safety in youth.

The story of who I am and who I am becoming is very much bound in these early adventures in literacy. Early on I found language both magical and powerful. I decided to teach so I could help children open their own worlds with words. All of my passions—politics, education, writing, reading—revolve around the impact language had on those formative experiences of growing. Reading led to writing, and writing enabled me not to escape the more painful realities of childhood, but to have the courage to envision them better. The world of books was not a better world but one which *could* be. Being a writer for me is having a particularly awkward date and consoling myself with the thought, "This would make a great Woody Allen script." It is living a beautiful moment and thinking simultaneously, "What will this moment look like later in words?" Vita Sackville-West said to write is "to clap the net over the butterfly of the moment." I think writers are like children collecting fireflies in a glass jar. We let them go in the shadows of dusk, but fall asleep with the memory of glowing jars. I still find libraries to be this safe place, with nooks of wonder, a place where nuns can compete ruthlessly for packages of Pepperidge Farm cookies, and the world of my parents can become real. My writing is what enables me to still be wandering in the lands beyond the wardrobe and above the bar in this my 21st year.

Thought and Innocence

James Bowman

James Bowman, when he wrote the following essay, was a sophomore humanities major concentrating on the study of philosophy. In this essay he explores the ways in which curiosity formed for him the linchpin in what Plato called the "examined life." Both his childhood and his chosen major illustrate the ways in which "just thinking about things" led him to the study of philosophy.

As a child, I enjoyed all of the various activities that are typically associated with young boys. I collected bugs, traded baseball cards, and played kickball or hide-and-go-seek with my friends. I rode my bike all over the neighborhood, and watched television, and took walks to the neighborhood pharmacy to buy candy. However, my favorite pastime is one that I have not outgrown since childhood; I always liked to think.

When I wasn't running around with my sister or the neighborhood kids, I liked to find some quiet place where I could spend time alone. I scaled the neatly stacked firewood and pulled myself on top of the tool shed in the back yard, where I lay on my back for hours. I used that time to ponder over many of the seemingly magical things that exist in the world as it is seen through the eyes of a kid. Soon, I lost the ability to distinguish between the vast sky and myself.

"What are you doing?" my mother asked me one day while I was in silent contemplation. In retrospect, she may have been concerned about the amount of time her son was spending in solitude.

"Oh, I'm just thinkin' about things," I replied matter-of-factly.

Curious as to what kind of "things" a three- or four-year-old child might have to think about, my mother then asked, "What kind of 'things'?"

Indeed, this was a question that deserved an answer. What was in my virginal mind that begged such lengthy pondering? I didn't have the vocabulary to explain to her that birds were able to fly through the air, and I wanted to know their secret so that I could fly too. How could I make her understand that when I stared at a cloud long enough it seemed to lower itself toward the earth as if drawn by my gaze, and I longed to touch one someday? I just knew that, if I thought about it for long enough, I could reason out some way to accomplish these feats.

With all of these observations and questions rolling through my mind at once I could not think of any way to sum it all up to Mother. "You know," I finally said dreamily, "just things." Somewhat bewildered, my mother left me to my thoughts in peace. My mother tells me that, though I could barely shape the letters to make a word—let alone compose a whole sentence!—I had a journal in which I wrote my thoughts and discoveries every night before bed. Eventually, I would drift off to sleep with the wonders of the world still whirling in my tiny head.

Soon enough, the world was in many ways demystified. No longer a child, I began to accept many of the fundamentals of our world. Flight was for birds and clouds would always be out of reach, so I resigned myself to a life on the ground. Much of my awe of the world immediately around me faded with experience. Still, there were questions pending, and I was fortunate enough to receive the encouragement to ask them.

My entire life has been spent trying to reason out some sort of answer or solution to that which is elusive in life. I wanted to remove the veil that left all of the secrets of the universe silhouetted and out of reach, but I never thought of myself as a philosopher. I have always liked to think, but never thought of actually becoming a certified thinker. It was my mother, knowing me better than I know myself, who suggested that I take an introductory course in philosophy. Once in the class I found myself again being swept away with the same wonderment that I possessed as a child. For the first time in my adult life, it seemed clear to me what I wanted to be when I grow up.

Of course, I know that all answers lead to new questions. Those new questions sometimes lead to more specific answers, but the chain of questions and answers is infinite. In the end, I am certain that I will have found little more by way of absolute truth than I had as a child. However, I feel the search is necessary in order to develop conviction, if only in lack of understanding. In the end, I am simply happy to be thinking about things. You know, just things.

Writing Application

Now that you've read other people's stories, it's your turn to consider your own talents and past experiences. If you've decided on a major, think about why you might have come to that field and the careers that it opens to you. If you're undecided, use this as a chance to consider what fields might fit best with your own talents and interests. Or, if you are a returning student, you might write about some of your on-the-job experiences and how they led you to consider further education. Write a narrative that describes a process of discovery, or perhaps a particular moment, that helped you to find your passion for a subject area, for a possible career field, or for a particular type of work. Show how that commitment developed and how deeply it helps to define who you are.

Use whatever style and structure that you think would fit the situation you are describing. You can either use a narrative style like the essays above, or, if you are more comfortable with it, use an essay format. In order to generate ideas for your piece, you might first use some of the inventional techniques discussed in Chapter 2.

Case 4 IMAGINING OCCUPATIONAL *ETHOS* THROUGH JOB DESCRIPTIONS

Because the primary purpose of job ads is to attract qualified individuals to the placing organization, such ads can be a useful way to learn about the work done by professionals in the field and the work done by specific companies. The ads are constructed carefully to describe not only the skills required but also to envision what a successful employee will bring to that position.

Writing to Respond

Read over the following job descriptions, adapted from actual job postings, and choose one or more that you find interesting. In your writer's notebook, write a brief interpretation of each, noting what the ad seems to indicate are the most important characteristics of someone doing this job—that is, some elements of the *ethos* of a person well suited for the position. Though some of the technical requirements of the jobs might be unfamiliar to you, you might also describe the types of educational experiences that seem to be primary in one's qualifications for such a job. Describe, in your own words and in as much detail as possible, the type of person the job seems to require.

Staffing Manager

Join one of the country's top personnel firms, located in Northern California. We're looking for motivated candidates with experience in the accounting or staffing industries. Excellent oral and written communication skills a must. Joining our team will allow you to work with some of the best in the business and give you the opportunity to increase your income through initiative and hard work.

Do you have:

- Experience in business fields?
- Excellent communication and organizational skills?
- The ability and desire to relocate to California?
- A motivated and self-driven desire to succeed?
- A desire to increase your earnings?
- An ability to work well with others?

If you can answer yes to these questions, then you should give us a call—today!

Analytical Chemist

We are currently in search of a highly motivated and independent candidate for the position of Analytical Chemist at a rapidly growing biomaterials and medical device company in Seattle, Washington.

Job Description: The Analytical Chemist must have hands-on experience in various analytical and instrumental methods.

Duties and Responsibilities: (in no particular order of importance)

- Quality Control of raw materials and finished product according to PTG Quality Systems protocols.

- Experience in Research & Development activities.
- Experience in industry research methodology.
- Experience with basic repair and maintenance of test equipment.
- Technical writing of reports and procedures (including revisions).
- Ability to keep PTG confidential laboratory notebooks current.
- Experience with calibration of instruments.
- Ability to develop and implement new test methods as required.

Secondary Duties:
- Attend training programs as needed.
- Inventory supplies and chemicals for lab.

Bachelor's Degree in Chemistry required.

Mortgage Processor

Needed for reviewing applications. This position will not have any customer contact. Responsibilities include fact-checking applications, preparing paperwork for settlements, and managing escrow payments and out-of-closing payments. Bachelor's degree in Accounting preferred. Experience helpful.

Entry-Level Manager, Testing Service

About our Company:

Our nationally based franchises have helped prepare students for a variety of standardized tests for the past 40 years. With offices and classrooms throughout the country, we prepare students for over 25 different standardized tests, including entrance exams for secondary school, college, and law school, as well as teacher licensing exams. We offer both classroom review sessions and private tutoring.

We are searching for an entry-level Manager based in suburban Pittsburgh, Pennsylvania.

Responsibilities:
- Hiring, training, and supervision of staff and teachers
- Managing specific shifts within the test center
- Assisting with bookkeeping and accounting procedures
- Promoting the center through advertising
- Occasionally teaching or tutoring, as necessary
- Delivering presentations to prospective students in area schools and businesses

Requirements:

- Bachelor's degree
- Solid organization and planning skills
- Attention to detail
- Team motivation abilities
- Marketing and customer service abilities
- Problem-solving, decision-making, and management skills
- Ability to work independently
- High energy level and ability to thrive in a fast-paced environment
- Ability to work during days, evenings, and weekends when required

Human Resources Generalist

Position available for a Human Resources Generalist who wishes to be part of our growing HR team. The generalist is responsible for monitoring and reporting any issues relating to employees to the proper management officials. The successful candidate should be ready to work closely with employees of the firm.

Job responsibilities will include: Generating reports for the HR manager relating to all HR issues; preparing and implementing employee surveys, questionnaires, and satisfaction interviews; remaining actively involved with employees to assure questions and concerns are being addressed; keeping current on issues and concerns related to the work environment; implementing procedure and policy of the firm; making certain all employment regulations are met; supplying information and forms to all employees; acting as a resource to the recruiting and training managers, acting as a liaison between area managers and their employees to resolve conflicts, maintaining workers' compensation files and managing claims, participating in new employee orientation; managing, tracing, and trending personnel data.

The ideal candidate will have a bachelor's degree, two or more years of experience in HR management, proficiency with the PeopleSoft HRIS system, knowledge of federal and state employment laws, benefits and payroll knowledge, and strong interpersonal and communication skills.

Security Specialist

Position available for a Security Specialist within a growing global organization. Security Specialist will assist with design and modification of security systems, investigations, and other issues on an as-needed basis. Candidates for our security teams must undergo a background check and have no criminal record.

Essential Duties and Responsibilities:

▓ 40%: Perform security reviews at select business locations globally.

▓ 25%: Prepare written reports with findings and recommendations.

▓ 25%: Assist in security awareness programs and policy development for each site.

▓ 10%: Assist in the design and modification of existing security systems.

Position Requirements:

Education: Bachelor's degree in Criminal Justice or related field

Preferred Attributes and Experience:

▓ 2–3 years' security experience

▓ Impeccable background and high ethical standards

▓ Excellent oral and written communication skills

▓ Knowledge of industry standards in security practices and systems

▓ Knowledge and experience in conducting investigations

▓ Working knowledge of PC applications including Microsoft Word and Excel

▓ Ability to travel 15 days per month

Fitness Professional

Opportunity available for fitness professional to lead the development and coordination of new Health and Fitness Center programs. As the Fitness Manager you will be responsible for developing programs that can help our members to achieve their fitness goals. You will also provide continuous training and educational opportunities for both clients and staff.

You will also be expected to help keep our fitness center at a state-of-the-art level. Currently, the facility conducts personal fitness assessments and training, with three swimming pools, a spa, track cardiovascular/weight equipment, and child care center.

Qualifications:

▓ Bachelor's degree in exercise science, exercise physiology, physical education, or related field

▓ ACSM or NSCA certification preferred

▓ Two years of staff supervisory experience in a health club environment

Wilderness Youth Counselor

Open spaces, fresh air, and the sky above: You won't find them in a 9–5 job! But as a wilderness-experience counselor, your office is the wild. You'll live year-round in one of the most beautiful natural locations in the western United States. Hiking, canoeing, sleeping in the open air. Does that sound like you?

And here's the best part: At the same time, you'll be helping at-risk kids learn how to dream about and plan their future.

Job Type: Full time/Live in

Purpose: The youth counselor works full time/year round and supervises a group of 7–10 at-risk youth 24 hours a day at a wilderness camp. Primary responsibilities are to ensure group members are safe, engage in positive activities, and developing useful life strategies.

Activities: Daily activities vary, but can include hiking, backpacking, low and high ropes work, outdoor games, and events such as cookouts and canoe trips. All activities are the framework for problem solving and developing basic life skills.

Schedule: Youth counselors typically work five consecutive days followed by two free days, but some activities may require extended coverage up to and including 14-day wilderness trips.

Physical requirements: Candidates must be able to perform several physical actions required in regular activities, including but not limited to supporting your body weight for 30 minutes on your hands and knees, twisting your torso 90 degrees from standing position, and getting off the ground from a kneeling position without touching the ground with your hands.

Education: Youth counselors have education and interests in diverse fields including human services, education, health, liberal arts, and science. All youth counselors must be at least 21 years of age.

Experience: Wilderness youth counselors have a wide variety of professional and volunteer experiences. Child care experience is preferred. Diverse outdoor experiences are also highly preferred. Interest in athletics and physical games and activities of all types a plus.

Compensation: The starting salary is $22,000 per year plus medical insurance, free room and board, and relocation assistance.

Writing Application 1

Choose one of the job ads above that you find particularly compelling and write an extended letter to a friend or relative detailing your reasons for applying for such a job. Describe what you take to be your special qualifications for the job, the talents and skills you would bring to it, the types of satisfaction you would expect to take from such a job, and how your college career will help you to achieve the necessary knowledge and skills to do the job.

To prepare yourself to write a detailed letter, find out what you can about this line of work; talk to individuals you know and/or teachers in the field, search the field on the Internet or in periodicals, learn as much as you can about the skills and education that are listed in the ad, etc. You might also do some private invention, brainstorming, and freewriting on your motivations and the things that most attract you to this type of work.

Writing Application 2

Investigate websites: If you have access to the World Wide Web, visit one of the many sites devoted to careers, such as http://www.votech.about.com/ or http://www.monster.com/, where you can navigate among various potential career fields and the skills associated with them. This will give you the chance to consider how your own résumé matches various career fields. It also will allow you to consider what this type of job makes of you—that is, the *ethos* that you occupy from within this job or career field.

Then, investigate three other websites related to this field of work. Write an essay that informs others who might have an interest in this field, providing details about the special skills, experience, and education required as well as a description of the lifestyle associated with this type of work. If you can, you might create an electronic essay (or even your own website) that provides hyperlinks to these sites and that analyzes and comments upon the various aspects of this type of work. This is meant to help your classmates and other interested parties develop a better idea of not only the work and skills required for such a career but also its most exciting aspects.

Investigating the Worlds of Work

Finding something to do with one's life is a complex task wrapped in a simple veneer. For a young child, proclaiming the desire to be a firefighter or a marine biologist is easy, since tomorrow she might choose to be a teacher or a basketball star. Even as you progress through middle school and high school, selecting an occupation is based in what seems to be a quite distant future. Then suddenly, that question ("What do you want to be?") grows teeth as it takes the form of selecting a major and envisioning a lifetime of work. Can I really be an astronaut?

But does our vision of work have to lose its luster just as it starts to take on some semblance of reality? Not necessarily. The first two chapters focused on the past and the future, asking you to use writing to explore ideas that have occupied you happily in the past and work that you might envision doing in a world without restrictions. In this chapter, you'll use another set of inventional strategies to explore some of the present realities of occupations.

Learning those realities need not come at the expense of childlike excitement about being a marine biologist (and so swimming with the dolphins and whales). To the contrary, you can consider many intriguing topics as you investigate the world of work in more substantive ways—the characteristics of workers in a particular field, the beliefs that bind them together, the variety of opinions and lifestyles their professions encompass, and the ways their work contributes to the wider community. But how can you gain access to, and better understand, the topics that occupy the lives of people engaged in productive work?

My answer: by listening closely. The expertise, values, and shared work that hold a group of people together as professionals are contained in the words that they use, words that represent them to other members of their occupation (as a sign of common values) as well as to those outside of their occupation (as a sign of their value to the community). As students, you can learn a great deal by inquiring into those words and their meanings in various fields of study and endeavor. To gain access to those shared values and ideas, you can look to what rhetoric might call the *commonplaces* of professions—the language used to represent each occupation's work. And since it is likely that at least one of your primary motives for attending college is to find satisfying work, knowing the commonplaces associated with fields that interest you can be an important part of the learning you do in college.

WHAT ARE COMMONPLACES?

In the simplest terms, commonplaces are commonly held beliefs, concepts, or ways of thinking. Of course, to have such commonality, they must exist within a specific group or community and must be communicated in words—that is, commonplaces define, *and are defined by,* specific groups of people speaking with one another.

For example, American society has commonplaces that help to define our culture. One such commonplace is self-government, the idea that U.S. citizens have the right to influence the laws under which they live. This democratic ideal is not only a founding concept of the American system of government but also a core belief that most Americans accept without question—because to deny that basic tenet (or commonplace) would suggest that they are not fully members of that culture. Many related commonplaces define the American people, commonplaces such as those guaranteed by the Bill of Rights. Though some citizens might question the scope of these rights or whether they are available in the same measure to all people (Do the poor have the same level of representation as the rich? minorities the same as the majority?), the *basic principles themselves* are still generally accepted without much debate.

WRITING TO EXPLORE 3.1

Consider some of the groups to which you belong and the commonplaces associated with them. Remember that commonplaces are not just the ideals themselves but the ways in which they are represented in words. (In #4 below, for example, the U.S. Marines use the slogan "The Few. The Proud. The Marines." What does that phrase suggest?) Here are some possibilities:

1. If you are an athlete, list commonplaces generally accepted by members of athletic teams.
2. What commonplaces are shared by college students at your college or university?
3. What shared beliefs help to define a religious group to which you belong?
4. What shared beliefs hold together members of the military? How do those beliefs influence their ability to perform their duties? What key phrases are used to express those beliefs?
5. What commonplace ideas define the Democratic Party? the Republican Party? the Green Party? Libertarians? (For this one, you might need to do a bit of research on the Internet.)
6. What commonplaces are held by environmentalists? by feminists? by social conservatives? by social liberals? Do any of these groups share values or commonplaces?

After you have listed commonplace ideas held by any of the groups listed above, go back through your list and (1) eliminate any of the ideas you listed that might be contested by a significant portion of that group, and (2) try to rank those commonplaces from most crucial to the group to the least crucial, asking yourself which of the beliefs are closest to the core values of that group of people.

COMMONPLACES AS SHARED VALUES

The above exercise illustrates ways that commonplaces hold a group together and articulate the foundation of ideas on which its decisions and actions are built. For example, if I accept the American commonplace of free speech, it would be difficult for me to argue for censorship of the press unless I could prove that it would serve a more important commonplace of our culture—say, the commonplace that the United States is "one nation under God." (That's why I asked you to rank those commonplaces once you had generated them—they sometimes conflict.) This is not to suggest that all members of a group always agree on the fine points of each of the commonplaces (as the censorship example, an oft-debated topic, illustrates). But it does suggest that knowing the commonplaces of a group helps you to better understand its values.

The values represented in commonplaces are rooted in language—that is, specific words, phrases, and even whole documents represent to members a group's most important ideologies. Some phrasings that capture American commonplaces or ideologies might be familiar to you:

- "Ask not what your country can do for you; ask what you can do for your country."
- "All men are created equal."
- "This country of the people, by the people, for the people, shall not perish from the earth."
- "the cradle of liberty"

Lines like these, and the concepts they portray (citizenship, equality, democracy, freedom), form the basis for identification with a specifically American ideology. They are recited or paraphrased again and again as a sign of belonging to that group. (You might note, for example, how many American commonplaces became a visible source of unity and stability after 9/11—on banners, bumper stickers, and in political speeches.) Of course, such commonplaces—when examined more carefully—can also be used to critique a culture. A writer or speaker might ask whether all men (and women) are really granted equality, whether most citizens do put their country first, whether the government does function of, by, and for the people on any given occasion. But few Americans would question the *concepts themselves,* and even fewer do so successfully. These ideas are at the heart of the culture's character—its group *ethos,* so to speak.

WRITING TO EXPLORE 3.2

Commonplaces are so powerful that they can, in and of themselves, cause a group to form around them. Here are a few more commonplaces. In your writer's notebook, try to identify what group or groups are most closely associated with each. Then, freewrite on why each phrase represents a particularly important commonplace for that group:

1. Do unto others as you would have them do unto you.
2. Women, as a group, have suffered much oppression over human history.
3. Life begins at conception.
4. Economic expansion must be subjugated to the demands of clean water and air.
5. All citizens of this country have the right to bear arms.
6. We must allow for diverse cultural beliefs and practices.

Each of the above commonplaces represents a key belief for a group, cultural movement, or organization. As such, the character or *ethos* of the group can be at least partially gauged by an understanding of its key commonplaces.

COMMONPLACES AS COMMUNITY *ETHOS*

As we discussed in Chapters 1 and 2, the actions people perform and the way they present themselves in words define much of their character or *ethos*—the self they present to the world in any given situation. But character is also created and portrayed by the company people keep. The communities with which people identify help to present them to others as well, and so are crucial to the formation of *ethos*. This is seen in many ways. You might list the clubs, organizations, or societies to which you belong on a résumé. Why? You didn't form that organization. You may not hold office in that group. You might not even be particularly active in that group's work. Then why, in a résumé that is meant to represent you to prospective employers, would you list things like the Physics Club, the Young Republicans, or the National Rifle Association? What do your associations say about you?

They can say many things. A résumé is not a full biography; it is a partial self-presentation that tells prospective employers those things that somehow reflect on your fitness for a specific position. It also is meant to give its readers a sense of you as a person, associating you with the commonplaces and the *ethos* of its members. For example, what commonplaces would you associate with membership in the National Rifle Association—even beyond the most basic one, the right to bear arms? Is there a group *ethos* that goes along with membership in that group? How about membership in People for the Ethical Treatment of Animals? the Biology Club?

There is a danger here, of course, of crossing the line between associating the commonplaces of a group with its members and stereotyping. That line is often unclear. Can I assume, with some certainty, that an NRA member believes in the right to bear arms? Of course. Can I assume that she believes in personal freedoms more strongly than those who stand for gun control do? Perhaps. Can I assume that she belongs to a militia group or believes that the government has too much power? No. At that point, I've clearly crossed a line between the commonplaces of the group and stereotyping its members.

WRITING TO EXPLORE 3.3

Consider the following groups or clubs, and list the *commonplaces* that you could fairly associate with each. Then, in your writer's notebook, list some of the *stereotypes* associated with that group. What distinguishes one from the other? If you're not immediately familiar with a group, you might check a website or other forms of publicity published by that group.

- Parent-Teacher Association
- National Association of University Women
- Lions Club
- NAACP
- NOW
- Sierra Club
- Arbor Day Society
- ACT UP
- Young Republicans

   As you completed the above exercise, you might have once again noticed that the line between commonplaces and stereotypes is sometimes a bit fuzzy. After all, associating any set of values with an entire group can be dangerous. But writers often base their ideas on such shared values, both when they are writing or speaking *as* a member of a particular group or community and when they are writing or speaking *to* a particular group or community. Doing so allows writers to develop an *ethos* that takes into account the values of that community and that, in a sense, speaks the language of that group.

COMMONPLACES AND OCCUPATIONAL *ETHOS*

What does it mean to be a "scientist" or a "businessperson" or a "psychologist"—not only in terms of the work such people do but also in terms of the core beliefs that inform the work done in that field? Examining the commonplaces of various occupations can help you to understand what it means to work within those fields—and what those fields make of their workers.

You might use your present occupation as a student to help you to become informed not only about the content of the field or fields you are considering for your life's work but also about the commonplace ideas that are shared by the people in that field. Doing so can help you to try on the set of ideas that are at the heart of that field and see if occupying that character (or *ethos*) fits your own talents, goals, and plans.

One of the ways that you might better understand various occupations is to notice how the words used by their practitioners define their profession's beliefs and work. As you saw above, the language used by any group helps you to understand the principles that inform it. This is true not only of social organizations and countries but also of academic disciplines and professional fields. For example, what would happen if instead of considering the commonplaces of the NRA or People for the Ethical Treatment of Animals you were to consider the commonplaces associated with being a business major, an English major, or a nursing major? What commonplaces do these fields seem to accept as a group? What commonly accepted principles help to define not only the professions but also the people who work in those professions?

WRITING TO EXPLORE 3.4

In your writer's notebook, try listing the commonplaces associated with the following disciplines of study and work.

- biology
- psychology
- literature
- nursing
- political science
- business management
- business marketing
- foreign languages
- history
- any other major that you are considering

Considering commonplaces can be a good start toward reflecting on the work of disciplines that help to define us. Learning what we *don't* know can be valuable too. By showing us the gaps in our knowledge ("I want to be a business major, but I'm not really sure about the differences between marketing, management, or economics"), this brainstorming can lead us to an important step in the writing process: the need for further inquiry.

INQUIRING FURTHER INTO AN OCCUPATION'S COMMONPLACES

Now that you have some sense of why investigating commonplaces can help you understand occupational communities, you might begin to think about the places occupational and academic commonplaces reside. You have already begun the process of interrogating yourself and your educational and occupational motives. Thinking back over what you've discovered so far about those motives, you might attempt to synthesize some of those ideas. For example, you might write something like this:

> After reading over my writings about my interests, I have begun to notice that each of the occupations that interest me involve physical work—work that takes me away from a desk and keeps me on my feet. Perhaps that suggests that I prefer not to do work that is office based and that might involve frequent travel or hands-on work. . . .

But such general observations are not substantive enough to facilitate deeper levels of learning. It is equally important that you consider the many questions that no doubt arose in your earlier writing or that arise now as you think over the personal motives you have established for your education. As you read over your earlier thoughts, you might add to it key questions like this:

> I see here that I've noted that business managers need many years of experience to effectively motivate their colleagues—but how does one get such experience? And what types of educational experiences can help me to find motivation techniques? Will psychological studies also be useful in understanding organizational behavior? I wonder what publications exist to bring me information on these issues.

By asking important questions like these, you can use your writer's notebook as a place where your rough ideas or offhand thoughts evolve into something more—lines of thought for further inquiry. Before you attempt to answer those questions, it is important that you find sources of information that can help you to develop your questions into more focused areas of inquiry.

ETHOS AND PROFESSIONAL COMMUNITIES

Most organizations do their best to let others know what they do, why they do it, and why their work is of value to the public. This process is usually referred to as *public relations*. Print publications and the Web provide access to a wealth of information about professional and disciplinary organizations, many of which publish their commonplaces in the form of mission statements, organizational or disciplinary principles, or constitutions. Examining these sites and publications can provide a rich array of words and ideas to enhance your memory of what its people stand for and do.

For example, the website for the National Council of Teachers of English (NCTE) looks like this:

FIGURE 3.1 The home page of the National Council of Teachers of English.

The first thing you might notice about this professional organization's site is the way it defines the profession and organizes its information. The tabs on the top right lead to sections devoted to "Elementary," "Middle," "Secondary," and "College" links. Many of the other links likewise deal with teaching—the act at the center of this profession and organization. You might also note that links to the organization's journals and other publications, as well as to affiliate organizations, are provided.

But to really gain access to some of the commonplaces of such sites, you must look a bit deeper. You might, for example, follow the link called "Issues/Positions," where you would find a wealth of information about what the organization and its members believe as a whole. NCTE and its affiliate, the Conference on College Composition and Communication (CCCC), lists positions on issues such as diversity and gender balance in English curricula, beneficial classroom conditions, standards for assessment, literacy education, tracking of students in high schools, and useful methods for teaching writing. The following position, for example, addresses the issue of African-American vernacular language, or Ebonics:

> The Conference on College Composition and Communication (CCCC), composed of 9,000 scholars who teach at colleges and universities across the nation, is deeply committed to the development of literacy for all students.
>
> News media reports and commentaries regarding the recent Ebonics controversy have been, for the most part, incomplete, uninformed, and, in some cases, purposefully distorted. The public deserves a statement reflective of the viewpoints of language and literacy scholars.
>
> Ebonics—also known as Black English Vernacular, African American Language, and by other names—is a distinctive language system that many African American students use in daily conversation and in the performance of academic tasks. Like every other linguistic system, Ebonics is systematic and rule-governed. It is not an obstacle to learning. The obstacle lies in negative attitudes towards the language, lack of information about the language, inefficient techniques for teaching language and literacy skills, and an unwillingness to adapt teaching styles to the needs of Ebonics speakers.
>
> Teachers, administrators, counselors, supervisors, and curriculum developers must undergo training to provide them with adequate knowledge about Ebonics and help them overcome the prevailing stereotypes about the language and learning potential of African American students and others who speak Ebonics. Teachers in particular must be equipped with the fundamental training and knowledge that will enable them to be effective in teaching language and literacy skills to Ebonics speakers.
>
> We strongly support the call for additional research on how educators can best build on existing knowledge about Ebonics to help students to expand their command of the Language of Wider Communication ("standard English") and master the essential skills of reading and writing.

What are some of the key commonplaces of this organization (and, at least partially, those of the people who choose to be members) as revealed in this position statement? This organization states its responsibility to inform the public about this issue, since NCTE and CCCC define themselves as organizations devoted to the teaching of language skills—that is, the organizations claim the right to speak based on their professional expertise (or *ethos*). And it states their commitment to diversity and respect, concepts that are evident in many of the organizations' other position statements as well.

WRITING TO EXPLORE 3.5

Read over the CCCC's statement on Ebonics once again and quote those lines you find crucial to defining the commonplaces of this professional organization. Then, use freewriting to react to each of the lines you have quoted. If you have access to the Web, you might also compare the ideologies or commonplaces of this statement with other position statements available at http://www.ncte.org/cccc.

Likewise, the American Psychological Association (APA) website provides public information about the discipline and occupation of psychology (at http://www.apa.org).

APA is, according to the site, "a scientific and professional organization that represents psychology in the United States. With more than 155,000 members, APA is the largest association of psychologists worldwide." What does it mean for this organization to claim to "represent psychology in the United States?" Why is this claim followed by the statistical information about its "more than 155,000 members" and the status of APA as "the largest association of psychologists worldwide?" Think especially about the *ethos* that those claims attempt to establish and how they lend credibility to the commonplaces of this organization as representative of the commonplaces of psychology in the United States more generally.

The internal or group *ethos* is furthered through its relationship with those outside of the profession. The APA provides a link from its home page entitled "Public Publications" that allows people to "access information for parents, teens, the media and others about: Parenting, Healthcare, Depression and more." Though this in some ways is an obvious attempt at public relations—an attempt to create a positive image of the discipline and the organization to the public—it can still help people to determine the commonplaces of the group. For example, if you followed the link for women's issues, you would find the following statement: "The Women's Program's Office (WPO) coordinates APA's efforts to ensure equal opportunities for women psychologists as practitioners, educators, and scientists and to eliminate gender bias in education and training, research, and diagnosis." As an office of the APA, this group falls under the umbrella of the organization, which here (on its official website and in the "Public Interest" section of that site) states its commitment to women's issues in the profession and in education.

FIGURE 3.2 The home page of the American Psychological Association.

WRITING TO EXPLORE 3.6

The APA, in keeping with the commitment of the discipline of psychology to scientific method, examines prejudice as a social phenomenon and with a scientist's eye:

Simply put, prejudice is bias. Prejudice refers to the negative opinions, judgments, beliefs, and feelings we hold about individuals because of their membership in certain groups or categories. When these negative views lead us to act in certain ways towards these individuals and groups, the result is discrimination. Racial prejudice is one form of prejudice. Racial prejudice is prejudice that is based on membership in racial groups. The issue of whether humans are grouped into "races" naturally, or whether "race" is a concept which we use to categorize people but which has no scientific basis, is addressed below.

How would you describe the style and tone of this piece? Does it openly take a moral position against racial prejudice? Why or why not? What commonplace ideas held in the social sciences or psychology are revealed here? Jot down what you take to be key passages in your writer's notebook and analyze the values they seem to suggest are held by APA members.

As you considered the questions above, you might have discovered a number of things. Here are things that struck me as an outsider to this field: First, I thought about how this set of ideas related to its sponsoring institution, the APA. More specifically, I considered how this statement fit within the commonplaces of the social science of psychology. As I looked closely at the way in which this introduction to racial prejudice was written, I noticed several commonplaces about the social sciences in general and psychology in particular. The final line, I noted, pointed out the method to be used in examining the issue: Race (and by implication, racial prejudice) will be examined for *whether or not there is a scientific basis to the concept*—that is, this statement is suited to the set of guiding ideas that helps to define the profession of psychology; conclusions are not drawn based on emotions or anecdotes but rather on science. Let's now return to the NCTE website and see how a similar issue is perceived within the commonplaces of English teachers.

Besides the statement on Ebonics included above, NCTE also provides position statements on issues such as the following:

- Guidelines for Nonsexist Use of Language in NCTE Publications, which "identifies common language usages which arbitrarily assign roles or characteristics on the basis of sex"

- Common Ground, which "features NCTE-IRA Joint Statement and principles of access, diversity, and fairness on intellectual freedom"

- Guidelines for a Gender Balanced curriculum (for both Pre-K to Grade 6 and Grades 7–12), which addresses "the issue of gendered literature," provides "several suggestions for promoting gender equality in the classroom," and "encourages all English teachers to integrate literature by and about women in the curriculum"

- Non-White Minorities in English and Language Arts Materials, which "offers guidelines for selecting materials that provide accurate, positive, and full representation of non-white minorities"

While each of these position statements, along with many others, address the issue of discrimination and bias—as does the APA paper included on its website—the principles that inform the NCTE deals specifically with issues related to the classroom. You might also note that many of the principles of discrimination and nondiscrimination addressed by NCTE deal with bias *through language and literature,* the province of professional English teachers. Rather than approach the topics of prejudice and diversity by investigating its scientific basis, the guidelines provide practical suggestions for avoiding biased language in the classroom. Thus, though each organization has a clear position in opposition to prejudiced ideas, each is expressed through a slightly different occupational *ethos.*

WRITING TO EXPLORE 3.7

If you have access to the Web, compare and contrast one of the NCTE position statements to one on the APA website. As you make the comparison, consider the reasons why an organization representing scientists (specifically, psychologists) might approach an issue the way it does. Compare the psychologists' approach to the approach taken by teachers generally, and English teachers specifically, as represented on the NCTE site.

As you proceed with your investigations of various professions, you should regularly react to the ideas you hear discussed, continuously adding your analyses of academic subjects (and their related occupations) to your notebook. You should regularly look over the material you collect there, freewriting in response to questions like:

- What would it mean to be a major in this field of study or member of this organization in terms of its common beliefs, values, and methods?
- What commonplaces of this field of study or profession seem closest to your own values? Which seem most difficult for you to accept, and why?
- What aspects of this profession or field of study seem to suit your talents and abilities particularly well?

While I was writing this book, I thought about questions like these. By doing so, I learned a good deal about the work done in various fields through reading—and by speaking to others about their work. One of those people was Eric Engle, a professional geologist (profiled in Reading and Writing Applications 1). Eric's work is to help land developers determine whether a plot of land is suitable for its planned use. To do this, Eric must investigate whether groundwater is adequate for the project and study the ways in which the proposed development would affect use by existing homeowners and businesses. This work requires Eric to collect and interpret data using techniques that he learned while studying natural sciences at Lock Haven University. He could not do his job without that basic knowledge base. Eric is also called on to form and defend the practical implications of the geological studies he performs. As he puts it, "In college, you learn straight geology. On the job, that part is about 25 percent of my job. The other 75 percent is based in decision-making, communication skills (both oral and written), and people skills."

Thus, though Eric's major did not correspond exactly to the work he eventually took on, it provided him with the knowledge to make subjective decisions from data, to write reports on matters of practical importance to his clients, and to negotiate differences with developers who might be disappointed by his informed decisions about land use. It is those aspects of the work world that we discover by examining the fields more closely.

One useful way to inquire into the common values and topics of various occupations is to read and analyze the way writers in those fields express themselves. If you read and reflect on phrasings that express important facets of occupations in which you have an interest, you can gain more extensive knowledge of what it would mean to be a member of that community. You can use your writer's notebook to help you to collect the commonplaces of the occupations you examine.

THE WRITER'S NOTEBOOK AS COMMONPLACE BOOK

Though called by many names, the commonplace book is a writer's tool that has been used for centuries as a place to record ideas that one encounters—ideas that are contained within key words, phrasings, and documents. It is useful because, as you've already begun to learn, inventing ideas involves more than simply brainstorming or freewriting—all ways to tease ideas out of our own minds. You also need to be a *collector,* using your notebook (and your memory) to store ideas and words that will enrich your ability to write in an informed way. Using your writer's notebook as a type of commonplace book gives you a place to collect and comment on ideas, words, and phrases that strike you as important perspectives on a specific topic, and to use that process of thoughtful collection as a heuristic toward developing your own informed thoughts.

So how does a commonplace book help you to generate ideas and organize your thoughts about those ideas? By writing down the words of others, you occupy a special place somewhere between reader and writer. For example, I'm especially fond of the following line written by a former teacher, Professor Elaine Scarry, that I ran across in *The New York Times Magazine* (November 19, 2000; 78–81) more than twenty years after I was enrolled in Professor Scarry's class in Victorian literature:

> There's nothing about being an English Professor that exempts you from the normal obligations of citizenship.

As I copy down the line in my own handwriting (or keyboarding), I am for the moment somewhere between reader and writer. I am forced to consider how it feels to "say" that line. Because of the things that I believe about my work (and since it was written by a former teacher), the line moved me even more as I wrote it down. In fact, writing it in my commonplace book was a start toward trying to understand its implications.

Then it was my task to figure out why I liked the line so much. Was it that I believe in its truth and wisdom? Did I like the way the line was phrased? Did it help to make my academic job seem less isolated from the rest of the world? In this way, the line became an impetus to respond. That, too, is part of the commonplace book. It is a place where the words of others and your own words mingle and interact; it is a place where you converse with what you hear and read. Here's what I wrote in response to finding the words of Professor Scarry after transcribing the words themselves:

"There's nothing about being an English Professor that exempts you from the normal obligations of citizenship." Precisely. The profession, like any profession, asks more of us than narrow self-interest. It requires citizenship. So rather than wondering where the Liberal Arts have *gone*, why not wonder what the Liberal Arts can *do* in the present moment. If we live in a time when higher education has its basis in a student's honest desire to find meaningful work, then why not make that desire, to borrow John Dewey's words, the "genuine motive" for study, and make the pursuit of satisfying work a truly liberalized education?

You might recognize in this commonplace book entry some of the ideas that inform this book. That's the way ideas can grow in response to other ideas—through the conversations you have with other writers and thinkers.

Of course, the conversations aren't always spurred by admiration. If I read something that particularly bothers me or with which I disagree on some visceral level—that is, it gives me a pain in my gut—then I might also bring that to my commonplace book and try to figure out where that pain or distaste originates. For example, if I read in the newspaper that a local school district has banned a book that I loved as a child, or one that my own children love (like *Harry Potter*), I might take a quotation from one of the proponents of that ban and try to figure out why I reacted so strongly to it. I might also try to articulate why I disagree—in terms that are less violent than that pain in my gut. I would, in a sense, look for available arguments against censorship (which I might also jot down if I can recall or locate them) or for reasons why the experience of this book might, to the contrary, be a positive experience for children. I should, of course, also consider whether there is something in the original statement that made sense. In this way, the commonplace book becomes a conversation involving many people whose words I recall and many examples that speak to the issue raised by that first piece of discourse—a conversation that I am moderating and from which I can learn a great deal.

Using the commonplace book, then, you can better understand how commonplaces are not only sets of ideas that are held by a particular group but also *the ways in which those ideas are verbalized*. It reminds you that commonplaces are not just ideas but ideas *contained in language*, often in a pithy or moving way. So, when the NRA uses the slogan "Guns don't kill people, people kill people," that wording not only contains one of the commonplaces of that organization but expresses it in a way that captures the emotions and the loyalties of its members; it also responds to gun control advocates who might claim that "guns kill people." By analyzing the phrasing of an idea as well as the idea itself, you can learn a good deal about how the phraser thinks.

WRITING TO EXPLORE 3.8

Use your writer's notebook as a place to collect commonplaces and to try out the process of informally responding to them. In your notebook, write three quotations to which you have a strong reaction. They can be song lyrics, quotations from a book, television show, film, or the newspaper—even something a friend or teacher said. Then, freewrite in response to each quotation, trying to develop the reasons why you find it in some way moving. As with other forms of freewriting, you should follow your ideas wherever they lead.

Throughout this chapter, we discussed ways that academic disciplines and professional communities leave a public record—the ways in which the writing and other discourses of particular occupations are accessible to you. We also discussed ways to collect and respond to those public statements in order to spur your own inventive thoughts.

In the Reading and Writing Applications section that follows this chapter, you'll be encouraged to begin collecting and analyzing the commonplaces of various academic and occupational communities. You'll have the opportunity to conduct interviews, investigate the commonplaces that groups express on their websites, and gauge the ways that your current occupation as a student can contribute to the occupations to which you aspire, those you have held in the past, or those within which you are currently engaged. Each of these writing activities will help you to engage with the work of various communities and to begin the process of situating your own values among those communities.

Work and Community

Case 1 INTERVIEWING—EXPLORING PROFESSIONAL *ETHOS* THROUGH ITS PEOPLE

Finding a life's work requires more than merely choosing a major or profession from a catalog or career guide. To understand more fully the work that is done in any occupation, it is also important that you consider its commonplaces—the values and ideas that inform that occupation's work. One natural source of such information is the people who already work in those disciplines or occupations. By speaking with them, you can learn how they feel about their work, why they are committed to it, and what they consider its most serious challenges. After all, if you are attempting to understand occupations as more than simply jobs but rather as lifestyles and modes of thinking, looking at them without listening to the people involved may not give you an accurate picture.

Fortunately, people usually are fond of talking about their work, and knowing that is a fine place to begin conducting interviews. If you think of an interview not as an interrogation—an attempt to gather specific information—but as an opportunity to have a conversation, you're on the right track.

Interviews can provide inside information about the real work done in an occupational field or discipline and can allow you to hear how professionals in those fields talk about their work—the commonplaces that they seem to hold, the *ethos* that they present, and the practices that they use on the job. By speaking to such professionals, you will gain a better sense of what it means to be a biologist or a nurse or a lawyer. Since I was interested in knowing how people write on the job, for example, I asked some of the people I interviewed about the ways that they invent ideas; I wanted to see if techniques like brainstorming, using a writer's notebook, or collaborative invention have applications in the work world. I found that similar techniques are indeed used on the job. For example, geologist Eric Engle always discusses a project or problem with one or two people "to get things rolling in the right direction. . . . Nearly everything we do," he noted, "is a collaborative effort."

I also learned about some commonplace practices through these interviews. For example, I found commonalities in business-related fields, where collaborative invention (see Chapter 2) is especially crucial. Robert Colleluori told me that in his marketing firm "we do lots of brainstorming sessions where my first rule is that no one's contribution is ever wrong and no one can make a negative comment about someone's suggestion." Likewise, in her work as a systems architect, Jane Whitaker's team used brainstorming sessions frequently:

> These were group sessions, usually five to eight people, with one person acting as a facilitator. . . . We'd have a large pad on an easel and lots of markers and masking tape, and as we'd fill up a sheet, it would be hung around the room, and we'd continue until we couldn't come up with any new thoughts. Then we'd go back and start going through the ideas, organizing them, combining related ones, eliminating some, working down to a manageable few or a workable several. . . . The facilitator played a critical role in keeping things moving and focused, encouraging off-the-wall ideas, shutting down criticism that came too early, and so forth.

From such interviews I was able to learn some of the commonplaces of business practices.

Conducting a successful interview requires a combination of careful preparation and a willingness to allow the conversation to move naturally. In order to help that process along, it is important that you be a good listener and active participant in a conversation rather than merely a researcher trying to gather specific information. One of the key factors in a successful interview is making your interviewee comfortable enough to speak frankly with you. Choose a pleasant setting in which you both feel able to speak, and will have few interruptions. It is also important to let your interviewee know the purpose of your conversation, your sincere interest in what she has to say, and your respect for that knowledge.

Since good conversations usually take place around shared interests, it is also important that you prepare for your interview. Think about the current state of the field, find out what you can about the work that the interviewee and her organization does, and learn about issues that her field currently faces. For example, if you were interviewing a journalist, issues like public attitudes toward the media might be of special interest. It would be even better if you had thought about recent instances of tough journalistic decisions; if there were a recent case reported in the newspapers in which the actions of a journalist were questioned (such as the story of Jayson Blair, who used false and sometimes plagiarized information in his *New York Times* articles), you might bring that up in the most nonconfrontational way you can. This will show your interviewee your sincere interest in her field and show your respect for her opinion on the topic.

Once the conversation begins, that's when good listening becomes important. Sticking to a prepared script of questions and spending most of your time referring to or jotting down notes is less likely to spur a frank discussion than careful listening and apt responses. This, too, requires careful planning, since you will need to make sparse notes during the interview and then flesh them out immediately afterward to avoid forgetting key moments in the conversation. During the interview, jot down just a few words that will jog your memory after you are done; be sure that you have at least an hour immediately after the interview to write down your recollections, key words and phrases used by your interviewee, and your general impressions.

Interview Tips

Before the Interview

- Set up your interview well in advance, at the convenience of your interviewee.
- Explain why you are conducting the interview.
- Choose a comfortable setting.
- Let your interviewee know about how long the interview will last.
- Let your interviewee know how you will use the information she provides. Consider offering to let her read what you write to check for accuracy.

On the Day of the Interview

- Prepare a set of questions, but don't feel obligated to stick to it; allow for spontaneity.
- Consider using a tape recorder, but consider the downsides of doing so as well: Transcribing takes time, and some interviewees may be intimidated by a recorder. Always ask permission in advance if you want to record an interview.
- Remain as neutral as possible, and keep your body language and reactions from interfering with an interviewee's willingness to talk.
- Ask open-ended questions and avoid influencing the answers; remain nonconfrontational.
- Begin with questions likely to make your interviewee comfortable with you.
- Be sure to allow the interviewee to answer questions fully; don't rush him.

- Try not to jump from topic to topic; provide transitions between questions.
- Before you conclude, allow the interviewee to add any information that he'd like to and to speak about final impressions.
- Plan for time after the interview in which to make careful notes.

After the Interview

Use your writer's notebook to reflect and record your observations, asking questions like:

- What new aspects of this occupation did I learn about?
- What parts of the job seem to bring a special joy to the practitioners I spoke with? What parts seemed to make them tired or concerned?
- Can I see myself doing this job? What aspects seem to be beyond my sphere of interests or talents? Are there ways that I might nurture those aspects of myself?
- What types of writing or communication skills seem to be most important in this profession?
- What type of lifestyle does this occupation offer its workers? Does it fit my character and goals?
- Does the work excite the interviewee in ways that also inform the other aspects of his life?
- How did this person find herself in this occupation? What logic or processes led her to it? What skills, talents, or interests seem to have informed those processes?
- Does the interviewee identify a definable role within the larger community? Does she carry that expertise back into her other interests and activities?
- How does what I learned from this interview correspond to aspects of this occupation that I learned from other sources?
- What questions do I still have?

These questions can act as guides as you develop the interview into an essay about the work of a profession. Below is a sample student essay that resulted from two interviews. Reading it might give you ideas for conducting and writing your own interview-based essay. Here's what Kristin Lease had to say about her interviewing and writing process:

> In my search for details about the nursing field, I interviewed two very successful women, Dr. Marian Condon, a Professor of Nursing at York College, and Mrs. Sue Walters, an RN working as a staff nurse at the Surgical Center of York. Each of these women has shed light on the various aspects of the nursing world throughout their own unique experiences. Not only have I learned about the basic requirements and expectations that one will encounter, but I have also gotten a taste of what pleasures and challenges one will face while pursuing a career

in this particular field. Research based on textbooks and curriculum guides provides necessary information, but hearing about others' mistakes and accomplishments is information coming from the best source available. Throughout the interviews, I focused on what it would mean to be a "good" nurse, yet by the time I finished writing my paper, I realized that being "good" is a natural part of the nursing job.

Taking the Challenge to Become "Good"

Kristin Lease

A number of talents, skills, and personality traits are needed in order to be a successful nursing student or professional. Both Dr. Marian Condon and Sue Walters have learned over the years that the most important of these qualities is one's ability to handle stress. Nurses are often forced to deal with unpredictable circumstances such as allergic reactions to medication by patients, sets of important files being misplaced, or temper tantrums being thrown by frustrated doctors. With these and many other complications erupting almost daily, Walters commented on how mandatory it is to be able to "go with the flow." Although a nurse cannot be totally carefree, Condon stressed the importance of a person's ability to stay calm and collected: "A rigid individual would most likely crumble under pressure and not perform up to the level that both the patients and other staff deserve."

Being able to handle stress is usually a trait that a person is born either with or without. But, in the nursing program, students are taught about almost any situation that could cause them some trouble. Learning about the possible scenarios that one may confront often helps a person to feel more confident and relaxed in such a hectic environment. The students are also ensured that, much of the time, things are not going to run perfectly, or even smoothly. Helping a student to realize that problems will arise and that they need to be treated in a calm manner is an important part of the training program in Nursing.

Being intelligent and having a strong motivation to learn are each imperative qualities as well. The nursing program's curriculum is both demanding and stimulating, mainly revolving around upper-level science courses and labs. Although book smarts are important, Walters describes the *effort* that should be made: "Obviously there is a large amount of class time and clinical time, but a student needs to put even more time into it at home. A rule that the other nursing students and myself went by was that every hour of work with the professor or in the hospital equals three hours of work on your own." Because so much studying, reviewing, and researching is done during an individual's "free" time, devotion and determination must be present as well.

With people and their care at the center of importance in this field, a nurse must have a very specific personality. Compassion, friendliness, interpersonal skills, sensitivity, and professionalism are just a few characteristics that can separate an average nurse from an outstanding, well-rounded nurse. Walters feels that her sociable and caring traits have helped her to connect with the patients quite easily. "I absolutely love people and apparently it shows. Not a day goes by that I don't make a new friend" (Walters). Condon is also aware of the importance of a patient's needs: "A person in your care must always come first. It's sad when they [patients] think a nurse is going out of their way to be kind because it should happen all the time; it's part of our job."

Condon described a unique prerequisite that is not listed in the requirement book. "Corporate culture is more of a necessity than a skill in all lines of work. It is having the proper appearance, speech, and attitude for the professional world." She remembered a student who excelled in all her classes, was involved in extracurricular activities, and had a wonderful, kind heart. She seemed to be well down the road to success. Unfortunately, she hit a bump in the road when Condon realized that she was lacking corporate culture. Condon recalled this student's appearance and style of language as unacceptable: "She dressed to impress and that is simply not needed. She wore too much makeup and low-cut, tight clothing. She also used a lot of slang in her speech. You have to speak properly if you want to be taken seriously and earn respect."

As a student goes through a nursing program, he or she will be trained extensively. Lectures and advice from the professors are both necessary and beneficial, but the actual knowledge of the treatment and medication are taught through three basic stages. The first step in the process is the completion of several upper-level science courses. Biology, psychology, chemistry, physics, and anatomy are just a few [features] of the required curriculum. The classes include hours of lab time and studying. They are designed to teach the students about the human body and all its functions. Walters recommends a love for science when entering this field: "Make sure you can say 'biology is my friend.'"

The second step is receiving hands-on experience through a large amount of clinical time. The number of hours that students are required to complete varies, depending on the college that he/she attends. Walters, who received her degree at Millersville University, engaged in clinical time for two years. Each semester she was required to work in the hospital for sixteen hours a week, or two eight-hour shifts. To an average person, juggling mandatory clinical time and a full-time college career may seem impossible. However, Walters feels that nursing students should be responsible for even more clinical time: "Connecting classroom theory to practice is a necessary experience, and this type of learning can only take place in the hospital setting."

Clinical time is also important because it is the first time the students are acquainted with the hospital and its environment. As Walters stated, clinical work provides a student with necessary experiences. Observations and knowledge that [students] gain during this time is something that they will need for the third stage of their training, and more importantly, throughout their career.

The final stage of this training occurs during the senior year. It is a unique program referred to as the "Nursing Practicum." Each student is paired up with a certified nurse, and for several weeks a shadowing atmosphere is created. Students are exposed to and engage in a variety of nursing situations. With an experienced nurse by his/her side, a student takes blood pressures, gives baths, administers medication, and bandages open wounds. As the practicum continues, students increase their participation and eventually perform almost all of the day-to-day basics of nursing. This senior activity finalizes the answers to any questions or concerns a student may have. It also enhances their confidence and knowledge to full capacity. Walters, who participated in a similar program during her schooling at Millersville University, "loved the experience": "I gained so much confidence and it really made me feel like a part of the group." This intense amount of training is needed for a nurse to succeed years down the road.

Both professionals and students face exhausting challenges throughout their careers and schooling. Although they are different types of obstacles, each and every one is still challenging. The main trouble spot that a student can expect to face is managing his or her time wisely. Condon has seen many potentially successful nurses waste away their opportunities by simply not realizing how much time is needed. A lot of pupils try to balance both their studies and a job. Condon stresses that in some cases, a job is not needed. "You have to ask yourself [as a nursing student] whether you are working to pay your tuition or to buy and wear nice clothing?" Obviously, one's priorities must be put in order.

Although one may think that becoming a professional means overcoming all obstacles, it is impossible to have a career that presents no challenges. Some of the harshest aspects of nursing are the physical and emotional effects it can have on an individual. Working long, unusual hours and dealing with very stressful situations can take its toll on a devoted employee. Working in the critical care unit for several years, Condon began to feel run down and emotionally drained. A lot of this emotional exhaustion was a product of working in a very understaffed area. She also carried extra emotional baggage home with her every evening, worrying about a patient's health and stability until morning. "I would go to bed tired and wake up tired. I realized this wasn't what I wanted to be doing the rest of my life" (Condon). Walters, on the other hand, is very happy with being an RN despite the fact that she gets worn out as well. She thinks the extent of one's aches and pains depends on the person and his/her attitude. "I get exhausted from time to time, but I feel my job is worth it" (Walters).

Another ongoing battle for nurses is the constant changes in medication. "You can't ever know everything about them; even the doctors don't know [about the medications]" (Walters). There are books with all the different medications listed that one can use to study, but it is just a constant learning process. Condon stresses the importance of making an effort to know the basics. "You have to pay attention to the changes and have some idea of what the different prescriptions are, otherwise you are going to make the patient nervous and uncomfortable, or worse yet, endanger their health" (Condon).

In every professional field, there are ethical issues present, each yielding their own problems and consequences. Condon and Walters agree that the issue most frequently encountered is a dispute between a dying patient's wishes and his/her family's wishes. Going to extra lengths, or engaging in "heroics," is something that many ill patients wish to avoid: "Oftentimes, a patient and their family will sign papers stating that they don't want to use heroics long before that person becomes very sick. The family then sees them lying in the hospital bed, sick, and panics" (Walters). Oftentimes the family's wishes are met, and the staff will revive [the patient]. But, if their health continues to deteriorate and they eventually go "code"—total systems failure—nature will be allowed to take its course.

Another issue that occurs from time to time is a question involving confidentiality. When nurses are helping a patient, they are required to see and use his/her medical chart. If an individual is HIV positive, the nurse will need to know immediately in order to take certain health precautions, but that nurse is not permitted to tell anybody else about that person's disease. Of course, that nurse should not have the right to notify anyone she feels suitable about this individual's disease, but what if that patient's boyfriend, girlfriend, husband, or wife is there with them and they don't know that their significant other has tested HIV positive? Is it fair to give that unknowing person the potential to become infected with the AIDS virus?

When addressing these and many other ethical issues present in the health-care environment, how should a nurse react? Although it may be extremely frustrating, nurses must remember that they are performing a job and not forget their duties. "You can't let your own feelings interfere when you are dealing with these type of issues; this is a part of your job" (Condon). The only weapon a nurse can use in these situations is the power of persuasion. Helping a family to see and understand the suffering an ill loved one is going through and making an HIV-infected individual realize the consequences that will come from keeping the secret are the most beneficial ways for a nurse to make a positive difference. At times, certain issues may be overwhelming, but one's good judgment will always pull one through. For this reason, many nursing programs have courses that deal with issues of ethics in healthcare. Many of the issues addressed in such courses examine medical legalities and malpractice along with issues of confidentiality and morals. An informed and open-minded approach can provide students and professionals with an advantage in these rough situations.

Nurses are incredible people. They are highly skilled, well-trained individuals who overcome mind-boggling obstacles and put their duties as a nurse above their own feelings. The most incredible part about them is the amount of respect, kindness, and love that they show to each and every person. This includes not just their patients, but their everyday acquaintances as well, like myself. Both Dr. Marian Condon and Mrs. Sue Walters have made me realize what an important job nursing is. Filling the shoes that they have helped to create is a challenge that I am willing to tackle. With a few words of advice, Walters has given me a head start down the road to success: "Keep your mind and eyes open, but most of all, follow your heart."

Works Cited

Condon, Marian. Personal interview. 10 October 2001.
Walters, Sue. Personal interview. 9 October 2001.
Walters, Sue. Phone interview. 7 November 2001.

Writing to Respond

One of the strengths of this essay is the wealth of insight provided by the nursing professionals interviewed by Kristin Lease. In your writer's notebook, consider the elements of successful interviews that Lease seems to have employed. How do you suppose she was able to gather so much information from these professionals? You might also brainstorm on what questions you would ask a professional in a career field you are considering—questions that are likely to spur the openness seen here.

Also note that gathering the information is only one part of the process. Lease's essay carefully incorporates the words and ideas of others into a clearly organized essay. Look back over the essay to determine how Lease organizes her ideas to help you to see the key issues of the nursing profession. How do individual paragraphs create a focus for her major points? How does she use transitions to move logically through the essay?

Writing Applications

Interview someone in a profession that interests you, and write an organized and focused essay that helps readers to understand that profession through the words of one its practitioners. You might also develop the essay with other research into the field or from other interviews. Before the interview, be sure to consider your interview questions carefully and to consider the techniques listed above. Then, try to focus your essay on the commonplace ideas and issues faced by people in this occupation.

Case 2 WEBSITE DISCOVERIES

With increasing frequency, the Web is used by organizations and institutions to make public the work that they do. For this reason, the Web can be an extremely valuable resource to you as you consider the fields of work that interest you. In Chapter 3, we examined the websites of two professional organizations, one devoted to the teaching of English, the other to the professional practice of psychology. Those examinations helped to uncover some of the key commonplaces that bring members of these fields together and that represent the work of each to the wider community.

But simply taking the information that you find on websites at face value is not sufficient; to be a critical thinker and an inventive writer, you should use the public presentations of occupations and institutions on the Web as a starting point for deeper inquiries into the values that are portrayed there. Using your writer's notebook as a place not only to collect but also to respond to the information you find online can help you to think more deeply about the occupations that interest you and the commonplaces that hold its practitioners together.

Below is an example of a website that has been annotated with a reader's inventive responses, responses that expose key commonplaces of this profession. You can use this example as a guide as to the inventive thinking you can do as you examine a professional site or brochure.

This sample website might lead to the following observations on the commonplaces of this profession:

- This organization is attempting to bring together professionals in scientific research and, more specifically, those who are involved in the publication of scientific findings as like-minded professionals. This establishes a group *ethos*.

- This organization is especially concerned with fostering communication among scientists and allowing for "a network of professional support" and "a continuous flow of cutting-edge information." It does so both by its focus on publication of information and by sponsoring conferences, "short courses," and "educational retreats."

- This organization takes on ethical issues. In particular, it is concerned with the issues of copyright and scientific conduct and misconduct.

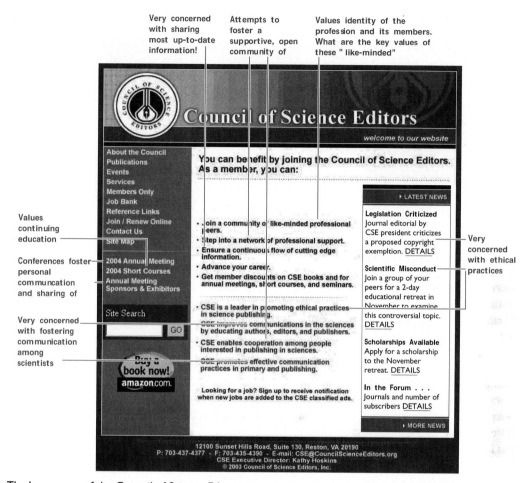

The home page of the Council of Science Editors.

▪ This organization feels that it is important to monitor and state its opinions on key political issues that affect members of this field of study and work. A current issue for people in this field involves the relationship between copyright protection for its members and free access to the latest scientific findings.

This last issue can be explored in greater depth by following the links to investigate the proposed legislation that would create open, free access to any research findings that are "substantially funded" by government monies. To state its position on this issue, the organization provides the following links:

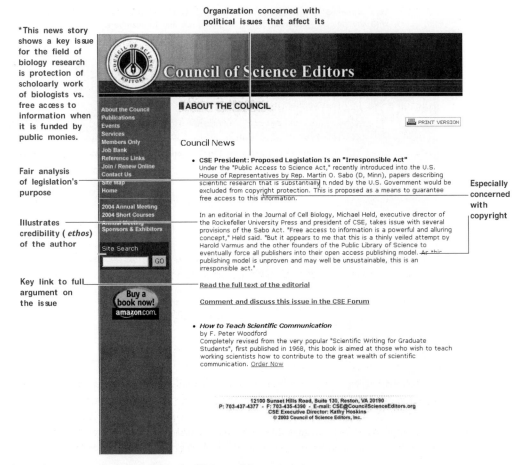

Council news page from the Council of Science Editors website.

By reading carefully and annotating these pages, we can uncover other key commonplaces and issues for this field of study:

- The organization is concerned with political issues that affect its work.

- The organization's spokesperson has a great deal of credibility (i.e., a strong *ethos*) because of his work and professional affiliations.

- Copyright is a key issue for both the editors of scientific journals and for the researcher/writers who contribute articles that detail their work.

The article itself carefully lays out the proposed legislation, acknowledging that free access to the latest information is important (after all, that is one of the commonplaces of the field, as stated on the home page). It concedes the point that providing free content is a valuable practice. But then, Michael J. Held goes on to present counterarguments that show why this organization and the scientists and editors that it represents must oppose this legislation:

- The journals need protection of information to be able to continue to function.
- The scientists themselves can share information without legislation to compel it.
- The legislation can break down a key commonplace of the field—that scientists wish to work collaboratively. This legislation, argues Held, "is already having the effect of splitting the community."
- Further study is needed of the effects of such legislation before it is instituted, since no one is sure "how a law such as the Sabo legislation would work."
- Removing key copyright protections and individual ownership of research ideas removes the part of the "incentive or value" for practitioners to continue their research.
- This issue is crucial for the field of scientific research and in particular for science editors.

Clearly, we can learn a great deal about this academic and occupational community by a careful examination of the materials that are posted to its site. This is true of many, many websites that represent the work of various fields of study and professions.

Writing to Respond

Based on a major or occupation you are considering, select websites and/or gather printed materials from your career counseling office that provide public presentations of institutions or organizations in that field. After you have carefully read, analyzed, and annotated your website or other materials (using the notes on the Council of Science Editors above as an example), in your writer's notebook make a list of commonplaces that inform this area of study and work. Think about the following questions as you read the materials you have collected, annotating them with your own ideas and reactions:

- How do members of this discipline or profession wish to present it to the public?
- What are the most important activities associated with this field of work or study? (For example, the NCTE website highlights teaching as its major topic area, rather than scholarship or research in English literature.)
- What current ideas or social practices most concern members of this field or organization? To what trends does the group seem to be responding? (For example, NCTE has position statements against censorship in schools.)
- What seem to be the most important issues facing members of this profession or discipline today?
- What phrases or terms seem to capture the values of this profession or institution—that is, what are some of the commonplaces that seem to inform this occupation's work?

Proposed legislation supports
an untested publishing model

Michael J. Held

Executive Director, The Rockefeller University Press

States the
goal of
proposed
legislation
Free access to information is a powerful and alluring concept. Under the "Public Access to Science Act," recently introduced into the U.S. House of Representatives by Representative Martin O. Sabo (Democrat, Minnesota), papers describing scientific research substantially funded by the U.S. Government would be excluded from copyright protection. This is proposed as a means to guarantee free access to this information.

Counterclaims
Representing the Rockefeller University Press (RUP), a nonprofit department of the Rockefeller University and publisher of The Journal of Cell Biology, I take issue with a number of the points made by the Sabo Act. It appears to me that this is a thinly veiled attempt by Harold Varmus and the other founders of the Public Library of Science (PLoS) to eventually force all publishers into their open access publishing model. As this publishing model is unproven and may well be unsustainable, this is an irresponsible act.

Science publishing: Models and costs

Concedes
this point
Introduces
problem
The mission of RUP includes the dissemination of scientific information to as broad an audience as possible as quickly as possible, so I am certainly not opposed to much of what the PLoS advocates. We at RUP welcome another player in the publishing field, and wish them well in their mission of providing free content by relying on upfront fees and charitable contributions. However, to attempt to legislate the demise of the time-honored subscription-based business model, prior to proving that another model works, does not seem wise. (The debut issue of PLoS Biology, the first journal from PLoS, is not due out until October, and the long-term financial health of the enterprise remains to be seen.) It is true that there are commercial publishers that reap profit for their shareholders from the sale of their journals, but there are also many not-for-profit society and university publishers that operate at little if any profit. In the cases where profit is made by the latter group, it is used to provide more features, more content, or educational programs that benefit society as a whole.

Proposed
solution

Practical issues
for the field
Print journals aside, the costs of producing an online journal are not trivial, and involve those of peer review, copyediting, production, and distribution (including costs in providing high speed access worldwide). New technologies are needed for the failsafe storage and secure maintenance of a large archive, and for the development of new features and search capabilities that make the material more readily available and of greater value to the researcher. In addition, many journals, including those at RUP, provide a valuable service in sifting through and interpreting (through news and commentary) a mountain of scientific data that is ever increasing. All this costs money. The RUP journals and many of the society journals exist by receiving revenue from a variety of sources: subscription and license fees, page and color charges to authors, advertising, and permissions for commercial use. In this manner, we are able to avoid charging any one participant in the process too much, and we keep our fees as low as possible. Ironically, an open access model may end up threatening the ability of some researchers to publish their research if all costs are lumped into a large upfront payment.

Call for
further testing

Stresses
collegiality and
cooperation
The various models for open access by groups such as PLoS, Scholarly Publishing and Academic Resources Coalition (SPARC), CreateChange, E-BioSci, and BioMed Central, among others, are honorable, noble experiments in dealing with the current publication dilemma. However, I see no reason at the present time to destroy the subscription model until we see that these new models can survive, any more than I see fit to kill off print immediately, solely because some want to, as opposed to waiting until the public says it is no longer needed. It is far better for all of us to work together cooperatively for the good of disseminating science, rather than to be in constant discord, thereby creating animosity among researchers, publishers, and librarians, and delaying progress.

Potential
problems
Those of us in the nonprofit sector are the natural allies of "open access." This is especially true for the large cadre of scientists who have for years donated extraordinary amounts of their expertise, time, and dedication to advancing the essential cause of free and open scientific communication, and done so long before PLoS appeared on the scene. The current effort, instigated by a small group and funded privately, is already having the effect of splitting the community. Their actions, embodied by the Sabo legislation, would

(continued)

Editorial link from the Council of Science Editors website.

appear to have a self-interested purpose of increasing the success of their own philosophy and business
Need for   model, to the possible detriment of all others. There are many other options to be explored, and indeed that
further study   already exist, to ensure "open access."

Existing free content

Many of the publishers (like RUP) that are in the middle of the publishing spectrum—the organizations
situated between the open access advocates and the commercial publishing conglomerates—have already
been instrumental in promoting free back content. These organizations publish a large percentage of the
most important scientific findings, asking for the advice of the already over-committed top researchers to
peer review the content prior to publication. Many of these publishers banded together with the assistance of
Key issue for   HighWire Press, a division of Stanford University Library System. This allows publishers with far fewer
the field   resources than the large commercial publishers to compete in the online arena.

An important feature of HighWire is its free content. To date 556,915 articles in 335 journals at HighWire are
available online for free, and this number grows daily. Currently, the RUP journals, and those of many HighWire
and some commercial publishers, make all of their content freely available to countries that are defined by the
World Health Organization as developing nations. For more advanced nations, the three RUP journals are also
available free after 6 months (The Journal of Cell Biology) or 12 months (The Journal of Experimental Medicine
and The Journal of General Physiology). HighWire publishers allow free full-text access to articles from the
references of one another's journals. Finally, RUP provides for free a fully searchable archive of pdfs back to 1975,
and within the year we expect to provide free pdfs all the way back to Volume 1, Issue 1 of each of our journals.

Open access and Sabo

The Sabo legislation would force scientific publishers into the PLoS open access model, because as soon as
we publish anything funded by the U.S. Government it would be available for anyone else to republish or
repurpose in any form once they gained access to our online or print editions. Anyone could then post it to any
open access site, or a commercial publisher could also post it, claiming huge amounts of data available at one
Key practical   location, clearly an advantage to the librarian. What would then be the incentive or value to publishers that
problem   need to rely on a proper business model rather than on charitable contributions as PLoS is currently doing?

Need for   Sabo's draft legislation is in effect overturning legislation that was put in place to protect an author's works,
copyright   i.e., copyright law. RUP continues to hold copyright to prevent misuse of the materials by third parties or
protection   commercial organizations, and as part of this duty we handle permissions on the authors' behalf. However,
we allow authors unrestricted use of their own materials for any purpose, and we encourage them to post
the pdfs of their articles on their or their university's web sites.

The U.S. Government supports both research and the writing of that research, just as it contributes to
research whose results are patented. As I understand it, the U.S. Government does not own that information
by virtue of providing grant funding, except in those cases where the work is performed at a government
agency, in which case the work is considered a work for hire and the government retains copyright, thereby
Practical   allowing free dissemination of that work. I cannot imagine how a law such as the Sabo legislation would
problem of   work, with some funds coming from the government, others from a university, and others from private
implementation   resources. There are frequently collaborations involving many sources and foreign governments. What is the
strategy for dealing with such cases?

Constructive thinking

The fact remains that a large swathe of papers are published by for-profit publishers. The more highly cited
of these journals offer a valuable product but negligible free material. Based on experience at RUP and
other nonprofit publishers, posting of older content for free holds no financial risks for the publisher and
huge benefit for the consumer, and yet the for-profit publishers continue to resist such ideas. Can we be
constructive in thinking of approaches to address this problem, so that we can influence these publishers in
ways that are less destructive to all publishers than the Sabo bill?

The power to coerce lies with those who pay the bills: the librarians. If librarians can act together they can
insist on solutions that are both financially viable for publishers and morally acceptable for consumers.
Meanwhile, authors who have work that is valid but of lower impact can vote with their words by publishing
in no-frills open access sites such as BioMed Central, rather than in obscure for-profit titles that are bundled
in large, expensive packages that libraries feel pressured to buy.

(continued)

Counterclaims

Finally, this draft legislation is named the "Public Access to Science Act" yet it really is about copyright. Copyright and public access are two entirely different entities, with one not necessarily affecting the other. As shown above, a copyright holder can still provide free access, and in fact granting copyright back to authors (as has also been proposed by PLoS) could prevent any form of free access because permission to post material would have to be obtained from each individual author. Publishers such as RUP seek to hold secure copyright so that we can ensure that we have both the legal right and the resources to guarantee free access, albeit after a brief interval.

Key problem for the field

The Internet bubble of the late 1990s showed that the obvious attraction of free content can flounder when faced with economic reality. The Sabo bill threatens to destroy a system that has become extremely efficient at disseminating scientific information in its many forms, without carefully examining the consequences of copyright prohibition. As such it is a hasty and ill-timed measure.

Writing Applications

Based on the information you have collected, write an informational essay that details what you take to be the key commonplaces of this profession. Try to help your audience—other students who share an interest in this field—understand what it means to be a professional in this field, what issues face the people who work in this profession, and the shared values or commonplaces that seem to be most important for workers in this profession. Be sure to support your claims with specifics from the site.

Case 3 ACADEMIC-OCCUPATIONAL CONNECTIONS

The sequence of courses (what educators call a curriculum) in any major is designed to prepare students for work in fields related to that academic discipline. Though some majors are more directly designed as career preparation (management, education, nursing) than others (English, philosophy, political science), each curriculum attempts to imagine the intellectual and physical work students might do in the future. For this reason, exploring the curriculum of a major that interests you can help you (and your audience) to understand the connections between your present occupation as a student, the work you may be doing now, and the potential future occupations associated with that field of study.

Though course catalogs and college websites are largely informational—they describe the nuts and bolts of attaining a degree—they can also be a useful source of information about the commonplaces of various disciplines and occupational fields. If you read closely and analytically, you can learn a great deal about your proposed area(s) of study.

The home page for Purdue University's Department of Communication is on page 111. I've annotated this page to illustrate commonplaces of the field of communication that are highlighted by this program. As with the organizational Web pages discussed in the previous case, careful reading and attention to the commonplace ideas that are embedded in a major's public presentation can help you to understand the work that is done there. It can also help you to see the connections between the course of studies and the occupations for which that course of studies prepares you.

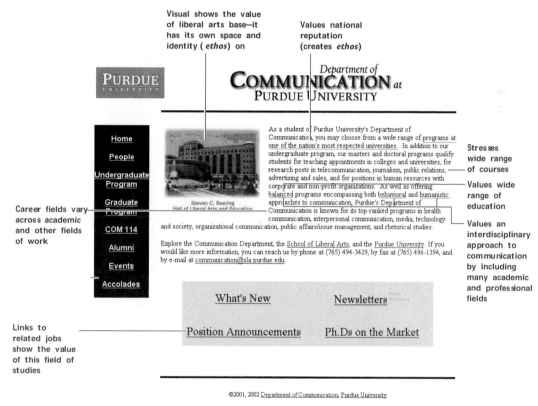

The home page for the Department of Communication, Purdue University.

The home page for the Department of Communication at Purdue offers an overview of the field's interests and commonplaces, including:

- The value of the educational institution itself
- The ways that communication as a field interacts with other disciplines and fields
- The fields and occupations for which the major prepares students, including "teaching appointments in colleges and universities, research posts in telecommunications, journalism, public relations, advertising and sales, and positions in human resources with corporate and non-profit organizations"
- The connection of the field of communication to both a liberal arts or "humanistic" and "behavioral" fields of study
- The areas of specialty that can be the focus of communication, including "health communication, interpersonal communication, media, technology and society," and so on
- The point that communication is not an isolated field but one that brings together many fields of study in an "interdisciplinary" way

Though the home page for a major provides a great deal of information about that field of study and work, detailed course information can give a more specific understanding of what the field encompasses. By reading individual course descriptions within a department or major, you can gain a much better understanding of how the courses are designed to provide you with a coherent experience in college. Take a look at some of the courses that are offered by the communications department at Purdue. On the following pages, I have annotated the material to point out what you can learn from each description.

The course descriptions flesh out the skeletal picture of the major that is provided by the communications home page, showing, for example, that:

- Critical thinking and writing are crucial for this major.
- A successful worker in this field must be able to work with specific types of information technology.
- Some subfields (like television, radio, and Web production) require specific practical skills and have their own set of problems and practical issues.
- Communications as a field is very much concerned with ethics, issues of gender, and minority issues.
- Communications is increasingly a global field of study and work.
- Each related career field has specific laws, concerns, and issues related to it.

Purdue University, as a large and diverse institution, offers a much wider range of courses than do communications departments in smaller schools. But no matter the size of your college, you can learn a good deal by a serious examination of your college catalog or website, paying special attention to the commonplaces of the field that it can reveal.

Courses

204 Critical Perspectives on Communication (formerly Communication and Social Knowledge). Introduction to critical thinking and writing about communication, focusing on strategic messages. Students will learn critical methods as they build thinking, analytic, and writing skills to help them become more sophisticated consumers and producers of messages. Involves mass lecture with recitation sections and numerous writing assignments to help students develop their abilities to analyze communication questions and construct coherent arguments about them in writing.

Both reading
and writing
are crucial

224 Communication in the Global Workplace. This introductory course is designed to provide students with a global perspective on the world of work by exploring communication issues that arise in the global workplace. The course will help students develop an appreciation of the relationship between culture, communication, and ways of organizing and doing business. Aimed at students across the curriculum, COM 224 fulfills the School of Liberal Arts global perspectives requirement.

Provides global
perspective

235 Information Resources & Technology. This course focuses on how students can use information technology and information resources to achieve their academic goals – how to access information, manipulate it, transmit it, and apply it to specific tasks. Introduces students to the use of various information technologies, including basic computer systems and software applications, with particular emphasis on information resources that are critical to the student of mass communication, journalism, and telecommunications.

Use of new
technologies

250 / 250H Mass Communication and Society. Introductory survey of mass communication. Principle topics include the history, function, managerial incentive structure, and regulation of media industries in the United States, the messages produced by media industries, and public concerns about the impact of media messages on individuals and society. The course is taught from a liberal arts perspective, and enhancement of media literacy is the overall course objective. Course Syllabus - Spring 2000 (Sparks)

Role of
communication
in wider
culture

256 Introduction to Advertising. An analysis of commercial persuasion from colonial times to the era of mass communication. The course examines the structure of advertising messages, how they are adapted to specific audiences, and the social settings in which they occur.

Practical
introduction
to methods
in the field

261 Introduction to Television Production. Introduction to the basic principles of television production. Through lecture, viewings, discussion, critiques, and a wide range of exercises, students will learn how television programs are designed, planned, and produced.

300 Introduction to Communication Research Methods. Introduction to empirical research methods as applied to answering questions about communication. Provides an overview of experimental and non-experimental research design and basic introduction to descriptive and inferential statistics including the use of statistical software for data analysis. Course Syllabus - Fall 2002 (MacGeorge) Course Syllabus - Spring 2000 (Roberts)

303 Intercultural Communication. A study of the complex relationship between culture and communication in a variety of interpersonal, group, organizational and computer-mediated settings. Explore the impact of perceptions, values, personal identity, beliefs, attitudes, cultural patterns, social institutions, culture shock, and

Linked

(continued)

Selected courses in Communications, Purdue University.

acculturation processes on people's ways of creating and interpreting verbal and nonverbal messages. The course focuses on the application of theory and current research for developing the knowledge, attitudes, and skills associated with intercultural communication competence.

324 Introduction to Organizational Communication. Prerequisite: COM 114 or equivalent. Introduction to communication, organizational, and management theories. Topics include symbolic exchange, message distortion, the rhetoric of work, and communication approaches to conflict and power, networks, organizational culture, negotiation, worker participation, technology, and superior-subordinate relations. Course Syllabus - Spring 2000 (Clair)

Communicating on the job!

Technologies for the field

334 Journalism for the Electronic Mass Media. Prerequisite: COM 256. Theory and practice of electronic journalism with projects relating to straight news, feature reports, commentary, editorial, interview, and documentary.

Use of technologies

336 Advertising in the Electronic Mass Media. Prerequisite: COM 256. Gives students an understanding of advertising processes through the planning, strategy, and execution of radio and TV advertising on behalf of clients and the presentation and analysis of client campaigns.

351 Mass Communication Ethics. A survey of various ethical approaches applied to situations confronting contemporary mass communicators, including misrepresentation in newsgathering, protection of sources, suppression of information, reporting of terror and violence, pressure from management and advertisers, and reporters.

Ethical issues in the field

Related legal issues

352 Mass Communication Law. Examines the American legal system along with the development of the First Amendment and numerous contemporary problems implicating the First Amendment. It also studies the current conditions in areas where communications practitioners should be well prepared, such as libel, privacy, access to public information, obscenity, copyright, advertising, the fair trial/free press concerns, and telecommunications regulations. The course will consider state and federal regulations along with court precedents.

Practical problem-solving

353 Problems in Public Relations. Public relations majors have priority. Students will design a PR campaign for a local client organization and execute the campaign during the semester within the agreed upon budget. The course pays special attention to conducting media relations (writing press releases and holding press conferences) and using other public relations tools such as newsletters, annual reports, etc. Course Syllabus - Fall 2002 (Botan)

356 Problems in Advertising. Prerequisite: COM 256; graduating advertising majors have priority. Focuses on the problem of analyzing and understanding advertising messages and their contribution to "social communication." Course Syllabus - Spring 2001 (Thompson)

358 Specialized Writing. Prerequisite: COM 252. Study of, and practice in, methods of journalistic research and presentation; preparation of in-depth newspaper stories based on student research. Course Syllabus - Spring 2002 (Natt)

Writing specialized by use in field

Gender ethics

376 Communication and Gender. Based on the assumption that studies of gender and communication are intertwined. Focus is on communication processes that create symbols of gender and how those processes recreate the meanings of gender in the lives of individual and groups. Course Syllabus - Spring 2000 (Webb)

(continued)

424 Communication in International Organizations. Explores the transformation from domestic to global forms of organizing in profit and non-profit contexts. Students will address the organizational and communication implications of increasing internationalization by focusing upon specific industries and regions of the world. Theoretical and practical approaches to understanding and interacting in culturally diverse systems will be highlighted.

Another course in global communication

435 / 435H Communication and Emerging Technologies. Prerequisites: COM 114 and 250. The history of the world has been marked by dramatic social change facilitated by communication technologies. This course addresses the implications of the newest of these technologies – digital media. First, we will examine the macro-social trends resulting from digital convergence of communication industries. Next, we will examine current and emerging technologies (e.g. the internet, virtual reality, etc.) and will look at how business is conducted in the new era of digital communication. Finally, we will examine current research about the ways which we communicate using technologies. These ideas will be the practical tools you will take with you into your professional lives as creators and facilitators of communication. Course Syllabus - Fall 2002 (Sherry)

Key focus = technology

442 Problems in Television Directing/Producing. A studio set atmosphere in which students address problems encountered in both dramatic and non-dramatic formats as they write, produce, and direct programs during the semester. Emphasis on organizational skills, program analysis, and aesthetic judgment.

Practical problem-solving

459 Public Editing. Study of and practice in the handling of graphic materials and page makeup techniques. A variety of publication formats, including standard and tabloid newspaper pages, will be dealt with.

462 Advanced Newswriting. Combines practical experience with classroom learning. Students will work 10-12 hours weekly at *The Journal and Courier* and attend a one-hour class weekly, during which J&C assignments are critiqued and readings discussed.

Skills for various fields

490 Internship in Communication. Open to students admitted to the Communication major (may be repeated for a maximum of 6 credits). Experiential, supervised training in advertising, journalism, public relations, organizational communication, or telecommunication. Usually offered in junior or senior year.

Practical on-the-job experience

491B Science: Its Practices and Its Publics. This course will consider how scientific information is created, disseminated, and evaluated and explore the role of professional and lay publics in these processes. In doing this, examine Bauer's assertion that "perhaps the central fallacy is that there exists an entity called 'science' about which sweeping generalizations can validly be made." One key to understanding this may be any differences we can discern between "frontier science" and "textbook science." Reach consensus on what is meant by "scientific literacy" and "scientific method(s)." Course Syllabus - Fall 2003 (Trachtman)

Communication in a specific discipline

491W Web Production. Provides students with an overview of the web production process. Learn basic web development skills including HTML, graphic and multimedia integration, and web site design. Get exposure to major web development software tools in current use. Views web development from a communication perspective, emphasizing audience analysis and site usability. No previous web development experience is expected, but students should be computer and Internet literate.

Practical use of technology

(continued)

Focus on career fields

Communication and Career Issues. This course provides an opportunity to explore careers and communication with emphases on lifelong career aspects and employability security. This course will discuss a variety of career topics including: assumptions about and definitions of careers in the U.S. and globally, vocational choice and implications, "managing your boss" and others with whom you interact in your career development, career uncertainty, employer-employee contracts, work-life issues, job loss, expatriate career issues, differing models for career communication (e.g., race/ethnicity issues, women's career development), and career fantasies and ways of making these fantasies happen.

Current issues

Communication Campaigns. The evaluation and assessment of existing public campaigns form the foundational structure of this course. Through the process of critiquing multiple commercial, political, and public health campaigns, students learn the key strategic elements involved in the creation of an effective campaign. Four areas of channel selection, content development, and campaign evaluation based on the knowledge developed in strategizing. Campaign topics include current and relevant areas of social change such as tobacco consumption, alcohol consumption, sexually transmitted diseases, birth control, environmental issues, nutrition and healthy eating, exercising, seat-belt usage, breast and cervical cancer screening, terrorism, biological and chemical warfare, etc.

Communications in specific fields

Communication in Health Organizations. Designed to introduce the student to a wide range of theory and practice about communication in health organizations. We will examine micro-level and macro-level interaction processes involved in cultural constructions of health and illness. Begins with a basic introduction to the field of health communication, ethical concerns in the health care environment, and the models that frame theory and empirical research in this area. Then address such issues as the creation of health meanings, health care socialization, naturalistic medicine, HMOs, health care teams, stress and burnout among health care workers, and social support at the dyadic, group, and community levels. The study of HIV/AIDS, occupational health and safety, and a CDC health communication campaign will serve as underlying empirical threads for grounding the theoretical and conceptual issues.

Cyber Law and Ethics for Media Practitioners. This class looks at both legal and ethical issues concerning the Web with which media practitioners should be well versed. The class examines some of the regulatory issues to get a background for the legal and ethical questions discussed in the class. It also includes some of the controversy over policy for the Web. It examines a number of legal and ethical issues that present specific problems on the Web, such as privacy (everything from cookies to information the government holds about each of us in their computer databases), libel (including how libel in cyberspace might have to play by different rules), access to information, copyright issues (such as framing, linking, Napster, the Digital Millennium Copyright Act), and numerous free speech issues (everything from hate speech sites to filters).

Ethical issues of minorities

Media and Minorities. Survey of some issues of race and gender in media products through the writings of a cross section of critical cultural scholars and an examination of contemporary perceptions of these issues in current media product.

Writing to Respond

Using our discussion of Purdue's communications major as an example, examine the course descriptions, catalog descriptions, and promotional materials of a field of study at your institution that interests you. You might also draw on resources on related career fields, including talking to professors and other workers in those fields. As you invent and plan for this essay, consider the following as you invent ideas in your writer's notebook:

- How do required courses contribute to the overall educational goals of the major?

- To what occupational goals and needs does each course contribute, directly or indirectly?

- Read the course descriptions for each required course, and the suggested sequence of courses. Try to imagine how the curriculum might prepare you for the work in that field. Consider both specific courses and the connections among them.

- In what ways do the general education courses that are required by your college contribute to the work of those in this major field or occupation?

- What seem to be the major issues that are faced by current professionals in this field?

Writing Application

Write an informational essay, brochure, or Web page for students at your college interested in this major. Though you may draw on the published materials from your college's catalog, website, and other materials, your goal should be to give prospective students a clearer vision of what this field entails, both for students and for future professionals. If you have work experience in this or a related field (as many returning adult students do), you might draw on that as well. You can focus on a specific professional goal or give a broad overview of the possible professions; in either case, help students to see the connections between the academic major and future work.

Case 4 COMMUNITY CONNECTIONS

Professionals in a field tend to work in groups distinct from the larger community—within corporations and companies, at trade shows, conferences, and conventions, and within professional publications. However, they are also very much part of the wider community, being called on as experts in a variety of community affairs. One of the ways you can learn about the work done in a particular occupational field is to notice the ways its professionals help their community to function—and how, in some cases, they can come into conflict with the larger community. Keeping an eye out for the ways that people in your areas of interest are represented in the news, local and national politics, and community groups can help you to see the interconnectedness of the work they do. By noting the public *ethos* of people in areas that concern you, you may develop a sense of how your field of study or potential field of work connects with a larger public.

The article that follows illustrates the ways in which workers in a specific field (in this case, pharmacists) can fill a community need:

The Community Pharmacy: A Canadian Health Care Success Story; Industry Report Shows Pharmacy Is Valuable Part of Community Life

Dateline: British Columbia, April 1

Every single day over eight million Canadians go to a community pharmacy in Canada for their health and personal care needs, making pharmacies the most frequently visited primary health care provider, says Christina Bisanz, President and CEO of the Canadian Association of Chain Drug Stores (CACDS), in releasing the Association's 2002 State of the Industry report.

Despite the economic uncertainty and turbulent health care environment of the past year, community chain pharmacies continued to expand their services and products for Canadians while creating secure jobs and investing in technology and training. CACDS members operate 1,278 stores in Western Canada, which is 57% of all pharmacies in the region. There are 506 community chain pharmacies located in British Columbia.

According to the 2002 State of the Industry, not only are community pharmacies providing more medication services, they have become neighborhood centers for health and wellness. One-hundred percent of CACDS' retail pharmacy members offer medication follow-up services and compliance programs, up from 83% and 92% respectively in 2001. Besides being prescription medication experts, pharmacists provide more counseling on over-the-counter (OTC) products than any other health professional. In 2002, 100% of CACDS members reported their pharmacists counsel patients on OTC and natural health products.

The community pharmacy infrastructure supports team-based primary health care. For example, community pharmacies are becoming common sites for nurses to provide flu vaccinations. Also, some pharmacies have nurses on staff working with pharmacists to provide testing and counseling for prevalent diseases, such as osteoporosis and diabetes.

The pharmacy's vital role in community life extends beyond the four walls of the drug store. Ninety-one percent of traditional drug stores and 75% of grocery and mass merchandisers with pharmacies offer pharmaceutical care to residents in long-term care and other facilities, including group homes and community centers.

The aging baby-boom generation who believes in prevention and quality of life is a driving force behind the surge in demand for pharmacy products and services.

"Canadians are taking a more active role in their health and are intensely interested in self-care. The community pharmacy is the ideal environment for the modern health consumer," says Bisanz. Not surprisingly, nutrition, anti-smoking, and cosmetic "camouflage" products, such as tooth polish kits, were among the fastest growing front-shop categories in 2002.

"Community pharmacies offer a highly accessible network of pharmacists that bring health and wellness products, services and care to Canadians, right in their own neighborhoods," says Bisanz.

Nearly three-quarters of CACDS's traditional drug store members were open extended hours (between 13 and 23 hours a day) in 2002. The vast majority of members (89%) increased investments in technology to enhance service levels for consumers. For the second year in a row, however, the State of the Industry report found that the pharmacist shortage is the greatest challenge limiting their ability to provide 24/7 access to primary health care services.

CACDS is the voice of community pharmacy in Canada. Its 22 members represent traditional chain drug stores, including national, regional and independently owned and operated pharmacies, and grocery chains and mass merchandisers with pharmacies. Its member pharmacies dispense some 75% of the nation's prescriptions each year through 4,151 stores—over 60% of the national total—and employ over 80,000 Canadians, including 14,730 pharmacists or some 60% of the pharmacist labor force.

The 2002 State of the Industry report highlights the results of the eighth annual CACDS member survey. It examines the latest economic and consumer trends influencing community pharmacy, the growing role of pharmacy in the health care system, and the economic contribution of Canada's retail pharmacy sector.

Writing to Respond

After reading the above article, freewrite in your writer's notebook about the ways that occupational/community interactions have functioned in this case to serve a specific need. What commonplaces of this profession help pharmacists to fulfill these needs? In what ways does the Canadian pharmacy function as a community center? Why is the pharmacy an important site for the distribution of healthcare information? Who are the beneficiaries of this relationship? Can you foresee any negative consequences in this relationship?

Writing Application

Read the newspaper and recent news magazines, watch local and/or cable news, and seek news outlets on the Internet. Look for public representations of people or issues related to your own areas of interest. In your writer's notebook, record your impressions about the public role played, and the public *ethos* portrayed, by people in your areas of interest. List the public concerns that fall within the sphere of influence of people in a profession or academic area that interests you. If you are a returning student who has worked in a career field in the past, this might also give you the opportunity to discuss the ways in which your present or past occupation interacted with your community in specific ways.

Using your own experiences, the experiences of others you know, and the sources of information listed above, write an informational essay, brochure, or Web page that describes how the work done in a specific career field is crucial to the wider community.

In order to help you think about style and audience, consider where you might publish an essay on your field; even if you have no intentions of formally publishing your essay, this exercise can help you to see the styles used in various venues—journals, popular magazines, and newspapers, for example. Using online resources and visiting your library's periodicals room (where you can browse recent editions of journals and magazines), try to find three publications that might be interested in publishing the essay on which you are currently working.

Drafting and Arranging Ideas for Your Readers

Much of the writing you have done so far in this book has been inventional—that is, for the purpose of generating and developing ideas. Though it is the first of the rhetorical canons, invention continues throughout all stages of your writing processes; after all, you are always trying to enrich your ideas. But if you wish to present those ideas to readers, you must consider other things as well: arranging your words and ideas in the most effective order, choosing a style that best communicates your message, and delivering your document in the form that will best suit your purpose and audience. These three activities are represented by the rhetorical canons of **arrangement, style,** and **delivery.**

The rhetorical canon of **arrangement** is a natural byproduct of the creative processes of invention. Though invention can help you to bring forth, collect, and develop ideas, those ideas rarely emerge in an organized form. For this reason, it is your task as a writer to find ways to arrange the ideas that you wish to express in a way that will seem reasonable to your readers and that best serves your goals as a writer. This chapter discusses strategies for taking that next step—searching for arrangement patterns that are logical, coherent, and suited to your audience. Since, like all facets of good writing, these strategies must be adapted to specific rhetorical situations, you'll also continue your inquiry into the ways various fields and occupations communicate among themselves and with the wider community, asking how to best arrange your ideas for each specific context.

As you begin drafting a document, you also must make decisions that are addressed by the rhetorical canon of **style.** Though difficult to define, style is largely about the words that you choose, about the sentence structures that you develop, and about the tone and voice that your words and sentences project. As you draft, you are choosing among many possible stylistic techniques. The stylistic choices you make will do a great deal to establish, or to undermine, your *ethos* in any given rhetorical situation. After all, those choices create the voice that your readers will hear—an important part of producing effective pieces of writing. This is especially true when you consider the many audiences for whom you are asked to write as a student, worker, and citizen.

The last of the rhetorical canons, **delivery,** provides strategies to help you to go public with your thoughts and words. As a speaker, that moment comes when you stand before an audience and *deliver* an oration. As a writer, similarly, the moment of delivery is when you present your written document to others. Since delivery is largely about final choices, about deciding among the arrangement patterns and styles that you invented in the processes of drafting and revising, we explore strategies to help you to make those choices with the rhetorical situation in mind. As a group, these three canons provide the rhetorical tools that are all used toward a single purpose: changing a reader's mind.

CHANGING A READER'S MIND

Whether or not you overtly attempt to influence your readers' position on a topic, your writing always aims at changing minds in a broader sense. Your writing presents new information, spurs deeper thought, and asks readers to imagine new possibilities—all likely to change their ways of thinking. One question you might ask as you begin to write is "In what ways do I want to change my readers?" The logical corollary is "*How* can I change my readers' thinking in those directions?"

Thinking about a direction for your writing is essential in drafting. It can help you to envision your writing as a pathway, a logically and/or emotionally constructed line of reasoning your reader can follow through your document. If you are to move your readers along a shared pathway of reasoning, of course, you must first meet them where they are *before* they read what you've written. Imagine, for example, that you are writing for readers who deeply believe in the right of citizens to disobey laws that are against their moral beliefs. You want to help them see that such actions are often counterproductive and dangerous to a society. In order to change their mind—which, at a minimum, means getting them to listen to your reasons why civil disobedience can be a dangerous practice—you must begin with your readers' assumptions and determine ways to reason with them about the relative value of each view. You can present new information, provide examples, describe or narrate scenarios, all attempting to expand a reader's perspective on the issue. But you cannot do so productively without considering the views that your audience likely holds coming into the conversation. Knowing where your readers stand on the topic, as well as where you wish to take them, can help you to imagine the logical steps from one position to another—and the rhetorical decisions that can help illuminate that path. But if you are doing this in a sincere and critical way, you must also be ready to revise and question your own paths of reasoning along the way.

In the discussions and writing opportunities that follow, we examine ways to discover and refine that imaginary pathway, to create a collaborative experience between reader and writer. We first approach the issues of arrangement, style, and delivery from a global perspective, asking questions about the shape of the whole document, such as:

- How can I discover ways to organize my essay?
- How can I choose among those ways?
- How can I anticipate my readers' reactions to various arrangement patterns?

We then consider smaller, more local (but no less important) issues:

- How will the order in which I present my ideas affect my audience's experience of my document?
- How can individual paragraphs, and the relationships among them, help me to create a logical pathway of reasoning?

■ How do various sentence structures allow me to show the relative importance of the ideas that I want to express?

By beginning with the larger, overarching questions of style and arrangement, you can focus first on finding a general pattern of reasoning and arrangement, and then refine that pattern by suiting individual paragraphs and sentences to serve that pattern. Many writers find this to be an efficient system, since there is little use in reconstructing and revising paragraphs and sentences that, in the end, don't fit the overall logic of your written document and so must be deleted.

DRAFTING AS DISCOVERY

You've probably been introduced before to the use of outlines as a method for organizing a piece of writing. Outlines are one method of arranging ideas, of imagining and planning a logical flow of ideas to help readers to move through your essay. In practice, however, it is sometimes difficult to imagine the precise arrangement of a document until you explore the thinking that connects the parts of your topic. Writing a discovery draft can help you to find lines of reasoning that can hold your essay together.

A discovery draft is, like other inventional writing, an attempt to come to grips with your ideas. There is one significant difference: A discovery draft comes *after* you have collected your thoughts through prewriting. It is more complex, incorporating not only your own ideas but also those ideas you have learned from other sources. While freewriting encourages you to follow your ideas wherever they lead, a discovery draft asks you to consciously *avoid* drifting; in fact, trying to construct a more logical order for your paper is one of its primary purposes. The process of writing the discovery draft is for this reason slower and more laborious than freewriting, because you should consistently be asking yourself questions: Where is this going? Am I staying on track toward my ultimate purpose? Does this information belong here or elsewhere? And my personal favorite question to myself: "What's your point? What *is* your point?"

Imagine that you are a fine arts student and that you are asked to write an informative essay on techniques of realism and how they compare with your own artistic techniques. Below is an example of what a discovery draft for that occasion might look like. Note how the writer drafts the essay with more than the topic in mind, interspersing comments and questions to herself (in brackets) throughout the piece as she searches for appropriate arrangement and stylistic choices. Her mind is not only on the information that she has collected but also on the best ways to convey that information. The resulting draft is a map of her thought processes, illustrating her attempts to discover possible patterns of logic and wordings that suit her goals. You can just *hear* the learning going on as this writer struggles to find her focus.

Realism in conjunction with photography captures the factual accuracy of life and its experiences. Realism stems for the French tradition of Romantic naturalism. [DO I NEED TO INCLUDE A DEFINITION OF ROMANTIC NATURALISM? WHICH SOURCES CAN HELP ME DO THAT?] Realism in all separate elements—landscape, portraits, narrative, historical and social, are based on the artists ability to represent the realities of life, in all its beauty and ugliness. [HOW SHOULD I DEFINE REALISM? WHAT DO THESE ELEMENTS HAVE IN COMMON?] The Realism of the 19th Century was largely spread due to the French Utopian socialist, Comte de Saint-Simon, who believed that with the aid of science he could facilitate the reconstruction of society, which he labeled the "Golden Age of Humanity." He believed that the artists of his day had a responsibility to function as an integral part of the proposed new social order. [TIE THIS INTO THE DEFINITIONS OF REALISM ABOVE]. Liberal critics began to embrace his theory of the role of the artists and in 1833 the critic, Gustave Planche first applied the term Realism to art. For him it meant that the artist was responsible to provide a moral dimension to a contemporary subject or theme, while also exhibiting distinct social intentions. Emile Zola, the author of several sociological novels, embraced and defended Manet's radical style. A literary critic, a Champfleury helped Courbet write his Realist Manifesto. With Courbet's statement: "To be in the position to translate the customs, the ideas, the appearance of my epoch, according to my own estimation; to be not only a painter, but a man as well; in short, to create living art—this is my goal," he demonstrates the belief that art and life are one in the same. Realists were predominately critics of the contemporary society. [IS THIS REPETITIOUS?] They showed the inequities of the human condition, in the dark setting of the industrial world and in the unindustrialized but difficult rural setting/world. [LIKE ALL REALISTS, THEY NEED TO SHOW THE REALITIES OF LIFE, BOTH POSITIVE AND NEGATIVE. COULD THAT POINT TIE TOGETHER MY ESSAY?] Realist painters concentrated on calmly and coolly depicting the difficulties/obstacles in achieving personal freedom. [PERSONAL FREEDOM—A KEY CONCEPT?] This freedom was unobtainable because of their heredity, their environment, and because of their own passions. Therefore Realist philosophies were based on the role of art in human life. [AGAIN, THE KEY SEEMS TO BE THE RELATION OF ART IN LIFE IN THE REALIST MOVEMENT. HOW CAN I FURTHER STRESS THAT?]

The deterioration of the Salon and Academy system began within the period of Realism. In 1863 the Salon of the Rejected painters was formed by Napoleon the III in response to the public's and artists' outcry for the over 4,000 Salon-rejected works. Although Napoleonic artistic tastes were more akin/similar to/related to the academy, he did realize the need for the public to critique/discard/agree on the rejected works.

This is significant because it set the foundation for an alternative exhibit that was not dictated by the tastes and standards of the academy jury and their definition of official art. [MAYBE I SHOULD MAKE THIS DISTINCTION SOONER, TO SET THE CONTEXT FOR THE PIECE?] The reasons for this event are perhaps even more significant than the event itself. [O. K. THAT'S A CRUCIAL POINT. HISTORY IS CRUCIAL IN UNDERSTANDING THE REALIST MOVEMENT. IS THAT MY POINT????] With the emergence of critics and with their published writings on art, art became an accessible to the general public. The academy was no longer the mediator between the painter and the public. [I'VE ALREADY TALKED ABOUT ZOLA'S ROLE AS CRITIC—TIE BACK INTO THAT?] The public, the critics, and the artists themselves now had a part in the definition of art and as it relates to the desires of the public, critics and artists. Therefore, it is the public and the critics who support the artists now, not the academy.

Also, with the Age of Enlightenment came the idea of aesthetics as an area of study. [EXPAND ON THIS—BUT WHERE DOES IT FIT IN?]

The foremost/most significant Realists of the 19th century were Gustave Courbet, Honore Daumier, Edouard Manet, Corot, and Millet. This group in their own individual styles were all united in the concept/theory of honoring the realities and the Heroes of Modern Life and/while portraying/exhibiting the current social and political comments they did follow the Realist sentiment that "Man should be of his own time." [GREAT QUOTATION. MAYBE THIS MIGHT HELP TO DEFINE REALISM FROM THE START. MIGHT EVEN MAKE A GOOD TITLE?] The heroes were for Manet the calm, dignified common presence of society's prostitute, the current entertainment trends of Paris— the exotic Spanish dancers and musicians. These works were composed of unmodeled, unidealized, flat outlined patches of color. [I HAVE A GOOD DEAL TO SAY ABOUT MANET—MAYBE THIS CAN BE ITS OWN PARAGRAPH?] Furthermore, as the photograph tends to emphasize the light and dark patches of a monochromatic work, so does Manet's portrait scenes of contemporary (realistic) life. Manet's figures/

subjects usually defiantly gaze directly at the viewer displaying their strength and comfort with their role/position in society.

Based on the above definitions of realism (as opposed to a simpler understanding of what is realistic) art participates in life, rather than reflecting a mirror image. It is a facilitator to /for art, rather than what? Art itself? Aesthetics? [To illustrate this I can use my own artistic development as an artist. As I first attempted to formally study art, self-portraits were the most difficult task/exercise to grasp. The concept was unreachable because I lacked the underlying/inner understanding of me as the subject. SHOULD I BEGIN WITH A STATEMENT ABOUT THAT? OR WOULD THAT MAKE IT TOO PERSONAL? WHAT WOULD MOST AFFECT MY AUDIENCE?]

Can you hear the writer looking for the lines of reasoning that will best serve the purposes of the paper? Finding that path is sometimes difficult, as you can tell from the writer's notes to herself: She is trying to come to grips with her own ideas, to find places where the ideas of others might fit in, and, at the same time, attempting to envision the way that the whole of the essay will eventually play itself out. Notice how the writer draws on ideas she has collected much in the way you have been collecting ideas in your writer's notebook; she recalls bits and pieces of information as she writes this discovery draft. She uses general statements about realism that she discovered in her reading and study. She uses historical examples. She uses quotations that help to explain the concept. If you trace the movements of the draft, they all share one thing—the attempt to discover a working definition.

In the process, the writer also attempts to find a logical arrangement or path of reasoning. As new ideas occur to her, she attempts to connect them with what she has already written. She recalls facts and characters from her reading that can serve as examples, and she searches for those phrases that seem to best capture her overall point. In all cases, rather than consider this draft something that can later just be cleaned up, she treats the first draft as discovery—something that will generate connections between ideas that can be the basis, eventually, for a clearer arrangement of ideas.

You might also note the writer's attention to stylistic choices as she attempts to find the right words and phrasings to express her thoughts on the topic. She writes, for example, "Although Napoleonic artistic tastes were more akin/similar to/related to the academy, he did realize the need for the public to critique/discard/agree on the rejected works." Rather than decide on the best word choice at this moment, she allows herself to speculate on several terms that might capture her point, knowing that she'll come back to this again to make decisions (including whether to include the line at all).

Once a discovery draft is complete, the writer can look over it and find those places where something coherent starts to emerge. If she manages to find one central point among the many she makes, things will start to fall into place as she cuts and pastes the movements of the essay into a logical sequence. Toward the end of this draft, you can hear the writer begin to find her central point, as she realizes that perhaps her own artworks can form the unifying element in explicating realism.

MINING FOR COHERENCE

One value of writing a discovery draft is that it helps you to search for coherence. Coherence means "the logically organized connection of parts." Searching for coherence involves two things:

- ▪ deciding on the most logical order in which to present your ideas, and
- ▪ helping *the reader* to see the progression of ideas from one to another.

Coherence can be plotted in an outline. But by writing a discovery draft, you allow yourself to play with your ideas, seeing how one might lead logically into another. The process is rarely perfect the first time through; you may go off on tangents (as the writer of the draft above did). But in many cases, by ruling out lines of reasoning that don't work, you can find an arrangement that does make sense.

After a draft (or partial draft) is written, you can stand back from it and mine for coherence. In mining, you try to separate the valuable minerals or gems from the material that needs to be chipped away and discarded. Sometimes all you find in a discovery draft is a single diamond—the moment of clarity in which you say, "Oh, that's it. That's my central point." You can hear that attempt to find the point in the above draft as the writer talks to herself: "Where does this fit in?" "How can I further stress that?" "Maybe I should make that distinction sooner." Though discarding words and ideas that you worked hard to generate can be difficult, it must be done to create a logically flowing essay. The good news is that once you find that central coherence, writing a mature outline (and the paper itself) can be much, much easier. What *seems* wasteful is really—to continue the mining metaphor—just part of the refining process.

So, using the above example, the next step is to create a functional outline. In this case, after thinking about her audience (art students) and her purpose (to help them to see how one's own work can fit into past traditions), the writer decided to focus her piece around a statement she made toward the end of her discovery draft: "To illustrate this, I can use my own artistic development as an artist." Her working outline then started to take shape:

1) Narrative of my own artistic development/ways that I have progressed from art that is just imitating styles and drawing pictures to my desire to have "content" (a social purpose? Ties to "real" life? What social concerns in particular concern me?)

2) Identify myself as a type of "realist" painter—because I want to "represent the realities of life, in all its beauty and ugliness." That will give me the reason to define realism. [I'll need to argue that knowing art history can help us develop personally as artists].

3) Describe various definitions of types of realism and move toward its essential elements. Then I can move on to specific examples.

4) Use historical examples to show how other artists, like me, developed toward using their art toward social concerns [that can, throughout the paper, keep my readers focused on my purpose]. Manet seems to be a central example. Are there other good ones? Tie together this section with the concept of "art for society's sake"? Distinguish this from aesthetics?

5) If I end the last section by distinguishing social concern from pure aesthetics, I can use the example of Napoleon and the Salon, or perhaps find other examples. What else do I have? I might also use the idea of Enlightenment to distinguish the purposes of art in various ages.

(continued)

6) I can transition back into the reasons why my own development moved away from just the formal study of art toward a more realistic focus.

7) End with some sort of argument for realism and social content, drawing again on the historical examples? Maybe end with "Man should be of his own time" quotation, or something like that?

THE CONVERSANT OUTLINE

You might notice that the above outline doesn't look like the conventional one, with Roman numerals and subsections. Instead, the above outline is *conversant*—the writer is talking (conversing) through the points she wants to make, considering ways to organize those points and looking for connections among them. Those are the fundamental principles of successful arrangement.

Conversational outlining can be productive because it *seeks* rather than *assumes* coherence. A linear outline suggests that your reasoning proceeds as a straight line and that planning an essay is just a matter of listing points to be covered. It assumes that because one point follows another, the connections will be clear to readers. In my experience, and that of most writers, inventive writing isn't that simple. Conversely, a "talking" or conversant outline makes no such assumption. It can be more effective because it is recursive rather than linear—it helps you to keep circling back to previous ideas and thinking about new ones, opening up many inventive options for arrangement.

Note, for example, the way the writer above seeks to find coherence between points 4 and 5:

4. . . . Manet seems to be a central example. Are there other good ones? Tie together this section with the concept of art for society's sake? Distinguish this from aesthetics?

5. If I end the last section by distinguishing social concern from pure aesthetics, I can use the example of Napoleon and the Salon, or perhaps find other examples. What else do I have?

Because you are constantly seeking ways that the various points cohere, you are at the same time finding places where they don't—where the logic breaks down, and where you have gaps that need to be filled. This, like the discovery draft, is a messy process—but whoever suggested that creativity was inspired by coloring inside the lines?

WRITING TO EXPLORE 4.1

Below is another student writer's attempt to find a coherent central point and a line of reasoning (other parts of the process, as well as the completed essay, is included later in this book). Read this piece, noting the way that Tracy Hanegraaf wrestles with both the issues and ways to *arrange* those issues into a coherent essay. Note especially the way that the topic develops as she writes from a general study on gender/wage issues to a discussion focusing on societal neglect of the family.

Imagine that you are working with Hanegraaf to help her to find an appropriate arrangement for her essay. In your writer's notebook, construct a conversant outline for this essay, much like the one on art history above. List the major points to be covered, suggesting an order for the ideas, supplying the logic that holds one point to another, and asking good questions about possible ways to bring coherence to the many ideas that she wishes to address.

When classified by gender, weekly medians of full-time, year-round workers can be alarming. However, reporters often neglect to mention statistics that indicate men work more hours per week and more weeks on average than women. In fact, most sources cited ignore various significant factors. Some researchers find that when wage comparisons are made between males and females in the same occupations, with the same amount of education, and working the same number of hours and weeks, the wage gap almost disappears. Additionally, some researchers suggest the gap almost disappears for childless females. What's more, "comparable worth" issues add another angle to the equal pay analysis, which has an entire group of followers who feel women are underpaid for jobs basically filled by the female population. The first part of my paper will concentrate on establishing the current position on the gender wage gap.

Next, I will present a brief history of the progression of the women's pay equity movement, focusing on landmarks and legal proposals of the past thirty years. Then, I will focus on main reasons for the gap as suggested by researchers and analysts, citing pertinent studies and statistics. Information concerning the intermittence of female workers and the saturation of women's occupational fields fits into this section. Additionally, the issues surrounding intermittence of female workers substantiate the fact that childless females appear to have equality in pay. Further illustrating this point, research addressing working mothers emphasizes the cost of mothering on careers. Focusing on reasons that suggest attitudes and choices contribute to the remaining gap, I will disclose surveys related to attitudes, choices, and values pertaining to work, marriage, and families.

The focal point of my argument will address society's values of success and its failure to acknowledge female, as well as male, priorities of family first. Results from surveys on attitudes and priorities regarding families and work will substantiate my appeal. I will advocate a respected and even admired status for women and men who choose to spend time with their families. Many women and men choose to value the nonmonetary work benefits of flexibility, less travel time, and a more family-oriented career. It is time for America to rate success through different venues—not the expensive car, house, and that annual Disney vacation (that most Americans cannot afford, anyway). Our children need us to listen, support, and share their lives more than a pair of designer jeans, a personal phone, and a television.

Finally, if society put more emphasis on the value of parents who devote time to raising their children, men and women with strong family values would feel supported and successful. I intend to support this part of my paper with details from the findings of a major study, conducted by the Families and Work Institute, that investigated job effects on life at home and, conversely, life at home effects on the job. This study examined the changing composition of the workforce and job performance relationships. Recent surveys indicate a continual increase of working families with young children; nevertheless, women remain identified as the main caregivers of their children. Stress from family demands was identified as the catalyst for employers to offer flexibility and support to workers juggling family responsibilities and careers. The gender wage gap has a legitimate reason for existing, and the alarm over this gap needs to be put into proper perspective, acknowledging society's family-first choice as the ultimate priority.

ARRANGING ARGUMENTS AND GAUGING READER REACTIONS

Deciding on the most effective way to arrange a piece of writing requires attention not only to what you wish to express but also to the rhetorical situation that inspired your desire to write—the purpose, audience, and exigency for the piece. Imagine that you work for a local chapter of the National Home Education Research Institution. You have been asked to write an informational brochure to dispel myths among parents about the effects of home schooling on children as they enter college and/or the workplace. Your audience is parents who may consider home schooling their children and teachers in public schools who may not recognize its benefits.

Once you place your writing within this specific rhetorical situation, you have more to consider. Where might you begin a discussion of home schooling? Members of the National Home Education Research Institution might have a set of values or commonplaces that inform their belief in this educational method; teachers in public schools might have sometimes competing commonplaces about education, as may parents who are considering what is best for their children.

WRITING TO EXPLORE 4.2

Using the techniques of invention (brainstorming, freewriting, commonplaces), imagine the likely concerns, level of information, and questions parents or public school teachers might bring to a discussion of home schooling. Consider the following questions about the audience: What commonplaces about home schooling are readers likely to carry with them into your essay? What do you imagine to be their initial attitudes toward the topic? What predispositions might present a problem for you as you attempt to show the value of home schooling? Considering your own position as a representative of the National Home Education Research Institution, what type of *ethos* must you project to make your presentation credible to readers?

Once you have considered your audience's initial positions on and levels of information about the topic, you can find ways to reason *together with your audience* toward your desired ends. Imagine a reader who is consistently nodding her head as she reads, mentally saying "Yes, I can see that," or "O.K., I follow where you're going with this." Even if your reader continues to disagree, you have still accomplished a good deal. You have at least created a situation in which ideas are exchanged rather than one in which the reader is consistently looking for reasons to reject your ideas. Such an attitude toward arrangement—seeing it as a process of reasoning together—can be both more effective and more civil than antagonistic or aggressive methods.

Real readers are not disembodied minds that meld with the disembodied thoughts that you present. Real readers come to what you write with mental capacities and functions, yes. But they also come to what you've written with emotions and with a sense of values—values through which they will judge not only your ideas but also you yourself. To remind yourself of this, you need only remember how passionate parents can be about assuring that their children receive the best education available. Effective styles of arrangement must account for the rhetorical situation you face, and successful communication takes place on these multiple levels—idea to idea, emotion to emotion, character to character.

WHAT TYPES OF READERS DO WE CREATE?

The rhetorical tradition identifies three basic means of persuasion or appeals: *ethos* (persuasion due to trustworthiness of character), *pathos* (persuasion by emotional appeals), and *logos* (persuasion by quality of the words and ideas themselves). Of course, separating one appeal from the others can only be done artificially. How can an idea be devoid of emotion or character? How can an emotion be separated from the person or what she thinks? How can character exist as separate from what human speakers or writers think and feel?

Though not fully separable, any one of these appeals can be emphasized by writers. If you discuss an issue from the standpoint of *pathos*, you might begin your writing with examples or anecdotes likely to produce an emotional response—a response that you can then analyze together with the reader. If you want to minimize the role of emotions and stress the factual or statistical evidence you have gathered, you might begin by moving the conversation in that direction. For example, consider the following opening for an essay on home schooling:

> Though we all want the best for our children, determining the educational methods most likely to produce positive results is a difficult affair. So many factors influence the quality of a child's education that it is crucial that *caring* parents also be *informed* parents. Many recent research studies have examined the relative successes and failures of home-schooled students in comparison with students in our public educational system. Those studies can help parents to make an informed decision about the best educational methods for assuring a successful future for their children.

An opening like this acknowledges the deep emotions involved in such a topic in its opening line ("Though we all want the best for our children"). But it then moves the reader toward the type of reasoning that the writer wants to share—one based on "findings of research."

Conversely, if the writer wished to build an argument based on *pathos*, the introduction might instead focus on the emotional reasons for parents to consider home schooling: Will my child be given enough opportunities to excel as an individual in a large school setting? What types of negative influences will he experience in a public school? Would home schooling stunt his social development? A writer who wished to stress the emotions that determine parenting decisions might begin as follows:

> You are standing at the bus stop with your five-year-old son, who is equipped with his new backpack and enough food to get him through, if need be, several days (all the food groups are represented!). You look suspiciously at the other children, wondering what will become of little Seth now that he will spend more of his waking hours among them than with you. You hope that the teacher that he meets will understand that Seth needs a bit of extra attention and that he is a perfectionist when he draws. What will the structure of 43-minute periods do to his creativity? What if he isn't ready to put aside his artwork when math class begins? What if he is the last one picked to play kickball at recess—what will become of his self-esteem? You wonder if you are sending your child off to a world of new learning and challenges or if you are simply abandoning your own responsibility to educate your child mentally, emotionally, and morally. Is there another way?

Unlike the previous introduction, which moves the reader beyond the pull of emotions toward a logical examination of "recent research studies," this introduction enhances the emotional investment of readers, painting a vivid mental picture of a deeply emotional moment. By drawing on shared emotions (worry, love, concern), it moves the reader toward the key question at the end: "Is there another way?" This question introduces what will follow—the examination of the emotional benefits for both child and parent of home schooling (the "other" way).

What if you wanted to build a case on *ethos*? How might you create a pattern of organization that stresses the good character or credibility of the author? In order to do so, you must illustrate the credentials you bring to the discussion. So, in this example, what if the writer was herself the product of home schooling or if she had done extensive research on the topic? Might that help the reader to accept her voice as credible and authoritative? Yes and no. This too involves arrangement. If the writer states, in effect, "Well, I've been there, and so I know and you don't," that won't encourage readers to accept the "good character" of the writer—haughtiness doesn't encourage open communication, no matter the level of expertise. But using that firsthand experience, especially in combination with a sincere attention to the audience's concerns, can be a powerful combination because it creates trust between reader and writer on a number of levels.

Consider the ways the author of the following essay develops her ethos, as well as the way in which she arranges her ideas throughout the piece.

Could Home Schooling Be Right for Your Family?

Sarah C. Threnhauser

I can still remember the day I realized that my siblings and I were truly different from everyone else. I was twelve years old and it was a typical Wednesday for my family. We had just finished our art class at the museum, and we were busy checking out all the new exhibits. My sister and I were pondering a recent addition in our favorite room—a tiny, dimly lit area with rich chocolate brown walls and massive paintings hung haphazardly from ceiling to floor—when our silence was interrupted by a frazzled tour guide, a frustrated teacher, and a sundry mix of children. Much to my surprise, these children were my former classmates. Some of them waved, some of them called out, and others simply whispered among themselves about my "strange" situation. But the tour guide took no notice; she brusquely pushed onward and with a quick summary of the room's content she swept away. The children followed closely and much to their chagrin, with the teacher in tow, threatening extra papers if they got out of line. My sister and I giggled at the awkwardness and then resumed our reflection. After half an hour or so in our little room, my mother reluctantly gathered us together to go home. I couldn't wait to get back and start researching my new favorite artist, but I paused for a moment and thought to myself, "I just spent two and a half exhilarating hours in that museum, all the while my former classmates rushed through in half that time. And now I'm going home, barely able to contain my excitement over my next school project, while they are drudgingly returning to their desks for a study hall with a looming threat of an extra report." It was right then that I knew I was different, but it was also then that I realized I was so glad that I was.

Yes, my education has taken a vastly different path than most people. I attended a public school in my younger years, but as my parents grew dissatisfied with the quality and content of our education, they made a radical decision that affected all of our lives: they took my brother, my sister, and me out of our elementary school and began to educate us at home. Most people have heard news reports, seen magazine articles here and there, or heard about a friend of a friend—but chances are, to most of them, home schooling is still a foreign topic that presents confusion and controversy whenever discussed. However, in today's ever-evolving society it is growing rapidly, and with this widespread popularity, more parents across America are seriously considering home schooling to be a viable option for their children's education. By drawing on my own experiences, countless studies, personal interviews, and expert opinions, I hope to interest you in the topic of home schooling, clear any misconceptions that you may have, and explain just what home schooling your own children would involve.

Why Would I Home School My Children?

There is a multitude of reasons as to why you may home school your children. Andrew S. Latham, a member of the Professional Education and Development Group at the Princeton Educational Testing Service, places home schoolers into two categories: ideologues, who adhere to traditional classroom styles but adapt the curriculum to their own personal beliefs, and pedagogues, who seek new styles and teaching methods. He explains that the pedagogues generated the home school revolution but that significant growth can now be attributed to ideological parents with religious beliefs (Latham).

Parents who are classified as pedagogues have a wide array of personal reasons for their decision. Many parents, like mine, are simply dissatisfied with the quality of their children's school and feel they can make an improvement. Sue McCallum, a confused mother from Wheaton, Illinois, removed her son from school when the administration placed him in both remedial and gifted classes (Barnes et al.). Others want to expand their child's horizons and feel a traditional curriculum and institutional nature is limiting a child's educational possibilities (Wingert and Kantrowitz). Still other parents choose to home school because their children have leaning disabilities that are not being addressed in the public education system. Jean and Jan Forbes of Alexandria, Virginia, felt that their two sons needed extra attention, which the school was not willing to provide. When they felt the teachers were not helping enough, they made the important decision to take their dyslexic son, Aaron, out of his elementary school and educate him themselves (Wingert and Kantrowitz).

Unlike the pedagogues, ideologues are more concerned about imparting personal beliefs and values than with changing the method of education. These parents are more concerned about positive social interaction and the moral well-being of their children. Sally Conrad, a long-time home schooler of four, declared, "I just wasn't happy with what my kids were being influenced by. They had mandatory sex education in fifth grade, and were being told that evolution was the only possible way for the world to have begun. That isn't what I wanted for my children" (personal interview). Many parents also have a fear that their children will become jaded in a school system where they are faced with violence, drugs, alcohol, promiscuity, and smoking (Wingert and Kantrowitz). Robert Phillips, a father who currently home schools, felt the need to remove his fifth-grade son, Bill, from his school when the child was exposed to too many fistfights (Time).

Although it is possible to classify home schoolers into these two groups, ideologues and the pedagogues, it would be fairly impossible to say two home-schooled families are the same. Home schoolers are diverse in every way imaginable; the parents are the deciding factors in how the education process will take place, and thus each family has its own system and techniques. One family may begin the day early with the Pledge of Allegiance and daily prayers, then go on to a standard structured curriculum, while another may create a relaxed setting and let the children focus on what topics they want whenever they are comfortable. This freedom and the ever-expanding possibilities make home schooling an appealing choice for all and a feasible possibility for any parent who takes the initiative—with the rapidly escalating numbers serving as proof.

Who Is Currently Home Schooling?

The number of home schoolers has been significantly increasing since the 1980s and has been growing at a rate of 7 to 15 percent per year, bringing the approximate total for 2000–2001 between 1.5 and 1.9 million children (Ray). Patricia M. Lines, a Senior Research Analyst with the National Institute on Governance, has stated that "At present, it is estimated that over 500,000 children are being educated at home on any given day." Although this growing population may be diverse in its methods, the majority of home schoolers are average Americans and undistinguishable from the rest of the population.

A study conducted by the National Household Education Survey in 1993 found that home schoolers varied very little, demographically, from the majority of individuals (Wagenaar). In areas such as regional disparity, emotional problems, and learning disabilities, home schoolers were found to be a very similar representation of the population as a whole (Wagenaar). This demolished a widely accepted conclusion that there was low minority involvement in home schooling (Wagenaar). It was, in fact, found that although the majority of home schooling families are Caucasian, one-fifth of the total number are of a minority group (Wagenaar). This study also found that the average home schooler will have a higher socioeconomic status than the general population (Wagenaar). It was observed that this was because "what [sic] makes the home school community different is its intense concern for the educational welfare of children" (Wagenaar).

What about My Children's Socialization and Academic Development?

The growing concern for the educational welfare of children is the point that most use to argue against home schooling. There are two very common stereotypes that accompany home schooling in every platform: poor academic standards and lack of necessary socialization. These are the most common arguments made against home schooling, and those who push them do so with such vigor and conviction that the stereotypes maintain their integrity—despite the overwhelming amount of evidence which proves otherwise.

The majority of studies and test scores have led to the conclusion that home-schooled children are academically above average (Lines). It was found in a nationwide study of 1,516 randomly chosen students that the standardized test scores of home schoolers were at, or above, the eightieth percentile, while the average publicly educated student's score was in the fiftieth percentile (Ray). In 1997, the president of the National Home Education Research Institute, Dr. Brian Ray, published a book entitled *Strengths of Their Own—Home Schoolers Across America,* which included the largest home schooling study ever conducted in the United States. He found that the home-educated students academically outperformed their peers, even though many parents did not have teaching certificates (Ray).

In the past, because of this ominous myth about the academic credentials of home schoolers, many parents found themselves in a predicament when it came time for their children to attend college. Currently, however, colleges have realized the previously unseen potential in home schoolers and are welcoming them with open arms. Cafi Cohen, the author of *The Homeschoolers' College Admissions Handbook,* has stated that nearly three-fourths of colleges have implemented admissions policies specifically meant to deal with home schoolers (Barnes et al.). While Rice and Stanford Universities are admitting home schoolers at equal to or greater rates than their public school applicants (Barnes et al.), Harvard University has seen a need to assign a special admissions officer, David Illingsworth, to deal specifically with the home schooled applicants (Wingert and Kantrowitz). Mr. Illingsworth has proclaimed that "Ten years ago, if you didn't have a diploma we didn't want you. Today we're always willing to look at different kinds of credentials" (Wingert and Kantrowitz).

Although there is currently only a limited amount of research on the long-term effects of home schooling, it has been shown that home schoolers fare very well as adults. One study conducted by J. Gary Knowles has reported that of all the adults in the study, none were on welfare or even unemployed (Ray). This same study has stated that "94% [of those surveyed] said home education prepared them to be independent persons, 79% said it helped them interact with individuals from different levels of society, and they strongly supported the home education method" (Ray).

Along with academics, a lack of socialization is the next important stereotype facing home schoolers. Many paint the picture of a home-schooled child as being passive, introverted, and unable to handle multifaceted social situations.

Yet, all the available research paints a very different picture. Sally Conrad has stated that her children "are always on their way somewhere." They participate in choir, the swim team, basketball, Odyssey of the Mind, art classes, a home-schooling co-op with another family, community service projects, Boy/Girl Scouts, and a variety of other activities (personal interview). Dr. Brian Ray has stated that "Ninety percent of these kids [home-schooled children] play with people outside their families" (Wingert and Kantrowitz). Author of *Growing with-out School* Pat Farenga has confirmed this with her personal research:

> Certainly group experiences are a big part of education, and home schoolers have plenty of them. Home schoolers write to us about how they form or join writing clubs, book discussion groups, and local home-schooling support groups. Home schoolers also take part in sports teams and musical groups, as well as the many public and private activities our communities provide. . . . Home schoolers can and do and experience other people and cultures with-out going to school (Jeub).

By being involved in these various activities, it has been shown that home schoolers are adequately socialized at home. Dr. Thomas Shyers has found that students who are educated at home have a positive self-concept, and they have considerably less behavioral problems than their peers who attend public school (Ray). Using the Piers-Harris Children's Self-Concept Scale, B.H. Ray found that home-schooled children generally scored higher than their publicly educated counterparts (Jeub). This led to the conclusion that "self-concept reflects socialization, [therefore] home schoolers are not socially deprived" (Jeub). This dispels the second most common stereotype associ-ated with home schooling.

Could Home Schooling Be the Right Choice for Your Family?

I hope the information that I have provided for you has interested you in the topic of home schooling and cleared any misconceptions you may have previ-ously held. Home schooling is a large task that will require extra effort and com-mitment on your part, but your children's education is a vital part of their growth and development; it determines their morals, values, work ethic, and it will shape them for their future. Home schooling may not be the right choice for every family, but ask yourself if it could be for yours.

Works Cited

Barnes, Steve, et al. "Home Sweet School: The New Home Schoolers Aren't Hermits: They Are Diverse Parents Who Are Getting Results—and Putting the Heat on Public Schools." *Time* 27 August 2001.

Conrad, Sally. Personal interview. 23 November 2001.

Jeub, Chris. "Why Parents Choose Home Schooling." *Educational Leadership Journal* 52.1 (1994). 10 October 2001.

Latham, Andrew S. "Home Schooling (Pros and Cons)." *Educational Leadership Journal* 55.8 (1998). 10 October 2001.

Lines, Patricia M. "Home Schooling Comes of Age." *Educational Leadership* 54:2 (1996). 18 November 2001.

Ray, Brian D. *National Home Education Research Institute* (2000). 30 October 2001. http://www.nheri.org/.

Wagenaar, Theodore C. "What Characterizes Home Schoolers? A National Study." *Education* 117: 3 (1997). 30 October 2001.

Wingert, Pat, and Barbara Kantrowitz. "Learning at Home: Does It Pass the Test?" *Newsweek* 5 October 1998.

WRITING TO EXPLORE 4.3

After reading Threnhauser's essay, consider the following questions in your writer's notebook. Share your responses with other members of the class to see what responses seem to be common—and to consider how the piece inspired those shared reactions.

- How does this essay encourage parents to consider the value of home schooling through the author's experiences?

- Are there any places where the essay presents a character likely to discourage a receptive reader?

- In what ways does the arrangement and presentation encourage *logos*-based reasoning (based on the facts of the case), and where does it invite *pathos*-driven (emotion-based) responses in the reader?

- How does the writer move the reader from one point to the other? Use your writer's notebook to track the key movements in this essay and respond to them by analyzing their likely effect on a reader.

So far, we've been discussing the overall impression or pattern of reasoning that you hope to create for a reader, and how different types of reasoning fit into various discourse communities. There are also many individual stylistic decisions to be made that can have a large effect on your reader's reaction to your writing. Let's examine some of those issues of arrangement.

WHY ORDER MATTERS

Readers read in a linear way, from left to right and from up to down. Though in some cases they might be willing to go back and reread part or all of your writing, in most cases they give your piece a single reading—and a single chance for it to succeed. Linear reading is also cumulative—each new idea builds on and is influenced by those that preceded it.

Imagine that you are writing a letter to your parents, asking them if it would be okay for you to stay in your college town over the summer to work rather than to come home. You have a great opportunity to work in your intended field of study, but you also know that your parents will be disappointed if you don't spend the summer at home. Your mom has already lined up a pretty good job for you, using connections that she has at work, and Dad's been talking about buying season tickets for the Cubs. But your advisors have been telling you how important it is for you to spend your summers getting the job experience you need in your field. All that baggage, those circumstances and predispositions, set an *external* context for your letter that you must take into account as you think about how to handle the issue in your letter.

But the letter itself will create an *internal* context, since each line your parents read will provide information and set the tone for the lines that follow. You don't want to deceive your parents, of course. Rather, you sincerely believe that this course of action is important, and you want your parents to understand why you need to take it—without hurting them. How can you accomplish this?

You can set the tone for the difficult news that you must bring out if you begin your letter by describing how much you've been learning in your major classes, how much the field is starting to intrigue you, and how much you appreciate the opportunity to attend college. This approach places the need to stay in your college town *within a context of reasons* that your audience will respect (your need for experience, your growing interest in your field of study) and not in a personal context (the fact that you won't be home for the summer). Setting a reasonable context about your need to gain practical experience early in the letter encourages your readers to consider what is best for your future—something that on an emotional level both you and your readers share.

Conversely, if you were to begin your letter with the news ("Mom, Dad, I'm thinking about not coming home this summer"), everything else they read in that letter will be tinged with the disappointment and sadness they might feel because they will miss you. Even though you might then go on to explain the reasons for your choice in much the same way as described above, the emotional reaction is already out there, making for less receptive readers.

This simple example illustrates a principle of arrangement that is true of academic and professional writing as well. The context for your writing is set again and again throughout the things you write. And that is true not only of the emotional reactions that your readers have; it also affects the *logos* (or line of factual reasoning) and *ethos* (the reactions your reader have to you as a credible source of information) of your document. Since readers rarely return to earlier parts of your document, the arrangement determines whether your writing will create the desired effect—an effect that is difficult to erase once the readers experience it.

PARAGRAPHS AS MICRO-UNITS OF ARGUMENT

The English language provides us with a variety of techniques for segmenting our writing into chunks of reasoning as well as methods of linking those chunks in a naturally flowing series of ideas. One of the most important techniques for arranging written English into logical segments is the careful use of paragraphs—a device of organization that you have been using since you started putting pen to paper. What does it tell a reader when you move from one paragraph to another—when you stop, indent, and begin again? The simplest answer to that question is that you tell your reader that you are moving on to a new topic. But that's not a wholly satisfactory way to look at paragraphs, because whole essays, even whole books, have (in the most general sense) a single controlling idea. Thinking, instead, about paragraphs as units of argument—each the presentation of one small but important facet of a larger case you are making—can help you to decide when to begin and end paragraphs.

There are many ways to effectively develop individual paragraphs. The most direct way to form a paragraph is to state its topic and then to provide explanation, illustration, or examples that develop that central idea, as in the following paragraph:

> Running a small business is much more complex than it might appear from the standpoint of a customer. As we enter the corner grocery store, we see the most simplified version of business—there are items on the shelf that the owner provides to us at a cost higher than that which he paid, hence breeding a profit. But that simplified sense of selling goods at a profit does not take into account the many cost factors involved in creating a profitable business. The entrepreneur must first consider start-up costs—money that will be laid out without immediate return: rent payments, advertising, purchasing inventory, renovation costs, and possible promotional activities all put the business in the red right from the start. Each time an item is sold, the costs include not only the purchase price of that item, but the labor costs of placing the item on display, restocking, and completing sales. Perishable items represent a particular challenge, since they can produce no income if they are not sold in a timely way, or less than anticipated income if the price must be reduced in order to move the item off the shelves. Utilities bills continue even through periods of slow sales. A successful entrepreneur must anticipate and plan for such hidden costs, and have sufficient resources to weather slow sales periods without damaging her credit with suppliers and other creditors. So, though a novice business owner might see the simple "buy and sell" formula as sufficient, an experienced businessperson is more likely to anticipate the many surrounding circumstances that will create a more stable financial plan.

This paragraph sets up a simple topic statement: setting up a small business is more complex than it seems. Then it seeks to illustrate that complexity by naming a series of mental activities that serious entrepreneurs must go through in order to create a successful business—moves that add up to a much more complex vision of the occupation than an outside observer might consider. But perhaps the writer would prefer to avoid stating the conclusion first; perhaps she is writing to a skeptical reader who will not be open to the idea that "running a small business is much more complex than it might appear from the standpoint of a customer." In that case, it might be best to develop this paragraph by first describing some of the complex thought processes of a business owner, and then lead up to that conclusion. Doing so might help readers draw their own conclusions ("Say, that's pretty complicated!") before you state the point yourself.

> The entrepreneur must first consider start-up costs—money that will be laid out without immediate return: rent payments, advertising, purchasing inventory, renovation costs, and possible promotional activities all put the business in the red right from the start. Each time an item is sold, the costs include not only the purchase price of that item, but the labor costs of placing the item on display, restocking, and completing sales. Perishable items represent a particular challenge, since they can produce no income if they are not sold in a timely way, or less than anticipated income if the price must be reduced in order to move the item off the shelves. Utilities bills continue even through periods of slow sales. A successful entrepreneur must anticipate and plan for such hidden costs, and have sufficient resources to weather slow sales periods without damaging her credit with suppliers and other creditors. Anticipating these hidden costs and risks will create a more stable financial plan. In short, we must remember that as we enter the corner grocery store, we see the most simplified version of business— there are items on the shelf that the owner provides to us at a cost higher than that which they paid, hence breeding a profit. Running a small business is much more complex than it might appear from the standpoint of a customer.

Though the individual sentences are nearly identical with those in the previous version, this paragraph develops incrementally, moving from a series of examples toward a conclusion or culminating statement. For particular situations and audiences, this technique can be effective.

Sometimes a question at the beginning of a paragraph can suggest a logical movement for the reader: from inquiry through a shared line of reasoning to a shared conclusion. You might begin the paragraph by asking, "Did you ever wish you could own a quaint little corner store, living the leisurely life of buying and selling everyday products that you loved when you ran that lemonade stand as a child?" Beginning with this interrogative sentence suggests that the goal is to "interrogate" a specific issue—to examine it with the shared goal of finding an answer to that question. This, too, creates a distinct pattern of reasoning.

There are many other ways to begin and develop paragraphs—too many to list, since the approaches to paragraph structure can be as diverse as the minds that create them. Sometimes, trying several possible paragraph styles can help you to find new approaches to the topic as well—that is, it can help you to invent new things to say.

WRITING TO EXPLORE 4.4

In order to practice your paragraphing skills, respond to the following scenario: You are a work-study assistant for one of your professors (choose the subject area based on your own interests). She has asked you to write, as part of a promotional brochure, a one-paragraph description of the goals of the program and how the program can prepare students for work in that particular field. First, consult descriptions of the program from your college catalog or website, gleaning what you take to be the most important facets of the program and the values and commonplaces that are important within this field of study. Then, develop three paragraphs—each with a different pattern of arrangement—to show to your professor. Finally, write a cover memo that explains which paragraph seems to work best, and why.

ARRANGING PARAGRAPHS INTO LARGER ARGUMENTS

Paragraphs are basic units of argument, but the way you arrange paragraphs within a letter, essay, or report is also important; paragraphs are building blocks of the whole. You begin a paragraph when you have a single, focused point to make and end it when you have sufficiently developed that point—and when you are ready to use that point as the starting point for another, related point. Thinking about your paragraphs in this progressive way can lead to a piece of writing that presents a logical flow of ideas.

WRITING TO EXPLORE 4.5

Carefully read the following article from *Adweek* by Chad Chadwick, president and creative director of Chadwick Communications in New York, paying special attention to the relationship between paragraphs—how one idea flows into the next. In the margins, or in your writer's notebook, try to describe the logic that moves the reader from one point to the next—how one assertion builds on the previous one. In what way does Chadwick help us to see the logic that holds one paragraph to another? Write a brief analysis of these techniques in your writer's notebook.

Brave New World

Chad Chadwick

"As work and play become one, advertising must change. It is a new world, ladies and gentlemen. You will be distinct, or you will be extinct." Such is the gauntlet thrown to the American worker by ads for the online employment directory Jobs.com. The message: The office is a radically different place than it was a few years ago.

Technology's promises—mostly unfulfilled hyperbole for much of the "information revolution"—are paying off in tangible ways. People "own" their careers as never before, in both real and metaphorical terms. According to *The New York Times*, only 200,000 Americans had equity in the companies for which they worked in 1974. Twenty-five years later, more than 10 million workers can claim a piece of the pie. Further, 6 million Americans left their jobs for other positions in 1998. In 1999, that number nearly tripled: to 17 million.

Fewer and fewer of us are willing to settle for work that merely pays the bills. Clearly, we seek employment that fulfills us as individuals. But liberation has not come without a price. The line between work and play has disappeared for many. From cell phones to telecommuting, technology has, in theory, given us the freedom to do what we want—when and where we want to do it. But in exchange, it has removed our safety net.

Though we can take advantage of new opportunities and create situations for which we believe ourselves best suited, we have no choice but to assume greater responsibility for the consequences of our actions. Who, beside ourselves, can shoulder the blame if we don't turn this unprecedented freedom to our advantage?

Consumers are challenged now to "become" themselves. For most, their work has become an indispensable part of the process. A change of this magnitude presents a real opportunity for advertisers and marketers.

Until recently, consumer culture was based on immediate gratification: a thirst for the 5 o'clock whistle and "Miller Time." Successful advertising reflected that reality. Now, however, people want to cast themselves as the heroes of their own lives. They no longer buy products or services; they buy self-image. To communicate with consumers, marketers must create a platform through which that self-actualization can occur.

Consider a new branding campaign for IntraLinks.com, an Internet business service. The tagline, "Is it work if you love it?" speaks to the new American worker. If you love what you do, you do it well; it becomes less work than personal growth. While others promise freedom from their jobs, IntraLinks is offering a way to build a career on one's own terms.

Of course, the most potent ad campaign of the last decade, Nike's "Just do it," also drives this point home. Nike recognized it wasn't selling the sole of the sneaker, but the soul of the wearer. "Just do it" speaks to the person in all of us who knows he or she is equal to the challenges implicit in the new economy. All we need is a little push.

It is, indeed, a brave new world. Distinct or extinct—it is as much a choice for marketers as it is for each of us in this new technological age.

WRITING TO EXPLORE 4.6

In your writer's notebook, recreate a conversant outline for Chadwick's essay. List the point he makes in each paragraph, and supply (in your own words) the logic that holds this piece together. You might also consider what appeals Chadwick makes to his audience: What values, priorities, and common beliefs about business does Chadwick seem to believe he and his audience share? How does he use questions and answers to create a logical pathway to share with his readers?

CREATING EMPHASIS THROUGH SENTENCE STRUCTURE AND STYLE

As with individual paragraphs, the arrangement of a document like the one above creates a structured process of thought designed to move readers toward a better understanding of a topic and a conclusion about that topic. Likewise, the way you arrange and structure individual sentences can help readers to follow your line of reasoning.

The arrangement and style of paragraphs within a written document, and the arrangement of sentences within paragraphs, are crucial to developing a shared line of reasoning. But good writers know that the structure of individual sentences can also demonstrate the relationship among our ideas. In the complex sentence styles you will use as a mature writer—sentences that contain more than one thought—you can arrange your words carefully in order to create just the effect you want. Choosing among these available styles—styles that function differently according to the arrangement of words—allows you to fine-tune your writing before you deliver it to your audience.

Much like paragraph structures, sentence styles not only convey information but also tell readers how to process that information, revealing the relative importance placed on various ideas. Though there are many, many possible sentence patterns, distinguishing between three types of sentence structure, and deciding when to use each, can be very helpful. These three styles are the **simple sentence**, the **coordinate construction,** and the **subordinate construction.**

Let's start with a simple example of a police report on an incident of truancy that occurred in a small town:

> It was a Monday. Schools were open. Three fourth-grade students were walking along the sidewalk. The students were not accompanied by any adults. The children were on their way to school. They saw the park. It was a clear spring day. They went to the park instead.

Though we can read the motives of the children into this group of **simple sentences,** the relationship between the beautiful day and their decision to skip school is not directly stated in the structure of these sentences. To illustrate this, we can just rearrange them:

> Three fourth-grade students were walking along the sidewalk. The children were on their way to school. Schools were open. It was a Monday. It was a clear spring day. The students were not accompanied by any adults. They saw the park. They went to the park instead.

In the second version, since the decision to go to the park immediately follows the statement that the students were not accompanied by any adults, the motivation of the children seems attributable to the lack of supervision. Or did they decide to go to the park and then notice the lovely day? Or does this passage suggest that the students, being fourth-graders, ought to have been accompanied by adults?

None of this is wholly clear because the simple sentences do not reveal the relationships among the various declarations of facts. Simple sentences, as you know, can be joined into compound or complex sentences. In fact, mature writers often create compound or complex sentences naturally, without really thinking much about the structures themselves. This is because it is sometimes difficult to contain complicated thoughts within the simple sentence structure, which is quite restrictive.

You can control the ways sentence structure influences emphasis and meaning. For example, let's say you combined sentences:

> Three fourth-grade students were walking along the sidewalk, and they were on their way to school. It was a Monday, and schools were open. It was a clear spring day, and they saw the park. The students were not accompanied by any adults, and they went to the park instead.

Joining pairs of sentences with *and* creates **coordinate constructions.** Coordinate constructions join two or more clauses with *and, or,* or *but,* and suggest that the ideas are closely enough related to be contained in a single sentence. But though coordinate sentences *imply* connections (it was a Monday, *so* schools were open; the students were unaccompanied, *so* they went to the park instead of school), they do not directly state a relationship between the ideas, and they do not suggest that one of the ideas is more important than the others. They merely say this happened, *and* that happened too. Or they say, this happened, *but* that happened too. Or they say that either this happened *or* that happened (or could happen, or might have happened). But how the various things that did happen relate with one another is largely left for the reader to decide.

One sentence now provides observations (Three fourth-grade students were walking along the sidewalk, and they were on their way to school); one sentence reports on the status of the schools (It was a Monday, and schools were open); the third reports on weather *and* the action of the children (It was a clear spring day, and they saw the park); and the fourth presents two further observations about the situation (The students were not accompanied by any adults, and they went to the park instead). The coordinate sentence structures, then, are used to organize the ideas into related groups and to *imply* connections among them.

But what if you wanted to indicate *how* the various facts are related? Then you need **subordinate constructions.** Subordination means "making one thing or idea less important than another." Of course, in the process, you are also making something *more* important than another. Let's look at another version of this group of sentences:

> Three fourth-grade students walking along the sidewalk were on their way to school. Although it was a Monday and schools were open, it was a clear spring day, and they saw the park. Since the students were not accompanied by any adults, they went to the park instead.

This example adds a new set of emphases to the collection of facts through the use of subordinate clauses. The first sentence emphasizes that the students were, at least at first, on their way to school. Beginning the second sentence with "although" subordinates the status of the schools (they were open) to the motivation of the students who decided to skip school (it was a clear spring day, and the park was inviting). The third sentence, now beginning with *since,* creates a cause-effect relationship, making the actions of the student the main clause ("they went to the park instead") and the lack of accompanying adults the cause of that action. Since the first clause is no longer self-sufficient ("Since the students were not accompanied by any adults"), readers anticipate a conclusion that will complete the sentence's reasoning, giving the cause-effect relationship extra emphasis. As such, the emphasis is placed not just on the effect of that lovely day—skipping school—but on the lack of supervision. The last sentence now clearly states that it is *because* of that lack of supervision that the children skipped school.

There is, of course, much more that could be done stylistically to enhance the effect of this paragraph. For example, we might write:

> The children were walking reluctantly toward their school when the park appeared before them, with its green field and shiny metallic structures. Noticing the warmth of the sun on their faces, looking up to the cloudless blue sky, and seeing no adults, they felt themselves pulled to the park instead.

Here, not only the subordinate structure, which builds toward a conclusion, but other features as well create the effect. The verb choices (the park "appeared," and they were "pulled" into it) and descriptive words ("reluctantly," "green," and "shiny") all add to the overall effect. But you might also consider whether such embellishments are appropriate to a police report ("Just the facts, ma'am")—and, conversely, what types of rhetorical situations would call for such descriptive wordings.

You can take two important lessons about writing from this simple example: (1) That the writer here needed to decide what the effects and emphases should be, and (2) That achieving those effects was accomplished through a series of revisions to the arrangement of the ideas within and among the sentences. Each of the above paragraphs contains precisely the same "facts." But each leaves its readers with a different overall impression, largely because of the arrangement of those ideas, how they are linked through coordinating or subordinating sentence structures, and the degree of detail they provide.

WRITING TO EXPLORE 4.7

Below you will find groupings of simple sentences. Try combining the simple sentences by using subordinate clauses to emphasize the point suggested after each group. You might even elaborate with descriptive words to stress the key element. *I have done the first two for you.*

1. The boy was smart. The boy was lazy. (Emphasize the boy's laziness.)

   ■ Though the boy was smart, he was lazy.

2. The boy was smart. The boy was lazy. (Emphasize the boy's intelligence.)

   ■ Even though the boy was lazy, he was certainly smart.

3. The game was long. The game was exciting. (Emphasize the excitement.)

4. The game was long. The game was exciting. (Emphasize the length of the game.)

5. Elephants are the largest of land animals. Elephants are intelligent. Elephants are gentle. (Emphasize the intelligence of elephants.)

6. Elephants are the largest of land animals. Elephants are intelligent. Elephants are gentle. (Emphasize the gentle nature and intelligence of elephants.)

7. Elephants are the largest of land animals. Elephants are intelligent. Elephants are gentle. (Emphasize just the intelligence of elephants.)

8. The supervisor was fair. The supervisor ran an efficient operation. The supervisor was strict. (Emphasize the efficiency of the operation.)

9. The supervisor was fair. The supervisor ran an efficient operation. The supervisor was strict. (Emphasize the strictness of the supervisor.)

10. The painting was Impressionist. The painting was from the nineteenth century. The painting has some characteristics not associated with Impressionism. (Emphasize that this painting fits into the Impressionist movement.)

11. The painting was Impressionist. The painting was from the nineteenth century. The painting has some characteristics not associated with Impressionism. (Emphasize that this painting has differences from those of the Impressionist movement.)

12. The painting was Impressionist. The painting was from the nineteenth century. The painting has some characteristics not associated with Impressionism. (Emphasize that the Impressionist movement was a nineteenth-century phenomenon.)

REVEALING THE ARRANGEMENT PATTERN THROUGH TRANSITIONS

In order to make writing work well, you must offer instructions to your readers—instructions that help them to understand where you are heading with your reasoning. Those instructions take the form of transitions.

For example, this book is about composing a life's work. However, the first words of this sentence ("However") and of the previous sentence ("For example") are not directly about that topic; they are instead a type of road sign for my readers as they negotiate my reasoning. "For example" tells my readers to read what follows as a specific case that illustrates the point I am trying to make in this paragraph. "However" tells my reader that what follows contrasts with what I just wrote. Without such transitions, writing would be much less readable, since readers would be completely on their own in trying to find the connections between ideas.

The most likely place for you to lose or confuse your readers is when you are trying to make connections between ideas. That happens most frequently between paragraphs—when you must help readers to see not only *that* you're moving from one topic or point to another related topic or point but also *why* and *how* you're doing so. You literally make a turn in the logic at that moment, and if you don't help your readers to negotiate the turn, it might be a while before you see them again.

Paragraph transitions do three things:

1. They announce a shift toward a new idea or point.
2. They show the relationship between the previous point and the new one.
3. They often (but not always) reiterate the connection that both the old and the new points have to your overall topic.

The goal is to help readers imagine the shape of your document. You are pointing out to your readers the way your ideas cohere—the way they relate both to each other and to your overall purpose.

Transitions have an additional benefit: They can point out places in your writing that are *not* properly arranged or organized. As you attempt to form a transition, you might find that the connection is extremely difficult to make. Those cases sometimes indicate a gap in your logic—either because something is missing, or because something is out of place. You may first need to reorganize your essay by cutting and pasting that paragraph into a better location or by deleting extraneous material.

Once you understand what is connecting one idea to another, you can reinforce and reveal that coherence through the use of transitions and other forms of metalanguage. Real readers, after all, do not necessarily all think like you do and therefore might need help to see the connections that you have found among the issues you discuss and the ideas you raise. For example, let's imagine that you are an engineer working for a local design firm. You have been asked to make suggestions about a local high school curriculum from your standpoint as a working scientist. You decide that you want to stress the idea that high school science education should spend less time on memorization of established facts and more time on honing the observation skills of students. You might, in a draft, write something like the following.

Students in high school learn about science in a way that seems more appropriate to the study of spelling or learning of multiplication tables. They are given a set of facts to memorize, as if they are always and everywhere true, and so use mental processes that are inappropriate to the work that real scientists do. In the process of memorizing "facts," students also learn something else. They learn that learning about science is a passive process.

Scientists in laboratories use past facts to determine the processes they use and to set the protocol for various experiments. It would be a tremendous waste of time to start from scratch every time that a new experiment was set up. Established facts provide the necessary base of past knowledge from which new discoveries can be made. Knowing the composition of elements—and the elements themselves through the periodic table—certainly must be accomplished. Does the process of accomplishing that task through memorization and objective tests also tend to create passive learners? And are passive learners likely to become good scientists?

The creativity that is involved in actual science is often overlooked. *Creativity* is a word that too often is limited to the processes used to produce art and literature—to painters and "creative" writers. Creativity informs all the things that scientists do as well. Scientists are not merely processing information through established methods; they are in the business of creating new methods, developing as yet unthought-of ways to approach natural or man-made processes.

After drafting the above paragraphs, the writer might reread them and discover that the central theme she is attempting to convey is the contrast between active, creative methods of learning and passive rote memorization. Once the writer articulates that central point to herself, she can go back and reinforce it for readers by means of a slight reorganization and through the addition of metalanguage that reinforces the key theme. On the next page, I've inserted possible transitions in italics, along with a description of the function of each transition.

This introductory phrase helps the reader see the point you are about to make.

This contrast word helps readers see that you are about to present information that partially contradicts the "creative" understanding of science you wish to forward.

This addition once again reinforces your central point; it also sets up your use of the opposing word *passive* at the end of the paragraph.

This introductory sentence acknowledges a potential counterargument, anticipating your readers' possible reactions—and so keeps them from finding you shortsighted.

This introductory phrase helps readers see a key logical connection—that active learning leads to a creative mind, and in turn, that a creative mind is required of good science.

The addition of this one contrast word helps readers see that, though creativity is necessary, the actual learning students do is in opposition to this attribute.

Though students often come to think of science as a rigid and unwavering set of facts, the profession of science really involves a great deal of creativity. However, students in high school learn about science in a way that seems more appropriate to the study of spelling or learning of multiplication tables. They are given a set of facts to memorize, as if they are always and everywhere true, and so use mental processes that are inappropriate to the work that real scientists do—*work that requires an active, creative mind.* In the process of memorizing "facts," students also learn something else. They learn that scientific information is learned by a passive process.

This is not to suggest that learning previously established facts is unnecessary, or that rote memorization can be wholly done away with. Scientists in laboratories use past facts to determine the processes they use and to set the protocol for various experiments. *After all,* it would be a tremendous waste of time to start from scratch every time that a new experiment was set up. Established facts, *then*, provide the necessary base of past knowledge from which new discoveries can be made. *Hence,* knowing the composition of elements—and the elements themselves through the periodic table—certainly must be accomplished. *But* does the process of accomplishing that task through memorization and objective tests also tend to create passive learners? And are passive learners likely to become good scientists?

Passive learners lack an important attribute of a successful and active scientist: creativity. Yet the creativity that is involved in actual science is often overlooked. *Creativity* is a word that too often is limited to the processes used to produce art and literature—to painters and "creative" writers. *But* creativity informs all the things that scientists do as well. Scientists are not merely processing information through established methods; they are in the business of creating new methods, developing as yet unthought-of ways to approach natural or man-made processes.

The addition of a few key transitional phrases can help you to discover the links between the points you are making and so can help you to move forward onto related topics. It can also help the reader to understand the intended path of reasoning that you are creating. If you clutter your writing with too many instructions to readers, you may obscure the topic itself. But the process of forming transitions can help you to reveal the logic of your piece to the reader—and hence help you to accomplish your purpose and to develop a reliable, logical *ethos* in the perception of your readers.

Most of the stylistic work we discussed in this chapter returns to *ethos*— the ways your writing represents you as a logical, professional, reliable authority on a topic. Part of that *ethos* comes from what you actually know about a topic. But the way you formulate, arrange, and present that knowledge is at least as important as what you know. The Reading and Writing Applications that follow give you the opportunity to practice these and other stylistic techniques before moving on to Part 2, where we discuss the types of writing that inform a variety of academic and professional fields.

Practicing Patterns of Arrangement

Writers do not have a single style that they use on all occasions but rather fit their stylistic technique to the situation. As we discussed in Chapter 4, the patterns of arrangement and stylistic techniques you choose are determined by each rhetorical situation you face. But in order to have the stylistic strengths to make such choices, good writers must first develop their rhetorical muscles through practice. Knowing this, rhetorical educators developed a set of exercises, called the *progymnasmata*, designed to improve prowess with language. The roots of this word, *gym* (as in "gymnasium") and *pro* (as in "before"), remind us that the *progymnasmata* was designed as a preparatory workout for students of rhetoric, exercises that helped them to face the various occasions within which they would be called on to use language. These rhetorical workouts functioned largely by (1) imitating and playing with stylistic patterns, and (2) considering how (and why) such patterns can be useful in writing.

In your own education, and as preparation for your life's work, you too must develop techniques that will serve you in good communication. And while each field has a preferred style, some basic patterns of communication (sometimes called *genres* or *modes*) can be useful in a variety of situations. Like a tennis player, who needs a variety of shots—forehand, backhand, drop-shot, and lob—in order to face each situation in a match, a good writer needs a wealth of stylistic techniques. The activities that follow are meant to extend your store of stylistic options, giving you a wider repertoire to draw on as you write within the rhetorical situations that you face as a student and as a professional.

DESCRIPTION

One of the most basic stylistic patterns allows you to create sensory images for your readers—helping them to see, feel, touch, taste, or hear some phenomenon by reading the words you have written. **Description** functions through word choices that create mental images. You can describe an apple as "delicious," which tells the reader that you enjoyed eating it. If you describe an apple as "tart," you come closer to a specific sense experience—the sensation of a sharp or sour taste. If you describe the apple as "bursting with sharpness," you add another element of sensation—the suddenness of that sour taste on your tongue. You also might want to describe tactile sensations, describing the apple as "firm and bursting with tartness," helping the reader to experience the *feel* of the apple as you bit into it (its firmness) as well as the sensation of *tasting* it (its tartness). You could add other sensations: the look of the shiny, green apple; the sharp smell it emitted as you bit into it; the loud crack you heard as you bit into its firm skin.

This basic stylistic skill has a range of uses that are crucial to many types of academic and occupational writing. If you want to provide readers with a clear understanding of the results of a scientific experiment, you may need to describe the phenomena you observed in careful detail. If you want to illustrate the conditions under which a group of people live, or their reactions to an event, you may need to paint a mental picture of those conditions or reactions for your readers. If you want to show changes in a phenomenon over time, you might need to describe what you observe in great detail in order to illustrate subtle or dramatic changes. In each case, careful description involves first observing the details of each situation and then finding the words that best capture those sensory details.

For example, read the following passage from Alice Munro's "Boys and Girls":

> Henry Bailey suffered from bronchial troubles. He would cough and cough until his narrow face turned scarlet, and his light blue, derisive eyes filled up with tears; then he took the lid off the stove, and standing well back, shot out a great clot of phlegm—hsss—straight into the heart of the flames. We admired him for this performance and for his ability to make his stomach growl at will, and for his laughter, which was full of high whistlings and gurglings and involved the whole faulty machinery of his chest.

This description begins with a simple declarative statement: "Henry Bailey suffered from bronchial troubles." That statement, however, carries little of the descriptive force of that which follows. It is the small details—the "scarlet" face, his tearing up, the "great clot of phlegm," and the "whistlings and gurglings"— that help us to truly experience his "bronchial troubles." Just as the observers became involved in the "whole faulty machinery of his chest," so do we through the verbal descriptions. These descriptions are enhanced by the careful diction (word choices): not just red but "scarlet"; not just mucus but a "great clot of phlegm"; not just a face but a "narrow" (and hence sickly) face. Though this description is designed to characterize Mr. Bailey within this piece of fiction, such descriptions (though likely in different words) might also be used for a medical assessment or to describe the results of poor social or housing conditions under which some people must live. The effect of the paragraph is to provide not only a mental picture but also a sensory one.

To understand how description might function in another type of document, read the following report. Gwen Anderson wrote it in a memo reporting on conditions she found in a Chicago public housing project:

> During inspection of basements of buildings (6) in Henry Horner Homes Project by the Manager, Assistant Manager, and Maintenance Superintendent, the following was found:
>
> An estimated two thousand (2000) appliances:
>
> Refrigerators—some new, with the insulation pulled out, missing motors, aluminum freeze compartments missing, electrical cords ripped out, some standing in pools of water and rusting away.
>
> Ranges—some stacked wall to wall—floor to ceiling and barring entry into the storage room, parts missing (doors, burners, grates, boiler trays, knobs, panels, etc.), standing in pools of water and rusting away.
>
> It should be noted also that the these appliances were heavily infested with roaches, fleas. Cats were bedding and walking the rafters (pipes) and dead rodents and animals were lying in storage areas, stench and putrid odor abounded. (The manager became nauseated to the point of intensely vomiting for relief, and could not continue the inspection until after being revived.) Soiled female undergarments and paraphernalia with foul odors were lying around. No equipment presently in use by staff could be used to withstand this odor beyond a minute! In most storage areas, the electrical fixtures had been ripped out and any security devices (locks, chains, gates, etc.) had been removed or severely damaged.
>
> Kitchen cabinets—new cabinets, with some still in cartons—were sitting in pools of water, rusted beyond use. These cabinets were amidst dead animals, rodents, human and animal excrement, garbage and junk items, and the odors were overwhelming. (qtd. in Kotlowitz, *There Are No Children Here* 240)

This memo, unlike the fictional example of Henry Bailey, was written with a specific occupational goal in mind: to remedy a serious health hazard in this housing project. However, despite the very different purpose, the goals and techniques of description are similar: to help the readers (Anderson's superiors at the Chicago Housing Authority) to understand and experience the level of danger and poor management that existed within these homes. Though the purpose of the memo is to report "facts," a good deal of that reporting involves careful sensory descriptions.

WRITING TO EXPLORE STYLE EXERCISE 1

As is illustrated by the diverse scenarios below, description is an important stylistic technique in a wide variety of situations. Practice your skills of description by writing on some of these topics. You can use these topics as brief exercises to develop your skills or extend your writing into larger projects.

- Write a description of a product that you particularly like, showing its physical, sensory features in ways that would make it attractive to other potential customers.
  - If you want to develop this further, you might create a larger advertising plan showing the facets of the project that you might stress through description.
- Go to a local museum or gallery and describe a single painting, sculpture, drawing, or photograph. Use details and description to help your readers to experience the work of art with you.
  - If you want to extend this description, you might write a review of an entire show or a group of works by a featured artist.
- Write a description of one place in your city or town that you feel helps to make the community unique.
  - If you want to extend this writing task, imagine that you have been hired by the local Chamber of Commerce to help attract people to your area. Use description to show why your hometown is a wonderful place to live.
- Write a description of a place in your community that you feel is neglected or in need of attention from citizens or government officials.
  - If you wish to develop this description, imagine that you are part of a citizen group that has decided to bring about change in a problem faced by your community. Focusing on some aspect (or aspects) of your community that needs change, use a key description (a dilapidated park, a rundown school, a dangerous intersection) to show the need.
- Describe some problem—and its effects—with a policy in a job you have held or in your high school or college. Use vivid language to illustrate it.
  - If you wish to develop this writing exercise, write an extended letter of complaint or letter to the editor that uses description to call for change in policies.
- Sit and observe either a natural setting or a place where people congregate. Using careful observation, write a vivid description of the place and the activities that take place there.
  - If you'd like to extend this, imagine yourself to be either a social scientist or a natural scientist. Write a description of the natural phenomena or the variety of social activity you see, using details as a field researcher might and making suggestions about why this place might be worth further study for professionals in your field. What important information might it provide? Why would others in this field be interested?

NARRATION

Though description is a powerful communication tool, it provides only a snapshot. On some occasions, you need to describe an event or experience as a "moving picture" in order for readers to gain the full experience. On such occasions,

narration or storytelling can be a valuable stylistic skill. There are many types of, and many uses for, stories. Some stories are fictional; others recount actual events, describing a past moment as accurately as possible.

Narration is one of the most effective stylistic options available to writers. People love to hear narratives because it is natural for them to think in terms of stories; their lives, after all, are made up of characters and events that take place over time. As a teacher, I know that each time I pause in class and begin to tell a story, the attention of my students heightens.

WRITING TO EXPLORE STYLE EXERCISE 2

In your writer's notebook, recall times you used stories as a form of communication. In what types of situations do you tend to rely on stories to make a point, interact with others, or illustrate concepts or ideas? What types of audiences seem to appreciate your stories most?

Narration, like description, takes many forms and can be used for a number of purposes. For example, the social sciences employ case studies to present the stories of specific people or situations and so to illustrate a human phenomenon (as in psychology) or a social situation (as in, say, criminal justice). Lab reports or protocols are also a form of narrative; they tell about a series of events or procedures over time. In business, narratives are used to describe the success (or failure) of companies and to advertise products (as in testimonials). These examples only begin to scratch the surface of the ways that narratives can be used to make a point.

Stories, or narratives, can be told in as many ways as there are storytellers, but some techniques of storytelling are universal. Here are key features of storytelling:

- Narratives are chronological—*chrono-logic* means "organized by time"—though not always in precise chronological order. Sometimes the unfolding of time can help you to create suspense or dramatic tension as the reader attempts to figure out what will happen next, or the relationship between events.

- Narratives need strong characterizations. In order to become invested in a story, readers must get to know the characters. It is not enough to say "I loved my friend"; you must help your readers to see why the emotion is warranted, letting them in on the details about the person that can inspire such love.

- Narratives rely on action. Aristotle suggested that plot, or action, was the crucial aspect of a good dramatic presentation. After all, characters reveal themselves to readers through their actions.

- Narratives organize experiences in a purposeful way—that is, though the events of life can be baffling and seem to lack substantive order, writers usually select details for their stories carefully. They don't include details just because they happened; they select details because they are relevant to the point of the story.

- ■ Readers look for meaning in narratives. As a writer, at least in most cases, it is your job to select and organize the events of a story in a way that makes meaning available to your readers.

- ■ Narratives use description and setting. In order to express action and character, writers need the language skills of description discussed above. One major element of a story that must be described is its setting; remember that in order to picture the action and characters of a narrative or story, readers must also be able to imagine the place in which the action occurs.

- ■ Narratives use varying points of view. The narrator, or storyteller, can be an outsider, describing the events from a third-person or omniscient perspective (using *he, she, they*), or the storyteller can be a character in the story and give a first-person account (using *I*). The latter style, of course, allows for less distance between the storyteller and the story—it has a sense of immediacy. But the third person has the advantage of a wider, and sometimes more diverse, set of perspectives on the situation (as well as a greater aura of objectivity). Point of view can be adjusted to fit the purposes for telling the story.

WRITING TO EXPLORE STYLE EXERCISE 3

Write a narrative or story that:

1. makes readers feel the need to contribute to a favorite charity.
   - ■ If you'd like to extend this, create a series of stories/anecdotes that might be used in a promotional brochure for that charity.

2. illustrates a general principle from your field of study. For example, if you are a psychology major, you might write a story that explains the effect on children of watching too much television, or shows that are too violent; if you are a biologist, you might narrate the ways in which humans interfere with natural processes.
   - ■ For a more extended approach, you might make your story part of a larger position statement about the topic.

3. breaks down a stereotype. For example, you might write a story that shows what professionals in a field that interests you or with which you have first-hand experience actually do: Show the exciting aspects of accounting or managerial work, the varied skills of teaching, the importance of nursing to primary caregiving, or the living nature of historical analyses.
   - ■ To extend this into a larger project, you might use your story as part of a promotional brochure for a particular occupation or academic department.

4. shows the need to change a policy at work. In this case, the goal of your story is to illustrate in narrative form how that policy affects the morale, the efficiency, or some other aspect of the work environment.

- After illustrating a specific effect of the policy in action, you might extend this into a more developed call for a change in the policy—adding, perhaps, more narrative moments.

5. introduces the importance of a topic. The goal of this story is to help readers realize that some area of concern that you and others in a particular field or profession see as important should also concern them—that is, you are writing a story that illustrates exigency. For example, you might tell a story about a special-needs child who has been mainstreamed into a classroom to illustrate how this integration can help (or harm) the child and/or the other students.

   - If you choose to develop this, write an essay that incorporates storytelling into a more complete explication of your topic.

ANALYSIS

Though it is natural to organize experiences and events chronologically, chronological order isn't always the best stylistic choice. On some occasions, you want your readers to focus not on events *as they occur over time* but on *some other way of reasoning through their significance.* In those cases, the goal is often to help readers to draw general principles from specific cases, or to make a decision about one case based on general principles. **Analysis** involves you and your reader in a shared process of examining experiences and/or events, asking, "Why is this significant?" or "What should we make of this?"

Analysis, like the other stylistic techniques, has identifiable features:

- Analytical writing reasons from specific examples toward more general principles (or vice versa).
- Analysis presents material in an order that promotes a logical pattern of reasoning or supports a main point rather than as a series of chronological events.
- Analysis relies on a claim/support structure—each assertion made comes from specific information presented.
- Analysis draws conclusions and asks readers to accept them based on the evidence presented.

Let's consider the example of the Chicago Housing Authority's description of the conditions at its Henry Horner Homes. If I wanted to use those descriptions within an analytical style, rather than simply list and embellish those sense experiences, I might structure my memo in a different way. You'll recall that the memo began this way: "During inspection of basements of buildings (6) in Henry Horner Homes Project by the Manager, Assistant Manager, and Maintenance Superintendent, the following was found." Such a stylistic patterning sets up what follows nicely: a description of the conditions.

But let's say that the information and observations collected were being used as part of a larger report on waste in government programs. In that case, rather than focusing the reader on what "was found" (a description), I might structure that information like this: "The effective management of Chicago housing projects is undermined by many instances of waste in the use of expensive resources." Readers of this sentence will expect to find evidence of this claim—evidence that very well might draw on description and storytelling but that is presented within a pattern of logic that analyzes the information collected and presents a carefully constructed interpretation of the "facts."

Writers employ many forms of analysis. One type frequently used in academic writing is the analysis of other people's writing. When you analyze the words of others, you use critical reading skills to dissect the implications of their ideas. To do so, you might *paraphrase* or *summarize* their words—pointing out what is significant in that piece of writing. You also frequently need to *quote* directly the piece of writing you are analyzing in order to illustrate the specific ways in which the writer makes points. When you quote directly, you allow your readers not only to hear the ideas of others but to experience directly their voice and style. For example, if you were citing the memo about the Henry Horner Homes, you could paraphrase the original text describing the government inspectors' inability to stay at the site for long due to the stench. But the writer's own words, "No equipment presently in use by staff could be used to withstand this odor beyond a minute!" capture not only the point but also the writer's tone and emotions. Depending on the situation, I might want to retain those emotional elements as well as the content.

WRITING TO EXPLORE STYLE EXERCISE 4

Read the two analyses of school-to-work programs below and, by annotating the articles and/or responding in your writer's notebook, describe how each argues its point—the types of evidence presented, the way that the argument is arranged, the assumptions made about audience, etc. The second article is a much more in-depth and systematic study than the first, which largely uses the testimony of a few individuals to make its point. Consider how audience and purpose may have influenced the choices made by each author, and list what you consider to be the most important points raised by each. Also, note how each author uses techniques we discussed—description, narrative, and analysis—to develop his ideas.

School-to-Career Programs Help Students Focus on Future

Patrick Healy

Patrick Healy is a staff writer for the *Boston Globe* who writes frequently on education for the *Globe* and other publications. This brief essay discusses the advantages of school-to-work programs—programs that attempt to make education more directly related to students' career possibilities.

The days when college graduates meander from job to job may be a convention of the past. School-to-work programs now in place at most Rhode Island high schools are trying to alleviate occupational indecision by helping students understand their career choices earlier in life.

Maryann Mitchell, a business teacher at Lincoln High School, is in her fourth year of teaching a school-to-work class. She said it's never too early to teach a person about his or her options. "Everybody goes from school to work," she said, "whether it's from college to work or from high school to work."

An elective class at Lincoln High School, Mitchell's school-to-work class would be part of a student's course requirement, if she had her way. "The average person works 92,000 hours in a lifetime," she said, "and if you're unhappy for a good portion of those 92,000 hours, that's a lot of frowning."

Mitchell is one of the pioneers of school to work training in Rhode Island. In 1997, along with Robert Delaney, who was then the coordinator of entrepreneurship skills training at the Community College of Rhode Island, she implemented the course at Lincoln High School. Delaney had had success with a similar program in Nova Scotia called Young Entrepreneurs Going Places, and when he joined the CCRI staff, the school had just received a national award to develop an entrepreneurship program. Funded through the Northern Rhode Island Business Education Alliance, the program has spread to nine area public high schools in northern Rhode Island. Delaney is now the development manager of workforce development at CCRI. He said school to work is not just an important program for aspiring entrepreneurs. "The program provides students with the opportunity to make a choice to start their own business," he said, but if they do not want to do that, "it gives them the skills that make them valuable employees, so when they enter the workforce they're that much more ready."

Jaime Nash is the current coordinator of entrepreneurship skills. His next step will be faxing a questionnaire to all Rhode Island high schools, encouraging them to offer entrepreneurship education if they don't already. "I think it's going great," he said of the program, "and frankly, I'm a little surprised that it's not going faster."

In the southern part of the state, school-to-work training is approached a bit differently. Instead of having specific entrepreneurial classes, the notion of school to work is implemented into the curriculum of most classes through teachers' externships with area businesses and guest speakers.

Southern Rhode Island Collaborative Assistant Coordinator of School-to-Career Program Development Joseph Potenza said this has a similar positive effect on students. "The point of asking a businessperson to be involved is to increase the competence of these kids who are eventually going to be knocking on your door for jobs," he said. "The goal is a more educated citizenry and some of the tools you can use to achieve that can be found in the business community."

School-based Coordinator for the program in Exeter, West Greenwich, North Kingstown and Coventry, Pam Betres was formerly a classroom teacher before she took this position two years ago. She said one advantage to the program is that students are no longer asking, "Why do we need to learn this?"

"If you can help answer that question by having the students apply what they're learning to the real world, then that's wonderful," she said. Betres said the program is not robbing the students of their childhood as much as it is helping them make the most of their lives. "I hate to say that we're here to produce skilled workers," she said. "We want to create well-rounded individuals who can apply what they're learning to many aspects of their life."

Nash agreed. "Students are able to see what they're capable of doing at such an early age," he said. "It is a reality."

Study of School-to-Work Initiatives: Studies of Education

Ivan Charter

Ivan Charter wrote this report as project director for a study of school-to-work initiatives sponsored by the U.S. Department of Education's Office of Educational Research and Improvement. It not only adds further perspectives on this topic but also demonstrates the ways in which in-depth studies are necessary to reveal the intricacies of a social phenomenon or program.

Introduction

The purpose of this report is to help practitioners, policy makers, and program developers create sound systems for school-to-work transition. Its approach to doing so is twofold: (1) presenting an analysis of how school-to-work reform affects its clients and participants, and (2) describing a set of twelve "critical elements" that our research indicates are essential to any sound school-to-work system. These findings are based on lessons learned from a series of case studies conducted by the Academy for Educational Development (AED) in fourteen communities across the United States, part of a four-year national study of school-to-work transition reform.

As part of that study, we undertook to discover and describe exemplary instances of reform: cities, suburbs, and rural communities creating new systems with the common intent of changing how high schools educate in order to improve the prospects young people face after high school. We sought out variety: different models of change, different kinds of communities, different emphases in approach.

In the end we selected fourteen communities for case studies. For those who believe in school-to-work reform, their variety is exciting, for it confirms that ingenuity and commitment will create many paths towards the same broad purpose. We saw examples of career academies, statewide and regional systems, school-based enterprises and off-site workplaces, systems that emphasize career guidance and others that emphasize the integration of academic and vocational study.

One purpose of national studies of school reform is to explore what difference the reform has made to students, but also to educational institutions and other partners in the reform. The AED/NIWL study discovered a wealth of positive outcomes for students, schools, businesses, colleges, and other community partners. We offer these in section III of this report, to affirm the practical benefits of the school-to-work strategy, but also to offer our readers evidence with which to advocate for the introduction of school-to-work reform.

Another purpose of studies such as this one is to identify best practices from which others may learn, through study and comparison of existing models. Yet those with whom we met often cautioned that to transfer any model wholesale from one community to another without major adjustments is a recipe for failure. As Richard De Lone (1990) observes in his study of model replication, this "cookie-cutter" approach to replication resembles franchising in the private sector, and features well-defined program models, detailed implementation plans, and specified components.

At the other end of the continuum, replication strategies allow for greater local adaptation, require less fidelity to the original model, and encourage more creativity in its reproduction. As the authors of the School-to-Work Act of 1994 understood, school-to-work reform, by definition, requires more flexible replication strategies. School-to-work is not a one-size-fits-all proposition. Local circumstances—including but not limited to the labor market, business base, school infrastructure, and personalities—require flexibility of those who hope to create a school-to-work system in any locality. Implementing school-to-work reform requires that reformers study a range of options, consider what transition pieces already exist, weigh local resources and barriers, and assemble a new combination of vision and programmatic pieces that, one hopes, will eventually evolve into a system.

So rather than select one or more models to recommend as the best practice for school-to-work, this report identifies "critical elements" or "building blocks" that appear to be essential to any sound school-to-work system. Our hope is that doing so will help practitioners, "architects" of school-to-work at both local and state levels, assemble these building blocks into new or reformed systems that make sense for local circumstances.

Case Study Reports

The advantage of case study methodology, characterized by intensive and focused field work, is that it provides for the collection of a rich amount of data from which to draw a comprehensive portrait of a reform initiative and its dynamics. The research teams wrote 25–30 page case studies of each initiative, describing their findings about its design, implementation, impact, and barriers faced by program developers. The case study reports reflect the emphasis on description rather than on evaluation. The primary purpose of AED's study was to document and analyze useful models and practices from which others could learn as they sought to reform education in their communities.

Cross-Site Analysis

Throughout the case study process, the research team convened to discuss cross-cutting elements, relating and synthesizing the findings of their individual case studies. The teams considered the elements identified as critical at each site, explored similarities across sites, defined variations, and arrived at agreement that an element was present and important in at least four or five sites.

The result of these discussions is this cross-case comparison report. Its basic purpose is twofold: (1) to document and analyze the outcomes of school-to-work reform, so as to educate practitioners and policy makers about the results that can be documented; and (2) to document and analyze the critical elements common to many or all of the communities studied, so as to make their models and practices accessible and useful to others seeking to reform education in their communities.

Outcomes of School-to-Work Reform

An educational reform that engages as many players and as many levels of the educational system as does school-to-work transition reform has the potential to achieve significant outcomes for many people and institutions. AED/NIWL's study documented evidence of such outcomes for students, business partners, schools (from elementary grades through college), and other partners to the STW collaboration.

Outcomes for Students

The genesis of the school-to-work movement was the widespread concern that students were leaving high school unprepared for work, lifelong learning, and citizenship. These undesirable "outcomes" remain the impetus behind the current movement. But is there evidence that school-to-work is making a difference?

Our findings suggest that it is important to look both at long-term outcomes for young people and at short-term outcomes—changes that occur while students are enrolled in a school-to-work program. A few sites in the AED/NIWL study had gathered sound data concerning long-term student outcomes in the categories of employment, postsecondary education, and income, and evidence of connections between these circumstances and their secondary school STW experiences. These studies indicated that, a few years after graduation, STW graduates were more likely to be employed, more likely to access postsecondary training, and had higher incomes and professional standing than their peers who did not experience STW. It is one of our recommendations for further research, however, to collect more data on these long-term outcomes for students: employment, independent living, postsecondary education, income, and professional standing.

While these long-term outcomes have an undeniable bottom-line importance, AED/NIWL urges that the short-term outcomes we have documented also be valued, both because of their intrinsic importance, and because they enable students to achieve the long-term outcomes that are the ultimate goal of STW. We found short-term outcomes for students in terms of skills and knowledge, career direction, motivation, and empowerment.

Teachers, administrators, employers, and students themselves at the case study sites reported skills development as a key outcome of STW programs. Most programs are reported to be effectively teaching occupational skills at a sufficient level to enable students to gain a foothold on the professional ladder within an occupation. Most programs also teach, through a combination of classroom instruction and experiential education, a range of "employability" skills: resume preparation, job searching, interviewing, and on-the-job roles, responsibilities, and human relations. Less commonly, gains in academic skills were reported, often by students who observed that their STW experience had motivated them to pay more attention to academics, because now they saw the connection between "book learning" and real world experience.

A new sense of career direction is another very important short-term outcome for students documented by the AED/NIWL study. STW students acquired both formal career plans and a personal, career-directed way of thinking about their futures. Most of the AED/NIWL sites had in place an individualized career planning process integrated with student course selection and postsecondary plans. These processes mean that every student has an individual plan to guide him or her through high school and beyond, in contrast to the traditional system of clumping students into college-going, vocational, or general tracks. Going through the formal process, however, also appears to have enabled many students to internalize career planning processes, a lifelong skill that enables them to weigh their plans against their goals and resources, and take responsibility for changing their plans as their goals shift.

Students in STW programs discussed their career plans thoughtfully and knowledgeably, demonstrating their acquisition of career planning skills and ability to apply these to their own lives. In particular, students talked about their own career paths, explaining step-by-step plans for acquiring the training, work experience, and sometimes even the financial resources they would need to achieve their career goals. They had an integrated vision of schooling and work, and an incremental view of building careers. Students and teachers also both observed that students who previously had shied away from college entirely were now planning at least some college course work.

Motivation is a broadly defined concept, but anyone familiar with high school students in the late 1990s knows how critical it is. Students in STW programs and the adults who work with them report remarkable improvements in motivation, both among students who do well in traditional classrooms and students who do not. Even students who have left school, or are on the verge of it, become motivated to return and to succeed in school. Students apply themselves in new ways to their studies, both on the job and in workplaces. They have an answer, as a principal at one site observed, to the question "Why am I studying this?" Various explanations are offered for the increased motivation: visible rewards in terms of career experience and prospective employment, opportunity to be treated as adults in an adult world, learning that is contextual rather than abstract, pedagogy more conducive to a range of learning styles, and the opportunity to escape from the high school building.

Closely related to motivation, but a more sweeping outcome, is the development of "empowered" students. By "empowered," we mean students who have the knowledge, freedom, self-esteem, and motivation, connected to a deep sense of individual responsibility, to make independent choices for themselves and play meaningful roles in setting the course of the STW program itself. A setting with empowered students has achieved a profound educational reform, because in many respects it is the mirror opposite of the traditional high school classroom.

Outcomes for Business and Industry

Although STW reform is primarily intended to benefit students, the AED/NIWL study found evidence of positive outcomes for business and industry as well. Businesses were pleased to have the immediate benefit of extra workers provided through STW internships, although some employers complained that, under short-term arrangements, by the time students were trained and up to speed, the internship had ended. We also found evidence that, besides providing an extra pair of trained hands, students can supplement an employer's work force in more sophisticated ways, performing tasks that otherwise would not be accomplished. Students apply problem-solving and technological skills, conducting a marketing survey in Sitka (Alaska), for example, or surveying fire safety systems in Dayton (Ohio), or training adult employees in the use of computer technology in Fort Pierce (Florida). In these examples, the educational system has supplied business with the latest or most sophisticated workplace techniques, rather than the other way around.

Some businesses also reported as a positive outcome the development of a better-trained pool of potential employees, who understood the industry and its needs. Business representatives on advisory groups, in particular, were pleased with the opportunity to shape the curriculum of occupational training in the high school, and believed they were having an influence on these programs and their graduates that would ultimately pay off for business in terms of a better qualified workforce. Indeed, the case studies found some evidence of businesses hiring graduates of STW programs.

The organizational structures of STW programs and systems create new roles for business and industry that together amount to a more continual and more substantive presence in the educational system. Business takes on leadership roles through representation in partnership steering committees and advisory groups, but it also plays face-to-face roles with students and instructors as employers work as mentors, trainers, and curriculum developers.

Face-to-face supervision and mentoring of students in the workplace at times produces practical and positive outcomes for business. Employees who supervise students gain supervisory, mentoring, and training skills. Analyzing tasks in order to convey them to students, and analyzing competencies in order to assess their accomplishment, has led to improved internal training for regular employees, and reexaminations of internal career paths, according to some businesses.

Collaborating with other community representatives on advisory groups and partnerships has the beneficial outcome for business partners of improved political and business connections. Businesses make new contacts and have opportunities to develop existing relationships that go beyond the STW initiative.

Participation in STW also provides a business with an avenue for good public relations. The role can bring the business more visibility in the community, specifically within the schools—often the heart of a community—and in a fashion that demonstrates commitment to children and to the community's future. AED/NIWL found, however, that many of the businesses participating in STW appeared to be motivated by a sincere commitment to community service, rooted in a sense of social responsibility. STW programs have many positive outcomes for businesses, but they also require a great deal in energy, time, and resources. Businesses that do participate, however, also appear to have their sense of commitment reinforced by their participation, both because they see results for their efforts, and because they see, firsthand, how serious the issues are. Such businesses often become advocates for school-to-work, encouraging other businesses to take part.

Outcomes for Schools

By definition, the outcome of STW reform is the transformation of the educational process itself: changed curriculum, pedagogy, standards, assessment, scheduling, even the physical location for learning. School-to-work is an educational reform so profound that it literally transforms every aspect of schooling, at least at the secondary level. This recognition goes a long way to explaining the complexity of implementing STW reform, and the resistance with which it often meets within schools.

Secondary Schools. One outcome is the introduction of new resources—usually brought about through business or other partnerships, sometimes through grants: equipment, funds, advice, speakers, mentors, staff development, student placements. These resources represent new opportunities for students, obviously, but also for school staff.

Which leads into the second outcome: opportunities for the professional development of instructional, counseling, and administrative staff. STW reform means new staffing configurations, new kinds of responsibilities, and new ways of thinking about existing roles and relationships within the school. Staff members who become committed to the reform will see these innovations as opportunities for personal growth as well as for an improved school. They pursue formal training introduced through STW reform and make their own opportunities for personal development.

When STW reform engages school staff in professional development in this manner, it has the further outcomes of creating a more knowledgeable and a more motivated staff. The AED/NIWL site visitors found many instructors who reported that STW had led them to understand and adopt more comprehensive views of student learning processes. Counselors tired of planning career days were reengaged by the opportunity to create more sophisticated career planning systems. Staff members who become engaged in STW reform bring renewed energy and creativity to their work, perhaps in part because, like their students, they have a new sense of purpose for what they are doing in school. Sometimes this also results in a new, formal mission statement; sometimes it is simply a new sense of mission.

As observed above, STW reform by definition leads to the outcomes of changed curriculum, pedagogy, assessment, and scheduling and location of learning. STW reforms in these areas tend to mean certain thematic outcomes as well: more individualized approaches to students and their learning, more flexibility in styles and structures, more competency-based and standards-based teaching and assessment. A transformation of the school's career counseling system—its structure and process—is also by definition an outcome of STW reform. The AED/NIWL case study process uncovered different models, which, in contrast to traditional guidance counseling, depend upon individual student career and educational planning processes, continual assessment, and up-to-date labor market information, and do not emphasize application to traditional four-year college programs.

Another outcome of STW reform is that it results in less isolated schools. STW brings schools into the community and invites a variety of community partners into the schools, who in turn bring new perspectives, resources, and connections. The STW processes in which they engage are likely to lead to a community that knows more about the schools and feels more commitment to what happens within them. In some cases, this sense of ownership has led to practical support, such as passage of a school bond issue.

A final outcome of STW reform is that it tends to reorient secondary-school thinking towards a K–14+ concept. High school graduation is no longer the goal towards which all activity in the school points: staff members are creating new articulation arrangements with postsecondary institutions and helping their students plan their futures with the years after high school graduation in view. High school graduation and college admission have become steps in a life-long learning process, rather than make-or-break hurdles.

Postsecondary Schools. Colleges and universities who engage in STW programs also reorient their thinking towards a K–14 or even K–16 model, making traditional college admission requirements more flexible, granting college credit for STW courses, and even admitting students still in high school to college courses. This reorientation is a significant outcome, but so is the reform in admission requirements, which may change both the process and the materials required, for example, waiving credit requirements or accepting student portfolios. We did find, however, instances in which postsecondary systems were not responsive to these new systems, even openly setting policies that blocked the admission of STW students.

On a practical level, articulation and other agreements may mean a new source of incoming students for colleges. Increased enrollment is usually reported to be a welcome outcome, but some colleges have had more students seeking to enroll than they could serve.

Another outcome is that engaging in STW programs enables colleges and universities to have an impact on prospective students. Through articulation processes, college faculty and staff shape curriculum, strengthen standards, and assist teachers at the secondary level. In these ways, they help determine the preparation that students will bring to the postsecondary classroom.

Elementary and Middle Schools. Not surprisingly, the AED/NIWL study found relatively few outcomes for elementary and middle schools as a result of STW reform, for two reasons. First, our study's focus was on secondary school reform initiatives rather than STW reforms in elementary and middle schools. Secondly, few secondary-level STW reforms reach even as far as the middle school. Where there was a STW presence in the middle school, the primary outcome tended to be a strengthened, more systematic career exploration/awareness process. We documented a few curricular changes in middle school classrooms as well.

Outcomes for Other Organizational Partners

STW systems must work with secondary school, business, and postsecondary partners, but often engage other organizations as well, including government agencies, job training entities, community-based organizations, human services organizations, labor unions, and research organizations. In many cases, these partners are being brought into the educational system for the first time, an outcome intended to benefit students that may have desirable outcomes for the partners as well. Collaboration on a STW agenda is likely to introduce people to each other for the first time, create relationships in a new and collaborative context, and suggest new ways of working together. The AED/NIWL research team found evidence of activities apparently spun-off from collaborative planning on STW.

Effective STW reform, like the proverbial pebble tossed into the pond, has a ripple effect that bears important outcomes for all the major players in the effort. Outcomes for students may be most crucial, but the system's survival is also influenced by how it affects the organizational partners.

Writing Application

Using information from the two articles above, write a position statement that might be presented to your school board, analyzing the most positive features or the weakest aspects of school-to-work. Be sure to organize your essay carefully, keeping in mind the specific features of your own school system and the reasoning that you are trying to create for your readers. Try using direct quotations and paraphrases to support your analysis of this issue. If you wish to enrich your essay, you might do more research on the topic, including collecting information about your own school system.

Evaluation 1: Developing Criteria

Oftentimes, you must decide on and demonstrate the value of something in your writing. Citizens who find a local issue that has not been dealt with sufficiently, consumers who find a product unsatisfactory, or students who find their rights have been violated might be compelled to express dissatisfaction. A community member who finds an action particularly laudable might be compelled to write a letter of praise.

Many situations and styles of writing focus on the value of something. What they all share is the comparison of some person, event, phenomena, or condition to an ideal. Those ideals don't always represent perfection; more often, they are based in commonplaces held by some group—the values that are at the core of that group. The base of values that are used as the measure for praising or blaming are called *criteria*. To reason with your audience about the value of something, you and they must first agree to the terms on which those judgments are based.

WRITING TO EXPLORE STYLE EXERCISE 5

List standards, criteria, and ideals by which you might judge

- a painting, novel, or poem
- the functionality of a machine (home appliance, automobile, etc.)
- a medical procedure
- a law
- a military action
- an advertising campaign
- a proposed methodology for studying a learning disorder

Then, with other students in small groups or via e-mail, negotiate a set of criteria that you all agree on.

Sometimes you must judge the relative value of two or more options rather than measure a single item against ideal criteria. For example, consider the choices an office manager must make when choosing computer equipment or software being sold by two different companies. This comparative judgment does not assign value based on closeness to an ideal as much as it seeks the alternative *closest* to an ideal.

WRITING TO EXPLORE STYLE EXERCISE 6

Write an essay that compares two alternative solutions to a problem, arguing for one solution or the other because it comes closer to achieving the ideal result. In order to do so, of course, you first identify a viable set of criteria (viable in that your readers are likely to agree with them) and then compare *both* alternatives to those criteria. Though you could choose a topic from your own sphere of interests and expertise, here are some examples:

1. *Education:* What is the best way to educate special needs students? Choose between mainstreaming (placing special needs students in a regular classroom setting) and providing a separate educational setting adapted specifically for such students.

2. *Biology:* Can students learn about animal anatomy more effectively through computer modeling or live dissection?

3. *Literary studies:* Should undergraduate curricula focus on primary literary texts, or should a significant amount of time be spent on critical essays and literary theory?

4. *Business:* Should small to midsize businesses develop their own computer networks with their own staff of experts or outsource the work to external companies?

5. *Nursing:* In light of the current nursing shortage, should hospitals improve pay and conditions for nurses or attempt to focus their energies on activities that do not require nursing expertise and hire more orderlies and unskilled employees to perform less skilled tasks?

Evaluation 2: Confirming and Refuting

Academic and professional writing frequently requires you not only to analyze or evaluate something based on your own observations but also to make judgments about the ideas presented by others. Such judgments are usually expressed as either confirmations or refutations of those ideas. When you represent the ideas of others, it is crucial that you do your best to capture the substance of those ideas as well as the spirit in which they were presented. Then, after you have done your best to fairly represent the ideas, you can use your analytical abilities to judge their value. Making such judgments can be enhanced by asking four questions:

■ Do any inaccuracies appear in the evidence presented?

■ Is there any evidence that the writer neglected to consider?

■ Did the writer connect the evidence logically to his conclusions—that is, are the interpretations of the evidence sound?

■ Can any other possible conclusions be drawn from the same evidence?

Asking these questions can help you to either confirm or refute the ideas contained in that piece of writing.

A well-designed confirmation involves more than simply acknowledging that one agrees. Instead, it should provide further evidence of a position's credibility. You might, for example, show the value of another person's ideas by showing their usefulness in related situations. Or you might add examples that illustrate the writer's point. Or you might use your own experiences to confirm the reasoning of that piece.

In a refutation, your job is to present new ideas that undermine the value of that which you have read—and to do so in ways that can be shared by your audience. Drawing once again on the four key analytical questions above, you might generate examples or situations that the writer ignored (remembering that such examples must be, in some way, typical). You can extend the reasoning of the piece you are judging and show how it might lead to undesirable consequences. Or you could present evidence that was ignored by the writer in his piece. In any case, the refutation should show why claims made by the author are flawed.

WRITING TO EXPLORE STYLE   EXERCISE 7

The following essay provides still another perspective on the school-to-work issue. Based on your reading of this essay and the two previous essays on the topic, confirm or refute the thesis of one of the essays. To do so, draw on your own experiences as well as the information in all three articles presented here.

School-to-Work Education Shortchanges Academic Knowledge

Virginia Miller

Virginia Miller is a Pennsylvania-based consultant on educational policy. She has worked with The Heritage Foundation, which describes itself as a "research and educational institute—a think tank—whose mission is to formulate and promote conservative public policies based on the principles of free enterprise, limited government, individual freedom, traditional American values, and a strong national defense." The article below, though not directly representing that organization, is based on work that Miller conducted through her affiliations with the foundation.

America is embroiled in a debate over how best to educate its students.

Throughout the past three decades, elementary and secondary students have been exposed to a sea of educational fads, from new math and whole language to outcome-based education and cooperative learning. Each new theory has been administered as a healing elixir for the failure of public schools to help American youth rise to the same heights as many foreign students on international achievement measures. As post-secondary schools increasingly assume the responsibilities of elementary and secondary education, and as employers and parents complain about the failure of schools to teach basic skills, the standards movement has become the latest attempt to remedy lagging performance.

Eager to improve the quality of education, policymakers at the Federal, state, and local levels are pressing for higher standards in education. Major corporations are calling for higher standards in schools as well and are partnering with educators to promote their strategies. Governors are instituting state standards and assessments, and many states are tying them to grade promotion and graduation. Federal funding of elementary and secondary education programs, through such legislation as the Improving America's Schools Act and Goals 2000, imposes state content and performance standards tied to state assessments as a condition of funding eligibility. The mantra of the day in education reform is high academic standards with accountability.

Underlying this effort is the assumption that linking high-stakes assessments to standards will motivate educators to higher levels of teaching and students to greater achievement. The success of the new standards and the assessment of students' progress in meeting them will hinge on the content and quality of the standards themselves. So far, however, policymakers have focused on the process of implementing standards, paying little attention to their actual content.

A new definition of education standards has emerged—one that places greater relevance on the world of work. All learning is to take place within the context of a work situation or real-world environment with emphasis on workplace competencies. It is argued that this will provide relevance for students that will foster in them a desire to achieve greater levels of learning. The result, though, has been a narrower education that focuses on practical skills to the detriment of a broader academic approach. The danger of the new education standards is that they may elevate workplace competencies above essential academic knowledge.

Schools should not be required or encouraged by Federal funding to narrow their focus to emphasize workplace skills. The failure of vocational education to provide a quality education for non-college-bound students into the world of work is no reason to infuse and impose workforce education throughout the American elementary and secondary education system. A better solution would be to rebuild a vibrant voluntary vocational system to provide proper transition to work and careers for non-college-bound youth. Policymakers should develop education standards that are academic, rigorous, specific, measurable, and non-prescriptive of methodology or ideology. Standards should focus on academic content and be free of workplace skills or competencies.

The major impetus for transforming academic standards came in the 1990s, when Secretary of Labor Lynn Martin convened the Secretary's Commission on Achieving Necessary Skills (SCANS). In 1992, the commission published a report entitled "Learning a Living: A Blueprint for High Performance." It identified the skills the commission believed a 21st-century high-performance workplace would require:

- SCANS foundational skills: basic reading, writing, and math skills; thinking skills and problem-solving; and personal qualities such as individual responsibility, self-esteem, and integrity.

- SCANS workplace competencies: knowing how to allocate time, money, and materials; interpersonal skills such as working on teams, teaching others, and negotiating; using, evaluating, and communicating information; understanding social, organizational, and technological systems; and effectively using technology.

The SCANS report recommended integrating these competencies into core academic subjects taught in kindergarten through 12th grade and beyond. Calls to integrate the SCANS skills and competencies into state standards and assessments of core academic subjects as well increased nationwide.

In 1994, Congress passed the School-to-Work Opportunities Act (STWOA) to address the failure of the nation's primary, secondary, and vocational education systems to graduate young adults with marketable knowledge and skills. Embodied in the act are the central tenets of the school-to-work (STW) philosophy—workplace relevance, integration of academic and vocational education, and workplace competencies. STW is not vocational education, nor does it build upon vocational education. It also is not a distinct program. Rather, it is an umbrella philosophy for many activities that are intended to restructure systematically all education for all students.

Proponents claim that, for students to attain higher levels of academic achievement, education must be relevant to the real world—that is, to the world of work. They assert that integrating academic and vocational education in every subject for all grades will produce this relevancy. Thus, STW is much more than career awareness and guidance counseling. It is career integration in every discipline, across all subjects, at all grade levels, in all schools.

To varying degrees, STW has been implemented in all 50 states, and its defining features have been absorbed in the comprehensive education reform programs currently underway at the state level. All of these encourage teaching and learning in the context of real-life applications and careers. Career development is being infused throughout the curriculum as academic and technical curricula are integrated across all subject areas and grade levels. These measures provide for the sustainability of STW despite the impending sun-setting of the STWOA in 2001 and the growing sentiment in Congress to halt the program.

Today, there is evidence across the nation that STW has integrated workplace competencies, many based on the SCANS report, in classrooms, core academic subjects, and state standards. States are implementing standards infused with the SCANS foundational skills and workplace competencies. As stand-alone career or technology standards are embedded in language arts, history, science, or mathematics, the focus on workforce development is replacing academic essentials.

Problems and concerns: Serious concerns have been raised over the adoption of the SCANS recommendations because their generalized workplace competencies have never been validated. A National Job Analysis Study begun by ACT, Inc., in 1995 to validate the SCANS skills was never completed. After the Office of Management and Budget refused to continue funding in 1996, the project died. The preliminary results based on Phase I of the study were published, but with no definitive conclusions. The study could not produce sufficient information on which to generalize the SCANS workplace competencies to high-performance jobs, and further research was necessary to validate the recommendations.

Nevertheless, states are implementing their own standards based on the SCANS competencies, which may have no correlation to job performance.

According to a 1998 report by the National Association of Manufacturers, "40% of all 17-year-olds do not have the necessary math skills—and more than 60% do not have the necessary reading skills—to work in a $33,000 per annum production job at a modern auto plant." The American Management Association reported that 38.3% of job applicants tested in 1999 lacked sufficient skills for the positions they sought.

The fact that many job applicants lack the literacy and math skills necessary to perform anything but rudimentary assignments on the job is not the result of the schools' failure to teach workplace skills. Rather, it is the result of their failure to teach essential academic knowledge and literacy skills. There is a widespread assumption that workplace skills and their corresponding standards are the same as basic academic skills. They are not.

Basic academic skills are reading, writing, and mathematics, and standards for these subjects can be defined and measured objectively. Workplace skills, on the other hand, range from skills and competencies common to broad occupational groups to those essential for specific jobs. Some can be defined and measured objectively, but many are affective in nature and subjective in evaluation. The skills or competencies that fall into the affective domain include ethics, interpersonal skills, integrity, and respect for diversity.

A number of studies have raised serious questions about the effectiveness of STW. While some have found higher student motivation and engagement, as well as slightly lower dropout rates, not one conducted to date has found that STW or any of its component learning theories has increased the academic achievement of students as measured by standardized test scores. Children may be more motivated to attend schools, but this still does not answer the question: What are they learning and how well?

Much of the research that claims STW is a success does not consider academic achievement to be the highest priority. Instead, these studies consider student satisfaction, enhanced self-esteem, and other nonacademic outcomes as equal or superior to academic achievement. If any positive outcome, academic or nonacademic, is produced, STW is considered successful.

However, Mathematica Policy Research's National Evaluation of School-to-Work Implementation—the largest study of STW conducted to date—found that efforts by states to raise academic standards are occurring independently of STW. According to the report, "It has been difficult in evaluation site visits to identify clear plans for promoting [academic] skills in workplace activities that STW partnerships have arranged." Other studies support the Mathematica findings:

A study of 100 students participating in the Cornell Youth Apprenticeship Demonstration Project found that the youths did gain job-related skills and knowledge, but there were no effects on academic achievement. A report produced by the Institute on Education and the Economy concluded that "research regarding STW students' achievement on standardized tests is inconclusive. The few existing studies indicate that there is little, if any, effect on test scores."

These studies reaffirm a conclusion reached in a 1996 U.S. Department of Education study that, while most STW "programs are reported to be effectively teaching occupational skills at a sufficient level . . . less commonly, gains in academic skills are reported."

The business community and institutions of higher education continually point to the lack of academic skills in applicants, not to a deficiency in their workplace skills. "We are not interested in public schools teaching work-related skills," stated IBM CEO Louis Gerstner at the 1996 National Education Summit. "We can teach them what they need to man a machine or develop a marketing plan. What is killing us is having to teach them to read, compute, communicate, and to think."

If businesses and parents are more concerned with literacy skills and academic achievement, one might ask why there is such a strong movement to integrate workplace skills into school curricula. The answer lies in the dominant educational philosophy of STW. As a utilitarian view of education, it prematurely places the value of work above the value of academic knowledge and skills, to the detriment of both the student and business.

The school-to-work strategy fails to raise academic achievement as measured by standardized tests because its underlying theories of learning are flawed. The roots of this strategy lie in constructivist education theory (the belief that students will better remember information they create for themselves) and contextual or applied learning (learning that must take place within the context of work). These theories imply that education is not concerned with the acquisition of an accepted body of knowledge transmitted by a teacher, but, rather, with the process of helping students discover and create their own understandings from personal experience.

The belief that students will learn by scurrying about seeking information to attain ill-defined goals lies at the heart of contextual learning and STW. By simply engaging in work-related processes, students are supposed to develop critical thinking. However, there is no evidence that complex procedures can be learned before a student has mastered the simpler components of those procedures. Alan Cromer of Cornell University notes that "Without knowledgeable guidance from their teacher, students are truly like mice in a maze. Each will arrive at his own version of the goal with his own set of errors and misconceptions."

John Anderson, Lynn Reder, and Herbert Simon of Carnegie Mellon University are among the foremost cognitive psychologists in the U.S. They conclude that constructivist education theory and contextual learning claims are unproven and, in several respects, at odds with well-known scientific findings. In fact, such methods may be detrimental to learning as knowledge becomes situation-bound and context-specific, leaving students unable to generalize and transfer their knowledge to new and different situations.

Many parents assume that the education standards currently being adopted by the states are of high quality and grounded in core academic subjects. This is not the case. The curriculum integration of academic and vocational skills, known as contextual or applied learning, has become a cornerstone of education reform. As a result, state education standards increasingly define questionable workplace competencies, and local school curricula are infused with workplace skills and assessments to meet those standards.

Across the country, workplace competencies and real-world situations are found within the core curriculum in the context of tasks in English, mathematics, and science. Actual curriculum examples include the following:

- Chemistry students are asked to determine the most effective, economical, and environmentally safe grass fertilizer for a school district. The students then are to produce an analytical report with detailed procedures and conclusions and make a recommendation to the school district's grounds and maintenance department.

- Middle school math students visit local car dealerships to determine the average cost of cars with similar features. Groups of four students then present what they think is the best car for a given amount of money allowed and justify their choice to the class.

■ Taking time away from academics, high school seniors are provided the opportunity to experience a manufacturing work environment while learning the fundamentals of basketmaking.

States and individual school districts are beginning to mandate that students take employability skills and workplace competency assessments as well. The most notable assessment test is WorkKeys, produced by ACT, Inc. Based on the SCANS, it assesses such workplace skills as applied mathematics, applied technology, listening, locating information, observation, reading for information, teamwork, and writing. Tasks range from taking phone messages to computing sale prices, reading instructions for filling a candy machine, troubleshooting a hydraulic lift, and/or repairing a refrigerator.

WorkKeys is one of the fastest-growing workplace skills assessments in use today. For example, it is a graduation requirement for all high school students in Wichita, Kan. Beginning with the class of 2002, Topeka, Kan., and Jefferson County, Ky., will require seniors to achieve a minimum score on the WorkKeys exam to graduate. Illinois' new Prairie State Achievement Exam will include WorkKeys tests. In upstate New York, a Syracuse University–Community Workforce Development Partnership has inspired more than 30 companies to use WorkKeys with at least seven high schools in the region.

Education always has had economic and work-based implications, but never before have states tied economic development and the needs of business so directly to education standards. To the extent that work-based standards crowd out rigorous academic standards, businesses will soon discover that high school graduates who walk through their doors tomorrow are no better prepared in reading, writing, and math than they are today.

They may also discover that the "trained" graduates arriving on their industries' doorsteps may require retraining at an even higher rate. Youth who learn contextually do not perform well when basic knowledge and theoretical thought are required. The more specific or situation-bound that knowledge becomes, the less a student is able to generalize and transfer knowledge to new and different situations. Those who experience a well-rounded liberal arts education, by comparison, usually adapt easily to contextual learning situations.

A Better Approach: The difficulties students have in making the transition from high school to work or college would disappear if education reforms were focused on strengthening core curricula, using proven teaching methods, setting high expectations for students and parents, and enabling local educators to improve classroom discipline. If primary and secondary schools concentrated on improving these key areas instead of on implementing STW strategies, students would realize greater academic achievement and be better prepared for work or higher education.

To strengthen academic achievement, Washington should ensure that efforts to promote standards focus on academic standards. More important, state legislators and education officials at both the state and local level should:

- Eliminate STW programs and activities from comprehensive elementary and secondary education.

- Develop and incorporate education standards that are academic, rigorous, specific, measurable, nonprescriptive of methodology or ideology, and focus on academic content, rather than on workplace skills or competencies.

- Phase out contextual learning and replace it with proven teaching methods.

- Resist the integration of workplace competencies and academics at all grade levels.

- Restore academic focus and rigor to all subjects for all students.

- Restrict the participation of students in workforce investment programs.

- Protect kindergarten through 12th grade curricula and standards from inordinate business influence.

- Rebuild a vibrant and voluntary vocational system for transition to work and careers for non-college-bound students.

Research shows that education oriented to specific workplace skills and job training produces graduates who are less versatile and unable to change occupations without substantial retraining. By contrast, graduates of a rigorous liberal arts education can readily learn new skills and adjust to new jobs. There is life-long value in gaining knowledge of history, literature, science, mathematics, and the arts far beyond the world of work. The most important purpose of schools is to educate Americans to be vigilant guardians of their freedom and to be able independently to take advantage of the social and economic opportunities a free society affords.

For too long, primary and secondary public education has retreated from teaching these core academic competencies. The success of the current effort in Washington to improve the quality of education by imposing higher standards and assessments will hinge not on the assessments, but on the content and quality of the standards themselves. If these standards are academic, rigorous, specific, measurable, and nonprescriptive of methodology or ideology, America's schools will graduate adults who are better prepared for the many opportunities of the 21st century.

Academic and Occupational Writing

Each of the stylistic techniques you explored and practiced earlier are really just pieces of most written documents you produce. In real-life applications, you use a combination of description, narration, and analysis, you use stylistic patterns that show value, and you use refutation and/or confirmation to illustrate the value of someone else's ideas—sometimes all in the same document. But to produce a coherent document, you must bind the whole together with a controlling idea, or thesis. Having that controlling point in mind as you write and revise can not only keep you on track as you create a written document but also help you to choose among the available stylistic patterns, deciding where a story might help you to illustrate an important facet of the thesis, where description is needed, or when you need to refute ideas that are contrary to your thesis. As you move more deeply into the discourse of your professional area, and as you fulfill the many community roles of an active citizen, you will find that maintaining a strong central point or thesis is useful in practical applications as well.

WRITING TO EXPLORE STYLE **EXERCISE 8**

The previous essays illustrate varied perspectives on the issue of school-to-work initiatives. To practice your ability to maintain a focused thesis and to demonstrate to your audience why that thesis is important, take a position on the following:

- Are current movements toward school-to-work beneficial to the education of the youth of America, or do they detract from the larger goals of education?

Write a brief essay on this topic, drawing on information from the essays above and illustrating to your readers the exigency of the topic for a specific audience: parents, legislators, school boards, or teachers. Use as many of the stylistic skills and techniques discussed in this chapter as you can in support of your thesis.

As a specific type of *progymnasmata,* the exercises you performed in this section gave you practice in basic stylistic patterns. While learning these patterns can help prepare you for the more specific situations you will face in college and on the job, the level of success you achieve in using them still depends on your ability to incorporate them on varied writing occasions. In Parts 2 and 3, you apply those stylistic patterns to various academic and professional situations you may face. In Part 2, you will practice techniques for reading academic and professional discourses actively and thoughtfully. In Part 3, you will practice methods for writing in a wide range of academic and professional communities. Throughout the process, you'll have the opportunity to enrich your reading and writing skills by observing—and practicing—the ways such patterns function in the context of academic and occupational writing.

PART II

Reading and Writing in Academic and Professional Communities

This part of the book is based on a simple premise: Good writers are first (and always) good readers. Of course, defining what it means to be a good reader can be just as difficult as defining what it means to be a good writer. Despite that difficulty, this part of the book suggests that good readers do share specific techniques and characteristics, that you can develop those characteristics through discipline and practice, and that good reading is an essential way to enter the academic and professional communities you will encounter in college.

You will hear again and again in this part of the book about two key characteristics of good reading. First, good readers are active readers—that is, good readers do not treat reading as merely a one-way activity: The writer speaks, I listen. Good readers, conversely, approach the act of reading as a conversation: The writer speaks, I listen and I respond, I ask questions, I expect reasons, I challenge premises, and so on. Good readers are at once open-minded and skeptical, ready to listen and ready to speak (or write).

Of course, knowing how to respond, what questions to ask, and how to bring forth the answers to those questions from a piece of writing requires both effort and technique. In Chapter 5, and the Reading and Writing Applications that follow it, you will learn techniques of active reading that are adapted from the rhetorical tradition. More specifically, you will learn about the "common topics"—a set of questions that can be used to interrogate a wide variety of reading material in ways that involve you in conversations with its writers. Practicing these techniques will make you a more active reader—a reader always ready to respond to that which you read in productive ways.

Second, good readers are critical readers. The word *critical* often has negative connotations, describing one who is always ready to find the bad in whatever he encounters. That's not how I mean it here. When I talk about critical reading or critical thinking, I refer to the original sense of the word, which is derived from the Greek *kritikos*, which means "able to discern." Being a discerning reader means that you are able to judge that which you read by a reasonable set of standards or *criteria* (a word that comes from the same Greek root as *critical*). Of course, the difficulty is that the standards of judgment can vary according to the type of reading we do. This is especially true of academic and professional writing, since each field or discipline has its own standards by which value and credibility are discerned.

For this reason, in Chapter 6 and the Reading and Writing Applications that follow we go on to discuss the "special topics" that various fields and professions use as benchmarks for judging the validity and credibility of any given piece of writing. We discuss the ways in which various academic disciplines and fields prefer to communicate, what they value in terms of proof, and how they vary from one another in their perspectives on the world. Learning about these "discourse communities" (communities that share values and methods of communication) will help you to become more able, active, and critical readers in the various disciplines that you will encounter in college.

This part of the book also prepares you to become a better writer, since reading is treated as a natural prelude to response—and since that response often takes the form of writing. If you read carefully, the responses you make as a writer will be richer, more informed, and better adapted to the writing situations you face in college and beyond.

Reading Actively and Critically

In previous chapters, you sought information about various groups through their public presentation (both in print and on websites) and through interviews with practitioners in those professions. Yet you can tell only so much about a discipline or occupation by examining its public presentation. If you are to truly learn about the topics, you must engage with the ongoing conversations that take place among experts, understand the motives for those conversations, and develop a working knowledge of how a particular academic or occupational field tends to communicate. Becoming a more active and critical reader can help you to accomplish all three of these goals.

Though we learned to read as young children, learning to read documents of increasing specificity and complexity is an ongoing activity. Like writing, reading actively and critically requires a repertoire of skills, skills that prepare you to take as much understanding and learning as possible from each document you read.

Becoming an active reader requires that you not only learn what is being discussed but also that you actively engage with the ideas you find there. This movement from spectator to participant also describes the relationship between your role as a reader and your role as a writer. The more you learn about an issue by careful, active reading, the more ready you are to act on that knowledge— that is, the more ready you are to write.

When you read actively, your goals should be twofold. First, you must do your best to *understand* the information being presented and the conclusions being drawn. At the same time, as an active reader, you must also ask whether the material is reliable: How well does the author substantiate the information or conclusions that she presents? Asking that question is not just about being a suspicious reader (although there is a little of that). It is also about achieving a deeper level of understanding, an understanding not only of the conclusion being drawn but also of the methodologies and assumptions that led to that conclusion. The reading techniques offered in this chapter can help you to uncover those deeper understandings.

TOPIC ANALYSIS AS ACTIVE READING

Ancient rhetoric provides methods of examining an issue that can be useful as you attempt to understand and validate that which you read or hear. These lines of inquiry were classified by ancient rhetoricians like Aristotle into two categories: *common topics* and *special topics. Special topics,* as the name suggests, are both more specialized and more limited; they help you to identify the lines of reasoning that are associated with *particular fields of study* or the analysis of *particular types of problems.* The special topics, which we discuss in the next chapter, can help you to understand the unique modes of thought and writing that are used in specific academic fields or professions. In contrast, the common topics provide useful questions for the investigation of any topic—for reading actively and for generating various possible responses.

The common topics were classified by Aristotle into three general categories, each of which is discussed below:

■ Questions of past, present, or future facts

- Questions of size or value
- Questions of possibility

Questions of past, present, or future facts: This area of investigation focuses on whether some "fact" or state of affairs really exists now, has existed in the past, or is likely to exist in the future. In order to understand the type of inquiry suggested by this common topic, you must first let go of your simplified understanding of "facts" as simply that which is "true." Many concepts that are introduced as facts are really *conjectures*—something *proposed* as true.

The first of the common topics asks us to investigate the "facts" of any case—to interrogate them as a lawyer would. Lawyers do not merely accept what is presented. They question what really happened, what really exists, what existed in the past, and what is most likely to exist in the future. In short, they don't accept the "facts" of a case as givens; they acknowledge that "facts" are really conjectures and so always subject to interpretation. Likewise, when you read actively, you go beyond memorizing facts or concepts that you can then restate; you look more deeply to the underlying reasoning that informs such "facts."

Consider, for example, the following "fact" presented again and again in the media: School violence is increasing. Both explicitly and implicitly, this message is frequently before you. But is it true? Was there less school violence in the past? Is the trend continuing in a way that suggests that the future is even bleaker? And what is meant by "school violence"? What counts as "violence"? Is bullying violence? Is verbal abuse? Are schoolyard fights? All of these questions lead not only to a more inquisitive style of reading but also can breed areas for your investigations as writers. Can you see subjects for further investigation arising in the above questions?

Sounds pretty combative, doesn't it, to always question what you read? But it need not be so. Questions can be asked without implying disbelief. Even if your questions are not adequately answered, that need not invalidate an argument; it might just lead to areas that require further investigation or the next step in the progression of inquiries. The most important aspect of these questions is that they help you to generate ideas—to invent more substantial things to say about the issues you investigate as a reader and as a writer.

Questions of size or value: This common topic asks you to consider not only the "facts" but also the *relative size or value of those facts.* That is, even if you accept that some phenomenon or state of affairs does indeed exist (or existed in the past or is likely to exist in the future), you might then go on to question how important or pressing that "fact" is in relation to the wider situation being examined. For example, even if you accept the statement that school violence has increased, you still might question whether the increase is significant enough to constitute the crisis that media reports seem to suggest it is. The summer of 2001 provided a fine example of how getting the question of size wrong (or exaggerating the size or importance of the "facts") can be dangerous. During that summer, shark attacks were the big news, giving rise to headlines like:

Shark Fright Spurs Warning

Shark Attacks Leave Beaches of Death

Shark Attack Sparks Kill Order

The Sharkman's Summer

Ban on Feeding Sharks Supported

Deaths, Sightings Turn Attention to Sea

These reports also led to actions designed to combat the attack of the "killer" sharks. *New York Newsday* reported that "sharks will be shot on sight if they pose a danger to humans in West Australian waters," while "scientists and conservation groups nationwide [who] have reacted angrily to new laws they say will further threaten the Great White, which is listed as vulnerable on the national threatened species list."

However, by February 2002 the headlines and accompanying facts were quite different. *New York Newsday* now provided the following headline and new set of facts:

Fewer Shark Bites (Really)

Miami—Shark attacks on humans, the subject of sensational summer headlines that made it seem the ocean predators were on a rampage, actually declined slightly last year, Florida researchers said yesterday. Researchers at the University of Florida's International Shark Attack File recorded 76 unprovoked shark attacks worldwide in 2001, down from 85 the previous year. Five attacks were fatal, down from 12 a year earlier, file Director George Burgess said.

So, did sharks attack in the summer of 2001? Certainly. But was it as large an event as many of us raised on the film *Jaws* came to believe? Certainly not. And considering the bans on feeding sharks and shoot-on-sight orders for a threatened species, we must conclude that size matters. (The summer of 2002 had its own exaggerations, this time about the abductions of children, which in fact were decreasing, despite media reports that seemed to indicate a plague of such occurrences.)

Asking questions about relative size and value as you read also teaches you about the values of specific academic and occupational fields. By gauging the relative importance of various topics within given fields, you can begin to formulate a picture of what a community of scholars and workers tends to value most, both in terms of topic and methodology.

Questions of possibility: The third category of common topics investigates the realm of what *is* (and therefore, what *is not*) possible. This area of investigation asks you to consider feasibility: whether a course of action or a future event has a reasonable likelihood of proceeding (and/or of succeeding). It also asks you to consider if an event or course of action is *likely* to take place. Some events or courses of action, after all, might be perfectly feasible—they *could* be carried out. But they still might be *unlikely* to happen.

One sobering example involves recent fears of terrorism. There is little doubt that the spread of chemical or biological weapons is a feasible possibility—it *can* be done, as has been illustrated in the seemingly endless flood of media reports following September 11, 2001. Still, you must investigate how *likely* it is that someone will in fact perform the actions necessary to bring about such an attack, and how likely such an attack is to happen in any given place. In this second question—about likelihood—you can find a good deal of room for questioning and debate, despite the established feasibility of carrying out such attacks. As you ask questions about possibility, you move beyond the theoretical realm and into the practical one. Asking questions like these can help you to read in ways that first raise theoretical issues about the feasibility of a course of action and then to follow that line of reasoning forward into specific and practical issues of implementation.

When you read actively, using the common topics to interrogate the "facts" of a case, you begin the process of moving from reader to writer, since you are always ready to respond to what you read. That willingness to respond, to engage in dialog, is another key feature of active reading, and it often takes the form of annotations in the margins. What follows is an example of how the common topics can be used to investigate an issue within the field of education and how you can make the texts you read more your own by questioning and annotating them.

THE TOPICS APPROACH: AN EXAMPLE

Let's say that you are interested in understanding (and testing the value of) an issue in a field that concerns you but in which you are not yet an expert. The issue here is the use of standardized tests in secondary education. You may be a stakeholder in this issue for many reasons. You may be an education major, giving you a vested interest in the topic as a prospective teacher. But you may have other perspectives from which to consider this an issue of concern: as a taxpaying citizen, a product of the American system of secondary education, a student in a civics course, and/or a parent or prospective parent. In all of these roles, the issue should be important to you.

In your studies, you encounter the following position statement issued by Northwest Regional Educational Laboratory at http://www.nwrel.org/cnorse/booklets/educate/11.html. What can you do with this piece? How are you to understand it, judge its validity, and respond to it? As you read the following essay, note the common topics that are broached here, especially (1) questions of past, present, and future fact; (2) questions of size or value; and (3) questions of possibility. To help you to determine the use of these topics, I've noted examples of each in the margin. But there are many more you could identify, and many other questions that, as an active reader, you might ask. As you read, ask as many good questions as you can, annotating the page with your own notes.

Student Assessment and Testing

Claim of size

In the current debate about nationwide educational restructuring, perhaps no issue is more central to the concerns of equity than that of student assessment. We have a long history of using questionably relevant tests to sort children for differential educational opportunities. Awareness of how standardized testing shapes curriculum and teaching highlights the link between assessment and educational quality. Yet, there is no consensus about how educational reform is to be achieved or what the role of student assessment should be. Politically powerful advocates of "outcome-based" education argue that high standards and a national system of testing will accomplish needed educational improvement.

Claim of future fact

We believe that neither excellence nor equity in education can be achieved as long as student assessment instruments, policies and practices limit opportunities to learn and narrow or dilute curricula and instruction. Both excellence and equity goals can, on the other hand, be served by assessments that help teachers to identify students' strengths as well as their needs and to determine the most appropriate and effective means of helping them to learn and grow.

Claim of possibility

Standardized Testing and At-Risk Students

Standardized tests have a disproportionate impact on students, teachers and curriculum in schools that serve low-income and minority students (Mitchell 1992; Tate 1993). Some widely found effects that are of particular consequence for equity in education are reviewed briefly below.

Testing and Ability Grouping

Both tracking and homogeneous "ability grouping" decisions, especially common in urban schools, are made primarily on the basis of standardized test results. Homogeneous grouping has often resulted in defeating school desegregation efforts by substituting within school segregation of minority groups and is, in addition, itself an unsound pedagogical practice. Even within the same classroom, "high" ability students are taught and expected to learn different content than are "low" ability or "low interest" students (Brown 1993).

Claim of past/present facts

Tracking and ability grouping are widespread and continue in spite of mounting evidence that is exposing "as fraudulent (or, at least, myopic) the claim that tracking is an appropriate response to differences in children's capacities and motivation" (Wheelock 1992).

Claim of past/present facts

Even if standardized, norm-referenced tests measured ability validly for all student groups (a claim that is widely contested), their use in sorting students for different educational opportunities is condemned even by the College Board in unequivocal terms: A substantial share of U.S. schools engage in ability grouping or tracking of students beginning at the elementary and middle grade levels according to presumed ability levels. As a number of studies have shown, tracking almost always means that those pupils who need the most support to raise their performance levels get the least, while those who need it the least have it showered on them. The consequence is a two-tiered system of education characterized by the following conditions: poor and minority students underrepresented in college preparatory classes such as algebra and geometry and overrepresented in dead-end classes such as consumer math and general math; guidance counselors who automatically presume that poor and minority students have neither the capability nor the inclination to attend college, and who therefore fail to provide adequate information to those students about college prerequisites and financial aid options; and teachers who fail to provide the necessary encouragement and enrichment to minority and poor students because their expectations of those students' success are low (Educational Testing Service 1991).

Series of claims of future facts/resultant problems

Testing and Curriculum

The pressure on school administrators, teachers and students to improve average school scores on norm-referenced, short-answer multiple choice tests has created a widespread tendency to ignore higher-order skills (since the tests elicit facts) and to put classroom emphasis on preparing students to take tests, especially at the elementary level—and more especially in low-income schools where drill has always been a more prevalent form of instruction than investigation has been. The

Claim of future fact and/or possibility

pressures of standardized testing on curriculum have decreased instruction in science, writing, problem solving and analytical reasoning; they are felt from kindergarten, where the pressure is to teach quantifiable math and reading skills and to prepare children for an educational career of "bubble test" taking, to high school, where minimum competencies for graduation may also mark the upper limits of instruction.

Claim of present fact

Sixty percent of early childhood educators recently surveyed reported that the pressure of year-end standardized tests caused them to teach in ways that were harmful to their children (Ascher 1990.

Claim of size

Arizona's recent experience in attempting to use testing to reinforce high standards curricula dramatically highlights the inadequacy of test-driven teaching. Arizona's researchers created a matrix and charted the items tested by the Iowa Test of Basic Skills (ITBS) and the frameworks, then charted the curricular framework items covered by the ITBS and TAP tests. While the curricular framework covered 100 percent of the ITBS and TAP items, only 26 to 30 percent of the curricular framework was assessed by the ITBS and the TAP. Using those standardized tests, Arizona could learn nothing about their students' mastery of 70 percent of their required school work (Mitchell 1992).

Claim of size

Testing and College

Claim of size

Standardized tests play an important role in determining whether or not students completing their secondary education will have an opportunity to attend college, what colleges they will attend, and the nature and extent of financial support they will receive (American Association of Collegiate Registrars and Admission Officers 1986). Culture and gender bias in college admissions examinations stack the deck in favor of white middle-class males (Crouse and Trusheim 1988). This continues in spite of the fact that the most widely used college admissions tests are, themselves, poor predictors of students' success in college (Allina 1987; Clark and Grandy 1984). Phyllis Rosser (1992), in collaboration with the National Center for Fair and Open Testing (FairTest), reports on the results of bias in college admissions testing:

Claim of future fact/possibility

> The test publishers claim that their exams predict students' future academic performance. Yet, while females consistently earn higher grades in both high school and college, they receive lower grades on all these exams. Reliance on such biased exams markedly diminishes chances for women to: obtain millions of dollars in college tuition aid awarded by the National Merit Scholarship Corporation, and over 150 private companies, government agencies and foundations; gain admission to over 1,500 colleges and universities; and enter many special education programs reserved for "gifted and talented" high school students.

Claim of future fact/size

All these factors can contribute to a real dollar loss for women in later life as they get less leadership opportunities. Members of minority groups and those from economically disadvantaged backgrounds are further penalized by the gender, race/ethnic and class biases of these exams. Given the obstacles that unfair testing, placement and assessment raise for so many in elementary and secondary schools, it seems particularly unfair that if they overcome the obstacles and graduate from high school they will then face a selection process that denies them equal access to higher education and its lifetime social, cultural, and economic benefits.

Alternatives

New work in cognition makes clear that both teaching and testing could be structured to better prepare students for the complex thinking required by life. Since current political trends make it unlikely that the power of testing will decline in our society, or that testing will cease to drive instruction, it is especially important to reformulate assessments so that they can help alter schooling in ways that will effectively and appropriately educate individual students to meet their personal needs as well as those of society (Ascher 1990).

Claim of possibility

A number of assessment approaches are currently being discussed and implemented as alternatives to the standardized, short-answer multiple-choice tests with which we are all so familiar. Whether referred to as "performance assessment," "situational testing," "authentic assessment," or "assessment in context," they identify a range of strategies that promotes instruction geared to complex thinking and problem solving. They provide both teachers and students with maximum feedback to demonstrate not only what they have learned about, but more importantly, what they have learned to do.

Claim of possibility

The important distinction is between "assessment" and "test." A test is a single-occasion, unidimensional, timed exercise, usually in multiple-choice or short-answer form. Assessment is an activity that can take many forms, can extend over time, and aims to capture the quality of a student's work or of an educational program. . . . [It is] a collection of ways to provide accurate information about what students know and are able to do or about the quality of educational programs. The principal forms of "authentic" or "performance" testing are portfolios, open-ended questions, observations and exhibitions. Portfolios, now used from kindergarten through graduate school, are the best known (Mitchell 1992).

They are collections of work actually done by the student, selected to demonstrate progress toward a stated aim. Their use in English/language arts, creative writing and mathematics programs is widespread, and, in several states, portfolio assessments are being developed in science programs.

Major differences between norm-referenced multiple-choice tests and performance-based assessments involve the extent to which performance-based assessments encourage students to construct their responses rather than select a right answer; solve a problem or work on a task using primary or authentic materials rather than prompts or passages taken out of context or devised specifically for the assessment;

apply basic and more complex skills in unison rather than in isolation; and pursue multiple approaches and solutions to a problem or task (Simmons and Resnick 1993). Problems with these approaches to assessment include difficulty in scoring; both Mitchell (1992) and Ascher (1990) report from research and personal experience the difficulty in developing reliable quantitative measures for writing assignments and the need for training if examiners are to score portfolios with a high degree of agreement. Nevertheless, Mitchell and Ascher find that alternative assessments yield better information about student progress.

Claims/questions of feasibility and possibility

Cost: Ascher (1990) argues that while such assessments are more expensive per pupil, testing need not be done as often as is done currently. Testing for accountability, in fact, can be done by sampling student populations, which would keep mandated testing costs within tolerable bounds. Mitchell (1992) argues that reducing the amount and frequency of testing will free time for instruction, and that properly designed assessments are, themselves, instructional tools—both of which considerations shift part of assessment costs into the "instructional cost" side of the ledger.

Claims of possibility and feasibility

Fairness: The National Coalition of Advocates for Students' concern about the historic use of testing to discriminate against children of the poor and of minorities is reflected in their caution against relying on any test/assessment in the absence of equitable resource and process restructuring:

> Nor are we captivated by claims made for a largely unproven set of "authentic" or "performance based" tests. As the National Council's (The National Council on Education Standards and Testing, chaired by Colorado's governor Roy Romer) own panel concluded, we lack evidence that these experimental tests can be widely deployed at a reasonable cost or that they will be fairer than traditional tests for at-risk students—especially when high stakes are attached to them (NCAS 1993).

Present facts questioned

Criteria for Assessment Recommendations

We recommend that any national, state or local student assessment standard or system meet the following Criteria for Evaluation of Student Assessment Systems, which has been endorsed by more than 100 national civil rights, education and advocacy organizations:

1. Educational standards specifying what students should know and be able to do be clearly defined before assessment procedures and exercises are developed. For assessment information to be valid

and useful, assessment must be based on a consensus definition of what students are expected to learn, and the expected level of performance, at various developmental stages. Such standards, which might also be called intellectual competencies, are not discrete pieces of information or isolated skills, but important abilities, such as the ability to solve various kinds of problems or to apply knowledge appropriately. The standards should be determined through open discussion among subject matter experts, educators, parents, policymakers and others, including those concerned with the relationship between school learning and life outside school. Without a consensus on standards, there is little likelihood of valid assessment.

Claims of possibility and feasibility

2. The primary purpose of the assessment systems should be to assist both educators and policymakers to improve education and advance student learning. Students, educators, parents, policymakers and others have different needs for assessments and different uses for assessment information. For example, teachers, students and their parents want information on individual achievements, while policymakers and the public want information for accountability purposes. In all cases, the system should be designed to provide not just numbers or ratings, but useful information on the particular abilities students have or have not developed.

   All purposes and uses of assessment should be beneficial to students. For example, the results should be used to overcome systemic inequalities. If assessments cannot be shown to be beneficial, they should not be used at all.

Claim of future fact (conjecture)

3. Assessment standards, tasks, procedures and uses should be fair to all students. Because individual assessment results often affect students' present situation and future opportunities, the assessment system, the standards on which it is based, and all its parts must treat students equally. Assessment tasks and procedures must be sensitive to cultural, racial, class and gender differences, and to disabilities, and must be valid for all and not penalize any, groups. To ensure fairness, students should have multiple opportunities to meet standards and should be able to meet them in different ways. No student's fate should depend upon a single test score. Assessment information should also be used fairly. It should be accompanied by information about access to curriculum and about opportunities to meet the standards. Students should not be held responsible for inequities in the system.

Claim of fact (conjecture)

Claim of fact based on commonplace

4. The assessment exercises or tasks should be valid and appropriate representations of the standards students are expected to achieve. A sound assessment system provides information about a full range of knowledge and abilities considered valuable and important for students to learn, and therefore requires a variety of assessment methods. Multiple-choice tests, the type of assessment most commonly used at present, are inadequate to measure many of the most important educational outcomes, and do not allow for diversity in learning styles or cultural differences. More appropriate tools include portfolios, open-ended questions, extended reading and writing experiences which include rough drafts and revisions, individual and group projects and exhibitions.

Claim of future fact and possibility

5. Assessment results should be reported in the context of other relevant information. Information about student performance should be one part of a system of multiple indicators of the quality of education. Multiple indicators permit educators and policy-makers to examine the relationship among context factors (such as type of community, socioeconomic status of students and school climate), resources (such as expenditures per students, plant, staffing and money for materials and equipment), programs and processes (such as curriculum, instructional methods, class size and grouping), and outcomes (such as student performance, dropout rates, employment and further education). Statements about educational quality should not be made without reference to this information.

Claim of possibility and/or future fact

6. Teachers should be involved in designing and using the assessment system. For an assessment system to help improve learning outcomes, teachers must fully understand its purposes and procedures and must be committed to, and use, the standards on which it is based. Therefore teachers should participate in the design, administration, scoring and use of assessment tasks and exercises.

Claim of possibility and/or future fact

Claim of present fact

7. Assessment procedures and results should be understandable. Assessment information should be in a form that is useful to those who need it: students, teachers, parents, legislators, employers, postsecondary institutions and the general public. At present, test results are often reported in technical terms that are confusing and misleading, such as grade-level equivalents, stanines, and percentiles. Instead, they should be reported in terms of educational standards.

8. The assessment system should be subject to continuous review and improvement. Large-scale, complex systems are rarely perfect, and even well-designed systems must be modified to adapt to changing conditions. Plans for the assessment system should provide for a continuing review process in which all concerned participate.

Conclusion

The nation's history of using tests to sort children for differential educational opportunities is a long one. It is time for schools, local education agencies and state and federal governments to ensure that no system of testing or student assessment be used except in the context of educational approaches that are based on standards for equity in educational resources and processes. Biased assessment instruments, policies and practices must not be allowed to limit opportunities to learn and narrow or dilute curricula and instruction. Unless preceded by an equitable restructuring of educational resources and processes, testing to meet National Student Outcomes Standards will leave students vulnerable to the discriminatory educational practices that deny 40 percent of students a meaningful opportunity to learn. More than 100 national civil rights, education and advocacy organizations have endorsed the Criteria for Evaluation of Student Assessment Systems presented above. By adopting these criteria as their basis for student assessment standards, states could ensure that student assessments create tools for—rather than barriers to—educational opportunity for all students.

Margin annotations:
- Claim of past/present fact
- Claim of possibility
- Claim of present fact
- Claims of size
- Claim of possibility

Works Cited

Allina, A. (1993). *Beyond standardized tests: Admissions alternatives that work.* Cambridge, Mass.: FairTest, 1987.

American Association of College Registrars and Admissions Officers, American College Testing Program (ACT), College Board (CEEB), Educational Testing Service (ETS), and the National Association of College Admissions Counselors (NACAC). (1986). *Demographics, standards and equity: Challenges in college admissions.* Iowa City, Iowa: American College Testing Program.

Ascher, C. (1990). *Testing students in urban schools: Current problems and new directions.* ERIC/CUE Urban Diversity Series, No. 100. New York: Clearinghouse on Urban Education, Teachers College, Columbia University.

Brown, R. G. (1993). *Schools of thought on how the politics of literacy shape thinking in the classroom.* San Francisco: Jossey-Bass.

Clark, M., and J. Grandy. (1984). *Sex differences in the academic performance of scholastic aptitude test takers.* College Board Report, No. 848. New York: College Entrance Examination Board.

Crouse, J., and D. Trusheim. (1988). *The case against the SAT*. Chicago: The University of Chicago Press, 1988.

Educational Testing Service. (1991). *The state of inequality: A policy information report*. Princeton, N.J.: Educational Testing Service.

FairTest. *The National Center for Fair and Open Testing*. Retrieved from the World Wide Web. http://www.fairtest.org/.

Mitchell, R. (1992). *Testing for learning: How new approaches to evaluation can improve American schools*. New York: The Free Press.

NCAS: National Coalition of Advocates for Students. (1993). *Cruel hoax*. New York: National Coalition of Advocates for Students.

Rosser, P. (1992). *Student assessment and testing*. Northwest Regional Educational Laboratory. Retrieved from the World Wide Web. http://www.nwrel.org/cnorse/booklets/educat/11.html.

Simmons, W., and D. Resnick. (1993). National standards and assessment: An equity research agenda. Paper presented to the National Symposium on Equity and Educational Testing and Assessment, Washington, D.C.

Tate, W. (1993). Economics, equity and the national mathematics assessment: Are we creating a national tollroad? In *New directions in equity for mathematics education*. Cambridge: Cambridge University Press.

Wheelock, A. (1992). *Crossing the tracks*. New York: The New Press.

Reading such a document is likely to spur some initial reactions. One such reaction might be, "Wow, I didn't know all that about standardized testing!" After all, the essay is rich with "facts" about assessment. Our reactions might also be influenced by our disposition on a topic *before* we read about it. I, for example, have been a teacher for the last twenty years, working both at the high school and college levels. As a result, I (like many other teachers) have a strong dislike for standardized testing because I don't believe such tests really measure the most important aspects of student learning. So, I might be tempted to say, "See, my intuition about the topic was just right!" Other citizens, especially those who feel that teachers aren't doing an adequate job, might react by saying, "Teachers don't like standardized tests because it makes them accountable for their work."

WRITING TO EXPLORE 5.1

What were your initial reactions to this piece as a whole? Without looking back at the piece or your annotations, freewrite in your writer's notebook on the points raised in this essay that you found to be most compelling and memorable, and the places where you tended to strongly agree or disagree (on a gut level).

All our reactions—yours, mine, and those who feel teachers have been acting irresponsibly—are very real, and so deserve your attention. However, none of these reactions are likely to get you very far toward developing your ideas. They are simply visceral or "gut" reactions, not in-depth examinations of a topic. In order to assess the validity of someone else's argument—to really try to understand what is at issue—you need a more carefully reasoned approach to critical reading.

As I noted in my annotations, the essay above expresses a number of ideas that are presented as *facts* and that support its eventual conclusions. Among those "facts" are claims that the present use of standardized tests is counterproductive to the goals of education and that it is discriminatory toward many groups (including minorities, lower-income people, and women). In the process, the essay also raises many questions of *size or value,* arguing that this is a large and important problem for the field of education and for the public more generally. The essay goes on to offer better systems of assessment, presenting us with questions of *what is, and is not, possible* for the future. Consider, for example, one conjecture presented:

> Standardized tests have a disproportionate impact on students, teachers and curriculum in schools that serve low-income and minority students.

This statement is proposed as a present fact—the fact that standardized tests harm low-income and minority students. Your judgment about its validity, of course, will come from a combination of careful scrutiny of the proofs presented in the essay itself and from further reading on the topic. But before beginning your research, you, as an active reader and effective writer, must first determine what the questions of fact really are.

Looked at from this perspective, the question does not remain as simple as "Do standardized tests discriminate?" That type of binary question doesn't really help you to develop your ideas, since binary questions have only two possible answers: true/false, yes/no, it does/it doesn't, good/bad. To read more critically, you might think about the issue in more complex ways, asking questions such as:

- What evidence exists in this field that standardized tests discriminate?

- Against whom do they discriminate?

- What is meant by "low income"? What income might be considered low?

Questions like these are not easily answered, but they provide a wealth of possibilities for your research and writing. Think of all the ways that such lines of inquiry could help you to respond to that single statement!

The statement also raises questions of *size or value* (Is this a large problem or an isolated one? What makes it "disproportionate"?). By noting key values that the piece raises (the tests discriminate, and discrimination is wrong), you can enter another area of possible investigation—and another way to formulate possible responses. Is this discrimination as widespread as is suggested (remember the shark example)? Do the problems with assessment standards represent a basic, systemic flaw, or are the problems just a minor glitch in an otherwise effective process? To investigate this topic, you might search the essay for evidence that addresses that question, and if you pursue the issue as a research topic, you might look to other sources as well to see if the impact is disproportionate based on income or minority status.

Asking questions about what is and what is not possible can yield further inquiries into the topic ("Is there a more proportionate way to assess students?" "Do students need to be assessed?"). If you accept the present fact (that the tests discriminate) and the values (that the problem is large and important), then you might go on to ask if anything can be done about it. Is there a better way that is feasible and possible? If so, why has the education system relied on standardized tests, as the essay tells us, for such a long time?

By generating good questions about this essay, you are reading in an active way that is likely to lead to further thinking, perhaps further research, and certainly richer writing. Remember that this type of critical questioning is not meant to be antagonistic or negative. Actually, active reading allows you to treat the writer's ideas more seriously, to come to terms with his thesis, his major line of argument, and his methods of investigation and proof. In short, inquisitive reading helps you to more fully *understand* the information being presented within a richer, more mature context. If you were to summarize this article now, after such active reading, you would have a much wider array of issues to discuss than you had when you simply assessed, as in the exercise above, your gut reaction to the essay.

WRITING TO EXPLORE 5.2

Above, I raised many questions that one might ask, based on the common topics. These topics generate questions about

- past, present, and future fact (What are the "facts" of the case, and are they accurate and complete, or must other things be considered?)
- size or value (Do the facts of the case really suggest a problem large enough to be worth our attention?)
- possibility (Are there alternative actions that can solve or ameliorate the problem or create a better situation?)

Following are several quotations from the article. In your writer's notebook, rewrite one of the quotations, or another that you select yourself. Then, drawing on the common topics, generate as many questions or approaches to the "facts" presented in the quotation as you can. Remember: The common topics are meant to help you to generate ideas and approaches to an issue—to invent. So don't feel that you need to answer each topic as if it were a question on a test. Instead, use it as a jumping-off point from which you can develop ways to approach the issue: See where the topics lead you, using the critical reasoning skills introduced above. Here are quotations for you to consider:

- Members of minority groups and those from economically disadvantaged backgrounds are further penalized by the gender, race/ethnic and class biases of these exams. (page 194)

- Standardized tests play an important role in determining whether or not students completing their secondary education will have an opportunity to attend college, what colleges they will attend, and the nature and extent of financial support they will receive (American Association of Collegiate Registrars and Admission Officers 1986). (page 194)

- We believe that neither excellence nor equity in education can be achieved as long as student assessment instruments, policies and practices limit opportunities to learn and narrow or dilute curricula and instruction. (page 192)

- Homogeneous grouping has often resulted in defeating school desegregation efforts by substituting within school segregation of minority groups and is, in addition, itself an unsound pedagogical practice. Even within the same classroom, "high" ability students are taught and expected to learn different content than are "low" ability or "low interest" students (Brown 1993). (page 192)

MORE APPROACHES TO ACTIVE READING

The types of critical reading that are suggested above have another important benefit: They keep you from quietly accepting all that the "experts" present us and saying simply, "Who am I to argue? They know more than I do." Instead, critical reading helps you to consider other possibilities—and to do so outside the box. This process of imagining other possibilities can result in a richer understanding of the issue, the quality of the writer's "facts," and possible areas for further research. As such, critical reading methods make you a more thoughtful writer, worker, and citizen because they help you to respond to material rather than just accept it.

Reading actively means, among other things, exploring alternatives. For example, this study suggests that "current political trends make it unlikely that the power of testing will decline in our society, or that testing will cease to drive instruction." You might, for the sake of generating ideas, refuse to accept that as a fact. You might instead attempt to imagine an educational system that isn't driven by grades or assessments. That would also raise all sorts of inventive questions: Are there alternatives to grading? Is it possible to motivate students without grades? Are students raised on tests able to accept the changes and still learn? What new pressures would that put on the formation of curricula? Would those pressures be positive?

WRITING TO EXPLORE 5.3

Drawing on the questions above, brainstorm or freewrite in your writer's notebook on the ways that an educational system without grades might function and how it has potential to overcome (or exacerbate) the problems raised in this article. Imagine as many possibilities for such a system as you can, and then develop in greater detail the one that you think has the most potential.

Another related way to read effectively is to consider the opposite of what is being proposed—using a technique that ancient rhetoricians called *dissoi logoi*, or "imagining the counterargument." For example, this essay argues that "biased assessment instruments, policies and practices must not be allowed to limit opportunities to learn and narrow or dilute curricula and instruction." In response, you might not only look at the potential for better methods but also at the available arguments *against* such a course of action. You might ask if in the process of attempting to create "unbiased" assessment structures, curricula and instruction might actually become "diluted." Could attempts to be inclusive also dumb down a curriculum (as some have argued)? And if assessment is not "standardized," might that invite even more bias? Even if you tend to agree with the original argument, imagining the counterargument will help you toward a richer understanding of the issue.

WRITING TO EXPLORE 5.4

In your writer's notebook, choose one conjecture or claim from the article above and do your best to construct reasonable counterarguments. Remember that your goal is to test a claim's validity by seeing how it bears up under critical pressure.

THE READING-WRITING CONNECTION

Identifying a set of questions—the points that need further examination—is only part of active reading. In fact, the initial product of the inventive and critical reading suggested above might be a bit chaotic and so lack real resolution. How does one take the next step?

Finding a reasonable way to respond to what you read requires finding common ground for discussion. One way to do so is to find points of **stasis**. Literally, the word *stasis* describes a condition of motionlessness where forces meet and so create a standstill. Similarly, in rhetorical terms, stasis describes a condition of disagreement on a specific issue—where two or more parties have not yet agreed on a particular "fact" of the case (recall our discussion of facts and conjectures above).

Though stasis arises from conflict—from at least two parties standing firm on a particular issue or set of issues—the result is more positive than it sounds. In order to understand why stasis is so important, you might consider its alternative. If a stasis point is not discovered, then you have gridlock; no conversation can ensue when the parties involved cannot even agree on the specific point of disagreement. In those cases, people present monologues on their beliefs but do not ever listen to, or engage with, the ideas presented by others.

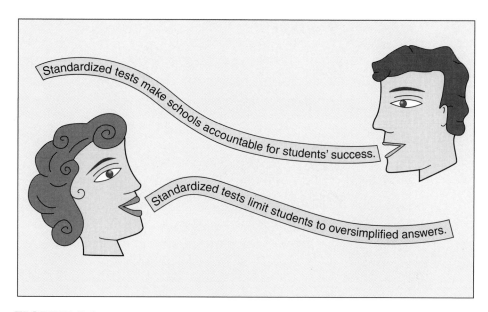

FIGURE 5.1 When people do not find stasis points—specific points of contact, and often disagreement—between their ideas, they are unable to have a true dialog. They talk past one another rather than to one another. Nothing develops.

On the other hand, stasis points are places where the real point of disagreement has been identified; as a result, stasis points not only identify previous points of contention, they also provide you, as an active reader, with an entry point into the conversation.

For example, if one writer argues that standardized multiple-choice testing is counterproductive because it teaches students to think in binary ways (right/wrong, true/false, yes/no), she has stated not only a general position on the topic (she's against it) but also has started to formulate specific reasoning on that topic (she's against it because it encourages binary thinking). Now imagine a position held by people in favor of standardized multiple-choice testing: It makes schools accountable for the learning achieved by their students, and does so through a measurable standard that can be compared across schools locally and nationally. Though there are two positions here, I don't see a stasis point yet. Why?

No stasis exists here (yet) because the arguments are, in effect, on two planes that don't intersect. That is, *it is possible for both of these statements to be true at the same time*. It is possible that standardized tests can *both* encourage binary thinking *and* provide easily measurable standards for judging a school's success. If a real discussion is to take place about the value of standardized tests, you need more suitable points of dialog, points that represent two identifiable positions on the same plane. In this case, you can discuss *either* the value of the tests as

FIGURE 5.2 When people do find stasis points—specific points of contact, and often disagreement—between their ideas, they are then able to begin a productive dialog. Beginning from the specific contact points, they can reason together to develop new, useful ideas, even if they continue to disagree.

standardized measures *or* the value of the tests as teaching tools. Until you decide which topic is really at issue, you can go no further.

Finding a point of stasis is crucial for your transition from active reading to responding with your own writing. In Chapter 4, we briefly discussed the process of formulating a thesis—the central point that you are trying to communicate when you write. That thesis is a place where you stand on an issue (e.g., standardized testing is discriminatory). However, as an active reader, you cannot formulate a thesis in a vacuum. When you read what others have written on a topic, you must not only consider where *you* "stand" but also where *people with other viewpoints* stand or are likely to stand on that topic (as we imagined in the *dissoi logoi* exercise). And when you imagine both your own "stand" (the English translation of the word *stasis*) and that of contesting parties—well, then you've entered a conversation as an active participant.

You might notice that achieving stasis comes (at least partially) from *limiting a topic* to a specific area of shared concern. That's because, as you discovered when you used the common topics, an almost infinite variety of approaches may be taken to an issue. But to move from the position of reader to that of writer, you must look for a specific place to respond. That's one of the reasons why finding a stasis point is so useful; it allows you to limit your topic to a specific area of concern. For example, the thesis that standardized testing is not useful "because it teaches students to think in binary ways" might be countered by this statement: "The thinking that a student does in order to choose a multiple-choice answer is not binary but rather complex; if a correct answer is reached, it evidences the fact that complex thought has been used to reach that answer. Thus, well-developed standardized tests can measure the products of complex thinking." Now, since both positions are limited to the issue of binary thinking, you have something to talk about and matters to study further: What kinds of thinking do students do while taking standardized tests? What are the goals of education? What are the best ways to test for their achievement? Can multiple-choice, easily measurable questions that breed complex types of thought be written? Such questions allow you to reason together with other writers, and with your audience, on a limited topic. If your writing tends to drift from one topic to another, identifying the stasis point—the crux of the matter— can help you to create more coherent and cohesive writing in response to that which you read.

WRITING TO EXPLORE 5.5

In order to practice finding stasis points, try the following:

1. Identify three claims or conjectures made by the authors of the article on standardized testing (or from another essay that you are reading).

2. Write at least one response to each of those claims that have been, or might be, made by others. (In many cases, the article itself discusses the points of contention with advocates of standardized tests; those are good places to look for stasis points.) Be sure that your responses are phrased in a way that engages directly with the claims that you have identified (as in the example I provided above) rather than introducing another area of concern.

3. Freewrite on specific points of disagreement that exist between the perspectives, and try to invent ways that you might investigate the relative value of both the original claim and the counterclaim.

Though finding stasis does not mean that you will be able to *resolve* areas of disagreement, it does provide you with ways to find a productive line of discussion about some limited issue, as your exploratory writing suggests (especially in Part 3). Just think about all the parties to the conversation in the article: teachers, administrators, parents, school boards, legislators, companies that produce standardized tests, and so on. If someone writes an article against the use of standardized testing, you can be pretty sure that others are talking about its advantages. But it is difficult to bring those positions together without identifying points of conflict. Rather than merely noting that one party accepts the value of standardized testing and another does not, an active reader looks for comparable points of discussion: One writer might argue that standardized testing is discriminatory, while another suggests that standardized tests are useful because they provide an equal measure of the skill sets of students nationally—and so avoids discrimination. Can you hear the professional conversations now?

This discussion of stasis suggests that critical reading involves a search for disagreement or argument. And though that is not always the case (at least not in obvious or simplistic ways), most forms of writing that you encounter in your academic and occupational lives do in fact discuss some disputed area. That is not to say that all such disputes are antagonistic; in fact, in most cases, rhetorical arguments arise because people have similar areas of concern. Two or more parties who share a great deal and who often have a common purpose simply disagree about the facts of a case, the ideas that surround a case, the importance of that case, or the best way to respond to it. In our example, people who favor standardized testing hold similar motives as those who wrote this article: improving the educational system. They disagree only about how that might be best accomplished.

In this chapter, you saw the ways that active reading and rich and informed writing share a great deal. By using the common topics and other techniques of critical reading, you practiced ways to engage with, rather than simply accept, the conjectures and claims made by other authors. This is a crucial step in your progress as a writer and, more generally, as a lifelong learner. By equipping you with techniques for inquiring deeply into that which you read, rhetorical reading can help you to identify and evaluate specific claims. It can help you to break down and analyze the quality of arguments in a systemic and coherent way rather than merely relying on your gut instincts and that which you've always believed. It is difficult to overestimate how important this skill can be to you as a student, as a professional, and as a citizen, since it gives you access to the deeper levels of thought that underlie arguments. Without this skill, your responses will remain superficial, and you will remain a mere consumer of other people's words; with it, you can enter the conversation as an active participant.

Likewise, seeking the stasis points that underlie positions can give you access to the most important issues being discussed in professional fields. Those stasis points proceed as much from commonality (shared motives and interests) as from disagreement. This commonality is one way to explain why people tend to group themselves into academic fields, occupational areas, or civic groups: They share things that they believe are worth talking about as well as basic rules for discussion. Thus, by reading actively, you can find an entry point into professional conversations by identifying what is at issue within professional communities and in the writing that helps to define those communities. In the next chapter, we investigate the ways in which these groups (what we call *discourse communities*) also share understandings of how communication among them can be best accomplished.

Before we move on to an investigation of how arguments are structured within specific fields, however, the Reading and Writing Applications section that follows encourages you to try out the active reading skills introduced in this chapter. They contain readings from various academic and professional fields, and you are asked to use techniques of critical reading to identify key areas of inquiry. As an active reader, you'll begin to hear the academic and occupational conversations and so find what people in those fields are currently talking about.

Reading Actively

As we discussed in the previous chapter, reading actively means being both inquisitive (asking questions) and disciplined (asking *useful* questions). The questions generated by the common topics and a search for stasis points can help you to develop active reading techniques that will help you to get the most out of your reading. The cases provided below give you the opportunity to further develop active reading skills that will serve you well as you enter any discipline or profession.

Case 1 IDENTIFYING POINTS OF DISAGREEMENT

Writing to Respond

Reading actively requires you to interrogate opinions surrounding current issues and to explore how those opinions come together at points of productive disagreement. Consider the following question:

> Should the National Endowment for the Arts deny funding for artworks that a large number of people might find offensive or obscene?

Your answer to this question can be based on your beliefs, morals, religious background, and personal experience. All of these are valid bases for response, but they are also largely private and visceral. To enter into public dialog, you also must consider the array of arguments that others might make—people who have professional as well as private interests in this question. Here are activities that you might use to force stasis—to make the key points of disagreement more visible:

1. State a working thesis that articulates what you believe about the issue. For example, "Funding art that many find obscene can harm our ability to raise morally sound children."

2. Identify the stakeholders in this conversation. What groups of people in what academic fields, occupations, or professional organizations are likely to have some stake in this issue? Here, of course, there are many: artists, museum and gallery owners, religious groups, teachers, government officials, and so on.

3. Drawing on the common topics, invent likely questions or areas of concern that surround that topic.

   - Questions of **fact:** What really are the circumstances surrounding this issue? With the arts funding question, for example, you might ask whether the National Endowment really is funding "obscene" art. You might ask whether the funding is encouraging the creation of offensive work. Or you might ask whether this funding is necessary for the art to be created.
   - Questions of **definition:** What category or area of concern does this issue fall into? So, continuing our example, you might ask what constitutes an artistic work. You might ask whether art is a public issue (here, asking how public issues are defined). You might ask how one is to define *obscenity* (that's a really tough one).
   - Questions of **value:** How serious is the issue? Would the funding of art that some consider obscene really hurt our society? Is artistic expression capable of undermining our public values? How much of our national budget really goes to funding the arts, and are there better ways to spend that money?
   - Questions of **procedure:** In this case, you might measure the possible responses to the question and begin the process of considering the effects of those potential actions. You might consider the constitutional and legal issues involved with free speech, public funding, censorship, and so forth.

   Each of these questions asks us to consider what specific areas of disagreement exist regarding a given issue.

4. Imagine possible stasis points among the stakeholders by limiting the issue to some specific facet of the wider discussion. For example: "Though artists have come to depend on public funding for their art, government officials have a wider constituency to consider in the spending of public funds." Such a statement identifies the way in which two groups might approach this question differently. There are, of course, many other stakeholders as well,

each with their own perspective on the issue: teachers, parents, ministers. What points of stasis might exist among them?

As you attempt to find stasis points, you will likely be forced to put aside some of the issues surrounding a topic in order to *focus on a single point of disagreement*. For example, the question about funding for the National Endowment for the Arts might be taken in a number of directions: What constitutes art? What is the purpose of public funding? Does a culture have a responsibility to support the work of its artists? Are public and religious morals at issue in artistic creation? Any of those questions might help to force a type of crisis or stasis point. The goal is to hem in a topic enough that you can create a focused and specific piece of writing.

Using the activities listed above, consider one of the following topics, or choose one of your own. Be sure to consider the key stakeholders in each issue:

- Should human cloning be permitted? What scientific arguments for or against it exist? philosophical arguments?

- Should we temporarily ease restrictions on law enforcement officials in times of crisis like that precipitated by the 9/11 attacks? How would law enforcement officials attempt to reach conclusions on this issue? political scientists? ethicists? What other groups are stakeholders in this matter?

- Should pharmaceutical companies be allowed to advertise prescription medicines on television? Who are the stakeholders here? What areas of concern can be raised by the common topics?

- Should special needs students be mainstreamed—placed in regular classrooms—or provided with special education classes separate from other students?

- Should the National Endowment for the Arts deny funding for artworks that some people might find offensive or obscene?

- Should government funds be available to charitable organizations that have a religious affiliation?

After you have identified the stakeholders in one of these areas of debate, and the likely stasis points about which those stakeholders will disagree, you might share your findings with other members of the class in person, or via a class listserv or e-mail exchange.

Writing Application

If you want to extend any of the above issues into an essay, you can use these inventional techniques and points of stasis as a starting point for an informational essay that helps readers to understand the complexity of the issue. To do so, detail the arguments that could be or have been made in relation to this issue. You might include information on the issue from other sources, or you might simply generate a variety of potentially important perspectives on the issue by using the common topics discussed in the previous chapter.

Case 2 WRITING SUMMARIES

Following are two articles that address questions of work, family, and community. Read both carefully and actively, using the common topics and other techniques discussed in the previous chapter as guides. Make careful notes in the margins and in your writer's notebook that detail the key issues that each article raises, and then use the prompts that follow to write accurate and mature summaries of each piece.

Writing to Respond

Sarah Ryan's essay, "Management by Stress," examines the ways in which changes in the work world have affected the private, family, and community lives of citizens. Since this author has served as vice president of the Greater Seattle Area Local of the American Postal Workers Union, she brings to this piece a hands-on knowledge of labor issues. Read Ryan's article carefully and, using the common topics, identify her main arguments. Annotate the article and take notes in your writer's notebook. You might also construct a list of questions to help you to further investigate this topic, should you choose to continue your study of it.

Management by Stress: The Reorganization of Work Hits Home in the 1990s

Sarah Ryan

When 185,000 United Parcel Service workers went on strike in August 1997 they may have been prepared to win their wage and pension demands. What they were not prepared for was the outpouring of public support that greeted them. While hundreds of union members and community supporters joined picket lines and rallies, they had also joined rallies for many losing strikes in the 1980s and 1990s, when the public consensus seemed to be against organized labor. This time, a Cable News Network poll showed solid support for the striking UPS workers—55 percent of those surveyed supported the union, while 27 percent supported the company position. Other polls showed similar results. For the first time in over two decades, a major strike succeeded in winning wage gains and job security and captured the public's imagination as well.

The problems of UPS workers sounded all too familiar to millions of American families, and they identified with the goals of the strike. The Teamsters Union members at UPS wanted to create 10,000 new full-time jobs from the tens of thousands of low-wage part-time jobs at the company that controlled 80 percent of the nation's package deliveries. About 57 percent of UPS's 185,000

Teamster workers labored part time—in many terminals two-thirds or even three-quarters of the employees. They made up 80 percent of new hires since 1993. The part-time workers' problems mirrored those of many Americans: They earned as little as $8 per hour as opposed to about $20 for full-timers; they often worked almost full time at their part-time wage; many needed a second job to get by; and few had any prospects for stable employment.[1] As more and more families have found themselves insecure about jobs and benefits, the dilemmas faced by part-time workers have grown.

In large part because of visible public support, the strikers won wage increases for part-timers totaling $4.10 per hour over the contract's term, raised the full-time wage by about 3 percent, and preserved the quality of their pension and medical plans. For the first time in many years, the public caught a glimpse of an alternative to the lean-and-mean workplace faced by so many. It was a glimmer of hope that was sorely needed.

An almost constant sense of insecurity haunts American families in the 1990s. Nearly half the population worries that someone in their household will be out of work in the next year. Parents no longer expect their children to have a higher standard of living than themselves. Most expect large-scale layoffs to be a permanent feature of the modern economy; meanwhile, they experience more stress while at work and are contributing more and more hours to the job.[2] No wonder nostalgia for more prosperous and predictable times is a recurring theme in politics and the arts, even among young people who have embraced the technology and values of the 1990s.

"Exiles in the promised land," Elizabeth Gilbert called them in 1996. A young reporter for a rock-music magazine, she described a sense of betrayal felt by many of her peers. There was supposed to be a reward for hard work in America—a rising standard of living based on growing productivity. Home ownership. The assurance that your children would have a better life than you had. "When my parents were young, America was unchallenged, cars looked great, a wife could raise her children safely, a husband could buy a home on a laborer's wage," Gilbert wrote, describing what many considered America's post–World War II social contract. While millions of African Americans and other United States minority populations were, for the most part, not included in the bargain, the contract has now been broken even for white families. A generation of workers is learning the hard lesson of the 1990s: Technology and the reengineering of work have changed almost every aspect of jobs, lowering compensation and expectations, increasing work hours, and deeply impacting family life.[3]

A fundamental reorganization of work has taken place in the last two decades. What the *Wall Street Journal* has labeled "the reengineering movement"[4] is not an accidental byproduct of technology or global competition. It is the result of a corporate political and economic strategy to abandon the old tactic of ensuring social peace by guaranteeing special privileges and security to some groups of workers. This has paid off on the stock market, as stock indexes hit record highs in 1996 and wealth distribution was dramatically altered.[5] Individual strategies for "coping with stress" have emerged, but social policy has not seriously addressed the nature of work reengineering or attempted to ameliorate its effects.

Consultants and psychologists retained by employers to help people cope with job and family stress usually deny the extent to which fear of job loss or overwork is engineered into workers' lives by real changes in the structure of the economy. They tell people that if they can change their attitudes, they can solve their problems. "People think of stress as something external," said Joel Haber, a White Plains, N.Y., clinical psychologist. "It's really our reaction to the events, rather than the events themselves, that causes stress." The president of the American Institute of Stress, a nonprofit research group, is quoted as advising: "The feeling of being out of control is always stressful, but very often that's a matter of perception. If you can't fight and you can't flee, you have to learn how to flow."[6]

The truth, however, is that very few workers have the resources or maneuvering room to either flee or flow. Corporate CEOs and highly paid professionals have the option of "downshifting"—cashing in their stock options or investments and seeking a simpler life. Underpaid and overworked production and service workers, male or female, cannot find relief in similar individual coping strategies.

The Families and Work Institute conducted a survey of 3,000 wage and salary workers in 1993 and found that 75 percent felt used up at the end of the workday, while 70 percent were still tired when they awoke to face another day on the job. Researcher Deborah Holmes explained: "One of the results of downsizing is that people are having heavier workloads. Not surprisingly, workers with heavier workloads report more job burnout."

What are the major aspects of work reengineering today?

1. *Lowering of worker compensation.* Real (adjusted for inflation) weekly earnings for nonsupervisory workers declined by 19 percent from 1972 to 1995.[7] When discussed as a "fall" or "decline" in wages, the use of the passive voice obscures the active attack on workers' living standards that has been underway for almost three decades. The grinding down of compensation levels represents a successful campaign by major businesses to avoid wage increases, hire new workers at lower levels, roll back previous gains, and defeat or restrain labor unions. Even over the past two years of rapid economic recovery and job growth, incomes continued to fall for the bottom 60 percent of households, while the gap between rich and poor did not narrow.[8]

Lower wages are not due to lack of worker productivity. Real Gross Domestic Product (a measure of how much each worker produces and a reliable index of the productivity of the average worker) *rose* by 19 percent per capita from 1970 through 1994.[9] In an unusually frank discussion of macroeconomic trends published in a February 1996 issue of the *New York Times*, Stephen Roach of Morgan Stanley, a Wall Street brokerage firm, acknowledged that corporations "have gone too far in squeezing the worker to boost corporate profitability and competitiveness. . . . Pay rates have now been squeezed so that they are running below the productivity curve and economic theory suggests that workers should be paid their marginal productivity contribution."[10]

Falling wages necessitate that families send more of their members into the workforce, spend more hours working, or get second or third jobs just to barely maintain their previous living standards. Or, of course, they must cope with economic hardship.

2. *Automation of production, information, and service work.* Technologies of the "information age" and automation of production have eliminated millions of jobs, and technology-based layoffs are feared by telephone workers and machinists alike. The steel industry is a prime example of the dramatic effect of technology on production and employment. U.S. Steel (now USX), the nation's largest steel company, employed 120,000 in 1980. By 1990, it produced roughly the same output with 20,000 workers.[11] Employment in the telephone industry, the economy's automation pacesetter, declined by 179,800 from 1981 to 1988.[12] AT&T alone announced 40,000 layoffs in early 1996.[13] While laid-off employees generally found other jobs, they most often received lower pay, and the insecurity generated by such experience clouds the lives of remaining workers.

3. *Internationalization of production, with manufacturing exported to low-wage areas.* Trade agreements like the North American Free Trade Agreement (NAFTA) and the Global Agreement on Tariffs and Trade (GATT) have loosened government restrictions and sped up the rate at which industries are moving production to countries like Mexico, where wages are about one-tenth of U.S. averages. The "maquiladora" program—the establishment of production factories along the U.S.-Mexican border—began in 1965. By 1992, half a million workers were employed on the Mexican side of the border in over 2,000 low-wage plants. Labor economist Harley Shaiken estimates that U.S. auto manufacturers could save $100 million annually in wages per plant, as Mexican automobile workers' total compensation averages $2 per hour as compared with U.S. auto workers' $30.[14] Thousands of Americans have watched their jobs head across the Mexican border in recent years.

4. *Corporate mergers and reorganization, with workforce "downsizing."* It became common for corporate CEOs in the 1990s to find their bonuses and stock prices increasing after the announcement of mass layoffs. Nearly three-quarters of all households have had a close encounter with layoffs since 1980.

The *New York Times'* 1996 feature series (and, later, book) "The Downsizing of America" examined the chaos, insecurity, and destruction in peoples' lives resulting from corporate downsizing. Workers who had staked their futures on the idea that their loyalty to the company would be returned told of their sense of loss and betrayal. One in ten adults said a lost job had precipitated a major crisis in their lives.[15]

Since 1979, 43 million jobs have been "extinguished." While manufacturing jobs have typically been thought of as those most vulnerable to layoffs, the *Times* researchers found that white-collar work was just as insecure in the 1990s. Workers typically find it difficult or impossible to replace their lost jobs with anything that would pay similar wages. The median pay drop in 1994 was $85 per week when new jobs were found.

5. *Newly created jobs are part-time and temporary as companies shift to "no-commitment" hiring.* "It's really a revolution" was how Gary Burtless, a labor economist with the Brookings Institution, described things in 1995. Temporary employment had tripled in only one decade, rising to include 2.1 million workers by May 1995.[16] Perhaps no statistic speaks as dramatically as this: Manpower Temporary Services, with 767,000 "employees," is now the nation's largest civilian employer, displacing the rapidly downsizing General Motors from the top spot.[17] Even government agencies have increased temporary employment. The U.S. Postal Service alone has over 70,000 contingent workers who have no job security, lower wages, and no health-care insurance.

Corporations face no additional cost or penalty for downsizing their permanent workforce and replacing long-term employees with temporaries, and they can hire and fire rapidly when business demands change. Temporary workers earn lower wages, usually have no benefits, and never know from one day to the next if they will be working. A Bureau of Labor Statistics (BLS) survey found that "most firms reported that less than ten percent of their temporary workers participated in a company-sponsored health-insurance program." Additionally, BLS found that temporary workers' real wages are declining. Between 1989 and 1994, wages for the employees of temporary agencies that employ twenty or more workers rose only 2 percent—before inflation.[18]

6. *Increased use of overtime and rotating shifts, particularly in manufacturing.* If you work for a major industrial employer, it's hard to "flee or flow" from management demands. While economic pressures sometimes compel workers to seek overtime, often there is nothing voluntary about longer work weeks. Workers may face firings or other disciplinary actions for refusing overtime to take care of their children. Bell Atlantic telephone, for example, after cutting 4,000 jobs in recent years, has been suspending workers who refuse overtime. Joe Bryant, a single father of two children, had worked overtime on weekends

but was unable to put in extra hours during the week due to child-care problems. He was given a suspension for refusing weekday overtime so that he could pick up his children at school. Another Bell Atlantic technician had worked sixty-nine of the previous seventy-three days and was suspended for three days for refusing additional overtime.[19]

In Decatur, Illinois, a corn-products plant, a tire factory, and a tractor manufacturer all demanded twelve-hour rotating schedules from their workers. In manufacturing operations like the A.E. Staley plant, twelve-hour days, with three days on and three days off, were imposed, and workers were switched from days to nights every thirty days. Staley workers Dick and Sandy Schable explained how their family life was severely disrupted by these schedules: "After the first day on twelve hours you were pretty much shot. The other problem was each week you'd have a different day off. And you could be called in during your time off at any shift at any time they deemed it necessary."

Some workers, unable to flee or flow, have been able to fight. In March 1996, twenty-six of General Motors Corporation's twenty-nine North American automobile manufacturing plants were idled as a result of a 3,000-person strike. The workers at a brake plant in Dayton, Ohio, had been required to work fifty-six-hour weeks. GM was demanding additional overtime, or it would contract the parts to low-wage shops. The strike, lasting seventeen days, won the hiring of 417 new workers.[20] GM had been a pioneer in "alternative work schedules," and excessive overtime has caused other recent strikes in GM plants.

7. *Team-concept and "total quality" management systems.* Worker/management cooperation plans swept the corporate world in the 1980s and 1990s. A 1992 survey of Fortune 1000 corporations found that 80 percent used management techniques such as Quality of Work Life, Quality Circles, or Employee Involvement.[21] While these techniques were initially presented as signs of a "new respect for the worker," they were accompanied by wage cutting, downsizing, and a new, intense pressure for more production, often applied by a worker's peers in addition to management. The Nissan Corporation was an early team concept, "lean production" leader. While company literature claimed the system was built on teamwork, cooperation and trust, declaring that "people are our most valued resource," workers described the job as "eight-hour aerobics. You feel like you've done three days' work at the end of the shift."

A former Nissan manager has described the long range results of such aerobics: "We hired exceptionally good people, people we thought we could keep for the rest of their working lives. I ran into one of them at the pharmacy the other day. He looked like he was dead. . . . He said to me, 'I think they've got us on a four- or five-year cycle. They'll wear us out and then hire new blood.' I think he may be right."[22]

While seemingly contradictory, team concept and high-pressure cost-cutting strategies are two sides of the same coin, according to labor journalists Jane Slaughter and Mike Parker, who say that the function of participation programs is to introduce management by stress.[23]

United Parcel Service, the target of the fifteen-day strike in 1997, calls itself "the tightest ship in the shipping business" and is well-known for a demanding and injurious work atmosphere. The rate of lost-time injuries in 1994 was 15 per 100 workers, compared to a shipping-industry average of eight or nine.[24] At the parcel sorting hubs, the system is designed to push the individual workers beyond normal capacity, as mechanized belt and box lines are operated at speeds with which virtually no worker can keep pace. When workers loading trucks inevitably fall behind, packages pile up, and extra "floaters" make rounds helping them catch up.[25] Work hours are often long for drivers. When a 1995 *Wall Street Journal* piece referred to UPS drivers as America's new sex symbol, the wife of a UPS driver wrote to the *Detroit Free Press*, "We are glad that someone has reminded us of what our husbands look like because, with the hours they work, you don't see a whole lot of them. That would also explain why they're being called 'Fantasy Men.' . . . No UPS wife has ever had an ache or tiredness that couldn't be topped by her husband."[26]

Consequences for Family Life

The reengineering of work occurs at the same time that family work patterns and gender roles are changing. Such work changes both accelerate these family changes and often deform their previously liberating possibilities for men and women. Few families fit the single-earner "Ozzie and Harriet" stereotype today, as more and more are supported by dual earner couples. In 1950, only 33.9 percent of working-age females were in the labor force; by 1993, 57.9 percent were working. By 1993, just over one-fifth of couples fit the single–male-earner model.[27] The rest were dual-earner couples or single-parent families, struggling to get by on one income in an economy that increasingly requires two.

Past generations of workers fought for a "family wage" and the eight-hour workday as policy solutions that would help them live with the industrial world. While the family wage was never paid to many workers, particularly African Americans, Latinos, and women, it was perceived as a reachable goal for many. The demand for a family wage was based on the assumption that every family could afford and would prefer to have a male full-time wage worker with a full-time, stay-at-home wife to tend to child care, housework, and family comfort. Many commentators feel that workers should fight to revive this family-wage system.

But social changes in recent decades have made the family-wage concept obsolete. Women do not want to, and often cannot be forced to, choose between work or family, even though they find that family life often turns into a "second shift" when housework and care of others is added to a demanding job schedule. Men also do not want to be forced into choosing between work and home. "I wish I could work part time," a male postal worker commented. "For men, it seems there's only a choice between full time or overtime."

Social solutions to the converging needs of men and women will not come out of the male-breadwinner–female-homemaker model. New solutions are being sought by labor organizations, women's groups, and others. While a consensus does not yet exist, ideas like shorter work time, business-tax penalties or incentives, corporate-shareholder activism, and militant labor organizing are being discussed. The very technologies that allow us to produce so much should allow us to have a richer life, not just a higher Dow Jones average. The quality of life in the future depends not on our ability to adapt our families to work, but to adapt work to our family, community, and individual needs.

A shorter work week with no pay cut is among the most promising solutions to the new realities of the work world. Shorter work time addresses the work, leisure, and family needs of both men and women. Proponents argue that since fewer workers are now needed to produce needed goods and services, the available work, income, and leisure should be shared by reducing the number of hours in a "full-time" job. Europe has had an active shorter-hours movement, and European countries have reduced work time through lengthened paid vacations and holidays. In the United States, we work about 200 hours more per year than workers do in Europe.[28]

In early 1995, a conference at the University of Iowa entitled "Our Time Famine: A Critical Look at the Culture of Work and a Reevaluation of 'Free' Time" drew together scholars, political leaders, labor activists, policy analysts, writers, business consultants, simple-living advocates, and exhausted workers in a search for solutions. The conference brought pioneering feminist writer Betty Friedan together with "war zone" labor strategist Jerry Tucker. Former senator and presidential candidate Eugene McCarthy conferred with Juliet Schor, author of *The Overworked American*.

The "Iowa City Declaration" adopted by the conference said that "the maldistribution of work and free time, with attendant inequality of incomes, has created a growing social problem. . . . We therefore urge the national governments of Canada and the United States to put in place before the year 2000 the legal arrangements to ensure that a thirty-two-hour workweek will become the norm for full-time workers in the first decade of the new millennium."[29]

Betty Friedan expressed the feelings of most participants when she commented that "it is obscene to continue in a culture of greed where the only people who benefit are the top 2 percent." Friedan's hometown of Peoria, Illinois, was the site of a bitter strike against Caterpillar Tractor's wage cutting and work reengineering. Seeing the results of falling wages, she warned that "a 20 percent drop in male income" could sow the seeds of political backlash against women's gains. To avoid such a counterproductive response, she argued, "it is necessary for women and men to work together to restructure work and restructure home." Such a backlash has already rolled back the gains that African-American and other workers made in the 1970s, and here too the shorter-work-week movement represents a promising alternative to attempts to reassert white privilege in order to gain a larger share of a shrinking pie. The conference, Friedan commented, was "part of a paradigm shift—which I can say with some authority, having been a part of one before."[30]

European unions and political bodies have adopted the goal of shortening work time and have negotiated twenty-seven- to thirty-four-hour work weeks with corporations like Volkswagen, Hewlett-Packard, and Digital Equipment.[31] "Time for living, loving, and laughter . . . that's what we want for our Saturdays," read a German strike banner at Volkswagen. The U.S. shorter-work-time movement is just beginning to revive after a decades-long sleep. In fits and spurts, progress toward a shorter work week is being made in some large American corporations. Oddly, it is in the course of fighting forced overtime, massive layoffs, and speedup that workers have proposed, and won, shorter hours with no cuts in pay.

In St. Louis, autoworkers producing top-selling minivans were faced with Chrysler demands for a ten-hour day. The union members voted down the company's schedule and proposed an alternative that would keep production going around-the-clock and create jobs: They won three thirty-four-hour shifts at forty hours pay and were able to recall 1,200 laid-off workers. "There was less stress, attendance was better, attitude was better," commented a local union officer.

Steelworkers at National Steel's Granite City, Illinois, mill had worked five eight-hour shifts a week for years. When the company demanded "alternative work schedules" involving up to sixteen hours per day with rotating shifts, the workers struck and shut down the mill. Their "Gold Mill Committee for a Decent Schedule" held public rallies involving spouses and children, claiming that the company's alternative schedule was "a family wrecker." The union proposed its own four-crew schedule and won a thirty-six-hour work week with forty hours pay and no forced overtime.[32]

The paradigm shift Betty Friedan referred to is happening in some labor struggles and in the individual choices of workers. It has not yet been reflected in social policy, but the emerging shorter-hours movement and the new energy among some labor unions make it possible to envision a future where families control their work, not the other way around.

Endnotes

1. David Bacon, "The UPS Strike—Unions Win When They Take the Offensive," August 24, 1997. "Polls Show UPS Strikers Have Wide Public Support," August 14, 1997, *Wall Street Journal Interactive Edition.*

2. "The Downsizing of America," *New York Times*, March 3, 1996, 16.

3. Elizabeth Gilbert, "Exiles in the Promised Land," *New York Times*, January 7, 1996, E19.

4. Al Ehrbahr, "'Reengineering' Gives Firms New Efficiency, Workers the Pink Slip," *Wall Street Journal*, March 16, 1993, 1.

5. For more background on wealth redistribution, social and tax policy, see Donald L. Bartlett and James B. Steele, *America: What Went Wrong?* (Kansas City: Andrews and McMeel, 1992); Thomas Byrne Edsall, *The New Politics of Inequality* (New York: W. W. Norton, 1984); Thomas Ferguson and Joel Rogers, *Right Turn: The Decline of the Democrats and the Future of American Politics* (Hill and Wang, 1986); U.S. Department of Labor, "Fact-finding Report: Commission on the Future of Worker-Management Relations," 1994.

6. Tim Donahue, "Workplace is becoming more stressful," *Seattle Times*, July 24, 1995, D4.

7. Labor Research Association, "Economic Notes," March 1996.

8. "The Tide Is Not Lifting Everyone," *New York Times*, October 2, 1997, A2.

9. "Rising Output. Falling Incomes," *Dollars and Sense*, May–June 1995, 43.

10. Floyd Norris, "Three Views, No Agreement," *New York Times*, February 4, 1996, F5.

11. Peter Drucker, *Post Capitalist Society* (New York: Harper Collins, 1993).

12. "Outlook for Technology and Labor in Telephone Communications," U.S. Department of Labor, Bureau of Labor Statistics, July 1990, Bulletin 2357, 1, 11–12.

13. Louis Uchitelle and N.R. Kleinfield, "The Downsizing of America: A National Heartache," *New York Times*, March 3, 1996, 15.

14. Dan Lallotz, "The Team in Mexico," *Working Smart,* Labor Education and Research Project, 1994, 239–240.

15. "The Downsizing of America," *New York Times*, March 3, 1996, 1.

16. "Job Insecurity: A Special Report," *New York Times*, July 3, 1995, 1.

17. "The Downsizing of America," *New York Times*, March 3, 1996, 16.

18. Labor Research Association, "Economic Notes," December 1995.

19. "Overtime Tyrant Gets Tough," *CWA News*, vol. 55, no. 9, October 1995, 7.

20. Keith Bradsher, "Showdown at GM Leaves Big Issues Still Unresolved," *New York Times*, March 23, 1996, 1.

21. Adrienne Eaton, "New Production Techniques, Employee Involvement and Unions," *Labor Studies Journal*, vol. 20, no. 3, Fall 1995.

22. John Junkerman, "Nissan, Tennessee: It Ain't What It's Cracked Up to Be," *The Progressive*, June 1987, 16–20.

23. Mike Parker and Jane Slaughter, "Working Smart: Guide to Participation Programs and Reengineering," Labor Education and Research Project, Detroit, Mich., 1994, Chapter 1, 1.

24. "In the Productivity Push, How Much Is Too Much?" *New York Times*, December 17, 1995, sec. 3, 1.

25. Interview with Tom Bernard, Business Agent, Teamsters Local 174, Seattle, May 1, 1996.
26. Letter to *Detroit Free Press* reproduced in a flyer by Teamsters Local 174, Seattle.
27. "Fact-Finding Report," Commission on the Future of Worker-Management Relations, U.S. Department of Labor, 1994, 10–11.
28. Ibid., 19.
29. "Iowa City Declaration," available from William McGaughey, 1702 Glenwood Ave., N. Minneapolis, MN 55405. Also, Shorter Work Time Group, 69 Dover Street #1, Somerville, MA 02144.
30. Betty Friedan, remarks to "Our Time Famine" conference, University of Iowa, March 10, 1996.
31. Jeremy Rifkin, *The End of Work* (New York: GB Putnam, 1995), 224–226.
32. Kim Moody and Simone Sagovac, "Time Out!" Labor Education and Research Project, Detroit, Mich., 1995, 40–42.

Writing Application

Write a mature summary of this essay that not only highlights Ryan's main points but also points out the claims of fact, size, and possibility that she makes. Use the common topics to uncover more subtle claims made and to begin the process of evaluating the article's value.

Writing to Respond

In the report that follows, Jenny Earle discusses practices in Australia that have attempted to encourage a "family-friendly" workplace. Earle is the director of the Work and Family Unit of the Department of Employment and Workplace Relations in Australia. The role of the Work and Family Unit "is to promote the implementation of family-friendly working arrangements, and to increase awareness of the opportunities available to include work and family provisions in workplace agreements." This governmental agency studies and makes recommendations for improving the relationship between work and family life. In the report below, Earle outlines positive results of such initiatives. Using the techniques of active reading we've been discussing, interrogate the claims being made in this essay.

Family-Friendly Workplaces: A Tale of Two Sectors

Jenny Earle

There are encouraging developments in the retail and public service sectors that indicate business is increasingly aware that it depends for its success on recognizing and accommodating the diverse needs of the people who make up the workforce. This is important if we are to address the problem of the current uneven spread of family-friendly workplaces across the economy.

Many factors are combining to shine the spotlight on workplace policies and programs that enable people to combine paid work with family responsibilities. The rise in dual earner families, associated especially with the increased labor force participation of mothers with young children, measures to increase the workforce participation of single mothers, and the increased involvement of fathers in child rearing, are all drivers of change.

Demographic factors such as declining fertility and the aging population are providing further impetus for progress in this area. There is growing recognition that Australia's competitiveness depends on the knowledge and skills of its people, and that to prosper, business needs to draw on a wide and diverse pool of talent. Work-family balance is thus increasingly important for long-term trends in labor supply, as the OECD (2001) has recognized.

A wide variety of provisions come under the general rubric of "family-friendly measures." However, they tend to fall into five main groups: leave provisions (such as parental and family or caregiver's leave); flexible working hours arrangements (including part-time work, job sharing, flexible start and finish times); child care provision or assistance; other support measures such as counseling and referral services; and information and training resources (Whitehouse 1999; Evans 2000).

These measures can be found in various sources—industrial relations legislation, provisions in industrial awards, state services, enterprise/workplace agreements, company policies, and a wide range of informal measures at workplace level. This article briefly outlines the federal industrial relations framework and then goes on to look in particular at recent developments in two very different sectors—the retail industry and the federal public service.

Implementing Work and Family Provisions

It is now widely acknowledged in the work/family policy arena that, beyond certain minimum conditions, approaches need to be tailored according to the characteristics of an organization and its workforce. One size does not fit all, either in terms of the range of employee needs and how these change over the life cycle, or in terms of the requirements of different industries and workplaces. This is because the challenges, opportunities and operational imperatives are different in different sectors and for organizations of different sizes.

In Australia, the federal legislative framework for workplace relations emphasizes the role of agreement-making in creating family-friendly working conditions, and the scope this offers for meeting both the business needs of the organization and the needs of the employees (Workplace Relations Act 1996).

At present, many family-friendly practices in the workplace are not formalized through the workplace relations system. While informal agreements, company policy or management practices may suit an organization in the short-term, there are good reasons to include family-friendly practices in formal agreements.

More and more companies do recognize the significant benefits that family-friendly work practices can bring to the workplace through increased staff morale, higher productivity, and reduced turnover of quality staff. The cost of providing a more flexible work environment will vary according to the specific measures adopted but does not have to be high (Russell 1997). The financial services giant AMP has calculated that its investment in family-friendly policies is yielding a 400 percent return in the form of lower staff turnover and higher productivity (Schwab 2001). It is also a recruitment aid for employers who want to position themselves as "employers of choice" in a competitive global labors market. A Price/Waterhouse/Coopers study of graduates worldwide found that work/life balance was key to choice of employer for 45 percent of graduates, compared with salary for only 22 percent (PSMPC 2001: 23).

However, the "business case" has always had more traction in relation to high-skilled occupations and industries, where training and replacement costs are high, and the recruitment and retention benefits of "best practice" provisions are easier to quantify. It has been harder to promote the business efficiency and cost effectiveness argument in sectors traditionally characterized as "low-skill" (such as retail), or where productivity is hard to measure (such as the public sector). This article reports on encouraging developments in the retail and public service sectors, which indicate that the scope of the business case may be broadening. This is important if we are to address the problem of the current uneven spread of family-friendly workplaces across the economy.

The Retail Sector: Family-Friendly Practices Add Up to Good Business Outcomes

Retail employs more people than any other industry sector in Australia—14 percent of the Australian labor force works in retail. Women make up over 50 percent of the retail workforce, and part-time workers constitute 46 percent of employees. The industry faces a number of challenges with the growth of extended opening hours and seven-day trading, increased competition and low profit margins. Today, many retail businesses operate at all hours of the day and night. We are surrounded by 24-hour convenience stores, have access to 24-hour banking, late night restaurants, and late night shopping. People's lifestyles and working habits are changing and these have particularly significant implications for the retail industry.

Its traditional image is of a low-skill, low-pay industry that is reliant on casual labor and offers little potential for building a career. Despite the extent of part-time employment it is not a sector renowned for its family-friendly work practices. In the Work and Family Unit's report (WFU 1999) "Work and Family: State of Play 1998," which analyzed developments in the spread of family-friendly working arrangements, the retail industry was identified as a "poor performer." Furthermore, according to AWIRS, retail employees were the least likely of any industry (except for "electricity, gas and water supply") to believe that they were given a fair chance to have a say at work (Morehead et al. 1997). Consultation with employees is a key factor in achieving a family-friendly working environment—see, for example, the Work and Family Unit's Resource Folder (WFU 1997–2001).

Against this background, retail industry leaders had begun to appreciate that the challenges facing the sector required a fresh approach. This led to the development of a partnership project between the Australian Retailers Association (which represents over 12,000 retailers who between them transact over 75 percent of the nation's retail sales), the Work and Family Unit in the Department of Employment and Workplace Relations, and the Equal Opportunity for Women in the Workplace Agency (EOWA).

The partnership worked with some of Australia's leading retailers to profile workplace practices in this sector, with a view to helping them improve business outcomes through better understanding and management of their workforce. Sixty retailers, representing 278,000 employees, participated in the study by responding to a postal survey, while 17 retailers hosted an extensive workplace visit, involving interviews with staff and managers. The project report, entitled "Balancing the Till: Report into Finding and Keeping Good People in the Retail Sector," has been published by the Work and Family Unit (WFU 2002). The "Balancing the Till" report, which also draws on international research and best practice, highlights 16 key messages for the industry. There is not the space here to discuss all the report's findings, so comment is restricted to some of the most significant.

The survey found that while employers place a very high priority on recruiting the right people, this contrasts with much lower priority given to keeping good employees. It also found that one of the principal reasons people may leave a job in retail is lack of flexibility and family-friendly working conditions. Almost a quarter of retailers who responded to the survey reported that a major reason for staff leaving their company was to seek more supportive work-life conditions. Nearly half of the retailers (44 percent) said staff left their business because they wanted more control over their working hours.

Some control over working hours is important to all employees but it is particularly valuable to those managing family care responsibilities (WFU 1999). Control can mean having a say in start and finish times, negotiating the number of hours worked per week, or being able to take time off to attend to family matters and make up the time later. Shops have to open and close at fixed times, and must be staffed to cover peaks and troughs in the trading cycle. Retail relies on rosters to cope with fluctuations in business and to cover extended trading.

While there are certainly models of "best practice" in the industry it is not yet the norm. For those who still regard the implementation of work and family provisions as too costly, the report presents some startling figures on the cost of replacing employees, even junior casual employees. A leading Australian super-market has estimated its costs per lost staff member as $3,800 per full-timer, and more than half that for a part-time worker.

Retailers who do the math should find that strategies to retain staff do pay off. The point made by Bill Healey, a former executive director of the Australian Retailers Association and one of the instigators of this project, is that "the retail industry is not an unskilled industry but it is an under-credentialed one, one in which many skills are not formally recognized." The under-valuing of skills can result in underestimates of the losses from staff turnover, and a corresponding failure to implement work-life provisions that would improve employee loyalty and retention. The clear message from this research is that there are gains to be achieved by providing an environment and conditions of employment that allow people to balance their work and family responsibilities. It increases their pro-ductivity at work and encourages them to be loyal long-term employees. This in turn fosters quality of service and customer loyalty.

While the majority of retail employees are women, less than a quarter of the managers are women. Providing flexibility for management and supervisory staff remains a key challenge for the Australian retail sector, as it does for many other organizations. It is a critical factor in capturing the untapped talent of the large female workforce. It is also important if family-friendly working arrange-ments are not to constitute a "mummy track", or a *cul de sac* for women's careers (Wajcman 1998). Part-time work is one of the principal methods used by women to balance paid employment with family responsibilities and commu-nity involvement. It can also give employers the flexibility they need to adjust working hours to business requirements while achieving higher productivity. However, it can prove to be a mixed blessing, often relegating women to the periphery of the labor market, with less training and promotion opportunities. In keeping with this, it is clear from this research that the vast majority of retail-ers are only too happy to provide part-time employment opportunities for their shop assistants but seem to have a mind-set against the possibility of providing such flexibilities for their shop managers.

Many of the key messages in the "Balancing the Till" report are echoed in other research. One of the retailers who hosted a workplace visit for the partner-ship's project, Eurest, has recently been recognized in the Australian Financial

Review's "Best Employer to Work for in Australia." That survey of 160 companies representing a cross-section of Australian corporate life found that:

- the top five factors affecting business results were acquisition and retention of talent, organizational culture, quality of leaders, customer loyalty, and employee motivation;

- a large number of the best employers had part-time workers, with some having more part-time than full-time people;

- the best employers see pay as part of a more holistic environment with flexible work practices and some work-life balance conditions;

- it is not "one size fits all": employers can't just go and copy others—they must communicate with their employees to work out what will fit their needs and those of the business; and

- the best employers receive nearly twice as many job applications as other employers and staff turnover is about 25 percent less.

As the "Balancing the Till" report emphasizes, contemporary work practices aligned with the needs of the 21st century workforce will significantly increase the management capability of the retail sector and increase its business competitiveness. Individuals are subject to changing demands and priorities as they move through the life cycle. They might start out balancing study and part-time work, or working full-time as young adults. There are times when developing a career and climbing the promotions ladder are the priority. When the responsibility of caring for young children, disabled relatives or aged parents arises, the focus shifts and needs are different.

The challenge for managers and employers is to enable employees to give the best they can as they move through life's phases.

The Public Services Sector

It should be the case that the federal government as employer best exemplifies its own workplace relations policy, and indeed this appears to be the case, since there is a high incidence of family-friendly provisions. Almost all APS employees are covered by either certified agreements (94.3 percent) or by Australian workplace agreements (5.2 percent) compared with the Australian workforce as a whole (35.2 percent and 1.8 percent respectively).

A new report on the Australian Public Service shows that family-friendly conditions are regarded as being very significant in both enhancing productivity and in delivering benefits to employees. The National Institute of Labor Studies conducted a survey in August/September 2001 on behalf of the Department of Employment and Workplace Relations. It follows up a similar one conducted in 1999 and indicates a substantial increase in awareness of work and family issues since then (Department of Employment and Workplace Relations 2001).

In the public sector, a key challenge is to find ways of enhancing productivity, so as to fund pay increases within APS agencies' budgets, but also to get better value for taxpayers' money.

Features were rated on the number of agencies recognizing them as important and on how important the agencies rated them. Most agencies (74 percent) reported performance management arrangements were the most important feature in enhancing productivity. Family-friendly working arrangements were also rated as an important feature by 74 percent of agencies, a dramatic rise since 1999 when only 22 percent of agencies said that family-friendly working arrangements were important in enhancing performance. Because this scored lower on the "how important" index, its overall importance ranking was reduced (to four). However, it is striking that three of the top ten ranked features relate to the provision of a family-friendly work environment.

"Flexible hours of work" covers a multitude of arrangements, from seven days a week rostering, to bandwidth hours (the range of hours within which employees may carry out their work), to part-time work. The survey found that about 45 percent of current APS agency agreements include specific provisions aimed at effectively managing extended hours. For example, the Department of Foreign Affairs and Trade has adopted a "Working Smarter" strategy, which discourages long working hours and rewards staff who show good judgment in setting priorities and maintaining work-life balance. This is a good illustration of committing to a process of workplace culture change with a practical initiative.

Pay increases were regarded as the most significant benefit to employees. However, there were many benefits ranked near equal in significance, including flexible working arrangements and family-friendly or work/life balance policies. These were considered to be a significant or a highly significant benefit in at least four out of five agencies. The survey report concludes that agreements are working for both agencies and employees. Importantly, it shows that flexible working arrangements and family-friendly measures are regarded as important features for enhancing performance in agencies.

Conclusion

It is encouraging to see the links developing between the work and family agenda, and the "employer of choice" and "managing diversity" agendas. This helps us to see that business depends for its success on recognizing and accommodating the diverse needs of the people who make up the workforce, and therefore that these programs should not be seen as optional extras but as integral to core business strategies in both the public and the private sectors.

References

ABS (2000), *Working arrangements of careers: managing caring responsibilities and paid employment,* Australian Bureau of Statistics, Canberra.

DEWR (2001), *Agreement-making in the Australian Public Service: 2001 Survey Results,* Department of Employment and Workplace Relations/National Institute of Labor Studies, Canberra. A full copy of the report can be found at www.dewr.gov.au/work-placeRelations/publicSector/default.asp. The site also contains links to a database of Innovative Clauses in Australian Public Service Certified Agreements.

Evans, J.M. (2000), *Firms' Contribution to the Reconciliation between Work and Family Life,* Occasional Papers No. 48, Labour Market and Social Policy, OECD, Paris, France.

Russell, G. (1997), *Guide to Evaluating Work and Family Strategies,* Work and Family Resources Folder, Department of Employment and Workplace Relations, Canberra.

Morehead, A., Steele, M., Alexander, M., Stephen, K. & Duffin, L. (1997), *Changes at Work: The 1995 Australian Workplace Industrial Relations Survey,* Longman, South Melbourne.

OECD (2001), Employment Outlook, Chapter 4, "Balancing work and family life: Helping parents into paid employment," OECD, Paris, France.

PSMPC (2001), *Workplace Diversity Report,* Public Service and Merit Protection Commission, Canberra, p. 23.

Schwab, P. (ed.) (2001), "HR Report," *The National Independent Newsletter on Employee Relations,* no. 239, p.2.

Wajcman, J. (1998), *Managing Like a Man: Women and Men in Corporate Management,* Allen & Unwin, Sydney.

Whitehouse, G. (1999), "Family-friendly policies: Distribution and implementation in Australian workplaces," *The Economic and Labour Relations Review,* vol. 10, no. 2, December.

WFU (1997–2001), *Work and Family Resources Folder,* Work and Family Unit, Department of Employment and Workplace Relations, Canberra.

WFU (2002), *Balancing the Till: Report into Finding and Keeping Good People in the Retail Sector,* Work and Family Unit, Department of Employment and Workplace Relations, Canberra.

WFU (1999), *Work and Family: State of Play 1998,* Work and Family Unit, Department of Employment and Workplace Relations, Canberra.

Writing Application

Write an extended summary of the piece, highlighting its main points, fairly explaining its key positions on family-work relations, and demonstrating what you take to be its most significant findings. You might also consider how this piece might have been influenced by the position of its author, its status as a governmental report, and its reliance on specific social policies. Is there a specific agenda here? Are there commonplaces about family and work on which this argument is based? Are there specific questions of fact, size, and feasibility that you might ask in order to interrogate this piece actively?

Writing to Respond

Though the topics of the previous two articles are different, the pieces share some key areas of interest. After you have read the articles, try to find stasis points in the perspectives offered by each. Ask yourself where there seem to be specific issues about work and family, the responsibilities of workers and employers, and possible ways to alleviate the competing demands of work and family in both articles—that is, ask what specific topics might provide points of comparison or stasis. You might, for example,

- Consider Sarah Ryan's call to "envision a future where families control their work, not the other way around." Do the programs by Australia's Work and Family Unit answer Ryan's call? Why or why not?
- Consider how the recommendations of Australia's Work and Family Unit correspond to the Families and Work Institute findings noted by Ryan. How is "work reengineering" similar to, or different from, the initiatives noted by Earle as she describes Australian business practices?
- Consider how gender is a factor in the argument made by each.

You might investigate many other sub-issues and stasis points—which your use of the common topics can help you to uncover.

Writing Application

Write an essay that (1) provides a clear summary of each article's most important points, and (2) shows how the two articles share common concerns and areas of agreement and disagreement (areas you've raised in the inventional exercises above). In order to organize your essay well, you will need to invent stasis points that allow the two readings to converse with one another. Your goal is to practice a key process of academic writing: learning to bring the ideas and words of others into a single conversation on a topic that interests your readers and yourself.

If you'd like to extend your essay, you might also speculate on the role of individuals, families, unions, and government agencies in promoting worker satisfaction and positive lifestyles. Who has the primary responsibility? Why?

Case 3 THE OCCUPATIONS AND THE CIVIC CONVERSATION

Though it is sometimes difficult to see connections between the fields you study in school and the issues that surround you in the "real world," recognizing those connections is crucial to becoming engaged students, informed workers, and active citizens. John Allen Paulos, a professor of mathematics at Temple

University and adjunct professor of journalism at Columbia University, is also a columnist for ABCNews.com. His books include the *New York Times* bestsellers *Innumeracy, Once Upon a Number*, and *A Mathematician Reads the Newspaper*, from which the following excerpt is taken. In this piece, Paulos demonstrates how a field that may seem to some, as he puts it, "a timeless discipline concerned with abstract truth" is in fact a crucial facet of understanding what goes on around us in the here and now. Paulos writes:

> It's time to let the secret out: Mathematics is not primarily a matter of plugging numbers into formulas and performing rote computations. It is a way of thinking and questioning that may be unfamiliar to many of us, but is available to almost all of us. . . . My aim is to leave the reader with a greater appreciation of the role of mathematics in understanding social issues and with a keener skepticism of its uses, nonuses, misuses, and abuses in the daily paper.

Paulos, then, is attempting to show about the academic field of mathematics that which is true of most academic fields: If you really understand its work, then you can see the ways in which activities that might be considered "merely academic" have real implications for your work and for culture more generally. In order to understand the ways that Paulos illustrates this claim, read the following excerpts from his book, noting the ways in which he identifies mathematical topics in everyday news that might otherwise be considered just for the classroom.

from A Mathematician Reads the Newspaper

John Allen Paulos

Company Charged with Ethnic Bias in Hiring

Test Disparities Need Not Imply Racism

The comedian Mort Sahl remarks that some newspapers might report a nuclear exchange between the United States and Russia with the headline WORLD ENDS: WOMEN AND MINORITIES HARDEST HIT. Sarcasm and hyperbole aside, victimization and the differential treatment of groups, whether intentional or not, are the basis for many a news story. The percentage of African-American students at elite colleges, the proportion of women in managerial positions, the ratio of Hispanic representatives in legislatures have all been written about extensively. Oddly enough, the shape of normal bell-shaped statistical curves sometimes has unexpected consequences for such situations. For example, even a slight divergence between the averages of different population groups is accentuated at the extreme ends of these curves, and these extremes often receive inordinate attention in the press. There are other inferences that have been drawn from this fact, some involving social policy issues such as affirmative action and jobs programs. The issue is a charged one, and I don't wish to endorse any dubious claims, but merely to clarify some mathematical points.

As an illustration, assume that two population groups vary along some dimension—height, for example. Although it is not essential to the argument, make the further assumption that the two groups' heights vary in a normal or bell-shaped manner (see diagram below). Then even if the average height of one group is only slightly greater than the average height of the other, people from the taller group will constitute a large majority among the very tall (the right tail of the curve). Likewise, people from the shorter group will constitute a large majority among the very short (the left tail of the curve). This is true even though *the bulk of the people from both groups are of roughly average stature.* Thus if group A has a mean height of 5' 8" and group B a mean height of 5' 7", then (depending on the exact variability of the heights) perhaps 90 percent or more of those over 6' 2" will be from group A. In general, any differences between two groups will always be greatly accentuated at the extremes.

These simple ideas can be used and misused by people of very different political persuasions. My concerns, as I've said, are only with some mathematical aspects of a very complicated story. Let me again illustrate with a somewhat idealized case. Many people submit their job applications to a large corporation. Some of these people are Mexican and some are Korean, and the corporation uses a single test to determine which jobs to offer to whom. For whatever reasons (good or bad, justifiable or not), let's assume that although the scores of both groups are normally distributed with similar variability, those of the Mexican applicants are slightly lower on average than those of the Korean applicants.

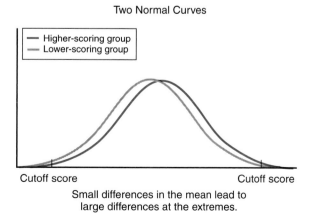

Two Normal Curves

Small differences in the mean lead to
large differences at the extremes.

The corporation's personnel officer notes the relatively small differences between the groups' means and observes with satisfaction that the many mid-level positions are occupied by both Mexicans and Koreans. She is puzzled, however, by the preponderance of Koreans assigned to the relatively few top jobs, those requiring an exceedingly high score on the qualifying test. The personnel officer does further research and discovers that most holders of the comparably few bottom jobs, assigned to applicants because of their very low scores on the qualifying test, are Mexican. She may suspect racism, but the result might just as well be an unforeseen consequence of the way the normal distribution works. Paradoxically, if she lowers the threshold for entrance to the mid-level jobs, she will actually end up *increasing* the percentage of Mexicans in the bottom category.

The fact is that groups differ in history, interests, and cultural values and along a whole host of other dimensions (which are impossible to disentangle). These differences constitute the group's identity and are what makes it possible even to talk about a collection of people as a group. Confronted with these social and historical dissimilarities, then, we shouldn't be astonished that members' scores on some standardized test are also likely to differ in the mean and, much more substantially, at the extremes of the test-score distribution. (Much of this discussion is valid even if the distribution is not the normal bell-shaped one.) Such statistical disparities are not necessarily evidence of racism or ethnic prejudice, although, without a doubt, they sometimes are. One can and should debate whether the tests in question are appropriate for the purpose at hand, but one shouldn't be surprised when normal curves behave normally. As long as I'm issuing pronouncements, let me make another: The basic unit upon which our society or, indeed, any liberal society ("indeed" is a sure sign of something pompous coming up) is founded is the individual, not the group; I think it should stay that way.

Aside from having a questionable rationale, schemes of strict proportional representation are impossible to implement. Another thought experiment illustrates this point. Imagine a company—let's call it PC Industries—operating in a community that is 25 percent black, 75 percent white, 5 percent homosexual, and 95 percent heterosexual. Unknown to PCI and the community is the fact that only 2 percent of the blacks are homosexual, whereas 6 percent of the whites are. Making a concerted attempt to assemble a workforce of 1,000 that "fairly" reflects the community, the company hires 750 whites and 250 blacks. However, just 5 of the blacks (or 2 percent) would be homosexual, whereas 45 of the whites (or 6 percent) would be (totaling 50, 5 percent of all workers). Despite these efforts, the company could still be accused by its black employees of being homophobic, since only 2 percent of the black employees would be homosexual, not the communitywide 5 percent. The company's homosexual employees could likewise claim that the company was racist, since only 10 percent of their members would be black, not the communitywide 25 percent. White heterosexuals would certainly make similar complaints.

To complete the *reductio ad absurdum,* factor in several other groups: Hispanics, women, Norwegians, even. Their memberships will likely also intersect to various unknown degrees.[1] People will identify with varying intensity with the various groups to which they belong (whose very definitions are vague at best). The backgrounds and training across these various cross sections and intersections are extremely unlikely to be uniform. Statistical disparities will necessarily result.

Racism and homophobia and all other forms of group hatreds are real enough without making them our unthinking first inference when confronted with such disparities.

SAT Top Quartile Score Declines

Correlation, Prediction, and Improvement

The Scholastic Assessment Test (SAT) is familiar to anyone who's ever attended high school in this country. Retaining the brand-name acronym, its new name is slightly less presuming than the former Scholastic Aptitude Test. Not surprisingly, some of the hundreds of news stories on the SAT spotlight those rare students who get a perfect 800 on the math section or a perfect 1600 on the test as a whole, much less frequently those who score 800 in the English section only. The standard newspaper filler describes the local student's high school activities, admirable qualities, college and career goals, and usually some endearing foible.

But most pieces are more substantive. A check of various newspaper databases reveals that in recent years, stories have dealt with the decline of scores since the early 1960s, the possible addition of essay questions to the heretofore exclusively multiple-choice format, the permission to use calculators, the poorer performance of girls and minorities on the test, the "renorming" of the test to inflate the average score to 1000, the extent to which scores can be raised by services that focus on test-taking strategies and heuristics, and, most important, the ability of the test to predict collegial success.

An amazing aspect of the ongoing coverage has been its breadth, detail, and tendentious slant. For what they're worth my brief reactions to the issues just mentioned: Scores have declined in part because a larger and more varied body of students is taking the test than ever before. Unfortunately, the scores in the top quartile have also declined, indicating a more general deterioration. The inclusion of essays on future tests would be a welcome modification. It doesn't require a score of 1600 to realize that the ability to organize and express one's thoughts in a coherent essay without misspellings or grammatical errors is at least as important as other skills the test measures.

Calculators will be of marginal help to test takers; the difficulty students have with the math questions is, popular opinion to the contrary, not computational. Girls consistently score lower than boys (only one-third of the highest scorers on the PSAT are girls), and minorities consistently score lower scores than whites. Nevertheless, the frequent charges of cultural and gender bias are, in my opinion, overstated (despite the rare question of the runner-is-to-marathon as oarsman-is-to-regatta type). The test is "biased," but only toward the educationally prepared, the physically healthy, and the psychologically receptive. And the gain from renorming the scores upward to achieve a symmetric distribution ranging between 200 and 1600 is outweighed by two factors: the loss of discriminatory power at the upper end of the distribution and the lack of easy comparability between future and past scores. Why not adjust the liveliness of baseballs so that the average hitter bats .500?

Studies do suggest that attending SAT preparation courses will raise one's scores to some degree. (More extensive and long-term intervention will raise them even more, of course.) Nevertheless, if students have sufficient self-discipline to practice on the sample tests supplied by the Educational Testing Service or to work with inexpensive software, I think they can derive a good deal of the benefit provided by these services on their own. (One striking hint some services offer is to learn how to darken circles quickly. Taking a second or two longer than is necessary on each answer can conceivably result in a noticeably lower score.) Since there is a natural and not insignificant variability in one's scores, taking the test several times and submitting only the highest scores in each section also makes very good sense.

The big question, however, is how predictive of success in college one's SAT score is. The answer is a resounding somewhat. There have been a variety of studies focusing on different groups of students and employing different protocols, controls, and assumptions. Most of them find that the correlation between SAT scores and college grades is not overwhelming. I surmise that the association appears rather weaker than it is because colleges usually accept students from a fairly narrow swath of the SAT spectrum. The SAT scores of students at Ivy League schools are considerably higher than those of community college students, yet both sets of students might have similar college grade distributions at their respective institutions. If both sets of students were admitted to Ivy League schools, however, I don't doubt there would be a considerably stronger correlation between SAT scores and college grades at these schools.

This is a general phenomenon: The degree of correlation between two variables depends critically on the range of the variables considered. Football players in the NFL are heavier, on average, than college football players. Weight is clearly significant in football, but one doesn't expect to see as close a correlation between weight and success within the NFL as there would be if college players and NFL players all played professional football.

And just as there are many dimensions of football ability that aren't measured by poundage, there are many dimensions of scholastic ability that aren't measured by the SAT. Concentrated work over an extended period is certainly one of them; the premium the SAT places on speed is especially difficult to defend. Anytime one tries to collapse a multifaceted, amorphous concept— physical beauty, political orientation, scholastic achievement, moral worth— along a linear scale, one is going to lose important information. I knew someone in graduate school in mathematics who scored around 400 in the math portion of the SAT (and comparably low on the Graduate Record Exam) and who now holds a prestigious endowed professorship in the subject. He is far from being alone, but if I knew only two things about a student—high school grades and SAT scores—I'd weigh the latter more heavily.

In the absence of a national curriculum or national standards, news coverage of the SAT helps provide a locus for discussion of educational policies and issues. Political reporters frequently build their stories around White House press releases, medical reporters wait for the latest edition of the *Journal of the American Medical Association*, and education reporters have the news on the latest SAT. Or as the statement might appear in the dreaded analogy segment of the test, political reporter : White House press release :: medical reporter : *JAMA* :: education reporter : SAT.

And those who think no discussion of the SAT is complete without a mathematics problem might consider the following, taken from the difficult portion of a recent test: In the correctly solved additions below, each of the five letters represents a different digit, EA being a two-digit number. What is the value of B + D if

$$
\begin{array}{cc}
A & C \\
+\underline{B} & +\underline{D} \\
C & E\,A?[2]
\end{array}
$$

Endnotes

1. A partially rhetorical question of tangential relevance: Assume that an organization wishes to "encourage" those having some characteristic C, but cannot directly inquire of anyone whether he or she possesses it. Assume further that Mr. X has a surname 20 percent of whose co-owners have characteristic C. If one knows nothing else about Mr. X, then it seems prudent to suppose that there is a 20 percent chance that Mr. X possesses C. If one later discovers that Mr. X comes from a neighborhood 70 percent of whose members have characteristic C, what should one's estimate now be of the likelihood that Mr. X posesses C? And what if one

subsequently learns that Mr. X is an active member of a nationwide organization only 3 percent of whose members possess characteristic C? With all this information, what can one now conclude about the chances that Mr. X has C?

2. Combining the two additions yields $A + B + C + D = C + EA$. If we cancel the C's from both sides of this equation, we obtain $A + B + D = EA$, and thus $B + D = EA - A$. The two-digit number EA equals $10 \times E + A$, and so $EA - A$ equals $(10 \times E + A) - A$, or simply $10 \times E$. Since the digit E must be 1, $(B + D) = 10 \times 1$, or just plain 10. (There are other approaches as well.)

Inventional Exercises

Seek out some "facts" being presented in the local newspaper or other popular periodicals, or on the radio or television, related to a field of studies in which you have an interest. If you are a biology student, for example, you might notice discussions of cloning, or environmental issues, or global warming. If you are a history major, you might note how discussions about various global conflicts are, in the popular media, related to past events and historical trends. If you are a management major, you might notice the ways in which economic trends or matters of ethics in business are addressed in the media. Spend a few days collecting potential topics and news stories that are written about them.

Use the common topics approach to generate as many things as you can to say about each argument—ways in which to discuss each issue through your particular field of studies or interest.

Writing Application

Write an informational essay that helps readers of popular magazines to understand the implications of the story you are analyzing. If you read an article on cloning, you might help other readers understand the science that informs this social issue; if you read an article on terrorism, you might enrich this discussion with a wider historical understanding of a particular conflict (say, between Islam and Christianity) or a specific historical trend (emerging nations, oppression by neighboring states, or arms races, for example).

CHAPTER SIX

Reading in Academic Disciplines

Have you ever attended a concert with a practicing musician? Have you ever been to a craft show with a carpenter, to a car show with a mechanic, or to an art museum with an artist? When craftspeople are surrounded by examples of the craft within which they work, they react differently than those who do not practice that craft themselves. Your musician friend is likely hearing chords and difficult riffs that to the rest of us might sound simply like enjoyable music. The carpenter is not looking at the chair as a place to sit but is likely circling it carefully, examining the joints and the quality of the design. The car mechanic isn't dazzled by the paint job on that 1968 Mustang—his head is already under the engine, remembering (or imagining) the days before catalytic converters and miles-per-gallon restrictions. And in the art museum, the artist is seeing the hand of Van Gogh in each brushstroke.

These people (and you might recognize yourself in one of them) share an important characteristic—they are experts in a particular area of concern. As such, they see, hear, and feel things that others with less interest in the topic might miss. They also possess a more keenly developed set of analytical tools to see, hear, and feel those things. Their areas of interest and experience also determine the communities within which they feel most comfortable and the language they use within those communities.

WRITING TO EXPLORE 6.1

In order to understand the differences in the ways that various groups communicate, consider the specialized communities to which you belong and/or those to which you aspire in your academic studies and career. In your writer's notebook, note at least two communities to which you belong or to which you would like to belong. Those communities can be based on your private interests (music, athletics, computer gaming, etc.) or your academic interests (physics, poetry, history, etc.). Then list some of the main concerns of those groups, the issues that they most often discuss, specific uses of language that help them to communicate with each other, and ways that members identify them as part of that community.

ACADEMIC DISCOURSE COMMUNITIES

Groups that are held together by shared interests, and by the preferred uses of language that allow them to talk productively about those shared interests, are sometimes called *discourse communities*. Discourse communities share a common language (or "discourse") and an identity that determines key areas of interest, specialized vocabularies, specific ways of reasoning through a problem, valid forms of evidence, and preferred styles of writing.

As you encounter the more complex writing in various fields, you will need tools that go beyond the general techniques suggested by the common topics approach discussed in the previous chapter. As you read journal articles and other writing that is written *by* experts *for* experts, you'll need to understand and participate in the reasoning style of any given piece—reading a scientific article like a scientist, a historical argument like a historian, or a marketing plan like a businessperson.

Colleges are, by one definition, a collection of *academic* discourse communities—groups of teachers and students who study similar topics, share interests, and

Shared interest / similar topics

use a language suited to the work that they do. As a student, you pass through many of these expert communities (sometimes called academic disciplines) in the course of a single day as part of your general education and major curricula. If you pay careful attention to the similarities and differences among these communities, your college education can provide you with a rare opportunity to experience many perspectives on learning. For that reason, it is important to develop strategies for reading and writing within these various discourse communities.

Eventually, as you narrow your focus to one occupational or disciplinary field, you will be called on to pay extra attention to specific topics, to reason in specific ways, and to adapt your forms of speech and writing to those that are accepted within your chosen field. That specialization will help you to become part of the ongoing conversations in the field—and, in the end, make you part of that community. But your ability to understand a wide range of fields will remain important, both as preparation for your specialty and as a way to communicate with people outside your chosen field.

Below, we explore some of the *special topics* that define the work of varied fields, helping you to begin the process of becoming an insider in the discourse of particular academic fields and professions. Learning about these special topics can help you to become more skilled in academic reading by discovering what disciplinary fields value, the ways their practitioners tend to reason through a problem, and the types of proof on which they rely. In the process, you'll also learn a good deal about yourself and the *ethos* that you are developing as an aspiring member of specific fields of study and work.

ACTIVE READING IN SPECIALIZED FIELDS

To prepare yourself to read specialized writing in a productive and active way, you might make two key assumptions: (1) whenever you read, you are entering a conversation that has been going on for some time, with or without you, and (2) when you enter that conversation, you are often entering a community of people with at least some shared concerns and values. Your first job as a writer, then, is to become a more informed reader and listener by learning about how this community reasons and writes.

Think about it this way. If you were to rush into a class or a meeting thirty minutes after it began and start to spout your opinions—not knowing what had been discussed before you arrived—you would be considered both rude and uninformed. In the same way, as you enter into discussions about various topics in your areas of study, it is important to know at least something about the participants in the conversation and the general content of the discussion that preceded you. Finding the balance between "inventive" thinking (thinking outside the box) and communicating within a given discourse community (acknowledging that the box exists) can be crucial for your work as a professional within various organizations and occupations.

WRITING TO EXPLORE 6.2

The textbooks for your current courses can teach you a good deal about the way people in academic areas or disciplines think and write. Just as I have been introducing you to key concepts and patterns of reasoning associated with the fields of rhetoric and composition, other textbooks introduce you to the concepts and styles of reasoning of their respective disciplines. Skim through an early chapter of three different textbooks from your courses (or those of your classmates) and, in your writer's notebook, identify features that seem to define the preferred modes of communication in those disciplines. Pay special attention to the word choices, the tone, the types of examples and proof used, the types of sentence structure—whatever differences you can identify.

READING ARGUMENTS IN ACADEMIC DISCIPLINES

As you no doubt discovered as you investigated the varied approaches taken in your textbooks, the ways different subject areas construct an argument vary. Let's begin by further defining a term we've been using quite a bit already: **argument**. Broadly defined, an argument is a condition wherein two or more parties are engaged in a dialog or discussion about a topic, a dialog from which might emerge productive discoveries that increase their knowledge of that issue. Rather than consider argument to be an unwillingness to accept ideas presented by others (the more antagonistic version), you might consider argument to be the willingness of two or more parties to engage in a dialog. In order to view argument in this way, you might remember some of the principles we have discussed thus far:

- that dialog can proceed productively when stasis is reached (the point at which participants agree to disagree upon specific aspects of an issue);
- that dialog can proceed most productively when parties to the conversation are speaking a similar language (often within a specific discourse community);
- that communication is facilitated when the dialog is based in a carefully arranged set of logical steps; and,
- that dialog proceeds most effectively when participants respect the many voices involved in ongoing conversations.

If you keep these points in mind, you can start to see that rhetorical argument is based in a set of concerns shared by speaker and audience, or writer and reader—concerns that are often defined by the academic discourse community.

Not only are the issues that practitioners in a field investigate based in shared values but so are the ways that specific audiences decide whether a proposed argument is credible—what that discourse community is willing to accept as "proof." In the textbooks you analyzed above, as well as in your many years as a student, you might have noticed that each subject area or discipline seems to have its own set of standards for what counts as proof.

WRITING TO EXPLORE 6.3

In your writer's notebook, freewrite on the forms of proof (evidence) that are most often used, and most acceptable, in each of the following areas of study. To gather ideas, consider the assignments that you have completed in these subject areas and the comments and directions of your teachers.

literary analysis

mathematical equation

psychology or sociology

biology

chemistry

business

As you no doubt began to notice in the above exercise, the proof necessary to make a convincing argument in each subject area varies quite a bit. For this reason, a working knowledge of the acceptable forms of proof in the discipline is crucial to active and critical academic reading. The analysis of a poem can rely on features of figurative language, the ambiguity of words, the careful construction of phrasing, an author's biography, or the social conditions that helped to inspire the work. Conversely, an analysis of a psychological condition or phenomenon might rely on case studies, physiological mechanisms, clinical or laboratory experimentation, empirical data collection—and not on the biography of the author of the study or the subtle connotations of the words chosen. Likewise, you might consider the necessary elements of a mathematical proof and how they differ from the proof for theories of evolution or political philosophies.

It is for this reason that the rhetorical tradition acknowledges that individual subject areas have their own *special topics*—areas of concern that arise from the nature of that field, as opposed to more generalized rhetorical principles. Unlike the common topics, which can be applied productively to almost any situation, the special topics can help you understand and write within specific subject areas. Just as you treated "facts" as proposed statements of truth rather than unchangeable or irrefutable ideas, so must you treat "proof" as a relative term that is often defined by the community in which the proof is offered.

Academic fields (or disciplines) vary in the amount and type of proof they require before accepting an argument as credible. In fact, a discipline or area of study is at least in part defined by what its practitioners consider to be solid evidence and what methodologies they consider to be most valid. Though there are many ways to organize the disciplinary work done in colleges, academic disciplines are often sorted into four basic categories: the humanities, the natural sciences, the social sciences, and business studies. In your present occupation as a student, these academic disciplines represent the discourse communities that you engage with daily and the languages you are learning to speak.

These categories, of course, are somewhat fluid. Nurses are engaged in both natural and social sciences; marketing majors and management majors share an interest in business fields; historians, literary scholars, and philosophers all consider their work to be within the humanities, though they often draw on knowledge from the social sciences; psychologists, sociologists, and criminal justice majors all share the issues and methodologies of the social sciences, whereas premedical students, geologists, and engineers rely on methodologies of the natural sciences. Still, understanding the basic assumptions made in each general area of study can help you be a more competent reader of academic discourse.

In the readings that follow, you are given the opportunity to think about the methods of reasoning, argument, and proof that are valued within each discipline. If you pay attention to the ways in which each field defines itself—its special topics of concern—you will hear the "argument" that each makes about the value of its discipline. That argument is made both explicitly, as each author describes his or her discourse community or field of interest, and implicitly, by the language and forms of proof that each author uses. As you read, note the methods used by each of the disciplines. Knowing more about each of these academic discourse communities can better prepare you for the academic reading that you will do throughout college, as well as the writing that you will do in response to that reading.

The Humanities

Generally, the humanities (as its name suggests) are concerned with human endeavors and culture. Of course, the social sciences also address human behavior, but their practitioners take a more quantified approach based on scientific methods. Some areas that are usually considered humanities are:

- literature
- rhetoric
- philosophy
- history

- political science
- fine arts
- foreign languages

Writing in the humanities shares the following characteristics:

- Humanities-based writing is analytical and text based, looking closely at primary texts or cultural objects to find meaning in them.
- Humanities-based writing values interpretation rather than quantifiable information.
- Humanities-based writing values aesthetics—the study of objects that are valued for their beauty or ability to move the emotion.
- Humanities-based writing often provides value judgments about the aesthetic or social value of various texts or objects.

WRITING TO EXPLORE 6.4

The following excerpt from Martha C. Nussbaum's *Cultivating Humanity* provides useful insights into what the disciplines within the humanities value. Nussbaum received her B.A. from New York University and her M.A. and Ph.D. from Harvard. She has taught at Harvard, Brown, and Oxford universities and is currently the Ernst Freund Professor of Law and Ethics in the Philosophy Department, the Law School, and the Divinity School at the University of Chicago. She has written many award-winning books and articles that use a humanistic perspective to examine law, politics, education, and a variety of other topics.

As you read Nussbaum's discussion of the importance of humanistic inquiry, consider the commonplaces and methods of this discourse community that it reveals—the types of beliefs that tie this group of thinkers together. Then, in order to understand the goals and methods of the humanities, respond in your writer's notebook to the questions that follow her essay.

The Narrative Imagination

Martha C. Nussbaum

[There] are many forms of thought and expression within the range of human communications from which the voter derives the knowledge, intelligence, sensitivity to human values: the capacity for sane and objective judgement which, so

*far as possible, a ballot should express. [The] people do need
novels and dramas and paintings and poems, "because they
will be called upon to vote."*

—Alexander Meiklejohn, "The First Amendment
Is an Absolute"

The world citizen needs knowledge of history and social fact.[1] We have begun
to see how those requirements can be met by curricula of different types. But
people who know many facts about lives other than their own are still not fully
equipped for citizenship. As Heraclitus said 2,500 years ago, "Learning about
many things does not produce understanding." Marcus Aurelius insisted that to
become world citizens we must not simply amass knowledge; we must also cultivate in ourselves a capacity for sympathetic imagination that will enable us to
comprehend the motives and choices of people different from ourselves, seeing
them not as forbiddingly alien and other, but as sharing many problems and possibilities with us. Differences of religion, gender, race, class, and national origin
make the task of understanding harder, since these differences shape not only
the practical choices people face but also their "insides," their desires, thoughts,
and ways of looking at the world.

Here the arts play a vital role, cultivating powers of imagination that are essential to citizenship. As Alexander Meiklejohn, the distinguished constitutional scholar
and theorist of "deliberative democracy," put it fifty years ago, arguing against an
opponent who had denied the political relevance of art, the people of the United
States need the arts precisely because they will be called upon to vote. That is not
the only reason why the arts are important, but it is one significant reason. The arts
cultivate capacities of judgment and sensitivity that can and should be expressed in
the choices a citizen makes. To some extent this is true of all the arts. Music, dance,
painting and sculpture, architecture—all have a role in shaping our understanding of
the people around us. But in a curriculum for world citizenship, literature, with its
ability to represent the specific circumstances and problems of people of many different sorts, makes an especially rich contribution. As Aristotle said in chapter 9 of
The Poetics, literature shows us "not something that has happened, but the kind of
thing that might happen." This knowledge of possibilities is an especially valuable
resource in the political life.

To begin to understand how literature can develop a citizen's imagination,
let us consider two literary works widely separated in place and time. In both
cases, the literary work refers to its own distinctive capacity to promote adequate civic perception.

Sophocles' *Philoctetes,* produced in 409 B.C., during a crisis in the Athenian
democracy, concerns the proper treatment of a citizen who has become an out-

cast, crippled by a disfiguring illness. On his way to Troy to fight with the Greeks in the Trojan War, Philoctetes stepped by mistake into a sacred shrine. His foot, bitten by the serpent who guards the shrine, began to ooze with an ulcerous sore, and his cries of pain disrupted the army's religious festivals. So the commanders abandoned him on the deserted island of Lemnos, with no companions and no resources but his bow and arrows. Ten years later, learning that they cannot win the war without his magical bow, they return, determined to ensnare him by a series of lies into participating in the war. The commander Odysseus shows no interest in Philoctetes as a person; he speaks of him only as a tool of public ends. The chorus of common soldiers has a different response (lines 169–176):

> For my part, I have compassion for him. Think how
> with no human company or care,
> no sight of a friendly face,
> wretched, always alone,
> he wastes away with that savage disease,
> with no way of meeting his daily needs.
> How, how in the world, does the poor man survive?

Unlike their leader, the men of the chorus vividly and sympathetically imagine the life of a man whom they have never seen, picturing his loneliness, his pain, his struggle for survival. In the process they stand in for, and allude to, the imaginative work of the audience, who are invited by the play as a whole to imagine the sort of needy, homeless life to which prosperous people rarely direct their attention. The drama as a whole, then, cultivates the type of sympathetic vision of which its characters speak. In the play, this kind of vivid imagining prompts a political decision against using Philoctetes as a means, and the audience is led to believe this to be a politically and morally valuable result. In this way, by showing the public benefits of the very sort of sympathy it is currently awakening in its spectators, the drama commends its own resources as valuable for the formation of decent citizenship and informed public choice. Although the good of the whole should not be neglected, that good will not be well served if human beings are seen simply as instruments of one another's purposes.

Ralph Ellison's *Invisible Man* (1952) develops this tradition of reflection about our failures of perception and recognition. Its hero describes himself as "invisible" because throughout the novel he is seen by those he encounters as a vehicle for various race-inflected stereotypes: the poor, humiliated black boy who snatches like an animal at the coins that lie on an electrified mat; the good student trusted to chauffeur a wealthy patron; the listening ear to whom this same patron unburdens his guilt and anxiety; the rabble-rousing activist who energizes an urban revolutionary movement; the violent rapist who gratifies the sexual imagination of a woman brought up on racially charged sexual images—always he is cast in a drama of someone else's making, "never more loved and appreciated" than when he plays his assigned role. The "others," meanwhile, are all "lost in a dream world"—in which they see only what their own minds have created, never the reality of the person who stands before them. "You go along for years knowing something is wrong, then suddenly you discover that you're as transparent as air." Invisibility is "a matter of the construction of their *inner eyes*, those eyes with which they look through their physical eyes upon reality."[2]

Ellison's grotesque, surreal world is very unlike the classical world of Sophocles' play. Its concerns, however, are closely linked: social stratification and injustice, manipulation and use, and above all invisibility and the condition of being transparent to and for one's fellow citizens. Like Sophocles' drama, it explores and savagely excoriates these refusals to see. Like that drama, it invites its readers to know and see more than the unseeing characters. "Being invisible and without substance, a disembodied voice, as it were, what else could I do? What else but try to tell you what was really happening when your eyes were looking through?"[3] In this way, it works upon the inner eyes of the very readers whose moral failures it castigates, although it refuses the easy notion that mutual visibility can be achieved in one heartfelt leap of brotherhood.

Ellison explicitly linked the novelist's art to the possibility of democracy. By representing both visibility and its evasions, both equality and its refusal, a novel, he wrote in an introduction, "could be fashioned as a raft of hope, perception and entertainment that might help keep us afloat as we tried to negotiate the snags and whirlpools that mark our nation's vacillating course toward and away from the democratic idea." This is not, he continued, the only goal for fiction; but it is one proper and urgent goal. For a democracy requires not only institutions and procedures; it also requires a particular quality of vision, in order "to defeat this national tendency to deny the common humanity shared by my character and those who might happen to read of his experience."[4] The novel's mordantly satirical treatment of stereotypes, its fantastic use of image and symbol (in, for example, the bizarre dreamlike sequence in the white-paint factory), and its poignant moments of disappointed hope, all contribute to this end.

As Ellison says, forming the civic imagination is not the only role for literature, but it is one salient role. Narrative art has the power to make us see the lives of the different with more than a casual tourist's interest—with involvement and sympathetic understanding, with anger at our society's refusals of visibility. We come to see how circumstances shape the lives of those who share with us some general goals and projects; and we see that circumstances shape not only people's possibilities for action, but also their aspirations and desires, hopes and fears. All of this seems highly pertinent to decisions we must make as citizens. Understanding, for example, how a history of racial stereotyping can affect self-esteem, achievement, and love enables us to make more informed judgments on issues relating to affirmative action and education.

. . .

When a child and a parent begin to tell stories together, the child is acquiring essential moral capacities. Even a simple nursery rhyme such as "Twinkle, twinkle little star, how I wonder what you are" leads children to feel wonder—a sense of mystery that mingles curiosity with awe.[5] Children wonder about the little star. In so doing they learn to imagine that a mere shape in the heavens has an inner world, in some ways mysterious, in some ways like their own. They learn to attribute life, emotion, and thought to a form whose insides are hidden. As time goes on, they do this in an increasingly sophisticated way, learning to hear and tell stories about animals and humans. These stories interact with their own attempts to explain the world and their own actions in it. A child deprived of stories is deprived, as well, of certain ways of viewing other people. For the insides of people, like the insides of stars, are not open to view. They must be wondered about. And the conclusion that this set of limbs in front of me has emotions and feelings and thoughts of the sort I attribute to myself will not be reached without the training of the imagination that storytelling promotes.

Narrative play does teach children to view a personlike shape as a house for hope and fear and love and anger, all of which they have known themselves. But the wonder involved in storytelling also makes evident the limits of each person's access to every other. "How I wonder what you are," goes the rhyme. In that simple expression is an acknowledgment of the lack of completeness in one's own grasp of the fear, the love, the sympathy, the anger, of the little star, or of any other creature or person. In fact the child adept at storytelling soon learns that people in stories are frequently easier to know than people in real life, who, as Proust puts it in *The Past Recaptured,* frequently offer "a dead weight that our sensitivity cannot remove," a closed exterior that cannot be penetrated even by a sensitive imagination. The child, wondering about its parents, soon learns about these obstacles, just as it also learns that its parents need not know everything that goes on in its own mind. The habits of wonder promoted by storytelling thus define the other person as spacious and deep, with qualitative differences from oneself and hidden places worthy of respect.

In these various ways, narrative imagination is an essential preparation for moral interaction. Habits of empathy and conjecture conduce to a certain type of citizenship and a certain form of community: one that cultivates a sympathetic responsiveness to another's needs, and understands the way circumstances shape those needs, while respecting separateness and privacy. This is so because of the way in which literary imagining both inspires intense concern with the fate of characters and defines those characters as containing a rich inner life, not all of which is open to view; in the process, the reader learns to have respect for the hidden contents of that inner world, seeing its importance in defining a creature as fully human.

Endnotes

1. The issues of this chapter are treated at greater length in Martha C. Nussbaum, *Poetic Justice: The Literary Imagination in Public Life* (Boston: Beacon Press, 1996).
2. Ralph Ellison, *Invisible Man* (New York: Random House, 1992), pp. 563, 566, 3.
3. Ibid., p. 572.
4. Ibid., pp. xxiv–xxv, xxvi.
5. See Nussbaum, *Poetic Justice,* for Dickens' discussion of this case.

1. Why does Nussbaum value the humanities, and literature in particular, as an important field of study?
2. According to Nussbaum, what types of educational value do the humanities hold?
3. What types of proof does Nussbaum offer for her claims about the value of humanities?
4. Based on Nussbaum's essay, what are some of the key characteristics of the humanities as an academic discipline or field of study?
5. What thinkers does Nussbaum most seem to value? What do they have in common?

The Natural Sciences

Practitioners of the natural sciences seek to bring order and reliability to their areas of study. That is not to say that natural scientists wholly accomplish that goal (or that they expect to). But these fields, generally speaking, tend toward this objective. For this reason, the sciences value empirical evidence. Empirical evidence is based in observable, repeatable phenomena. Though interpretation of that evidence does allow for a variety of conclusions, scientific method attempts to limit the role of individual interpretation and relies more on that which can be asserted with a fair amount of reliability—based on experimentation, experience, and repeatability. Some of the areas that are usually considered natural sciences are:

- mathematics
- physical science

- biology/life science
- chemistry
- geology
- astronomy

The writing done in the sciences is designed to remove as much interpretive bias and varying perspectives as possible. To do so, practitioners agree on the types of methodologies that are most likely to yield observable, sharable, and repeatable data—sometimes data that can be reduced to formulae. That is why the natural sciences rely on "controls" that attempt to isolate specific factors as crucial in natural processes.

WRITING TO EXPLORE 6.5

Below is an excerpt from a scientist who was also a prolific and influential writer. The name of Carl Sagan carries with it the type of situated *ethos* we discussed in Chapter 1 of this book—he was well known even beyond his own discourse community. Sagan was an astronomer, a NASA researcher (and public spokesman), a teacher at Cornell University, and an extremely popular writer and media personality. He published more than 600 scientific papers and popular articles and more than twenty books before his death in 1996.

In this excerpt, Sagan attempts to illustrate key facets of scientific methodology and to illustrate why the natural sciences are so crucial to the work of humanity. As you read the passage below, written by a well-known figure in the scientific community, you will likely find a great many possible stasis points with the conclusions that Martha Nussbaum draws from her observations of the humanities. Annotate as you read, marking what you take to be key passages that help to define this discourse community, and then respond in your writer's notebook to the series of questions that follow the reading.

Science and Hope

Carl Sagan

There is much that science doesn't understand, many mysteries still to be resolved. In a Universe tens of billions of light-years across and some ten or fifteen billion years old, this may be the case forever. We are constantly stumbling on surprises. Yet some New Age and religious writers assert that scientists believe that "what they find is all there is." Scientists may reject mystic revelations for which there is no evidence except somebody's say-so, but they hardly believe their knowledge of Nature to be complete.

Science is far from a perfect instrument of knowledge. It's just the best we have. In this respect, as in many others, it's like democracy. Science by itself cannot advocate courses of human action, but it can certainly illuminate the possible consequences of alternative courses of action.

The scientific way of thinking is at once imaginative and disciplined. This is central to its success. Science invites us to let the facts in, even when they don't conform to our preconceptions. It counsels us to carry alternative hypotheses in our heads and see which best fit the facts. It urges on us a delicate balance between no-holds-barred openness to new ideas, however heretical, and the most rigorous skeptical scrutiny of everything—new ideas and established wisdom. This kind of thinking is also an essential tool for a democracy in an age of change.

One of the reasons for its success is that science has built-in, error-correcting machinery at its very heart. Some may consider this an overbroad characterization, but to me every time we exercise self-criticism, every time we test our ideas against the outside world, we are doing science. When we are self-indulgent and uncritical, when we confuse hopes and facts, we slide into pseudoscience and superstition.

Every time a scientific paper presents a bit of data, it's accompanied by an error bar—a quiet but insistent reminder that no knowledge is complete or perfect. It's a calibration of how much we trust what we think we know. If the error bars are small, the accuracy of our empirical knowledge is high; if the error bars are large, then so is the uncertainty in our knowledge. Except in pure mathematics, nothing is known for certain (although much is certainly false).

Moreover, scientists are usually careful to characterize the veridical status of their attempts to understand the world—ranging from conjectures and hypotheses, which are highly tentative, all the way up to laws of Nature which are repeatedly and systematically confirmed through many interrogations of how the world works. But even laws of Nature are not absolutely certain. There may be new circumstances never before examined—inside black holes, say, or within the electron, or close to the speed of light—where even our vaunted laws of Nature break down and, however valid they may be in ordinary circumstances, need correction.

Humans may crave absolute certainty; they may aspire to it; they may pretend, as partisans of certain religions do, to have attained it. But the history of science—by far the most successful claim to knowledge accessible to humans— teaches that the most we can hope for is successive improvement in our understanding, learning from our mistakes, an asymptotic approach to the Universe, but with the proviso that absolute certainty will always elude us.

We will always be mired in error. The most each generation can hope for is to reduce the error bars a little, and to add to the body of data to which error bars apply. The error bar is a pervasive, visible self-assessment of the reliability of our knowledge. You can often see error bars in public opinion polls ("an uncertainty of plus or minus 3 percent," say). Imagine a society in which every speech in the *Congressional Record,* every television commercial, every sermon had an accompanying error bar or its equivalent.

One of the great commandments of science is, "Mistrust arguments from authority." (Scientists, being primates, and thus given to dominance hierarchies, of course do not always follow this commandment.) Too many such arguments have proved too painfully wrong. Authorities must prove their contentions like everybody else. This independence of science, its occasional unwillingness to accept conventional wisdom, makes it dangerous to doctrines less self-critical, or with pretensions to certitude.

Because science carries us toward an understanding of how the world is, rather than how we would wish it to be, its findings may not in all cases be immediately comprehensible or satisfying. It may take a little work to restructure our mindsets. Some of science is very simple. When it gets complicated, that's usually because the world is complicated—or because we're complicated. When we shy away from it because it seems too difficult (or because we've been taught so poorly), we surrender the ability to take charge of our future. We are disenfranchised. Our self-confidence erodes.

But when we pass beyond the barrier, when the findings and methods of science get through to us, when we understand and put this knowledge to use, many feel deep satisfaction. This is true for everyone, but especially for children—born with a zest for knowledge, aware that they must live in a future molded by science, but so often convinced in their adolescence that science is not for them. I know personally, both from having science explained to me and from my attempts to explain it to others, how gratifying it is when we get it, when obscure terms suddenly take on meaning, when we grasp what all the fuss is about, when deep wonders are revealed.

In its encounter with Nature, science invariably elicits a sense of reverence and awe. The very act of understanding is a celebration of joining, merging, even if on a very modest scale, with the magnificence of the Cosmos. And the cumulative worldwide buildup of knowledge over time converts science into something only a little short of a transnational, transgenerational meta-mind.

"Spirit" comes from the Latin word "to breathe." What we breathe is air, which is certainly matter, however thin. Despite usage to the contrary, there is no necessary implication in the word "spiritual" that we are talking of anything other than matter (including the matter of which the brain is made), or anything outside the realm of science. On occasion, I will feel free to use the word. Science is not only compatible with spirituality; it is a profound source of spirituality. When we recognize our place in an immensity of light-years and in the passage of ages, when we grasp the intricacy, beauty, and subtlety of life, then that soaring feeling, that sense of elation and humility combined, is surely spiritual. So are our emotions in the presence of great art or music or literature, or of acts of exemplary selfless courage such as those of Mohandas Gandhi or Martin Luther King, Jr. The notion that science and spirituality are somehow mutually exclusive does a disservice to both.

Science may be hard to understand. It may challenge cherished beliefs. When its products are placed at the disposal of politicians or industrialists, it may lead to weapons of mass destruction and grave threats to the environment. But one thing you have to say about it: It delivers the goods.

Not every branch of science can foretell the future—paleontology can't—but many can and with stunning accuracy. If you want to know when the next eclipse of the Sun will be, you might try magicians or mystics, but you'll do much better with scientists. They will tell you where on Earth to stand, when you have to be there, and whether it will be a partial eclipse, a total eclipse, or an annular eclipse. They can routinely predict a solar eclipse, to the minute, a millennium in advance. You can go to the witch doctor to lift the spell that causes your pernicious anemia, or you can take vitamin B12. If you want to save your child from polio, you can pray or you can inoculate. If you're interested in the sex of your unborn child, you can consult plumb-bob danglers all you want (left-right, a boy; forward-back, a girl—or maybe it's the other way around), but they'll be right, on average, only one time in two. If you want real accuracy (here, 99 percent accuracy), try amniocentesis and sonograms. Try science.

Think of how many religions attempt to validate themselves with prophecy. Think of how many people rely on these prophecies, however vague, however unfulfilled, to support or prop up their beliefs. Yet has there ever been a religion with the prophetic accuracy and reliability of science? There isn't a religion on the planet that doesn't long for a comparable ability—precise, and repeatedly demonstrated before committed skeptics—to foretell future events. No other human institution comes close.

Is this worshiping at the altar of science? Is this replacing one faith by another, equally arbitrary? In my view, not at all. The directly observed success of science is the reason I advocate its use. If something else worked better, I would advocate the something else. Does science insulate itself from philosophical criticism? Does it define itself as having a monopoly on the "truth"? Think again of that eclipse a thousand years in the future. Compare as many doctrines as you can think of, note what predictions they make of the future, which ones are vague, which ones are precise, and which doctrines—every one of them subject to human fallibility—have error-correcting mechanisms built in. Take account of the fact that not one of them is perfect. Then simply pick the one that in a fair comparison works (as opposed to feels) best. If different doctrines are superior in quite separate and independent fields, we are of course free to choose several—but not if they contradict one another. Far from being idolatry, this is the means by which we can distinguish the false idols from the real thing.

Again, the reason science works so well is partly that built-in error-correcting machinery. There are no forbidden questions in science, no matters too sensitive or delicate to be probed, no scared truths. That openness to new ideas, combined with the most rigorous, skeptical scrutiny of all ideas, sifts the wheat from the chaff. It makes no difference how smart, august, or beloved you are. You must prove your case in the face of determined, expert criticism. Diversity and debate are valued. Opinions are encouraged to contend—substantively and in depth.

The process of science may sound messy and disorderly. In a way, it is. If you examine science in its everyday aspect, of course you find that scientists run the gamut of human emotion, personality, and character. But there's one facet that is really striking to the outsider, and that is the gauntlet of criticism considered acceptable or even desirable. There is much warm and inspired encouragement of apprentice scientists by their mentors. But the poor graduate student at his or her Ph.D. oral exam is subjected to a withering crossfire of questions from the very professors who have the candidate's future in their grasp. Naturally the students are nervous; who wouldn't be? True, they've prepared for it for years. But they understand that at this critical moment, they have to be able to answer searching questions posed by experts. So in preparing to defend their theses, they must practice a very useful habit of thought: They must anticipate questions; they have to ask: Where in my dissertation is there a weakness that someone else might find? I'd better identify it before they do.

You sit in at contentious scientific meetings. You find university colloquia in which the speaker has hardly gotten 30 seconds into the talk before there are devastating questions and comments from the audience. You examine the conventions in which a written report is submitted to a scientific journal, for possible publication, then is conveyed by the editor to anonymous referees whose job it is to ask: Did the author do anything stupid? Is there anything in here that is sufficiently interesting to be published? What are the deficiencies of this paper? Have the main results been found by anybody else? Is the argument adequate, or should the paper be resubmitted after the author has actually demonstrated what is here only speculated on? And it's anonymous: The author doesn't know who the critics are. This is the everyday expectation in the scientific community.

Why do we put up with it? Do we like to be criticized? No, no scientist enjoys it. Every scientist feels a proprietary affection for his or her ideas and findings. Even so, you don't reply to critics. Wait a minute; this is a really good idea; I'm very fond of it; it's done you no harm; please leave it alone. Instead, the hard but just rule is that if the ideas don't work, you must throw them away. Don't waste neurons on what doesn't work. Devote those neurons to new ideas that better explain the data. The British physicist Michael Faraday warned of the powerful temptation

> to seek for such evidence and appearances as are in the favour of our desires, and to disregard those which oppose them. . . . We receive as friendly that which agrees with [us], we resist with dislike that which opposes us; whereas the very reverse is required by every dictate of common sense.

Valid criticism does you a favor.

Some people consider science arrogant—especially when it purports to contradict beliefs of long standing or when it introduces bizarre concepts that seem contradictory to common sense. Like an earthquake that rattles our faith in the very ground we're standing on, challenging our accustomed beliefs, shaking the doctrines we have grown to rely upon can be profoundly disturbing. Nevertheless, I maintain that science is part and parcel humility. Scientists do not seek to impose their needs and wants on Nature, but instead humbly interrogate Nature and take seriously what they find. We are aware that revered scientists have been wrong. We understand human imperfection. We insist on independent and—to the extent possible—quantitative verification of proposed tenets of belief. We are constantly prodding, challenging, seeking contradictions or small, persistent residual errors, proposing alternative explanations, encouraging heresy. We give our highest rewards to those who convincingly disprove established beliefs.

. . .

Read the following two paragraphs—not to understand the science described, but to get a feeling for the author's style of thinking. He is facing anomalies, apparent paradoxes in physics: "asymmetries" he calls them. What can we learn from them?

> It is known that Maxwell's electrodynamics—as usually understood at the present time—when applied to moving bodies, leads to asymmetries which do not appear to be inherent in the phenomena. Take, for example, the reciprocal electrodynamic action of a magnet and a conductor. The observable phenomenon here depends only on the relative motion of the conductor and the magnet, whereas the customary view draws a sharp distinction between the two cases in which either the one or the other of these bodies is in motion. For if the magnet is in motion and the conductor at rest, there arises in the neigh-

bourhood of the magnet an electric field with a certain definite energy, producing a current at the places where parts of the conductor are situated. But if the magnet is stationary and the conductor in motion, no electric field arises in the neighbourhood of the magnet. In the conductor, however, we find an electromotive force, to which in itself there is no corresponding energy, but which gives rise—assuming equality of relative motion in the two cases discussed—to electric currents of the same path and intensity as those produced by the electric forces in the former case.

Examples of this sort, together with the unsuccessful attempts to discover any motion of the earth relative to the "ether," suggest that the phenomena of electrodynamics as well as of mechanics possess no properties corresponding to the idea of absolute rest. They suggest rather that, as has already been shown to the first order of small quantities, the same laws of electrodynamics and optics will be valid for all frames of reference for which the equations of mechanics hold good.

What is the author trying to tell us here? . . . [W]e can perhaps recognize that the language is spare, technical, cautious, clear, and not a jot more complicated than it need be. You would not offhand guess from how it's phrased (or from its unostentatious title, "On the Electrodynamics of Moving Bodies") that this article represents the crucial arrival of the theory of Special Relativity into the world, the gateway to the triumphant announcement of the equivalence of mass and energy, the deflation of the conceit that our small world occupies some "privileged reference frame" in the Universe, and in several different ways an epochal event in human history. The opening words of Albert Einstein's 1905 paper are characteristic of the scientific report. It is refreshingly unself-serving, circumspect, understated. Contrast its restrained tone with, say, the products of modern advertising, political speeches, authoritative theological pronouncements—or for that matter the blurb on the cover of this book.

Notice how Einstein's paper begins by trying to make sense of experimental results. Wherever possible, scientists experiment. Which experiments suggest themselves often depends on which theories currently prevail. Scientists are intent on testing those theories to the breaking point. They do not trust what is intuitively obvious. That the Earth is flat was once obvious. That heavy bodies fall faster than light ones was once obvious. That bloodsucking leeches cure most diseases was once obvious. That some people are naturally and by divine decree slaves was once obvious. That there is such a place as the center of the Universe, and that the Earth sits in that exalted spot was once obvious. That there is an absolute standard of rest was once obvious. The truth may be puzzling or counterintuitive. It may contradict deeply held beliefs. Experiment is how we get a handle on it.

At a dinner many decades ago, the physicist Robert W. Wood was asked to respond to the toast, "To physics and metaphysics." By "metaphysics," people then meant something like philosophy, or truths you could recognize just by thinking about them. They could also have included pseudoscience. Wood answered along these lines:

The physicist has an idea. The more he thinks it through, the more sense it seems to make. He consults the scientific literature. The more he reads, the more promising the idea becomes. Thus prepared, he goes to the laboratory and devises an experiment to test it. The experiment is painstaking. Many possibilities are checked. The accuracy of measurement is refined, the error bars reduced. He lets the chips fall where they may. He is devoted only to what the experiment teaches. At the end of all this work, through careful experimentation, the idea is found to be worthless. So the physicist discards it, frees his mind from the clutter of error, and moves on to something else.[1]

The difference between physics and metaphysics, Wood concluded as he raised his glass high, is not that the practitioners of one are smarter than the practitioners of the other. The difference is that the metaphysicist has no laboratory.

For me, there are four main reasons for a concerted effort to convey science—in radio, TV, movies, newspapers, books, computer programs, theme parks, and classrooms—to every citizen. In all uses of science, it is insufficient—indeed it is dangerous—to produce only a small, highly competent, well-rewarded priesthood of professionals. Instead, some fundamental understanding of the findings and methods of science must be available on the broadest scale.

- Despite plentiful opportunities for misuse, science can be the golden road out of poverty and backwardness for emerging nations. It makes national economies and the global civilization run. Many nations understand this. It is why so many graduate students in science and engineering at American universities—still the best in the world—are from other countries. The corollary, one that the United States sometimes fails to grasp, is that abandoning science is the road back into poverty and backwardness.

- Science alerts us to the perils introduced by our world-altering technologies, especially to the global environment on which our lives depend. Science provides an essential early warning system.

- Science teaches us about the deepest issues of origins, natures, and fates—of our species, of life, of our planet, of the Universe. For the first time in human history we are able to secure a real understanding of some of these matters. Every culture on Earth has addressed such issues and valued their importance. All of us feel goosebumps when we approach these grand questions. In the long run, the greatest gift of science may be in teaching us, in ways no other human endeavor has been able, something about our cosmic context, about where, when, and who we are.

- The values of science and the values of democracy are concordant, in many cases indistinguishable. Science and democracy began—in their civilized incarnations—in the same time and place. Greece in the seventh and sixth centuries B.C. Science confers power on anyone who takes the trouble to learn it (although too many have been systematically prevented from doing so). Science thrives on, indeed requires, the free exchange of ideas; its values are antithetical to secrecy. Science holds to no special vantage points or privileged positions. Both science and democracy encourage unconventional opinions and vigorous debate. Both demand adequate reason, coherent argument, rigorous standards of evidence and honesty. Science is a way to call the bluff of those who only pretend to knowledge. It is a bulwark against mysticism, against superstition, against religion misapplied to where it has no business being. If we're true to its values, it can tell us when we're being lied to. It provides a mid-course correction to our mistakes. The more widespread its language, rules, and methods, the better chance we have of preserving what Thomas Jefferson and his colleagues had in mind. But democracy can also be subverted more thoroughly through the products of science than any pre-industrial demagogue ever dreamed.

Finding the occasional straw of truth awash in a great ocean of confusion and bamboozle requires vigilance, dedication, and courage. But if we don't practice these tough habits of thought, we cannot hope to solve the truly serious problems that face us—and we risk becoming a nation of suckers, a world of suckers, up for grabs by the next charlatan who saunters along.

Endnotes

1. As the pioneering physicist Benjamin Franklin put it, "In going on with these experiments, how many pretty systems do we build, which we soon find ourselves obliged to destroy?" At the very least, he thought, the experience sufficed to "help to make a vain Man humble."

---

1. Based on your reading of Sagan, develop a definition of *science* that you believe Sagan (and other scientists) would accept.

2. According to Sagan, what types of evidence are valued by the natural sciences?

3. In what ways is science, despite its empirical basis, a creative discipline? How is that creativity illustrated in this reading selection?

4. Imagine a dialog between Nussbaum and Sagan about the relative values of science and humanities. What might each say about the value of his or her discipline in relation to other disciplines?

5. Both Nussbaum and Sagan relate their discipline's work to the success of democracy. According to each author, why is their discipline especially crucial to a democratic society? Do they seem to have the same definition of democracy and its goals?

6. What conclusions can you draw about the differences between the modes of proof that are most important in the sciences and those that are in the humanities? What can those differences tell you about how you might read differently depending on the discourse community?

The Social Sciences

As a study of human behavior (and the behavior of humans in groups), practitioners of the social sciences share concerns with the humanities. But in their attempt to bring order and predictability to behavior and to study it through observable (empirical) evidence, these professionals share a good deal with natural scientists as well.

Some of the areas that are usually considered social sciences are:

- sociology
- psychology
- criminal justice
- education
- anthropology

The first thing to note about the social sciences is that they do identify themselves as *sciences*—that is, the social sciences are "scientific" in their methodologies. Either through observation of naturally occurring phenomena among humans (case studies) or through laboratory experiments, social scientists attempt to find patterns in human behavior, to isolate and control for specific factors, and to find correlations among behaviors—that is, to find the influence of some stimulus or cause on human reactions. What causes a person to become a criminal? What social influences cause a student to succeed in school? What factors about urban life define the way people behave in cities? Questions like these are studied systematically in order to increase knowledge of human motivation and, in some cases, to improve the quality of human interactions (or individual lives).

The writing done in the social sciences, then, shows characteristics of both humanistic and scientific writing. The writing in the social sciences, like that in the natural sciences, is concerned with proper method—with formulating and describing studies that are less likely to create biased or individualized observations. It values reliability over personal interpretation. However, like writing in the humanities, much of the writing in the social sciences is narrative: It tells stories, uses descriptive details, and provides in-depth characterizations of individuals and groups.

WRITING TO EXPLORE 6.6

Below is an excerpt from Juliet B. Schor's *The Overspent American*. Schor, a sociologist and the director of studies for Harvard's Women's Studies program, has written and lectured extensively on the topic of work. Annotate as you read, considering the ways in which Schor demonstrates the reliability of her conclusions through carefully collected data. Also note the ways in which she uses stories and description to illustrate the human element within the subjects she discusses.

A Test of Status Consumption: Women's Cosmetics

Juliet B. Schor

A few years ago, a student and I designed a test that can differentiate between consuming with and without a "status" element. We look at buying patterns across products that are similar in most respects but differ in their social visibility. We test to see whether people pay more for products with higher social visibility. The reason: visible goods give status that invisibles do not. For example, we predict that people will spend more money on furnishings for the living room than for the bedroom. Or that they will buy a notch above their usual price range for a coat (the most visible apparel item), or that they are more likely to wear underwear than shirts from WalMart. In tests of this sort, it is important to control for differences in quality and functional requirements. So, in looking at home furnishings, we would compare purchasing patterns for two functionally similar items, such as living room and bedroom curtains. (When discussing this project with a colleague, he reported that he decided not to buy curtains for the bedroom at all, because no one would know they were missing!)

Our test is from women's cosmetics, a multibillion-dollar business. This industry provides a fascinating look into the workings of appearance, illusion, and status. In many ways, the cosmetics companies are not too different from the snake oil peddlers of the nineteenth century. Despite the white coats of the salespeople (to make them look scientific), the hype about company "laboratories," and the promises made in the advertising, it's hard to take the effectiveness claims too seriously. Names like "Eye Repair Diffusion Zone," "Ceramide Time

Complex Capsules," and "Extrait Vital, Multi-Active Revitalizer with Apple Alpha-Acids" don't help the products' credibility either.

But despite its dubious effectiveness, women keep on buying the stuff. They shell out hundreds, even thousands, for wrinkle cream, moisturizers, eye shadows and powders, lipsticks, and facial makeup. And why? One explanation is that they are looking for affordable luxury, the thrill of buying at the expensive department store, indulging in a fantasy of beauty and sexiness, buying "hope in a bottle." Cosmetics are an escape from an otherwise all too drab everyday existence.

While there is undoubtedly truth in this explanation, it is by no means the whole story. Even in cosmetics—which is hardly the first product line that comes to mind as a status symbol—there's a structure of "one-up-womanship." It turns out that women are looking for prestige in their makeup case. Why do they pay twenty dollars for a Chanel lipstick when they could buy the same product for a fraction of the cost? They want the name. As *Mademoiselle*'s publisher, Catherine Viscardi Johnston, explains, "If they can't afford a Chanel suit, they'll buy a Chanel lipstick or nail polish and move up later." Crude as it may sound, many women want or need to be seen with an acceptable brand. A caption describing a Chanel lipstick in a recent newspaper article puts it bluntly: "A classic shade of scarlet, scented with essential oil of roses, in Chanel's signature black and gold case. Perfect for preening in public." One of my downshifters has less expensive taste (and less money than the typical Chanel buyer), but she conforms to the same principle: "I have a fifteen dollar lipstick I only take out in company," she tells me.

The status component in cosmetics purchasing comes out clearly in our research. We have looked at brand purchasing patterns for four cosmetics products: lipsticks, eye shadows, mascaras, and facial cleansers. Facial cleansers are the least socially visible of the four because they are almost always used at home in the bathroom. After a woman applies makeup in the morning, she doesn't clean her face again until she takes the makeup off. Eye shadows and mascaras are in an intermediate category. Women do reapply them during the day, typically in semipublic "powder rooms" (note the name). Lipsticks are the most visible of the four products. They are applied not only in the semipublic rooms but in public itself, at the end of a meal, in an elevator, on an airplane. The visibility difference can also be seen in the packaging strategies of the companies. Lipstick containers are quite distinctive and recognizable from across a table, while containers for mascara and facial cleansers are less so. (Eye shadows are often packaged to match lipsticks.) If you are skeptical, try this experiment, possible only with upscale women, and most naturally done over dinner. When the lipsticks start appearing after the dessert, ask each person how many of the brands they can recognize from across the table. When I tried this, the level of recognition was impressive.

To test our assumptions about the relative visibilities of the four products, my former Harvard student and coauthor Angela Chao conducted an informal survey among Harvard students, who reproduced our rankings nearly to a woman. Lipsticks are most visible, facial cleansers are least visible, and eye shadows and mascaras are intermediate. Having established the differences in social visibility across this group of cosmetics products, we then tested two propositions. The first was that socially visible products deliver less quality for a given price. And the second was that people buy top-end brands of visible products far more than high-quality invisible ones.

Independent quality tests conducted by *Consumer Reports* reveal that among a range of brand lipsticks consumers did not find systematic quality differences. Of course, there are different types of lipsticks. But within types, the lipsticks tend to be chemically similar, and users rated none of them better than any other in terms of quality, despite prices ranging from a few dollars to twenty-five dollars (see figure on page 264). By contrast, users can distinguish between the qualities of facial cleansers, thereby supporting our prediction that with visible products price is less connected to quality. The fraction of expensive brands purchased also varies systematically with visibility, as shown in the figure on page 265. Women are far more likely to buy expensive lipsticks than they are to buy expensive facial cleansers. In fact, with lipsticks, the higher the price, the more consumers tend to purchase them. This finding flies in the face of the received wisdom that a higher price discourages buyers. (Regression analyses contained in Chao and Schor [1998] make these points in more detail.)

This perverse relation between price and demand has been called the snob effect, to highlight the role of social status in such purchasing. How else can we explain the results of the cosmetics study? If women were merely in search of quality, attractive packaging, the chance to buy something at a swanky department store, the illusion that they could look like a model, or any of the many other explanations that have been offered for the success of this industry, we would not have found the patterns of purchasing across these four products that we did. Women would be buying expensive facial cleansers at the same rate that they buy expensive lipsticks. They would be getting all their cosmetics in the department store and not picking up the facial cleanser at the local druggist. Buying patterns across the four products would not differ.

Of course, this test does not explain what is going on in consumers' heads, that is, whether they desire social status or are trying to avoid social humiliation. We cannot say whether they are even conscious of the buying pattern we have found, and we can infer nothing concerning their feelings—for example, whether they enjoy consuming status goods or feel oppressed by a perceived need to do so. However, the absence of direct information on the inner life of the consumer

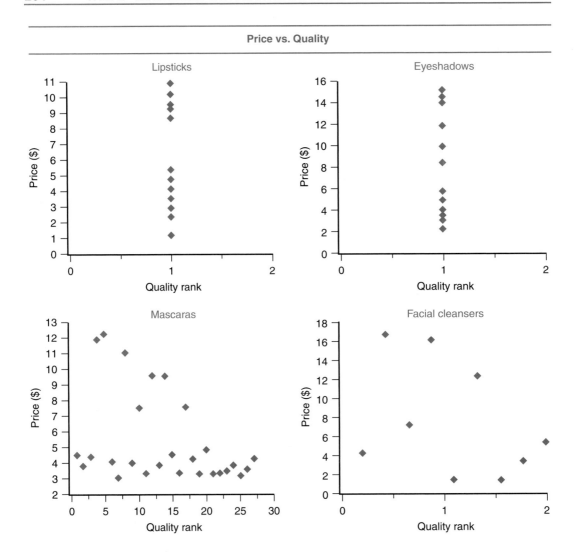

should not detract from these findings. Unlike other approaches, this is a decisive test. There is no other plausible explanation for the marked differences in brand buying by the public-ness of the product.

Of course, there is more to status than visibility. As I argued earlier, nonvisible commodities do become status symbols—foreign travel, a particular hairdresser, or a vacation home that none of your colleagues have actually seen. Information about your nonvisible possessions is typically passed verbally—in the first instance by yourself, and secondarily by others. Talking is an imperfect but

Product Distribution Graphs

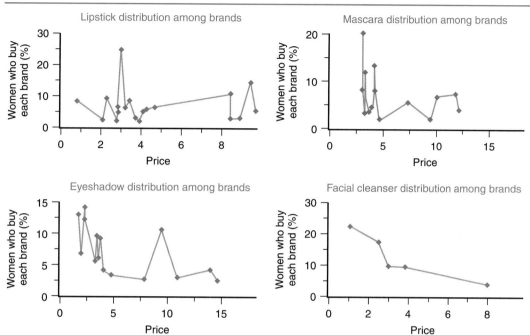

Lipstick distribution among brands

Mascara distribution among brands

Eyeshadow distribution among brands

Facial cleanser distribution among brands

somewhat effective method of creating desire and emulative behavior. There is also the possibility of private approaches to status symbolism, particularly for people whose values or personality make them reluctant to participate publicly. These people can join in by purchasing less conspicuous products or refraining from advertising what they have. A woman can derive inner satisfaction from buying unknown but expensive designer clothes, knowing they are luxury items that would confer status if others knew about them. At the same time, she does not have to contend with the negative psychic consequences associated with flaunting wealth, besting others, or trying to impress. But these exceptions aside, visibility and status do go together.

1. In what ways does Schor's writing illustrate her use of scientific method (observation of empirical evidence, statistics and other quantified information, careful description of methodology) to show reliability? List and comment on examples. Would Sagan accept her work as science?

2. In what ways does Schor's writing use description and narrative to illustrate the human characteristics that are crucial to the social sciences? List and comment on examples.

3. In what ways does Schor rely on previous knowledge and studies to support her contentions? List and comment on examples.

4. Schor addresses some of the limitations of the social sciences when she notes that "Of course, this test does not explain what is going on in consumers' heads, that is, whether they desire social status or are trying to avoid social humiliation. . . . However, the absence of direct information on the inner life of the consumer should not detract from these findings." What does this tell you about the work of the social sciences? Can you identify other passages where Schor addresses the value and/or shortcomings of the methods of the social sciences?

5. Though, unlike Nussbaum and Sagan, Schor does not directly address the importance of the social sciences within the wider community, her essay clearly does have implications for our society. What are some of those implications?

6. In what ways might the research done by this social scientist be interesting and useful to those in the field of business? In what ways can the methods of the social sciences contribute to the goals of business?

Business

Though the fields of business are clearly practical—they are devoted to creating financially successful endeavors—they are also areas of academic study. Areas of study in business include:

- marketing
- management
- organizational behavior
- economics
- advertising
- information systems
- accounting
- industrial engineering

Business encompasses many of the other fields we already discussed. It requires a solid understanding of human behavior; it requires a scientific and quantifiable methodology that breeds predictable and reliable results; and it often requires (in marketing and advertising, for example) a solid understanding of human emotions and a strong sense of the emotional and interpretive.

The academic study of business, and the writing done in conjunction with it, ranges widely among the other disciplines. People interested in organizational behavior cross the line into the social sciences. Accountants are "scientific" in their analytical methods and rely heavily on mathematics. Communication skills nurtured in the humanities become extremely important in the workplace and in customer relations, as can narratives and case studies of successful business ventures. Above all, professionals in the business fields are practical. They seek solutions to problems that can interfere with the success of businesses, both internally and externally. The types of writing done in business is as diverse as its concerns.

WRITING TO EXPLORE 6.7

Below is an excerpt from Tom Kelley's book *The Art of Innovation*. This description of the work done by one of America's most successful design firms provides insight into the types of thinking that inform the business fields. Though businesspeople can expect to do many other types of writing, this piece illustrates well the ways in which invention, a concept we have discussed at great length, informs this discipline. Annotate this piece, focusing on unique aspects of this community's work.

Building in Creativity and Innovation

Tom Kelley

Why should business care about creativity? Visit your local mall or trade show and you'll see that creativity sells. We're all searching for the next Mac or VW Beetle—any worthwhile innovation that captures the public's imagination and strengthens the company's brand. But many companies shy away from novel solutions. Moreover, they tend to believe that truly creative individuals are few and far between. We believe the opposite. We *all* have a creative side, and it can flourish if you spawn a culture to encourage it, one that embraces risks and wild ideas and tolerates the occasional failure. We've seen it happen.

. . .

What do stand-up toothpaste tubes, all-in-one fishing kits, high-tech blood analyzers, flexible office shelves, and self-sealing sports bottles have in common? Nothing actually, except that they're all IDEO-designed products that were inspired by watching real people.

We're not big fans of focus groups. We don't much care for traditional market research either. We go to the source. Not the "experts" inside a company, but the actual people who use the product or something similar to what we're hoping to create.

Plenty of well-meaning clients duly inform us what a new product needs to do. They already "know" how people use their products. They're so familiar with their customers and existing product line that they can rattle off half a dozen good reasons why an innovation is impractical. Of course, we listen to these concerns. Then we get in the operating room, so to speak, and see for ourselves.

A few years back, for example, Silicon Valley–based Advanced Cardiovascular Systems asked us to help it redesign a critical medical instrument used on heart patients during balloon angioplasty. The company sold an inflation device for the tiny balloon that the doctor inserts with a catheter through the femoral artery in a patient's leg. The balloon is guided up into the obstructed coronary artery and inflated, compressing the plaque and stretching the artery. ACS told us that the new inflation device—like the existing one—had to be suitable for one-handed use.

But when we went into the operating room—literally—that's not what we saw. Although the current product could theoretically be used with one hand, it really worked that way only if you had a hand the size of Michael Jordan's. In actual practice, medical technicians almost always used both hands with the device, since, as we observed, they weren't doing anything else with their "spare" hand. So why not design the new "Indeflator," we thought, for a two-handed technician? Why fight human instinct?

It's precisely this sort of observation-fueled insight that makes innovation possible. Uncovering what comes naturally to people. And having the strength to change the rules. From the simple observation that technicians used both hands flowed distinct improvements. We added ribs to the base of the pumplike device so that technicians could hold it steady in one hand while they inflated the balloon with the other hand. We tilted the pressure gauge upward so that it was easy to read during inflation. We increased control and precision. We made it easier to deflate the balloon too. And we made one other big change.

There's a critical moment in an angioplasty procedure when the surgeon instructs a technician to inflate the balloon. During the next sixty seconds or so, the balloon obstructs the artery, creating, in effect, a heart attack. At that point, with the patient still awake, the old device would make a loud clicking noise as it ratcheted into place.

Our new design lost that scary ratcheting sound.

Time in the Jungle

Clicks-and-mortar brokerage founder Charles Schwab has talked about his effort to assume the perspective of his customers. "I am like a chef. I like to taste the food. If it tastes bad. I don't serve it. I'm constantly monitoring what we do, and I'm always looking for better ways we can provide financial services, ways that would make me happy if I were a client."

Noble aspirations, and you can't argue with Schwab's track record, but we believe you have to go beyond putting yourself in your customers' shoes. Indeed, we believe it's not even enough to ask people what they think about a product or idea.

One reason is the same factor that prevents you from learning that your meat loaf tastes like sawdust. Your dinner guests are too polite to tell you the unvarnished truth, too wrapped up in trying to give you the expected answer. How's the meat loaf? "Fine," they say, "Delicious," if they care about you or think it will make you happy. How many people volunteer that they're having a lousy day? It's human nature to put a bright face on a dismal situation. Because there's no information, no value, no content to the "fine" response, we sometimes say, "Fine is a four-letter word."

A second reason for the "fine" response is that your guests don't know or can't articulate the "true" answer. Maybe the meat loaf needs more salt or less onion. The problem is that your guests may like to eat, but they're probably not food critics. In business, too, your customers may lack the vocabulary or the palate to explain what's wrong, and especially what's *missing*.

Companies shouldn't ask them to.

This is particularly true of new-to-the-world products or services. A user of a new type of remote control may not be able to recognize that it has too many buttons. Inexperienced computer users may not be able to explain that your Website lacks navigational clues. And they shouldn't have to. We saw this first-hand when a software company asked us to find out how users would react to one of their new applications. We set up a few computers and observed people struggling with the program. More than a couple were having a terrible time, grimacing and sighing audibly as they fumbled with the keyboard and mouse. But in exit interviews, the software company was given a different story. Those same people swore that they'd had no trouble with the new application and couldn't imagine a single improvement.

Customers mean well—and they're trying to be helpful—but it's not their job to be visionaries. Indeed, former 3Com CEO Bob Metcalfe tells the story of how, in the early eighties, his customers and salespeople practically *demanded* that he dedicate their R&D efforts to making a new version of its networking card for multibus-compatible computers. Metcalfe balked, and some of his salespeople quit in protest, disgusted that the company seemed to be ignoring the requests of its own customers. Instead, 3Com chose to develop an EtherLink card that worked with the new IBM PC. Today there are *no* multibus computers left in the world, but 3Com ships more than 20 million EtherLink cards a year.

Seeing and hearing things with your own eyes and ears is a critical first step in improving or creating a breakthrough product. We typically call this process "human factors." I prefer "human inspiration" or, as IDEO human factors expert

Leon Segal says, "Innovation begins with an eye." It is a general principle of humankind. Scientists, industrialists, anthropologists, artists, and writers have understood this for centuries, and many entrepreneurs understand it intuitively.

Once you start observing carefully, all kinds of insights and opportunities can open up. For example, the hugely popular elliptical crosstrainer exercise machines in your local health club got started from a simple human observation. Larry Miller, a human-factors-savvy person working at General Motors, was videotaping his daughter running one day and noticed the elliptical path traced by her feet as she went through her exercise. From that observation-based spark, Miller set about building a prototype of a device that would mimic his daughter's elliptical movement—without the jarring impact of feet hitting the ground. He sold his idea to Seattle-based fitness equipment maker Precor, Inc., which developed it into its EFX line of elliptical trainers. Thanks in part to Miller's epiphany, Precor is now the fastest-growing equipment company in the health club industry.

Netting a Bug List

Sometimes—if you're lucky—you can find inspiration for innovation by observing yourself. In many parts of your life, you go through steps so mechanically, so unconsciously, that this is not possible. When you're off your own beaten path, however, you are more open to discovery: when you travel, especially overseas; when you rent an unfamiliar car; when you try a new sport or experience a new activity. At those times, you are more open to ask the childlike "Why?" and "Why not?" questions that lead to innovation. Whenever you are in that new-to-the-experience mode, I would urge you to pay close attention and even take notes about your impressions, reactions, and questions. Especially the problems, the things that bug you. We call these mental and jotted-down observations "bug lists," and they can change your life. That's what happened one day to twenty-six-year-old Perry Klebahn on a visit to a Lake Tahoe ski resort.

Klebahn was recovering from an ankle fracture, and although he could walk without pain, his doctor had warned that skiing was inadvisable. Still wanting to meet his friends for lunch on the slopes, Klebahn discovered that the resort had some snowshoes available to help him traverse the snowy terrain. Using snowshoes for the first time, he was struck by how incredibly awkward they were to use. For one thing, they weighed more than ten pounds, turning what would have been a pleasant walk into serious exercise. On level or uphill terrain, the front of the snowshoes would fill up with snow, making them even heavier and causing you to trip over your own feet. Whenever there was a downhill slope, the shoes were hard to control and would sometimes slip out from under you. All in all, a pretty unpleasant experience, and a product category that had not seen much innovation since Lewis and Clark. A fatalist would have just written off snowshoes as awkward, antiquated equipment, but Klebahn was a Stanford product design student at the time, learning how to sharpen his observation skills, keeping bug lists, and asking a lot of "why?/why not?" questions.

Inspired by observing his own difficulties with the existing technology, Klebahn—while still a student—formed Atlas Snowshoe Company, which almost single-handedly created today's snowshoe industry. Using a clever design and high-tech materials, he cut the weight of the snowshoes by 70 percent and made them easy to use on any terrain. That left the small task of creating an industry around his new product, but within a few years, Atlas had partnered with ski resorts from Vancouver to Sun Valley in creating snowshoeing areas. Resorts initially worried "if we build one, will they come?" but a single snowshoe area at Vail boasted more than 100,000 visitors by its second season. Perry Klebahn, starting with a single observation, then following up with a lot of creativity and hard work, grew Atlas Snowshoe Company to more than $10 million in sales and then sold the company.

Anecdotal? Yes, but hardly an isolated case. Ask around, and you'll find that many entrepreneurs got started by observing humans struggling with tired routines and asking themselves what they could do about it. Scott Cook, cofounder of Intuit, got the idea for the company's first product by observing his wife paying the bills in the slightly tedious manual way. He wondered whether there wasn't a way to "quicken" that process. Intuit had sales of almost a billion dollars in 1999, and Quicken is still the company's most successful product.

Keeping Close to the Action

Whether it's art, science, technology, or business, inspiration often comes from being close to the action. That's part of why geography, even in the Internet age, counts. And why so many high-tech companies have emerged from Silicon Valley—and not Connecticut or even New York. New ideas come from seeing, smelling, hearing—being there.

This sensory immersion is why people still fly to other parts of the country for face-to-face meetings with clients, customers, and colleagues, even in the information age: why phone or videoconferencing often doesn't do it. It's also why people still go to museums, to be inspired in the presence of original artwork, though a digital image may be easily available on their home computer screen.

Asking questions of people who were there, who should know, often isn't enough. It doesn't matter how smart they are, how well they know the product or the opportunities. It doesn't matter how many astute questions you ask. If you're not in the jungle, you're not going to know the tiger.

1. What commonplaces of business fields are reflected in this description of the work done by IDEO?

2. How are narratives of other businesses used to illustrate the principles Kelley is presenting? In what ways does business rely on some of the same types of invention that we discussed in relation to effective writing?

3. How is success measured in this excerpt? Is it purely financial? What other types of success are valued here?

4. What methods are used by successful product engineers? What types of research and studies do they seem to value most?

5. Near the end of this passage, Kelley writes, "Whether it's art, science, technology, or business, inspiration comes from being close to the action." In what ways is the work that Kelley describes an art? a science? Consider this discourse community's methods in relation to those described in the essays on humanities and sciences above. What are the similarities and differences? How can those similarities and differences influence the way you read the discourse of this field of study?

EXIGENCY IN PROFESSIONAL AND ACADEMIC FIELDS

Academic work is, in some ways, isolated from direct concerns of the workplace (though as the above example from IDEO illustrates, some areas of business study tend toward practical applications). In order to maintain its objectivity and interest in "pure" research, some disciplines avoid direct connections with the work done outside the walls of a campus or research institution. But most academic research eventually informs the work of occupations in important ways.

As you continue your education, it will become increasingly important for you to learn how academic discourse communities interact with the wider world. One way to begin thinking about those connections is to recognize that in most situations, writing is done in response to some problem, issue, or topic that caused its writer to "speak up." Individual citizens or citizen groups who believe that a local issue has not been dealt with sufficiently, consumers who find a product unsatisfactory, or students who find their rights have been violated—all might be compelled to express that dissatisfaction and investigate alternatives.

In the information age, for example, the need for continuous learning is heightened. As systems architect Jane Whittaker notes: "As anyone with a PC knows, technology changes very quickly. Determining the direction that things are moving can be very difficult. The firm did not want to spend millions of dollars on, as an analogy, the equivalent of Betamax to find that the rest of the world had gone with VHS. If our computers in New York could not communicate with our computers in London or Tokyo, we had major problems." Technology has affected the work of Robert Colleluori's marketing firm as well: "The avenues for marketing a client's product or service have dramatically changed with the introduction of the Internet. There's online advertising, website marketing, online selling, online registration for conferences we plan, online banking—the list seems endless. All of this adds up to expertise, and as a small agency, we can no longer be everything to everyone, and must constantly evaluate our competencies and form alliances with experts in various fields to be able to offer the services our clients need."

Situations like these, which call for your attention, are said to possess *exigency*. It is not difficult to imagine why exigency is such an important attribute of good writing; after all, if a topic does not require the attention of its proposed audience or community, then why should it be written (and who will read it?). Sometimes that exigency is already present for the readers, because they know that the issue needs immediate attention; sometimes, however, the writer must create exigency by illustrating why a particular topic, despite previous neglect, should be discussed.

For example, though genetic research has been going on for many, many years, it receives a great deal of attention whenever it addresses cloning—especially cloning human embryos and even grown human beings. Likewise, the widespread use of home computers has brought many issues regarding the Internet into the foreground of public discussions—questions of censorship, privacy rights, and plagiarism, especially. And the potential for continuing violence in the Middle East, the source of much of our imported oil, has made questions regarding the widespread drilling for oil here at home and the ethics of inefficient SUVs exigent for people in a wide variety of fields—geologists, engineers, environmentalists, economists, and other businesspeople. Just as public issues go through time-based cycles of importance, so do the most important topics within any academic field or profession. For this reason, a major goal of your education should be to learn what issues are particularly exigent within the fields that you are studying.

Exigency also forms an important link between academic and occupational discourse communities. Academic research is conducted in order to learn more about an area of study that promises to add important new knowledge to the work of that field. Occupational research and writing attempt to make the work of a profession more effective, productive, and profitable. In each case, writing usually comes from a desire to study, and in some cases cause change in, a current situation.

For example, in the wake of the events of 9/11, many communities began to consider that day's impact on their field of interest. Those events have played an enormous role in new research and work in computer security, in protecting businesses (and stimulating new ones), in government agencies, in the psychology of terror and its aftermath, and in a wealth of studies and creative pieces that measure and express that moment's impact on humanity.

One community that has been significantly affected is criminal justice, a field intrinsically interested in the protection of citizens against terrorism. Law enforcement officials, criminal justice professionals, and students in the field all have found a special exigency to reexamine their methods in light of 9/11. Some law enforcement officials have argued for a wider range of powers in detaining and questioning suspects—arguments that would have had much less chance of being accepted before the 9/11 attacks. At the same time, civil liberties groups have found in the widespread detention of possible terrorists another exigency— the need to address the rights of people to freedom from unlawful accosting and searches. This exigency is raised indirectly by the events of 9/11 and more directly by law enforcement's response to those events. In sum, this is a moment worth seizing for a variety of communities—communities that are at once academic and professional.

As you read and write in college, you might attempt to make similar connections among the academic work you are doing, the types of thinking and writing done there, and the thinking and writing done in the occupational worlds that are based on those fields.

In Reading and Writing Applications 5, you have the opportunity to do reading and writing that will help you to apply what you've learned about discourse communities to the types of expert-to-expert reading that you do in your classes and on the job. This reading and writing will also give you a chance to see how it feels to "occupy" the particular *ethos* of an academic discipline or profession. Doing so might help you to think about the wide of array of choices that face you as you consider your life's work.

Exploring Academic and Professional Journals

In Chapter 6, you learned about discourse communities—groups of people who

- are interested in similar topics,
- agree on methods of examining those topics,
- value specific types of evidence and proof that they accept as reliable, and
- use language in ways suited to those inquiries.

Those discourse communities are often formed around academic disciplines and/or professions. Much of the most reliable and current information that is generated and read by discourse communities is found in **journals.**

Journals are a unique type of periodical. They are usually discipline- or profession-specific, written *by* people who do research in the field and *for* other academic researchers or practitioners. Journals are *refereed*—that is, their articles are reviewed before publication by experts for accuracy of findings and methodology and for pertinence to the particular field of concern. For this reason, the information that is found in journal articles is particularly authoritative—it has been accepted by the community's experts as credible.

Journals can be separated into two subgroups. **Academic journals** publish studies based in academic disciplines such as biology, literary studies, and economics. **Trade journals** publish information based in the work of particular professions, such as policing, computer technology, and education. There is a good deal of overlap in these groups, however, as some journals appeal to both academic and professional audiences; articles in journals like the *New England Journal of Medicine* and *Yale Law Review* may be written and read by both academic researchers and practitioners of law or medicine. Whether trade or academic, however, all journals share the role of providing timely, reliable information to people who want to do serious research on a topic. As college students, then, you will have many occasions to consult journal articles as you do research for your classes and to prepare yourself for your future occupations.

As we discussed in the previous chapter, reading expert discourse like that found in journals requires an understanding of the special topics that are of concern to each discourse community. To read this type of writing well, you must read in ways that members of this discourse community would expect—that is, to know the ways that people in this community prefer to communicate, what they value in terms of proof, and the assumptions that inform the research that they consider credible. For example, in reading a scientific article, you should look for empirical evidence: quantifiable, reliable, repeatable information. Reading an article in the humanities, however, might require you to consider quite different forms of proof. In the set of reading and writing activities that follow, you will practice the skills necessary to read expert discourse as it is found in journal articles.

Case 1 THE MISSION AND EDITORIAL POLICIES OF JOURNALS

We can learn a good deal about discourse communities not only by examining individual articles in credible journals but also by considering the work done by the journal itself. One place to learn about a journal's purposes is in its editorial policies—the guidelines it applies to invite, critique, and accept articles for publication. Here are some examples of journals and their editorial statements and policies.

■ *PMLA* is the journal of the Modern Language Association of America. Since 1884, *PMLA* has published members' essays judged to be of interest to scholars and teachers of language and literature. *PMLA* welcomes essays of interest to those concerned with the study of language and literature. As the publication of a large and heterogeneous association, the journal is receptive to a variety of topics, whether general or specific, and to all scholarly methods and theoretical perspectives. The ideal *PMLA* essay exemplifies the best of its kind, whatever the kind, addresses a significant problem, draws out clearly the implications of its findings, and engages the attention of its audience through a concise, readable presentation. . . . Each article submitted is sent to two reviewers, usually one consultant reader and one member of the Advisory Committee. Articles recommended by these readers are then sent to the members of the Editorial Board, who meet periodically with the editor to make final decisions. Until a final decision is reached, the author's name is not made known to consultant readers, to members of the Advisory Committee and the Editorial Board, or to the editor. Because the submission of an article simultaneously to more than one refereed journal can result in duplication of the demanding task of reviewing the manuscript, it is *PMLA*'s policy not to review articles that are under consideration by other journals. An article found to have been simultaneously submitted elsewhere will not be published in *PMLA* even if it has already been accepted for publication by the Editorial Board.

The Academy of Management Review (*AMR*) is a theory development journal for management and organization scholars around the world. *AMR* publishes novel, insightful and carefully crafted conceptual articles that challenge conventional wisdom concerning all aspects of organizations and their role in society. The journal is open to a variety of perspectives, including those that seek to improve the effectiveness of, as well as those critical of, management and organizations.

Although *AMR* seeks a variety of perspectives, each manuscript published in *AMR* must provide new theoretical insights that can advance our understanding of management and organizations. Authors can achieve this objective by developing new management and organization theory, significantly challenging or clarifying current theory, synthesizing recent advances and ideas into fresh (if not entirely new) theory, or initiating a search for new theory by pointing out and carefully delineating a novel type of problem. The management and organization theory contributions present in *AMR* articles often are grounded in "normal science disciplines" of economics, psychology, sociology, or social psychology, but the journal welcomes submissions that approach organization and management theory from nontraditional perspectives, such as the liberal arts and humanities.

AMR articles must meet the highest standards of academic excellence, as judged by expert scholars who serve as part of the *AMR* Editorial Board. Therefore, the typical *AMR* article is comprehensive and original in analysis, accurately grounded in extant theory and literature, innovative in propositions and structure, and timely in terms of cutting-edge ideas. The journal seeks discussions that take a provocative or controversial position and/or that are distinct in terms of style of exhibition over guarded positions or generic presentations. Regardless of position or style, authors should argue research implications and ramifications for practice explicitly and persuasively.

Contributors will find *AMR* open to many different formats, including theoretical syntheses, new and exploratory conceptual models, point-counterpoint debates, theoretically grounded discussions of methodology, historical essays with clear implications for current and future theory, discussion of timely and important social issues, and comprehensive literature reviews with strong theoretical implications. The journal is also receptive to alternative styles of presentation. However, when the purpose is to develop new theory, research propositions are often desirable. Alternatively, when the purpose of an article is to shift the way scholars view the world or the scientific enterprise, specific propositions may not be appropriate. Authors of such articles might propose new taxonomies, trace broad developments within or across fields, espouse new philosophical or analytical perspectives, or discuss the theory development process itself.

AMR does not publish reports of empirical investigations, including empirical tests of theory, case analyses, or articles primarily about data or the testing of data. These are published in the *Academy of Management Journal*. *AMR* also does not publish articles primarily for practicing managers, including articles that develop new managerial tools, "best practices" pieces that instruct managers, or interviews with influential people. These are published in the *Academy of Management Executive*.

■ *BioScience* publishes articles in three categories: news and features, overview articles, and departments.

   News and features: Articles in news and features are typically written by the American Institute of Biological Sciences (AIBS) staff or by professional science writers. The category includes Features, Washington Watch, AIBS News, BioBriefs, and Eye on Education.

   Overview articles: Overview articles review significant scientific findings in an area of interest to a broad range of biologists. All overview articles, whether invited or independently submitted, are peer reviewed for accuracy, applicability to the field of biological sciences, and readability. Overview articles should include background information for biologists in a variety of fields, and they should be free of jargon. Articles must be no longer than 20 double-spaced pages, excluding figures, tables, and references. Limit references to 50. Please include an abstract of up to 150 words and list up to five keywords.

   Departments: BioScience contains four standing departments: Editorial, Letters, Books, and Calendar. Editorials may be submitted without solicitation and may cover any topic of interest to biologists, from science policy to technical controversy. Editorials should be no longer than 500 words; they are opinion pieces, and thus references or footnotes are inappropriate. The word limit for Letters is 300.

   Other BioScience departments are

   ■ Biology in History: Essays on the history of biological thought
   ■ Biologist's Toolbox: Articles about technology's contributions to the practice of biology

- Education: Essays about the teaching of biology in schools and to the public
- Forum: Essays specifically related to policy issues that affect or result from biological research
- Professional Biologist: Essays discussing issues in the practice of biological professions
- Roundtable: Essays on a broad range of subjects of interest to biologists
- Thinking of Biology: Essays on the philosophy of biology
- Viewpoint: Opinion pieces on subjects of concern to biologists in general or to AIBS in particular

As you can see from the above editorial policies, journals have specific missions and audiences to whom they write—audiences that generally fall within a specific discourse community. Learning about the professional journals in the disciplines you will study can serve you in several ways:

- It can help you to understand the way each discipline thinks about issues that concern it;
- It can help you to learn preferred modes of writing for each discipline;
- It can help you to understand what is required to become a member of this discourse community as a student and/or professional.

Writing to Respond

Above, we provide a few examples of the editorial policies of professional journals. Examining those policies can help you to understand the types of research specific disciplines value. You can gain even more information by dipping into the journals themselves in search of a deeper understanding of what types of topics are discussed in academic and professional fields.

First, identify at least two academic or professional journals that are important to a field of study that interests you. You can do so in a number of ways: talk to teachers in those disciplines; ask your reference librarian; use your college's electronic library resources to see what paper and electronic journals are offered in that field; talk with professionals in the field of study or related work. Be sure to note information about these journals that you accumulate.

Examine the editorial policies and other front matter of those journals. Your task is to gain a general sense of each journal's mission, the areas of expertise it values, the types of research that it considers viable for inclusion. Make careful notes of those policies and editorial statements, collecting particularly apt wordings and explications in direct quotations (using your writer's notebook or notecards). Try to make generalizations about the work of each journal.

Then, using either electronic resources or paper copies, skim the tables of contents, abstracts, and some of the articles themselves, looking at the past year or two of issues. Doing so will deepen your understanding of not only the most current topics that are included in this journal but also the methodologies, writing styles, and modes of evidence used within this field.

Writing Application

After you have collected as much information as you can through the above activities, write an **informational essay** that describes the importance of this set of journals to work in the particular disciplinary area. Your audience should be other students interested in this area, so be sure to explain in as much detail as possible how the journals play an important role in the knowledge base of the discipline, the types of information that they are likely to find there, and the styles of research, evidence, and writing used. Your purpose is to inform others about the importance of these journals to specific areas of research. For example, in examining the description of *PMLA* above, you might note the following:

- This journal is intended to be "of interest to scholars and teachers of language and literature."
- *PMLA* "is receptive to a variety of topics, general and specific, and to all scholarly methods and theoretical perspectives" in the field of literary studies—that is, it does not focus on a particular period of literature or theory of reading literature.
- Because each article submitted "is sent to two reviewers, usually one consultant reader and one member of the Advisory Committee," you might conclude that readers can be assured that the content of the journal is closely scrutinized before it is published.

Then, by skimming the table of contents and perhaps a few articles that are found in this journal, you might draw additional conclusions:

- Recent articles in the journal frequently examine issues of gender, social class, and sexuality in literature.
- Recent articles often draw comparisons among literary works from various periods of history.
- Articles tend to cite both primary literary texts and other literary experts as a major form of evidence.
- Articles seem to assume some knowledge of literary history's major works.
- The methodologies used by literary experts vary and are sometimes borrowed from other disciplines like anthropology, history, and psychology.

After you have collected as many of these observations as you can, organize the information into a clear essay that shows key features of the discipline that these journals represent and how the journals help to advance those areas of study. Feel free to include information that you have gathered from teachers or other experts regarding these journals.

Case 2 ANALYZING JOURNAL ARTICLES

Reading academic and professional journals represents a special challenge for students. On one hand, journals publish each discourse community's most current information and so are crucial to becoming informed about a field's special topics. On the other hand, since those articles assume some expertise on the part of their readers, they can often be difficult reading for students who are new to the field. Overcoming the difficulties presented by expert-to-expert discourse can take a good deal of time and requires you to practice effective and specialized reading strategies. In this project, you are asked to begin developing those strategies by learning about the methodologies, commonplaces, and writing styles of articles in a specific field of study.

For example, let's imagine that you are in an introductory psychology course and are seeking the most current literature on the treatment of schizophrenia. Though you might find information on this topic in popular magazines (*Time, Psychology Today, Smithsonian*), it is also important that you learn to read more comprehensive expert-to-expert discourse. Based on the recommendations of experts in this field or your reference librarian, you seek information from reputable, refereed journals. You locate the following two articles and the authors' abstracts.

Symptom Factors in Early-Onset Psychotic Disorders

Jon McClellan, Chris McCurry, Matthew L. Speltz, and Karen Jones

Objective: To examine the factor structure of symptom ratings in early-onset psychotic illnesses.

Method: Subjects were drawn from a 2-year prospective study of early-onset psychotic disorders. Principal components analysis with orthogonal (varimax) rotation was used to create factors from baseline ratings on the Schedule for Positive Symptoms, the Schedule for Negative Symptoms, and the Brief Psychiatric Rating Scale for Children.

Results: Youths with schizophrenia (n = 27), bipolar disorder (n = 22), and psychosis not otherwise specified (n = 20) were included. Four symptom factors were identified: negative symptoms, positive symptoms, behavioral problems, and dysphoria. Negative symptoms were predictive of the diagnosis of schizophrenia and treatment with antipsychotic medications. Neither behavior problems nor dysphoria were predictive of diagnosis. In subjects who completed follow-up assessments at year 1 (n = 49) and year 2 (n = 39), negative symptoms and behavioral problems predicted poorer functioning.

Conclusions: The four factors are clinically relevant, with both treatment planning and prognostic implications. Negative symptoms best differentiated schizophrenia from the other disorders. Behavior problems and dysphoria were nonspecific problems that occurred in all three disorders, which likely leads to misdiagnosis in community settings.

Neurocognitive Enhancement Therapy with Work Therapy

Morris Bell, Gary Bryson, Tamasine Greig, Cheryl Corcoran, and Bruce E. Wexler

Background: Cognitive deficits are a major determinant of social and occupational dysfunction in schizophrenia. In this study, we determined whether neurocognitive enhancement therapy (NET) in combination with work therapy (WT) would improve performance on neuropsychological tests related to but different from the training tasks.

Methods: Sixty-five patients with schizophrenia or schizoaffective disorder were randomly assigned to NET plus WT or WT alone. Neurocognitive enhancement therapy included computer-based training on attention, memory, and executive function tasks; an information processing group; and feedback on cognitive performance in the workplace. Work therapy included paid work activity in job placements at the medical center (eg, mail room, grounds, library) with accompanying supports. Neuropsychological testing was performed at intake and 5 months later.

Results: Prior to enrollment, both groups did poorly on neuropsychological testing. Patients receiving NET + WT showed greater improvements on pretest-posttest variables of executive function, working memory, and affect recognition. As many as 60% in the NET + WT group improved on some measures and were 4 to 5 times more likely to show large effect-size improvements. The number of patients with normal working memory performance increased significantly with NET + WT, from 45% to 77%, compared with a decrease from 56% to 45% for those receiving WT.

Conclusions: Computer training for cognitive dysfunction in patients with schizophrenia can have benefits that generalize to independent outcome measures. Efficacy may result from a synergy between NET, which encourages mental activity, and WT, which allows a natural context for mental activity to be exercised, generalized, and reinforced.

Your first reaction might be "I just don't have the knowledge of this field to understand this article." And since I'm not an expert in psychology, I share that frustration. But if you—and I—leave it at that, you also leave yourself on the outside of all of the important information that might be contained there. So where do you begin? If you look closely at these abstracts, you can learn about the methods of proof and writing styles associated with this field—things that can help you to interpret the information contained in the abstracts and the articles that describes them.

You might, for example, note that both articles provide information about scientific method. Each article, for example, gives information about the group of people that was tested. The first article tells you that "subjects were drawn from a 2-year prospective study of early-onset psychotic disorders." The second notes that "sixty-five patients with schizophrenia or schizoaffective disorder were randomly assigned to NET plus WT or WT alone." Even without intimate knowledge of these methods, you can clearly see that this discourse community values knowing and, in many cases, controlling the group of subjects that was tested.

Each article also describes methodologies in some detail. The first article reports that "principal components analysis with orthogonal (varimax) rotation was used to create factors from baseline ratings on the Schedule for Positive Symptoms, the Schedule for Negative Symptoms, and the Brief Psychiatric Rating Scale for Children," and the second that "neurocognitive enhancement therapy included computer-based training on attention, memory, and executive function tasks; an information processing group; and feedback on cognitive performance in the workplace. Work therapy included paid work activity in job placements at the medical center (eg, mail room, grounds, library) with accompanying supports. Neuropsychological testing was performed at intake and 5 months later." Despite the jargon, it is clear that this discourse community asks its members to carefully describe the experimental method that was used—a method that is described in greater detail in the article itself.

As you consider other facets of these abstracts, you can find other shared values: the reporting of results, the discussion of those results, the formulation of conclusions from those results, etc. Already, even with a brief look, you've begun to understand what is valued in this discipline-specific form of writing. As you read more frequently and more deeply within each disciplinary field, you can collect information about these preferred academic styles and so learn to better participate in these discourse communities as a reader. In many ways, that's the process of reading (and writing) that is required of you both in your major and in your general education courses—learning how to read each field's discourses.

Writing to Respond

Locate two articles in reputable, refereed journals from a field that interests you. Using the model above, consider not only the subjects discussed but also the ways that the argument is presented. Remember: you will likely need to read the articles more than once, and actively, in order to discover the author's goals and methods of argument. Here are questions that can help you to be an active reader, seeking specific information, rather than a passive one. Respond to each question in your writer's notebook.

- What is the central point, thesis, or argument that each article attempts to make? Try to capture that central point in a sentence or two.

- What is the stated purpose of each article? In what way does each article attempt to advance knowledge in this particular subject area?

- What method of analysis, experimentation, or argument does each writer use? What types of evidence are offered as proof of the writer's thesis? Be sure to provide specific examples.

- What types of reasoning are used to interpret the subject matter? Show how the examples are used to prove the thesis and/or to support the conclusions.

- How does each writer draw on the work of other experts in the field? Provide specific examples of the ways that information from previous work in this area is presented within each article.

- What prior knowledge of the field is expected of the reader? In order to fully understand its points, what further information might you need to seek?

- Into what academic areas (natural sciences, social sciences, humanities, business) would you classify these articles? What shared facets of the two articles might suggest general principles about writing in this field of study? What do experts in these fields seem to value most? In order to draw these conclusions, you might review the principles of academic disciplines outlined in Chapter 6.

Writing Application

Write an informative essay that introduces the discourse methods of this field. Your audience is other students who are new to the field. Using examples from the articles, illustrate the field's basics assumptions (or commonplaces), the methods of research that seem most common, the most acceptable modes of proof, and as many features of the writing style that the articles share. Your goal is to help others (as well as yourself) learn about what to look for when reading journal articles in a specific discipline. Remember: Though the reading will be difficult, try to focus on what you *can* learn about the field and its discourse rather than what you *can't*; learning to read expert discourse can take some time.

Case 3 INTERDISCIPLINARY CONNECTIONS

Though much work is contained within specific disciplines or professional fields, some issues cross disciplinary boundaries and are shared by many fields. One such area of concern is the natural environment and its protection. This topic is an interdisciplinary one—a topic that can be addressed through the discourses of many fields and occupations. It is also a "real-world" issue that has serious implications for the lives of citizens. As you read the articles that follow, note how different discourse communities address a similar issue through their own special topics—the areas of investigation and evidence for that particular field.

Writing to Respond

As you read the article excerpts on pages 286–299, consider the following general topics as well as the specific questions accompanying each piece. Respond in your writer's notebook. You can also consider the guiding questions following each excerpt.

- What seem to be the major concerns on this issue shared by the writer and readers?

- What can you learn about audience from the publication in which each article originally appeared?

- What commonplace ideas inform each writer's perspective (and the perspective of his discourse community) on the natural environment?

- How is each article arranged logically—that is, what line of reasoning does the writer use to inform or persuade the audience?

- How do those methodologies, in effect, define the special topics or key questions raised in each discipline or profession? How can understanding each article's perspective on the environment help you to determine the questions or topics that are encouraged within a given area of concern or discourse community?

- What types of evidence or proof seem to be most important in this discourse community? List evidence presented in each article and analyze the logic that makes this evidence reliable within this discourse community.

- In what ways do the articles, though written from the perspective of different disciplines or professions, speak to one another? Can you identify stasis points at which the various disciplines intersect?

Social Sciences

Below is an excerpt from an article that explores the effect of gender on environmental attitudes. (Since I am assuming no prior expertise on your part, I deleted some of the evidence presented in the original article.) As you read, recall the features of the social sciences that were outlined in Chapter 6. Consider specifically:

- the methodologies used by these authors to study the issue and on which conclusions are drawn;

- the quantitative elements of the social sciences that are evident here;

- the ways that the authors set up a scientifically valid study; and
- the ways in which the authors draw on past work in the field.

from Elaborating on Gender Differences in Environmentalism

Lynnette C. Zelezny, Poh-Pheng Chua, and Christina Aldrich

A review of recent research (1988 to 1998) on gender differences in environmental attitudes and behaviors found that, contrary to past inconsistencies, a clearer picture has emerged: Women report stronger environmental attitudes and behaviors than men. Additional evidence of gender differences in environmental attitudes and behaviors was also supported across age. As a single variable, the effect of gender on proenvironmental behavior was consistently stronger than on environmental attitudes. It was found that compared to males, females had higher levels of socialization to be other-oriented and socially responsible. Implications for theory, social action, and policy are discussed.

One of the ways psychologists can promote environmentalism is to understand the relationship between demographic variables and environmental attitudes and behaviors and the implications these human-environment relationships may have on theory, social action, and policy. Numerous studies have examined the relationship between demographic variables (e.g., age, education, ethnicity, socioeconomic status) and environmental attitudes and behaviors. Research on environmentalism and gender has been somewhat limited, however, and "surprisingly little has been done to examine the . . . environmental activity of women and factors related to it" (Mohai, 1992, p. 2).

Why Are Females More Environmental?

A variety of theories have been used to explain gender differences in environmentalism. One widely used approach is based on gender roles and socialization (Eagly, 1987; Howard & Hollander, 1996; Miller, 1993; Unger & Crawford, 1996; Wilkinson & Kitzinger, 1996). Socialization theory posits that behavior is predicted by the process of socialization, whereby individuals are shaped by gender expectations within the context of cultural norms. Females across cultures are socialized to be more expressive, to have a stronger "ethic of care," and to be more interdependent, compassionate, nurturing, cooperative, and helpful in caregiving roles (Beutel & Marini, 1995; Chodorow, 1974; Eagly, 1987; Gilligan, 1982). On the other hand, males are socialized to be more independent and competitive (Chodorow, 1974; Gilligan, 1982; Keller, 1985).

Theoretically, gender differences in environmentalism imply links between socialization and values (Stern, Dietz, & Kalof, 1993). As guiding principles, values (Rokeach, 1973) predict attitudes and behaviors (Olson & Zanna, 1994); therefore, because females, compared to males, are socialized to value the needs of others, women exhibit more helping behavior and altruism (Gilligan, 1982).

Individuals who help possess an "other" value orientation according to Schwartz's (1968, 1977) norm activation model. This model suggests that helping behavior is most likely to occur when individuals are aware of harmful consequences (awareness of consequences—AC) and of their actions and feel responsible for these consequences (ascribed responsibility—AR). Thus, individuals may act proenvironmentally but they may have different values. For example, individuals may protest agricultural pollution (e.g., spraying pesticides) because it affects the air they breathe (i.e., egocentric orientation) or because it affects the air their children breathe (i.e., anthropocentric orientation) or because it affects the ecosystem (i.e., ecocentric orientation). Stern, Dietz, and Kalof (1993) proposed that individuals may have environmental attitudes that reflect a combination of these three value orientations. They found that women have stronger beliefs about the harmful consequences of poor environmental conditions for others, the biosphere, and self and that these beliefs predicted more proenvironmental behavior (Stern, Dietz, & Kalof, 1993).

For this article, we were particularly interested in ecocentrism, which is a fundamental belief in the inherent value of nature, the biosphere, and all living things. By definition ecocentrism suggests an extended "other" orientation, which, according to gender socialization theory, is characteristic of feminine socialization. Numerous studies have found that gender socialization significantly influences individual behavior very early in life, and these findings have been supported across cultures (Block, 1973; Williams & Best, 1990). In a recent study on gender and the environmental risk concerns, however, Davidson and Freudenberg (1996) suggested that gender differences in environmentalism are not universal. Therefore, we wondered whether gender differences in environmentalism could be found in children and across countries.

We examined gender differences in environmental attitudes and behaviors among primary and secondary school children. Based on socialization theory, we predicted that, compared to males, female students in primary and secondary schools would report significantly stronger environmental attitudes and greater participation in proenvironmental behaviors.

Gender Differences in Environmentalism Among Children

A stratified sample of primary and secondary school students ([N.sub.1994] = 584; [N.sub.1995] = 709) from diverse socioeconomic strata in California were systematically surveyed over a 2-year period. A 35-item questionnaire was designed to assess students' (1) general environmental attitudes (measured by separate items and an adapted NEP Scale; Dunlap & Van Liere, 1978), (2) self-reported knowledge about the environment, (3) feelings of personal responsibility for improving the environment, (4) specific environmental attitudes, (5) specific recycling attitudes, (6) interest and intention to participate in school recycling, (7) participation in school recycling after the initiation of district-wide school recycling (1995 survey only), and (8) demographic characteristics. The questionnaire included both closed-ended questions (n = 32) and open-ended questions (n = 3). The closed-ended questions, designed by the current authors, included 6-point Likert-type response scales (e.g., in response to question 6, "How would you rate your overall personal responsibility to improve the environment?" the response choices were 1—Extremely responsible, 2—Very responsible, 3—Somewhat responsible, 4—Slightly responsible, 5—Not at all responsible, and 6—I don't know).

The survey was pilot tested twice on elementary school students to revise the wording of the survey items so that they were appropriate for children. In the pilot testing, half of the items from the full 12-item scale of the NEP (Dunlap & Van Liere, 1978) were not understood by younger elementary students, and those items were not included in the final questionnaire. A shortened six-item NEP Scale assessed students' general environmental concern using the following items: (1) The balance of nature is very delicate and easily upset; (2) People must live in harmony with nature in order to survive; (3) Pollution is not personally affecting my life; (4) Courses focusing on conservation of natural resources should be taught in the public schools; (5) Although there is contamination of our lakes, streams, and air, nature will soon return them to normal; and (6) Because government rules are so effective, it is not likely that pollution will become too bad. The shortened NEP included Likert response choices as follows: (1) Strongly agree, (2) Agree, (3) No opinion, (4) Disagree, and (5) Strongly disagree. It was also determined, because of the reading level required to adequately comprehend this questionnaire, that the minimum grade level of students in the study would be fifth grade.

The reliabilities of the student environmental questionnaire were assessed separately using the 1994 and 1995 data. The reliability coefficients for this questionnaire remained relatively stable across ages, schools, ethnicities, gender, and socioeconomic status; the most consistent responses for these particular environmental items, however, came from Anglo high school students of middle or high socioeconomic status.

The relationships between students' demographic characteristics (e.g., age and gender) and their general environmental concern, specific environmental attitudes, and participation in school recycling were analyzed. The environmental attitudes and behaviors of girls and boys were compared by year. In addition, the effect of gender on NEP attitudes and proenvironmental behavior was assessed using effect size (r) calculations. Finally, gender differences in concern about specific environmental issues—air pollution, animal extinction, cutting down trees, wasting energy, water pollution, and trash in the environment—were qualitatively compared by year.

In 1994, with regard to general attitudes, girls reported significantly stronger overall concern about the environment than boys. Further, girls reported significantly stronger general environmental concerns than boys on the NEP and more personal responsibility to improve the environment. In terms of specific attitudes, girls expressed greater proenvironmental attitudes than did boys on concern about trash, interest in recycling, and interest in school recycling. Finally, girls reported stronger intentions to participate in school recycling than did boys.

In 1995, the pattern was identical. Girls reported stronger overall concern for the environment, general NEP environmental concern, and personal responsibility for improving the environment than boys. Further, girls reported stronger concern about trash, interest in recycling, and interest in school recycling. Finally, girls reported significantly more participation in school recycling.

Qualitatively, with regard to specific environmental issues, girls reported in both 1994 and 1995 that the issue that they cared the most about was animal extinction. Boys, however, reported in 1994 that their top concern was animal extinction, whereas in 1995, they reported that they were most concerned about water pollution. On the other hand, girls and boys consistently reported, across both years, that they were least concerned about wasting energy.

In summary, compared to boys, girls reported stronger proenvironmental responses on all environmental variables in this study, and this pattern was consistent across 2 years. The findings in Study 1 strongly suggest that environmentalism does not begin in adulthood, thus debunking the argument that gender differences in environmentalism arise with motherhood and protecting children from environmental threats (Hamilton, 1985a; Levine, 1982). The study's findings are consistent with the adult studies that were reviewed earlier in this article. Females, regardless of age (i.e., youth or adult) reported more concern for the environment and proenvironmental behaviors than males. Also, identical patterns emerged with respect to effect sizes. In both adults and youth, the effect of gender (female) was stronger on proenvironmental behaviors than NEP environmental concerns.

We are careful to note the limitations of our investigation. We did not directly compare the environmental attitudes and behaviors of children and adults, nor did we examine environmental attitudes and behaviors longitudinally within individuals. Future research is needed to understand the development of environmentalism, the stability of environmentalism across the life span, the interaction between age and gender on environmental attitudes and behaviors, and how environmentalism is related to cognitive, moral, and social development. Finally, research on gender differences and environmentalism is needed to address the generalizability and the universality of these findings.

References

Beutel, A., & Marini, M. (1995). Gender and values. *American Sociological Review, 60,* 436–448.

Block, J. H. (1973). Conceptions of sex roles: Some cross-cultural and longitudinal perspectives. *American Psychologist, 28,* 512–526.

Chodorow, N. (1974). Family structure and feminine perspective. In M. Rosaldo & L. Lamphere (Eds.), *Women in culture and society* (pp. 41–48). Stanford, CA: Stanford University Press.

Dunlap, R., & Van Liere, K. (1978). The new environmental paradigm. *Journal of Environmental Education, 9,* 10–19.

Eagly, A. (1987). *Sex differences in social behavior: A social role interpretation.* Hillsdale, NJ: Erlbaum.

Gilligan, C. (1982). *In a different voice.* Cambridge, MA: Harvard University Press.

Hamilton, L. (1985a). Concerns about toxic wastes: Three demographic predictors. *Sociological Perspectives, 28,* 463–486.

Keller, E. (1985). *Reflections on gender and science.* New Haven, CT: Yale University Press.

Levine, A. (1982). *Love Canal.* Lexington, MA: Lexington Books.

Mohai, P. (1992). Men, women, and the environment. *Society and Natural Resources, 5,* 1–19.

Olson, J., & Zanna, M. (1994). Attitudes and attitude change. *Annual Review of Psychology, 44,* 117–154.

Stern, P., Dietz, T., & Kalof, L. (1993). Value orientations, gender, and environmental concern. *Environment and Behavior, 25,* 322–348.

Van Liere, K., & Dunlap, R. (1978). Moral norms and environmental behavior: An application of Schwartz's norm-activation model to yard burning. *Journal of Applied Social Psychology, 8,* 174–188.

Williams, J. E., & Best, D. L. (1990). *Sex and psyche: Gender and self viewed cross-culturally.* Newbury Park, CA: Sage.

Wolkomir, M., Futreal, M., Woodrum, E., & Hoban, T. (1997). Substantive religious belief and environmentalism. *Social Science Quarterly, 78,* 96–108.

Zelezny, L. C., & Yelverton, J. A. (2000, April). *Feminine identity, collectivism, and environmental attitudes and behaviors.* Paper presented at the meeting of the Western Psychological Association, Portland, OR.

Here are some questions to consider as you plan your summary of this piece:

▪ In what ways do the authors avoid bias in choosing the group that was sampled to gather information on environmental attitudes?

▪ Why do the authors explain their rationale for the questions asked?

▪ How does this article demonstrate the importance of quantifiable information in the social sciences? How is that information collected and processed?

▪ According to these authors, what additional research is necessary to test their results?

Natural Sciences

The following excerpt is taken from an article that appeared in *BioScience*, an online journal. It takes a life sciences approach to the issue of environmental laws and programs. The article examines the type of knowledge that is necessary to inform such laws. Pay special attention to the way that this article first situates the problem within societal concerns (and so creates exigency) and then applies the disciplinary methods of the natural sciences to point out potential problems with implementation of this environmental policy. As you read, consider how the authors' scientific community influences their approach to the topic (and how it differs from the approaches that might be taken in other disciplines). Note especially the careful use of scientific definition that forms a key part of the argument.

Providing a Regional Context for Local Conservation Action: A Natural Community Conservation Plan for the Southern California Coastal Sage Scrub

Thomas S. Reid and Dennis D. Murphy

Abstract: Conservation biologists have come up with principles that address a wide range of conservation issues. In particular, biologists helped formulate a plan to conserve the California coastal sage scrub using a process known as conservation planning.

When the Secretary of the Interior for a Democratic administration embraces a conservation program developed by a Republican governor, it suggests that the idea may have real promise. The idea, Natural Community Conservation Planning, involves application of the modern tools of conservation biology in local land-use planning. A wedding of federal and state endangered species programs, the model integrates conservation and planning in a method that links social and economic considerations to biological concerns. The promise offered is a new means of conservation planning that Bruce Babbitt has called "the model for avoiding future environmental and economic trainwrecks." Right now, this program is being put to the toughest of field tests in southern California's coastal sage scrub community. Because the lands in question are mostly privately owned, and because the value of those lands is among the highest in the nation, the circumstances of this conservation planning exercise merit special attention.

The field of conservation biology has evolved rapidly in recent years and now offers general principles that can be applied in meeting a wide range of conservation challenges. In this article the term conservation planning is used to mean the process by which conservation biology is applied in the political, legal, and social context that leads to actual implementation of a land-use plan.

Land Ownership and Conservation Planning

Conservation planning on public lands is primarily a matter of determining goals and priorities of stewardship. While problems of competing interests on public lands can frustrate implementation of a full conservation agenda, the fundamental ability to control the use of public land lies within the legal authority of the public landowner.

By contrast, private landownership in the United States is afforded substantial protection from government control. Under the Fifth Amendment to the US Constitution, a property owner is protected from uncompensated governmental use of his property (referred to as a taking), and courts have interpreted governmental establishment of regulations or restrictions on land uses that essentially confiscate private property as a prohibited taking. Under US law, the states and their legal subdivisions of local government (i.e., cities and counties) have the most intimate connection with land-use regulation. The legality of local government zoning or general planning is well established and is practiced throughout most of the United States. The federal or state government may establish a Species Act, but if the lands affected are privately owned, then the practical implementation of conservation programs inevitably requires the involvement of local government.

Where conservation programs affect a relatively small geographic area or lands controlled by relatively few property owners, then landowners themselves can participate directly in cooperative planning activities. To be successful, this approach requires extraordinary amounts of time and human resources. Many view such parcel-by-parcel approaches as being too slow to address the vast conservation needs of the nation and too unresponsive to species needs on appropriate spatial scales.

Where conservation programs attempt to address resources on more appropriate regional scales, numerous property owners are inevitably affected, and it therefore becomes impractical to negotiate plans with individual owners.

That impracticality reflects core conflicts facing conservation planners: the daunting task of dealing with hundreds or even thousands of landowners and the significant differences in the readiness of individual landowners to contemplate the fundamental trade-offs between conservation and development.

While local government has the most direct statutory authority to deal with land-use designations and issues, its ability to resolve conflicts has critical limitations. Indeed, local government is seldom prepared to develop the policies necessary to provide for effective, scientifically defensible conservation programs. Local government traditionally serves urban needs and often lacks staff trained in conservation planning. Moreover, its authority is by definition limited to a specific jurisdiction, and local government simply cannot provide the regional coordination of plans necessary to meet effective conservation goals.

The Natural Community Conservation Planning Act

In 1991, California put into law a conservation program that attempts to provide ecosystem-based planning on a regional scale. California's Natural Community Conservation Planning Act emphasizes habitat conservation rather than species-focused conservation. However, politically and legally, the state has been constrained in its attempts to give itself strict regulatory authority to protect ecological communities, because, among other distinctly more political reasons, even scientists disagree about the explicit definition of an ecological community and its identity, distribution, and extent. The act provides for guidance and cooperative efforts, but it is nonregulatory, therefore lacks the enforcement provisions of the federal Endangered Species Act.

Despite its current lack of prohibitive power, many view the Natural Community Conservation Planning Act's breadth as its strength. While the federal Endangered Species Act has catalyzed laudable conservation planning efforts on both public and private lands, its species-by-species approach often falls far short of protecting the ecosystems upon which endangered species depend. Furthermore, the Endangered Species Act is fairly viewed as fostering so-called crisis planning, wherein conservation efforts begin only after species have become truly imperiled and have passed through a formal listing process. Even after conservation planning under the act has begun, critical marginal habitats, buffer lands, or landscape linkages that are not strictly occupied by a listed species are often left unprotected. California's Natural Community Conservation Planning Act intends to address such shortcomings of the Endangered Species Act.

The Southern California Coastal Sage Scrub Example

As a first trial of the program, California boldly undertook comprehensive planning to conserve the coastal sage scrub ecological community in southern California.

Much of the destruction of coastal sage scrub occurred decades ago with agricultural expansion, but more recent additional losses of natural habitat to urbanization have compelled conservation planning. The 6000-square-mile planning area includes all or part of five counties–Los Angeles, San Bernardino, Orange, Riverside, and San Diego. The planning area includes nearly half of the state's human population and accounts for the majority of the state's population growth in the past decade. Coastal sage scrub is sometimes referred to as soft chaparral. It comprises low-growing shrub species such as Artemesia californica, Eriogonom fasciculatum, Salvia leucophylla, and Salvia mellifera.

Originally, coastal sage scrub occupied coastal terraces, alluvial fans, and the foothills of the coast range below 1000 meters elevation, and it extended from Baja California to north of San Francisco Bay. The sage scrub is not a particularly homogeneous plant community—it differs in species composition depending on latitude, slope, aspect, soil type, and history of disturbances, particularly fire and grazing. Furthermore, sage scrub occurs naturally in mosaics with chamise chaparral, oak woodland, and introduced and native grasslands. On low-elevation terrain in southern California, agriculture and urban development have eliminated more than 80% of the prehistoric coastal sage scrub area, leaving perhaps 160,000 to 200,000 hectares.

Although few animal species are obligate inhabitants of coastal sage scrub, several species are strongly associated with it and are considered at risk because of its decline in southern California. Among some two dozen vertebrate candidates for federal protection, the coastal California gnatcatcher (Polioptila californica californica) and the coastal cactus wren (Campyl-orhynchus brunnecapillus sandie-gensis) have emerged as regulatory symbols of the community and are serving as target species for conservation planning. The California gnatcatcher was afforded protection under the federal Endangered Species Act in 1993; however, in a recent decision by the US Fish and Wildlife Service (USFWS) the coastal cactus wren was denied listing, ostensibly because it did not meet the federal criterion for a distinct population segment.

The flagship species for the Natural Community Conservation Planning program thus remains the California gnatcatcher, a species almost exclusively restricted to coastal sage scrub habitats at low elevations in southern California and northern Baja California. While the bird is not at imminent risk of extinction throughout its historical distribution, a vast majority of what must have constituted its prime habitat along the coast was converted to agriculture decades ago and has more recently given way to urbanization. Without a novel approach to conservation planning, the protection of currently occupied gnatcatcher habitat alone is not likely to assure the persistence of the species. Its highly disjunct, remnant distribution demands conservation of ample amounts of the remaining, currently unoccupied coastal sage scrub habitat, as well as conservation of other habitat types to provide landscape corridors for dispersal by the bird. Furthermore, without a regional, community-level conservation plan, other sage scrub-dependent species will inevitably become imperiled.

Planning Challenges

Several other factors frame the challenge faced by the State of California in implementing its Natural Community Conservation Planning program. These factors range from the difficulty of defining coastal sage scrub to the limited protection afforded species and their habitats by existing laws.

Coastal sage scrub is difficult to define. The sage scrub is an extraordinarily variable ecological community—it appears as dramatically distinct subcommunities and occurs in complex mosaics with neighboring communities.

As a result of this diversity, different mapping efforts usually produce differing interpretations of the distribution and extent of sage scrub. It thus can be ambiguous whether or not an individual parcel of land should be subject to planning. Additionally, coastal sage scrub can be highly variable over time in its response to fire, grazing, and agricultural practices, so that vegetation maps based on aerial photographs or satellite thematic imagery frequently miss areas that may have long-term conservation value.

The remaining sage scrub is highly fragmented. Although the planning areas still contain more than 160,000 hectares of coastal sage scrub, its distribution is highly fragmented as a consequence of both its naturally patchy occurrence and the urban and agricultural encroachment along coastal drainages. Habitat patch sizes are highly variable. The high intergradation exhibited by the plant communities in coastal southern California has the effect that the concept of patch size has less meaning for coastal sage scrub than it does for other biological communities. Analyses of the distribution and extent of sage scrub have considered its relative density within geographic neighborhoods of varying sizes; areas with the highest neighborhood densities are considered prime conservation targets. Most of the larger remnants of habitat are found at the higher elevations and farthest from the coast, a distribution that makes the design of interpatch linkages as challenging as the establishment of large reserves.

Private Landownership Predominates

Nearly three-fourths of the remaining coastal sage scrub is on privately owned land. US Forest Service holdings in the planning area are located for the most part above the upper elevation of the range of sage scrub, hence lack many species that are restricted to lower elevations. The largest single public landowner of sage scrub is the US Department of Defense (Camp Pendleton and Miramar Naval Air Station); conservation objectives must compete with the military mission on these lands.

A regional conservation strategy for sage scrub thus requires the cooperation of the stewards of public lands but unfortunately cannot rely on public land for major land contributions to a reserve system. Multiple jurisdictions are involved. The five-county planning area includes some 50 cities, one third of which include large areas of undeveloped coastal sage scrub subject to ongoing land-use approval processes, and, of course, pressure for immediate development. Involving all of the active jurisdictions in one comprehensive planning effort would impose substantial logistical and financial burdens on all governmental entities.

    . . .

Lack of a reliable scientific framework is a major hindrance to any program. With the coastal sage scrub Natural Community Conservation Planning program, it took two years to assemble even the basic resource information in some portions of the region. Most private land is poorly surveyed for biological resources. Regional planning efforts are likely to be most productive where inventory efforts—such as those conducted by The Nature Conservancy, state natural heritage programs, and the newly created National Biological Survey are already well underway. Although policy makers are accustomed to proceeding with scant information, adequate scientific information pays off by allowing increased efficiency and confidence in planning.

Here are inventional questions to consider as you plan your summary.

- What relationship between the scientific community and the environmental movement can be inferred from this article?

- How might the scientific studies introduced in this article influence environmental programs, according to its authors?

- One of the most important ways that this article illustrates its point is by scientific definition. What key definitions must the authors establish? How do they use those definitions to make specific arguments?

- What other modes of evidence are used in this article? Provide specific examples.

- Find three places where specific values held by scientists are illustrated in this article.

The Humanities

The following article explores the issue of environmentalism through the lens of the humanities, and more specifically as an issue related to religious studies. As you read, note the way that issues concerning human beings' relationship with the natural environment are contextualized in a larger discussion of spirituality and humanism. More specifically, note the ways in which the author sets up the argument as an issue for religious studies, how he discusses the environment as part of a larger web of humanistic concerns (as discussed in Chapter 6), and the types of evidence and reasoning he presents in order to forward his ideas.

The Fish That Will Not Take Our Hooks

Roger G. Kennedy

Abstract: Both religion and wilderness involve a confrontation between man and a force that cannot be comprehended or controlled. Conservationists and people with deep religious beliefs are natural allies.

Let us consider wilderness as a religious concept. Religion is the recognition of the limits of human competence in the presence of the unknowable and the uncontrollable before which all humans stand in awe. So is wilderness. Like the unknowable and sacred, it exists whether or not humans exist. It pre-exists humans. Therefore, we should conceive of wilderness as part of our religious life. Religion admits that we humans are not masters of the universe; we are not even masters of this earth. We are, instead, co-inhabitants of the earth with a multitude of other creatures, and we cannot even dream of controlling it.

If we cannot dream of controlling the earth, then, we certainly cannot control wilderness. It is essentially beyond control. It may have been abused, its vegetation destroyed, its animals brought close to extinction, but after we have restored it to health and while we continue to manage the way people act upon it, we should thereafter leave wilderness itself alone. Wilderness is that which we do not command. Wilderness is that which lies beyond our anxious self-assertion as humans. It is the present, proximate metaphor for that wide universe which, when we pray, we acknowledge to be beyond even our understanding.

Wilderness is a religious concept because it requires reverence from us and also because it is a deeply serious idea. Reinhold Neibuhr defined religion as that which we take most seriously. What could possibly be more serious than an awed response to the unknown and uncontrollable? What is more serious than a reverence for the health of this earth? Furthermore, wilderness legislation is an acknowledgment of our sins—our delinquencies as managers of those portions of the wild earth over which we have presumed to take control—and of our parallel responsibility to retain, restore, and preserve that which we have not yet corrupted.

To meet our sacred responsibility to both revere and protect the wild is too great a task to be left to the conservation community alone. If there is anything upon which conservationists can all agree, it is that there are not enough of us. While each of us may believe himself or herself to be a multitude, taken all together our ranks remain too thin for us to achieve the protection of the earth and of those places revered by humans, which is our task.

We are all trying hard, none of us gets enough thanks, and there aren't enough of us. We must bring new recruits to the cause, beginning with one group of fellow citizens who have, in their way, been part of our alliance all along but who have not heard much from us in the way of invitation. These natural allies are, I believe, religious people. The central concept of religious life is the same as the central concept of wilderness preservation. That concept is a sense of scale, of human scale, in the presence of larger things and larger matters. We are less than God, less important, less capacious, less knowing. Religious people speak of themselves as humbled in the presence of God; even the most secular of conservationists would admit, I think, that they often feel humbled in the presence of wilderness—part of God's world with its wondrous gifts. This feeling goes beyond awe to reverence. Most religious people think of the universe as intentional, as a Creation—not necessarily all at once, nor necessarily taking only a week's time, but intentional. Therefore, all its parts have value, all its species, all its mountains, waters, fields, and oceans. Humans, in the religious tradition, are not the only significant species on this earth. Our orchards, farms, woodlots, towns, and cities are not the only places worthy of respect. All Creation is worthy of respect.

The Wilderness Act of 1964 was the legislative expression of that respectful idea. That is why imbedded in the preamble to the act is the term "untrammelled." A trammel is a net. Untrammelled means unfettered, unnetted. The preservation of the "untrammelled," then, is a simple recognition that outside any of our snares or traps or cages there are forms of life deserving our respect. Wilderness puts all this on a map. Its borders, fetters, and trammels are limits to human pretension, limits easily understood and accepted by religious people because they merely affirm in geography what has been affirmed all along in theology. In theology it is said that beyond the boundaries of the known there is a realm denied to science, to history, to all the ordinary apparatus of knowing. In wilderness geography it is affirmed that when we come to the edge of wilderness we may know something of what lies beyond, but we shall not cross that border with the intention of controlling it.

Although we do not ordinarily genuflect as we pass a sign labeled "wilderness area," it would not be odd if we were to do so. Wilderness is a place, but it also is a mystery, a profound mystery. It is more than a gene pool—it is a fund of fathomless truths. We are constantly surprised by life in unexpected forms.

When microbes new to us, but known to themselves for millions of years, are suddenly discovered by us in densely visited Yellowstone National Park, it is not their monetary value that is most significant but their religious value: imbedded in them is the mystery of life, in its perpetually changing, infinitely various affirmations. To be guilty of snuffing out life by heedless or foolish intrusion is one kind of sin against which we must be on our guard.

Another sin of which to beware is to fail to allow enough space for the unknown to flourish, unmanaged, so that it may fulfill itself. Our proud, willful, often heedless and foolish species is learning all the time how little it really does know, how little it does control. All the essentials of life—birth, death, the sacraments—are intrusions by the unknown and by the essentially unpredictable into our well-planned, scrupulously managed, manicured lives. Wilderness areas are not big zoos; we are in the zoos, wilderness areas are outside the zoos. That is why they must be big enough to permit the full range of life within them. Wilderness is a fish that will not take our hooks.

Wilderness is necessary to us biologically. It is necessary to us spiritually. It also is necessary to us psychologically, increasingly so, and this need, too, has its religious character. Wilderness is a sort of physical, geographical sabbath. In wilderness we can find surcease from the consequences of our bad management elsewhere, of what we have done to the world and to ourselves during "the rest of the week," so to speak.

Here are questions to help you plan for your summary of this article:

1. What connections between the natural environment and religion does this article attempt to construct?

2. What does Reinhold Neibuhr's definition of religion add to Kennedy's argument?

3. What types of proof are offered here, and how do the proofs differ from those accepted in other discourse communities? Does one form of proof seem more valid than others? Why?

4. How does Kennedy use definitions to forward his argument? How is his use of definition similar to, or different from, that in the article on sage scrub above?

5. What types of philosophical ideas does this argument rely on? Point out specific philosophical assumptions that are made here.

Writing Applications

After reading the preceding articles on environmental issues, each drawn from the work of a different discipline, either:

1. Choose the article that comes from the discipline closest to your own field of interest, summarize its argument, and analyze the ways in which it uses methods and styles that are typical of that discipline's work. Use specific examples from the article that you believe can help others to understand the way professionals in this discipline write—and so can inform the reading they do in this field; or

2. Write a comparative essay that describes differences in methodology, writing style, and purpose among the three articles. Use examples that illustrate key similarities and differences among the disciplines in style, method of proof, and valid reasoning.

In either case, as you read and write on these articles, be sure to consider the influence of the discipline that informs each—that is, consider how writing from the perspective of the social sciences ("Elaborating on Gender Differences"), natural sciences ("Providing a Regional Context for Local Conservation Action: A Natural Community Conservation Plan for the Southern California Coastal Sage Scrub"), or humanities ("The Fish That Will Not Take Our Hooks") changes the writing style, the concerns examined, and the types of evidence included.

PART III

The Process of Research

THE ACTIVE READING TECHNIQUES DISCUSSED in Part 2 provided you with strategies for getting the most out of your reading. They can help you to read critically and so to better form (and inform) your own ideas. But as you attempt to become a literate member of academic, occupational, and civic communities, you face an additional challenge: You must locate, evaluate, and compare sources of information. These activities are all part of the research process.

In this section of the book, we treat research as a set of related activities, not a single one. Too often, *research* is defined simply as a search for "sources" and inspired by little more than fulfilling requirements. To develop as a student and a professional, you must go beyond this limited (and limiting) understanding of research and treat it as a sincere desire to learn more about a topic. This is why professionals do research: because it helps them to become informed enough to speak or write with a credible voice—and because speaking or writing on the topic really matters to them and to a specific audience. This type of productive research process requires an inquiring and curious mind as well as specific skills and techniques.

In Chapter 7, we discuss techniques for developing research questions that are likely to lead you toward the most useful information and that can help you to focus the information that you find. You'll practice techniques for translating those questions into focused search terms so as to take advantage of the powerful information technologies that now exist (without becoming overwhelmed by them). We also discuss ways to develop your initial thoughts on a topic into a research proposal—a document that can help you to plan and complete your task.

Chapter 8 then offers advice on incorporating the information you find (and will continue to seek as new questions arise) into your own purposes for writing. There are two difficulties in doing so: First, your voice can get lost amid those of the experts whose work you have read; and, second, the researched information that you encounter, though useful, may not be written for the same purpose and the same audience that you have in mind. This chapter provides you with strategies for maintaining your own voice as you incorporate the ideas of others and for adapting the information you find in ways that suit your audience and reasons for writing. The Reading and Writing Applications that follow the chapter reinforce these skills through practice, giving you the opportunity to practice forming effective search terms, to write a formal research proposal, and to write a summary of the available research on a topic (often called a *review of the literature*).

Chapter 9 describes techniques for developing, drafting, and revising a researched essay. The chapter offers strategies for developing a thesis, for finding a reasonable and logical organization for your ideas, and for revising productively, both on your own and in collaboration with your peers.

Finally, Chapter 10 helps you to deliver the goods—to present your researched argument to your audience in a polished form. Polishing your presentation can involve a variety of activities, depending on the form you choose. First we explore possible formats and designs for written presentations and the situations in which each is most useful. We also explore techniques that can help you to plan and deliver oral presentations. No matter which form of delivery you choose, you must edit your work (or plan your presentation) carefully to be sure that your language is appropriate to the situation and that it is as error-free as possible. To help with that final polish, Chapter 10 provides ideas on how to identify your own rough spots as a writer and ways to begin to smooth them out.

Taken as a group, these chapters and the accompanying Reading and Writing Applications section allow you to develop your own research processes. They also allow you to use your research to write with a more confident voice—a voice that is made credible by the information and arguments you find and learn about but is not overshadowed by them.

Research as Inquiry

Why do we do research?

Based on the work you've done in school up to this point, you might be tempted to answer "because it is required." You've likely done many academic exercises that looked something like this:

> Write a paper about the Cold War between the United States and the Soviet Union that followed World War II. Describe its root causes and later events that influenced its continued escalation. Your paper should be 7 to 9 pages long and must include 7 secondary or primary sources.

The expectations for such an assignment are largely that of a **report.** A report gathers, summarizes, and, in some cases, synthesizes information from other sources. Assignments like this are meant not only to help you to learn about the topic itself but also to extend your learning capacity by insisting that elementary exercises like copying information from a single encyclopedia or website are no longer adequate. The requirement for a specific number of sources and a minimum length are not random; they suggest the degree of detail and the variety of perspectives that

Teaching Academic Research

My job is to help students find and develop research topics. I see so many teenagers with so much to say, but with no facts to back up their opinions. It is my job to teach them how to use the resources that are available to them in order to obtain the knowledge that they want. My job also includes re-training students to think of research as a search for truth instead of the support for a previous assertion. The struggle lies in the sifting of an enormous amount of information in order to find your own answers to life's pertinent questions. In my own research, I would not survive without my computer. It is my world. It is my dictionary, my thesaurus, my grade book, my co-teacher, my inspirational speaker, and my access to a world of information. I use the Internet to find interesting activities and writing prompts for my students.

—*Jodi Heller (High School English teacher)*

the instructor feels is necessary for students to learn—both about the topic and about the process of doing research.

Even in college, you are given instructions that describe research expectations for many of the assignments that you do. Assignments developed by your professors provide guidelines for success, discuss necessary steps toward producing a strong paper, and make specific demands much like the one above—number of pages, number of sources, and so on. The guidelines are meant to show you what the teacher considers an adequate treatment of the assignment. But you know *me* well enough by now (if you've been reading carefully) to know that I'm not going to let you rest on "adequate." So allow me to let you in on a little secret: Teachers give you guidelines for "adequate," but what they really want is something beyond that, especially when it comes to writing. What teachers really want is to have their socks knocked off.

Knocking socks off is largely about *ethos*—the character you portray to your readers (in this case, your teachers). Creating an *ethos* that will make your readers confident in your conclusions and that will make them read what you've written with real interest begins with knowing a good deal about your topic. But don't confuse *having* a great deal of information on your topic with *knowing* a great deal about your topic. Though becoming a true expert in a topic might take years, forming a voice viable enough to speak or write confidently on a topic can be accomplished much more expeditiously than you think. If your research is properly limited, focused, and disciplined, it can certainly make you conversant on a topic and so allow you into the dialog surrounding it.

What elements are necessary to becoming conversant on a topic? You need vocabulary—the words that capture the key concepts involved in a topic. You need to know the commonplaces surrounding the topic—the generally accepted aspects of work being done on that topic. You need to know the main characters— the people whose *ethos* on the topic is most firmly established. And you need to know the most important issues surrounding the topic—what most people involved in this conversation are talking about. What flashpoints or key items are debated—the stases? You will, of course, also benefit by learning as many established "facts" on the issue as possible, making sure that they come from credible (and usually multiple) sources.

So, let's start again: Why do we do research?

Because in doing research we learn more about our topic and fields of interest, because research helps us to uncover useful and interesting things to say about our topic, and because, in many cases, research helps us to learn a great deal about ourselves and our predispositions, challenging us to see the world in new ways. We do research to become capable participants in a discussion.

RESEARCH AS A MEANS, NOT AN END

In Chapters 5 and 6, you learned reading techniques designed to help you to listen to the professional conversations in various academic disciplines and professions. If you wish to also enter into those conversations as a participant, more developed research methods will be your entry point. Though college-level researching draws on skills of information collection that you already learned, you also need new skills that can help you to speak with authority on a topic. Those skills emerge from our motivation to perform research.

One of the misconceptions that students often have about academic research is that finding and relaying information is the *goal* of the process. Real research, rather, is motivated by a sincere need to learn more about a topic so as to speak or write credibly about it, and to draw substantive and reasonable conclusions; finding information is the means to that end. Consider, for example, how Jane Whittaker approached research in her work as a computer systems architect:

> Research in my field is multi-faceted. There is internal and external information to be gathered and analyzed. And there are very definite right and wrong conclusions to be drawn, and hefty consequences to be paid for bad research or bad conclusions.
>
> The information is very current—in some cases so current, it's not published and we have to go to the sources for conversations with researchers or developers. Our internal research involved measuring the usage of our technical resources: how many trades were processed, in what time frames, how many people are using the system at any point in a 24-hour period, a week, a month, a quarter, a year, how many jobs run, how much memory is used, when, how much data is stored, on what media, how long are we required by the SEC to keep that data, how often is it accessed, and so on. These are all empirical questions, but there are many schools of thought on what information to capture and how to calculate the necessary statistics. This changed regularly and required constant research to be sure we were not using outdated or disgraced methods.
>
> The really difficult information to gather and make decisions about was the direction of technology. A firm as large as mine had to be cutting edge—but not bleeding edge. It needed to know what new technology was on the horizon, who was using it, how was it faring, and what other vendors were offering. And I had to look ahead: I had to consider whether deciding on A would make choosing B impossible next year, what's compatible with what we've got, with what the firms we communicate with have, etc. Wrong decisions can cost the firm hundreds of millions of dollars, either in replacement costs, upgrades, or lost business.

Research Goals on the Job

The difference between academic research and the research I do now? Time and resources. In school, no matter what field you're in, you have lots of time to learn what types of sources are out there and how to get them. In the work world, with time and budget constraints, you really don't have the option to spend hours and hours researching. Your focus needs to be on getting the job done.

—*Eric Engle, Geologist, Del Val Soil*

The high-stakes research that faced Jane Whittaker was approached as a series of problems to be solved and decisions to be made. The process was also creative, since not all of the information necessary to act knowledgeably on the topic was available in a single location or through a single form of research. No set of guidelines was available on how to conduct this research; what needed to done and how much information was necessary was dictated by the goals and needs of the situation. How much research did Whitaker need to do? Enough to make reasonable, considered conclusions about the issues she faced.

Though academic research has somewhat different ends than that done by a professional on the job, the two types do share one key characteristic: Research must be motivated by a sincere desire and need to locate the most useful information that can serve a specific goal. After all, the information people remember best is that which they treat as most useful (touching a hot stove is a bad idea; Lorenzo's has the best pizza; John is an excellent proofreader; Terry owns a set of jumper cables). Information like this rarely slips our mind because it is *contextualized*—it responds to a real need. In order for the information you collect for researched writing to have that same staying power in your mind, you must prepare for research in ways likely to create that effect. To treat research as a means to an end that you really wish to achieve, you must first imagine the ends that are being sought, asking questions like these:

- What question am I trying to answer, or what problem am I trying to solve, or what phenomenon or process am I trying to explain?
- What specific information do I need to speak authoritatively?
- What information does my *audience* need to understand the issue and to find me a credible voice on the topic?

By asking such questions, you do not just seek information on a topic but search for ways to solve a problem, to fill a gap, and to prepare yourself to speak or write knowledgeably. The inventional research activities discussed below can help you to generate those questions and so to set your research on a productive path.

FOCUSING RESEARCH GOALS

To make your research process as focused as possible, you can look at it not as a task of collecting "facts" but as a process of collecting what Aristotle called "available arguments"—gathering and thinking through existing approaches to an issue that others have used and that might be useful to you. In an information age, the problem is rarely finding enough "facts." The real problem is finding *useful* facts—those that help you to complete your research goals. That, of course, requires you to approach research in focused and organized ways, even before you go out to seek information. Consider the following scenarios, which illustrate very different approaches to researching:

John is assigned a paper on school violence. He starts online with several search engines, using subject and key word searches to locate articles and websites on "school violence," and he finds many potential sources of information. He does his best to choose ten sources that seem to be reliable: All the websites have the .edu, .gov, or .org domain, indicating that they are from the websites of educational, government, or nonprofit institutions (which are not trying to "sell" us anything). All the articles are from reputable refereed journals and established magazines. He also finds three recent books on the topic—recent enough to be applicable. He now has a list of potential sources for his paper.

Jennifer is also writing a paper on school violence. She spends her first week writing informally on a number of inventional questions: What do I already know about school violence? What do I classify as violence in school (is violence in schools related to guns and other weapons, or is bullying violence as well? Are teacher-student relations ever violent? Are fights after football games a form of school violence?)? She also finds herself freewriting on related topics: Is violence a recent phenomenon, or is it something that has simply gotten more press recently due to a few isolated but severe incidents? Are other forms of violence also growing? Is there any relation between school violence and the number of latchkey children? As she writes, other questions occur to her as well: Is school violence more likely to happen in specific areas of the country or in specific types of communities? Does it usually take place among specific races (or between them)? By using these inventional techniques, Jennifer identifies a range of questions that are of interest to her and might be of interest to her readers. She has, to this point, done no formal searches.

Which of these students is further along in the process of writing a researched essay? John has clearly gathered more information: He already has isolated ten pieces of seemingly reliable information. Jennifer has only a list of questions. However, as Aesop noted in his fable of the tortoise and the hare, the race does not always go to the swift. As this process continues, John will not only need to make sense of the articles and books he has collected but he will likely have a hard time bringing them together in a coherent way, because what he has collected lacks a focus and a limited topic. He has information; but he will likely have a difficult time learning about a specific aspect of school violence because he has not developed ways to organize that information.

In contrast, Jennifer has not collected any information yet. But when she does, the fruits of that research will be focused on specific questions and so will be easier to organize around a single, limited thesis question, or at least a limited series of related questions. If, for example, she decides the key question to explore is whether school violence is related to students' race, she will have a much smaller number of sources, but the source materials will be closely enough related to allow for more intensive and focused learning and so give her the chance to discuss her topic in credible ways—to become an expert.

These scenarios illustrate general principles about doing research—and especially the value of writing activities that can help you to seek specific, contextualized information. Clearly a combination of the two techniques is possible. You might begin by writing informally in order to focus your research questions and to consider likely sources of information and opinions on those questions. You might also perform an initial search and, based on the general information you collect, generate new, more complex questions and lines of inquiry. In this way, the process is *recursive*—you think and do inventional writing, you search, you think and do more inventional writing, and you re-search. That cycle can continue quite productively throughout the process of writing a researched project.

WRITING TO EXPLORE 7.1

Early in this book, we discussed the rhetorical canon of invention—the many available techniques for generating and developing ideas. Inventional activities are important for writing researched papers as well. This initial writing can help you, like Jennifer, to focus the goals of your research.

In order to practice focusing your research, imagine that you are interested in the topic of affirmative action and, more specifically, in whether affirmative action programs are still serving a useful purpose in our country. (Or, if you are currently beginning a researched project on some other topic, you can use that topic instead.) This topic has a good deal of exigency, as legislators and citizens consider whether to continue these longstanding programs that were designed to bring equity to higher education and the workplace. But the topic is also large and diffuse—so large that researching just the topic of affirmative action is likely to be extremely frustrating as you attempt to sort through the bundles of information available

To prepare yourself to research a facet of this topic, you must use the inventional techniques that you've learned about in this book and that were illustrated by Jennifer's processes in the above example. In your writer's notebook,

- Develop as many good questions and approaches as you can about the general topic of affirmative action (or on your own topic), thinking about the many groups of people that affirmative action can affect.

- Choose a question that particularly interests you and develop it by considering what information you might need to investigate that topic.

- Consider what audiences might be interested in such a topic, and write questions that they might be likely to ask. Consider also the academic disciplines or other discourse communities that might be involved in this area of research.

- Make a list of the types of information that you might need in order to begin a serious investigation of your more limited topic; be creative in developing this list, moving beyond general types of information to more specific ones. For example, you might determine that you need information on the percentage of African Americans who attended college before and after affirmative action laws were instituted.

- Share your questions with others in your class. In small groups or via e-mail, create a list of possible approaches to research on affirmative action.

The goals of inventional writing activities like those above are first to open up the possibilities for an investigation of this broad topic and then to begin focusing on narrower questions that can not only help you to begin your search but also to organize and contextualize the information as you locate it.

But the questions that you generate by inventional writing of this type are limited to the issues that you can develop on your own. In order to enrich your list of possible lines of inquiry—ways to thoroughly investigate and learn about a topic—you might also see what others have identified as key issues surrounding your topic.

WRITING TO EXPLORE 7.2

Imagine that you have done an initial search for information on the topic of affirmative action and have located the following article. Annotate this article with notes in the margins and, using the techniques of active reading discussed in Chapters 5 and 6, isolate key issues, areas of interest, stasis points, and conjectures made by the author.

    Use the article as a way to collect possible approaches to further inquiry into the topic, asking what questions it raises and what aspects of the topic seem most worth pursuing. That is, let the reading help you toward more focused, more specific areas for investigation. (If you are beginning research on another topic, find one article that overviews that topic and use it instead.)

The Contextualization of Affirmative Action: A Historical and Political Analysis

Fayneese Miller, Xae Alicia Reyes, and Elizabeth Shaffer

Affirmative action is defined as a determined effort to ensure that ethnic groups that are significantly underrepresented in colleges and/or in the workplace are more equitably represented. Over the years, the definition has been expanded to include women, people with disabilities, and other groups that have been historically underrepresented in certain fields and educational institutions. It was never the intent of affirmative action to force unqualified individuals into any institution (Lorber, 1994, pp. 216–217). This latter point, however, serves as the basis for the disgruntlement that many Americans have with affirmative action. The purpose of this article is to describe the historical journey of affirmative action and to show how it has become the political piranha of the 1990s. Another purpose is to show how affirmative action has benefited most Americans and that its effects in changing the status quo have not been as great in some areas as had been hoped.

Historical Origins of Affirmative Action

Affirmative action programs were designed in the context of laws prohibiting discrimination against racial and ethnic minorities. Drawn up in the crisis atmosphere of World War II and the subsequent optimism of the Civil Rights Movement, presidentially issued regulations and federal laws prohibited employers from automatically excluding potential employees solely on the basis of race or ethnicity (Hacker, 1992, pp. 118–119).

Affirmative action was enacted to end discrimination in the workforce. The problem that affirmative action was supposed to eliminate was the systematic exclusion of workers from consideration for jobs. Although Blacks were trained for particular jobs, when they applied for jobs commensurate with their training, they would not be hired. One reason for not hiring qualified Blacks was many employers did not think a Black person should earn the high wages that accompanied skilled labor positions. Specifically, it was thought that Blacks should not earn more than Whites, regardless of the skill level of the White employee. Another reason for not hiring a Black person was White employers thought their White employees would refuse to work with "coloreds." Initially, these employers were not interested in affirmative action in the workplace, they simply wanted government protection of their freedom to choose.

The government refused to protect the free choices of those who did not want to work with people of color, since this was considered antithetical to the interests of a nation mobilizing its entire population for a war effort. Additionally, the request to protect employers' freedom to choose was in direct conflict with the government's attempt to put forth a model of human freedom to challenge Nazi Germany and the Soviet Union. Demonstrating that the United States cared about justice for all, including the ability to compete fairly for a job, was considered a more significant national interest than protecting White workers' racial comfort (Takaki, 1993, pp. 397–400). Such justice arguably increased the national ability to fight wars and to produce goods and offered a working model of the liberal principle that freedom and power are synonymous. However, when it became apparent that Whites might no longer benefit from inclusionary practices, governmental policies reverted back to exclusionary practices.

Although employment discrimination was eventually outlawed, exclusionary practices continued, and it soon became apparent that the historical legacy of racial and ethnic exclusions could be corrected only by taking affirmative actions in education and training programs, job testing, and promotions. Modes of recruitment and channels of family and community knowledge about job availability had to be opened up. Job tests and promotion criteria, designed according to the experiences of White workers, had to be rethought to include the experiences of African American workers (Freeman, 1978, p. 109).

Similarly, sex discrimination was thought to be parallel to race discrimination. It was assumed that women, given the chance, would have work aspirations and abilities similar to those of men, would get jobs for which they had not previously been considered, and would push to have the labor force integrated by gender. Congressional passage of the Equal Pay Act (1963) and inclusion of "sex" as a prohibited category for job discrimination in the 1964 Civil Rights Act worked to alleviate both sex and race discrimination (Evans, 1989, pp. 275–276).

The Civil Rights Act of 1964 forbade discrimination in education, training, hiring, promotion, and salaries on the basis of race and gender. Following the passage of this act, affirmative action was formally established by President Lyndon Johnson in 1965.

Affirmative action guidelines instructed organizations that the proportion of students, apprentices, new workers, and workers at every level should reflect the proportion of people of every race and gender in the general population, provided they had suitable qualifications (Lorber, 1994, p. 217). It was never the intent of affirmative action to hire based on such nebulous characteristics as race or gender. The legislation clearly dealt with proportionality and qualifications.

Blacks and women were clearly underrepresented in the labor force prior to the legislation in the 1960s. In many areas, the underrepresentation continues. The underrepresentation is often due to biased perceptions of the ability of women and their "place" within society. The scope of discrimination regarding women's economic independence relative to that of men's should not be underestimated. This is especially so during the time prior to the passage of legislation in the 1960s. As numerous histories of professional women have shown, women were systematically excluded from formal education programs and from various jobs and career ladders even though they had struggled to achieve the necessary credentials (Evans, 1989, pp. 261–262). The breakdown of overt discrimination worked to dismantle barriers to free choice for people of color and women. The notion of affirmative action served as a protection from exclusion (Goldin, 1990, pp. 201–202; Kirp, Yudof, & Franks, 1986, pp. 9–10).

The struggle for equality has been notable not only in the workforce but in our educational system. Public education policy in the United States reflects society's struggle to balance the values of individualism and equality. Equality requires that everyone in our society have equal access to a quality education, regardless of background. Because of the history of discrimination in this country, it has been necessary to remove or minimize the barriers to education for large segments of the population who have been denied equal access to schooling. Excluded populations have included new immigrants, Blacks, working-class people, people living in poverty, and women. These populations have been excluded or denied access to secondary and higher education institutions (Hacker, 1992, p. 135).

Large segments of the population were virtually excluded from secondary and postsecondary education in the United States. This continued until well after World War II. Two of the most significant changes in American education after World War II were the adoption of the G.I. Bill of Rights, which gave all returning veterans financial support for college, and the 1954 Supreme Court decision Brown v. Board of Education. This landmark decision declared that the prior "separate but equal" statute was unconstitutional, and with this legal support, African Americans began to demand access to equal educational programs (Hacker, 1992, p. 161).

A major effort was made in the 1960s and 1970s to bring the level of schooling to an equal standard for African Americans, Latinos, and women. However, beginning in the 1980s, the argument was reignited that educational excellence had been sacrificed in the pursuit of equality (Sowell, 1994, p. 177). Nevertheless, affirmative action was one of the methods used to assist previously excluded populations in achieving equal access to educational opportunity.

Current Political Climate in Relation to Affirmative Action

Currently, affirmative action is under siege. The election of 1994 brought a sweeping change in our political climate. Conservatives have, for some time, expressed opposition to affirmative action policies (Roberts & Stratton, 1995, p. 80). With new political clout, that opposition is being argued more forcefully and will, no doubt, result in continued and protracted debates on affirmative action and possibly a reversal of the policy. During this past year, the Supreme Court ruled in Adarand Constructors, Inc. v. Pena that tough and uniform rules need to be used to examine race-conscious programs. This decision serves to question all affirmative action programs and to subject them to strict guidelines. Under this standard, many federal work and education programs that in the past have given aid to racial and ethnic minorities will be disallowed. The University of Texas at Austin's law school was legally forbidden to use race as an admission criteria. The Clinton administration's recent review of federal affirmative action policies led to the decision to amend rather than rescind the policy (Fineman, 1995, p. 25). The University of California recently voted to eliminate affirmative action procedures from its admission guidelines. The majority of the citizens in the state of California who voted in the fall of 1996 supported Proposition 209, which eliminates affirmative action in California. All of these incidents are examples of the kind of fundamental change we are likely to see in the future. By institutionalizing preferential treatment, many people believe affirmative action results in reverse discrimination, and, therefore, affirmative action as a policy is seen by some as a direct contradiction to the American ideal of meritocracy (Cose, 1995, p. 34). Millions of Americans believe in the American Dream and view the United States as a country in which, for the most part, hard work and merit determine who prospers and who does not (Oliver & Shapiro, 1995, p. 6). These Americans deny, in whole or in part, that racism and sexism result in discrimination (Hacker, 1992, p. 60). These Americans see merit as color and gender coded. That is, people of color, more so than women, are not as meritorious as men, especially White men.

Asian Americans are the only group—of those that can be classified as an ethnic minority—who are viewed as meritorious. Some Asian Americans have even come to believe that they are more meritorious than other ethnic minority group members. Simply put, they have bought into the "model minority myth," a myth that serves to alienate them from other ethnic minorities and affect their ability to take advantage of psychological and social welfare services, even when it is clear that the services would benefit their mental health. The myth has also led to a backlash against Asian Americans. During the economic difficulties of the early 1980s, Asian Americans were beaten to death or accused of taking away jobs from "Americans." This myth has also created inertia among Asian Americans about affirmative action or misplaced resentment of Blacks and Latinos. According to Matthews (1995), former executive director of the Asian American Resource Workshop, "Asian Americans have suffered from being the 'model minority.' As a group, we have not taken a formal side. Our community has continued to be complacent on this issue." The model minority myth has created and will continue to create conflict among ethnic minorities. More important, the conflict will have a greater effect on the determination of future policies on the topic than any other event. It would therefore seem that instead of conflict, compromise is needed.

Many Asian Americans believe that if racial quotas are used, they may be hurt by affirmative action policies. Specifically, they believe they will lose coveted spots in the professional schools, and their place in college admissions will be taken by Latinos and African Americans. According to preliminary data that we have collected on college students' attitudes toward affirmative action, Asian Americans would prefer that admission to college be based on merit or what they perceive as "the regular admissions criteria." At the University of California at Berkeley and Los Angeles, Asian students have complained that they have been hurt because the number of places they were qualified for had been greatly reduced (Shea, 1995, p. 12). According to Hacker (1992), "The fear of having 'too many' Asians seemed to many a replay of policies colleges once had concerning Jews" (pp. 138–139). Because Asian students would be allocated most of the "race-blind" places because of their academic records, there is potential conflict between Asian American students and other students of color (Hacker, 1992, p. 141). Average SAT scores among low-income students, for example, reflect that Asians score almost 100 points higher than Latinos and 140 points higher than African Americans (Hacker, 1992, p. 138). Although some might argue that for Asian American students, affirmative action can both create and negate opportunity, as Katal (1996) argued, affirmative action has many benefits for Asian Americans. The problem with Asian Americans' denigration of affirmative action and embracement of a system is that they are assuming they are perceived as equals by the American population. They are assuming that they will not be the victims of discrimination.

Perceptions about America

America is often seen as a country that preaches the ideals of equality but practices the hypocrisy of privilege based on race, gender, and class (Hacker, 1992, p. 129). Preferential treatment for Whites is so successfully institutionalized that most White people are unaware of it (Hacker, 1992, p. 32). There is also the belief that White men are being hurt and discriminated against because of affirmative action policies (Hacker, 1992, p. 51).

However, this belief does not reflect reality. White males are the most educated and the most politically powerful, and occupy the most prestigious occupations in this country (Swoboda, 1995, pp. A1, A18). White males constitute 33% of the population but make up 80% of tenured professors, 80% of the U.S. House of Representatives, 90% of the U.S. Senate, 97% of school superintendents, and 95% of top management at Fortune 2000 industry and service firms (Hacker, 1992, p. 124; Kaufman-Rosen & Kalb, 1995, p. 24; Swoboda, 1992, pp. A1, A18; U.S. Department of Labor, 1995, pp. 1–3). White males may claim to be hurt by affirmative action, but affirmative action has not yet come near to equalizing their preferential treatment.

Naison (1995), in a review of Roberts and Stratton's book *The New Color Line: How Quotas and Privilege Destroy Democracy,* stated: "To equate the inequities and inconveniences white males face today to the poverty, disfranchisement and raw physical terror Blacks experienced in the first half of the 20th century shows an astonishing capacity for historical amnesia" (p. 5). The only way one can hold to a belief in a meritocracy, in the light of this status, is to believe in the biological superiority of White men. Such is the philosophy espoused by the popular book *The Bell Curve* (Herrnstein & Murray, 1994).

Contemporary Outcomes: Challenges and Problems

The positive results of affirmative action can be seen in the increase of African Americans and females in every sector of middle-class professional life—from pilots to newscasters (Hacker, 1992, pp. 112–113, 146). There has been an increase in the number of Asian Americans and women business owners. Affirmative action has especially benefited women, who have enjoyed a 57% increase in the number of women-owned businesses and who have become 43% of workforce managers (Kaufman-Rosen & Kalb, 1995, p. 23). Affirmative action has helped to create a new Black middle class and to transform the role of women. Affirmative action, however, is still needed to continue leveling the playing field. For example, although Harvard University states that last year 6 out of

18 tenure positions were offered to women, "Harvard has averaged only one woman for every 250 positions over the last 24 years. At that rate it will take up to 80 years before the faculty looks truly coed" (Hancock & Kalb, 1995, p. 81). On average, nationwide only 23% of college faculty members are women (Hancock & Kalb, 1995, p. 81). According to Lawrence Bussey, chief of the Reports and Analysis Branch at the Office for Civil Rights (OCR) at the U.S. Department of Education, 4,976 complaints of racial discrimination were received by OCR in the federal fiscal year 1995. Preliminary figures show 5,852 hate crime incidents were reported to the FBI during 1994. The incidents were reported by more than 7,200 law enforcement agencies in 43 states and the District of Columbia (U.S. Department of Justice, 1995, p. 1). Sexual harassment, until recently, was an acceptable American practice. In 1991, the Urban Institute sent out young Blacks and young Whites with equivalent resumes and references. They were trained to behave identically in their application for entry level jobs. The Whites were hired at a statistically higher rate (Littwin, 1995, p. 7).

The effect of affirmative action rollbacks on students of color will cause a significant decrease in educational and job opportunities. It will cause a decrease in labor force diversity, which will mean a decrease in role models and an increase in the attractiveness of alternative roads to success. It will cause a decrease in collaborative efforts to address institutional racism and sexism, which will mean decreased collaboration between high school teachers and counselors and college recruiters to increase the pool of qualified applicants. There will be less opportunity to prove that nontraditional applicants can succeed in a college environment. There will be less motivation on the part of teachers, college professors, and school administrators to identify and modify factors within the school and college environment that discourage minority and female student achievement. There will be an increased reliance on tests as the significant indicator of merit. A reliance on biased standardized tests will fail to identify large numbers of talented youth (Sowell, 1994, p. 175). Finally, the negation of racism and sexism and the assertion of the belief that America is indeed a meritocracy flies in the face of the experience of students of color and women and will, undoubtedly, further alienate already disenfranchised students.

Affirmative action is necessary for our country's economic survival. As two-career families become an economic necessity and single-parent homes steadily increase, all families are helped by policies that discourage discrimination against women. As children of color look at their options in society, affirmative action will result in their seeing people of color in a wider variety of careers—from police officers to congressional representatives. As corporate America looks to expand its markets and maintain its workforce, diversity is essential. By the year 2000, 85% of the new entrants to the workforce will be women and minorities

(U.S. Department of Labor, 1995, p. 3). To succeed economically, American demographics require a diverse workforce.

Racism and sexism are no longer profitable. Legislated integration and affirmative action help us rid ourselves of an ideology that has outlived its usefulness. affirmative action not only benefits a majority of workforce, it is necessary for the prosperity of the economy as a whole. Continuing to blame Blacks, Latinos, Asians, and women for life's frustrations provides an easy but expensive scapegoat.

In sum, although the moral issue is that affirmative action is one vehicle to mitigate the impact of past and present discrimination, the economic issue is that the combination of demographic changes and the increased need for skilled workers requires us to better use the human resources that have, until recently, been underused. It is at this critical time in our society that affirmative action is under siege. Some argue that affirmative action is necessary to level the playing field and ensure that minorities and females have equal access to education and careers. Others argue that affirmative action is a biased system that unfairly discriminates against the most qualified applicants. As Cose (1995) states, "It's easy, and politically expedient, to pretend that everything would be fine if affirmative action weren't screwing things up. The truth, of course, is much more complicated. Even if the movement to ban affirmative action succeeds, there is every reason to believe we will find ourselves pondering how to deal with the same difficult questions of racial estrangement and inequality that spawned affirmative action in the first place" (p. 34).

Affirmative action is by no means a perfect public policy. It is, however, the only means currently available to ensure that all people are created equal and have the opportunity to succeed.

References

Cose, E. (1995, April 3). The myth of meritocracy. *Newsweek.*

Evans, S. (1989). *Born for liberty: A history of women in America.* New York: Macmillan.

Fineman, H. (1995, April 3). Race and rage. *Newsweek.*

Freeman, A.D. (1978). Legitimizing racial discrimination through antidiscrimination law: A critical review of Supreme Court doctrine. *Minnesota Law Review, 62,* 109.

Goldin, C. (1990). *Understanding the gender gap: An economic history of American women.* New York: Oxford University Press.

Hacker, A. (1992). *Two nations: Black and White, separate, hostile, unequal.* New York: Ballantine.

Hancock, L., & Kalb, C. (1995, December 11). Harvard held up. *Newsweek.*

Herrnstein, R., & Murray, C. (1994). *The bell curve: Intelligence and class structure in American life.* New York: Free Press.

Katal, N. (1996). *Affirmative action and Asian American.* Unpublished paper presented at a conference on affirmative action, Brown University, Providence, RI.

Kaufman-Rosen, L., & Kalb, C. (1995, March 27). What about women? Affirmative action: The White House searches for ways to regain control of a treacherous issue. *Newsweek.*

Kirp, D.L., Yudof, M.G., & Franks, M.S. (1986). *Gender justice.* Chicago: University of Chicago Press.

Littwin, A. (1995, October 19). Remedying a current injustice. *The Brown Daily Herald,* p. 7.

Lorber, J. (1994). *Paradoxes of gender.* New Haven, CT: Yale University Press.

Naison, M. (1995, December 3). Assessing affirmative action [Book World]. *Washington Post,* p. 5.

Oliver, M.L., & Shapiro, T.M. (1995). Race, wealth and inequality in America. *Race, Wealth and Inequality in America,* 4(6).

Roberts, P.C., & Stratton, L.M., Jr. (1995). How we got quotas: The color code. *National Review.*

Shea, C. (1995). Affirmative action on the line: Under UCLA's elaborate system race makes a big difference. *Chronicle of Higher Education.*

Sowell, T. (1994). *Race and culture: A world view.* New York: Basic Books.

Swoboda, F. (1995, March 16). Glass ceiling firmly in place. Panel finds minority, women are rare in management. *Washington Post,* p. A18.

Takaki, R. (1993). *A different mirror: A history of multicultural America.* Boston: Little, Brown.

U.S. Department of Justice. (1995). *Uniform crime reports: Hate crime 1994.* Washington, DC: Federal Bureau of Investigation.

U.S. Department of Labor. (1995, May). *Facts on working women (No. 95-1).* Washington, DC: Women's Bureau.

Follow-up: After reading and annotating this article, go back to the questions you developed in Writing to Explore 7.1 and add to the concerns you raised in those notes any new issues that reading this article raised for you. What additional research areas does this article suggest? What new audiences? What new approaches to the topic?

WRITING A RESEARCH PROPOSAL

Though the thinking, reading, and writing done early in the research process is often informal and reflective, formalizing research goals can also be useful. Doing so forces you to convince an audience (as well as yourself) that the research you are about to undertake is worthwhile, well conceived, well planned, and feasible. It also compels you to begin developing a professional voice and *ethos*—to think and write as a member of a particular discourse community, and to articulate the goals for your research in ways that members of that community and your audience will consider credible. At this point in the research process, you begin moving from areas of *interest* to areas of *study*. Rather than generalizing about matters that interest you or relate to your professional or personal interests, you now need a more disciplined and focused process of acquiring, evaluating, and synthesizing information.

In academic and professional writing situations, this articulation of goals and processes often takes the form of a **proposal.** In the simplest terms, a proposal is a piece of writing that seeks permission to proceed with a project. On the job, professionals write proposals to ask for time, money, or both to pursue a project that they feel is worthwhile and that they hope others will consider worthwhile as well. Though they vary with circumstances, all proposals share common purposes—to convince others that the project is worth the resources devoted to it, that the plan is feasible, and that the personal resources (mental and physical) are available to make it work.

More specifically, writing a proposal for research you are about to undertake can serve a number of purposes. It forces you to articulate the value of your research to a real audience. In academic writing, your audience is your classmates or teachers; on the job, the audience is your superiors. Writing a proposal also forces you to envision the process through which the work can be accomplished well. Further, it requires you to articulate the specific areas that you will investigate—both to show the feasibility of the study (that it can be done) and to argue for your own *ethos* (that you can do it, that you know the right questions to ask).

This kind of planning is useful because, as with other forms of work, an organized and disciplined process gets the job done more effectively and, in many cases, more efficiently. Of course, *efficient* doesn't just mean *fast*. It means making the best use of time. Second, the *process* can help you to define the process of inquiry that you are undertaking, a process that requires discipline, time management, and the ability to sustain a long-term project through the long term—all skills that will help you in both your academic and professional careers.

As you develop a proposal, you must mold the ideas you've been considering as potential topics into a more cohesive topic question, along with a specific purpose and audience. What exactly is it that you are trying to learn? What exactly is the purpose to which you will put that information? And exactly what audience will be—or should be—interested in that topic and purpose? If, as discussed in Chapter 4, you think about writing as an action that moves readers from one point (what they think and/or know *now*) to another (what you want them to think and/or know *after* they read your essay), that will be a good starting point. However, before you can influence your audience, you need to do some learning yourself.

WRITING TO EXPLORE 7.3

To understand the mental work that leads to focused research methods, consider the thought that went into the student research proposal below. Though this proposal is unusual in approach—it is more personal and lengthier than the proposals you might construct—it illustrates nicely the mental processes that inform the early stages of the research process. As you read, annotate and make notes on the ways that this proposal makes the case that this research is necessary—and that the writer is the one to do it. Then, use your writer's notebook to consider the questions that follow.

Can She Do It? My Reality and a Proposal

Audra Shearer

My Reality: A new boy arrives at my high school near the end of the school year in 1999. He seems quirky and eccentric, qualities that most people use to describe my friends and I, so we befriend him. After a while he gets stranger and eventually scary—he threatens to rape a friend of ours, he says that he spies on some of us, and he develops an elaborate plan for the best ways to blow up the school to maximize destruction and death, complete with illustrations. My friends and I look to each other, unsure of how to handle it. The answer comes when the rest of the country wakes up to the reality of school violence on April 20th 1999, when we learn of a place called Columbine.

Proposal: What do all parents and educators like (and unlike) yourself have in common? A desire to protect and teach children in order to better their lives. This wish becomes harder to fulfill as we encounter a new kind of terror in modern society—school violence. We witness this monster on the news; we see it in our hometown schools. It has become an inescapable part of everyday life. For these reasons, it has become so important to protect the mental health and sense of security of the youth of today as they walk into classrooms that could erupt into violence at any moment. In order for children to grow and progress past these violent episodes in schools, we need to know what happens inside the minds of the children who are forced to witness or be harmed by the violence. What effect will it have psychologically to these future leaders of our country? These are questions that must be answered because we have a developing need to help our children through the changing times that bring violence directly into the school system. We need to know the psychological effects and repercussions of school violence on children in modern society. We need to know what society can do to help children cope with these tragedies. The topic question that I will address in my paper will be—"what effect does school or classroom violence have on children psychologically, and what are the best ways to cope with it?"

The purpose of writing this paper is to alert school officials, administrators, teachers and parents to the importance of following up on instances of school violence to protect the needs of children psychologically, and also to find ways to help children cope with school violence through constant psychological support. It would also serve as a way for me to learn about this topic. As a potential 'School Psychologist' in my future, I need to be aware of the methods to deal with violence and have an understanding about what I could do to help children through these hard times.

The topic of school violence is constantly in the news, yet the attention needs to be directed to helping children psychologically after the events have occurred instead of glorifying the tragedy for the violent offenders and the morbid public. The subject of the children involved should be the utmost concern, and everyone needs to know how to deal and cope with school violence. We need to help our children, and in order to do this we need to know what happens to these kids after being subjected to this kind of violence. We live in a constantly evolving society in which children need help along the course of their lives. Will school violence ever stop now that it has become almost commonplace and much publicized? Everyone needs to know about the research out there because we all will be future parents, educators or mentors, with children in our lives. In fact, as I revise this, an 'NBC News Special Report' interrupts the program I'm watching to report a school shooting that occurred minutes ago in San Diego with two children losing their lives and thirteen wounded. Every life involved is affected; we are affected merely by hearing about it. School violence has become so prevalent that we need to know how to help children who have been victims to it.

My paper will be addressed directly to school officials, administrators, teachers and parents (or basically anyone involved in the field of education or the lives of children). I can target my paper towards them by invoking their concern and love for children's well-being. These people would be eager to learn about this topic, and I can appeal to them through their love for children. I think it is safe to make a general characterization about this audience that they are passionate people. They put the lives of children first and would welcome any chance to read a paper like mine to help the kids that they hold dear. I hope to move my audience from a passive attitude to an active one about what they can do themselves to help children.

My present experience in Psychology, my major area of study, has prepared me for this project. We have read Psychology Journals in my classes, and this will help me to understand some of the material that I will find. My background in this field will help with psychological terminology to write this paper, and will also put me in contact with more experienced people than I in this field.

In order to construct this paper, I will continue my searching for resources that I started in class. I would love to find primary sources from an actual survivor, from Columbine maybe, or the recent event in California. Schools typically change their rules and regulations after a violent incident, and I would like to find research on the psychological effects of adding metal detectors etc. to school life. Do security measures like this cause fear? To become a credible writer on this subject I will also have to research the kinds of counseling available to students after violence, how many students return back to a previously violent school, a drop in grades or attendance, and the ways that students have become desensitized to incidents of violence.

The aftermath of writing a paper, for me, is like coming out of a dark cave with only one tunnel or direction, so establishing a timeline of events before I start is hard. A tried-and-true procrastinator, I will undoubtedly give myself unneeded pressure to finish up. Knowing that I have about two weeks between each paper in order to research, create and revise will help to keep me somewhat on track. Time is, of course, always an issue. This is a project that I will have to devote a lot of time to, and between my job and other classes, this is hard to come by. I have this game plan in mind for the near future:

- I want to have all source material collected by the end of this weekend, or before Monday 3/12. To this end I will go to the library and get the journals and books that I need articles out of that I discovered during our in class searching.

- During the week of 3/12–3/16 I would like to have all material read and annotated so that I can begin drafting with relative ease. I will have at least one good draft by the end of the weekend.

- The remaining time up to 3/22 I will revise my paper until I think I can do no more; I'll get up early the Thursday it is due and do more.

- I'll probably do a similar process for seeking additional information.

I am confident that I can do this. I am passionate to learning about this, and it has captured my attention because I believe that the information I present in my paper could promote so much learning to help children from suffering. It is a project worth my time; I have planned and looked ahead realistically to have enough time to write a strong piece, and I have found resources and credible information already to get me started on researching. I am ready to go and think that I am likely to succeed. So can I do it? I'll put myself up to the challenge and do the best that I can. The results will remain to be seen.

In order to understand the thinking that underlies a research proposal, consider the following questions in your writer's notebook:

- What is motivating Audra Shearer to undertake this research project?

- How does the research she is planning to undertake arise from personal concerns? What part of it is related to her life's work?

- What disciplines and discourse communities will Shearer enter as she conducts her research?

- What questions does she isolate in this proposal?

- What audience does Shearer imagine for this project? How does the knowledge of this audience's needs help to guide the research she is proposing?

- Does Shearer's proposal make its readers confident in its potential for success? How so?

The techniques for developing your lines of inquiry that we have been discussing in this chapter illustrate how important careful planning can be to successful research. Early research activities can also remind you of the many disciplinary and occupational stakeholders involved in the topics you examine. Consider, in this case, the affects of school violence on colleges, children, parents, school boards, security companies, weapons manufacturers, and so on. Then consider the academic stakeholders—those interested in the topic from a research standpoint: sociologists, political scientists, behavioral scientists, and education specialists, all interested in the phenomenon from a wide range of research perspectives.

The techniques we have been discussing also suggest that the process of formulating good research questions is recursive; research does not always proceed in simplistic or linear ways—finding a topic, finding sources, reading them, and then writing. You must come back again and again to the questions you are asking, developing and enriching them as you continue to learn more; good research always breeds more questions. Still, doing this early work can help you to stay focused on your areas of concern as you enter the sometimes overwhelming world of twenty-first-century information technologies—technologies that can provide floods of facts, conjectures, case studies, experiments, statistics, and so on. Finding your way through this wealth of information requires a combination of curiosity and discipline.

MEMORY, TECHNOLOGY, AND THE ORGANIZATION OF INFORMATION

As we begin our discussion of ways to efficiently gather information on your focused topic, you might recall the definition of "facts" that we developed as we discussed the common topics: When you examine complex issues, what you call facts are often really conjectures or *proposed* explications of some condition or

Technology and Research on the Job

The Internet has dramatically changed the research world in both the academy and in profession. Searches are so much easier—less time in the library and more time on the Net. In the medical arena, the copywriting we do needs to be completely backed by carefully documented references, so we do use research much like that in academia. Additionally, when we are researching for competitive intelligence reasons, we also use this form of research. We frequently handle custom research for clients, both qualitative and quantitative, depending on what we need to learn to get the job done. We use the results of research to develop positioning for a company, a product, or a service—to help us to understand perceptions that are out there, and with which we need to contend.

—*Robert Colleluori (Owner/operator, Robert Michael Communications, Inc., Marketing and Advertising Firm)*

phenomenon rather than unchanging and universally accepted ideas. That is one of the reasons for collecting ideas from many sources—to compare the conjectures and see what agreements and disagreements (or stasis points) exist. But in an information age, accessing varied and pertinent sources of information is often less difficult than managing that information.

Before computers, information-gathering was different. The collection and use of information was a physical process wherein you literally got your hands on information through books and periodicals in libraries. You paged through them manually, made photocopies and notecards, and worked to make sense of mounds of paper. Of course, some of those activities are still useful and necessary, but there's no doubt that things have changed significantly in a relatively short time. Many of us still remember the days when *searching* meant something quite different, and quite a bit more physical, than it does now.

Though the ways that we collect and use information have changed, some principles derived from the rhetorical canon of memory might help to avoid the negative repercussions of an information age—especially the problems that arise from information overload. For ancient rhetoricians, memory was important because a good speaker needed a ready supply of available arguments and stylistic techniques on which he could draw on any occasion. Since people now have powerful technologies for storing and accessing information, it might seem that human memory is no longer so important—but be careful before you jump to that conclusion.

Though the media through which you can obtain information has never been more powerful or more diverse, the availability of information doesn't necessarily translate into usefulness. Bombarded by "facts," you face new difficulties in selecting and evaluating the information that comes your way. And despite the existence of the information "out there," let's be honest—it doesn't do much good until it's "in here"—in your mind, that is. Just a look at a typical news network screen or an Internet site home page can illustrate the challenges that face you as a consumer or receiver of this information:

You are not only bombarded by this series of images, the bits and bytes of information on each new screen whenever you turn on the television or computer, but you also must choose among the seemingly endless stream of hits that can arrive when you search the World Wide Web or online subscription services for locating journal articles or books. Try it out yourself. Pick a general

(continued)

FIGURE 7.1 In order to see how much information bombards you from various sources, you need only look at your computer screen. The typical news network site features scrolling copy, numerous images, commentary, on-site reports, and news updates—often all at once. How much can be comprehended at once?

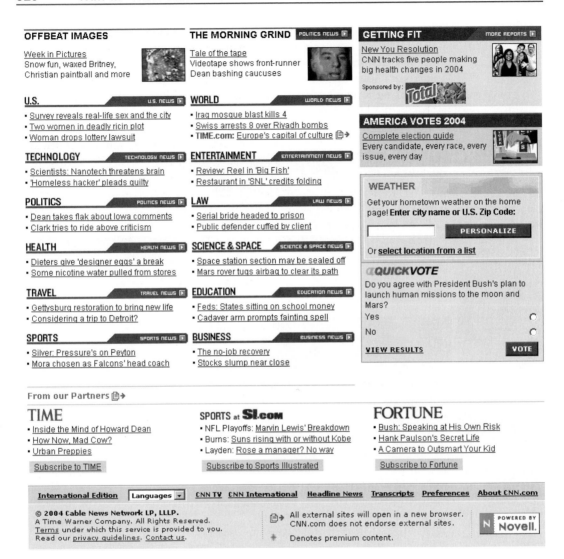

FIGURE 7.1 Continued

topic that interests you (baseball or cloning or Shakespeare) and perform a computer search; you'll be overwhelmed by a glut of information that can discourage the most voracious learner.

So where do you start? How do you resist the temptation to draw on the first
five or ten items delivered and to ignore the hundreds of others that might contain information that is more pertinent, more reliable, or more complex? The
work you've already done in understanding the goals of writing and the early

stages of communication can be useful as you enter the world of researching. However, in order to use technology effectively, you can also benefit by considering how information is stored in the virtual public memory systems.

Electronic resources are both like and unlike the public lending library. Both store information that you can access systematically. The organization of a library is based on particular subject areas. However, since libraries must shelve *physical* books, the Dewey Decimal and Library of Congress systems that organize them are one-dimensional—they are based on decisions about whether a particular book about the Middle East and its religions belongs, for example, in the area of philosophy/religion (classified in the B section of the Library of Congress shelves) or that of Eastern history (classified in the D section of the Library of Congress shelves). In that system, human knowledge is organized by predetermined subject areas, though some flexibility, of course, exists. Those physical spaces, defined by areas of knowledge, can also be physically browsed.

MAP OF LIBRARY OF CONGRESS SHELVING

Some Examples

A. General Works

AE Encyclopedias

AI Indexes

AP Periodicals

AY Yearbooks

B. Philosophy and Religion

B General philosophy

BC Logic

BF Psychology

BJ Ethics

BL-BX Religion

BM Judaism

BP Islam

BQ Buddhism

BR-BX Christianity

C. Auxiliary Sciences of History

C General Works

G. Geography and Anthropology

G Geography (general)

GB Physical geography

GC Oceanography

GN-GT Anthropology; Manners and customs

GV Recreation; Sports, games, and amusements

H. Social sciences (general)

HA Statistics

HB-HJ Economics

HB-HD Economic history and theory

HE Transportation and communication

HF-HJ Commerce, business, and finance

HM-HX Sociology

HQ Marriage and family; Women's studies

HV Crime and justice

L. Education

L Education (general)

LA History of education

LB Theory and practice; Teaching

LD-LJ Education in the United States

Q. General science

QA-QB Mathematics; Astronomy

QC Physics

QD Chemistry

QE Geology

QH Natural history

QK Botany

QL Zoology

QM-QP Human anatomy; Physiology

These physical spaces, of course, did not wholly define the way that people searched for information; even before computer technology, knowledge was cross-referenced in card catalogs so that the same book could be found by asking different questions (about the author, about the subject, about the title). So if you sought information on Islam, you would be directed to items in books about the Middle East as well as books about religion and philosophy.

Electronic library access systems have retained many of the principles of card catalog searches, but computer technology has broadened the ways in which you can search for information. The way in which information is arranged and recalled is now much more complex, much quicker, and much more flexible—both in the library and on the Internet. That is because rather than residing on a specific shelf, information also exists as electronic documents. These electronic documents are, in a sense, *shuffled each time you perform a search*. Rather than lying in distinct, predetermined areas, the information is fluid and moves to you as you create topic questions—as you invent ways to access the information you seek.

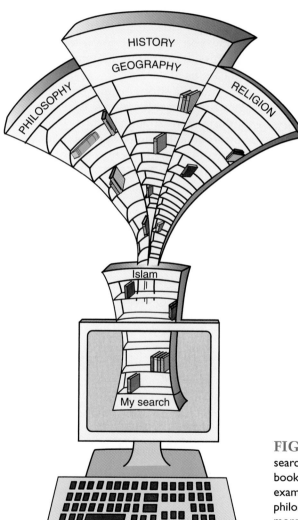

FIGURE 7.2 When you perform an electronic search, in effect, you create your own virtual bookshelf. A search for information on Islam, for example, pulls from electronic documents on philosophy, history, geography, religion, and many more areas. How your new shelf is arranged depends on the questions you ask.

You should also recall that all electronic documents are not the same. Though they all might wind up, one way or another, on your computer screen, they have gone through very different procedures to get there. For example, your college likely has subscription services that allow you access to refereed journals (discussed in Chapter 6 and Reading and Writing Applications 5). These journal articles are just like the print versions in credibility and authority because they have been refereed, or judged for accuracy and quality by experts. But not all websites are equally reliable. Some have a great deal of credibility by virtue of their sponsoring institution (the U.S. Government, the Folger Shakespeare Library, or university sites, for example), whereas others are simply web pages, created by individuals, that may or may not provide authoritative and reliable information and opinions. So, no matter how you search, it is important to assess the value of the source carefully (as is discussed further in reference to writing a proposal in Reading and Writing Applications 6).

With all these sources of information, your questions need to be really good ones—specific enough not to turn up too many unusable sources. They also must be well thought out to turn up the *right* information. Though the arrival of oodles of information on your desktop can be instantaneous, preparing good questions can take some time. That's why active approaches to the early stages of research are important, as illustrated in the scenario of Jennifer and John, Audra Shearer's proposal to write about school violence, and your own activities in the exercise involving affirmative action.

The most frequent way you turn up electronic information is through subject or keyword searches. You can turn a search engine or subscription service into a public library, browsing the virtual shelves on "cloning" or "baseball." But you can also be more efficient and more inventive by asking questions that yield data organized in ways that are more useful. The joy of computer searching, then, is manipulating information *before it even arrives* (that's also the challenge). By asking good questions, you can let the technology help you to limit and focus information; you create your own virtual bookshelves.

But the questions you ask when actually searching for materials must be written in a way that computers can understand. Though some search engines (Ask Jeeves, for example), purport to use natural language as the basis for searches—that is, you can ask a question in the way you would ask a person—most search engines (both Internet and periodical searches) use some form of Boolean logic or a version of library subject categories to function.

Boolean logic, named after mathematician George Boole, is a system of logic that can expand or limit the amount of information you receive based on the operators you use to create sets of information. Boolean operators are "AND," "OR," and "NOT." These terms function to manipulate the sets of information you receive—in effect, as we noted above, they help to reshuffle the pool of public information based on your search. They do so using a logic that you probably studied at some point in your mathematics classes, based on the Venn diagram. Though each search engine, and each college library, has its own set of electronic searching parameters, you can keep these general principles in mind.

If you use the operator AND, you are telling the search engine to find all the information filed by the combination of two or more keywords—that is, you want the engine to list all entries that include all the keywords you've joined by AND. So, if you were searching for items on affirmative action and hiring practices, you have several options.

You could search for "affirmative action," and the search would generally only find locations that have both these words joined together in that way—the word *affirmative* and the word *action*. If you found that this search returned too many hits, and hits that weren't organized according to your needs, you might limit the search by adding another operator.

Using the Boolean operator AND reduces the number of entries the computer will turn up. For example, if you wanted to focus the previous search, you might enter "affirmative action AND hiring AND United States." The resulting list would include only entries that had all three items as keywords. But you also must realize that it would *exclude* all entries that didn't explicitly mention the United States—even if the article or site happened to discuss *American* affirmative action programs. That's why it's sometimes important to search using several configurations of words until you find the best grouping.

Another Boolean operator that you can use is OR. Using OR expands the number of entries you'll retrieve, since it expands the question to retrieve items that use *any* of the terms your search includes. So, whereas "affirmative action AND hiring" will yield all entries that have both those keywords, "affirmative action OR hiring" will yield all entries that have *either* term. In this case, the logic of such a search is probably faulty—do you really want all entries that mention "affirmative action" *or* "hiring"? Think about all the unnecessary hits that "hiring" might produce.

However, the operator OR can be useful *in combination with* AND because it allows you to consider synonyms for words that might appear in articles (remember the example of America and United States above). For example, you

The Venn diagram below represents the results of a search using the Boolean operator "AND." The search returns only sites that include all three terms.

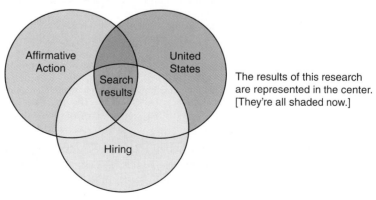

The results of this research are represented in the center. [They're all shaded now.]

FIGURE 7.3

Results of the search for "Affirmative Action OR hiring." This search will return all entries that include either of the two terms–a much larger set of results than with the search "Affirmative Action AND hiring," which includes only results that have both terms.

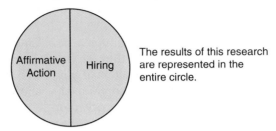

The results of this research are represented in the entire circle.

FIGURE 7.4

might search "affirmative action AND hiring OR employment." This will capture all entries that discuss both hiring and affirmative action, including those that use the term *employment* rather than *hiring*. (On many search engines, you can also use truncations like "employ*." The asterisk tells the computer to retrieve all entries that start with "employ" but that might have a variety of endings: employers, employment, etc.)

NOT is an operator that can help you to exclude false hits—returns of information that are clearly not what you are looking for. If, for example, you were searching for information on rapid eye movement, a physical phenomenon that occurs during deep sleep and is referred to as R.E.M., you might also turn up information on the musical group R.E.M. In order to perform this search more efficiently, you might search for "R.E.M. NOT music." That will tell the engine to exclude entries that include the keyword "music" as well as "R.E.M. " (Of course, an article about how music can enhance deep sleep, and so rapid eye movement, would be excluded. So be careful what you ask for—or don't ask for.)

This diagram shows how the Boolean operator "NOT" functions. The large circle represents all the hits from a search for "R.E.M." The smaller circle with the X represents the part of the search that is excluded by using the operator "NOT" (here, "not music"). The operator "NOT," then, is used to limit the number of false hits–hits that are on a topic that does not apply to the research you are doing.

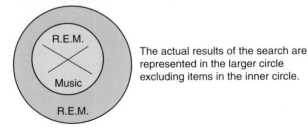

The actual results of the search are represented in the larger circle excluding items in the inner circle.

FIGURE 7.5

Knowing the Library of Congress headings (discussed above) can also be useful, since you can do "subject" searches on many search engines. Subject searches use the library classification categories to return information. Doing a subject search, in effect, asks the computer to let you browse the virtual shelves for books and/or periodicals that fit within those predetermined categories rather than creating your own combination of keywords, as you do with Boolean logic. So, in our example, searching "affirmative action" as a subject search will seek all information that has been categorized in that way by the Library of Congress, regardless of whether the words appear in the title. Each of these methods has enough advantages that, in most cases, it is worthwhile to try both types in order to refine your research base.

Knowing the logic of how a computer forms searches can help you to formulate your research more effectively. Instead of just punching in whatever terms or topic you are researching, take a few minutes to consider the Boolean logic or subject areas for your search; this simple step can not only provide more focused returns but also help to enrich your understanding of the concepts and topics that are related to your general topic. In Reading and Writing Applications 6, you'll have opportunities to try out these techniques.

To summarize, mature research methods require the following activities:

- Beginning from "the research impulse"—a sincere desire to learn about a topic;
- Viewing research as a means to that learning, not an end in and of itself;
- Treating research as a recursive process in which you don't merely collect everything, read it, and then write, but rather move back and forth among the parts of the research process;
- Using invention techniques to formulate good research questions;
- Formulating search terms from those research questions;
- Treating the collection of information as a search not just for "facts" or opinions but rather as a search for available arguments—ways to approach the issue or topic;
- Using information technology maturely—as a means controlling the machines and the information they access for you through limited and focused searches;
- Contextualizing your research as you search and as you read—that is, considering the material you find in light of your specific purposes, research questions, discourse communities, and rhetorical situations. This requires you to use the active reading techniques discussed in the previous two chapters.

Though the processes of accessing information efficiently that we have been discussing in this chapter are crucial, they are not ends in themselves. The real learning comes about not merely in shaking the information tree and seeing what falls; the real learning comes when you start to digest that information and make it your own. That's what we discuss in Chapter 8.

CHAPTER EIGHT

Building Credibility and Confidence through Researched Writing

Chapter 7 presented a method for collecting information meant to meet the needs of specific rhetorical situations. That process involved asking good questions and evaluating the information we collect for reliability and relevancy to our topic. But as we noted, "having" information isn't the same as understanding it. A mature research process must also help us to feel comfortable entering ongoing discussions about our topic.

WRITING TO EXPLORE 8.1

What are some topics you find comfortable discussing? Perhaps you feel conversant on a particular sport. Perhaps you know a good deal about mystery novels. Perhaps you've worked as an environmental volunteer and so are able to confidently discuss issues of conservation or recycling. Or perhaps you have already established yourself in a profession or career field and so have a strong working knowledge of that occupation.

Explain to a nonexpert audience some feature of an activity that you know a good deal about. Explain a fine point of a sport. Describe a position you have on a community issue. Or describe the challenges and pleasures of an occupation that you are currently engaged in or have held in the past. Help others to share your experiences.

Then, try writing the same information to people who know as much about the topic as you do, accommodating your style to the higher level of expertise.

The above exercise allowed you to assume an expert position, a comfortable *ethos* from which you could write without notes or references. Though your writing was not formal or polished, you probably did not lack ideas or language to describe the topic, and so the material flowed from your head rather naturally. Possessing that type of expert voice breeds confident, focused, and effective writing. Knowing the level of expertise of those to whom you write can also help you to decide how to express your ideas, as you may have noticed as you wrote to a more expert audience. Chapter 8 considers how your present occupation as a student can help you to move toward that same level of credibility in the academic and professional roles to which you aspire.

In order to test the validity of your ideas, you must enter into written and spoken conversations with other experts. "Entering into conversations with other experts" might sound a bit intimidating. But as a learner, you are striving to invent an expert *ethos* on each topic that you investigate, and if you have already spent time in a career field, as many current college students have, you bring a good deal of that experience with you. In any case, as you research a topic, you are not only attempting to learn and understand the "facts" but also to find ways to be comfortable discussing those "facts" with other experts.

Over years of reading student papers, I have noticed that when students write short, impromptu pieces on topics with which they are familiar, their style is readable, interesting, and inventive. However, when they write on topics about which they feel less expert, their writing becomes strained and lifeless—the essays become mere reports, listing the information and leaving the writer's voice behind. That change in style, I surmise, comes from a sort of inferiority complex—what can I say about a topic in the midst of experts who have studied a topic much more intensively than I have?

That inferiority complex and the related problems with style, I suggest, come from skipping an important step in the writing process: reflection. As you write academic papers, sometimes you merely collect and then regurgitate information. Since you don't feel confident with the topic, you act as a mere conduit of information collected from others. Good writers, conversely, pause to reflect on what they have learned in advance of going public with their thoughts. They continue to ask questions after collecting information—questions that can help them to feel comfortable going beyond the role of observer to entering into an ongoing conversation.

Before you can write confidently, then, you must go beyond overt reliance on outside sources. Despite the great usefulness of the library and computer as virtual public memory systems, you must still make use of the most powerful tool of all—your own mind. If you read actively during the research process, and if you pause to consider what you've learned, you will find that you have many new things to say about your topic. In this chapter, we discuss strategies for finding the credible voice with which to express those things.

Perhaps the most challenging aspect of writing academic papers that rely heavily on researched information is the retention of your own voice as a writer as you incorporate many other expert voices. Let's start with reasons why keeping your own voice in control is important. The truth is that when you write academic papers, the experts you cite often do know a good deal more about your topic than you do. That will be the case when you enter a profession as well; everyone will at least *seem* to know more than you do about that field of work. But in either case, simply to assume a subordinate position and so to let your position as a learner keep you from entering the conversation will not help you to move toward the professional voice and status that you seek; it will, to the contrary, teach you to subordinate your ideas to those of others.

Finding a more confident voice can be nurtured through your approach to the reading and research that you do. First, listen closely to the ways in which any given topic is discussed by experts—listening not only to the information itself but also to the terms of the conversation. Reading actively (as discussed in Chapters 5 and 6) and researching in the ways suggested in Chapter 7—researching to really learn about a topic rather than merely to gather information that will be transcribed in your essay—can increase the fluency and confidence with which you can discuss a topic. Like any initial attempt, your first steps might be tentative and reliant on the work of others. But those steps still must be taken as part of the liberal education that colleges provide and that your future work will require of you. You must learn how to converse with professionals in your field(s) of interest.

INVENTING *ETHOS* THROUGH EXPERTISE

Though the library and computer are indispensable tools in the learning process, it is important that we don't mistake them for learning itself. As we discussed in Chapter 7, the Internet and the library serve as a type of *public* memory to which you can look for information and informed opinions. But real learning takes place through your *individual* memory, as you recall what you have learned and attempt to make sense of the information you have collected—without the aid of your notes or source material. At this point in the writing process, as you stand poised between your role as reader/listener and your role as writer/speaker, you must take some time to see what you really know about your topic. In this moment, you can survey all the information you have collected and ask a simple (yet difficult) question: "What's your point?"

That question is really at the heart of a concept we discussed briefly in Reading and Writing Applications 3: the thesis. Though this concept is in some ways fairly straightforward (the thesis is the main point you are attempting to make), formulating a mature thesis in the context of the great deal of information you collect when writing a researched essay is no easy process. It requires you to bring together all that you have learned on a topic and to forge from that amassed information a central idea—*your* central idea—that will hold your writing together. We might use a related word to describe this process: **synthesis** ("syn-thesis": combining separate elements into a coherent whole or thesis).

One of the ways that writers construct a thesis is by finding their place within a dialog of others who have written on a topic. In fact, a good deal of the work you do as you prepare a draft is to situate yourself amid the experts and to find the gaps in the literature that you hope to fill through your own writing. For example, read the following introduction to an article on urban planning, written for a group of professionals in the field.

Putting the Future in Planning

Dowell Myers

Introduction

The future is generally considered to be a core concern of the planning profession. A central purpose of planning is to make decisions in the present that will guide future activities designed to make improvements for the benefit of the future community.

Two difficulties constrain planners' roles in shaping the future. First, the future consequences of planning actions are not knowable with much certainty. The context is often complex, with many interconnected elements, and planning actions such as those regarding land use or major public works often will have consequences many decades ahead. Second, amidst this uncertainty, decisions about the future require gaining agreement among a great many stakeholders, many of whom hold markedly different valuations of key factors, often backed by passionate, vigorously asserted views.

The twin hazards of uncertainty and disagreement form an essential context for planning's ambitions of shaping the future. In practice, planners may retreat to shorter-range decisions with more limited consequences. Or they may resort to public relations devices that may gain agreement in superficial ways. Still another response is to hide behind technical analyses that are not fully shared with the public, neither revealing the true level of uncertainty nor exposing judgments to potential disagreement. *Better methods are clearly desired for professional leadership regarding the future* [emphasis added].

Professionalism Regarding the Future

A decade and a half ago, Andrew Isserman (1985) issued his plea, "Dare to Plan," where he declared that planning had lost sight of the future and abandoned its role as both visionary and creator of better alternatives. Indeed, the search for political relevance and the burden of daily "firefighting" has focused the city planning profession on shorter-range events. Among academics, an even greater handicap has been restrictions imposed by social science that direct attention only where data exist—in the past, not the future.

There is an additional explanation for our neglect of the future. Planning is concerned with the two universal dimensions, space and time, but it is often difficult to address both at once. The planning profession's attention is focused on spatial area differences at a single moment in time, in part because of our focus on land use maps and on the now-ubiquitous geographic information systems. Certainly, the future has consequences for these spatial patterns, *but the future is a process unfolding in time, and that time dimension is much less visible in maps or in practice. At present, our methods for addressing the time dimension of planning are far less developed than those for space* [emphasis added].

In recent years, a resurgent awareness of the future has sprung forth, expressed through 2020 vision plans (Helling, 1998) and debates over smart growth, New Urbanism, and the like. Challenges faced in many U.S. universities to explain the importance of the small but vital planning field—if it's not architecture, public administration, geography, or engineering, what then?—have led to renewed reflections on professional identity and to rediscovery of the future. The Strategic Marketing Committee established by the Association of Collegiate Schools of Planning (ACSP) recently identified six key topics that anchor the identity of planning: human settlements, interconnections, the future, diversity, open participation, and connecting knowledge and action (ACSP Strategic Marketing Committee, 1997). Two of these six topics—interconnections and the future—are likely the most particular to the planning profession.

Interdisciplinary connections lie at the heart of planning, but this topic also exposes the field to criticism from more narrowly trained experts in the contributing fields. The future is the only topic that other professions have ceded to planners as relatively uncontested turf. Perhaps because it is uncontested, planners take this topic for granted. *We assume that the future is what we are about. But we give very little attention to sharpening our tools and inventing new procedures to address this vital aspect of our practice* [emphasis added].

Regrettably, we also exercise less leadership regarding the future than society deserves from us. A recent review identifies a sizable set of theories and tools useful for constructing the future in planning (Myers & Kitsuse, 2000). That review surveys methods of temporal analysis that link past, present, and future, and it discusses the relationships among projections, forecasts, and plans. Also addressed is the tension between activist shaping of the future and the unethical manipulation of projections to support desired objectives. Methods for representing the future are critical, and the review discusses envisioning, scenario building, and persuasive storytelling.

Admittedly incomplete, the planners' toolkit for addressing the future needs to be expanded and upgraded. It is important for planners to be knowledgeable about a wide range of existing methods, instead of relying on only a limited subset about which there is local knowledge. Often planners engage in reinventing the proverbial wheel, making up rather mediocre methods, rather than drawing upon the collective expertise of the profession. *Professional planners should be able to draw upon established methods for constructing the future as needed, improving those methods in the course of local adaptation, and then returning the upgraded methods to the toolkit for other members of the profession to use. Only in this way can planners truly develop the professionalism needed to approach the topic of the future with authority* [emphasis added].

References

ACSP Strategic Marketing Committee. (1997). Anchor points for planning's identification. *Journal of Planning Education and Research, 16,* 223–224.

Helling, A. (1998). Collaborative visioning: Proceed with caution! Results from evaluating Atlanta's Vision 2020 project. *Journal of the American Planning Association, 64,* 335–349.

Isserman, A. (1985). Dare to plan: An essay on the role of the future in planning practice and education. *Town Planning Review, 56,* 483–491.

Myers, D., & Kitsuse, A. (2000). Constructing the future in planning: A survey of theories and tools. *Journal of Planning Education and Research, 19,* 221–231.

This introduction accomplishes a number of things. It summarizes pertinent research on a specific topic and refers the reader to the variety of approaches that have been taken to that topic. But it also is self-assertive, establishing the *ethos* of the author as well by showing the space or gaps in the ways that this topic has been approached that the present article attempts to fill. That is, it says "one author has said this, another that, but I will look at this (new) way."

I have italicized places in the essay where the writer attempted to find his own place in the conversation. For example, after discussing ways community planners do their work, the writer asserts that "better methods are clearly desired for professional leadership regarding the future," opening up a space for what follows. More specifically, Myers notes that "at present, our methods for addressing the time dimension of planning are far less developed than those for space," illustrating the exigency or timeliness of this study. He also shows ways that past thinking has been shortsighted and how the new perspectives he offers might overcome that deficit.

This recounting of work done by others on an issue is called a review of the literature. Though not all types of researched writing use a literature review, the process it represents—collecting, summarizing, and synthesizing the existing ideas on a topic—is a necessary part of all research. The review of the literature has a specific rhetorical aim: to show why past work on a topic, though useful and important, is not yet adequate. In that way, it creates the exigency for the writer's contribution, and it identifies the specific area within which that contribution can be made.

If you imagine the thinking that informed the above introduction and review of the literature, you'll find that it is a product of the reflection and real learning that we have been discussing. In order to find his place in the conversation, Myers reflected on all that he had learned about the topic as he did his research and then paused to consider what else still needed to be said. That moment required a powerful act of memory—not merely transcribing what others had said but *synthesizing* that information in a way that organized it and so revealed what remained to be said on the topic.

This dialogic moment, the moment when you imagine yourself in dialog with other experts on a topic, is an indispensable part of any researched writing task. Without it, you are likely to produce just a report of what others have said. You are also less likely to nurture your own professional *ethos*, since what you present is less likely to stay with you. This type of thinking is also crucial to finding your life's work, since entering into a profession really means entering into *a community of people* who share specific concerns. Below are a number of exercises that can be useful to you in the reflective learning process between the collection of information and the writing of a draft, between acting as a listener and then acting as a speaker.

The exercises (and those in the Reading and Writing Applications section that follows) can be used in two ways.

- If you are currently working on a researched essay, you can use them as ways to enrich and develop your work on that project.

- If you are not currently working on a researched essay, you can use them to hone your skills as a writer and to help you to find a place for yourself within a discipline or occupation to which you aspire.

ASSESSING AUDIENCE LEVEL

One productive way to answer the question "What do I have to say on this topic?" might be another question: "What do I have to say *to whom*?" Placing your researched writing within a context of audience can help you to focus. It changes the question from "What do I know?" to "What do I know *that my audience needs to hear*?" This reflective process is a way to test your understanding of a topic. Determining the usefulness of your approach to the topic is nearly impossible without considering your audience, since different audiences require specific information and specific methods of presenting that information. For instance, in the example above, Myers acknowledges that his audience comprises community planners in the way that he organizes his review of the literature and identifies the gaps in that research that he hopes to fill.

Audience becomes especially crucial as you consider your life's work, or as you extend the work that you are currently doing through continuing education. Continuous development of your professional *ethos* requires you to consider what has already been said as well as what needs to be said. Knowing the discourse community to whom you are writing can help you to make important decisions as a writer:

- what can be *assumed*, because your audience already knows and accepts it;
- what needs to be *explained* (because it is unfamiliar); and
- what needs to be *argued* (because it is contentious).

As you move further into your discipline and toward the areas of knowledge that will inform your life's work, you will become more and more comfortable with knowing the difference between that which is already accepted, that which is contested, and that which is new. But even now, on any topic that you research, you can make such determinations by carefully reflecting on what you learn.

WRITING TO EXPLORE 8.2

To better understand the importance of audience to the drafting process, read the three brief essays that follow. Though all three articles address the issue of computer security, each does so with a different audience and purpose in mind, and so makes use of the available information in ways suited to its rhetorical situation. After reading the articles, discuss the ways in which each writer addresses a specific audience and how the information that is selected and presented is focused on the likely needs and interests of that audience. Think about the following as you read:

- What level of knowledge, expertise, and concern does the writer assume in the audience?
- How is the author's occupation and field of expertise evident in each article?
- How would you describe the tone and style of the piece?
- Note places where each author has made decisions about what to assume, what needs to be explained or defined, and what needs to be argued.

- Note also that though all of these essays draw on researched information, the information does not control or restrict the writer's voice. Find places in each article where the author incorporates ideas that were likely gathered through research, and others where the author presents his or her own conclusions.

Then, in your writer's notebook, respond to the questions that follow each article.

The first essay was published in *Police Chief*, a trade journal for criminal justice professionals. It addresses ways that criminal justice professionals can protect their own technology by providing them with the basics of computer security.

Network Security: Safeguarding Systems against the Latest Threats

Eric Moore

In the past several years, security breaches of individual computers, networks, and the information they hold and transmit have reached epidemic proportions. The number of known computer viruses surpassed 70,000 in January 2002. Worldwide reports of Web site defacements reached an all-time high in September 2002—more than 9,000 attacks—according to the London security consultant agency mi2g Limited, and that figure is 54 percent higher than August's previous record-breaking tally of 5,830 defacements.[1] Numbers just released from the Computer Security Institute (CSI) put computer crime losses at an estimated $455 million in 2001, up from $377 million in 2000.

Breaches in cybersecurity can lead to vulnerability and embarrassment for any organization that finds itself a target, but security risks come at a much higher cost for law enforcement. In addition to confidential data that law enforcement agencies must safeguard—incident information, investigation reports, arrest records and warrants, criminal history databases, and so on—police departments and law enforcement agencies have the added responsibility of presenting a secure image to the public. Any compromise to that image can diminish public confidence in the affected law enforcement department or agency.

Another concern stems from the fact that police have traditionally been targeted by those who want to rebel against authority.[2] A police presence on the Internet can tempt an angry hacker or underground group into anonymous remote attempts to deface police properly (in the form of obscenities and slurs posted to a Web site, for instance) or steal electronic information for criminal gain. Attacks of this kind against law enforcement Web servers have been occurring with greater regularity in recent years. Although high-profile cases make news reports, many other attacks go unreported due to lack of media interest or the potential negative repercussions to a particular law enforcement agency's image.[3] And countless others go undetected and could ultimately pose the worst threat of all.

Law enforcement networks—the same ones that provide law enforcement personnel with e-mail and messaging capabilities, automated searching of databases of photographs and fingerprints, and remote access from field investigations—are vulnerable to intrusion by malicious outsiders looking to gain an upper hand on the law. Attacks on police and law enforcement networks can lead to losses of money, time, reputation, sensitive information, and even lives. As the Internet and other national information infrastructures become larger, more complex, and more interdependent, the frequency and severity of unauthorized intrusions will escalate.[4]

Like other entities on the Web that are facing the reality of electronic compromise, law enforcement must increasingly assess and plan the protection and security of its networked systems.

Defining Network Security

Network security is the protection of networks, their services, and their connections from unauthorized access, modification, destruction, or disclosure. The primary goal in network security is the prevention of unauthorized entry to the system, although completely preventing breaches in security currently appear unrealistic. For this reason, the idea of network security must be extended to include the limiting of damage from attacks that may occur, and ensuring system capabilities in spite of compromises or failures.

Although the day-to-day assessments and technical maintenance of network security are typically handled by an organization's network administrator and information technology staff, every system user in an organization has a role to play in keeping security breaches to a minimum.

Securing information on networks requires far more than the latest tool or technology.[5] It involves multiple tiers of security practices in addition to ongoing planning, the cooperation of every person in an organization, and good communication. Organizations must understand exactly what they are trying to protect, and why, before selecting specific solutions. In addition to safeguarding their electronic databases and reputations, organizations must also ensure that users of their systems can count on those systems being there when they need them.

Today, a variety of methods must be employed to protect the security infrastructure of your systems and critical data. Threats can be minimized through a combination of awareness, effective security technologies, and implementation of practical system security procedures.

Determining Your Network's Security Needs

There are many types of law enforcement networks that hold varying amounts and levels of secure information. National or regional networks often house vast databases of criminal information from multiple jurisdictions. State and local police networks are typically used to store more day-to-day working case files and specific criminal case histories relevant to a particular jurisdiction and its surroundings.

Although there are basic network security standards that every organization must follow, specific needs will differ. Each organization should assess the data and systems it wishes to guard and the best practices available to protect them. Primary points to consider include the following:

- Value of the assets that must be protected
- Consequences of loss of confidentiality or operational capability
- Vulnerabilities that could bring about a loss
- Existing threats that could exploit vulnerabilities
- Likelihood that a threat might occur
- Availability and appropriateness of options and resources to address risk[6]

Vulnerabilities to network systems are ever changing, but the top security concerns that plague organizations—as indicated by headlines, reports, and survey results—seem to remain constant. To help thwart system compromise, network managers and users should familiarize themselves with current security tactics and technologies.

Think Like a Hacker

Knowing who could compromise your network—and why they would want to—is one of the first steps toward network security for your organization. Law enforcement faces many challenges in securing networks from persons and groups whose intent can range from pranks to system crashes to theft of sensitive information for criminal use. Thinking like a hacker can help an organization see which avenues a real hacker might take to gain unauthorized access and what the hacker might attempt to steal or destroy.

Apply Available Patches

In the rush to get their products to market, software vendors have traditionally overlooked many security vulnerabilities that are inevitably discovered by users. These vulnerabilities are often communicated through underground channels and exploited for potential entry points into a network before a software vendor can release an updated version of the application.

This problem ultimately affects nearly every software product or application created and can usually be temporarily fixed by the software vendor through the release of new code in the form of a patch. This code can then be provided to customers to "patch" or alternately correct the software vulnerability until a new version of the software is made available. The most popular and secure way to repair a software vulnerability is to download a patch from the software manufacturer's Web site. Most patches automatically place the proper code in the affected program or application on the user's computer.

Downloading a patch may sound simple, but this security solution can be daunting for network administrators managing an array of software applications requiring patches on perhaps hundreds of individual desktops. Still, updating patches is one of the most important things an administrator can do, according to many security consultants.

Scott Blake, director of security product strategy at Razor, the research arm of security company Bindview, says that many computer crimes are successful because the attackers find well-known software vulnerabilities that make it easy to bypass network defenses. "Nine times out of ten, they take advantage of old security problems that have been known about for a long time and that patches exist for, but people have not bothered to apply," Blake says.[7]

Firewalls: The Most Popular Form of Security

Firewall protection is now ranked as the most popular applied method of security technology, according to current market reports. Simply put, a firewall protects a computer network from unauthorized access. By examining and filtering network traffic at the network boundary, firewalls have become an essential element of network security. Firewalls may be hardware devices, software programs, or a combination of the two. Though firewalls are most often used to guard internal networks from outside attack, they can also be configured to limit outside access by internal users.[8]

Firewalls primarily allow access control. A network administrator can use the firewall to create a set of rules defining which ports to keep open, which to disallow, and any IP (Internet Protocol) addresses or entire networks to block. Firewalls can also be utilized to control in-network traffic. They can and should be used to control access from one part of your internal network to another. A firewall on the edge of your network can be a powerful deterrent against breaches in security, but only if it is configured correctly.[9]

Software firewalls have increased in popularity because they enable the network manager to put security on machines where it is needed, whether desktop or laptop. Laptops not equipped with firewall software pose enormous threats to an organization's network security. First, if not protected while operating remotely, the laptop allows an obvious threat to unsecured files and folders. Secondly, if allowed to connect to a network without protection, laptops have the potential to introduce a host of malicious code (in the form of viruses) once reintroduced to the network. Network managers are increasingly encouraged to identify where software firewall protection is needed and think about adding this extra layer of security.[10]

Guard against Viruses, Worms, and Trojan Horses

A virus is an unwanted self-replicating program that attaches itself to other programs. Viruses can infect program files or macros that are used in word-processing and spreadsheet documents. Viruses are spread when you open programs or documents that have been infected. As the program or document opens, the virus will run and try to infect other programs or documents on the same computer or, if available, computers connected to it in a network. Any of these newly infected programs or documents will try to infect more programs or documents, and a perpetual cycle can continue. Viruses can be designed to do a number of disruptive activities such as delete or damage files, clog mail systems, and even use e-mail to send your documents or saved passwords to another person.

A worm is a more powerful and destructive type of virus that exists independently as a program. Unlike a virus, a worm doesn't require any action (such as clicking or downloading) by the user to launch itself. Recent worms have been capable of installing backdoors that allowed free access to infected computers. Recent worm programs include Code Red and Nimda. Code Red spread to 300,000 machines in 14 hours in 2001.[11]

A Trojan horse program is often falsely believed to be a virus. Instead, the Trojan horse is an independent program that pretends to be something else while running harmful operations in the background. For example, you might download a program from the Internet and, when you run it, it deletes files from your hard drive. Antivirus software is not good at detecting Trojan horse programs, so be especially cautious when downloading or opening programs and files from the Internet and unknown sources.[12]

You can generally protect yourself against viruses in the following ways:

- If you are using an unsecured operating system, install antivirus software (secure operating systems such as Unix or Windows NT inherently guard against traditional, as opposed to e-mail, viruses).

- Avoid downloading programs from unknown sources (such as those found on the Internet). Restricting software use to purchased CDs eliminates almost all risk from traditional viruses.

- Make sure macro virus protection is enabled in all Microsoft applications. Never run macros in a document unless you know what they do. There is seldom a good reason to add macros to a document, so avoiding all macros is a good policy.

- Use virus protection software to scan any new programs or files that may contain executable code.
- Avoid opening files, programs, or attachments from unknown sources (especially Word or Excel documents or files with .exe or .vbs extensions).
- Viruses and Trojan horse programs are often exchanged in online chat sessions. Do not accept any files while using chat.
- Regularly back up your system. Recent backups may help you recover information in the event that data is lost to a virus.[13]

Intrusion Detection

An intrusion detection system (IDS) allows network administrators an additional automated tool for discovering unauthorized network access. These systems can help administrators discover not only when the intrusion occurred but also what actions need to be taken to repair damage.

Rather than take preventive measures when an attack is detected, an IDS is used to alert a system administrator of unauthorized activity. An IDS simply monitors the audit data (activity log) of an operating system. This same data log could be viewed manually by a network manager, but the IDS automation offers a more accurate and timely option. An IDS can help alert administrators of much more than a system break-in; it can detect internal intrusion of limited-access areas of a network, atypical use of system resources, or network violations of special user privileges.

Encryption

Encryption is the encoding of information in such a way that only a person (or computer) with a key can decode it. Although encryption is typically more applicable to information security than network security, it can be utilized across networks to secure information transfer. Encryption's use of coded messages is especially useful for conducting secret communications often required by law enforcement and the military in planning and carrying out undercover investigations or covert operations. Encryption is one of the most popular forms of information security utilized today, and two types of encryption are especially popular.

- Symmetric-key encryption requires a secret key (code) to be installed on the computers sending and receiving the encrypted messages, and it requires administrators to know which computers will be involved in transmissions so the secret key code can be installed on each one.

- Public-key encryption requires the use of both private and public keys. Each computer involved holds a private key and exchanges a public key to any other computer that wants to communicate securely. The public key from a transmitting computer is used with the receiving computer's private key to decode the encrypted message.

Penetration Testing

Penetration testing is the evaluation of a network system's security based on non-malicious but actual attempts to circumvent its security features. A penetration test analyzes a system for design weaknesses, technical flaws, and procedural failings. Close examination is made of all technical and procedural security measures to ensure not only that they comply with the requirements of the organization but also that they are being followed by connected networks (such as multiple office locations, partners, and remote systems).[14]

Essentially a systems security audit, a penetration test is administered by an outside security testing company that can offer unbiased assessment of a network and informed recommendations for needed improvements. Penetration testing programs are also available for self-analyzing the security of networks.

Insider Attacks

According to InterGov, an international organization that works with police agencies to combat cybercrime, insiders commit about 80 percent of all computer- and Internet-related crime, and these crimes cause an average loss of about $110,000 per corporate victim.[15]

CERT, a prominent national center of Internet security expertise, defines "insider intrusion" as any compromise or penetration of a network, system, or database that is committed by someone who has or formerly had legitimate access to the network, system, or database. Insiders include current and former full-time employees, part-time employees, and contractors.[16]

Insider attacks are more of a threat because they are better conceived, due mostly to direct system access and knowledge of a system's architecture. An insider can learn of known security weaknesses in an organization's network to steal sensitive information or commit other illegal activity. To cut down on the number of insider threats, network administrators should not assign group access or generic authorization to entire departments. Allow access only to those persons who need it.

Law enforcement networks store and transmit information that could be used to aid and abet criminals or otherwise be traded or used for personal gain. The temptation to steal or sabotage information can come early or late in a career, and can be motivated by any number of life situations such as reprimand, termination, or financial setback. In other cases, even a positive event such as a promotion can place an individual in a position of greater responsibility with greater access to information that could be compromised.

Network security managers should encourage all personnel to develop a heightened internal awareness and promptly report employees demonstrating any suspicious behavior, especially while conducting activities on workstations and systems.

Guidelines for Network Security

Reinforcing commonsense ground rules for both network users and network administrators can help keep systems secure. Following are lists of do's and don'ts:

Do's

- Use the latest technologies to protect the network
- Use virus detection software
- Close any excess connections to the Internet and the network
- Use strong passwords that contain alphanumeric and upper- and lowercase characters
- Encourage employees to create strong passwords and change them regularly
- Respond to breaches of security in a timely manner, encouraging good security practices
- Regularly back up the system to help recover from possible loss
- Create written security policy that is followed and updated as needed

Don'ts

- Share passwords
- Use former privileges after transfer or termination
- Download software from the Internet without prior permission and virus scanning
- Attempt to use unauthorized access methods
- Use anyone else's user account for system sign-on or general purposes
- Open e-mail attachments if the sender is not known or cannot be verified

Law Enforcement Networks

The success of many law enforcement networks today has proven that vital, secure systems can be maintained. In 2002 the Regional Information Sharing System (RISS) intelligence network, which supports investigative and prosecution efforts involving narcotics trafficking, criminal gangs, and organized and violent crime across jurisdictional boundaries, received the Second Annual Computer Security and Information Assurance Award for Law Enforcement and Public Service, sponsored by Potomac Forum Limited, in recognition of its outstanding security practices.

The RISS program, funded through a grant from the U.S. Department of Justice's Bureau of Justice Assistance, was chosen because it exemplifies government computer security best practices by enabling the sharing of law enforcement information among thousands of professionals across the United States.

The RISS intranet, using V-One's SmartGate VPN technology, enables officers from more than 5,000 member agencies to securely access criminal intelligence databases. U.S. Attorney General John Ashcroft has described RISS as "the only secure Internet-based national network for sharing of criminal intelligence among federal, state, and local law enforcement agencies."[17]

New advancements in secure law enforcement networking will soon be realized in the form of a single Web interface linking RISS and the FBI's Law Enforcement Online (LEO) network. George March, director of the RISS Office of Information Technology, recently said that users of the linked networks will have access to computing resources as well as people and expertise across the entire spectrum. "One of LEO's biggest advantages is the ability to offer a secure online space for specific interest groups to work and share information," March said. "RISS excels in providing Web access to multiple databases in local jurisdictions across the country."[18]

Both networks will continue to operate separately, with the Web interface serving as a connection for those users who need it. A single directory and e-mail system is planned to allow easy contact between members of either network. The directory will enable full security on the network by setting access according to personal identity.[19]

As law enforcement and intelligence agencies show a growing interest in and need for networked communications, standards for network security must become a primary initiative. Although no network is immune to attack, much can be done to keep breaches in network security to a minimum. By keeping informed of the latest security threats and safeguards, law enforcement agencies can use networking technologies to operate more effectively while maintaining a safe Web presence. Secure network connections enable law enforcement agencies to work together on many levels, sharing information safely across jurisdictions and without boundaries.

Endnotes

1. David Legard, "Web site defacements rise to all-time high in September," *IDG News Service,* September 30, 2002.

2. Deb Zaborav, "Trusting the Security of Law Enforcement," *Unix Insider,* May 3, 2001.
3. Zaborav, "Trusting the Security."
4. Julia Allen, Christopher Alberts, Sandi Behrens, Barbara Laswell, and William Wilson, "Improving the Security of Networked Systems," Networked Systems Survivability Program, Software Engineering Institute, Camegie Mellon University, October 2000.
5. CERT, www.cert.org.
6. CERT, www.cert.org.
7. Andrew Conry-Murray, "New Public Network: Network Security's Not So Secret Ingredients," *Network Magazine,* August 3, 2001.
8. Jeff Tyson, "How Firewalls Work," December 19, 2002, www.howstuffworks.com/firewall.htm.
9. Mike DeMaris, "A Rookie's Guide to Defensive Blocks," *Network Computing,* June 24, 2002, www.nwc.com.
10. Dave Mitchell, "Firewalls: The Soft Option," *VNU Net,* July 25, 2002, www.vnunet.com.
11. Yona Hollander, "The Threat of Internet Worms," *SC Magazine,* July 2002, www.scmagazine.com.
12. Marshall Brain, "How Computer Viruses Work," December 19, 2002, www.howstuffworks.com/virus.htm.
13. Brain, "How Computer Viruses Work."
14. Corsaire Ltd., "Penetration Testing Guide," December 19, 2002, www.penetration-testing.com/penetration-testing-guide.html.
15. Jim Carr, "Strategies and Issues: Thwarting Insider Attacks," *Network Magazine,* September 4, 2002.
16. CERT Coordination Center, "2002 Survey of Network Security and Insider Threats," www.cert.org.
17. "RISS Program Wins Award for Computer Network Security," www.riss.net.
18. Diane Frank, "Web Links Law Enforcement Nets," *Government e-Business,* August 20, 2002, www.fcw.com/geb/articles/2002/0819/web-leo-08-20-02.asp.
19. Frank, "Web Links Law Enforcement Nets."

1. How does Moore create *exigency*? That is, how does he motivate his readers by illustrating the importance of this topic for the profession?

2. What research does the author seem to have done in order to write this piece?

3. What is the central point that Moore is trying to make? How does he wish to influence his audience? Try restating his thesis in your own words.

4. What types of knowledge and expertise on the part of the audience does Moore assume? What types of knowledge does he feel the need to define or explain?

5. How does Moore use definitions to help make his audience understand his message? List a few examples.

The second article, published in *Computer Weekly*, presents the issue of computer security to a quite different audience, and with a much more limited scope. As you read, try to compare and contrast this piece with the one published in *Police Chief*, once again focusing on the assumptions that the writer seems to make about the level of expertise of his audience.

How Effective Are Gigabit Intrusion Detection Systems?

Anthony Adshead

In a recent survey commissioned by VanDyke Software, 66% of the companies questioned said they perceive system penetration to be the biggest threat to their business.

The survey revealed the top seven threats experienced by companies to be:

- Viruses (78%)
- System penetration (50%)
- Denial of service attacks (40%)
- Insider abuse (29%)
- Spoofing (28%)
- Data/network sabotage (20%)
- Unauthorized staff access (16%).

Although 86% of respondents use firewalls—a disturbingly low figure—it is clear that firewalls are not always effective against intrusion attempts. The average firewall is designed to deny clearly suspicious traffic—such as an attempt to telnet to a device when corporate security policy forbids telnet access. But is also designed to allow some traffic through—web traffic to an internal web server, for example.

The problem is that many exploits attempt to take advantage of weaknesses in the protocols that are allowed through perimeter firewalls, and once the web server has been compromised, this can often be used as a springboard to launch additional attacks on other internal servers. Once a "rootkit" or "back door" has been installed on a server, the hacker will have unfettered access to that machine at any point in the future.

Business Case

The business case for installing intrusion detection systems (IDS) has never been clearer. The computer world's equivalent to the burglar alarm, an IDS provides valuable back-up to the beleaguered firewall system.

As in the physical world, this "burglar alarm" provides valuable notification that someone has managed to breach perimeter security measures. It should allow IT staff to determine exactly what happened during the attack, and hopefully provide indications of how the security weakness might be addressed. In some circumstances, the IDS can even retaliate by tearing down the TCP connection being used by the attacker before any serious damage is done. This is the equivalent of picking the intruder up by the scruff of the neck and drop-kicking him out of the door.

When discussing IDS in this article we will be concentrating exclusively on network IDS (NIDS), rather than host-based IDS (HIDS). The latter relies on agents installed on each host to be protected in order to watch for such trigger conditions as changes in file permissions, unauthorized or suspicious log file entries, or alterations to critical system files.

The NIDS, on the other hand, monitors traffic on the wire in real time, examining packets in detail in order to detect patterns of misuse—perhaps spotting denial of service attacks or dangerous payloads—before the packets reach their destination and do the damage. They do this by matching one or more packets against a database of known "attack signatures," or performing protocol decodes to detect anomalies, or both. These signature databases are updated regularly by system suppliers as new attacks are discovered.

Resource-Intensive

Most of the network-based IDS currently available work in what is known as "promiscuous mode." This means they examine every packet on the local segment, whether or not those packets are destined for the IDS machine (much like a network monitor, such as Sniffer). Given that they have a lot of work to do in examining every packet and tracking active sessions, they usually require a dedicated host on which to run.

One of the biggest problems faced by NIDS products in recent times has been the rapid increase in affordable bandwidth. When IDS products first appeared, 10mbps was the fastest network around. Very quickly, however, network speeds have increased to 100mbps, and now 1gbps and beyond. And each increase in network speed seems to take less time to become affordable.

Unfortunately, IDS have had a tough time keeping up, and tests run over the past two years have highlighted several products that had serious problems acquiring even 100Mbit of traffic without dropping packets. Gigabit has proved a real challenge—so much so that even though some IDS appliances sport 1Gbit interfaces, the suppliers are only rating them at multi-100Mbit speeds.

Dropped packets are the IDS designer's biggest nightmare, since if even one of those dropped packets is one of those used in the exploit data stream, it is possible that the entire exploit could be missed. It has rapidly become apparent that in order to achieve 100% detection rates at all network loads using all packet sizes, some custom hardware is required.

Today's network cards—and especially the default drivers that come with them and the default packet capture mechanisms in most operating systems—are simply unable to handle a full gigabit of traffic at wire speed in promiscuous mode. High-performance network cards with custom drivers or custom, application-specific integrated circuits are the only real solution—anything less is unlikely to be able to handle extreme loads.

Of course, this does not necessarily mean that a gigabit IDS appliance that uses standard gigabit network cards is useless. Far from it—when it comes to custom hardware, the main aim is to ensure that the appliance can handle the most extreme traffic loads, or even multiple gigabit segments in a single device.

However, the majority of network administrators currently deploying gigabit networks will find that they are seeing far less than a full 100Mbps of traffic moving over the wire, and for these implementations even a standard PC with an off-the-shelf gigabit network card will be able to cope quite easily. It is vitally important for the administrator to be able to characterize the traffic on the network as accurately as possible. They must ask:

- What is the average bandwidth?
- What are the peaks (remember, even one dropped packet during peak activity could allow an exploit to slip through unnoticed)?
- Is the traffic mainly one protocol (there are so many HTTP exploits that need to be covered by the IDS that some IDS engines struggle on networks that are predominantly HTTP traffic) or a mix?
- What is the average packet size and level of new connections established every second—both critical parameters that can have detrimental effects on some IDS engines, especially if the packet size is small and the connections per second figure is high?

Deployment issues too become more complex as network speeds increase. Most 10mbps networks used shared hubs, and it was a simple matter to install a promiscuous-mode IDS device on the hub in order to see all the traffic on the network. Gigabit networks require a pure switched environment, which means that if the IDS is attached to a switch port it will only see the traffic on its own port—not really much use.

Deployment Issues

One solution is to connect the IDS to a Span or mirror port on the switch, to which is copied all the traffic from all the other ports. Now, however, we revisit an earlier problem—what if the switch is the consolidation point for several other switched networks within the corporate network?

You might think that would be the ideal point to place an IDS, since it would ensure that all traffic is seen. But if the administrator is mirroring just four segments and each segment has just 300mbps of traffic—well within the capabilities of almost any gigabit IDS product—the total traffic being mirrored on a single 1,000mbps port is 1,200mbps. Something has to give, and the result is more dropped packets.

Even where traffic levels are kept within 1,000mbps and the IDS engine is geared up to handle it, some switches are unable to mirror that amount of traffic effectively—once again the result is dropped packets, but now it is the fault of the switch.

Other possible solutions involve the use of network taps and load-balancing switches, but the fact remains that it is critically important to match the traffic levels presented to the IDS to the capabilities of both the IDS sensor itself and the switch on which it is installed. In some respects, detection performance is the least of the problems facing the administrator tasked with deploying these devices. The problem with any gigabit IDS product is, by its very nature and capabilities, the amount of alert data it is likely to generate. With 1gbps of traffic passing through the IDS, the number of alerts could reasonably be expected to be 10 times that generated by the typical 100mbps product.

Overburdening Staff

How many members of staff would be needed to process, investigate and resolve that number of alerts? And how long before the IDS becomes just another device in the corner that is largely ignored thanks to its insistence on overloading the administrator on a daily basis?

It is vitally important that the signature set is tuned to match the traffic on the network being protected in order to eliminate as many false positives as possible. Automated centralized correlation systems can also be of huge benefit when it comes to sifting through masses of data from multiple IDS sensors to identify the most urgent threats. There is a clear case for implementing an IDS, but network managers must be aware of the potential pitfalls to be avoided when deploying gigabit IDS products.

As with most network technologies, the higher the speeds, the more complicated the deployment. Security is no exception, but if approached with sufficient thought, care and planning, gigabit IDS can be a highly effective weapon against a wide range of network intruders.

1. Who is the most likely audience for this piece?
2. Based on its audience, does this article need to create exigency in the same way that the article from *Police Chief* did? Why or why not?

3. What types of expertise does Adshead assume on the part of the reader? List a few examples, illustrating how his tone and style reflect his assumptions. What terms might a nonexpert audience need defined?

4. In what parts of the article does the writer need to educate his readers, even beyond the assumed expertise? List a few examples in which he must explain or define.

5. On what types of research does this piece seem to draw? Is that research acknowledged in any way?

6. Does this article have a thesis or main point that the author is arguing? Is it merely informational? Or is it both? Support your answer with specific examples from the article.

The third article on computer security was published in *Issues in Science and Technology*, published by the National Academy of Sciences. Its authors, Bruce Berkowitz and Robert W. Hahn, are both researchers at widely respected institutions (the Hoover Institution at Stanford University and the American Enterprise Institute–Brookings Joint Center for Regulatory Studies, respectively). As you read, consider the ways in which this article places the issue of computer security in the public forum as an issue for government authorities.

from Cybersecurity: Who's Watching the Store?

Bruce Berkowitz and Robert W. Hahn

The most important question to ask in addressing any public policy issue is: What problem needs to be solved? Yet despite all the attention that cyber-attacks receive in the media, there is little hard data for estimating the size of the cybersecurity threat or for calculating how much money is already being spent to counter it.

The data gap begins with the government. According to the General Accounting Office, the federal government spent $938 million on IT security in 2000, just over $1 billion in 2001, and $2.71 billion in 2002. However, the data do not tell us how much is being spent on different kinds of security measures. Moreover, there is no way to determine from the data whether all government agencies keep track of IT security spending in the same way.

Publicly available data on private IT security spending is, if anything, even less reliable and harder to come by. According to the Gartner Group, a leading IT consulting firm, worldwide spending on security software alone totaled $2.5 billion in 1999, $3.3 billion in 2000, and $3.6 billion in 2001. Once spending on personnel, training, and other aspects of information security is considered, total IT security spending could be substantially more. But the bottom line is that neither government nor private sector statistics on IT security spending are terribly useful for the kind of analysis that is common in most other policy sectors.

The most often cited source for IT security data is probably the FBI-sponsored survey published by the Computer Security Institute (CSI), a San Francisco-based membership organization for information security professionals. In 2002, CSI sent its survey to 503 computer security practitioners in U.S. corporations, government agencies, and financial institutions. The survey asked respondents about the security technology they use, the types and frequency of attacks they had experienced, and the losses associated with these attacks.

Needless to say, this is a very small percentage of all computer networks and hardly a scientific sample. Yet the greatest shortcoming of the CSI survey is that it lacked reliable procedures for uniformity and quality control. Each respondent decided for itself how to respond. One company might estimate financial damages from cybercrime with data from its accounting department, using insurance claims and actual write-offs on its balance sheets. Another might provide a gut estimate from a systems operator who monitors network intrusions. In either case, CSI did not require substantiation.

Even so, fewer than half the respondents in the 2002 CSI survey (44 percent) were willing or able to quantify financial losses due to attacks, which means that the data that are provided are almost certainly statistically biased. This is suggested by the results of the survey, which should raise questions even at face value. For example, survey responses from 1997 to 2002 indicate that the number of attacks in some categories has been constant or falling, even though the number of potential targets during this time grew exponentially. Similarly, the total cost of these attacks soared, despite the fact that companies were more aware of the cyberthreat and were spending more to protect themselves.

In recent years CSI has conceded weaknesses in its approach and has suggested that its survey may be more illustrative than systematic. Nevertheless, government officials and media experts alike freely cite these and other statistics on the supposed costs of cybercrime, even when the estimates fail the test of basic plausibility. For example, in May 2000 Jeri Clausing of the *New York Times* reported that the Love Letter virus caused $15 billion in damage. Yet the most costly natural disaster in U.S. history—Hurricane Andrew, which in 1991 swept across Florida and the Gulf Coast—caused $19 billion in damages. Moreover, this figure reflected 750,000 documented insurance claims, plus tangible evidence of 26 lost lives along with the near-total destruction of Homestead Air Force Base and an F-16 fighter aircraft. Are we to believe that one virus has almost the same destructive power of a Class 1 hurricane? Similarly, during a February 2002 committee hearing, Sen. Charles Schumer (D-N.Y.) cited a report claiming that the four most recent viruses caused $12 billion in damage. By comparison, the Boeing 757 that crashed into the Pentagon on September

11 caused $800 million in damages. Could the four viruses cited by Schumer really cause 15 times as much damage?

In reality, analyzing the damage of most network intrusions is time-consuming and expensive, which is why it has rarely been done on a large scale. To analyze an attack on a computer network, someone must review logs and recreate the event. Even then, sophisticated attackers are likely to stretch their attacks over time, use multiple cutouts so a series of probes cannot be traced to a single attacker, or leave agents that can reside in a system for an extended time—all making analysis harder. Logically, the trivial attackers are the ones most likely to be detected and the sophisticated ones are most likely to go unrecorded.

Without an exhaustive research program, which has not been carried out, the exact scope and nature of the cyberthreat contains enormous uncertainty. The current strategy proposes to identify threats, but it does not propose to collect reliable data that would define the threat. This lack of data is not an argument for ignoring cyberthreats. However, when the available data contain this much uncertainty, dealing with the uncertainty of the threat must be an integral part of the strategy. A prudent policy will focus on the most certain threats that have high probability and high potential costs. It will hedge against the less certain, less dire threats, and include mechanisms that direct efforts toward those areas with the greatest payoff and limit the resources that might inadvertently be spent on wild goose chases.

In our view, the greatest threat may simply be the economic harm that would result if the public loses confidence in the security of information technology in general. A threat that is only slightly less pressing is the possibility that a foreign military power or terrorist group might use the vulnerability of an information system to facilitate a conventional attack.

The possibility that a purely electronic attack might cause a widespread collapse of information systems for a prolonged period with large costs and mayhem is possible, but a second-order concern, if only because potential attackers have other alternatives that are easier to use, cheaper, and more likely to be effective in wreaking havoc.

The Government Role

The most significant feature of the role set forth for government in the current cybersecurity strategy is that it arbitrarily precludes action common in other regulatory domains. It also defines a role that is dubious at best. For example, the strategy states, "In general, the private sector is best equipped and structured to respond to an evolving cyberthreat." This is also true in other regulatory domains such as occupational safety. No government body is responsible for issuing grounding straps and face goggles. Unfortunately, the strategy ignores a basic fact of regulation: Although implementation is left to the private sector, the government has a large role in setting standards, designing regulations, and enforcing these measures.

The strategy goes on to say that the federal government should concentrate on "ensuring the safety of its own cyberinfrastructure and those assets required for supporting its essential missions and services." It also says that the federal government should focus on "cases where high transaction costs or legal barriers lead to significant coordination problems; cases in which governments operate in the absence of private sector forces; resolution of incentive problems . . . and raising awareness." Alas, the government itself has a dubious record. As recently as February 2002 the Office of Management and Budget identified six common government-wide security gaps. These weaknesses included lack of senior management attention, lack of performance measurement, poor security education and awareness, failure to fully fund and integrate security into capital planning, failure to ensure that contractor services are secure, and failure to detect and share information on vulnerabilities.

In other words, more than six years after the Defense Science Board's IW-D study and three years after the government's first cybersecurity plan, most government agencies have yet to take effective action. This is hardly an argument for making government the trailblazer in security. The reality of the situation is that the government is poorly suited for providing a model for the private sector. Government bureaucracies (not necessarily through any fault of their own) have too much inertia to act decisively and quickly, which is what acting as a model requires. Because of civil service tenure, government agencies lack an important engine of change found in the private sector, namely the ability to replace people inclined to act one way with people who are inclined to act another. Also, government agencies are locked into a budget cycle. In most cases, a year is required for an agency to formulate its plan, another year is needed for Congress to pass an appropriation, and a third year is required for an agency to implement the plan—at a minimum. This is why government agencies today are rarely at the leading edge of information technology. There is no reason to believe cybersecurity will be an exception to the rule.

The bulk of the responsibility for "securing the nets" will inevitably fall to the private sector because it designs, builds, and operates most of the hardware and software that form the nation's information infrastructure. This is why the strategy's determined avoidance of regulation and incentives is so misguided. Organizations such as the information security analysis centers that the government has encouraged industries to establish are valuable for coordinating action against common threats, such as viruses and software holes. Larger response centers such as the Computer Emergency Response Team/Clearance Center at

Carnegie Mellon University can play a similar role for the information infrastructure as a whole. However, the ownership and operation of the information is simply too diffuse to deal with real-time hacking and more serious cyberthreats through any kind of centralized organization. Cybersecurity is a problem requiring the active participation of scores of companies, hundreds of service providers, thousands of operating technicians, and millions of individual users.

The most effective way to shape the behavior of this many people is by setting broad ground rules and making sure people play by them. Anything else amounts to trying to micromanage a significant portion of the national economy via central control. Two central questions must be addressed. First, what kind of incentives will be effective at providing additional security? Second, how can we begin to design systems that will provide an efficient level of security—that is, one that yields a level of security where the difference between benefits and costs is maximized?

Policy Options

A number of options should be on the table for designing more effective cybersecurity.

Better Use of Standards by the Government and the Private Sector

The government may consider developing standards for software protocols for the future Internet that are more secure. These could include, for example, software that limits anonymity or requires "trust relationships" in multiple components of a network. (A trust relationship is one in which a user must identify herself and demonstrate compliance with technical standards before, say, she can gain entry to a database or use software.)

At a minimum, the government should consider playing a more active role than it does now in setting standards. Currently government policy is biased against intervening in the standard-setting process. Yet that is exactly what it should be doing when market forces left to themselves do not provide sufficient security to the country as a whole, which many experts believe is the case at present. Despite the claims of critics who want to "keep the information frontier free," the government, in fact, was a main contributor to the development of the current Internet, including the processes that resulted in current standards.

In addition to developing standards for software that are more secure, the IT industry should also consider developing more rigorous security standards for operations and software development. These should address both outside threats, such as hackers, and inside threats, such as sabotage and vandalism inside a company. After the rise in virus attacks and hacking incidents in 2000–01, some companies (most notably, Microsoft) announced that they would make security a higher priority in the design of their products. Critics of these efforts have complained that they were inadequate and were often disguises for marketing strategies designed to impede competition. Whatever the merits of these criticisms, they illustrate how government could serve as an honest broker—if it takes a more active role. Such standards could be voluntary or enforced through regulations. The more important point is to ensure that someone establishes "best practices" for industry and government that can be flexible for a variety of users but still provide a legal hook for liability.

Better Use of Regulation

In some cases the government may want to issue regulations to establish minimal acceptable security standards for operators and products. These would be cases in which the market has clearly failed and government action is required to address situations in which there are inadequate incentives or other factors preventing the private sector from developing these standards by itself. It may also want to develop an approach that requires firms to certify in their annual reports that they have complied with industry best practices.

Liability

Many computer and software makers have generally fought changes in the liability laws. A key argument is that an increase in liability has the potential to reduce innovation in the fast-moving IT sector: true enough, but only if the changes are poorly crafted or go too far. There is a good economic rationale to consider changes in liability law that would give software and hardware companies some responsibility, so that they have an incentive to increase the amount of attention paid to security issues. Liability represents a big step over many of the voluntary measures that are being advocated now, which we doubt in most cases are likely to be adequate in addressing the problem. The strength of liability is that it is a market mechanism that is much more efficient in shaping the behavior of millions. Reforming IT liability is, in effect, a market-style measure to promote better security by providing those best positioned to take action with the incentive to do so. In this same vein, the government should consider measures that would require corporations to tell their stockholders whether there are significant cybersecurity risks in their business and to certify that they are complying with industry standards and best practices to address them.

Clearly, one size does not fit all when it comes to cybersecurity. The kinds of measures appropriate for a Fortune 500 corporation are probably inappropriate for a start-up company operating out of a garage. The best approach is probably to let the market, combined with reasonably defined roles of legal responsibility, to tailor an optimal solution. But for this to happen, government will need to remove the obstacles that prevent the market from doing this currently, and to play a role in those cases in which a "public goods" problem dissuades companies and consumers from acting.

Research

Most important, we need to recognize that we are largely flying blind at this point in a public policy sense, because we have such a limited understanding of the costs of cybersecurity attacks and the benefits of preventive measures. The government should sponsor research on this subject—research that, up to this point anyway, the private sector has been unwilling or unable to conduct. It should also develop mechanisms for systematically collecting information from firms (with appropriate privacy protections) that would allow the government to help develop a better strategy for addressing cybersecurity in the future.

Security and Privacy

Finally, public officials must learn how to balance privacy and security, and public policy analysts must do a better job of explaining the balance between these two goals. Simply put, technology often leaves no practical means to reconcile privacy and security. For example, a trusted IT architecture, in which only identified or identifiable users can gain access to parts of a computer or network, inherently comes at the expense of privacy. A user must provide a unique identifier to gain access in such a system, and this naturally compromises privacy. Even worse, the data that a network uses to recognize a trusted user often can be used to identify and track the user in many other situations.

On the other hand, technology that guarantees privacy usually presents some insurmountable problems for security. The classic example is strong encryption. Because it is impossible for all practical purposes to break strong encryption, a person using it can conceal his communications, thus ensuring privacy. But such protection also can make it impossible to trace criminals, terrorists, hostile military forces, or others who would attack computer networks.

One way of addressing this problem is to concede the technical threat to privacy and use strict laws and regulation to compensate. This, of course, was the idea behind key escrow, which government authorities proposed in the mid-1990s as an alternative to completely eliminating restrictions on encryption. Under the proposed system, third parties would hold the "keys" to a cipher (actually, the means to break the cipher via a back door). Under certain specified conditions, the third parties could be ordered to provide the keys.

The U.S. government (in particular, law enforcement and intelligence organizations) took an imperious approach to the issue, which proved foolhardy because, in fact, they could not control the spread of encryption even if they tried. At the same time, the IT industry adamantly resisted the proposal arguing that foreign customers would not buy "crippled" U.S. software or hardware, and thus opposed any restrictions. In the end, the technology did prove beyond control, and the net result was soured relations between government and industry, which continue even today.

Rather than focus on whether or not to control a particular technology, society would often be better off addressing the consequences of abuse of the technology. There are numerous precedents for such an approach. For example, technology allows people to track their own rental records at the local Blockbuster, but laws provide assurances that such use carries substantial penalties. Similarly, trusted systems could be required in specific applications (e.g., financial institutions, critical infrastructure). Then people could be given the choice of whether they wished to use those networks. Other systems could be non-regulated (common e-mail). Laws could ensure that privacy was protected—and that users who tried to enter a system without complying with disclosure requirements were criminally liable. These regulations should be enforced in a way that engenders public support. One approach is to have a non-political, bipartisan governing body that makes sure government enforces these standards and does not abuse its own access to personal data.

A Leadership Role

Designing a cybersecurity policy is not simple. There is very little good information on the costs of cybersecurity attacks and the benefits of proposed policy measures. The problem is extremely complicated because of the IT infrastructure, the large number of users, and the diverse nature of potential attackers.

Addressing this problem will take economic insight and political courage. Given the complexity of the problem, we think a variety of policy instruments should be used, including voluntary standards, regulation, and liability. The challenge for policy research is to develop deeper insights about the precise nature of the cybersecurity problem and the costs and possible benefits of different policy interventions.

The challenge for politicians is to give more than lip service to this issue. That means taking a leadership role in communicating the importance of the problem and defining a mix of government and private-sector strategies for dealing with it in a manner comparable to that found routinely in other areas of public safety and homeland security.

At a minimum, funding of serious, comprehensive research on the size of the problem and the benefits and costs of policy measures should be relatively noncontroversial and beneficial. Somewhat harder is educating the public about difficult tradeoffs that need to be faced. At some point, we are likely to find, for example, that security cannot be enhanced without making some sacrifice in other features, such as ease of use or total assurance of privacy and anonymity.

Such tradeoffs should not be swept under the rug but rather discussed as part of a continuing dialogue over the best way to approach this difficult problem.

1. How is the audience for this piece like or unlike that of the other two articles? Who does the audience seem to be?

2. How do the authors attempt to provide a historical context for their discussion? How does that context help to create exigency?

3. How much expertise is necessary to understand this piece? In what parts do the authors assume specific types of expertise?

4. What types of research are used to support these writers' main point? How is the research that is used within this piece different from the research in the two articles above?

5. What types of research do the authors suggest is yet to be done?

CONSTRUCTING A DIALOG

Another useful way to nurture your understanding of a topic, and so your confidence in writing about it, is to construct a dialog among the experts whose work you have been reading. Doing so requires you to imagine the positions and ideas that might be expressed about your topic by the experts whose work you have read.

WRITING TO EXPLORE 8.3

Let's assume that you are researching cybersecurity. In your research process, you have located the three above essays and determined which parts of those essays are most relevant and useful to your project. Read them again carefully, trying to determine the position taken by each author on the topic, and make a few notes on each.

Then, imagine that you are writing an essay for a general readership—say, something for the business column of *Time, Newsweek,* or *U.S. News and World Report*— or an academic essay for a class. Your goal is to inform readers about the current state of cybersecurity in this country. Your key topic questions are "What new measures are available for combating cybercrime?" and "Who is responsible for instituting such measures?" Open up that question to the three experts whose work you have read. Without looking back at the essays, use what you remember of each author's essay to imagine a conversation among the three. Asked to comment on your topic questions, what might each author say? Act as a moderator of the conversation, asking questions or for clarification from each. Use this inventional writing to come to terms with each author's position—but without your own opinions.

Then, after you have written this dialog, join in yourself. At what points in the conversation do you feel compelled to respond? Where might you tend to agree with one author rather than another? Where might you ask further questions or demand more evidence?

By writing this dialog, and then including yourself in it, you accomplish several things. You attempt to listen with an open mind to the ideas expressed by these experts. You focus the evidence and opinions of the experts around your own key point of focus. And, by trying to keep each writer's position in your memory as you create the dialog, you begin coming to terms with the key questions and arguments that surround the issue. In the end, you come closer to being ready to respond not only to the issue but also to the approaches that others have taken to it. You've entered the conversation.

Further, if you approach your research in this dialogic way (what are the terms of this conversation, and how can I enter it?), you will likely remember the various positions for much longer. By consistently imagining yourself in the midst of these ongoing conversations, you begin to find your own professional *ethos*.

ANALYZING DECORUM AND TONE

Another benefit of reading many sources is that you can learn the styles writers prefer to use to approach that topic. That is, you can learn about *decorum*—the appropriate style for the rhetorical situation. We might pause to note that *decorum* (using appropriate styles and approaches to a topic) does not have the same meaning as *mimicking*. At the same time, being inventive does not mean being disrespectful. Though there are times when simply throwing aside the usual discourses on a topic can be effective (for shock value or in writing fiction or poetry), there are many more situations in which knowing the appropriate style and tone can bring you more credibility and enhance your *ethos*. You might recall that a shared discourse community can make communication more effective and efficient because the speakers, writers, and audiences have agreed to modes of communication that best serve the ends of the community. By participating in these modes, you show your willingness to be a cooperative and collaborative member of that occupational or academic community.

WRITING TO EXPLORE 8.4

To understand how tone and appropriateness influence writing styles, look back over the three articles above. What writing techniques are common to all three? What techniques seem specific to each article's rhetorical situation and discourse community? How does the article from *Police Chief* differ in style from the others? How is the article written by academic researchers, "Cybersecurity: Who's Watching the

Store?" similar to journal articles discussed earlier in this book? Note, for example, the use of quotations, the use of subheadings and other forms of arrangement, and the analysis of governmental action or inaction. In your writer's notebook, describe the tone of each article—and compare and contrast it with the tone, style, and use of researched information employed in the other pieces. Then, try writing a paragraph-long summary of each article, addressing the same audience as the original piece and so using a similar style. This will give you practice in adapting style to the specific rhetorical situation.

ACKNOWLEDGING THE IDEAS OF OTHERS

Your *ethos* is enhanced by the ease and grace with which you discuss your topic, both orally and in writing. But that ease and grace must also include your ability to discuss how others have approached the topic in the past (and, eventually, your ability to situate your ideas among those of others). There are several ways to demonstrate what you have learned about a topic (as opposed to recorded in your notes and source material). These exercises ask you to express what you've learned from others in digested form.

As you write, you consistently look toward a synthesis of ideas, a synthesis that can demonstrate that you truly understand your topic. Remember the first exercise in this chapter, when you wrote on a topic with which you are familiar? It's that type of familiarity that will allow you to write clear, effective prose—prose that reflects your own clear thinking on a topic. In order to prime your memory for the task of writing, taking time to express the many things you've learned—and doing so from memory—can help you to see the big picture.

Of course, whenever you use the ideas and words of others, you must be wary of plagiarism. In academic and workplace writing, it is important to acknowledge those ideas that you have learned from others and to distinguish your own ideas from those you took from other sources.

There are, of course, many reasons why you should acknowledge the work of others. First, demonstrating your knowledge of the work of others increases your own credibility, since it shows that you have done your homework on the topic. That credibility is even stronger when you demonstrate a real understanding of the arguments made by others rather than merely letting those arguments stand on their own. And acknowledging the work of others gives credit where it is due, creating a logical trail of ideas that will help your readers to see how the topic has been handled in the past. As you synthesize the ideas of others, of course, the line between your own ideas and those of the experts whose work you have read can become difficult to define.

You must make many judgments as you decide to whom a thought or words belong. It's relatively easy to know that you must document a source when you quote from it directly. But if you have gathered information from a number of sources and combined them with your own ideas, how can you tell who really "owns" an idea and so deserves credit? There's no easy answer to that one. But here are two pieces of advice:

First, you should acknowledge the thinkers and writers who have influenced your ideas. You can do that in a number of ways. Even when you paraphrase or summarize someone else's ideas, you can include parenthetical citations, pointing to specific pages of source articles, like this:

> It is likely that the business of the cybersecurity industry will double within the next few years (*Business Week* 191).

You can include the name of the author or the source in the text of your essay, like this:

> According to a recent prediction by *Business Week*, the cybersecurity industry is likely to double within the next two years (191).

In either case, you acknowledge the influence that this writer's work has had on your own. Acknowledging contributions that others have made does not reduce the value of your own thoughts, nor does it suggest that the idea is precisely the same as it was stated in the source. Quite to the contrary! Mature incorporation of other people's ideas situates them in the service of *your* main points. This, in turn, can help you to avoid merely reporting on other people's ideas and to keep your own voice in control. For example,

> With each new accomplishment in technology, it seems, comes a consequent problem. Though the ability to gather, store, and use information has never been greater, so are its perils. For example, in just a three-month period, one health insurance company was the victim of over 145,000 attempts to illegally access the company's computer system (*Business Week* 191).

In this case, I used information provided in the cited article but incorporated it for my own purposes. Though the article was written to show the potential for growth in this security industry, I used it to illustrate my own point: Technology not only has benefits but also breeds problems. In this way, my own point—not the source author's—stays central to the writing.

WRITING TO EXPLORE 8.5

Using the three articles above as sources, write a paragraph on each of the following topics. Incorporate one piece of information from *each article* into your paragraph, but keep your own opinion on the topic primary.

- The newest and best technology for combating cybercrime
- The weaknesses in security methods that exist in our country
- The obstacles to creating secure computer networks in the workplace

The techniques above represent just some of the ways that you can fully digest the ideas of others, and so prepare yourself to write with authority; there are many others. Each of the techniques below is designed to help you to move from the mechanical collection and restating of information toward a more confident control of your topic—a confidence that will show up in your writing style. If you are currently engaged in a researched project, try out some of the following:

WRITING TO EXPLORE 8.6

- **Hold peer partner conversations:** After doing initial research on your topic, have a face-to-face conversation with another student, explaining to him what you have learned. Articulating what you have learned orally, and then answering your partner's questions, can help you to not only recall information but also to find ways to express it to others. The process will also help you to identify your weak spots. If several members of the class share a topic, you might even set up a panel to present to the rest of the class, followed by questions and answers.

- **Deliver an informative speech or monologue:** Deliver a brief, extemporaneous speech designed to give basic information on your topic to an uninformed audience. Doing so will not only test your knowledge of the topic but also will help you to formulate key definitions in your own words.

- **Imagine a FAQ:** Develop a series of Frequently Asked Questions, considering what an uninformed audience would most likely want to know about. Then, attempt to answer each question. This exercise can help you to become conversant on your topic and to anticipate the types of information your audience will need.

- **Develop a list of terms and concepts:** Make a list of the most important terms and concepts pertaining to your topic and write clear, cogent definitions of each. This, too, will help you to understand your topic and increase your ability to address it clearly.

- **Paraphrase the experts:** Without looking at your research materials, do your best to recall the perspectives on your issue provided by experts whose work you have read. Doing so will help you to come to grips with the arguments and key players in the discussion—and to develop your own words for explaining those concepts for when you begin to draft.

All of these activities share a single purpose: to make you more conversant on a topic you are examining—and so readier to present your ideas in your own words.

WRITING MULTIPLE INTRODUCTIONS

Writing isn't always an efficient process; sometimes what you write in a first try leads you right into a dead end—and no matter what you do, it isn't going to lead you out of that dead end. The writing itself blocks the development of a rich and inventive essay. One way to avoid this trap is to simply produce *several introductions*, each taking as different an approach to the topic as you can conceive. Doing this forces you to decide which approach is most likely to lead to a productive piece of writing; the alternative is the sense that you need to go with the first approach that occurs to you. Though writing multiple introductions might *seem* inefficient, the technique can save you lots of time in the long run by giving you the chance to choose among various approaches to a topic.

You might begin a report on the effects of literacy on economic well-being as follows:

> The inverse correlation between literacy rates and poverty rates has long been established. In areas with especially low literacy rates, the poverty rates are far above the national norms. Further, poverty in low literacy rate areas has proven to be especially persistent. The rate of families and individuals whose incomes rise above the poverty level for families who are functionally illiterate is extremely low, further reinforcing the link between these factors. But few studies have illustrated the effect of community literacy programs upon the future economic well-being of communities.

This opening has many advantages, clarity and focus among them. It also fits nicely into the academic discipline of the social sciences, proposing to study a societal phenomenon by seeking correlations among data. It also uses styles that are acceptable within this discipline, such as the objective passive voice common to the sciences.

But there are many other ways to begin the report, ways that will be determined partially by the rhetorical situation. Since introductions play such an important role in moving the writer in a specific direction with the remainder of the essay, it is worthwhile to consider a variety of possible introductions—not by revising but by setting one aside and trying a wholly different tack. In this case, you might try, for example, a narrative:

> Imagine a family whose legacy is poverty, a poverty fueled by the inability to communicate. The Cortez family of North Philadelphia is such a family. For three generations. . . .

Beginning with a case study or narrative sets a different tone and establishes a different relationship with the reader. Choosing between the two, then, is about decorum or appropriateness. But generating several possible approaches can really help you to begin the drafting process with a bit of momentum. You might even involve a peer in the process.

> **WRITING TO EXPLORE 8.7**
>
> Try writing an introduction for a paper that you are writing or are considering writing, or that has been suggested by an instructor. Then, pass your introduction along to a peer via e-mail or in class. Ask your partner to read your introduction and then to write her own wholly original version. You can do this with several partners so as to generate a variety of possible approaches to your topic.

WRITING A WORKING ABSTRACT

Another way to test your knowledge of a topic and to begin finding the language to express it is to write an **abstract.** An abstract is a brief summary of a longer work that captures the thesis and the main details of that work. Its purpose is, as you likely know, to help potential readers know whether the article is worth reading—whether it contains the type of information that they seek. For this reason, an abstract must accurately capture both the content and the spirit of the piece of writing it describes. Consider, for example, the following abstract taken from the field of social sciences:

The Lowdown on Literacy

Abstract: The National Center for Education Statistics' (NCES) report "Adult Literacy in America" reveals that low levels of literacy are linked with poverty. Over 40% of people with the lowest literacy skills are poor, while only 10% of the people with the highest literacy skills are poor. The NCES ranks people into five literacy skill categories, with level 1 being the lowest. Slightly more than 20% of the population falls into level 1, two-thirds of whom never completed high school, and one-quarter of whom are recent immigrants.

Consider what this abstract accomplishes: It manages to describe the conclusions drawn in the piece; it provides information on the method; and it indicates the importance of the findings. The author was able to compress the crucial facets of the piece into a few words.

Though the abstract is generally written *after* the piece is completed, sometimes it is written as a proposal for future work. In any case, attempting to write an abstract *before* you draft an essay can be a useful exercise; you must cut through all the material that you have collected and get quickly to your point—and how you intend to support it.

WRITING TO EXPLORE 8.8

For an essay or paper you are currently writing, envision an abstract. Be sure that the abstract is no longer than about 100 words and that it captures the key features and approach of your proposed essay.

FINDING COMMON GROUND

Earlier, we discussed the concept of stasis—the place where the arguments on an issue come together and share basic points of disagreement. Once you have searched for information and begun the process of increasing your expertise on a topic, search for stasis points.

Since stasis is at the heart of an issue—in a sense, it *is* what is at issue—trying to articulate where various authors stand or reach stasis can be helpful in coming to grips with the most important areas to discuss in a draft. Begin by articulating the key stasis point or points and then use that point to help you to plan your essay.

WRITING TO EXPLORE 8.9

Read the following three statements on Ebonics and identify the key stasis points (points of contention or key disagreement) among them. For example, you might note that one point of stasis involves the effects of allowing Ebonics credibility in the classroom. Imagine what each of these authors might say in response to that point of stasis. Many more stasis points can be identified by considering the dialog represented in these three pieces. Develop as many stases as possible, looking beyond the most obvious ones.

1. In an interview with Georgia State University professor Lisa Delpit, coeditor of *The Real Ebonics Debate: Power, Language, and the Education of African-American Children*, Michelle Tucker asked, "What are the lessons from the Ebonics debate?" Delpit responded as follows: "Rather than see this language as just something to be fixed, we as a larger society have to understand its beauty. Then we can then acknowledge it as a wonderful language form, while we also teach 'edited' English. If kids want to fit in, if they want to be part of the group, they'll learn the language. But if they feel rejected by it, they'll resist it." Michelle Tucker, *NEA Today,* 17.2 (1998): 17.

2. Mark Gura, in an article for *Educational Leadership,* wrote: "Whether Ebonics is ultimately classified as a dialect, a true language, or plain old street slang, it's clearly not the language itself that is so offensive. Our nation accepts this language as the *lingua franca* that is pressed into service in so many movies and TV shows—family entertainment eagerly gobbled up by the masses. Is it

that we are offended by the effort to grant legitimacy to what many of us merely tolerate—and do so from a position of superiority?" *Educational Leadership*, 54.7 (1997): 87.

3. In "Ebonics Is Defective Speech and a Handicap for Black Children," Leon W. Todd wrote: "Ebonics is a politically correct term for dysfunctional speech. Legitimizing poor language habits will not help children find a job nor take control of their affairs later in life. The commerce of American society is based on standard English, and placing alternate language at the center of a child's school experience will lead to inhibited learning once the child leaves that isolated environment. Let us face it, ebonics is a fancy political cover for abnormal, defective, or dysfunctional speech. Students and their families who use these unfortunate speech patterns often are in need of a speech therapist to help treat their group reinforced speech pathology if they are to function effectively in the usual mainstream society." *Education*, 118.2 (1997): 177–81.

Building a confident and credible voice as a writer is crucial to your progress as a student and toward becoming a professional. In many ways, your confidence in your ability to speak and write on a topic signals your entry into a discourse community (or discipline or occupation). A member of a discourse community not only listens and reads well but is also ready and willing to speak or write.

The work you do in a first-year writing course can take you only so far in that direction; it takes many years to fully enter into a discipline or profession. But what you are learning is the process of getting there—the process of finding a life's work, and the process of composing your own thoughts on that area or knowledge and work. It is really at the moment when you feel qualified to discuss the ideas of a discipline or profession with other experts—even if they seem to know more than you do—that you enter into that community. Conversely, nothing can exclude you from a community more readily than your silence or inability to speak confidently. It is for this reason that your communication skills are so crucial to your successful entry into a discipline or profession. People are valued by the quality of their ideas; but separating the quality of their ideas from their ability to express them is all but impossible.

The Reading and Writing Applications that follow give you opportunities to practice developing a researched essay, drawing on the techniques we've been discussing. These techniques will move you toward the final stage of the writing (or speaking process): delivery. Delivery constitutes the moment in which you move from reader/learner to speaker/writer. That last canon of rhetoric brings together the others, asking you to use all the language skills you've been amassing toward creating an informed and polished presentation of ideas.

Inquiry and the Research Process

As we discussed in Chapters 7 and 8, becoming informed means more than having information; it involves understanding that information. It also involves using information within a rhetorical situation, including:

- having a reason to write (purpose)
- having an audience that agrees that there is a reason to discuss this topic or that can be convinced that there is a good reason (exigency)
- having knowledge of the conversation on this topic that preceded your entry into the conversation (through a review of the literature)
- having something new to say (finding gaps in the literature)

In the cases that follow, you will have the opportunity to practice these concepts through your own reading and writing. The cases give you guided practice in the skills and techniques associated with doing mature research. They can also help you through those processes in the context of research that you may currently be conducting.

Case 1 FOCUSING A TOPIC AND FINDING SEARCH TERMS

The process of finding usable and pertinent information requires a good deal of preparation and planning. The invention you do as you enter a conversation on

373

a topic, and within a specific discourse community, is crucial to a focused search for information and opinions on that topic.

Imagine you are interested in studying the so-called gender-wage gap—the difference in salaries paid to men and women who do similar work. Though you have a topic, it is a large one, touching on a wide range of discourse communities: politics, business, women's studies, and law, among others. For you to gain enough expertise to write intelligently about it, you must narrow the topic. Finding the most useful lines of inquiry is an important first step because when you confront the glut of information and opinion on this topic, you must ask specific questions to guide your search. In Chapter 4, you looked at Tracy Hanegraaf's attempts to develop and focus her work on this topic. Below are her attempts to take the next step in the process, finding her line of inquiry through inventive thought and initial reading as well as a consideration of the disciplines involved in this research.

Inquiring into the Gender-Wage Gap

Tracy Hanegraaf

Females in their late teens and twenties seem to have clearer career goals than males, according to a study done in 1999 by Rutgers Marriage Project Study. One-tenth of these career women train for careers in the health professions, an area still predominantly female. But the gap has narrowed, and many women do go into the fields of science, engineering, or business. Unfortunately, these educational equities have failed to progress beyond the schools. Women continue to be undervalued in the workplace, excluded for promotions, and paid $15,000 a year less than their equally educated male counterparts. Where is the outrage here? Has our women's rights movement become stagnant? Females have had to take the largest steps in the battle toward equality. Women had to fight for the right to vote and serve as elected officials. Shirley Chisholm said her greatest obstacle was not being black, but being a woman. The gaps in education pale next to the gaps in salaries. We have fought a battle for equal opportunities, but do we stop here? What is a highly successful, career-oriented female facing upon entering the real world of business?

When I looked at a study conducted to identify very important life values by gender, I found that even though values regarding being successful in work for the last thirty years have remained proportionately equal, males regard having lots of money as much more important than females. What does being successful in work mean for males versus females? Do the traditional philosophies of males supporting the wife and family still play a major role in this gender gap? As Friedan said in "The Quiet Movement of American Man," "both man and woman have to confront the conflict between their human needs—for love, for family, for meaning in work and purpose in life." However, do males and females confront this conflict with differing degrees of commitment reflected by society's view of stereotypical roles? I hope to find an answer to some of these puzzling questions.

This issue deals with sociological, business, and economic philosophies. As an education major, mother of four children, and someone who has worked in education for the past six years, I understand the gender equity situation well. I have already done much research on gender equality in education. Through research reports for my psychology class, I learned to read and draw unbiased conclusions from scientific research studies.

Studies in sociology, business, and economic journals that focus on gender gaps in salaries may provide a valuable resource for my paper. Studies focused on social expectations of males and females may show how this effects stereotyping. These gender gaps may possibly be narrowing, adjusting to an ever-slow rippling effect. Attitudes and behaviors reinforcing the stereotyping roles may be unconscious; our society is a product of sex role stereotyping. Though I will not restrict my research to primary journals, I may find pertinent surveys in secondary journals.

Expanding on various resources, I intend to use some relevant lines from works by D. H. Lawrence, Betty Friedan, and perhaps Mary Wollstonecraft. These pieces, though dated, reflect on the ageless plight of male versus female roles and contain passages that adapt to my topic. There may also be some pertinent information in video or film, but not necessarily primary information. For example, the theme from a recent movie, *What Planet Are You From?*, explores gender differences and could be used to add a lighter tone to my paper.

This is what I intend to do. I plan to start my research concentrating on sociology and business articles in primary and secondary journals. Also, I will search for any books that would have insight into differences in gender values and sexual discrimination. The reference department has texts that contain government statistics and surveys that focus on gender differences in educational goals, career goals, and family values. I will keep a large notecard of information and bibliography for each source used.

This proposal allows Hanegraaf to begin an important set of processes. She tries to situate her own areas of interest among those of other writers:

- "Shirley Chisholm said her greatest obstacle was not being black, but being a woman."

- "As Friedan said in 'The Quiet Movement of American Man,' 'both man and woman have to confront the conflict between their human needs—for love, for family, for meaning in work and purpose in life.'"

▪ "I intend to use some relevant lines from works by D. H. Lawrence, Betty Friedan, and perhaps Mary Wollstonecraft. These pieces, though dated, reflect on the ageless plight of male versus female roles and contain passages that adapt to my topic."

Hanegraaf also attempts to isolate the issues or points of stasis that exist on this topic, looking for specific ways into the conversation. She notes that:

▪ "Females in their late teens and twenties seem to have clearer career goals than males, according to a study done in 1999 by Rutgers Marriage Project Study. One-tenth of these career women train for careers in the health professions, an area still predominantly female."

At the same time, she concedes that there are other perspectives on the issue that must be accounted for:

▪ "But the gap has narrowed, and many women do go into the fields of science, engineering, or business. Unfortunately, these educational equities have failed to progress beyond the schools."

Hanegraaf also acknowledges that a problem still exists:

▪ "Women continue to be undervalued in the workplace, excluded for promotions, and paid $15,000 a year less than their equally educated male counterparts."

Hanegraaf uses this initial writing on the topic to create a set of important questions that can help her to formulate search terms for the collection of information. For example, she writes:

▪ "What does being successful in work mean for males versus females? Do our traditional philosophies of males supporting the wife and family still play a major role in this gender gap?"

▪ "Where is the outrage here? Has our women's rights movement become stagnant?"

▪ "We have fought a battle for equal opportunities, but do we stop here? What is a highly successful, career-oriented female facing upon entering the real world of business?"

▪ "Do males and females confront this conflict with differing degrees of commitment reflected by society's view of stereotypical roles?"

In these pointed questions, you can hear Hanegraaf begin to develop the lines of inquiry that can guide her through the research process and so lead her to specific search terms. Though her topic is still not fully focused, she has certainly made great strides toward finding her way into the conversation, at least as a listener.

Hanegraaf also considers the types of learning she is doing in other classes (such as psychology) and the discourse communities, the fields of study, most likely to be concerned with this issue:

- "Studies in sociology, business, and economic journals that focus on gender gaps in salaries may provide a valuable resource for my paper. Studies focused on social expectations of males and females may show how this effects stereotyping. These gender gaps may possibly be narrowing, adjusting to an ever-slow rippling effect. Attitudes and behaviors reinforcing the stereotyping roles may be unconscious; our society is a product of sex role stereotyping."

And you can hear Hanegraaf begin to find the methods through which she can find answers to her questions in the current literature on the topic:

- "I plan to start my research concentrating on sociology and business articles in primary and secondary journals. Also, I will search for any books that would have insight into differences in gender values and sexual discrimination. The reference department has texts that contain government statistics and surveys that focus on gender differences in educational goals, career goals, and family values."

This planning bodes well for the project that follows. Hanegraaf has created a line of inquiry and research that identifies specific issues within the overall topic. Her initial thinking and reading can now form the basis for well-thought-out searches using Boolean operators that limit and focus the return of information in books, periodicals, and websites. Her search may have become overwhelming and unfocused had she simply searched for information on "gender and wages."

The above version of Hanegraaf's initial proposal was the product of many of the inventional activities we've been discussing—brainstorming, freewriting, and peer conversations—all involving a good deal of mental work. In the exercise below, you can practice that mental work as you consider how you might think through, and so hem in, the following topics. Remember: the goal is to focus your search and so understand the topic better. The important side effect of such thought is finding useful search terms.

Writing to Respond

- Consider the following situations and write what you would consider to be useful search strings, using Boolean operators (and, or, but).
- Go back and brainstorm, freewrite, and discuss the topic with others. What new possibilities for search terms or keywords arise in your writing or in those conversations? Do your best to limit the topic to narrow areas of interest and to expand the number of potential keywords you might use in a search.

Say you are writing on the influence of U.S. corporations on the rainforest. In your freewriting and discussions, you might discover that the rainforest needs to be identified (South American?); you might search for information about specific corporations (McDonald's? Pepsi?); you might consider whether you are looking for biological information, statistics, importance of the rainforest, and so forth. You might think about specific discourse communities involved in this debate in ways that would limit the search by subject area (based on the Library of Congress headings discussed in the previous chapter).

Try limiting the following broad topics, using the processes discussed above to find facets of the topic that might be explored. As you think about each topic, develop search terms that would help you to gather information on those limited facets of the topic, try them out, and use new search terms to focus to your process. In your writer's notebook, keep track of the terms and approaches you use.

- The history of gun rights
- The types of work that are done by people in business fields
- The work of early women authors
- The latest innovations on cloning
- Ways that community action groups can be formed
- Why certain people seem prone to addictive behaviors
- Choose your own topic, or use one suggested by your teacher or classmates

Case 2 WRITING A FORMAL PROPOSAL AND ANNOTATED BIBLIOGRAPHY

The processes of inquiry explored above represent crucial starting points in coming to terms with research projects. But even the solid proposal by Hanegraaf above was largely self-reflective as she struggled to find ways into the topic: "However, do males and females confront this conflict with differing degrees of commitment reflected by society's view of stereotypical roles? I hope to find an answer to some of these puzzling questions."

Eventually, you should begin thinking of your research in terms of potential audiences, considering how your inquiry will find its way into a larger discourse community. This part of the research process not only further limits your inquiry in useful ways, it also helps you to find your own voice amid those of experts. Of course, as we've noted, research is a recursive process, not a linear one. One way to ensure that your research gets off to a productive start is to formulate your plan into a formal proposal on which you seek feedback.

There are many ways to write a successful proposal. Here are elements that might be included as you attempt to detail your goals to a reader who will provide feedback (a teacher, a colleague, a superior at work):

1. A focused topic question: What specifically is it that you (and your audience) need to know more about?

2. A specific audience to whom you will present this information, along with:

   - Your initial characterization of that audience and their likely attitude toward your topic.
   - A statement of how you expect to appeal to this audience on this topic.

3. A specific purpose statement: What do you want to accomplish? How do you wish to affect your audience's views? What is the goal of your writing? Include:

   - Your reasons for wanting to affect this change.
   - A statement and argument about the exigency of this topic for this audience.
   - A statement about the timeliness of the topic.

4. A proposed line of inquiry: Present ways you intend to research this topic.

   - What are some of the questions that you will need to answer or find out about if you are to become a credible writer on the topic?
   - What types of sources, primary and secondary, do you expect to be most useful?

5. A statement about your qualifications to do this research:

   - In what ways does your previous experience or training prepare you to do this research? For example, if you plan to research a scientific topic, what qualifies you to read the work in scientific journals? What do you know about scientific method? What do you know about the area of inquiry? Though you will, of course, learn new things along the way, what will prepare you to do so?

6. A proposed timetable. To project this, you'll need to look carefully at deadlines, consider lead time for interlibrary loaning, allow time to schedule interviews or do primary research such as questionnaires or surveys, etc. Try to lay out a viable timetable that will help you keep on schedule.

Though these considerations are necessary for most proposals, they need not be addressed in the order listed. There are many ways to be creative in your presentation of the topic to sell readers on the idea (recall Audra Shearer's proposal on studying school violence in Chapter 7). As long as the writing suits the audience, you should feel free to incorporate various styles—full paragraphs, bulleted items, charts, graphics—whatever best characterizes the work you plan to do and gives it credibility. Be sure to consider style, tone, and voice, remembering the key element of every proposal: credibility.

A good proposal makes your reader feel sure that your topic will interest your audience and that you are capable of making good on what you propose to do. A proposal often also includes evidence that you have already invested time into the topic—that you didn't ask for permission to proceed until you were relatively sure that the resources for your work are available. To further add credibility to your proposal, you might give an assessment of the state of research in this area. What aspects of the issue are people writing about most? What seem to be the key concerns? Are there areas that seem to be neglected—and if so, why? Your goal in this discussion is to characterize generally the types of information that you have found, the key issues that seem to be most discussed in relation to your topic, and to highlight what you take to be the most exciting research you have found.

To illustrate the accessibility of the necessary information (and your own ability to find it), you can include an **annotated working bibliography.** An annotated bibliography presents, in digested form, information that you have found that indicates your topic is worth pursuing; it is a "working" bibliography because it will continue to change over the research process as you add and subtract items. An annotated bibliography can be presented in many forms. To make it work best, and to help you to not only list items but learn about them as well, you might include the following:

1. A correctly formatted citation (using accurate MLA or APA style, unless another format is preferred in your field).

2. A brief summary of the source's main point (or thesis), with just enough detail to let your reader know what she would find there should she look.

3. A brief statement regarding the value of this source to your research. How, specifically, will it be useful? How do you expect to make use of it? What information or point of view does it supply? Is it one of the more valuable sources?

4. A brief statement assessing the source's credibility. In order to evaluate the credibility of each item, you can identify the source as scholarly (journals written expert to expert), popular (magazines meant for the general public), or trade (magazines meant for members of a particular occupation). You might consider whether the information is primary (gathered or generated by the writer himself) or secondary. You can also evaluate the source for authority by evaluating its objectivity, accuracy, and the references it includes.

Below is an example of a typical bibliographic entry:

The citation will be useful as you later prepare the Works Cited or Reference page for your essay. This citation is MLA style; you might use whatever style is most often used in your own field. See Chapter 10 for details.

Morsch, James. "The Problem of Motive in Hate Crimes: The Argument against Presumptions of Racial Motivation." Journal of Criminal Law and Criminology. 8.2. (1991): 659–689. Expanded Academic ASAP. Gale Group. Schmidt Library, York College of PA, York, PA. 5 Mar. 2001 <http://web2.infotrac.galegroup.com>.

Lays out the main topic or thesis.

Morsch investigates who has the burden of proof (prosecutor or defendant) in proving racial motivation in hate crime court cases.

Indicates why the author — He provides details about how difficult such motivation is to prove, citing case
and his work are credible.   studies and specific legal issues that have arisen in those cases.

Shows the author's key ¬   These details will help me to explain the complexity of the legal issues
sources of evidence and   surrounding hate crimes.
his scholarly approach
to the topic.

Shows how the article —   This, in turn, might help to show how difficult it is to define hate crimes. This article
will be used toward the   is a scholarly, secondary article because Morsch builds his argument on primary
writer's own purposes.   sources like state laws and other commentator's ideas.

Further explains the ———   Morsch, a professor of law at Temple, supports his argument with 20+ references
author's approach to   and presents each side of the issue equally before making his judgment.
that topic.

This annotated bibliography entry is more than part of a list of sources. It is the beginning of a dialog that you will continue both privately—as you consider the information available on your topic—and publicly with your teacher, peers, and perhaps other experts in this topic area. Each entry asks you to do more than just collect information; it asks you to "digest" it. To digest can mean not only to shorten and summarize but also to process the information through your mind. That is, in the process of writing good summaries and evaluating the usefulness of each item to your topic, you are *learning*—you are moving knowledge from the public memory to your own individual memory (as we discussed in the last chapter).

Following is a revised proposal Tracy Hanegraaf wrote as she continued her research on the gender-wage gap. Note how her topic has changed, developed, and/or continued the work of the earlier proposal. Also note the ways in which this proposal argues for the importance and exigency of this topic.

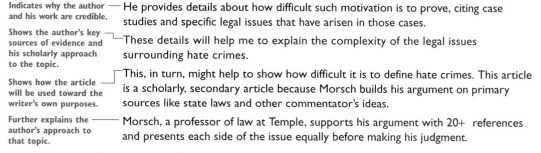

Exploration of the Gender-Wage Gap

Tracy Hanegraaf

The first part of my paper will concentrate on establishing the current state of the gender-wage gap. Current studies on the gender-wage gap involve several interrelated issues. First, there are disagreements concerning various methods of calculating wage disparity. Consequently, the media has been inclined to inflate and distort the situation, arousing public emotion with alarming figures. Some analysts simply use the median of all female annual salaries and the median of male annual salaries to create a ratio. This method used by the U.S. Census Bureau is most often cited by the media and ignores many variables. Another method of calculating the wage gap uses weekly medians of full-time, year-round workers, and produces even more alarming results. Reporters often neglect to mention statistics that indicate men work more hours per week and more weeks on average than women.

In fact, most sources cited ignore various significant factors. Some researchers find that when wage comparisons are made between males and females in the same occupations, with the same amount of education, and working the same number of hours and weeks, the wage gap almost disappears. Additionally, some researchers suggest the gap almost disappears for childless females. What's more, "comparable worth" issues add another angle to the equal pay analysis, which has an entire group of followers who feel women are underpaid for jobs basically filled by the female population.

After establishing the current position of the gender-wage gap, I will present a brief history of the progression of the women's pay equity movement, focusing on landmarks and legal proposals of the past thirty years. Then, I will focus on main reasons for the gap, as suggested by researchers and analysts, citing pertinent studies and statistics. Information concerning the intermittence of female workers and the saturation of women's occupational fields fits into this section. Additionally, information regarding these issues substantiates results that indicate childless females appear to have equality in pay. Further illustrating this point, research addressing working mothers emphasizes the cost of mothering on careers. Focusing on reasons that suggest attitudes and choices contribute to the remaining gap, I will disclose surveys related to attitudes, choices, and values pertaining to work, marriage, and families.

The focal point of my argument will address society's values of success and its failure to acknowledge female, as well as male, priorities of family first. Results from surveys on attitudes and priorities regarding families and work will substantiate my appeal. I will advocate a respected and even admired status for women and men who choose to spend time with their families. Many women and men choose to value the non-monetary work benefits of flexibility, less travel time, and a more family-oriented career. It is time for America to rate success through different venues—not the expensive car, house, and that annual Disney vacation (that most Americans cannot afford, anyway). Our children need us to listen, support, and share their lives more than a pair of designer jeans, a personal phone, and a television.

Finally, if society put more emphasis on the value of parents who devote time to raising their children, men and women with strong family values would feel supported and successful. I intend to support this part of my paper with details from the findings of a major study conducted by the Families and Work Institute, that investigated job effects on life at home and, conversely, life at home effects on the job. This study examined the changing composition of the workforce and job performance relationships. Recent surveys indicate a continual increase of working families with young children; nevertheless, women remain identified as the main caregivers of their children. Stress from family demands was identified as the catalyst for employers to offer flexibility and support to workers juggling family responsibilities and careers. The gender-wage gap has a legitimate reason for existing, and the alarm over this gap needs to be put into proper perspective, acknowledging society's family-first choice as the ultimate priority.

Since I am focusing my paper on issues of social concern, I have chosen *The Humanist* as my source of possible publication. This magazine supports human rights, social justice, and goals of life from human need and interest. The editors stress their position supporting individual liberty and opportunity consonant with social and planetary responsibility. As a result of information I obtained, I feel my paper will be in philosophical accordance to the audience and editors of this publication. The "glass ceiling," equal pay legislation, and "comparable worth" add perspectives on the issue, as well as the discovery of several articles, mostly newspaper and secondary periodicals, from the UK and Canada that lend an international flair to my topic.

I found my topic covered thoroughly in many disciplines; even an entire issue of *The Quarterly Review of Economics and Finance* at the end of 1999 was dedicated entirely to women and their progress in the past century. Unfortunately, the interlibrary loan system denied my request for the entire journal, and I have since requested several separate articles from this special issue. I chose these articles based on the authors' names that I recognized as scholars who conducted surveys and studies mentioned in other sources. I selected material by establishing the significance of the articles, choosing only those I felt came from credible, competent sources. I chose works written in a scholarly fashion, that cite scholarly sources, and which were written by notable authors. I also chose some articles that came from trade journals. These allowed me to compare and contrast information between the different occupational fields.

I found conflicting interpretations on the severity of the gender-wage gap and disagreement concerning methods of statistically comparing male and female salaries. Most of the studies I found in primary, scholarly journals focused on this computation and really did not address the disparity between same occupation, level of education, and level of seniority wages, sometimes referred to as "equal job, equal pay." Although pay equity laws and "comparable worth" argue the issue from an overall wage-gender bias (not an apples-to-apples comparison), these issues point to the same conclusions of work commitment and family values that factor into the gender-wage gap for comparable job situations. They are valuable in explaining the history and issues that create the current gender gap situation we face.

To further educate my audience on the history of legal and social issues that define woman's progress in the past century, *Women and Public Policy: A Revolution in Progress* will be very useful. Sorensen's book explains the results of the

Urban Institute's study on the narrowing wage gap and provides a thorough analysis of factors influencing women's salaries through the 1980s. Likewise, Ida Castro's article from *National Forum* captures the history of the women's pay battle, and goes even further into the undervaluing of traditional "women's work" which I will want to include as a major reason for discontent, and a factor in gender-wage disparities.

One factor in the gender-wage battle is the cost of woman's mothering role. Two articles, Mallon's "The Cost of Being a Woman" (lending an UK perspective to my paper) and Hewlett's "Have a Child and Experience the Wage Gap," address the working mother's side of the issue. Considering the mothering role cause, Art Pine in "Pay Problems" uses results from Women's Policy Research and economists' opinions to prove that the pay gap is the result of choices, not a gender bias issue.

Summing it all up, the most exciting article I found, Lynch and Post's report "What Glass Ceiling?" exposes an accurate, researched picture of female career concentrations, hours spent working, and career aspirations, showing the overall effect of these on the gender gap. The authors cite credible, unique surveys and studies that I had not encountered in my previous research. Also, they balance their information with interesting statistics on women who have broken past the "glass ceiling" and female entrepreneurs. This shows that if women want to be highly successful, if they have this motivation rather than family-first priorities, they can accomplish their goals and dispel the gender-wage myth. Research from "Meek Women Lose Out in Battle for Pay" fits into this picture, illustrating another perspective that suggests women cause their own gender bias; women are less assertive in regards to promotions and pay.

To finalize my studies, I may want to research some of these specific studies such as "The New Providers" study that found women defined success more in regards to home and family than males, as cited in Lynch and Post's article. These studies may provide me with more pertinent support for my argument. Finally, in assessing the breadth of material I have accumulated, I may dispose of current news articles from *USA News* and *Fox News*, although the *Fox News* article provides recent legislation pending Congress. These two articles show that my topic is very current, but for the most part reiterate the information I found from other sources. The articles from *Advertising Age* and *Enterprise* are not my most valuable sources, but they may be used to lend a focus of actual statistics from predominately male professions, and show that the facts remain constant regardless of the profession. Additionally, the opinions and attitudes expressed by executives in these industries reflect those permeating all areas of business and professions.

I will finish this research by March 16, and start writing the rough draft of Paper #3 (the research progress report and annotated bibliography). This rough draft will be completed by March 20, in time for finalizing by March 22. For the next two weeks I will work on Paper #4, rereading my original topic and purpose. I will explore how my research findings expand on my original ideas, and possibly confirm or contradict them. I will consider how to best organize my information, include my own ideas, and draw conclusions. By April 7, I will begin the rough draft of my final paper, incorporating the information from Paper #3 (my viewpoint), and conclusions from Paper #4 into a culminating essay that will awaken anyone, male or female, about the gender gap. This paper should be very enlightening to young women entering the workforce for the first time. By April 24, I will begin polishing and revising my final paper with a May 3 completion date.

Annotated Bibliography

Castro, Ida L. "Worth More Than We Earn: Fair Pay as a Step Toward Gender Equity." *National Forum* 77 (1997): 17. Expanded Academic ASAP. Gale Group. Schmidt Library, York College of PA, York. 20 Feb. 2001. Castro presents many facts concerning attitudes that affect the gender-wage gap, as well as statistics to provide an overview of the changes in the women's job market for the past fifty years. She reports on the results of a 1994 Working Women Count! Survey done by the Women's Bureau of the U.S. Department of Labor, a brief history of the Equal Pay Act, and offers solutions for what women can do to alleviate the inequity problems. Castro, director of the Women's Bureau of the U.S. Department of Labor, the only federal agency designed to advocate for women in the workforce, gives an interesting view of the narrowing changes in the women's workforce since 1950, along with reasons for the existing gap. This is a secondary, researched news article and how-to article with focus more on the undervaluing of traditional "women's work," an angle I may want to use in my paper to explain the difference in the wage gap and its progression over the years.

Conway, M. Margaret, David W. Ahern, and Gertrude A. Steuernagel. "Chapter 4: Equal Employment Opportunity Policy." *Women and Public Policy: A Revolution in Progress.* Washington, D.C.: *Congressional Quarterly,* 1995. Chapter four of this book has historical information on "Patterns of Employment," as well as the history of the Equal Pay Act, definitions of the "glass ceiling," and the latest "comparable worth" concept and its legal implications. This background information will be valuable to educate the reader on the history of the equal pay battle. Although this is a secondary source, this book is a current (1995) publication by a scholarly publisher citing and translating specific legislation with documentation. The authors represent renowned universities as professors of political science, government, and law; scholars from various universities reviewed their writing.

Hewlett, Sylvia Ann. "Have a Child, and Experience the Wage Gap." *New York Times* 16 May 2000: A31. Hewlett addresses the issue of working mothers versus working women. She cites a study and survey with figures supporting the existence of the wage gap with probable cause. This is a fairly current news report in a reputable newspaper by Hewlett, a fellow at Harvard's Center for the Study of Values in Public Life, and Chairman of the National Parenting Association.

Lynch, Michael, and Katherine Post. "What Glass Ceiling?" *The Public Interest* Summer 1996: 27. Expanded Academic Index ASAP. Gale Group. Schmidt Library, York College of PA, York. 16 Mar. 2001 <http://web2.infotrac.galegroup.com>. Lynch and Post provide a very thorough investigation into the gender-wage gap, proving the very narrow gap is mostly due to personal career choices and disappears when all factors are considered. Many surveys and studies are cited with supporting details and statistics on career concentrations, salaries, hours worked, the "glass ceiling," and women entrepreneurs in this all-encompassing researched article. The authors provide data from several studies that support views that women intend to work intermittently and retire sooner than males, as well as results from surveys on gender definitions of success and differences in long-term work commitments. This researched, secondary article is credible because the authors base their opinions on the examination of studies done by the Census Bureau, National Bureau of Economic Research, and other government committees.

Mand, Adrienne. "Good New (Sort Of): Male-Female Wage Gap Narrowing (Maybe)." 18 Aug. 2000. *Fox News* 7 Mar. 2001 http://www.foxnews.com. Mand gives a thorough report of the narrowing gender-wage gap, citing statistics and survey graphs from several government sources. Additionally, she provides current legislation before Congress (the Fair Pay Act, and Paycheck Fairness Act) and several comments from renowned scholars and business people. This fairly recent news article provides me with some pertinent figures on the wage gap in specific work fields and statistics supporting the one main factor believed to contribute to the pay gap. Recent legislation and activity focused on the gender-wage gap issue are specified, providing me with information from the legal side of the issue.

Pine, Art. "Pay Problems." *Los Angeles Business Journal* 4 Dec. 2000: 47. Business Index ASAP. Gale Group. Schmidt Library, York College of PA, York. 28 Feb. 2001 <http://web2.infotrac.galegroup.com>. Pine first addresses the argument of the wage-gender gap, contending the salary gap figures are not calculated fairly. He uses statistics to establish an accurate measurement of the gap and discusses the factors influencing the remaining gap. He quotes a researcher from Women's Policy Research on the discrimination problem, pitted against an economist who feels there is no discrimination, but rather choices. These two different perspectives will be helpful in presenting various sides of my issue. This is a very current, secondary news article written by a news columnist in a business oriented, popular newspaper.

Sorensen, Elaine. *Exploring the Reasons Behind the Narrowing Gender Gap in Earnings.* Washington, D.C.: Urban Institute Press, 1991. Sorensen reports on a research study conducted by the Urban Institute, a non-profit government policy and educational organization, that studied the narrowing wage gap in the 1980's, potential for females in high-growth jobs, and analysis of factors influencing women's low pay. The results of this research are crucial, primary pieces of information in establishing cause and effects of the gender-wage gap. Though Sorensen's report is a secondary source, the Urban Institute Press published the report, and for the most part, it is a primary source by a research and educational foundation. It is ten years old, but the majority of the narrowing occurred prior to the 1980's, and the research results are still relevant in today's labor market.

Swiss, Deborah J. *Women Breaking Through: Overcoming the Final 10 Obstacles at Work.* Princeton: Peterson's Pacesetter Books, 1996. Swiss's book, written as a result of 325 surveys of women in the prime of their careers, reports on the current gender gap in the work environment and provides suggestions to women for overcoming the major gender barriers in the workplace. Swiss offers a personable view with many real-life success stories and suggestions that will enable me to show a personal perspective to my paper, enlightening the reader to true values and attitudes of modern women. This 1996 book is a secondary source, though Swiss's surveys (her credentials are not given) would be considered primary information.

Wood, Lisa. "Income Gap Far From Closed." *The Financial Times* 22 Jan. 2001: 10. Business Index ASAP. Gale Group. Schmidt Library, York College of PA, York. 28 Feb. 2001 <http://web2.infotrac.galegroup.com>. Wood reports on a *Financial Times* survey of women in the Master's of Business program and the wage gap. She provides legitimate reasons for this gap from several researchers and institutions. These concrete facts are very valuable for my paper, offering more than just attitudes and opinions on the causes of the pay gap. This is a very recent (Jan. 2001), secondary news article in a business trade journal.

Tracy Hanegraaf's topic proposal illustrates the ways in which you might use a proposal to clarify your thinking on a topic. But it accomplishes more than that. As Hanegraaf explains the topic, she also argues for its importance as well, helping her to develop viable ways to discuss it with her audience. Much of what she writes might find its way, in some altered form, into the researched essay itself because she has clearly become conversant on the subject—she knows enough about it to explain what she has learned to someone else.

Writing Application

If you are currently engaged in a research project, prepare a proposal and annotated bibliography, following the previous advice and examples. Be sure to think about your audience for the proposal as well as the ultimate audience for the researched essay you are proposing.

Case 3 WRITING A REVIEW OF THE LITERATURE

Preparing a review of the literature is a process driven by several purposes:

- To demonstrate your awareness of the important previous research on a topic and hence enhance your own *ethos;*

- To demonstrate your understanding of how that research fits together as context and background for your own project;

- To demonstrate how your research can fill a perceived gap in the work done up until this point—a place for you to jump into the conversation and extend it;

- To serve as a sophisticated introduction to your researched essay, and to clear a space for the ideas to follow.

Writing to Respond

The literature review is useful not only as you write a proposal but also as part of your introduction to the researched essay itself. To see how various academic fields use the literature review, read one or more of the following excerpts from scholarly, refereed articles, all dealing with questions related to gender roles. (In the original, these literature reviews were accompanied by references, notes, and/or Works Cited lists; I have not included these here.) In your writer's notebook, discuss the following:

- What do all of these literature reviews have in common in terms of presentation of past research?

- How do the reviews of the literature vary by academic discipline or field?

- How does each author use past research to introduce the present topic?

- How are the studies cited organized by the authors of the articles excerpted below?

- For what purposes does each author quote articles directly? When are paraphrases or summaries used?

Social Sciences (Social Psychology)

Jealousy as a Function of Rival Characteristics: An Evolutionary Perspective

Pieternel Dijkstra & Bram P. Buunk

Jealousy is generated by a threat to or the actual loss of a valued relationship with another person due to an actual or imagined rival for one's partner's attention (Buunk, 1991; DeSteno & Salovey, 1996; Heider, 1958; Parrot, 1991; Salovey, 1991). Because the presence of a rival is a necessary and defining condition for jealousy, feelings of jealousy are assumed to be competitive in nature. The person who notices that his or her partner is attracted to a third person is likely to see that person as a rival and will experience a sense of competition, because both are vying for the partner's exclusive love and attention. If a person perceives his or her partner paying attention to the rival, the rival will become a very salient target for social comparison, and the jealous person will compare his or her qualities with those of the rival (Buunk & Bringle, 1987). Social comparison with the rival will mainly take place on those dimensions that are believed to be important to the partner (Mathes, 1991; White, 1981). A rival who is perceived to have superior qualities on these dimensions will evoke more feelings of jealousy than a rival who is perceived to have inferior qualities on these dimensions (DeSteno & Salovey, 1996).

Following from evolutionary psychology, males and females will differ in the rival characteristics that evoke feelings of jealousy. These differences are linked to the different resources males and females invest in their offspring. Females invest relatively more direct physiological resources (contributing their own bodily nutrients to the fetus and nursing the child), whereas males invest relatively more indirect resources (such as food, money, protection, and security) (Buss, 1994). Because humans value those characteristics in a mate that maximize an offspring's chances of survival, males and females will be guided by different characteristics in a mate (Kenrick, Groth, Trost, & Sadalla, 1993; Kenrick, Neuberg, Zierk, & Krones, 1994). Females who are selecting mates will desire males who are able to provide resources. The ability to provide resources is related to a man's level of dominance (Buss, 1994). A dominant male is characterized by self-confidence, initiative, assertiveness, extroversion, ascendance, and authoritativeness (Luteijn, Starren, & Van Dijk, 1985; Sadalla, Kenrick, & Vershure, 1987). Because of these characteristics, a dominant male will in general achieve a higher position in the social hierarchy and therefore obtain more resources than a nondominant male. Females, therefore, more than males will value a potential mate's dominance and will prefer a dominant male more than a nondominant male. A number of researchers have found support for this assumption. For instance, Kenrick, Sadalla, Groth, and Trost (1990) found that characteristics related to dominance were more central criteria for a woman's choice than for a man's choice of partner. Likewise, Buss (1989) found that a potential mate's social status was more important for women than for men across a number of cultures. . . .

In the present study, each participant is asked how he or she would respond to a scenario in which the participant's partner is flirting with an individual of the opposite sex who is either high or low in dominance and either high or low in physical attractiveness. Because jealousy is aroused by characteristics of the rival that are believed to be important to the other sex (Mathes, 1991; White, 1981), it was predicted that among males the degree of jealousy in response to the scenario will be influenced particularly by the rival's dominance (Hypothesis 1), whereas among females the degree of jealousy will be influenced particularly by the rival's physical attractiveness (Hypothesis 2). We therefore predicted two interactions: a physical attractiveness by sex interaction and a dominance by sex interaction. Because it was expected that the perception of one's own physical attractiveness to the other sex (in other words, one's "mate value") would be related to feelings of jealousy (Bush, Bush, & Jennings, 1988), mate value was assessed as a control variable.

Natural Sciences (Genetics)

The New Genetics and Women

Mary B. Mahowald, Dana Levinson, & Christine Cassel

The Human Genome Project (HGP) is a worldwide effort to map and sequence all of the 100,000 or so genes that are found in the 47 chromosomes of human beings. Each gene comprises a sequence of four chemicals called nucleotides. These link together to form long, complex molecules of deoxyribonucleic acid, commonly known as DNA. The totality of genetic information in each organism is called its genome. To map the human genome means to locate each gene on a particular chromosome. To sequence the human genome means to determine the order in which the four nucleotides are arranged in each gene.

Specific genes, or combinations of genes, are associated with specific conditions: diseases and susceptibility to diseases, particular abilities, and distinguishing characteristics like eye color or height. Except for identical twins, each individual's genome is unique. Knowledge of our genetic makeup thus encompasses knowledge of what is personally unique about us. Information generated by the HGP will result in a greater understanding of genetic variation and disease, and has the potential to make available an increased number of genetic tests for screening and diagnosis of diseases, as well as other biological characteristics of humans.

Recognizing that the HGP raises fundamental issues of bioethics (Annas 1992), the U.S. Congress designated from 3 to 5 percent of the three billion dollars originally allotted to human genome research for studies of the ethical, legal, and social implications (ELSI) of the project and created a working group for this task (Roberts 1993). A novel aspect of the HGP is that it studies these issues alongside the scientific ones in the hope that problems can be anticipated and policy options developed. Three principal areas have been identified for initial study: privacy and confidentiality of genetic information; protection from discrimination based on genetics; and safe introduction of genetic tests into mainstream medical practice (Collins and Galas 1993).

Although all of these issues are relevant to individuals, families, and society at large, women, because of their central role in reproduction and caregiving, are affected not only differently but also more significantly than men by the information emerging from the HGP. Nonetheless, women have seldom been the focus of studies emerging from the ELSI program of the National Center for Human Genome Research. Accordingly, the goal of this article is to document the distinct impact of "the new genetics" on women. By identifying gender differences not only in research and clinical practice, but also in the psychosocial, legal, and ethical implications of the HGP, we hope both to evoke and to inform public discussion and policies that may be generated by these issues.

A Typology of Gender Differences

Women are recipients of genetic services not only in their capacity as patients, but also as participants in prenatal diagnosis, treatment, research, and, frequently, as primary caregivers of those affected with genetic conditions. Women also predominate among health care providers for those who utilize genetic services; their predominance, however, is limited to those areas of health care that are held in less regard and are less remunerative than others (Weaver 1978). For example, only one-third of doctorally prepared medical geneticists are women, but 94 percent of master's-prepared genetic counselors are women (Wertz and Fletcher 1988a; Pencarinha et al. 1992). The difference between male and female roles in reproduction accounts for the predominance of women as recipients of genetic services even when they are not personally affected by genetic conditions. Because some diseases are treatable in utero, pregnant women already undergo treatment for the sake of their fetuses. As gene therapies develop, they may be encouraged even more to participate in therapies for the sake of their offspring. Political and social pressures are sometimes brought to bear on women who are carriers of genetic diseases, particularly those women who do not have independent financial resources to care for affected children. Such women may be challenged about becoming pregnant or criticized for continuing a pregnancy after prenatal diagnosis confirms the presence of fetal abnormality or genetic condition (Purdy 1978). Conversely, the ongoing controversy over abortion might lead to increased social criticism of women who wish to terminate affected pregnancies. Businesses may limit options of women in the workplace, and insurance companies may curtail their access to coverage based on genetic knowledge relevant to women's reproductive capacities.

Five Questions Based on Gender

To facilitate examination of ethical issues raised by gender differences in genetics, it is necessary to identify the differences that arise in research, the clinical applications of that research, and the nonmedical aspects of people's lives that are or may be affected by advances in genetics. This article addresses five empirical questions as a guide in that determination:

1. Of the genetic conditions that the HGP investigates, which ones mainly affect women, and to what extent?

2. To what extent are women needed to fulfill the goals of the HGP—for example, by supplying genetic materials, undergoing preconception or prenatal testing or procedures, or by contributing to the process of research?

3. To what extent, if any, does availability of genetic information, including decisions about prenatal counseling and testing, influence women's decisions regarding reproduction and decisions to continue or terminate a pregnancy?

4. In what ways, and to what extent, have women been differentially affected through employment or insurance practices because of genetic information available to themselves or to others?

5. What impact does caregiving of those affected by genetic diseases have on the lives of women?

Humanities (History)
Gender and Working Class Identity in Britain during the 1950's

Stephen Brooke

Recent scholarship has emphasized the place of gender in the formation of British working class identity during the late eighteenth and early nineteenth centuries. If gender attended the birth of the English working classes, was it also present at their (apparent) death? Some aspects of the history and culture of gender in the 1950s have attracted scholarly attention. The particular relationship between gender and class within the post-war working classes remains less well-explored. Nicky Hart provides an exception to this with a contribution which stresses the centrality of gender to changes in class outlook in the post-war period. Hart argues that the gender inequality crucial to class formation declined, replaced by gender "convergency" (largely in wages): "one concomitant of the diminution of class consciousness which accompanied the growing affluence of manual workers was a decline in gender inequality." Just as "[g]ender inequality is the missed ingredient in the rise of class politics," Hart writes, "gender convergence is the secret of its decline" in the post-war period. The value of Hart's contribution is in its insistence that gender and class were interconnected in the fifties. Its specific arguments overstate the gender convergence of the fifties. The growth of part-time work for women certainly offered material gains for women, but in other spheres, it is hard to see a clear empirical case for any convergence between male and female workers. This is particularly true in terms of the wage differential between men and women. If we look at the period between 1924 and 1970, the largest gap between male and female earnings came in 1940, when women earned 42% of men's wages; the smallest difference came in 1946, when women earned 55% of men's wages. The average wage differential was fairly consistent at approximately 50.4%. Thus in material terms, convergence was not very great. The persistence of wage disparity would have been much more obvious. Strikes by female workers at Ford's Dagenham plant in 1968 and Lucas' Acton factory the following year brought this disparity to the public eye. One might also say that Hart treats the decline of class-consciousness as a given: class may not, however, have disappeared, but simply been felt and expressed differently.

The present article adopts another approach to understand the relationship between gender and class in the 1950s. It suggests that more complicated and less certain gender identities emerged at the work-place and in the home during this period. In this, femininity became less firmly tied to motherhood, while work gradually became accepted as a province of both men and women and masculinity was seen as reformed. This destabilized established understandings of working class masculinity and femininity. Thus, alongside changes in working class experience and outlook (such as the enjoyment of affluence and economic security), we might place significant changes in working class gender identities. . . .

The present article examines this question first by discussing changes in patterns of work and maternity for working class women in the fifties. It then uses texts of social observation and sociology such as *Coal Is Our Life* (1956) and *Family and Kinship in East London* (1957) to explore observations of working class family life and masculinity. It concludes with a brief examination of nostalgia and misogyny in a variety of texts, from Richard Hoggart's *The Uses of Literacy* (1957) to literary and cinematic texts of the "Angry Young Men" and "social realist" movements. There are particular qualifications which guide this discussion. Some limitations have, first of all, been imposed upon its canvas: for the most part, it looks at texts published between 1950 and 1962. As well, this article is principally concerned with the discursive representation of gender within the working classes, but it does suggest that such representations had a relationship to material changes in working class life in the 1950s. Within the confines of the present examination, it is impossible to address in any detail one of the most important of those changes: the large-scale slum clearance and rehousing which helped transform the physical environment of life for many working-class people. Though changes in masculinity are considered, the initial focus is upon changes in femininity. This has particular purchase in relation to work and sexuality. Such changes were apprehended by some contemporaries as the catalysts for wider transformations of femininity, masculinity and family life. Finally, a qualification regarding the evidence must be made: unsurprisingly, contemporary works of sociology and social observation often helped constitute what they sought to discover—the shift in working-class life and identity. Placing this process in an historical context is one of the foci of the article; another is examining the ciphers produced by this literature as a means of understanding social change in the 1950s. The article first considers changes in femininity with relationship to work and sexuality, then examines changing reflections upon masculinity and family life and concludes with a consideration of the cultural representation of changes in gender identities in the fifties.

Writing Application

The literature reviews excerpted in the previous selections illustrate some of the goals of this important aspect of academic writing. Though they are likely much more detailed than the writing you are currently engaged in, they still provide useful models for academic writing that can help you to develop a credible *ethos* by demonstrating your knowledge of previous work done on a topic that interests you. The literature review can also help you to situate your own work among that done previously, helping you to find your way into the conversation among experts.

If you are engaged in a research project, write one to three paragraphs of a literature review that helps your readers understand the state of research on a given topic, drawing on the advice and examples above. In the process, attempt to find some area of knowledge or some key question that has not yet been adequately considered in relation to this topic.

Case 4 PROPOSALS IN THE WORKPLACE AND COMMUNITY

Though the proposals we've been discussing are largely ways to discover and learn more about your topics and purposes, proposals are also frequently written in occupational settings. Robert Colleluori's business, for example, all but depends on successful proposals:

> Effective proposals are the only way that we are awarded business. We primarily handle business-to-business accounts, and so our proposals are more technical writing than creative. Once we are awarded the account, we then do

further proposals, this time through a live presentation of findings or proposed course of action and recommendations. It's important on these occasions to know the basics of this form of presentation, and not try to be too creative with what is expected in a clear proposal. It is crucial to be clear, correct expression and as concise as possible.

Jane Whittaker, in her role as a senior systems architect, was also called on to write proposals:

> I write proposals to buy certain computer hardware or software, justifying why we need to spend millions of dollars (one mainframe computer can cost around 5 to 10 million dollars before any software is purchased for it). I think the most effective proposals are those that respect the reader's intelligence. Explain the problem as clearly and concisely as possible, without using emotionally-charged terms. Lay out the options for solving the problem, and the pros and cons of each. Identify the proposed solution and why it was selected. I think the most important thing is the tone of the proposal. It should not sound pleading nor should it sound imperious. It should strike the reader as a carefully considered suggestion coming from a thoughtful, intelligent colleague. I think of transactional analysis—don't write like a whining child or a demanding parent; write like a mature adult and your audience will respond in kind.

Eric Engle, in his work as an environmental geologist, also acknowledges that "each project requires a signed proposal before we start any work. The most important thing in producing our proposals is that we are honest about costs and time lines—we need to be able to live up to what we propose."

Proposals, then, are not always used as means to develop a writing project but often have specific ends in mind; in occupations, and in civic affairs, proposals are often written to initiate action. You may already be in an occupation where you are called on to write proposals; if not, it is likely that you will be someday. Even now, you can use proposals to initiate changes in the community in which you live and work, asking your audience to consider a course of action that you believe can improve that community.

Though proposals take many forms, they all have characteristics in common. Proposals for action usually must do all the following:

- Illustrate a real need.
- Show how that need affects a specific audience and community (or how not acting can negatively impact this community).
- Address not only the benefits of the proposed course of action but the feasibility of the plan and your ability to accomplish its goals.
- Offer a potential solution or way to alleviate that need.
- Suggest specific details for action.
- Propose an initial course of action.
- Ask for permission to proceed with the project.

Writing to Respond

Below is an excerpt from a proposal that I wrote with the help of my colleagues to suggest a new major in professional writing at the college where I work. Read it, considering the above list of issues usually addressed in a proposal, and, in your writer's notebook, decide whether the proposal makes its case, which arguments seem to be the most compelling, what might have been left out and what might have been expanded, and what suggestions you might make for improving it.

DATE: 21 January 2001
TO: Professor Susan James, Curriculum Committee Chairperson
FROM: Dominic Delli Carpini, Department of English and Humanities
RE: Proposed Major in Professional Writing

The Department of English and Humanities proposes that a major in professional writing be established at York College. The major in professional writing would be designed to prepare students for a wide range of careers as writers and communications specialists in fields such as publishing, government and non-governmental organizations (N.G.O.'s), corporate communications, non-profit and social-service organizations, health care, finance, the arts, etc. The major would provide students with:

- A foundation in the study of English and Humanities
- A wide range of critical thinking and problem solving skills
- Marketable communication skills such as editing, electronic communication, and collaborative writing
- A background in the history and theory of language usage
- Guided experience with a wide range of writing situations and stylistic options
- A minor or area of concentration in an area related to students' career interests
- Experiential learning through on-site work in professional writing
- A portfolio of written work that students can use in their search for work as a professional writer or a writing specialist within an organization

Rationale

The need for skilled writers and communicators within various organizations continues to grow, both nationally and locally (statistical information available upon request). As a result, professional writing has become one of the fastest growing areas of English studies. Professional writing programs have been, and continue to be, instituted at a wide range of colleges and universities (a partial list of colleges and universities with professional writing majors and a summary of how such programs have affected English department enrollments is available upon request). These programs have been extremely successful in attracting motivated students.

The English and Humanities Department currently offers a concentration in writing for its majors, a concentration chosen by over half the English majors in the department (the other two concentrations are Literature and Theater). The increasing number of our writing concentration students who have completed successful writing-based internships has made the potential for careers in the field more evident. Our students have interned at such locations as *Baltimore* magazine, the York Chamber of Commerce, *Central PA* magazine, Junior Achievement, York Newspapers, *Harrisburg* magazine, the American Red Cross, York Literacy Council, York Inn and Restaurant, Harley-Davidson, and Aventis Pharmaceuticals. Further, recent graduates have found that potential employers in publishing as well as in various other professional fields have particularly valued their writing skills.

However, the current curriculum does not provide a structured experience for students interested in a career in professional writing. In our most recent departmental assessment, students and writing faculty alike recognized the need for a more coherent, focused, and current course of studies to prepare them for the wide range of job opportunities for professional writers.

The English and Humanities Department have endorsed this major. Our external reviewer has also commended plans for the major during his recent assessment process. In his assessment report, our outside assessor wrote, "The establishment of a Professional Writing major seems to be an excellent idea, both for the strengths of the Department faculty who teach writing courses and for the nature of YCP itself." He went on to note that "the department is to be commended for moving in this direction," and includes the planned major among the commendations in his summary (full report available upon request). Plans for the major were also commended by a well-respected authority on professional writing and technology who visited our campus last academic year.

Recently hired faculty in the English and Humanities Department bring with them a wide range of education and experience in writing pedagogy. Most recently, our department was fortunate enough to hire a graduate of Purdue's highly regarded Rhetoric and Composition program who also brings with him three years of experience in James Madison University's program in Professional and Technical Writing, and experience with Miami University's long-standing writing program as well. Other faculty members bring with them recent experiences with some of the strongest Rhetoric and Composition programs in the country: The University of Massachusetts, Amherst; The University of North Carolina; The Pennsylvania State University; The State University of New York; Syracuse University; Tulane University. Our faculty members are also represented as frequent presenters and in various positions of leadership in national organizations such as the Conference on College Composition and Communication, The Council of Writing Program Administrators, and The Association for Business Communication.

Description of the Program

Undergraduate programs in professional writing are generally divided into two types. One group of such programs specializes in technical writing fields, preparing students to prepare technical documents in fields such as engineering, science and industry. The other group of programs provides broader, less specialized experience in writing.[1] Though the proposed program belongs to this second group, it also offers the potential for specializations in technical fields through formal minors, special topics courses, or areas of concentration. In this way, our program is adaptable to a wide variety of career paths or graduate education.

The curriculum will help students recognize that good writing is always grounded in rhetorical situations—it is always writing "about" something and writing "to" someone. As such, the program is designed to nurture students' general critical thinking and problem solving skills, while also asking them to consider the needs of specific professional writing situations and sites. Each of these goals, as discussed below, is served by specific parts of the proposed writing curriculum. The program will also require students to study a single field or discipline more intensively; students will be required to complete a formal minor related to their proposed career path, giving them essential experience with the way that various occupational fields communicate. So a student interested in writing for industry may minor in business; a student interested in web-based writing may choose visual communication; and a student interested in writing for pharmaceutical firms might choose biology or chemistry. Students interested in creative or freelance writing will also have the opportunity to work with one of our published creative writers on the skills necessary to revise, submit, and market their writing.

Students completing this program will have a number of career and educational options:

- They will be prepared for a variety of entry-level positions as writing specialists with various organizations and businesses.
- They will have the solid background in rhetoric and composition that would make them attractive candidates for graduate study in these areas: towards the Ph.D. in Rhetoric/Composition (the fastest growing area of English stud-

ies); an M.A. in Rhetoric/Composition; an M.A. in Professional/Technical Writing; or an M.F.A. in Creative Writing.

- They will have a strong background towards the practical applications of writing skills in both freelance and organizationally based writing, and so may find work as an independent contractor, editor, or consultant.

Writing Program Curriculum

Though we have not completed work upon our curriculum, we can outline a potential course of studies at this time. The courses for the proposed major would be organized into five broad categories: Courses in the liberal arts, courses in language theory, courses in practical application of writing skills, courses giving students a hands-on career experience and asking them to reflect upon that experience, and courses in a field related to their career aspirations. Though some of the courses clearly could fit within several categories, they might be organized as follows:

Liberal Arts Foundation Courses

- Foundations of English and Humanities
- English Humanities Electives (at least 2 in literature)
- Advanced Composition

Writing Theory Courses

- Rhetorical Theory
- Language and Linguistics
- Interdisciplinary Writing
- Special Topics in Professional Writing

Writing Application Courses

- Writing in Professional Cultures
- Professional Editing
- Writing for the Web
- Advanced Non-Fiction
- Creative Writing
- Creative Writing Electives
- Special Topics in Professional Writing

Experiential Learning and Career Preparation Courses

- Experiential Learning (w/ 3–6 credits of on-site experience)
- Freelance Writing for the Marketplace

- Special Topics in Professional Writing
- Senior Seminar (w/ portfolio development)

Area Specialization Courses: Minor in Career-Related Area

- The requirement for a formal minor is designed to prepare students for work within various organizations, and to help them to gain experience with the types of discourse used in various disciplinary and occupational fields. In conjunction with the minor, and through available electives such as Freelance Writing for the Marketplace, students will also have the opportunity to gain experience with published authors in writing, revising, and submitting manuscripts for publication, preparing them for freelance work or work as writing consultants.

We request permission to proceed with work upon this major. In order to begin the process, it would be useful to have some specific resources devoted to development of the program:

- Funding for a student assistant to research other similar programs
- Establishment of a task force to further study the viability of such a program for our college
- Consideration of possible further positions to facilitate the major
- Consideration of an administrative position to oversee the development and ongoing work of the new major

We ask that the Curriculum Committee, at its next scheduled meeting, consider this initial proposal and forward to us its recommendations for proceeding with the proposed major.

Notes

1. Carnegie-Mellon University, for example, offers specializations in either area. Notable programs in technical and scientific communications are housed at James Madison University, Michigan Technological University, Miami University of Ohio, Eastern Michigan University, and Arizona State University East. Many other programs offer the more broad-based "professional writing" major or concentration; these are more in keeping with what we are proposing for York College, and include, among others, Youngstown State, SUNY Cortland, Elon College, Moravian College, Purdue University, Eastern Oregon University, Eastern Kansas University, Grand Valley State, The University of Massachusetts, Briarcliff College.

Writing Application

Consider the skills that you have accumulated and your aspirations for the future. Then imagine how that set of skills and interests might benefit a community to which you belong: a workplace, your hometown, your college, or an organization to which you belong. Drawing on those skills and talents, write a proposal for some course of action that might benefit that group. If you currently hold a job or have worked in a career field in the past, you might consider ways that your workplace might function more efficiently or effectively and then propose new procedures, the purchase of new resources, or the hiring of new experts to help do the work of that company. If you are an engineering student, you might, for example, propose a summer camp to teach problem-solving skills to young people. If you are an artist, you might propose a beautification project for campus. If you are a historian, you might propose researching and writing the story of your college's founding or that of the organization to which you belong. Or you might propose a new course that would enhance the curriculum of your school.

CHAPTER NINE

Developing Researched Arguments

Nearly everything you write in academic and occupational settings is, to some extent, an argument. Sometimes arguing means taking a position on an issue; sometimes it merely means illustrating that you know what those positions are. But in all cases, you are at least arguing for your own credibility to speak with some degree of authority on a topic.

As discussed in previous chapters, writing with authority begins with becoming informed not only about your topic but also about the preferred modes of writing in any given rhetorical situation and discourse community. In this chapter, we discuss ways to apply that knowledge as you draft academic and occupational documents.

ETHOS REVISITED

As students, a good deal of your job is to develop an *ethos* that will serve you in your academic field and, later, in your profession. Recall that *ethos* refers to the public character you develop as you learn through reading and writing. Your credibility comes from having information, understanding that information, and being able to clearly communicate that information to your audience *logically*. That last word—logically—is central to developing a credible *ethos*. There are, of course, many forms of logic (as has been demonstrated by our examination of the methodologies adopted by various academic disciplines). But at its most basic, your logic is demonstrated through the ability to create a flow of ideas that readers recognize as reasonable. Readers should be able to perceive how each new piece of information you present both builds on the previous point and moves toward a new one. If at any point in your document the reader is unable to follow (or unwilling to accept) the connections among the ideas you present, your credibility suffers, and your argument is less likely to succeed.

Remember the task that faces every reader: making sense of the words and ideas the writer presents. In Chapter 4, we discussed methods of developing this logical flow of ideas, using a conversant outline that not only creates a list of topics to cover but also reveals the logic that moves readers from point to point. That technique applies to all forms of written argument, including researched essays, and is worth reviewing as you draft your researched essay.

Additional techniques are specific to researched projects that ask the writer to synthesize significant amounts of information and opinions. For this reason, writing and revising a logical draft of a researched document demands your staying in control, never allowing your own voice to be overwhelmed by the voices you invite into your paper. Allowing researched information to dominate your writing has two unhappy consequences: First, since the information you collect may be disparate, presenting the ideas of a variety of writers can disrupt your own flow of thought; and, second, if you take a position too far in the background, your *ethos* all but disappears.

Both of these problems can be overcome if you incorporate judiciously the information you collect—if you think of the information you collect as contributing to your own purposes in writing rather than an end in itself. This protectiveness of your own *ethos* is accomplished at a number of levels:

- by your careful construction of a thesis
- by your careful construction of a logical sequence of ideas, a sequence dictated by your own purposes in writing and not the purposes of the writers whose work you draw on

- by your attention to the preferred modes of organizing and supporting an argument within a given academic or occupational field
- by the judicious use of summaries, syntheses, paraphrases, quotations, and citations
- by ensuring that your argument progresses from one point to another with a sense of coherence and by using modes of proof acceptable to your discourse community
- by using style, tone, and diction appropriate to your rhetorical situation

The remainder of this chapter examines each of these strategies for producing a credible, logical draft of your researched document. Like all aspects of the writing process, this series of guidelines is best considered as recursive rather than linear—there is no simple recipe. Yet each of the guidelines can help you to maintain your focus as you go through the difficult process of situating your own voice among the voices of other experts.

ESTABLISHING A THESIS

Though not all types of writing require you to take a side on some contested issue, all writing *does* require that you establish a coherent and credible position. Stating a thesis is valuable because: (1) it limits your treatment of a topic, allowing you to present a thorough, rather than cursory, examination ("I'm doing this, but I'm not doing that"); (2) it allows you to enter into a conversation by situating your voice among others (by revealing key points of stasis); and, (3) it allows you to tell your reader what to expect from the writing that follows. In this way, it helps you to establish a line of reasoning within which you want to involve your readers.

Let's imagine that you are writing an informational essay. Consider the following thesis statement:

- In this essay, I will discuss sexual harassment.

This statement of topic reveals to the reader, in the most general sense, the issue you will examine. But it is unlikely to help your reader to know the parameters of the study. Further, it does not help you to create a specific line of reasoning for what will follow. But it is a start, and a clear one. This stripped-down statement allows you to start the process of thesis development on solid ground. How might this general statement be developed into a more detailed thesis?

First, you must consider scope. In reality, no single essay can "discuss sexual harassment" in its entirety. As you develop a thesis statement, then, you want to be as clear as you can in stating the parameters or limits of the study. The statement might then develop incrementally as follows:

- In this essay, I will discuss sexual harassment in the workplace.
- In this essay, I will discuss laws that govern sexual harassment in the workplace.

- In this essay, I will discuss the history and development of laws that govern sexual harassment in the workplace.

- In this essay, I will discuss the history and development of recent laws that govern sexual harassment in the workplace.

- In this essay, I will discuss the changes in sexual harassment laws affecting the workplace that have occurred over the past decade.

Each of these statements creates a more limited topic that more clearly reflects, both to the reader and the writer—you—the information that will be discussed. That thesis, of course, is also influenced by the information you uncovered in the process of researching the topic. Through a careful consideration of the materials gathered, your research has come to center on recent changes in workplace harassment law. You have also told your reader (and yourself) what you will *not* be discussing—for example, sexual harassment in schools, sexual harassment in the nineteenth century, and the psychological effects of sexual harassment.

Beyond limiting the scope, an effective thesis may also situate your own perspectives on the topic amid those of the other writers whose work you have read. If you have completed the type of mature research processes that we discussed in the previous two chapters, you have not only collected a good deal of information but also have reflected on its implications and synthesized its relationship to your research goals (through writing activities like the proposal, annotated bibliography, and review of the literature). Now, as you begin formulating a thesis, you can use that learning to find your own position. You may find it in perceived gaps in the research—points that have not yet been adequately covered in the literature. So, your thesis might continue as below. Note that this writer uses two sentences; a developed thesis need not be restricted to a single sentence.

- In this essay, I will discuss changes in sexual harassment over the past decade that have affected the workplace. I will focus in particular on the lack of involvement of businesspeople in the writing of harassment legislation.

In this case, the writer noticed that not enough attention has been paid to businesspersons' opinions in the formulation of laws that may affect them greatly. But even if you do not locate such a specific gap in the research on a topic, you can at least situate yourself in terms of your approach.

- In this essay, I will discuss the changes in sexual harassment laws over the past decade that affect the workplace. I will attend particularly to whether the ways that these laws define illegal behaviors are sufficiently clear to be enforceable.

Here, though the thesis does not address a specific deficiency in the literature, it does point to a particular perspective on the question, offering to study whether or not the laws are clear enough to be usefully applied. That type of thesis, though not really stating an opinion, does state a position: that examining the language of the laws and their consequent enforceability is an important facet of the topic. Not only will this help the *reader* to know the specific topics that will be addressed in the paper, but it also will help the *writer* to develop a reasonable plan for organizing those topics logically.

A solid thesis also reveals to its readers *how* the present document will approach its limited topic—that is, the thesis (and, in more detail, the surrounding introduction) should provide readers with a sense of your document's proposed method of reasoning. So, to continue the example, your thesis might now state:

- In this essay, I will discuss the changes in sexual harassment laws over the past decade that affect the workplace. I will present landmark legislation on this topic and **analyze not only its clarity (or lack of clarity) in defining illegal behaviors but also its enforceability within specific court cases.**

This thesis continues to develop the writer's sense of the document's purpose and focus, now not only limiting the topic to be broached but also outlining (in the part I have highlighted) the types of evidence that will be examined in reasoning through this issue—legislation and court cases.

The incremental development of a thesis can force you, as a writer, to consider key issues of arrangement and focus, issues that are likely to start you toward a more limited topic, a more clearly defined perspective on the topic, and more directly articulated statement of your methods of reasoning. You must then, of course, decide how that logical line of reasoning will play out across the document as a whole.

WRITING TO EXPLORE 9.1

Drawing on a topic that you are currently researching, use the methods above to create a focused and limited thesis. Begin with a simple statement of topic, as above ("In this essay, I will discuss sexual harassment"). Then, incrementally develop your thesis, bringing to it increasing focus, ruling out the areas you will not discuss, and so centering your goals on that which will be primary in your essay.

WRITING A SKELETAL DRAFT

A good draft develops a line of reasoning that not only makes sense to you as the writer but also reveals your reasoning to the reader. This attention to shared reasoning can allow your reader to follow the line of logic you develop in support of your thesis. It also helps you to feel more comfortable with the topic you are investigating, nurturing your own credible and logical *ethos*.

The difficulty is that the books, articles, and other sources that you have found do not necessarily speak directly to one another. It is your job, then, to help your reader to see how the pieces of this research puzzle fit together, how they intersect with and affect one another within the context you have set up. Setting the context is also a key part of the development process.

One way to establish this clear and sharable line of reasoning is to draft a skeletal version of your researched document. Much like the conversant outline discussed in Chapter 4, this skeletal draft establishes a series of logical movements for your paper as well as the connections between those movements. Practically, producing a skeletal draft is often best accomplished by, for the time, putting aside the source information you have collected. Instead, in this draft, you rely on *your memory of what you learned so far* and the major points that you must discuss to develop a document that serves your purpose. Rather than trying to force each piece of evidence you have collected into your draft—and so letting the information control the organization of your essay—begin by imagining the steps of logic necessary for a thorough examination of your topic.

This skeletal draft should grow from your carefully constructed thesis. For instance, in the above example, we developed the following thesis:

> ▪ In this essay, I will discuss the changes in sexual harassment laws over the past decade that affect the workplace. I will present landmark legislation on this topic and analyze not only its clarity (or lack of clarity) in defining illegal behaviors, but also its enforceability within specific court cases.

We now must decide how to play out the claims and methods of analysis we establish in this thesis over the course of our essay. The thesis suggests several points: (1) that sexual harassment laws have changed over the last decade; (2) that there are specific legislative actions that are particularly important; (3) that such legislation has attempted to define illegal behaviors as regards sexual harassment; (4) that these definitions have influenced particular court cases; and (5) that an examination of those court cases can help us to make value judgments about the value and enforceability of such definitions. Already we can see a shape for the essay emerging, a shape that can be developed into a working draft with identifiable and logically connected movements.

The next step, then, is to begin the drafting process, following this set of connected movements, and establishing from memory our sense of the key elements of each part of this argument. As we write as much as we can recall about each of the issues, we are also searching for the way to transition toward the next logically related topic. If we know the next point we need to raise within the pattern of reasoning that we are developing, we can keep writing *in that direction*, searching for a logical connection that can get us there; we move on to that next point when we find it. Then, only after we have decided on the lines of logic necessary for our purpose (lines of logic that are *influenced* by what we have read and digested but not *controlled* by them) can we make decisions about what we need to import from those outside sources.

WRITING TO EXPLORE 9.2

Building on the focused thesis you established in the previous exercise, write a skeletal draft of your essay that pays particular attention to the logical connections leading from one point to the next. Consider what you have learned about your topic, but don't refer to the researched materials; rely on your memory of what you have read. Pay special attention to creating strong transitions from one point to the next—transitions that allow the reader to see how the introduction of a new subtopic flows naturally from the previous subtopic.

CONSIDERING DISCIPLINARY EXPECTATIONS

Writing a skeletal draft can help you to establish the points that are most important to your argument, but you must also take into consideration the preferred methods of proof for the disciplinary or occupational field within which you are writing. That is, you must remind yourself that you are not writing in a vacuum; quite to the contrary, you are entering into a conversation whose parameters are already established. And though your writing may extend those parameters, it is generally unwise to ignore them altogether. For example, if you were writing the essay on sexual harassment that we've been discussing for a criminal justice class (or as a criminal justice professional), you would focus largely on the enforceability of the laws: finding ways of detecting if and how these laws are violated, considering whether the laws allow criminal justice professionals the necessary bases to do their job, determining methods of gathering evidence, and so on. However, if you were to write about the same issue from the perspective of social psychology, women's studies, business management, or history, your approach (and your methods of proof) might be quite different. And if you were writing a policy for a company for which you worked, your document would surely be quite different, since the rhetorical situation has many new exigencies.

That is not to say that information from one field cannot be imported into another; it certainly can be. However, to do so, you must translate the information you have collected into the discursive style expected by professionals in that field. For this reason, you must extend your understanding of what it means to create a logical argument by asking a key question: "Logical to whom?"

ual harassment was virtually verbatim that of the EEOC in its own Guidelines on Sex Discrimination—in the excerpt provided at the beginning of this article. The ramification for employers is that anti-harassment policies stated in this way can be declared to be "defective or dysfunctional" and can therefore open the employer to liability. The Smith decision indicates that federal courts are likely to require more stringent definitional standards. Of further concern is that anti-harassment policy statements, which just a few years ago were sufficient to establish the employer's good faith effort to prevent harassment, may no longer satisfy the new stricter judicial standard of review being developed in some circuits.

This article examines the current state of employer liability in light of these recent federal court rulings. Additionally we analyze their impact on increasing the standard of judicial review of organizational anti-harassment policies. Key related issues, including actionable sexual harassment, the Faragher/Ellerth affirmative defense, and the Kolstad good faith defense, are briefly reviewed. Finally, in response to the growth of harassment claims based on protected classes other than sex, we consider the need to extend current sexual harassment policies to also encompass harassment based on race, national origin, and religion.

Sleazy Courtroom Tactics Hit Harassment Cases

National NOW Times

Abstract: The National Organization for Women vowed to work for the passage of laws that will protect women who file sexual harassment suits from attacks on their sexual history. The passage of the Civil Rights Acts of 1991 as an offshoot of the landmark sexual harassment case filed by Anita Hill has raised some negative effects. With the rise in damages given to victims of work-based sexual harassment, defense lawyers of companies utilized increasingly aggressive tactics for breaking down the credibility of women.

Surveying Sexual Harassment in the Law Enforcement Workplace

Timothy L. Fuss

Abstract: Issues concerning the control and prevention of sexual harassment in the law enforcement service are presented. Techniques include survey methodology, analysis and reporting of results. A sample sexual harassment questionnaire is included.

A Brief History of Sexual-Harassment Law

Susan Crawford

Abstract: Sexual-harassment law grew from the Civil Rights Act of 1964. This Act prohibits employment discrimination against any individual on the basis of the person's race, color, religion, sex or national origin. Unfortunately, the law failed to protect women from sexual harassment for the most part of 1970s. In 1975, the first-ever sexual harassment case was dismissed, with the court seeming to suggest that discrimination against women could be reasonably expected in the workplace. The courts began to take a different view in the latter part the decade. In 1977, appellate courts proceeded to reverse many lower-court decisions that rejected sexual harassment claims. The US Supreme Court finally spoke on the issue in 1986 when it heard its first sexual harassment case. Among other things, it reaffirmed the unlawfulness of sexual harassment under Title VII. In 1991, the Court ruled that victims do not have to show psychological injury to back their claims.

What Is a Gender Norm and Why Should We Care? Implementing a New Theory in Sexual Harassment Law

Linda B. Epstein

Abstract: Many scholars have recently suggested a reconceptualization of sexual harassment as gender harassment. In this note, Linda Epstein examines some of their theories and concludes that a unified theory of gender harassment based on gender norms should indeed be adopted by the courts. Focusing on cases involving male-female sexual harassment, Epstein argues that this approach is superior to current judicial practice because it encompasses nonsexual but sex-based harms to women. Epstein then proffers a practical definition of what constitutes a gender norm: The adoption of such a definition by the courts would enable them to successfully implement a gender-based theory that includes harms beyond those that are "sexual" in nature.

WRITING TO EXPLORE 9.4

To develop your understanding of how the shape and line of reasoning need to be taken into consideration as you draft, try the following: Choose one of the abstracts above—the one that most interests you or that represents a field in which you are majoring. Based on the methods of discourse analysis discussed in previous chapters, consider the abstracts and, perhaps looking at academic and/or professional journals in this field, imagine a likely organization for an essay on this topic. What are the likely parts of such an argument? What sections are usually included in articles in this field (a review of the literature? a methods section? a presentation of data? a discussion of theoretical backgrounds? case studies?)? In doing this, you should be imagining approaches to the topic that would help you appeal to the logical modes used in a particular field of study— that is, what will your audience consider to be a reasonable examination of a topic and sufficient proof?

INCORPORATING RESEARCHED INFORMATION

Once you have established the shape of your essay, based on own goals for writing, the learning you have done through mature research processes, and the preferred methods of the discourse community within which you are writing, you are ready to incorporate the materials you have collected. Though there are many ways to bring those materials to bear upon the argument that you are building, we might separate them into three distinct categories: summarizing, paraphrasing, and quoting.

In all cases, the goals of incorporating researched materials are similar. Though we often consider the material we have collected as "evidence" or "support" for our claims, there are other ways to think about how researched material can be used. For example,

- You can use that material to illustrate the generally accepted commonplaces on a topic, either accepting those commonplaces or showing how they are in some way deficient.

- You can use that material to show disputed areas, illustrating how the work of other experts identifies stasis points and so establishes topics that require the analysis and judgments—both your own and those of your audience.

- You can use that material to illustrate the need for further examination of a topic, showing how what others have already accomplished has neglected or skirted key facets.

- You can use data, statistics, or case studies that were meant for one purpose to illustrate some new ground that *you* wish to establish. For instance, a study of hiring practices meant as training for personnel managers might be used to illustrate the subtle gender inequities in such practices.

- You can use the words of others to illustrate emotional, disciplinary, or occupational attitudes toward a topic.

Though the above list is clearly not complete, it does illustrate that the processes of active reading—truly engaging with the material—are important as you incorporate that material into your writing.

You provide a context for the information you include in your draft when you introduce a summary, paraphrase, or quotation. For example, imagine that you are writing an essay that argues that the concept of sexual harassment is too often immediately associated with male harassment of women. In support of that claim, you might decide to incorporate the work of Linda B. Epstein, whose essay on sexual harassment is abstracted above. You have several choices on how to incorporate that information.

You might **summarize** her article, providing your readers with an overview of the claims that she seems to be making and her support for those claims. Note how the following example places Epstein's work in the context of your own essay's goals:

> Sexual harassment is too often considered to be only an issue that affects women's roles in the workplace, leaving those (albeit less frequent) cases for female to male or same-sex harassment to fall through the legal cracks. Linda B. Epstein has suggested that one practicable way to widen our legal and social understanding of harassment in the workplace is to rename, and so redefine, this concept as gender harassment. Using perspectives both from law and social sciences, she argues that such a redefinition can provide many benefits for better dealing with this workplace problem.

Rather than detail one specific facet of the argument, this provides a global view. In this case, it allows you to examine how such a concept (and others that might be incorporated) could alleviate the problem of seeing harassment as male to female only. That is, you maintain control of the purpose of your essay and use the summary to suggest one potential solution to the problem you are examining.

But summaries are, by their nature, general. Since they take into account the entire argument made by another expert, what is gained in breadth is sometimes lost in depth. Sometimes you need more in-depth information from your sources. In those cases, you might choose to paraphrase or quote segments of your source material.

First, a few general notes about paraphrasing or quoting. In each case, since you are taking material from one context (the original piece of writing) and importing it to a new contexts (your own document), it is important that you are both ethical and careful in the use of that material. Quoting or paraphrasing out of context, either intentionally or unintentionally, is a serious rights violation. For example, Epstein's article is designed to argue that a reconsideration of "sexual harassment" as "gender harassment" may be more socially equitable. However, if you chose one of the questions that Epstein raises in her essay's introduction and, in the process of paraphrasing or quoting it, misrepresented her overall perspective, that would be both inaccurate and unethical.

Thus, whether paraphrasing or quoting, your introductory or tag phrase must accurately provide two things:

1. the context of the argument from which this specific information is taken, and
2. the relationship between this quotation or paraphrase and your own argument.

For example, let's continue the above example as follows:

> More specifically, my study will examine the ways in which cases of male/male or female harassment are particularly problematic. Epstein's article, which is largely concerned with harms to women from this mis-definition, also suggests that same-sex harassment can provide particular challenges for litigation. She suggests that recent court decisions leave a dangerous loophole when it comes to same-sex cases of harassment (1).

This example illustrates how a writer can paraphrase—summarize a *particular claim or piece of evidence* from a source—to translate the source's ideas into his own words. However, as in this example, the writer must be careful to provide a context for his claim; note the observation that Epstein's article is "largely concerned with harms to women from this mis-definition." Doing so (1) avoids misrepresenting the article's overall purposes and (2) allows the writer to import and translate useful information for his own purposes.

Sometimes it may be more effective to cite source material word for word and so quote directly. The disadvantages of doing so are (1) that it is sometimes difficult to smoothly incorporate the words of others into the tone and flow of your own paragraph and sentence structure, and (2) that it is sometimes more difficult to show how the words of another author fit directly into your purposes. But there are also gains. Sometimes the words of another are so eloquent that they are worth quoting for effect; sometimes they state something so succinctly that you can't really do better. And on some occasions, you may want to retain the tone of the original, either because it amplifies your own argument or because you want to comment on the author's tone, attitude, or perspective. (This is often the case, for example, with literary analyses, where the voice and style of the author is often as important as the point that he is making.)

So, for example, in the above example, instead of the paraphrase, we might incorporate the following quotation:

> More specifically, my study will examine the ways in which cases of male/male or female harassment are particularly problematic. Epstein, in an article largely concerned with harms to women from this mis-definition, also notes that "however helpful the Court's decisions will be in terms of how the law will work, one unanswered question of substance remains as troublesome as ever: why same-sex harassment constitutes sex discrimination" (1).

In this example, the paraphrase has been replaced by a direct quotation. By quoting directly, we allow our audience to hear the author's tone in words like "troublesome" and "unanswered questions," words that portray the author's attitudes and that support our own essay's concerns with the problem of same-sex harassment. You might also note that in order to incorporate the direct quotation, adjustments to the sentence structure were necessary to allow for a smoother transition into the quotation. The context of the article from which the quotation is taken, however, is still clear.

There are, of course, other types of information that need to be incorporated into researched essays, depending on the purpose of the document and its discipline: statistics, charts, definitions, case studies, experimental results, and the like. You will, as you become more familiar with your chosen field of study and profession, learn its specific guidelines. However, the general principles are similar; you must decide in any given case whether it is more effective to summarize general findings or claims, to paraphrase specific parts of a source document, or to quote those parts precisely and directly.

RE-VISIONING AND REVISING

At the learning, planning, and drafting stages, you envision a piece of writing, imagining what it might look like. You draft an essay that attempts to find focus, to remain consistent with your purposes, and to incorporate the ideas of other experts. But it is unlikely that your first attempts will be polished enough for public consumption.

After you have a draft to work with, you can really focus on the craft of style—on finding just the right words, just the right phrasings, just the right punctuation, to make our points. At that stage, you can "re-vision" the piece based on the many acts of invention that produced the draft. For people who take writing seriously, revision is the most satisfying part of the process. It is the time for chipping away at the rough edges of what you have written and see clarity—and, in some cases, brilliance—emerge.

I like to think of the craft of revision as similar to that of finishing a piece of carpentry. You've given the object shape (whether it be a table or a piece of correspondence); some function and purpose (to hold objects, or to convey a policy); and some style (four-legged colonial dining table, or a memo). But though the design and purpose are emerging, the product remains rough. Here's where you need to get out the sandpaper (in varying grits) and the wood putty. First you do the rough sanding, knocking off the unnecessary elements, filling in the big holes (with more evidence or logic to link claim to support). As you continue to polish your draft, you work your way through a series of finer revisions, considering facets of your writing such as paragraph structure, transitions, sentence structure, diction (word choice), and punctuation choices. Finally, you apply the final polish by proofreading. Though concentrating on one item at a time seems like it would make the revision process less efficient, most writers find this is a productive approach and, often, *more* efficient. Rather than treating the revision stage as the time to "fix" or "correct" a piece of writing, you can use a more organized process to take on one issue at a time.

READING AND EDITING YOUR OWN WRITING

To extend the analogy of revising and sanding furniture, the "rough sanding" is the first stage. That rough sanding can be effective only, however, if you are willing to see the blemishes and imperfections of your work—to read your own work critically, carefully, and with some distance. Sometimes this first revision, if you've really drifted while writing your draft, takes a chisel.

A good writer learns to read his or her own writing as a good (critical) reader. One way to do so is to allow some time between drafting and revising. You can rarely gain critical distance or objectivity on a piece of writing immediately after you have written it. Ideally, you should try to come back to a draft the next day, or even a few days later. When you do so, it will look different—it will be less familiar, and you'll be able to read it with a fresh set of eyes. But, of course, you don't always have the luxury of waiting a day or two; your boss might want that memo on her desk today. Even in that case, taking a walk to the coffee cart after you've written a first draft and then coming back to it can be useful. Then, when you read the piece, you've changed roles from writer to reader/commentator.

To do this new job, you can continue the conversant model of writing. You can *literally* talk to your draft by reading it aloud and telling it when you're confused ("Wait a minute, I don't follow that point") or unconvinced ("Where's your support for this?"). Another way to talk to your writing is through written comments, making notes in the margins or using the electronic commenting feature of your word-processing program to write yourself notes.

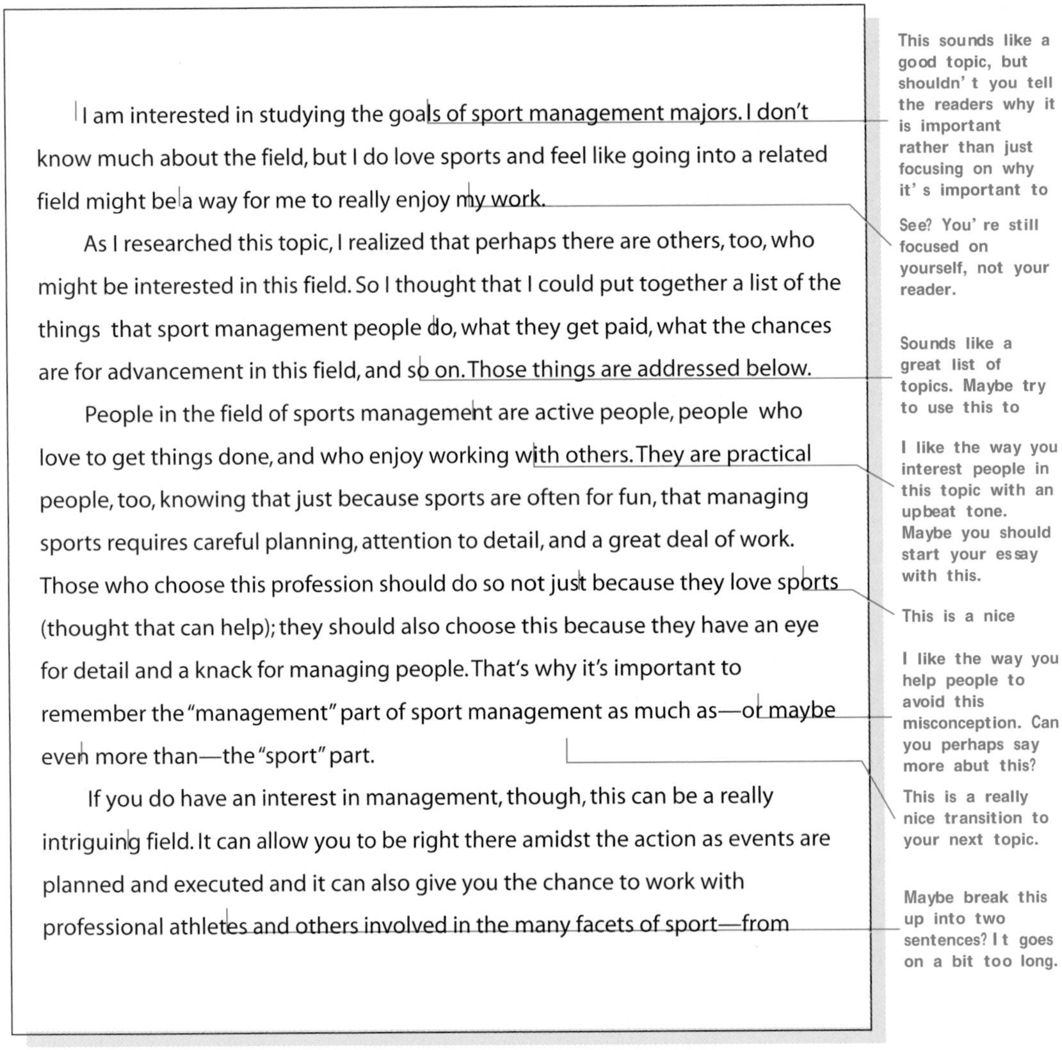

I am interested in studying the goals of sport management majors. I don't know much about the field, but I do love sports and feel like going into a related field might be a way for me to really enjoy my work.

As I researched this topic, I realized that perhaps there are others, too, who might be interested in this field. So I thought that I could put together a list of the things that sport management people do, what they get paid, what the chances are for advancement in this field, and so on. Those things are addressed below.

People in the field of sports management are active people, people who love to get things done, and who enjoy working with others. They are practical people, too, knowing that just because sports are often for fun, that managing sports requires careful planning, attention to detail, and a great deal of work. Those who choose this profession should do so not just because they love sports (thought that can help); they should also choose this because they have an eye for detail and a knack for managing people. That's why it's important to remember the "management" part of sport management as much as—or maybe even more than—the "sport" part.

If you do have an interest in management, though, this can be a really intriguing field. It can allow you to be right there amidst the action as events are planned and executed and it can also give you the chance to work with professional athletes and others involved in the many facets of sport—from

Comments in margin:

This sounds like a good topic, but shouldn't you tell the readers why it is important rather than just focusing on why it's important to

See? You're still focused on yourself, not your reader.

Sounds like a great list of topics. Maybe try to use this to

I like the way you interest people in this topic with an upbeat tone. Maybe you should start your essay with this.

This is a nice

I like the way you help people to avoid this misconception. Can you perhaps say more abut this?

This is a really nice transition to your next topic.

Maybe break this up into two sentences? It goes on a bit too long.

FIGURE 9.1 Using the Comment function to write notes in a draft manuscript.

Then you can summarize and prioritize the notes you make to yourself. Set up a triage that lists the most important issues for you to improve in your next draft—your biggest concerns. One way to create such a list of revision issues is to work your way through your document several times, each time concentrating on a specific set of concerns. Though there are many possible ways to divide the concerns you face during the revision process, following is one process that many of my students and I have found useful.

1. Read over your document once without stopping, just as a reader would. As you read, pay special attention to

   - the amount of support provided for your claims,
   - the overall logic of the piece (is there a logical connection between the claim and support?), and
   - whether one point follows from, and leads logically to, the next.

   That is, consider whether you have created a logical flow of ideas. After you've read through the draft, write yourself a note about your general impressions.

   - Is there enough support?
   - Do any spots seem thin or underdeveloped?
   - Did you get lost anywhere in the draft? Where exactly?
   - Did the tone seem appropriate?
   - Did you enjoy the reading?

   Questions like these, and others that you might come up with on your own, give you the chance to respond as a reader might—so be as objective as you can. Then, respond to each of your concerns by planning the best revision strategy (for example, doing a bit more research or developing one of the issues more thoroughly) and then carrying it out.

2. Read your document again, this time paragraph by paragraph. In the margins, make brief notes about the topic and purpose of each paragraph. Then, check to see if

   - the information contained in each paragraph all relates to its topic, or if some of it might be better addressed elsewhere or developed into its own topic, and
   - the information provided is sufficient to complete the paragraph's purpose, or if more development is necessary.

   You should also check to see if each paragraph is connected to the one that precedes it and the one that follows it with useful transitions. In some cases, though you may have planned an internal organization for your essay, the reader might not follow the organization unless you help her to see the connections among your ideas.

3. Read your document a third time, this time considering just sentence structure and word choice. Consider whether each sentence is clear, focused, and grammatically correct. Also consider if the sentence boundaries best express the connections between your ideas, drawing on the techniques of coordination and subordination discussed below. Would some of the longer sentences be clearer if they were broken into shorter ones or made more concise? Would the point of some of the sentences be clearer if they were combined into compound or complex sentences using coordination or subordination?

This stage may be best accomplished by using your word processor to try out a variety of sentence configurations so you can see which one is most effective for your purposes.

It is at this stage that you are beginning the "fine sanding," trying to find the best ways to capture your point through inventive uses of language, playing with the sentence order and the diction (word choices) to create memorable phrasings. Of course, you may not have the time (or the need) to spend time on every sentence. But the wording and phrasing of any sentence that seems unclear to you and the sentences that are most important (thesis sentence, introductory sentences, expression of your most crucial points) deserve extra attention. Remember: real readers can remember only so much of anything they read. If you pay special attention to the sentence structure and wording of the most important parts of your essay, they'll remember what you want them to.

4. In your final revision of the document, you are polishing—looking for grammatical and typographical errors, final stylistic changes, and opportunities to make your document as professional as possible. We discuss advanced techniques for polishing your documents and using design techniques in the next chapter. But no matter the level of complexity, the final stage is always about delivering a product of which you can be proud.

At each stage of revision, gathering input from others can be valuable, since you are not always able to be wholly objective about your own writing. This part of the revision process is important in your occupational writing as well. As Eric Engle notes, from his perspective as an environmental geologist, "Having someone proof your work is extremely important. My boss is an excellent writer/editor, and I have learned a great deal from him. Having someone review my writing also increases my confidence level." But whereas Engle treats peer review as a chance to bring polish and correctness to his work, Jane Whittaker's work as a systems architect has led her to invite the reviews of her colleagues at an earlier stage, based more on the content:

> Depending on the subject and the nature of the communication, I have other people look it over. This is often helpful, but could be a mixed blessing. These read-throughs were not proofreadings; they were mainly to check for substantive errors and politically sensitive things. And that's where the mixed blessing is. There are lots of opinions about what's sensitive or not. Also, very few people I work with are capable of or interested in reading for correct grammar, punctuation, or spelling.

The work done by Robert Colleluori and his colleagues in his ad agency also rely on such collaborative revision:

> It's all about what the reader hears or "sees" in the writing. If it's a proposal for our business clients and not creative writing aimed at consumers, we typ-

ically have three people in the agency review it for proofing purposes and flow. If it's creative, I like to have a group read it and give comments. You never know what may trigger a better word, stronger images, etc. that could make something come more alive, tell a better story, paint a better picture, deliver a better message. We sometimes use a formal, professional focus group to test two or three concepts, verbal and graphical, to understand how a document is perceived before placing an ad or doing a mail campaign.

Clearly, working with others as you write is an important skill, not only for your present academic writing but also to become a better colleague of others in your profession. In order to obtain the best responses from your peer readers, and to establish grounds for honest responses (both those you get and those you give), you must show your openness to such input.

INVITING PEER RESPONSE

Since many high school English classes use peer response workshops, you may have used this technique before. You may also have used peer response more informally, just asking friends or relatives to look over something you've written and respond to it. If your experiences are like those of most others, you've probably had mixed success with the process. Why is the process sometimes successful and sometimes less so?

You might be inclined to think that perhaps the success depends on those who review your work; clearly, some of your peers are more motivated and serious about the work than others. But it may not be enough to simply *hope* that the person with whom you work will perform well; there are ways to invite better responses from peers. I use the word *invite* specifically because it is important to make peer reviewers, like guests, feel comfortable within your space. Inviting peer readers into your writing, after all, is difficult for both parties. You are wondering whether what you have written makes any (or at least enough) sense, and your reviewer is caught somewhere between the responsibilities of honesty and collegiality and the desire not to offend the writer. In short, the interpersonal dynamics at work in a peer review can't be ignored. Inviting useful responses, then, is partially about creating critical readers for your writing and partially about developing good working relationships with the people involved.

Just as you needed to make yourself a better reader of your own writing— by reading aloud, allowing time and space between yourself and your drafts, and by talking to your drafts—so do you need to help your peer reviewers become better and more critically insightful readers. The two are not unrelated, since the critical reading you've done of your own work can be used to establish a model for your readers. Good peer review sessions often result from the way in which the writer presents herself to the reviewer.

For example, you might hand over your paper to a reviewer with the following words:

> I'm really feeling awful about this piece. It was so hard for me to get going, and I know it didn't come out right. I have a really hard time with writing, and it seems like I'm never able to give the teacher what he wants. I make so many mistakes, and he always seems to hate what I write. I don't know. What do you think?

Though this introduction purports to invite response ("What do you think?"), it also does a lot to make the reviewer wary of critical reading. Consider what it says between the lines: "I'm nervous about other people's responses to my writing, and I've had my feelings hurt in the past." Since it focuses on your sensitivity to past responses, and focuses more on "mistakes" than on the collaborative development of the piece of writing, this introduction is not likely to create a willing and critical respondent. In fact, it seems to request that the respondent not be overly critical and so further damage your self-esteem. This, of course, is understandable; we're all a bit sensitive about our writing.

But readers are usually sensitive too, and nervous about pointing out weak spots. Creating good peers, like creating good colleagues at work, requires you to inspire a sense of openness, trust, and shared responsibility. You can do so by letting your peer reader know (1) the issues that most concern *you* about your writing, and (2) that you welcome a reader who is willing to make critical comments and substantive suggestions.

You can accomplish this in a number of ways. First, you can tell your peer readers about the critical responses you've already made to your own work. By speaking first about your writing's rough spots, you show your readers that you consider it to still be in process. This can be done in many ways, but here are two suggestions: You could write a cover memo to your reader before you arrive for the peer review session, or you could simply take notes about your own work in advance of the session and talk through them with your reviewer. In either case, you can frame your remarks in ways that invite serious responses:

- **Invite critique as helpful.** Rather than show the kind of trepidation exhibited above, do your best to set your peer reader at ease about critical comments. Let her know that you need such comments in order to improve your work. Let your reader know that though the work is still in process, you believe in its potential. So, rather than a comment like "I'm really feeling awful about this piece," you might write "I really think that the idea here is solid, but I'm concerned about whether the main point is coming through. Could you let me know whether my point is clear? Where do you get confused? I really want this to be a strong statement, because the topic is very important to me." This type of invitation focuses on the quality of your work, not your personal feelings. It displays seriousness in your attitude toward your work. And it asks for collaborative effort toward improvement rather than assurances that the work has potential.

- **Clarify your goals/purpose.** Help your reader to understand your topic, purpose, and audience, and the effect you want to have on that audience. If you give your reader a strong sense of your intentions, he will be better able to consider the parts of the draft that contribute to those goals and those that detract from them. This approach also focuses your conversation around the issues that most concern you as a writer.

- **Model the type of critique you expect.** Drawing on your own reading of your draft, discuss facets of the work with which you are still dissatisfied or struggling. By doing so, you alert your reader to specific concerns you have about the draft; you also model the amount of criticism you welcome (and expect) from your readers.

- **Mention facets of your writing with which you have struggled in the past.** If in past essays you have not provided sufficient evidence, if you tend to jump from point to point without adequate organization and transitions, if you tend to write overly long sentences, and so on, tell your reader. Then she can be on the lookout for known weak spots.

- **Thank your respondent.** Though "please" and "thank you" might seem like lessons from your childhood, they are still at the heart of collegial human relations. Either in the cover memo or in person, it is important to express your gratitude both before and after the session. Of course, one of the most sincere ways you can show your appreciation is to treat your colleagues' work with respect and seriousness as well; put real effort into the critiques that you do for them.

Creating good peer readers is, like so much else in writing, a process—that is, your first attempts may not be as successful as later attempts. But you will be practicing a skill that is absolutely crucial on the job—your ability to balance honest assessment of colleagues' work with the emotions and attitudes that go with being human. If you develop this type of collegial attitude, your chances of succeeding in the workplace are enhanced greatly.

USING PEER COMMENTS

Though you want to encourage as much response as you can, and though you want to do your best to assure that the comments are honest and incisive, you also need to use what you hear judiciously. In the end, the decision whether to accept the advice you get is your own. As Whittaker notes above, peer review is "often helpful, but could be a mixed blessing. These read-throughs were not proofreadings; they were mainly to check for substantive errors and politically sensitive things. And that's where the mixed blessing is. There are lots of opinions about what's sensitive or not."

Interpreting the comments of peer readers requires care. Sometimes peer readers can identify a problem but aren't able to propose a solution. Sometimes they hear a lack of clarity but misidentify the cause. Their comments can still be valuable, however. If a reader points you to a spot in your paper that seems problematic, and if on reading it over again, you agree, then it is often up to you to find the best way to address the problem. Peer reviewers provide reactions and, sometimes, suggestions. But it is up to you to make the effort to address the issues they identify.

Perhaps the best way to make such decisions, as with other aspects of writing, is to try them out. With word processing, doing so is rather easy and low-risk. Copy or rename your file (being sure to save the original), and see where your reader's advice takes you. Don't feel that you must follow the advice slavishly, but try to work with the spirit of the comments. If a reader suggested that you need more examples, try to find where such a revision makes sense. If a reader suggested changing your tone to make it less formal, see if that better serves your goals. If she suggested that some of your sentences are too long, try revising for conciseness. And so on. As you incorporate this advice, you'll likely discover other possible revisions as well; be ready to respond to them. Or, if you disagree with a peer's comment on some facet of your draft, you might leave it be or run it by someone else. In any case, if you have saved the original, you can compare the new version to the old to see which revisions actually improve the paper—and you can also see which changes were counterproductive. Revisions don't always improve matters, at least not on the first try. So, as with other stages of the writing process, your time and patience are required.

The final effort that you must make as we move from *writing as a process* to *writing as a product*—a finished document—should respond to what you learned in your peer reviews. In particular, you should realize that readers expect your presentation draft—the one that you give to your audience—to be your highest and best effort, a polished presentation that captures what you know in the most readable and moving language you have available. The activities of this chapter can help you address that expectation with care. That care extends to the physical form of your documents as well—to issues of correctness, to issues of document design, and, in the case of oral presentations, to the ways that you help your listeners follow complex arguments without the opportunity to read along. Chapter 10 provides advice on adding that final polish.

CHAPTER TEN

Delivering Researched Arguments

In ancient rhetoric, *delivery*, the fifth and final canon, comprised the moment within which the orator (or writer) went public with his ideas. Though composing is an activity, a process that involves continuous revision, the canon of delivery reminds you that at some point most writing becomes a product, a polished delivery of your ideas and words. Joseph Williams puts it well: "Perfection is an admirable goal, but it is the enemy of done" (*Style: Ten Lessons in Clarity and Grace*, 6th ed.: 12). Deadlines and the desire to position your thoughts and words within an ongoing dialog require that you, at least for a time, call your work "finished." And that's a good thing, too; if perfect is indeed "the enemy of done," then deadlines are its friend.

So, as you move toward delivery, you must consider the physical form in which you will present your words and ideas to others. Doing so asks you to consider questions like:

- Is my message best contained within an oral presentation, a written document, or both?

- What will the presentation of my ideas sound or look like?

- Is there a preferred form for such communications (letter, memo, report, oral briefing)?

- What experience of my oral or written text do I want my audience to have (and/or what will they expect it to look like)?

As you consider how to publish (i.e., make public) your writing, you will ask questions that can help you to decide on a polished format for your work:

- What are the most innovative and effective ways to deliver this communication to an audience?

- What facets of my *ethos* or character do I want my document or presentation to stress—and what visual or auditory *ethos* is most appropriate to the rhetorical situation?

- How can I physically arrange my document or oral presentation so as to move my reader along the desired path of reasoning?

- What styles of presentation (oral or written, academic or popular, expert-to-expert or expert-to-novice, etc.) can best serve my purpose and audience?

- How can the physical document or presentation stress the key stasis points of my topic?

All these questions remind us that in the twenty-first century, the fifth canon of rhetoric, delivery, is more exciting (and more complex) than ever. Delivering your message takes place not only through words and their "meanings" and nuances (alphabetic rhetoric) but also by means of the images that accompany those words—and by the physical shape and size of those words through the use of fonts and layout (visual rhetoric). Though this was always true to a certain extent, the possibilities are far more numerous than before because of new media and enhanced capabilities in word processing and document design. Even oral presentations bring with them new visual expectations—not just of charts and other visual aids but also of dynamic electronic enhancements that capture the eye as well as the ear (as with PowerPoint). As a communicator, it becomes your job to choose among the vast array of available technologies and to deliver a document or presentation with decorum, with effectiveness, and with a consistent *ethos*. You have access to many bells and whistles; but bells and whistles can both enhance and detract from the message that you seek to deliver depending on how you use them.

Amid all the available technologies, there is still a place for the relatively unadorned academic paper—a document based on something called *manuscript form*. Manuscript form is, by contemporary standards, a very plain style whereby words are presented without elaborate design techniques, instead conforming to the strictures of APA, MLA, CBE, or other relatively strict manuscript formats. This is true for good reasons—not to restrict creativity but to create consistency and rigor in the presentation of carefully researched ideas and to allow the editors and reviewers of such journals to do their job efficiently.

So what is a twenty-first century student writer to do? Clearly, it is important in your life as a writer, a worker, and a citizen to have a working knowledge of *both* academic and professional formats as well as some skills of document enhancement. In addition, you need to learn how to choose among the available modes of delivery according to the situation. In this chapter, we explore some of the available techniques and the situations that influence their use. Of course, we cannot pretend that this chapter is a comprehensive discussion of every potential oral and visual presentation. Rather, it is meant to give you strategies for *choosing wisely among the possibilities that exist*—how to think through rhetorical situations and to find the most effective ways to polish your document or presentation for delivery.

We first discuss the need for the careful editing and proofreading that assures a document free of basic errors. Then we discuss the possibilities for delivering your message to an audience as effectively as possible, considering principles that apply to both oral and written communications. The goal is to explore and practice ways in which you might be inventive while still attending to the call of decorum in various rhetorical situations.

EDITING

As you think about your writing as a finished product, you must first consider the basics. Despite the powerful effects you can achieve through new document design technologies, your first task is to be sure that you have carefully revised and edited the text itself. No matter how visually attractive you make a document, if it contains errors in spelling or basic rules of edited American English (sentence structure errors, punctuation mistakes, lack of grammatical precision) or typographical mistakes (leaving out words, errors in margins, poor proofreading), your credibility as a writer will suffer. In fact, it can suffer even more due to the possibilities of document design: Consider the effects of a PowerPoint presentation in which a misspelled word is boldfaced and blown up to 48-point type! That's pretty difficult to ignore.

There are many handbooks that can assist you with the processes of proofreading and editing, but perhaps most importantly, you need to be aware of your own recurring demons—those types of errors that you have, in the past, struggled with most frequently. I tend to write long sentences that are some-times difficult to read. I know there are certain words that I consistently mis-spell. I tend, in early drafts, to overuse commas and sometimes switch point of view too frequently. Knowing these things about myself, when I proofread, I look for such errors especially carefully.

WRITING TO EXPLORE 10.1

In your writer's notebook, make a list of the types of errors that seem to recur in your writing. Recall comments that you have received on papers this semester and from past teachers. Consider the rules of grammar that seem most difficult for you to incorporate or get right. After making this list and using a handbook or reference guide, try to restate in your own words the relevant guidelines of edited American English that most apply. As you continue your writing, it will be useful for you to continue adding to this personal list of common errors, each time seeking the related guidelines.

Though we each need to be aware of those facets of edited American Eng-lish that are most difficult for us to conquer, some errors seem to plague many of us. Below is a list of some of those frequent errors, errors that I have noticed in my own students' writing. I consider these errors to be growing pains—the types of things that can go wrong with writing when the writer attempts to move from a simple, mechanical style to one that suits the more complex work done at a college level.

Run-ons and Comma Splices

A run-on sentence results from the failure to provide the proper punctuation or conjunctions to connect two complete thoughts. For example:

> The effects of affirmative action have been both negative and positive it is difficult to assess its overall level of success.

In this case, two separate thoughts that are closely related in topic have not been joined properly in sentence structure. This error is frequent among college writers as they attempt to capture complex ideas; writers "run on" as they draft because they are continuously trying to explicate complex ideas, have lots to say, and are doing their best to get it all onto the page.

But as you proofread, it is important to polish your punctuation or con-junction use so as to create from run-ons either one compound or complex sen-tence, or two simple sentences. The above example needs something to connect the first clause, "The effects of affirmative action have been both negative and positive," and the second, "it is difficult to gauge its effects." There are many possible ways to accomplish this, including a period, a semicolon, or a coordinating conjunction (*and* or *but* might work here). You could also create a subordinate construction by placing "since" or "because" at the start of this sentence:

> Since the effects of affirmative action have been both positive and negative, it is difficult to assess its overall level of success.

The subordinating word *since* makes the first clause dependent and so ties it grammatically to the second thought, which completes it; the first can no longer stand alone as an independent clause.

You might also be tempted simply to place a comma between the two clauses. This, however, does not solve the problem, since a comma is not a strong enough mark of punctuation to connect two independent clauses. Doing so here would create what is called a *comma splice*. As the name suggests, a comma splice attempts to "splice" or connect two independent clauses with a comma. However, a comma cannot provide the strong pause needed between two complete thoughts. If you find that you have, in a draft, connected two independent clauses with a comma, you can correct the error in the same way that you correct run-ons: Find stronger and more grammatically sound ways to show the relationship between those thoughts.

Subject-Verb Agreement Problems

Another common error arises when a subject and its verb do not agree in number—that is, a singular subject is used with the plural form of a verb, or vice versa. For example:

> Affirmative action cases is a real problem for American business.

The problem here, of course, is that the subject (cases) is plural, and the verb (is) is singular. For this reason, the sentence above may sound wrong to your ear. But even with a good ear, you might make agreement errors when the subject and verb are separated by interrupting phrases. Hence, as we become more mature writers and create more complex sentence structures, agreement errors can be more difficult to hear. For example:

> The many problems associated with affirmative action has become a frequent subject of conversation for businesspeople.

Though your ear for correctness may have caught this one too, the discord likely wasn't quite as loud as with the first. That's because the phrase that immediately precedes the verb, "with affirmative action," has a singular object (action). The proximity of that word to the verb "has" increases your chances of missing the agreement problem: "affirmative action has" can sound okay.

So, as maturity of sentence structure grows, even good writers may fail to hear errors in agreement. If you know that you have struggled with this in the past, the best way to make decisions about a singular or plural verb is to read the sentence without the interrupting phrase. Here, read the sentence *without* the bracketed phrase:

> The many problems [associated with affirmative action] has become a frequent subject of conversation for businesspeople.

Easier to hear the error this time, isn't it? As you proofread, especially if you know you have had agreement problems in the past, check to see if subjects and verbs agree by locating the two and reading them without the words that separate them. That gives your ear for standard English a better chance of helping you out.

Punctuation Errors with Direct Quotations

Another common error that arises in college writing is misplaced punctuation used in conjunction with quotation marks. Because you will be using more and more researched information in your writing, you will be faced with more occasions on which you quote from outside sources. The rules governing proper punctuation surrounding direct quotations can seem pretty complex, and so you might need to check your reference handbook for individual cases and more complete explications. But there are a few simple guidelines that can help you to check for correct usage.

First, remember that periods and commas generally go before the end quotation mark. Hence, the correct punctuation looks like this:

> Affirmative action laws are "the most useful pieces of legislation this country has ever seen toward greater civil rights."
>
> Though affirmative action laws are "the most useful pieces of civil rights legislation this country has ever seen," they are also the most hotly contested.

The exception to this rule is when we use parenthetical citations; in those cases, the punctuation *follows* the parentheses. Hence,

> Affirmative action laws are "the most useful pieces of civil rights legislation this country has ever seen" (Smith 24).

In the other case, you would likely cite the quotation at the end of the sentence:

> Though affirmative action laws are "the most useful pieces of civil rights legislation this country has ever seen," they are also the most hotly contested (Smith 24).

But if you wanted to attribute the quotation to Smith while suggesting that the end of the sentence represents your own ideas, you might need to punctuate as follows:

> Though affirmative action laws are "the most useful pieces of civil rights legislation this country has ever seen" (Smith 24), they are also the most hotly contested.

> In short, periods and commas go before the end quotation mark except when a parenthetical citation appears immediately following the quotation.

Conversely, colons and semicolons are placed *after* quotation marks:

> Affirmative action laws are "the most useful pieces of civil rights legislation this country has ever seen"; they are also the most hotly contested.

Question marks and exclamation points vary according to the situation. You include them *before* the quotation mark (1) if they apply only to the material within the quotation marks, or (2) if they refer to both the quotation itself and the sentence as a whole:

> Affirmative action has created many questions, such as "Do these laws violate the rights of citizens who are members of the majority?"

> How are we to answer questions like "Do these laws violate the rights of citizens who are members of the majority?"

However, if the question mark or exclamation mark only refers to the sentence as a whole and not to the quoted material individually, the punctuation goes *after* the quotation mark.

> How is one to gauge the effect of "the most useful pieces of civil rights legislation this country has ever seen"?

If you, in the past, have had problems with punctuating around direct quotations, be sure to check your usage carefully whenever you use them, considering these guidelines.

> In short, determine the placement of question marks and exclamation points by considering whether the punctuation applies to the whole sentence (in which case you should place the punctuation after the end quotation mark) or only to the material included within the quotation (in which case you should place the punctuation before the end quotation mark).

Another common error associated with quotations involves block or inset quotations. Quotations that have five lines or more should be set off from the text by indenting the entire passage ten spaces (you may also sometimes inset shorter quotations for emphasis). The common errors are as follows:

Common Errors in Use of Block Quotations

- Using quotation marks along with indentation: Quotation marks should not be used around indented quotations.
- Centering quotations: Long quotations are indented on the left margin only, not the right. On the right side, continue the quotation all the way to the standard margin.
- Not introducing the quotation properly: Usually, the best way to introduce an indented quotation is with a colon following the introductory phrase or sentence.

So, an inset block quotation looks like this:

> The long history of affirmative action has attested to many things. Affirmative action laws are the most useful pieces of legislation this country has ever seen toward greater civil rights. Still, the laws have raised many questions about the rights of those who are in the majority. Those questions sometimes come to us as claims of reverse discrimination and practices that are unfair to business owners. (Smith 24)

Aside from the layout of the above quotation, you might also note

- the colon following my introductory phrase ("So, an inset block quotation looks like this:") and
- the parenthetical citation that comes *after* the final period.

Misplaced Modifiers

Though the term *misplaced modifier* has several definitions, the concept is really pretty simple: You've not made it clear enough what a descriptive or modifying phrase is meant to describe or modify. For example:

> Patriots in their own right, affirmative action laws have a set of heroes whose work should be noted.

The writer meant the phrase "patriots in their own right" to refer to the "heroes" of affirmative action. But the structure of the sentence gives the impression that the opening phrase refers to "affirmative action laws." The solution? As far as possible, keep related words together. Here you might write:

> Affirmative action laws have a set of heroes, patriots in their own right, whose work should be noted.

or

> Patriots in their own right, the heroes of affirmative action laws deserve to have their work noted.

There are many other ways that I might have revised the above sentence. But no matter how you define *misplaced modifiers*, keeping words that are related to one another together makes your prose much more readable.

Pronoun References

Pronouns have a particular use. They are used to replace nouns that you have used earlier (as in this sentence, "they" replaces the word "pronouns" from the previous sentence). Sloppy use of pronouns leads to confusion among readers. This is a common problem.

Note the way that I used "this" in the previous sentence. To what does it refer? Does it refer to sloppy pronoun usage? to the confusion that it can cause? to usage of pronouns generally? It can be difficult to determine the antecedent of "this." Assuming that your readers can figure things out is not a good strategy for writing; you want to make your writing as clear and precise as you can.

As you revise, pay special attention to your use of these generic pronouns, also called "relative pronouns," since they are meant to show the *relationships* between concepts. Be sure that such relationships are made clear to your readers. In the above sentence, for example, I might have written "This generic pronoun usage is a common problem."

Though there are many guidelines to pronoun usage, as you revise, you might simply check carefully that readers will be able to see the relationship that you are trying to establish between one word and another whenever you use such pronouns.

WORD CHOICES

As you draft, you work hard to capture complex thoughts in appropriate language. Chapter 9 discussed the connotations that words carry within specific discourse communities. However, sometimes the right word just doesn't appear in your mind immediately, and, in an attempt to maintain the flow of your ideas, you may settle for words that are close to your meaning but that aren't as precise or effective as they might be. Further, in your attempts to vary word choices and so enrich your writing, you may turn to a thesaurus to find synonyms—a wonderful way to learn new vocabulary, but one that can also cause you to use words that you don't know very well and so might use inappropriately.

As you revise, it is important to assure that your word choices are appropriate not only in meaning (denotation) but also in connotation. For example, you might describe the effects of affirmative action laws as discriminatory, inequitable, biased, uneven, or bigoted. Though each of those words has a similar meaning (and is therefore listed as synonymous in a thesaurus), each has its own tone, implication, and connotation. *Discriminatory* means that the laws show bias but also suggest that the bias is unfair to some group. *Uneven* suggests that the laws do not affect all parties equally, but it does not carry the same connotation of unfairness. *Bigoted*, on the other hand, has a strong connotation of intentional bias. As you revise, then, it is important that you consider which word most accurately expresses your meaning, both in definition and in tone.

You should also be careful of words that sound similar but that carry different meanings. *Discriminating*, for example, when used as an adjective, is a positive word meaning "making judicious and fair decisions"—quite different than "discriminatory." *Judicial* means something quite different than *judicious*; *economic* and *economical* have wholly different meanings as well. (Check your dictionary on each of those word pairs.)

Though the above list of common errors and accompanying guidelines is by no means complete, it does point out common areas of concern that you should attend to as you work to make your writing as precise and effective as possible. Before you dress your language in attractive fonts and surround it with accompanying visuals, you must acknowledge that the words, phrases, and sentences you use carry with them the potential to enhance, or detract from, the credible *ethos* required of good students and successful professionals. With that said, you must also acknowledge that though the basics of edited American English specify guidelines—that is, stated rules for formal writing—the decisions you make as a twenty-first-century writer also require you to be sensitive to many types of document delivery.

Imitation is a time-tested way to acclimate to the rhetorical situations and discourse communities you enter each time you write with specific audiences and purposes in mind. As a writer, the decisions you make represent a meeting of minds—a way to foster communication by presenting documents that conform to the preferred formats of that discourse community. That, of course, does not preclude inventiveness; it just suggests that your job in delivering documents or presentations involves not only your own preferences but those of your audience as well. As urged throughout this book, the *ethos* you present should acknowledge the common communication modes of members of the community within which you are writing.

PREPARING MANUSCRIPTS IN ACADEMIC FORMATS

The most basic, and likely the most familiar, form for presentation of your written work is the academic format. Academic papers have specific guidelines for style and the presentation of evidence; some of these cross academic disciplines, while others are discipline-specific. In addition, there are *modes of delivery* that are preferred in academic environments, most of which involve page design, source citation, and references lists. Though we cannot cover all the intricacies of the various formatting systems here (again, many handbooks are available for such specifics), we can describe the reasoning behind academic formats more generally. Following this reasoning will help you to understand its purposes and so to use academic formats in the spirit in which they are meant.

The American Psychological Association (APA), for example, has developed a style of documentation that is used widely in the social sciences and often in business programs as well. On its website, the APA states that

> When editors or teachers ask you to write in "APA style," they do not mean writing style. They are referring to the editorial style that many of the social and behavioral sciences have adopted to present written material in the field. Editorial style consists of rules or guidelines that a publisher observes to ensure clear and consistent presentation of written material. Editorial style concerns uniform use of such elements as
>
> ■ punctuation and abbreviations
>
> ■ construction of tables
>
> ■ selection of headings
>
> ■ citation of references
>
> ■ presentation of statistics
>
> ■ as well as many other elements that are a part of every manuscript.
>
> The American Psychological Association has established a style that it uses in all of the books and journals that it publishes. Many others working in the social and behavioral sciences have adopted this style as their standard as well.
>
> Much of the APA's style guidance covers fairly clear-cut issues, such as punctuation and formula presentation. There also exists a large segment of information that deals with the style and function of more complex expression. Knowing how to write without bias, for instance, or what constitutes ethical publication can elude newcomers and long-time authors alike. (http://www.apastyle.org/)

In this description, the APA makes an important distinction between "style" as we referred to it in earlier chapters and "editorial style that many of the social and behavioral sciences have adopted to present written material in the field," a preferred method of *document design and delivery* that "consists of rules or guidelines that a publisher observes to ensure clear and consistent presentation of written material." That is, the purpose of observing the rules of APA style (and here they are truly *rules* that require rigid observance!) is to establish a standard formatting for presentation of scholarly work—work like that you will do in many of your classes, as well as the work you will do if you continue in graduate school or in many areas of research. The APA also notes that this agreed-upon formatting helps to define this discourse community in a number of ways. By establishing "a style that it uses in all of the books and journals that it publishes," a style that "many others working in the social and behavioral sciences have adopted" as a standard as well, this formatting, citation, and document design system identifies its users as members of a defined academic and scholarly community. When you write as a student within classes that require APA style, you are, in a sense, being invited into that academic community, and so you are asked to observe the modes that will foster effective communication with others in that field.

Academic formatting defines its discourse community in more subtle and significant ways as well. As the APA notes, though "much of the APA's style guidance covers fairly clear-cut issues, such as punctuation and formula presentation," it also addresses "the style and function of more complex expression. Knowing how to write without bias, for instance, or what constitutes ethical publication can elude newcomers and long-time authors alike." This statement suggests that participation in this discourse community involves more than simple formatting items like punctuation or citation style; it is part of a larger system of scholarly work that addresses issues such as bias and ethics. Think, for example, about the ethics of documentation; you document sources not only to create a trail of ideas for your readers but also to give credit where it is due (and so to avoid committing plagiarism). If you think about rules of documentation in this way, you realize that the rules exist for important reasons and so deserve strict adherence.

In the humanities, as well as in many other disciplines, the Modern Language Association (MLA) style is the standard. Like the APA, the MLA notes that "The style recommended by the association for preparing scholarly manuscripts and student research papers concerns itself with the mechanics of writing, such as punctuation, quotation, and documentation of sources" and goes on to identify its discourse community:

> MLA style has been widely adopted by schools, academic departments, and instructors for nearly half a century. MLA guidelines are also currently used by over 125 scholarly and literary journals, newsletters, and magazines with circulations over one thousand; by hundreds of smaller periodicals; and by many university and commercial presses. MLA style is commonly followed not only in the United States but in Canada and other countries as well.
>
> *http://www.mla.org/www_mla_org/style/style_index.asp?mode=section*

In your high school writing classes, it is likely that you used MLA format for preparing documents, including the Works Cited system designed and maintained by the MLA. Now that you are a college writer, it is important that you continue to develop your familiarity with this system or learn the system that is most frequently used in your academic discipline. Your academic advisor and instructors in classes in your major field can help you to determine what style or styles are most important for you to master.

Though APA and MLA are the most common formatting systems you will encounter, there are others. For example, the Council of Science Editors (formerly the Council of Biology Editors, or CBE) presents its formatting system, designed for publication of scientific work, in *The CBE Manual for Authors, Editors, and Publishers*. This group also identifies its discourse community with some care: "Many writers in the natural sciences use the citation style recommended in the *CBE Manual,* which also gives advice for styling and formatting scientific papers, journals, and books for publication." CSE's website is http://www.councilscienceeditors.org/pubs_citing_internet.shtml.

WRITING TO EXPLORE 10.2

A review of the *CBE Manual,* from *Booklist,* December 1, 1994, can further develop your understanding of CBE's discourse community. Read the excerpt from the review below. Then, in your writer's notebook, list the conventions of the scientific disciplines that are addressed in this review. Note also the ways in which the CBE formatting system seems, according to this review, to address those commonplaces, and how it differs from APA and MLA styles. Try to be as specific as possible.

Earlier editions [of the *CBE Manual*] focused on style for those publishing in the plant sciences, zoology, microbiology, and the medical sciences. This quite expanded sixth edition covers all scientific disciplines, excluding only a few technological areas that are not experimental or observational. In order to include new disciplines, the sections on how to write and submit papers to scientific journals have been omitted. This was a sensible change, since each journal already publishes its own procedures.

The Style Manual Committee of the Council of Biology Editors had five aims in producing this excellent book: to support convergence in style in an international framework, to simplify formats for citations and references, to simplify style rules, to offer options based on the deeply rooted conventions of some disciplines, and to reduce work at the keyboard. The major parts of the book are "General Style Conventions," "Special Scientific Conventions," "Journals and Books," and "Publishing Process." Of these parts, the first two make up the bulk of the book. "General Style Conventions" covers every possible aspect, including alphabets, symbols, punctuation, capitalization, abbreviations, and geographic descriptions. Most of these conventions are also used outside the scientific community, so this manual can serve as a style reference for all writers, although some conventions are unique to science. For example, this section recommends the use of Arabic numerals instead of spelled-out words for the numbers one to nine. The "Special Scientific Conventions" section is comprehensive, covering the electromagnetic spectrum, subatomic particles, chemical elements, chemical names and formulas, analytical methods, drugs and pharmacokinetics, chromosomes, viruses, bacteria, plants, algae, human and animal life, the earth, and astronomical objects and time systems. . . . There is no other book like this for the scientific and technological community. It should be the major desk reference for anyone writing a scientific article or book. Students should be made aware of the manual early in their educational career so that old habits can be broken and correct procedures adhered to.

Though they feature many different manuscript styles, academic formats share a great deal as well. Foremost among these similarities is a relatively simple document design—a design that allows for ease of editorial review (both by teachers and, later in your career, journal editors) and an attention to careful citation of your sources.

The use of a simple document design acknowledges several key points:

- Editors (and teachers) need room to make comments on your text, and so the documents are usually double-spaced. Margins and other white space should be observed carefully and according to your teacher's prescriptions or the journal's editorial statement for contributors.

- Editors, not the author, make decisions about the physical layout of the text, and so manuscript forms use few word-processing techniques, with the exception of necessary graphics, tables, charts, etc. Since such visual aids are used frequently in the sciences and social sciences, APA and CBE formats are relatively specific on this.

- Fonts should be chosen for readability, and a minimum of word-processing commands should be included in electronic texts; manipulation of the electronic documents is easier for editors if they contain no page or line breaks, fancy styles/formats, or complex layouts.

Following are two student papers, one prepared in APA style, the other in MLA style. Read them, noting the marginal comments that describe disciplinary differences, differences in formatting, and differences in documentation styles for each. In your writer's notebook, jot down the general principles that inform each style, focusing on key areas of similarity and difference, and speculating on the reasons why each makes sense for this academic discipline. (For example, you might consider why MLA in-text citations use a page number when available, whereas APA uses the date of publication.) You might also attempt to draw general conclusions about the relationship between each system and the disciplines that use it. Finally, consider which of the methods is more frequently used in each of your classes (or in your major) and why.

Psychological Effects 1

Title is centered on page. Titles
in APA style should be clear and
focused, and should reveal the
topic as precisely and concisely
as possible.
Byline and course information
centered below title.

The Psychological Effects of School Violence on Children

Audra Shearer

Professor Dominic Delli Carpini

WRT 200

May 1, 2001

Psychological Effects 2

Title is centered on first page of the paper's body.

                    The Psychological Effects of School Violence on Children

Nearly *a million* students took guns into their schools in 1998

If more than one work by the same author(s) and published in same year is cited, you must include a lowercase letter to identify that article more specifically. That letter helps the reader find the proper article on the Reference page.

(American Academy, 1999b) and students carry an estimated 270,000 guns

to school every day according to the Centers for Disease Control and

Prevention (Children and Violence, 2001).

As frightening as these figures are, they should not surprise you.

Unlike MLA style, APA cites the year rather than the page.

School violence has become so prevalent in our society that it is evident

that no one is safe from it.

Introduction lays out the topic of the essay.

This violence afflicts large and small schools, urban and rural areas. In

fact, 52% of teenagers from relatively small "benign" communities now live

with the daily fear that an attack like the Columbine shootings could occur

in their school (Aronson, 2000). It has become an inescapable part of

everyday life. Although the annual number of school shootings is on the

decline, the number of shootings involving multiple victims is on the rise

(Aronson, 2000). Research by Singer, Anglin, Song, and Lunghofer (1995)

has revealed that 34% of students reported being threatened and 13%

Note use of statistical information in social sciences.

reported being attacked at school, while 23% had been victims of gun-

related violence in 1995.

Children who experience catastrophic events like school violence will

show a wide range of reactions. Some will have bad memories or worries

and fears that will fade with emotional support and the passing of time.

However, children who have experienced school violence are vulnerable to

serious long-term problems and mental disorders. Helping children avoid or

overcome emotional distress in the wake of violence is one of the most

important challenges that a parent, teacher, or psychologist can face

(National Institute, 1999b). All children and adolescents exposed to

violence, even if only through graphic news reports, should be observed for

signs of emotional distress (National Institute, 1999a).

Psychological Effects 3

Problem

The problem section sets up the exigency or purpose for writing, as well as the research problem that is being investigated.

The more direct the exposure to violence, the higher the risk for emotional harm (National Institute, 1999a). As an example, the National Institute of Mental Health (1999b), or NIMH, urges, "In a school shooting, the student who is injured will be most severely affected emotionally. And the student who sees a classmate shot, even killed, probably will be more emotionally affected than the student who was in another part of the school when the violence occurred. But even the second-hand exposure to violence can be traumatic." Violence exposure has a destructive effect on children's peer relationships, and this is especially important because an early compromise of peer relationships is a strong predictor for later mental health problems. The difference in witnessing school violence or being directly, physically harmed by it can lead to either a positive or negative effect (Schwarz, 2000).

Witnessed violence, unlike violent victimization, is not always associated with unpleasant consequences for the child. Children can develop positive evaluations of violence and may even learn to accept the differences of other students more readily. In most circumstances, witnessed violence represents a less extreme compromise of children's feelings of safety and well being. On the other hand, violent victimization has negative effects on emotion regulation and can lead to peer rejection, bullying, and aggression. Yet both of these ways to experience school violence can ultimately harm a child's mental health. Children who experience school violence often develop symptoms similar to post-traumatic stress disorder, which will be covered later in the article. These children will experience intense anger, sadness, and anxiety. Victims of violence will have more difficulties with emotion regulation than a mere witness will. The ways that emotion regulation is tested is usually based on the ability of the child to recover quickly from episodes of distress, to control their excitement in "emotionally arousing situations," and to

Psychological Effects 4

respond appropriately when peers are aggressive or hostile (Schwarz, 2000). The findings of the Schwarz and Proctor (2000) article show a substantial link between community or school violence and negative peer reaction in social situations for children. The violence is associated with many levels of risk for mental disorders that will lead to difficulties in social situations with peers. The study conducted in this article shows that victimization in the school will have a negative influence on a child's social adjustment. With all these consequences, it is important to have an understanding of the common mental disorders that develop after school violence so as to know how to help children. In a report of the Surgeon General, Donna E. Shalala, Secretary of Health and Human Services (2001), delivered this message. "The world remains a threatening, often dangerous place for children and youths. And in our country today, the greatest threat to the lives of children and adolescents is not disease or starvation or abandonment, but the terrible reality of violence." For reasons such as these, it has become so important to protect the mental health and sense of security of the youth of today as they walk into classrooms that could erupt into violence at any moment. In order for children to grow and progress past these violent episodes in schools, we need to know what happens inside the minds of the children who are forced to witness or be harmed by the violence. What effect does school violence have on them psychologically?

School officials, administrators, teachers, parents, mentors, or anyone with children in their lives, this article is meant to alert you to the importance of following up on school violence to protect the needs of children psychologically. Knowing how to treat mental health after violence may lead to the development of other treatment strategies and prevention programs (Singer, M. I., Anglin, T. M., Song, L. Y., Lunghofer, L., 1995). School violence is constantly being broadcasted on our local and national news programs, yet the attention needs to be directed to helping children emotionally, as well as physically, after the [events] have occurred. The

Reference here shows the dependence of claims and information throughout the first part of the paragraph upon this author's work. Avoid overusing parenthetical references when a long series of claims is based upon the same source.

Since the authors are named in the paragraph itself, there is no need for a parenthetical citation here. It's clear that the information cited comes from that study.

Since this web source has no page numbers, it need not be cited by page as direct quotations usually are.

With less than six authors, all authors are named in the first in-text citation. After the first citation, it can be cited by including just the first author's name (here, Singer) and *et al.*, which means "and other." If there are more than six authors you can use et al. even with the first citation.

children in your lives should be your utmost concern because we live in a constantly evolving society in which children need help along the course of their lives. Will school violence ever stop now that it has become almost commonplace and much publicized? The national high school death toll over the last two years is 27 students and teachers killed (Vatz, 1999). We all need to know of the research out there so that this number does not continue to rise and so that we can help the children that we hold dear.

Note how the author reinforces the exigency of her argument.

Every life is affected by school violence; we are affected merely by hearing about it. Everyone becomes anxious because "Who will be the next target?" is always the question; the environment is changed because it does not offer the safety expected of it (Hazler, 1996). In 1996–97, 10% of all public schools reported at least one serious violent crime to police or law enforcement (Bureau of Justice Statistics and Office of Juvenile Justice and Delinquency Prevention, U.S. Department of Justice as cited in American Academy, 1999). Children are aware that they are no longer safe in schools.

Children and adolescents who experience a violent event like school violence have difficulties in mental health and cognitive functioning (Mazza, 1999). Victims have common experiences that require assistance and treatment, but it is important to remember that as each child is unique; so is their reaction because children have a lot less life experience than adults in which to evaluate their personal trauma (Hazler, 1996). This is a significant concern because of the complex relationship between violence exposure and adolescent mental health. This article will show you some of the most common after-effects, as well as offer some advice on how to help your children cope. Psychologists also stress the importance of recognizing the "hidden damage they see lurking just below the surface" (DeAngelis, 2000), and we should also be aware of it.

A Findings or Results section usually follows the Problem section, reporting on results of the research—in this case, the secondary information gathered by the author. In other cases, the Results section reports the results of primary research conducted by the author herself.

Subheadings help to organize the information for a reader.

This citation refers to information reported throughout the second half of this paragraph.

Psychological Effects 6

Findings on the Effects of School Violence

Violence exposure is associated with mental health problems. Some of the most common psychological effects are:

Depression

Depression is a common reaction by victims because they can see no escape from their problems and little opportunity to fix what is left. Depression includes self-punishment; victims will bad-mouth themselves, which can lead to physical mutilation or potentially to suicide (Hazler, 1996). In a sample of 3,735 high school students, it was determined that depression is a significant factor in the development of the relationship between psychological trauma symptoms and exposure to violence (Mazza, 1999). Sadness is a normal reaction for children to experience after the loss of a classmate or the witnessing of school violence. However, if this sadness occurs continuously for two weeks, causes functional impairment or physical symptoms like sleeping disturbances, appetite changes, and difference in energy levels, as well as psychological symptoms like apathy, suicidal ideas, or feeling of worthlessness, the sadness may be diagnosed as major depressive disorder. Children may describe their feelings as depressed, "down in the dumps," hopeless, empty, "blah," or discouraged. An early sign that a child may be beginning to develop this disorder is poor concentration. He/she will typically be forgetful and will become easily fatigued when asked to concentrate on difficult problems. Most commonly among children with this disorder, rather than adults, irritability develops. Sadly, this irritability often alienates loved ones because of a constantly "cranky" mood (Long, 2001).

Major depressive disorder is the most frequently diagnosed mood disorder in children and adolescents, and this is especially important because death from suicide is the third leading cause of death for teens. Depressed kids are sad—they feel pessimistic about their futures and

Psychological Effects 7

unloved by their family and friends. Dr. Philip Long (2001) provides some other thought-provoking statistics about depression:

This bulleted list allows the writer to highlight and organize key information.

- At any time, between 10 and 15 percent of the child and adolescent population has *some* symptoms of depression
- Twenty to 40 percent relapse within 2 years, and 70 percent will do so by adulthood
- Children who first become depressed before puberty are at risk for some form of mental disorder in adulthood, while teenagers who first become depressed after puberty are most likely to experience another episode of depression
- Twenty to 40 percent of adolescents with depression eventually develop bipolar disorder
- In a 10– to 15–year follow-up study of 73 adolescents diagnosed with major depression, 7 percent of the adolescents had committed suicide sometime later

Stressful life events like school violence are precipitating factors of depressive disorders and suicide attempts. Adolescent girls are most vulnerable—studies prove that the coping methods they use cause more "focused and repetitive thinking about the event" and thus develop more stress and sadness (Long, 2001).

Post-Traumatic Stress Disorder (or PTSD)

Within the first month of an extreme trauma, anxiety and behavioral disturbances may occur; this is called acute stress disorder, which is closely related to post-traumatic stress disorder (or PTSD). This psychological damage can develop because of witnessing, experiencing, or participating in an "overwhelmingly traumatic (frightening) event" (American Academy, 2000a). Extreme trauma can be felt in school violence because of severe physical assault, near-death experiences, or witnessing a murder. PTSD and acute stress disorder are characterized by a poor memory of the event,

Psychological Effects 8

general anxiety, avoidance of the situation or anything that could cause memories of the event, and intense and vivid recollections through dreams, flashbacks, or recurring thoughts or visual images (Long, 2001). The re-experiencing of the event in this manner may lead to feelings of helplessness and hopelessness at not being able to change what happened (Mazza, 1999). Children will also re-experience the event when the media covers its anniversary (National Institute, 1999a). Specifically, children will often relive the violence through repetitive play. Young children will typically have nightmares about the traumatic event that involve monsters, themes of rescuing people, or threats to themselves or others (American Academy, 2000a).

People differ in their vulnerability to PTSD. Recent brain imaging has also shown that this disorder causes altered metabolism and blood flow in the brain (National Institute, 1999b). In a sample of 221 inner-city youths, it was determined that a strong predictor for the development of PTSD is exposure to violence (Mazza, 1999). According to Mazza, violent events may cause "an intense physiological reaction and feelings of intense fear, helplessness, or horror" (p. 205).

Page numbers are included when available for direct quotations.

Nine percent of people exposed to trauma will develop such a disorder. About half of the cases will remit or diminish within 6 months, but for the remainder of the cases the disorder will persist for years and can eventually come to dominate their lives (Long, 2001).

These disorders can be diagnosed by signs of:

The bulleted list helps the writer to emphasize key factors in diagnosis of depression.

- Abnormal depressed mood during the day
- Abnormal loss of all interest and pleasure
- Irritable mood
- Abnormal appetite or weight disturbance, either weight loss or weight gain
- Sleep disturbances
- Fatigue or loss of energy
- Abnormal self-reproach or inappropriate guilt

Psychological Effects 9

- Poor concentration or indecisiveness
- Abnormal morbid thoughts of death or suicide
- Refusal to return to school and "clinging" behavior, like shadowing the mother or father around the house
- Being easily startled or jumpy
- Physical complaints like stomach aches, headaches, or dizziness for which a physical cause cannot be located
- Withdrawal from family or friends, listlessness, decreased activity, and preoccupation with the events of the violence

Note the transition to a discussion of treatment options.

Understanding all of the potential dangers of psychological effects is the only way to begin to treat them. Author and psychologist Barbara Coloroso, a resident of Littleton whose children attended Columbine High at the time of the infamous shootings there, said this about overcoming school violence: "You keep doing your work, but there's this intense sorrow, a gray veil covering it all. And as you go through your own grief, you help your children. You start with 'Oh, no, life is unfair,' then there's a long period of 'life hurts,' [and] Eventually you come back to 'life is good.' (Simons, 2000). The National Institute of Mental Health (1999a) suggests a substantial early education, success in academic situations and a nurturing social environment as good tools to overcoming incidents of violence. Denial, however, can be a force that hinders healing. Students and their families who don't express grief and instead function normally in their everyday lives may be suffering more, and therefore are more of a concern to psychologists.

More people have begun to realize the complexity of psychological after-effects, especially after the Columbine shootings in April 1999. Two days after the six-month anniversary of the shootings, Carla Hochhalter, a mother of a girl paralyzed in the shootings, walked into a pawn shop, asked to see a gun and shot herself after battling with depression. On February 14, 2000, two other Columbine students were shot and killed at a sandwich shop by an unidentified killer. And recently a talented

Psychological Effects 10

Columbine basketball star hanged himself because of the grief he felt at having witnessed the murder. Incidents like these are not uncommon and occur mainly because of the psychological side effects of school violence. Many organizations and psychologists offer advice for coping with school violence and some of the best ways are explained below.

Note how the social sciences rely on specific cases to support their argument as well as on more quantified statistical evidence.

Discussion

The Discussion section allows the writer to illustrate the significance of the findings and results to her own topic.

One of the best ways to help children avoid developing a mental disorder from school violence is to help them directly at the scene of violence as it occurs (National Institute, 1999b). According to NIMH (1999), any adult at a disaster scene can:

- Find ways to protect children further from danger by creating a "safe haven" or sheltering them from onlookers and media coverage
- Stay with any children who seem to be in acute distress like panicking or trembling, intense grief or loud crying or rage until they can be calmed
- Reassure children verbally or non-verbally (like a hug) to make them feel safe

The family is typically the first resource that can help a child after school violence has occurred. The child who has the most family support will be the one to recover more fully. Parents should let their children know that it is okay to feel upset, while reassuring any fears, allowing them to cry or be sad, and letting them feel that they have some control in their lives. One of the worst mistakes that parents can make is rushing their child back to school too soon. This is because children need time to talk about their feelings and feel reassured before they return to the previously violent atmosphere (National Institute, 1999b).

The responsibility to help children psychologically after school violence also goes beyond the home. It is a parental and community responsibility for all parents to look out for their children, and also their children's friends. In a CNN special program entitled *Listening After*

Psychological Effects 11

Littleton, adolescents as well as some survivors of the Columbine shootings offer their advice to parents in supporting their children and helping them to cope. They suggest that parents "open dialogue and listen, don't be judging or accusatory," and "don't authorize; go to their level and be open to listening." Alisha Basore, a Columbine survivor whose best friend died in the tragedy, had this to say in the program: "What made these kids feel that death was the only way out?" (CNN, 1999). For this reason alone, the manner in which parents react in front of their children is very important. The AACAP (2000a) stresses that minimizing the danger will not ease the concern of children; instead, they (the parents) should stress that they are also able to cope with the situation.

Note use of specific cases—typical of the social sciences.

Conclusion

Hopefully this article has helped to show you how important it is for all of those dedicated to the lives and futures of children—family, peers, teachers, and innumerable others—to come together to form a protective barrier to help children both physically and mentally after school violence. Treating students who experience the emotional and psychological consequences of violence should be a team effort. Steve Davolt (1999) stresses, "Students who escape violent events physically unscathed often present school-based providers with injuries not so readily apparent. Treatment of these students is crucial, because it goes to the heart of the culture that allows violent tendencies to flourish." Meanwhile, Hazler (1996) urges that "families of victims tend to put significantly more energy into protection and guidance of the child than they place on encouraging independence of thought and action so they will be able to function on their own when not with the family." Whether supporters of children suffering from the after-effects of school violence are understanding, helpful, and instructive, disappointed, respectful, angry, rejecting or degrading during the early stages of coping will have a significant impact on the child's future progress (Hazler, 1996). Hazler again urges, "Victims

The conclusion allows the writer to present her own summation of the findings and discussion, relating both to her specific topic.

Psychological Effects 12

need to know that they are not in this alone." Children will gain confidence from overcoming their grief from school violence, and this increases the likelihood that they will seek new challenges in their lives and have less fears associated with the violence.

Given all these findings, physicians can also screen for the effects of violence exposure during routine check-ups, or similar checking can be done in guidance offices (Singer et al., 1995). Services like these could really help children. Singer et al. insist, "We must consider exposure to violence a public health epidemic worthy of our most comprehensive and well-reasoned efforts" (p. 480).

References

American Academy of Child and Adolescent Psychiatry. (2000a).
    Helping children after a disaster. [online] Retrieved March 7,
    2001, from the World Wide Web:
    http://www.aacap.org/publications/factsfam/disaster.htm.
American Academy of Child and Adolescent Psychiatry. (2000b).
    AACAP home: 1999 violence fact sheet. Retrieved March 9, 2001,
    from the World Wide Web: http://www.aacap.org/info
    families/NationalFacts/99violFctsh.htm.
Aronson, E. (2000). Nobody left to hate: Teaching compassion after
    Columbine. New York: Worth Publishers.
Baldwin, D. (1999). You are not alone: By the American Red Cross.
    Retrieved March 11, 2001, from the World Wide Web:
    http://www.trauma-pages.com/notalone.htm.
Center for Mental Health Service. (2000). School violence prevention.
    Retrieved March 7, 2001, from the World Wide Web:
    http://www.mentalhealth.org/schoolviolence/index.htm.

List of sources in APA style is titled "References" and centered on the page.

Since there are two articles by this author in the same year, the *a* allows the writer to distinguish one from the other.

When citing electronic sources, include the date of retrieval.

Electronic sources include URL or Web address.

In APA style, article titles are not in quotation marks, and only the first word and proper nouns are capitalized.

Psychological Effects 13

Chandras, K. V. (1999). Coping with adolescent school violence: Implications for counseling. <u>College Student Journal, 33,</u> 302–312.

CNN. (1999). <u>A CNN town meeting: Listening after Littleton.</u> Turning Learning, Inc.

Davolt, S. (1999). School tragedies alter clinician's roles. <u>ASHA Leader, 4,</u> 1.

DeAngelis, T. (2000). In the aftermath of Columbine. Retrieved March 5, 2001, from the World Wide Web: http://www.apa.org/monitor/sep00/columbine.html.

Hazler, R. J. (1996). <u>Breaking the Cycle of Violence: Interventions for Bullying and Victimization.</u> Washington, D. C.: Accelerated Development.

Mazza, J. J., Reynolds, W. M. (1999). Exposure to violence in young inner-city adolescents: Relationship with suicidal ideation, depression, and PTSD symptomatology. <u>Journal of Abnormal Child Psychology, 27,</u> 203–218.

National Institute of Mental Health. (1999a). Child and adolescent violence research at the NIMH. Retrieved March 7, 2001, from the World Wide Web: http://www.nimh.nih.gov.publicat/violencerestfact.cfm.

National Institute of Mental Health. (1999b). Helping children and adolescents cope with violence and disasters. Retrieved March 4, 2001, from the World Wide Web: http:/www/nimh.nih.gov/publicat/violence.cfm.

Schwartz, D., Proctor, L. J. (2000). Community violence exposure and children's social adjustment in the school peer group: The mediating roles of emotion regulation and social cognition. <u>Journal of Consulting and Clinical Psychology, 68,</u> 670–683.

Precise page numbers from paper journals should be included.

In APA style, book titles are underlined or italicized as in MLA style. Each important word is also capitalized.

Journal names are underlined, and the underlining continues under the volume number, unlike MLA style.

Note the use of authoritative refereed journals for credibility.

Psychological Effects 14

Shalala, D. E. (2000). Youth violence: A report of the Surgeon General. Retrieved March 12, 2001, from the World Wide Web: http://www.surgeongeneral.gov/library/youthviolence/report. html.

Simons, J. (2000, September 17). New books emerge after Columbine shooting. <u>Denver Rocky Mountain News,</u> p. F14.

Singer, M. I., Anglin, T. M., Song, L. Y., Lunghofer, L. (1995). Adolescents' exposure to violence and associated symptoms of psychological trauma. <u>Journal of the American Medical Association, 273,</u> 477–482.

Vatz, R. E., Weinberg, L. S. (1999, September 15). School murders and the limits of psychiatry. <u>USA Today,</u> 58–59.

Citations of newspapers and weekly magazines include the month and year as shown.

With less than six authors, all are named on the reference page.

Popular sources like newspapers can add details to a researched paper, but they are not sufficient in themselves to make your case within academic disciplines or specialized fields.

Rebecca Delli Carpini

Dr. Patricia Johnson

HUM 500

Essay #2: "Jenny" and Pre-Raphaelite Painting

Interart Analogies: The Space between Rossetti's
"Sister Arts" in "Jenny" and *Found*

The Pre-Raphaelite period in Victorian England, a turbulent time both socially and morally, gave rise to a new female icon as prostitutes became labeled "fallen women" in a society that on its surface was laced-up and prudish. These women, who represented a "recognizable and sizable segment of the population" (Lee 1), became an object of fascination for artists and writers of the time. They explored the more intricate levels of this social phenomenon, complicating simplistic moral judgments by portraying the "fallen woman" within a deeper social and personal context. Recognizing the artist's role as social critic, the Pre-Raphaelite artists not only addressed the complex issues and emotions that surround "fallen women," but they strove to depict this complex situation in written and visual art forms with an apparent degree of sympathy.

This essay will explore the analogous treatment of the idea of the "fallen woman" in two Pre-Raphaelite artworks of Dante Gabriel Rossetti—the 1869 poem "Jenny" and the unfinished painting *Found* (1853–59). Extending the theory of interart analogy set forth in Troy Thomas' "Interart Analogy: Practice and Theory in Comparing the Arts," this essay will examine how analogous techniques in painting and poetry are especially vivid when the two works are produced by the same hand.

Thomas' method recognizes the structural differences of varied art forms, and argues that rather than focusing upon the "similar" methods of these "sister arts" (poetry and painting) one might more accurately focus upon the analogical translation that takes place when "reading" a painting as opposed to "reading" a poem or other written text. That is, "analogous

Delli Carpini 2

relationships may be defined as ones in which comparisons of similar features, characteristics, attributes, or effects are made between otherwise unlike things, that is different arts" (18).

Page number is cited, but not the author, since the author is named in the opening of the paragraph.

This paragraph discusses the theoretical methodology that will be used in this analysis. This is typical of essays in the humanities.

Because these different arts, by their very nature, involve varied artistic processes and techniques, the most viable form of interdisciplinary critique must be "subsumed under analogy" rather than mere "structural similarity of form" (18). Briefly, this reliance upon "analogy" rather than "equivalence" among formal features requires an intermediate step in the process of interdisciplinary critique—a step that allows for "the differences that arise when the crucial factor of artistic medium is taken into account" (18). The process of accounting for such differences analogically is termed "translation."

For example, one might consider poetic symbolism to be "similar" to a painter's use of iconography; however, the arts involved are different enough to require a more elaborate system of interpretation. Using analogy, one might instead attempt to account for the "different characters of the media" involved (21). Thus, the mediating factor in this analogy would ask us to account not only for the similarities in the forms, but for the differences that arise due to the unique features of each form. In effect, we would need to consider the following logical formula:

Theory is explicated in more detail through example.

Symbol : poetry :: iconography : painting

This system of "translation," goes beyond showing similarity; instead, it produces richer interpretations because they not only try to examine the works involved, but also to uncover the nature of the analogy that ties one art form to the other. Using Thomas' method, then, we might ask how Rossetti translates the Victorian cultural notion of the "fallen woman" in the space between poetry and painting; specifically, this analysis will focus upon a series of key analogies that represent the fallen woman within two opposing worlds: the pure world of the country versus the treacherous world of the city.

Delli Carpini 3

Subheadings allow the writer to organize the argument that follows for her readers.

Analogy 1: Characterization: Poetry:: Value: Painting

In "Jenny," the narrator of the poem makes value judgments about the sleeping, inactive character of a prostitute whose services he has enlisted. The narrative value judgments cast upon Jenny contrast with judgments he holds about his betrothed cousin, Nell, "the girl that he is proudest of" and who possesses "lips that tell the truth." The narrator introduces a metaphor to capture the difference between Nell and Jenny's character.

The first time line numbers from a poem are cited, they are preceded with "lines." This tells the reader that the numbers refer to lines, not pages.

> The potter's power over the clay!
> Of the same lump (it has been said)
> For honour and dishonour made,
> Two sister vessels. Here is one. (lines 181–84)

Though Jenny performs no actions in the poem, the narrator weaves Jenny's "fallenness" into the fabric of the poem through his comparative assessments of her character.

Substantial portions of a poem (more than a line or two) are cited in block quotation, retaining the original line structure.

After a long description of Nell's purity and truth, he turns metaphorically to what has been made of the other "lump" of clay, Jenny:

Close analysis and interpretation of text is offered, as is often the case with articles in the humanities and especially in literary studies.

> Of the same lump (as it is said)
> For honour and dishonour made,
> Two sister vessels. Here is one.
> It makes a goblin of the sun.
> So pure—so fall'n (203–07)

Line numbers are usually used to cite poetry. After the first citation, you need not include the word "lines."

The narrator's characterizations of Jenny, however, are balanced by his own self-evaluation. His focus shifts back and forth between judgments upon his own character, "like a toad within a stone" (282), and his critical vision of the sleeping Jenny. His opinion of her is hence erratic—it continuously shifts from "compassion to condescension" (Noclin 73), from lust to disgust with man's role in creating the fallen woman. He is, for example, somewhat penitent in "having used you at

In the humanities, direct quotations from both primary and secondary sources are more frequent than in the sciences.

Titles of paintings are italicized or underlined.

Studies in the humanities frequently explore aesthetic methods. Here, the painter's techniques and their effect upon the viewer are explored in detail.

Writer uses secondary evidence as support for her argument.

Delli Carpini 4

his will" (86). In this way, the narrator assigns moral value through his use of characterization.

In *Found*, Rossetti uses a visual translation of value (the comparative degree of light to darkness) as a formal-artistic element to perform a similar type of character evaluation of the female subject. He has chosen to depict the background setting, her previous home amidst the pure and moral country life, as filled with light; this (visual and temporal) background is set against the darkened, urban setting of the "fallen" woman. As Noclin notes, this use of value functions as a visual "metaphor of despair" for Rossetti's "fallen woman" (73). In the visual art form, the artist only has a single "still" frame to depict both past and present, morality and fallenness. Therefore, he must rely on the viewer to play the role assumed by the narrator in the poem, and to employ the visual cues that Rossetti has set forth for interpretation. In this way, the value judgments upon character presented in the poem, through interart analogical translation, are presented in the form of the painting's use of value.

Analogy 2: Composition : Painting :: Stanza : Poetry

Rossetti is adept at depicting the narrative element in his visual works through his use of deliberate compositional choices. As discussed above, he uses visual metaphors to separate and divide the "fallen" women's previous "moral" life with her current "sinful" life. These compositional elements effectively present the dichotomy of her life using the foreground as her darkened city life while choosing to express her former (morally) brighter country life through an intricate, but far away, photographic background. Rossetti has successfully used this technique of "multiple planes" within other works such as *Beata Beatrix 1877*, as has been noted by Susan P. Casteras (143), who also recognizes the deliberate compositional choices of Rossetti. This view of multiple

Delli Carpini 5

planes not only implies the two contrasting worlds of the woman, but it also demonstrates the passage of time.

Rossetti employs visual formal elements that emphasize the "fallen" woman's separation and division from the urban setting—a setting in which Rossetti himself lives. These divisional elements (the wall, the bridge, the strong use of value) may be interpreted as a visual clue as to the woman's position, or "dis-position," within the Victorian Society.

Cultural analysis is a frequently used method in recent essays in the humanities.

Also, although she appears to be in the marketplace, she seems isolated from the normal happenings of the urban society. And even further away from her is the past—the honest, simple country life that is clearly of the "other" world (the more brightly lit world) beyond the Blackfriars Bridge. Further, Rossetti has placed her slumped-fallen body against a wall that has been identified as the church wall—further emphasizing the division that separates her from the moral society.

Note careful description of details that are used to support the argument.

Weathers, for example, sees these compositional elements as deliberate, calculated details drawn from the geography of Rossetti's London: The painting's backdrop is "near Blackfriars Bridge (a frequent place for a prostitute) in London" and the "brick wall is modeled after one found in Chiswick" (100).

In the poetic version of the fallen woman, Rossetti effectively depicts this division of worlds and the temporally based "falling" of Jenny through the division of stanzas within the poem (so, though Jenny is "fallen," we can also see her "falling").

Note the attention to wordplay—a key element of literary works and interpretation.

First, we are presented with a vision of Jenny's past countrified life, "old days" that she can remember "haply at times" (124–25):

Note how frequently that primary sources are referred to and analyzed in literary studies.

> Much older that any history
> That is written in any book:
> When she would lie in fields and look
> Along the ground through the blown grass,

> And wonder where the city was.
> Far out of sight, whose broil and bale
> They told her then for a child's tale. (126–34)

This stanza shows, in retrospect, the linguistic division between the "old days" (previous simple, honest country life) and the current city life where the "market-lists are bought and sold" (138) and where Jenny herself has become commodified, bought and sold on "Saturday night . . . Market-night" (140). This dichotomy, supported by the division in stanzas in ways analogous to the compositional divisions in *Found*, suggests that Jenny has lost the "goodness" of the old days and has become a "fallen" woman within the urban society. This division is further amplified as the stanza continues:

> Our Learned London children know,
> Poor Jenny, all your pride and woe;
> Have seen your lifted silken skirt
> Advertise dainties through the dirt; (143–46)

Analogous to the compositional divisions in *Found*, these details, separated both temporally and spatially (by the stanza break), detail the two worlds of Jenny and the moral white space between them.

Analogy 3: Rhythm : Painting :: Plot : Poem

Among the effects created by a painting's compositional elements is rhythm. Created in a variety of ways (line, color, shape, etc.), it moves the viewer's attention across a canvas in the ways determined by the painter. Used carefully, this rhythm can simulate a temporal movement analogous to a verbally based plot, which moves a reader's attentions from moment to moment.

In *Found*, a two-dimensional, single frame artwork manages to create a plot-like rhythm despite the restrictions of the form. For

Consistent section titles and numbering can create an organized essay for the reader, though subheadings are usually reserved for longer papers.

Note the attention to technique in fine arts analysis.

Delli Carpini 7

example, the cart suggests earlier actions of the male figure—he has come to town (crossing the Blackfriars Bridge); he has come to town for a purpose (selling his calf at market as indicated by the netted calf); he has discovered a fallen woman; and he is in the process of lifting her from that state. All these formal elements provide a temporal rhythm for the painting. That "plot" has given rise to many interpretations of the story depicted: like her, he came from the country to do business; the woman he had "found" is perhaps a past lover from the country; the woman he has found is morally fallen into prostitution; and so on.

Rossetti analogously depicts the narrative passage of time in the poem through his use of verbal plot devices. He first creates a frame for the narrative through the story of the prostitute, Jenny, who has fallen asleep on his lap. This frame tale allows Rossetti to move his narrator through a series of thoughts regarding his past, present, and future life. Through this series of thoughts, the narrator provides the reader with the contexts of this single moment. Earlier, he has met her in a dance hall; they have gone back to her room; she falls asleep; while she sleeps, he compares her room to his room "so full of books" (23); and given this time alone, he ponders on his absence from his own room and his own immorality "as to-night [his] work was left;" (29).

This reverie continues to unfold until the morning when, the narrator muses,

> I think I see you when you wake,
> And rub your eyes for me, and shake
> My gold, in rising, from your hair (376–78)

This internal monologue, analogous to the rhythm of the painting, guides the reader through a series of temporal moments that are all contained in this single scenario.

Careful attention to visual details is crucial to analysis of the fine arts.

Writer shows the relationships between the paragraphs with this transition.

Note the careful attention to diction necessary for the study of poetry.

Delli Carpini 8

Both painter and poet, Rossetti provides an intriguing example of artistic commitment to the contemporary themes of the Pre-Raphaelite Victorian period, a complicated period in England's history socially, politically, and morally.

The writer begins her conclusion by returning to the original topic. In a short paper, there is no need to label it as "conclusion," though the voice should make it clear that a summation has begun.

Rossetti's engagement with these complex issues was made all the more effective through the analogous links made between and within Rossetti's two art forms. The concept of the "fallen" woman as it existed within his society was portrayed all the more effectively in the space between the visual and the verbal. And, in turn, that space becomes both more accessible, and richer, when one employs principles and practices of interart analogy suggested by Thomas.

Through the translation process (from written to visual art forms) we can locate and explore the analogous elements of each work.

Reiteration of methods used.

Having two common bases, Rossetti himself and the cultural theme of the fallen woman, makes such a translation of the sister arts even more cohesive, and extends the capabilities of Thomas' interart analogy. As illustrated in the above examination of Rossetti's companion pieces, "Jenny" and *Found*, interart analogy provides a richer field of interpretation from which to feel the traces of the Victorian "fallen" woman (and so to move closer to Stephen Greenblatt's new historicist goals of hearing from the dead).

Notes larger implications of the methods for future work in this area.

In MLA style, the list of sources can be titled "Works Cited," which indicates that all sources on the list are directly referenced in the paper itself, or it can be titled "Works Consulted," which indicates that the list contains both sources that are directly cited and others that influenced the author but are not cited directly in the paper.

Book titles are underlined or italicized.

"Ed." indicates a book's editor.

URL or web address listed.

Title of article or book chapter is in quotation marks, and all major words are capitalized.

Titles of paintings are underlined or italicized. The electronic site from which the image was taken is also identified.

Delli Carpini 9

Works Consulted

Casteras, Susan P. "Pre-Raphaelite Portraiture: A Strangely Disordered Vision." In <u>Collecting the Pre-Raphaelites: The Anglo-American Enchantment.</u> Ed. Margaretta Frederick Watson. Brookfield, VT: Ashgate, 1997: 139–148.

Lee, Elizabeth. "Fallen Women in Victorian Art." <u>The Victorian Web.</u> Brown University. 9 Sept. 2002 http://www.artchive.com/artchive/R/Rossetti/rossetti_found.jog.html

Nochlin, Linda. "Lost and Found: Once More the Fallen Woman." In <u>Women, Art, and Power and Other Essays.</u> New York: Harper & Row. 1988: 57–85.

Rossetti, Dante Gabriel. <u>Found.</u> 1856. <u>The Artchive.</u> 18 Sept. 2002 http://www.artchive.com/artchive/R/Rossetti/rossetti_found.jog. html.

Sheets, Robin. "Pornography and Art: The Case of 'Jenny.'" In <u>Critical Essays on Dante Gabriel Rossetti.</u> Ed. David G. Riede. New York: Macmillan, 1992: 149–168.

Thomas, Troy. "Interart Analogy: Practice and Theory in Comparing the Arts." <u>The Journal of Aesthetic Education</u> 252 (1991): 17–36.

Weathers, Rachel. "The Pre-Raphaelite Movement and Nineteenth-Century Ladies' Dress: A Study in Victorian Views of the Female Body." In <u>Collecting the Pre-Raphaelites: The Anglo-American Enchantment.</u> Ed. Margaretta Frederick Watson. Brookfield, VT: Ashgate, 1997: 95–108.

Citations are separated by using hanging indents for all lines other than the first.

Journal titles are italicized, and journals are cited by volume number, year, and page number.

Date the electronic document was accessed.

Source of material collected electronically is noted. In this case, the affiliation lends credibility.

VISUAL RHETORIC

Though as students you must learn the academic styles noted above, you should also consider other available formats. Those who use writing in the workplace can help you to understand how visual rhetoric generally, and document design specifically, is used in professional discourse—and why it is important for you to learn some of the available techniques as you practice writing in college. Jane Whittaker, in her role as systems architect, writes:

> I use many of the design features in Word, mainly font changes, bolding, italicizing, bullets—lots of bullets. I change color, indent sections, and insert graphics. All of this is to highlight important concepts, draw attention to the logical progression of an argument and its conclusions, or make it easy for a busy senior executive to run her (oh, alright, his) eyes down the page and get the major points without having to read every word.

Even more directly, Robert Colleluori's work as owner of an advertising firm forces him to consider the persuasive capabilities of visual rhetoric:

> In our business, look and feel has a lot to do with what we say. It helps to express how we want our message to be heard. Sometimes, when I write something, I put side notes to the creative department to "add bells and whistles" like "bold this," "use a script font here," "make this certain letter smaller or larger," "italicize," etc. It helps deliver the word or set of words more effectively. This has always been true in the advertising business. There was always that control of enhancement opportunity. Now technology allows this to happen in word documents for those outside of the advertising or graphic design fields as well. Despite those technologies, however, I feel that the first test is whether the writing could be received in the way it's intended without all those bells and whistles—that's strong writing.
>
> With that said, there is no doubt that pictures, illustrations, and images "are worth a thousand words." It all starts with writing, though. We put in words that which we want to say, what message we want to deliver. But we also know that we have a limited amount of time to deliver that message, for example, on a billboard. On average, there are only a few seconds that a driver has to read or get the message from a billboard. After it's all written out, then I ask, "What image can eliminate the words to get the message across in the given amount of time that the viewer has? And with impact! What color is more readable and applies to the feel that we want to portray? What font and style will add to the consistent message?"

WRITING TO EXPLORE 10.3

Over the next few days, pay special attention to the design, message, and effectiveness of bulletin boards, bumper stickers, and posters you encounter. In your writer's notebook, list the uses of design, color, and images that you find particularly effective.

In technical fields, the enhancements available with new technologies are equally important. Eric Engle's work as a geologist requires him to produce lengthy reports that very much rely on specific document formats:

> All of our reports are done on Word. The old acronym KISS ("Keep It Simple, Stupid"), used by one of my geology professors at Lock Haven University, is good advice. Since most of the work and reporting we do is very similar (just different results), we can use boilerplates of former reports. I use Excel to make attractive data tables and charts. In addition, our drafting department creates maps and figures to help show what we are talking about. Usually, the text portion of the report is around 30 pages; the supporting data tables, charts and figures add up closer to 100–200 pages.

PRINCIPLES OF DOCUMENT DESIGN

Give a young child a new box of crayons or a set of paints, and there is little that he won't try to create with them. Children are fearless, and so invent some of the most fantastical of color combinations, creatures, and scenarios. It is this playfulness that allows them to learn so quickly. This is also one of the reasons that young children learn the possibilities of computer technology with such facility; they are unconcerned with limits and have no fear of going down blind alleyways. My own children are constantly teaching me capabilities of my computer that they discovered simply by happy accident.

Such inventiveness is crucial to document design. But, of course, there is more to it than that. Once you have explored the possibilities, you must be judicious choosing among them, since your documents usually have serious purposes that can be undermined by overly garish document enhancement. Web designers have learned this. They remind us that sites that use all the available bells and whistles (and so obscure the actual message) may not, in the end, be as effective as the simpler designs that choose carefully among available technologies based on the purpose of the site.

You might apply this same thinking to document design. We have suddenly, as a culture, been given access to a wealth of document enhancement possibilities that two decades ago were available only through the most advanced of print shops. Now we can incorporate images, change fonts, develop hyperlinks, and even use color. It's difficult to imagine for those who did not live in the time before affordable word processing, but not that long ago we could not even italicize or boldface a passage. We were left with underlining and techniques of punctuation to control emphasis and tone.

The sudden onslaught of available design techniques, unfortunately, does not come with an equally sudden understanding of how to use them decorously and with audience and purpose in mind. That's something that you need to continue to develop as a communicator, and something about which you must make decisions each time you are asked to deliver a document or oral presentation.

You can make such individual decisions, like other rhetorical choices, by considering audience, purpose, discourse community, exigency, and so on, but there are general guidelines that can help to guide those decisions as well. Let's explore some of those principles of document design, realizing that they are just rules of thumb that must be customized to fit any given situation.

Keep It Simple

Since, as Colleluori notes above, visual rhetoric is a relatively quick and often subliminal form of communication, it is important that your designs are simple enough to be taken in by the viewer at a glance—and that they don't, in the process, distract the reader from your purposes. When the visual rhetoric is meant to *supplement* your message rather than *be* the message (which it sometimes is, as in billboards), it is crucial that the design be used as a type of punctuation. Though the word *punctuation*, in writing talk, means the marks like commas and periods, it also means "stress or emphasis." The two meanings are not unrelated. The use of punctuation marks is designed to stress to readers the points the writer is making, the message he is delivering. Document design functions as a form of punctuation as well, providing readers with visual cues to the ways you want them to read your document. When you boldface, for example, you draw extra attention to a word, phrase, or longer passage. That can be effective. But if I were to boldface this entire page, would that bring any emphasis to it? Not likely. By emphasizing everything, I lose the key power of boldfacing—contrasting a heavy font with surrounding lighter fonts.

This same principle applies more generally to other principles of design. Multiple design techniques can compete with one another, causing a type of overload that distracts the reader from what might be your most important messages. So keeping your designs simple can allow you to choose more precisely what it is you wish to emphasize.

Keep It Clear

As difficult as it is to keep your words, sentences, and paragraphs logical and focused, controlling the design of your page and its effects can be even more difficult. Gauging the subliminal and visceral reactions that your graphics and page design will inspire in readers is much like considering which jacket or shoes to wear for a big interview.

One thing to keep in mind with serious writing tasks—the kinds of writing you do in school or on the job—is that an audience is unlikely to be impressed purely by design or graphics. Though such enhancements can certainly improve the effectiveness of your message, the key is still clarity. Your document design and visuals should neither obscure the written text nor draw attention from it. Instead, they should subtly reinforce your message, and therefore make that message clearer. Here are several ways that your design can help to simplify and clarify, rather than obscure, your message.

First, consider when something you need to communicate might be digested more easily by your audience in a bulleted list, graph, or chart than in a paragraph. In many cases, such types of communication combine words and design to help readers remember information or claims. You might, to consider this issue, look back over the places in this book where I and the editors decided to use bullets, images, charts, and so on to make our point. Then consider why we made such choices.

Keep It Limited and Consistent

Logical flow also requires you to consider document design, to keep a consistent message and focus. As Whittaker suggests, the goal of document design techniques is to "highlight important concepts, draw attention to the logical progression of an argument and its conclusions, or make it easy for a busy senior executive to run her eyes down the page and get the major points without having to read every word." You can also help to clarify your message by using headings and subheadings to emphasize the relationships among your ideas. As we discussed in the context of transitions, readers often need help following the line of logic that you are attempting to establish within a document. Especially if the document is relatively long, using headings and subheadings can help readers to see the hierarchy of your ideas, much as in an outline.

When you group ideas under a heading, you provide a context for those ideas. For example, if you title a section "Potential Solutions," you alert your readers that what follows should be read in the context of problems raised earlier and ask them to consider the viability of each possible solution you present. Within that section, you might have subheadings for each of the potential solutions, or use verbal cues to indicate the relationship of the ideas: "First," "Another possible approach to solving the problem," etc. In either case, the goal is to keep the message clear by helping readers to see the relationships among your ideas, the hierarchy that relates one idea to another, and the overall structure of the piece. Note the use of headings, bullets, and numbering to organize information in the excerpt that follows.

Getting the Most from the Entry-Level Job

George Adderley

As we've been discussing, the entry-level job is a necessity for most professionals—a place to start and a way to gain experience. But if you treat the entry-level job as a kind of purgatory—a place where you suffer until you're allowed into heaven—the wait can be long.

A more productive way to look at the entry-level job is to explore its possibilities, and to take careful note of every new skill, technique, or responsibility you gain. By keeping track of the various learning experiences, you are at the same time developing a tool kit of skills and a road map to other potential jobs. More importantly, you are learning to be an inventive, innovative, and engaged worker. Rather than view the job as "beneath you" or "not what you went to school for," you should consider it a chance to gain the valuable experiences that will make you ready for the right job—in that organization or in another—when it comes along.

Moving Beyond the Entry-Level Job

Though you should always strive to get the most from entry-level jobs, you should also be ready when a better job comes along. One way to do so is to regularly check classified ads and on-line job services like Monster.com. But there are more subtle ways to "keep your eyes open" when it comes to the job market.

In most professional positions, you are not isolated within your own work-space. People who represent other firms that do business with yours, clients who are in other related lines of work, business associates, professionals with whom you have regular contact in doing your job—they are all potential sources of that first move. So, doing your work well in an entry-level job not only shows your current employer the value you have, but it also shows other potential employers that you are a good worker.

Of course, asking those various people about possible openings can some-times be a bit uncomfortable. But if you do your job well, and you listen closely, you will sometimes hear the right moment when it comes:

- you are complimented on your work and told "I wish my employees had your commitment"
- you are processing an order for art supplies, and mention to the client—a graphic designer—what you know about that work, and how you enjoy it
- you are at a meeting with superiors, and find just the right moment to make a suggestion that shows your expertise.

Moments like these are the ones that can help you make that first big move beyond the entry-level job. Be sure that you're ready for them.

Keeping an Updated Credentials File

Being "ready" for the moment when it comes requires some work and planning. If a person that you encounter in your current job says to you, "You know, I'd love to see your résumé," you don't want to have to scamper home at the end of a long day and start from scratch (though you will always have to customize).

And you don't want to rush others either—others who may need to write you a letter of recommendation. So be prepared with that credentials file.

Contents of a Credentials File

1. **An up-to date resume template:** Résumés need to be customized for every job for which we apply. But that doesn't mean we're starting from scratch each time. If you have a skeletal résumé as an electronic file, it is much quicker and easier to add to it, cut and paste to rearrange, add new skills, etc.

2. **A cover letter template:** Like the résumé, the cover letter also needs to be customized for the occasion. But there are certain elements of a good cover letter that you can prepare in advance, and so be ready when the right opportunity comes up.

Another way to make your document's message clear is by the visual look of your page and, specifically, by the use of contrast and white space. When we discussed the arrangement of ideas in your writing, I noted that readers read from left to right and up to down. And they do—*except when we ask them not to.* In order to keep the organization of your ideas as clear and focused as possible, you must use the principles of contrast and white space.

White space has always been crucial to writing—think about how paragraph or section breaks indicate to readers a pause and shift in topics simply by leaving blank space. But with new word-processing capabilities, you can design in ways that draw attention to those elements on a page that you most want readers to notice. You can do so by surrounding those elements with white space and by adding extra contrast with the white space (more emphatic fonts, boldfacing, borders, etc.). When you create such contrasts, you draw your reader's eye to a specific part of the page—a part that you, as a writer, have decided ought to receive special (and immediate) attention. As with other parts of this process, however, be careful what you ask for, and don't sacrifice clarity to garish design.

When you don't want to distract readers, be sure that your inclusion of charts, tables, or other graphics looks just like business as usual—using the same or a similar font as the body text, less bolding, thinner borders, less white space. This matter-of-fact presentation is common in journal articles and internal occupational documents, where the goal is to maintain a professional and understated demeanor. The most obvious case where you ask readers *not* to follow their usual reading technique is when you design a page that draws the eye to somewhere other than the top of the page. Imagine, for example, that you are reading an article; you turn from a page that is wholly text to the following page.

from Racial Trends in Satisfaction with Police

Matthew V. Robinson

The relationship between race and satisfaction with police is well documented. Numerous studies have proven that African Americans are less satisfied with the police than whites (Murphy & Worrall, 1999; Brown & Benedict, 2002; Reisig & Parks, 2000; Brandl & Frank & Worden & Bynum, 1994). However, there are also studies that prove that African Americans are just as satisfied or more satisfied with the police than whites (Sims & Hooper & Peterson, 1999; Brandl & Frank & Worden & Bynum, 1994; Reisig, & Correia, 1997). In a study in Detroit, African Americans were found to be more satisfied with police than whites (Frank & Brandl & Cullen & Stichman, 1996). This could be attributed to the fact that in Detroit, African Americans make up the majority of the police force. Contradictions such as these show that other factors are playing a role in satisfaction with police. Furthermore, little research has been conducted on other races such as Alaska Natives; for instance, when other races are included they are all grouped into one "other" category (Klaus, 2000).

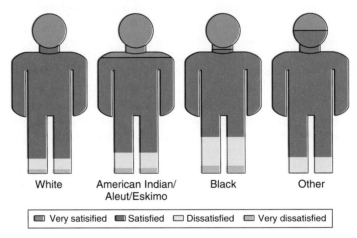

Results of Anchorage, Alaska study showed
no significant difference in satisfaction with
police due to race, questioning past assumptions

Using data collected by the Anchorage Adult Crime Victimization Survey (AACVS), a telephone survey was administered using a random-digit dialing (RDD) method. After the RDD method produced a list of numbers, the list was given to an agency which eliminated the non-working and non-residential numbers. This lowered the amount of numbers from 6,000 to 3,460. The surveyors then called those 3,460 numbers between the hours 10:00 am and 5:00 pm and between the hours of 7:00 pm and 9:00 pm. Of the numbers called, 733 produced completed interviews for a response rate of 32 percent (Giblin & Robinson, 2003).

The dependent variable was satisfaction. It was measured by asking the question, "In general, how satisfied are you with the police who serve your neighborhood? Are you very satisfied, satisfied, dissatisfied, or very satisfied?" The independent variable examined was race. Participants were allowed to choose from "White, Black, American Indian/Aleut/Eskimo, and Other" (Giblin & Robinson, 2003).

This study, conducted in urban Anchorage, found that race had no affect on satisfaction with police, contradicting other studies that showed a large difference in satisfaction amongst the different racial groups.

Your eye is drawn immediately away from the top of the page and toward the graphic, which asks you to interrupt the flow of your reading and to notice the visual reinforcement of the message contained within the text itself. Such interruptions can be effective or ineffective, depending on the goals of the publication. In some cases, a well-placed visual can be just the thing to remind the readers of your overall purpose in writing, functioning much like a transition that reminds the reader of the big picture.

But, as with all facets of effective writing, you must consider how the design will keep your message clear. In some cases, an interruption from the flow of your text is not useful; it might be best to keep your reader's eye moving along consistently from up to down. Thus you would place your graphic within the borders of the body text and so indicate the precise spot in the reading process where readers should encounter the visual, whether it be graph, chart, image, text box, or table.

In these examples, though the graphics are separate from the text itself, they are meant to supplement the main article's text, not draw the reader into a related but separate piece.

Effect of Habitat Fragmentation on Red Fox (*Vulpes vulpes*) Population Health in Northern York County

Jeremy M. Hamsher

The ever increasing suburbanization of the rural countryside of America leaves many questions about the future of wildlife in these areas. An effect of this rapid population increase is habitat fragmentation. Fragmentation separates populations of organisms from food sources, water and other con-specifics (Gaines 1997). However, while fragmentation detrimentally affects some species, it may allow others to exploit new resources (Gehring 2003). The organisms that can exploit a fragmented landscape can move from a population under control to an overpopulated burden on the ecosystem (DeStefano 2003). A species which is adapted over a wide variety of environments may be better able to respond to landscape changes from human impact. In northern York County, Pennsylvania, little is known about the effect of fragmentation on the red fox (*Vulpes vulpes*). Along with the effects of fragmentation, little is known about the population structure and overall health. The effect of fragmentation in York County is important because it could be used as a management model for other similar areas. The niche breadth of the red fox has yet to be characterized for this broken landscape. By determining the population dynamics in response to human-induced fragmentation, management plans can be developed to help maintain healthy populations of this species in human rich environments (Gehring 2003). This study attempts to assess population health and determine if habitat fragmentation has a detrimental effect on red fox distributions and densities.

Methods

Various trapping locations were located by habitat type and levels of habitat fragmentation using digital photo-orthoquads. We then trapped foxes at each location using #1 1/2 foothold traps and dirt hole sets. Morphological measurements of foxes captured were taken, and incidence of mange and degree to which the animal is affected was recorded. A canine tooth was removed for age analysis and stomach contents were examined. Rodents were trapped using a mark-recapture survey to determine food availability at each location.

Results

The frequency distribution of body weights and frequency distribution of femur lengths were first determined.

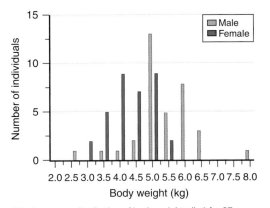

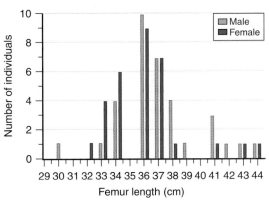

The frequency distribution of body weights (kg) for 37 female and 34 male foxes.
Female mean body weight = 4.273 kg
Male mean body weight = 5.462 kg
When analyzed using an unpaired T test, the means were not found to be significantly different.

The frequency distribution of femur lengths (cm) for 32 female and 34 male foxes as an index of growth and maturity.
Female mean femur length = 35.88 cm
Male mean femur length = 36.998 cm
When tested using an unpaired T test, the means were found to be not significantly different.

Then, the relationship between femur length and body weight for both males and females was studied to determine current trends in growth and development.

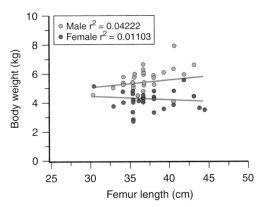

Correlation between femur length (cm) and body weight (kg) for both male and female red fox to show current trends of growth and development. Both r^2 values show little correlation between femur length and body weight.

Keep It Tasteful, Audience-Centered, and Appropriate

The previous example relates a simple but important point. Like the way you dress, the way you dress *your documents* says a great deal about you. The design of your documents carries with it visual cues about your tone and your understanding of what it means to be part of a disciplinary or professional discourse community. Those communities not only have preferred styles of argumentation but preferred styles of visual presentation as well.

Decisions you make about visual design, then, are not merely based on personal preferences but on the expectations of your audience and their sense of what is credible and appropriate in arguing a point. Since we have spent a good deal of time discussing ways to analyze the work done in various fields, you have likely already accumulated solid information on what various disciplines and occupational fields tend to value. The natural and social sciences, for example, share a concern with reliability of data and empirical (repeatable and observable) proof. For this reason, graphs, charts, and tables can be used to present in a clear and orderly fashion the results that you have garnered from primary research (your own experiments or studies) and secondary research (reporting and developing the results of experiments or studies done by others). You might then expect to see documents that look like this:

Methylation of an Upstream Alu Sequence on the Imprinted H19 Gene During Spermatogenesis in Rhesus Monkeys

Amanda Stafford

Introduction

Genomic imprinting involves "marking" parental alleles as either maternal or paternal. Such imprints are established during gamete production and involve differential DNA methylation. Unfortunately, however, the exact imprinting mechanism is unknown. DNA methylation is aided by the enzyme DNA methyltransferase, which adds methyl groups to 5'-cytosine residues of CpG islands; this methylation results in gene silencing. Previous studies have shown that differential DNA methylation patterns exist in the genome of sperm and eggs (Kierszenbaum 2002). One highly studied methylated/imprinted gene is H19. Research shows that H19 is methylated in sperm but not eggs. The paternal H19 allele is silenced due to hypermethylation. In contrast, the maternal allele is hypomethylated and, thus, expressed. How the paternal H19 imprint is made, however, is not fully understood. The upstream region of the H19 gene in primates contains an Alu sequence.

```
5' CTGGGTGCGG    TGGCTCACGA    CCAACCTGGC
   TAACACGGTG    AAACCCCATC    TCTACTAAAA
   ATACAAAAAA    TTAGCCGGGT    GAGGTGGTGG
   GCGCCTGTAG    TCCCACCTAC    TTGGGAGGCT
   GAGGCAGGAG    AATGGTGTGA    ACCCGGGAGG
   CGGAGCCTGC    AGTGAGCCGA    GATCATGCCA
   CTGCACTCCA    GCCTAGGGGA    CAGAGCGAGA
   CTCAAAAAAC    AAAAAACAAA    CAAAAA 3'
```

Upstream Alu sequence of the H19 gene. Highlighted areas indicate methylation sites. Pink is MspI/HpaII and blue is HhaI.

Expected results were determined based upon previous experiments by Davis et al. and Rubin et al., as shown in the following table.

Expected results based upon previous experimentation.			
	Upstream Alu	H19 (Davis et al.)	Alu (Rubin et al.)
Spermatogonia	hypomethylated	hypomethylated	—
Primary Spermatocyte	increased methylation	increased methylation	
Secondary Spermatocyte	methylation increase	methylation increase	
Round Spermatids	methylation increase	methylation increase	
Elongated Spermatids	hypermethylation	hypermethylation	hypermethylation

The social sciences and business fields also rely on a specific type of narrative evidence: case studies that illustrate how general principles can be demonstrated by or gleaned from actual cases. Case studies might involve individuals or groups. In some publications, then, you might find cases set off from the principles discussed in the body text. Such a page might look like this:

Not Another Essay! 20 Alternatives for English Teachers to Use in the Classroom

Stacy Crist

For many students, the assigning of an academic essay can be their worst nightmare. Let's face it, a great number of students just hate essays (and English teachers *love* essays). Sometimes it is hard for teachers to consider alternatives to the traditional essay. After all, essays assess a student's logic and how they synthesize information.

However, some students just do not succeed on essays. Studies on learning styles and various types of intelligence have suggested that for some students, positive learning experiences don't need to begin and end with the traditional essay. Though these students may work as hard as other students, they are simply not as capable of learning—and showing that learning—through essays. This is why other projects such as the twenty discussed here can be important in helping those students who are not as capable in the essay form.

But perhaps more importantly, allowing for a variety of formats and outlets for creativity, students can better discover both the joy of learning and the joy of writing. Though writing is most often thought of in the classroom in terms of the traditional essay, that is certainly not the only way that students can learn language skills. All the projects suggested in this study not only allow students to work to their strength and so allow them to have positive learning experiences. They also give students a great deal of practice in reading retention and writing creatively.

Sometimes, the graphics are designed to provide practical instructions or ways of putting the knowledge to use. For example, educational and other trade journals often include articles that provide strategies that can be applied at work. In such cases, the graphics can help readers to visualize the technique in practice. Following are examples.

When the Essay Impedes Learning: A Case Study

From the beginning, both James and Ari, sixth graders at Shrewsbury Middle School, were intrigued by the story of Huck Finn. They could each imagine what it felt like to be constrained by the teachings of a strict and confining education, and felt the longing that Huck felt to explore. They knew how hard it was to be "civilized," to be inside those cinder block walls of the school on a warm spring day. Huck's story touched each of them deeply, capturing their imagination as literature should.

But then came the assignment: a 3–5 page paper describing Huck's moral dilemmas.

James got right to work, using his reading as a basis for constructing his own ideas and words, which flowed easily as he considered the experiences of Huck Finn. But for Ari, this is where the learning stopped. For her, the joy she first took in the story, her real affection for that reading, was undermined by the analytical essay she was assigned. Instead, she felt dread.

Note how the graphic from a paper about teaching helps to illustrate the product of the technique discussed:

Alternatives to Essays for English Teachers
Stacy Crist

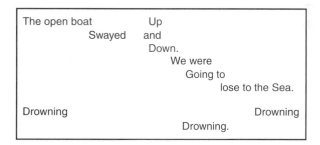

Poetry

- Allows students to express feelings
- Helps students experiment with different writing styles

This is an example poem about Stephen Crane's "The Open Boat," where men are lost at sea and are ready to abandon ship and swim to shore, with one man drowning.

> The open boat   Up
>   Swayed   and
>   Down.
>   We were
>   Going to
>   lose to the Sea.
> Drowning   Drowning
>   Drowning.

Vernacular

- Students emulate writing style of specific author
- Shows understanding of style

An example writing in the style of Mark Twain:

> One day I wuz walkin down the road when outta th corna of my eye I seed the biggest rabit ever sittin' in the brush. Me bein' so hungry that my big insides wuz eatin' my little insides he looked like a rite tasty supper. I wuz a creapin' up on that rabit just silent as a full blood injun. Just afore I got to him Bam! he wuz off like a streek a litenin. Well I shot after that rabit. Well, I put my eye up to a tiny not hole in the trunk and seed nothin' more than a whole passel a rabits!

Diagram

- Used to brainstorm, trace events and character development
- Requires students to know and understand main points of a novel or issue
- Can be drawn and hung on bulletin board

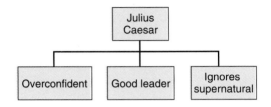

Letters to Author

- Have students write a letter to an author
- Pair students and have them switch letters and answer them
- Demonstrates a working knowledge of author
- Requires rudimentary research

An example of letters to and from Mark Twain:

Dear Mr. Twain,
I enjoyed your book *Huck Finn,* but I have a question. How did you feel about slavery when you were living through it? Thanks for your help!
Sincerely,
Pete James

Dear Mr. James,
I greatly abhor slavery. My character Huck goes on to learn that slavery is an abomination to the world. He also learns that black people are human beings too. This reflects my beliefs.
Sincerely,
Mark Twain

Journal

- Promotes regular writing habits
- Kept for one or two weeks
- Includes feelings, thoughts, reactions
- Reflects personality of the student

Example of transcendental journal:

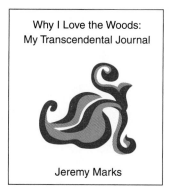

Why I Love the Woods:
My Transcendental Journal

Jeremy Marks

Games

- Engages students in reading a novel
- Students create cards with questions about the novel
- Game board, game pieces, and instructions created by students

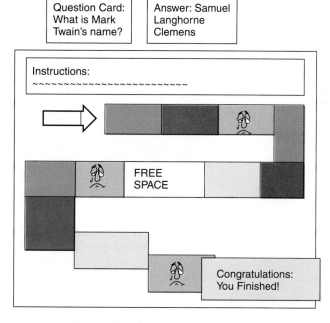

Question Card:
What is Mark
Twain's name?

Answer: Samuel
Langhorne
Clemens

Instructions:
~~~~~~~~~~~~~~~~~~~~~~~~~

FREE
SPACE

Congratulations:
You Finished!

Literary Pursuits: A Learning Game

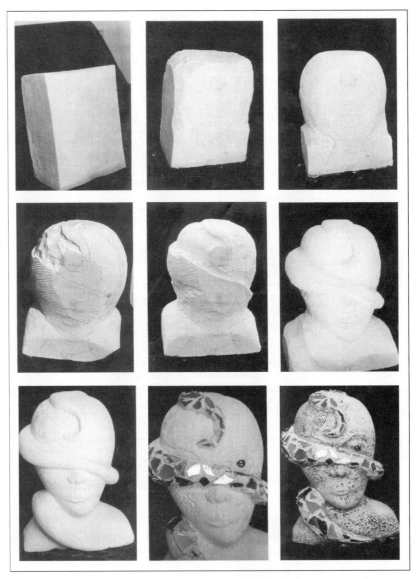

FIGURE 10.1   Some sculptures are carved from plaster. The artist begins with a plaster block, formed by pouring plaster into a rectangular form or mold. When the plaster dries, the mold is stripped away, leaving the raw material for sculpting. The process of carving and finishing a sculpture from a plaster block is called a "subtractive method," since this process requires the artist to remove part of the plaster in order to create the art object. In effect, the artist is creating both the negative space (that which is removed) and the positive space (that which is left). The subtractive process is documented above (Figure 10.1), showing the sculpture as it takes shape and is finished with other materials such as mirrors and marbles. Finally, the sculpture is "washed" with shoe polish applied over acrylic paint. The wash remains only in the indentations, revealing and heightening textural details of the sculpture.

The humanities, which rely to a large degree on interpretation of other texts, can stress those types of concerns by means of inset quotations that are surrounded by white space, visual representations of cultural or aesthetic "texts" (a drawing, a painting, a page from a seventeenth-century journal) as artifacts that illustrate artistic principles, philosophical ideas, or cultural nuances to be interpreted. The presentation of such primary source materials allows the reader to follow along with the writer in the process of interpreting those materials.

Business-related documents vary widely. Documents that are meant as advertising or public relations use graphic design to influence, and sometimes sell, ideas or products. Expert-to-expert discourses, usually found in scholarly and trade journals or in business-to-business correspondence, use graphics, charts, and tables to present quantitative information in support of claims about the viability of principles of management, marketing, human resource management, accounting, and so on.

In each case, the visual design of a page can immediately and forcefully reinforce your participation in a particular discourse community and so increase the likelihood of your written documents' success and the acceptance of your own *ethos* as credible. Conversely, if you prepare documents that violate key commonplaces or principles of those discourse communities, your design can damage your credibility and, with it, the persuasive effect of the document. Thus, to create an effective visual design, it is important that you study carefully the types of documents that are considered standard within your field of work and do your best to balance inventive presentation with the tried and true methods of the field.

WRITING TO EXPLORE 10.4

Examine documents from at least three sources in your major or in a field of study that interests you. You might look at books, websites, professional or trade journals, promotional materials, or popular magazines. Scan the pages of each and, in your writer's notebook, list the principles of design that seem to apply to the visual presentation of information within that field.

Keep It Correct

Despite the practices of individual fields and disciplines, all fields share a common concern with accuracy and correctness. In this way, visual and verbal presentation of ideas are not wholly separate. After all, many of the graphic elements of your documents also include words: the text that is included in text boxes, charts, and graphs; the captions that accompany pictures; the labels that accompany diagrams. In order to make the most of such visually enhanced presentations of information, then, you must make those graphic elements as readable as possible. Here are a few guidelines that can help to make your visuals readable:

- As with paragraph structure, it is important that the content be as focused and organized as possible. Select the information you will include by considering its direct pertinence to the overall purpose of both the individual visual and the document as a whole. Be sure that the material included is organized within a reasonable and apparent structure; as with a paragraph of text, readers should be able to readily see the connection among the ideas and each individual idea's connection to an overall point.

- Graphics used, especially in conjunction with oral presentations, should be sequenced logically—that is, readers should be able to perceive how the introduction of a new slide, diagram, chart, or table relates to the previous information presented. Readers should be able to perceive a logical progression of ideas among your graphic elements.

- Visuals must be created in ways that do not frustrate the reader. Unreadable fonts (because of size or design), inconsistency of design, large blocks of text, color that lacks contrast (yellow, light green, or light orange print against white background, for example), or haphazard placement within a visual actually work counter to the benefits of visual aids: Rather than providing at-a-glance arguments, they slow the reader and make her less likely to attend carefully to the visual.

- Check graphics for parallel structure and consistent verb tenses, especially with lists or bulleted items. It is quite difficult to read lists that shift the structure of phrases or the tense of verbs that often introduce those phrases. Consider the following list of points to consider in résumé writing:
  - Project a positive image
  - You should list any related job experience
  - Extracurricular activities
  - Items that don't relate to the job you applied for shouldn't have been included

In this list, the writer shifts structure (from the clear imperative of the first item, to a second person directive in the second, to simply naming something to be included in the third bullet, to a full sentence in the last item). The last item also disorients the reader by using an odd mixture of present and past tenses. Here is a more effective and readable list:

- Project a positive image.
- List any related job experience.
- Include pertinent extracurricular activities.
- Exclude experiences that don't relate to the particular job.

In this list, each item is parallel in structure and consistent in tense, making the logic of the list more apparent to the reader.

Proofreading and careful editing are equally important to the visual presentation of information as they are to the body of your document—perhaps even more so, because document design draws attention to these parts of your document through techniques like use of white space, contrast, font size, borders, and so on.

Here are a few more general pieces of advice that can make your document more effective:

- Use clear, readable fonts, especially for body text; in visual aids, be sure that fonts are large enough to be read easily at a glance. This is crucial in slides and when using PowerPoint; consider the viewer in the back of the room.
- Don't use large blocks of text on slides or in visual aids. Rules of thumb suggest using fewer than twenty-five words per visual aid, four to six lines of text, and no more than six words per line.
- Avoid using ALL CAPS. It's like SCREAMING AT YOUR READERS; nobody likes that.
- Don't underline text for emphasis; underlining is reserved for elements like book titles and website URLs.
- Leave ample margins; white space is often as important as the type itself.
- Contrast creates a strong effect. Use dark text against light background or vice versa.
- Use appropriate graphics; humor is often useful, but be sure that it does not detract from the tone you are trying to project in your document as a whole. Here, too, consider the appropriate *ethos*.

THE WRITING-SPEAKING CONNECTION

There is no doubt that the oral presentation of an argument to an audience involves a different set of skills than a written presentation. In fact, oral presentations themselves differ widely depending on the occasion, its degree of formality, the length of the presentation, the technologies available to enhance the speech, and, as always, the audience. Since this book is largely concerned with written communication, I'll begin by admitting that what follows is not all there is to know about oral argumentation—not by a long shot.

However, I *can* suggest with confidence that many principles of written communication can inform the oral presentation of ideas as well. After all, the rhetorical principles on which this book are based, including the canons of rhetoric (invention, arrangement, style, memory, and delivery), have their roots in the principles of ancient oratory and so were designed to inform public speakers.

For this reason, preparing to deliver an effective oral presentation involves many of the same activities that we have discussed in this book. You must invent—collect ideas both from your own mind and from appropriate outside sources. You must arrange those ideas in an order that is reasonable both to you and to your audience, taking into consideration the methods of proof that are acceptable to given discourse communities. You must choose language styles carefully—words, terminology, style of presentation, and level of assumed expertise—based on the occasion. And you must use memory—both the public memory available in books, periodicals, and electronic sources, and individual memory and learning—to digest the information that you collect. Further, as a speaker, it is important that you use your memory to organize information in ways that allow you to speak with an audience without too great a reliance on a written text. That is, you should be comfortable enough with your material to interact with your audience rather than appear absorbed in your notes or text—neither reading from a prepared type-script nor from slides or other visual aids.

This last point suggests the key difference between written and oral communication: the live audience. While in the preparation and delivery of a written text you can become wholly absorbed with your text, in oral communication, an audience wants to be included in an actual dialog with you. Written occasions are also dialogs with your readers—but those dialogs are imagined. Oral occasions compel you to engage in actual dialog; even if the communication is largely one-way as you speak to an audience, it is crucial that you tend toward speaking *with* members of your audience rather than *at* them.

Once again, you can learn a good deal from the professionals. Robert Colleluori's oral presentations are his bread and butter; if he cannot convince a live audience of the validity of his ideas, and in a limited amount of time, his business can't remain viable:

> Impact, Impact, Impact. That's what is important! The only way you create impact is to know your objectives going in. I set goals and objectives before any presentation, and more importantly, a way to measure those goals and objectives. I don't like to give an oral presentation that doesn't at least allow a Q and A to see what questions are out there. Did I deliver the goods effectively and make an impact? I can only tell that by the measurability factor. I don't like to wait until the end to see if the applause is sincere or not. Then it's too late. I even like some Q and A or interactive substance during my presentations. My presentations are not about me looking smart and talking at people. My presentations are about helping clients understand more clearly their challenges and helping them to solve their problems.

As a high school teacher, Jodi Heller knows that "every day for me is an oral presentation." She goes on to suggest that

> the most important aspect of an oral presentation is often visual—using graphs and symbols in order to emphasize the knowledge that you are trying to convey. The excitement with which you present information is crucial. If you are bored, your students are *definitely* going to be bored.

You all likely know about what types of oral communication are effective, as Heller suggests, because of your experiences in classes. You are much more likely to become engaged in a class when a teacher, even within a lecture format, engages with you, looking for signs that you are following along, pausing for questions, stopping to qualify or clarify when the looks on the faces of students suggest a lack of understanding or engagement (something that Colleluori notes as crucial as well). The ability and willingness to acknowledge that communication involves not only a speaker (or writer) presenting information or an argument but also the audience's reception of that information or argument. The real joy of oral presentation is the possibility of immediate feedback, both verbal (questions, comments, calls for elaboration) and nonverbal (nodding heads, smiles, rapt attention). Effective speakers draw energy from their audience and are flexible enough to follow the audience's feedback toward a successful act of communication.

There are many occasions on which you are asked to speak *extemporaneously*—informally and without a prepared script. Such occasions include the times in class when you are asked to respond to questions or discussion points raised by your teachers. On those occasions, you are most prepared if you have literally done your homework. Doing your homework in the figurative sense is important in more formal speaking occasions as well. Even when you will speak without written notes (or with minimal notes), you do a great deal of composing, often in writing, in advance of the actual oral presentation.

COMPOSING FOR ORAL PRESENTATIONS

As with written communication, careful preparation is crucial to successful oral presentation. However, you have likely been told at some point that you can be overprepared for oral presentations—so tied to your script that you are not prepared for the inevitable variability that the live audience brings to the situation. But being overprepared doesn't mean that you know too much about a topic; quite to the contrary, the more you know about a topic, the more likely you are to be able to speak about it with grace, confidence, and flexibility. If you merely collected information to transfer wholesale to the minds of your audience, you have not taken full advantage of the wonderful potential of any speaking occasion. But if you really understand your material and its implications for the audience you will address, you are prepared to speak with them, not at them. Those speakers who seem the most nonchalant about their presentations—they *really* know their stuff.

So, the composing process that precedes an oral presentation is largely dependent on individual memory and the real learning we discussed in Chapter 8. If you are able to digest the information that you have collected, to see the connections between the ideas that you have studied, you will be capable of adjusting your speech to the occasion as it presents itself on the day you deliver your presentation. This involves thinking relationally—thinking about how one idea connects logically to another. For this reason, the inventional work that you do in preparation for an oral presentation frequently involves composing in writing, even if, in the end, you put aside what you have written and speak with few, or even without, notes.

Freewriting on a topic that you have been studying can be an excellent way of preparing for an oral presentation, since it helps you to find natural relationships between ideas, relationships that occur to you as you think through your subject in writing. But after you have done your freewriting, it is also important that you find in it the potential for bringing order to the set of ideas that you want to communicate. Just as you attempt to arrange your ideas in the processes of writing early drafts, as you prepare for oral communication you search for logical connections that can help you (and eventually your audience) to progress through the series of points you have to make.

Likewise, the process of preparing an oral presentation requires you to consider the words and styles that are most likely to capture your audience's interest and attention. So, even though you will likely not read verbatim from a page, experimenting with phrasings can certainly help you to find the right words within which to capture your point, phrasings that will come back to you as you face your audience.

Much of this stylistic preparation can be worked out in writing as you draft phrasings and sentences that bring clarity and liveliness to your expression. But since the occasion that you face is an oral one, it is also important that you do some of the work of inventing and composing orally—by speaking with others about your topic. Once you have a general idea of where you plan to go in your oral presentation, it can be very useful for you to then chat informally with others to see what comes out of your mouth when you are asked to talk about the topic, to see what formulations of the idea seem to sound best to you and your listener, to gauge your listener's response (quizzical, disturbed, intrigued), and to listen to the questions and comments that your presentation raises in this practice situation. There is simply no substitute for these informal moments of preparation.

All of these preparatory steps of composing have strong parallels with the techniques of writing that we have discussed, and especially with perhaps the simplest but most crucial point I have made in this book's treatment of research: You need to know what you're talking about to compose an effective presentation, whether oral or written. Getting to know what you're talking about involves reading, study, and talking with others.

ORAL PRESENTATION AND *ETHOS*

Though your academic and occupational *ethos* is highly dependent on your ability to communicate well in writing, there is something particularly important about your ability to communicate orally, and to do so with ease, comfort, and self-confidence. Though the act of writing can show what you know about a topic, it is also an act that often involves multiple revisions and many chances to get it right. When you communicate orally, you are also faced with the challenge of getting it right; but you are asked to get it right *right then!* Since that can be challenging, it also comes with great rewards in terms of *ethos*. In academic settings (class participation as well as formal oral presentations), on the job (in meetings and presentations), and in civic affairs (in speeches, debates, and press conferences), people earn respect for their ability to convey a message. It is difficult to overestimate the value of this skill for success in college, for job advancement, and for civic participation.

All effective communication means reasoning together with your audience and allowing for multiple viewpoints, as we discussed in relation to planning written documents. But in oral delivery, the two-way nature of communication is all the more obvious because your audience is physically present and will display their reactions to you immediately, either directly (through questions and comments) or indirectly (through body language). If you invite your audience to actively participate in your oral presentation and take their reactions into account, they are more likely to be with you when the presentation ends—they may agree or disagree, but they will be with you.

DELIVERING AN EXPERT VOICE

The above occasions illustrate the ways in which trust between speaker and audience can be developed through two-way communication. But that trust comes not only from your willingness to acknowledge the views and attitudes of your audience but also from their willingness to accept your character or *ethos* as informed and reasonable. As with written communication, certain techniques make earning that trust at the moment of delivery more likely.

The first of those techniques involves memory. As with all forms of communication, it is important to establish a logical flow of ideas that allows your readers to follow your reasoning from start to finish. This can be even more difficult, of course, when speaking than when writing because you must be willing to respond to formal and informal feedback you receive from your audience.

Finding the balance between getting your message out and being flexible enough to adjust that message to the reception you are receiving is a skill that takes a good deal of practice. Memorizing a speech, or reading it from a prepared script, can assure that you will cover all of your points in a carefully planned order. Conversely, having just a rough idea of the points that you wish to cover can allow you to find those parts of your presentation that strike a chord with the audience and play them up to great effect. But the former approach can make you seem rather antiseptic and cold, and the latter can make you seem disorganized or unprepared. Balance is the key. If you have a solid idea of the points you want to cover and anticipate the places in your presentation that are most likely to inspire response, you can achieve a useful middle ground between the two.

In order to perceive an expert *ethos,* your audience must associate your message with you directly, and when you simply read at them from notecards or a prepared script, you don't project that what you say comes directly from you. As such, your presentation notes should be as skeletal as possible; they should be reminders, memory devices, that help you to remember the key points that will be delivered with our eyes looking directly at your audience. Glancing down at notes or at visual aids that you have prepared can allow for useful pauses, interims when your audience can digest your message; but the message itself should be delivered with eye contact, with confidence, and with a sincere interest in the response it generates.

For this reason, careful preparation involves many components. Here are basic activities that can help you to prepare for oral presentations:

1. Consider the rhetorical situation: In order to plan an effective oral presentation, just as you do for written communication, you should begin with questions about the rhetorical situation:

    - What is the purpose? What do you want to accomplish?

    - What do you know about the audience? What special needs as listeners do they have? How much knowledge do they have of the topic? What definitions must you supply, and what knowledge can you assume? What level of technicality can you use in the language? What are the demographics of the audience (age, gender, educational level, likely number of attendees, political and religious views, etc.)?

    - What is the level of exigency of this topic for this audience? Will your audience already understand the timeliness and importance of the topic, or do you need to establish it? If it must be established, what arguments for exigency are they most likely to accept?

2. Consider the content that you must cover in order to serve your purpose in speaking, and how to emphasize the most crucial content:

    - What are the crucial facets of the issue for listeners?

    - What examples, statistics, or other evidence are likely to have the most impact on this audience?

    - What topics that you must cover are most likely to be misunderstood or will be difficult to explain? How can you make these topics easier to follow in an oral presentation?

    - What details might you exclude and still accomplish your purpose? What can you leave for the question and answer period?

    - What questions do you want to prompt in your audience?

    - What larger concerns might your audience have in relation to your topic?

■ If the presentation is being given to a certain organization, what concerns specific to that group (and what commonplaces that they hold) do you need to take into account? Are you considered an insider or an outsider within this group?

3. What is the most appropriate tone and style for your presentation? In considering the *ethos* that you want to project, you must consider the following questions:

■ What level of formality or informality is appropriate to this occasion? What will your audience expect? Do you wish to fulfill those expectations, or alter them?

■ What will your audience consider to be a respectful and appropriate attitude toward sensitive topics?

■ What level of expertise and specific vocabulary should your presentation use, considering the audience?

■ What predispositions about you or your topic can you develop, or alter, by your style? Do any of these predispositions stand in the way of effective communication (e.g., your audience will consider the topic dull or banal, when you wish to make it exciting and interesting)?

4. An effective oral presentation must also quickly and effectively set up a context within which the rest of the presentation will be received. To do so, you should consider the following questions:

■ How can you quickly and effectively communicate your most important points and purposes? Can you capture your point in a single sentence? Can you repeat that sentence periodically to stress your central message?

■ How can you alert the listeners to the structure of your talk? That is, can you prepare your listeners for what is to follow by outlining the structure of your talk, and so make them better listeners?

■ What organizing techniques can you use to help your audience stay with you through the progression of ideas? At what points should you pause and review your main point, or points that have been covered already, so as to support the logical connections between your various topics?

5. An effective oral presentation is also largely dependent on the order in which you broach topics, especially sensitive ones. As we discussed in reference to the arrangement in written documents in Chapter 4, it is difficult to get an audience back once you have made them resistant. Since this is even more true on oral occasions, you should consider the following questions:

■ What parts of your presentation are most likely to create resistance or, if not handled delicately, offend your audience?

■ In order to make resistance or offense less likely, what preparatory work must be done in your talk? That is, what points must you establish first to allow for the most receptive audience? What details might you provide to break down possible points of resistance *before* you get to the sensitive issues?

■ And, with the two above points in mind, what is the most reasonable, audience-sensitive order in which to organize your presentation?

6. Because listening for extended periods is in some ways more difficult than reading, oral presentations require techniques that can hold a reader's interest. In order to invent such techniques, ask yourself the following questions:

■ Can you personalize the more mundane statistics or data that you need to present by relating it to audience concerns?

■ Can you find ways to use narrative to draw in audience interest? Should you use case studies? recount personal anecdotes?

■ Can you find appropriate places to pause and, as Robert Colleluori suggested, "not wait until the end to see if the applause is sincere or not"? In what ways can you use audience feedback to gauge your success and involve audience members in active listening?

■ In what places will your audience need to see, as well as hear, the information you are presenting? That is, where will you require visual aids to keep your audience with you?

Clearly, many, many questions must be considered in preparation for an oral presentation. But don't let the length of the list intimidate you. Many of these considerations are related and so can be dealt with quite efficiently. But whereas ignoring these elements can make for a shaky presentation, attending carefully to them can have an extremely important benefit: It can make you confident in advance of the presentation—confident that you are ready for the oral occasion you are entering. And nothing is as important for effective oral communication as confidence.

In general, oral presentations benefit from a relatively simple structure:

■ An introduction that states your main purpose in addressing this group and previews what your listeners can expect

■ A body that covers each of the points promised (though, of course, a responsive speaker might make slight alterations to that organization based on audience feedback)

■ A conclusion that not only reiterates the main point but also speaks to its importance, answering the key question: So what? Why should this audience care? What do you want them to understand differently now, or what actions do you want them to perform? How should they be changed?

USING VISUAL AIDS AND TECHNOLOGY

It is not hard to imagine the importance of visual rhetoric on oral occasions—especially when you have little time to make your case and when your audience is challenged to understand sometimes complex ideas simply by listening. Including visuals and other enhancements can, in such situations, be crucial. With the many technologies now available, choosing appropriate visual aids, like choosing any form of visual rhetoric, requires the same combination of inventiveness, decorum, and restraint that was discussed in reference to document design. In fact, reviewing those sections of this chapter with oral presentations in mind will give you a very good start toward creating effective and appropriate visual aids.

As you consider the use of visual aids in oral presentations, keep these additional guidelines in mind:

- Use visual aids to enhance the major points you need to cover.
- Use visual aids to present data that is more easily understood in graphic than in oral form.
- Use visual aids to provide a graphic representation of the relationship between ideas that you are presenting. Sometimes, a map of your ideas or an outline of points you plan to cover can help to strengthen logical connections.
- Be careful that visual aids do not distract your audience from points that you are making verbally.
- Don't merely read from visual aids; keep the message simple enough that your audience can read them in conjunction with your spoken delivery.
- Pause long enough for the audience to read or digest the visual aid, and then help them to understand its importance. Remember that the visual aid will likely gather more attention than you will, at least when it is first unveiled, so be sure to allow for this momentary loss of attention.
- Consider using drawings, graphs, charts, cartoons, statistics, photographs, maps—whatever visual can help to reinforce your point or keep your audience's attention in the right place.
- Be sure that your visual aids conform to the stylistic advice provided earlier in this chapter in relation to fonts, lines of text, and so on. With oral presentations, you must pay special attention to font size, since a font that is hard to read or not large enough can really distract your audience.

POWERPOINT AND POSTERS

The visual and technological culture in which we live has increased audience expectations for visual aids. Whereas not long ago a marker, poster board, and (if we wanted to be especially polished) stencils might have sufficed, in many fields and organizations, electronic enhancement of visual aids is all but expected. Two technologies that have been especially influential are PowerPoint (and similar programs) and professionally prepared posters.

These PowerPoint slides, prepared by Audra Shearer and Tracy Hanegraaf, whose essays are included earlier in this book, represent graphically the key findings of their research. As a supplement to the oral presentation that accompanied them, they are meant to suggest key ideas, not explicate them. They make an impact quickly and allow the listeners to focus on the speaker's oral presentation.

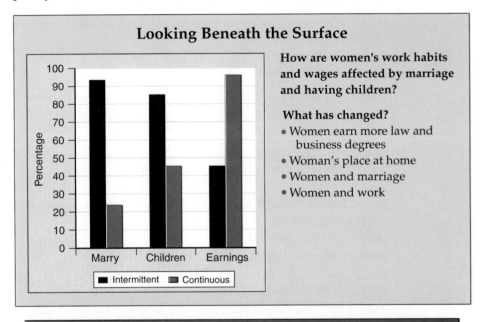

FIGURE 10.2   PowerPoint slides.

Recent Events

- Nearly a **million** US students took guns to school during 1998.
- National high school death tolls over the last 2 years are **27** students and teachers killed (1999).
- These are the facts, but where do we go from here?

FIGURE 10.2 Continued

Another aid to oral communication is the poster. Posters contain a great deal of information that can be supplemented by oral explication but that is much more self-sufficient than the bulleted items on a PowerPoint slide. This representation of ideas is largely visuals and text, and it requires careful layout. Posters are usually printed for very large formats, and although they were once the province of business presentations, they are becoming commonplace in many academic disciplines. The sample posters that follow illustrates how a full argument can be built into a poster presentation.

Oral presentations, whether long and formal or brief and informal, reflect on you in ways that are even more direct and immediate than responses to your writing. Because you are physically present, you are associated all the more closely with your message, with your tone, and with the credibility you project or fail to project. In order to become a successful communicator, then, it is important that you extend the principles of rhetoric discussed throughout this book to what are, in fact, the bases of rhetoric in oratory. One way to do so is to extend the work you are doing in writing to oral occasions. How would the change in format affect organization? word choices? exposition of topics? use of various styles (narrative, analytical, etc.)? By considering the oral situation carefully, you can enhance your rhetorical sensitivity to audience, purpose, and occasion—making you both a better speaker and a better writer.

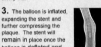

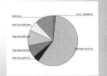

FIGURE 10.3   Samples of posters.

Casebooks for Further Reading and Research

THE READING AND WRITING YOU have done throughout this book was aimed at helping you to become an informed and educated worker with a real stake in the work of disciplinary fields and occupations. We have discussed ways to become informed, ways to use the information you collect to make strong arguments, and the reasons why involvement in ongoing disciplinary and professional conversations is so crucial. As you continue to learn about specific fields and occupations, you will find that workers in individual fields must face many issues. These issues frequently cross the boundaries between public and private life; they create dialogs between one discipline and another; and they require negotiation among your own goals, the goals of your workplace, and the goals of the larger society.

Below, you will find a series of such issues introduced in "casebooks"—readings and suggestions for writing that provide material for thought, further research, and writing. Their purpose is, like much of what we have done in this book, heuristic: They provide ways of opening or uncovering areas for further investigation.

Each of the casebooks

- Introduces a general topic;
- Provides introductory discussion of that topic;
- Provides documents that are useful starting points for your consideration of that topic; and

- Provides ideas on how you might use this "case" as an occasion to write.

Each case can be used in a number of ways:

- It can provide a topic for classroom discussion or for discussion with interested peers;
- It can help you to understand issues that exist in the contemporary world of work;
- It can give you occasion to practice the skills of active, critical reading; and
- It can provide you with topics for further research and writing.

In some cases, the material I provide might lead you to develop related topics that apply more directly to your own occupational or civic concerns. You should feel free to do so, customizing these cases in ways that allow you to research and write on topics in which you have a sincere interest.

The cases also call for a wide variety of types of writing—informational and persuasive, academic and popular, traditional format and formats that allow for innovative designs or technologies. That too is part of your task as a writer: to consider the genres within which your communication is best expressed. Use these cases to discuss with your teacher and peers your options for responding in writing and/or orally to each issue raised.

Finally, remember that these cases are meant to supplement the thinking and writing strategies that are discussed throughout this book. Use these cases as ways to practice the techniques discussed in this book— techniques like inventive writing, active reading, critical thinking, careful research, and, in all cases, attention to rhetorical situation. These rhetorical skills will continue to serve you personally as you compose a life's work, and publicly as you consider your place within a community of fellow workers and citizens.

Casebook 1 FAMILY, MATERIALISM, AND RESPONSIBILITY

In a culture that values work as much as ours does, some people question whether work has become too central to our lives, overshadowing things like spirituality, leisure, family, relationships, and so on. In response, some people have learned to live with less in the hope of reducing hours spent at work and finding more time for other things in their lives. This phenomenon, recently dubbed *downshifting*, is not wholly new. Henry David Thoreau, an American Transcendental philosopher and author, and the Romantic poet William Wordsworth both suggested many years ago that work can interfere with those things that really make us human. Others, conversely, might counter that the work we do is a large part of what makes us feel complete—as is argued by Richard Reeves in "The Joy of Work," included in Reading and Writing Applications 1. The discussions that follow can help you to think through the role of work in the context of other things that are important in your life.

Writing to Respond

In order to begin thinking about this topic, read the following pieces, annotating them carefully in the margins. Use your writer's notebook and the analytical skills discussed in Chapters 5 and 6 to find stasis points and to invent your own approaches to the topic. As you read, you should also consider ways that you might further investigate this or related topics. Try to develop informed responses to these perspectives on the relationship between work and leisure, between spiritual growth and career ambition, between responsibilities to work and responsibilities to family and friends, and so on.

You should also look ahead to ways that you could use the research processes discussed in Part 3 of this book to further investigate this topic. In order to develop a project on a topic like this, you should consider a variety of approaches. For example, you could (as in Juliet Schor's work below) collect case studies or statistical information. Or you might perform interviews. Or you might use the writings of others, both scholarly and imaginative, to investigate possible perspectives on the topic. Choosing the type of research you do depends on the audience and purpose of the piece you choose to write. But as you read and prepare to respond with your own writing, keep the key research questions in mind: What more do I need to know in order to respond credibly, and how can I go about learning those things?

The World Is Too Much with Us

William Wordsworth

William Wordsworth (1770–1850) was a British Romantic poet who believed deeply in the importance of nature, and who saw industrialization as in some ways destructive to the human spirit. William Wordsworth's 1807 sonnet, though written almost 200 years ago, suggests that the desire for goods is sometimes antithetical to the desire for personal fulfillment and spiritual growth.

The world is too much with us; late and soon,
Getting and spending, we lay waste our powers;
Little we see in nature that is ours;
We have given our hearts away, a sordid boon.
This sea that bares her bosom to the moon,
The winds that will be howling at all hours,

And are up-gathered now like sleeping flowers,
For this, for everything, we are out of tune;
It moves us not.—Great God! I'd rather be
A pagan suckled in a creed outworn;
So might I, standing on this pleasant lea,
Have glimpses that would make me less forlorn;
Have sight of Proteus rising from the sea;
Or hear old Triton blow his wreathed horn.

from The Overspent American

Juliet Schor

Juliet Schor is a senior lecturer at Harvard University and the author of *The Overworked American: The Unexpected Decline of Leisure* (1991). In that book, she questions the increasing amount of time Americans are spending on the job, beginning with a startling demographic: "[W]hen surveyed, Americans report that they have only sixteen and a half hours of leisure a week, after the obligations of job and household are taken care of." Schor also has a larger purpose, as she goes on to suggest that "by understanding how we came to be caught up in the cycle of work-and-spend, perhaps we can regain a reasonable balance between work and leisure." In this excerpt from her 1998 book, *The Overspent American: Why We Want What We Don't Need*, Schor continues that project, providing case studies of "downshifters"—citizens who have decided to put aside their need for "luxuries" (a tough concept to define) so that they can work less and so find more time for other facets of their life. As you read this piece, consider whether the attitude toward work and leisure expressed here seems to be a positive one, or whether the actions of these citizens are irresponsible to themselves and family. Have they found the "reasonable balance" that Schor called for in her earlier book, or has the pendulum swung too far away from the fulfillment of occupational and civic goals? You might also compare the ideas expressed here with those of William Wordsworth and Henry David Thoreau, included in this casebook.

The Path to "Freedom": Alice Kline

There is no typical downshifter profile, but Alice Kline's mentality (although not her income level) is just about as representative as any that I encountered. Alice, along with her husband (a chemical engineer) and two children, lives in a well-to-do

Boston suburb. In her mid-fifties, she is an attractive, articulate professional in the advertising business—hardly a countercultural type. Alice stayed home to raise her children, and when they reached junior high, she took the first full-time position she'd ever had, at a high-fashion company that made handbags and women's accessories. She adored it. "My job was my identity. That's what made me important, and that's what confirmed my skills." In the ten years she worked for the company, she moved up the ranks, to the position of merchandising director. It was a fast-paced and exciting life. But eventually she found it somewhat disquieting. "I was in the Orient twice a year. I was in Europe once a year. I was never not on a plane. And I had children, and I was married, and, I mean, my lifestyle was really pretty strange." She came to realize this strangeness while "walking down a main street in Hong Kong, which is hung with flags and signs and lights all in Chinese. And I felt very much at home. It didn't feel like a strange place. I was halfway around the world. And I didn't miss anything, and I didn't miss anybody."

Everything changed when Alice was laid off, after her company was sold. First she grieved. Then she picked up the pieces and went into job-search mode (counseling, group support, Monday morning meetings dressed for work). She ended up taking a job at a public relations firm, but the price was a $20,000 salary cut, one-third of her former earnings. The PR job didn't work out, but it did teach her about her psychological makeup. When her supervisor let her go, "it was, like, 'Fine, I'm on unemployment, don't bother me for a while. I need to think, about what I want and what I need.'" So she did a little networking, made some contacts, and began freelancing for an advertising company. "Situation assessment kind of writing, which I can do in my sleep. And I was happy as a clam. I could write at midnight, I could write in my jeans. I thought, this is wonderful, this is what I want to do. I want to be left alone." The company liked what she was doing and wanted her on board full-time.

"They had to beg me, because I had cut loose psychologically and emotionally from the working world. I really had." She agreed to work full-time, but only if she could work a four-day week. "I'm not invested, I'm not attached. If they fire me, I will go write. And because I'm not so anxiety-ridden about, am I going to succeed here or not? I think I'm doing good stuff." On the practical side, things have also changed enormously. "My commute is three minutes. I don't travel. Little by little, I've been getting closer to what I want to do. I still haven't figured out how to leave before seven, seven-thirty at night, because yes, I'm certainly cramming five days' work into four days. But padding around in my nightgown on Friday mornings is worth anything." Although Alice was originally downshifted involuntarily, she is among the nearly one-quarter of job losers for whom the experience has been a blessing. She wouldn't even consider going back to the kind of life she had. "I'm not willing to take that pressure anymore—absolutely not willing."

Like most downshifters, Alice has undergone a major change in her relationship to money, time, and work. "Four years ago, if somebody had said to [me], 'What will you do in five years?' that question would have terrified me, because I had no plan, I couldn't see what the future held. And now I do. So the prospect of more time and less money is much more comfortable now for me than it was a couple of years ago." She believes there's an inevitable trade-off between time and money. "That's just it. You know, pick one."

There is no question that Alice Kline has paid a high price for what she has gained. "I've given up money, and I've given up striving to reach top management. I will never be a vice president of a company, I, like, stopped, you know, mid-climb. And bailed out."

So how has she been managing, making $20,000 less, putting two children through college? Granted, the Klines are comfortable, and her husband still has his job. But her salary was one-third of the family income. When she lost her first job, her son panicked. Her husband was "hyperventilating, because he didn't really know if we could manage. They couldn't see they wouldn't starve." The family is more relaxed now, but they have had to make significant changes in their spending habits. Alice used to do a lot more impulse buying. "Clothes. Kids. Gadgets, whether it was a VCR or things like that." At the time of our interview with one child still in college, vacations were limited to nearby Maine. Financially the Klines are doing more thinking about what they spend, more budgeting. "It's like we've let go. We've let go of a lot of things."

Does she feel financially deprived? "In a sense. I can't do things for my kids the way I could without thinking. If somebody wants a piece of stereo equipment, that has to be thought about. It's not like they're never going to get it. There are no extraneous expenses. It's just a much more planned life." Of course, her job-related expenses are lower. As almost all downshifters attest, working costs money, whether it's transportation expenses, child care, takeout food because you're too tired to cook, or a shrink to deal with the pressure.

And for women especially there are always the clothes. Alice's job was in fashion, so her expenditures on clothes were particularly high. "I had to dress. And I had to spend money on clothes because I had to look a certain way." Not that she didn't enjoy buying clothes. "I wasn't in that business by accident. I'm always going to have a funky pair of earrings on. I think it's fun to dress, I love clothes. But like to do it on my terms, not because of pressure to look a certain way. I have to spend all money on clothes? I don't really want to do that. I'd rather buy something pretty for the house. [Now] the pressure is gone. I don't know when the last time was I bought something." Like many downshifters, Alice is "living off a wardrobe that's fairly deep. But I buy very little for myself. And probably can't afford to buy a lot of stuff for myself."

Learning to live on less is a process. "I think it's like going on a diet. When you're used to spending at a certain level, or you're used to eating at a certain level—which I'm also trying to deal with—I don't know that you can make huge transitions all at once, unless you have to. You kind of do it in stages. So I think that I will keep transitioning to different ways of spending my money or finding certain things that are important. I'm more willing to spend money to entertain people in my home than to put something on my back. So there's changing values within the money."

Alice Kline didn't begin her lifestyle change by questioning her consumer values. "I can't say that I don't think it's fun to do things or that I don't think material things are important. But"—and here I believe Alice describes the quintessential change that most downshifters go through—"*what I'm willing to do to get there has totally changed.*" The importance of money has fallen relative to "quality of life, what I do for a living, the actual content of what I do, connection with friends, connection with other people, connecting up on a personal level even with people that I work with. The quality of my life at work was terrible. It was so tense." Now she is excited about her work, and although she hasn't perfected the routine, "it's coming, little by little."

Alice strongly believes that money is freedom. She found total financial dependence on her husband demeaning and confining. But she has gained other freedoms that she will cling to just as tenaciously as the financial liberation she gained when she went to work. "I really can say no. I can say, 'I want to do it this way.' I believe that I can structure my life and my work life on my terms. I never believed that." Now she's finding out "how little money can I live on and still have what I define as freedom. It's like finding out how little food can I eat." She laughs.

The Work-and-Spend Cycle *in Extremis:* Jennifer Lawson

Jennifer Lawson was forty-one when we met and had some months earlier taken a voluntary layoff from a prestigious computer software and consulting firm. She lived with her boyfriend in a condominium in Cambridge. While she was not a typical yuppie—she didn't have a college degree—she was definitely in flight from the excesses of the work-and-spend cycle. She was living on unemployment, doing no extraneous spending, and thrilled to be out of the working world.

Jennifer had grown up in a middle-class family, but as a rebellious teenager, she married a man her parents hated, had a child, and missed out on college. Finding herself a single parent early on, she was forced into low-paid women's factory work in the upstate New York town where she grew up. She fought the company for a higher-paid (male) job driving trucks, but after more than a decade she wanted a change. She moved to the Boston area and serendipitously landed a job at the software firm. She worked there thirteen years, moving up the ranks, despite her lack of a credential, in various technical positions. By the time she left, she was making just over $40,000 a year. She'd come to a dead end in her job, had never really cared about software or computers, and, after so many years, was tired of the weekly grind. Her son was out of college, so she asked for, and was given, the company severance package.

For Jennifer, the upward creep of desire was at the root of her problem. She thinks back to 1980. "At that time, I was thinking that if only I could make $10,000 a year, I'd be fine. And there I was, thirteen years later, making $42,000 a year, and I still wasn't breaking even. I was just about exactly as much in debt as I was when I was making $10,000 a year. It just didn't make any difference. And I'm sure if they had given me a raise to $60,000, I would've managed to spend $65,000. That's just the way I've always been about it. And many people I know are the same way. Once you get to $40,000 a year, then you develop a lifestyle that requires $40,000 a year to support it. And if you keep doing that, then every year when they give you raises you just adjust your spending upward, and it doesn't really help anything."

Like many of the women she knows, Jennifer frequently spent her lunch hour doing recreational shopping. "I'd be in a bad mood, I'd go shopping at lunchtime, I'd try on a dress, I'd say, 'Well, I kind of like it, you know, it's only $89, I'll buy it.' I buy it, I bring it home, and never wear it. I didn't really like it." Or she'd go for one item and return with "seven or eight other things, because I'm easily distracted and I'm not very good at making quick judgments. And so I'd stand there and waffle for a minute, and I'd say, 'Ehh, do we really need another sofa pillow? Oh, all right, I'll take it!' Because it was easier than walking away from it."

If an item cost less than a few hundred dollars, Jennifer would buy it without thinking very long. They'd go to California every year to visit her brother. Eat out. See first-run movies. Like the other dual-earner couples in her building, she and her boyfriend kept the UPS man busy with mail-order shopping. What did she buy? "Small household accessories. There's a company called Horchow that sells gifts and trinkets and objects to put on your bookshelves. Lots of books, lots of records, almost anything you can think of that isn't a major appliance comes mail-order now." My favorite examples were on her terrace. "Even though we don't have a yard, that hasn't kept me from populating the entire porch with expensive gardening accessories. Because I like to garden, so I buy things from Smith and Hawken and Dwight Flower Farms."

Her boyfriend was into consumer electronics. "He loves the Sharper Image catalog and the *Electronics Digest*. He always wants a newer DVD. It's certainly not necessary. I mean, it's the same kind of machine as a VCR—like, the picture quality is better. And you know, a few people have them. And the discs for them are very expensive, and you can't record your own, but he's a programmer. We have a nice home Macintosh that we mostly just use as a toy. We have a nice printer for it. He likes to mail-order software for it; he's been talking about a new, faster modem to add to it. We don't have a fax machine yet, but he really thinks we need one."

Naturally she was maxed out on her credit cards. "Everyone else I know lives like this too. I mean, I was surrounded by people who do things like using reserve credit to pay their VISA bill at the end of the month, juggling one form of credit, and people kind of laugh about it. Everybody was in way over their heads, and the object of the game was to sort of tread water. Barring disaster, we were all paying.

"So, I felt like I was spending all of my life's energies doing something that I didn't much care about just to get a check every two weeks so that I could go out and buy some more books that I never had the time to read and some more records that I never had the time to listen to. And one of the things that sort of set off alarms was that I realized I had several occasions where I brought home either a new book or a new record and found out that I'd already bought that book or record. Which is really pathetic, you know. I've got stuff stacked up all over the house, and I'm never going to get to read any of them unless I'm in a major car accident."

Quitting her job was a blessing. She was able to calm down and quit smoking. She took up Russian and started to exercise. She no longer collapses into bed Friday evenings, spending the next two days vegging out and spending money. She goes into stores only to buy food. "And it's amazing how painless that has been, because, you see, I'm surrounded by nice objects. I already have a house full of things. I have equipment and supplies for crafts that I was planning to take up years ago and hobbies I was going to try, all carefully mail-ordered and stashed away and never unwrapped. I have hundreds and hundreds of books. I have a television with cable. Unless you insist on seeing something the week that it opens, you can see it on TV a month later anyway. I haven't had any trouble amusing myself at all."

She finds her situation a little scary sometimes, although she realizes that with her boyfriend still earning a good salary she isn't going to be "sleeping on the subway grates." And, she says, their standard of living is still probably better than that of 99% percent of the population, "so we ought to be able to do fine."

from Walden

Henry David Thoreau

Henry David Thoreau (1817–1862) was a American essayist and poet who believed deeply in the need for "transcendence"—for moving beyond the reliance on material goods toward a reliance on one's self and spiritual needs. While at Walden Pond, where he lived for just over two years on what nature provided, Thoreau considered human economies—what we need, what we don't, and how to work less. As you read this excerpt from *Walden*, consider how his feelings about work compare to others we have discussed in this book.

When I wrote the following pages, or rather the bulk of them, I lived alone, in the woods, a mile from any neighbor, in a house which I had built myself, on the shore of Walden Pond, in Concord, Massachusetts, and earned my living by the labor of my hands only. I lived there two years and two months. At present I am a sojourner in civilized life again. . . . I see young men, my townsmen, whose misfortune it is to have inherited farms, houses, barns, cattle, and farming tools; for these are more easily acquired than got rid of. Better if they had been born in the open pasture and suckled by a wolf, that they might have seen with clearer eyes what field they were called to labor in. Who made them serfs of the soil? Why should they eat their sixty acres, when man is condemned to eat only his peck of dirt? Why should they begin digging their graves as soon as they are born? They have got to live a man's life, pushing all these things before them, and get on as well as they can. How many a poor immortal soul have I met well-nigh crushed and smothered under its load, creeping down the road of life, pushing before it a barn seventy-five feet by forty, its Augean stables never cleansed, and one hundred acres of land, tillage, mowing, pasture, and woodlot! The portionless, who struggle with no such unnecessary inherited encumbrances, find it labor enough to subdue and cultivate a few cubic feet of flesh.

But men labor under a mistake. The better part of the man is soon plowed into the soil for compost. By a seeming fate, commonly called necessity, they are employed, as it says in an old book, laying up treasures which moth and rust will corrupt and thieves break through and steal. It is a fool's life, as they will find when they get to the end of it, if not before. . . . Most men, even in this comparatively free country, through mere ignorance and mistake, are so occupied with the factitious cares and superfluously coarse labors of life that its finer fruits cannot be plucked by them. Their fingers, from excessive toil, are too clumsy and tremble too much for that. Actually, the laboring man has not leisure for a true integrity day by day; he cannot afford to sustain the manliest relations to men;

his labor would be depreciated in the market. He has no time to be anything but a machine. How can he remember well his ignorance—which his growth requires—who has so often to use his knowledge? We should feed and clothe him gratuitously sometimes, and recruit him with our cordials, before we judge of him. The finest qualities of our nature, like the bloom on fruits, can be preserved only by the most delicate handling. Yet we do not treat ourselves nor one another thus tenderly. . . .

The mass of men lead lives of quiet desperation. What is called resignation is confirmed desperation. From the desperate city you go into the desperate country, and have to console yourself with the bravery of minks and muskrats. A stereotyped but unconscious despair is concealed even under what are called the games and amusements of mankind. There is no play in them, for this comes after work. But it is a characteristic of wisdom not to do desperate things. . . .

Let us consider for a moment what most of the trouble and anxiety which I have referred to is about, and how much it is necessary that we be troubled, or at least careful. It would be some advantage to live a primitive and frontier life, though in the midst of an outward civilization, if only to learn what are the gross necessaries of life and what methods have been taken to obtain them; or even to look over the old day-books of the merchants, to see what it was that men most commonly bought at the stores, what they stored, that is, what are the grossest groceries. For the improvements of ages have had but little influence on the essential laws of man's existence: as our skeletons, probably, are not to be distinguished from those of our ancestors.

By the words, necessary of life, I mean whatever, of all that man obtains by his own exertions, has been from the first, or from long use has become, so important to human life that few, if any, whether from savageness, or poverty, or philosophy, ever attempt to do without it. To many creatures there is in this sense but one necessary of life, Food. To the bison of the prairie it is a few inches of palatable grass, with water to drink; unless he seeks the Shelter of the forest or the mountain's shadow. None of the brute creation requires more than Food and Shelter. The necessaries of life for man in this climate may, accurately enough, be distributed under the several heads of Food, Shelter, Clothing, and Fuel; for not till we have secured these are we prepared to entertain the true problems of life with freedom and a prospect of success. Man has invented, not only houses, but clothes and cooked food; and possibly from the accidental discovery of the warmth of fire, and the consequent use of it, at first a luxury, arose the present necessity to sit by it. We observe cats and dogs acquiring the same second nature. By proper Shelter and Clothing we legitimately retain our own internal heat; but with an excess of these, or of Fuel, that is, with an external heat greater than our own internal, may not cookery properly be said to begin?

Darwin, the naturalist, says of the inhabitants of Tierra del Fuego, that while his own party, who were well clothed and sitting close to a fire, were far from too warm, these naked savages, who were farther off, were observed, to his great surprise, "to be streaming with perspiration at undergoing such a roasting." So, we are told, the New Hollander goes naked with impunity, while the European shivers in his clothes. Is it impossible to combine the hardiness of these savages with the intellectualness of the civilized man? According to Liebig, man's body is a stove, and food the fuel which keeps up the internal combustion in the lungs. In cold weather we eat more, in warm less. The animal heat is the result of a slow combustion, and disease and death take place when this is too rapid; or for want of fuel, or from some defect in the draught, the fire goes out. Of course the vital heat is not to be confounded with fire; but so much for analogy. It appears, therefore, from the above list, that the expression, animal life, is nearly synonymous with the expression, animal heat; for while Food may be regarded as the Fuel which keeps up the fire within us—and Fuel serves only to prepare that Food or to increase the warmth of our bodies by addition from without—Shelter and Clothing also serve only to retain the heat thus generated and absorbed. . . .

I do not mean to prescribe rules to strong and valiant natures, who will mind their own affairs whether in heaven or hell, and perchance build more magnificently and spend more lavishly than the richest, without ever impoverishing themselves, not knowing how they live—if, indeed, there are any such, as has been dreamed; nor to those who find their encouragement and inspiration in precisely the present condition of things, and cherish it with the fondness and enthusiasm of lovers—and, to some extent, I reckon myself in this number; I do not speak to those who are well employed, in whatever circumstances, and they know whether they are well employed or not; but mainly to the mass of men who are discontented, and idly complaining of the hardness of their lot or of the times, when they might improve them. There are some who complain most energetically and inconsolably of any, because they are, as they say, doing their duty. I also have in my mind that seemingly wealthy, but most terribly impoverished class of all, who have accumulated dross, but know not how to use it, or get rid of it, and thus have forged their own golden or silver fetters. . . .

A man who has at length found something to do will not need to get a new suit to do it in; for him the old will do, that has lain dusty in the garret for an indeterminate period. Old shoes will serve a hero longer than they have served his valet—if a hero ever has a valet—bare feet are older than shoes, and he can make them do. Only they who go to soirees and legislative balls must have new coats, coats to change as often as the man changes in them. But if my jacket and trousers, my hat and shoes, are fit to worship God in, they will do; will they not? Who ever saw his old clothes—his old coat, actually worn out, resolved into its primitive elements, so that it was not a deed of charity to bestow it on some poor boy, by him perchance to be bestowed on some poorer still, or shall we say richer, who could do with less? I say, beware of all enterprises that require new clothes, and not rather a new wearer of clothes. If there is not a new man, how can the new clothes be made to fit? If you have any enterprise before you, try it in your old clothes. All men want, not something to do with, but something to do, or rather something to be.

Casebook 2 WORK AS A CIVIL RIGHT: ISSUES OF RACE AND GENDER

Equal pay for equal work: it is a reasonable ideal, and one that few would question in a culture like ours, where equality forms one of our key commonplaces. But translated from the marketplace of ideas into the actual marketplace, this ideal may or may not be carried out. The relationship between one's race, gender, or ethnicity and the chances for career advancement (both in wages and authority) has long been a concern for underrepresented workers. As you consider your own future, you might benefit by seeking sources of information and argument on this crucial topic for the American workforce—because it may affect you personally, because you may be asked to participate in or to effect change in systems of compensation for workers, because you have strong ethical beliefs about the topic, or because it affects our culture more widely.

The Equal Rights Amendment (ERA) passed the U.S. Senate and then the House of Representatives, and on March 22, 1972, proposed as the 27th Amendment to the Constitution, the ERA was sent to the states for ratification. It was ratified by twenty-two of the necessary thirty-eight states in the first year. It however failed to receive full ratification within the requisite seven years due to fears that it would change basic features of U.S. culture. One argument suggested that the amendment would undermine a woman's right to be supported by her husband, which some people believe is a foundational feature of the nuclear family as well as of their religious beliefs. Some states also feared that the ERA would place too much authority in the federal government.

By 1977, thirty-five votes had been collected, but as the 1979 deadline approached, it became clear that the ERA was not likely to be ratified by the last three states needed. In July 1978, following a march of 100,000 supporters in Washington, D.C., that was organized by the National Organization for Women (NOW), Congress extended the deadline for ratification to June 30, 1982. Still the amendment did not receive ratification, and though it has been reintroduced again and again, the ERA still is not law.

The text of the ERA is printed below. Read this proposed amendment to the U.S. constitution—a surprisingly simple document—and consider what it is meant to suggest about our commonplaces and beliefs. But also look beyond its philosophical and ethical dimensions and consider its practical implications: How would this amendment change our culture? To whom would enforcement power go? What would the enforcement process be like? What specific actions does the ERA seem aimed at supporting? What actions does it wish to curtail? Can you identify possible undesired or unintended consequences of this amendment? Why do you suppose that it has failed to be ratified? In answering such questions, of course, you would do well to investigate the history of the ERA and of the debate surrounding it. Use the research skills discussed in this book, as well as the activities of engaged reading and writing, to learn more about the ERA and to prepare yourself to take a position on its ratification.

The Proposed Equal Rights Amendment:

Section 1. Equality of rights under the law shall not be denied or abridged by the United States or by any state on account of sex.

Section 2. The Congress shall have the power to enforce, by appropriate legislation, the provisions of this article.

Section 3. This amendment shall take effect two years after the date of ratification.

Attempts to legislate on behalf of the civil rights of underrepresented workers, including both racial and gender groups, began well before the ERA was proposed. In 1964, the Civil Rights Act, aimed at eliminating discrimination based on race, color, religion, sex, and national origin became law. A brief excerpt from the Civil Rights Act of 1964 is included below. As you read this piece of legislation, consider the following questions, responding in the margins and in your writer's notebook:

- Why is the Act written as it is? Why is the legal language so thick and complex? Try to cut through the difficulties and imagine what this use of language is meant to accomplish.

- How does this Act compare with the ERA? What purposes are different in this type of legislation, as compared with a constitutional amendment?

- We discussed the importance of definitions earlier in this book. Why are careful definitions of terms and concepts especially crucial in a legal document? Why are specific terms (*person, employer,* etc.) defined in this Act?

from **The Civil Rights Act of 1964**

The Civil Rights Act of 1964's purpose is defined in its preamble as follows:

To enforce the constitutional right to vote, to confer jurisdiction upon the district courts of the United States, to provide injunctive relief against discrimination in public accommodations, to authorize the Attorney General to institute suits to protect constitutional rights in public facilities and public education, to extend the Commission on Civil Rights, to prevent discrimination in federally assisted programs, to establish a Commission on Equal Employment Opportunity, and for other purposes.

Be it enacted by the Senate and House of Representatives of the United States of America in Congress assembled, that this Act may be cited as the "Civil Rights Act of 1964."

SEC. 2000e. [Section 701]: DEFINITIONS

(a)   The term "person" includes one or more individuals, governments, governmental agencies, political subdivisions, labor unions, partnerships, associations, corporations, legal representatives, mutual companies, joint-stock companies, trusts, unincorporated organizations, trustees, trustees in cases under Title 11 [bankruptcy], or receivers.

(b)   The term "employer" means a person engaged in an industry affecting commerce who has fifteen or more employees for each working day in each of twenty or more calendar weeks in the current or preceding calendar year, and any agent of such a person, but such term does not include

　　(1)   the United States, a corporation wholly owned by the Government of the United States, an Indian tribe, or any department or agency of the District of Columbia subject by statute to procedures of the competitive service (as defined in section 2102 of title 5 [of the United States Code]), or

　　(2)   a bona fide private membership club (other than a labor organization) which is exempt from taxation under section 501(c) of title 26 [the Internal Revenue Code of 1954], except that during the first year after March 24, 1972 [the date of enactment of the Equal Employment Opportunity Act of 1972], persons having fewer than twenty-five employees (and their agents) shall not be considered employers.

(c)   The term "employment agency" means any person regularly undertaking with or without compensation to procure employees for an employer or to procure for employees opportunities to work for an employer and includes an agent of such a person.

...

(f) The term "employee" means an individual employed by an employer, except that the term "employee" shall not include any person elected to public office in any State or political subdivision of any State by the qualified voters thereof, or any person chosen by such officer to be on such officer's personal staff, or an appointee on the policy making level or an immediate adviser with respect to the exercise of the constitutional or legal powers of the office. The exemption set forth in the preceding sentence shall not include employees subject to the civil service laws of a State government, governmental agency or political subdivision. With respect to employment in a foreign country, such term includes an individual who is a citizen of the United States.

...

(j) The term "religion" includes all aspects of religious observance and practice, as well as belief, unless an employer demonstrates that he is unable to reasonably accommodate to an employee's or prospective employee's religious observance or practice without undue hardship on the conduct of the employer's business.

(k) The terms "because of sex" or "on the basis of sex" include, but are not limited to, because of or on the basis of pregnancy, childbirth, or related medical conditions; and women affected by pregnancy, childbirth, or related medical conditions shall be treated the same for all employment-related purposes, including receipt of benefits under fringe benefit programs, as other persons not so affected but similar in their ability or inability to work, and nothing in section 2000e-2(h) of this title [section 703(h)] shall be interpreted to permit otherwise. This subsection shall not require an employer to pay for health insurance benefits for abortion, except where the life of the mother would be endangered if the fetus were carried to term, or except where medical complications have arisen from an abortion: Provided, that nothing herein shall preclude an employer from providing abortion benefits or otherwise affect bargaining agreements in regard to abortion.

SEC. 2000e-2. [Section 703]: UNLAWFUL EMPLOYMENT PRACTICES

It shall be an unlawful employment practice for an employer

(1) to fail or refuse to hire or to discharge any individual, or otherwise to discriminate against any individual with respect to his compensation, terms, conditions, or privileges of employment, because of such individual's race, color, religion, sex, or national origin; or

(2) to limit, segregate, or classify his employees or applicants for employment in any way which would deprive or tend to deprive any individual of employment opportunities or otherwise adversely affect his status as an employee, because of such individual's race, color, religion, sex, or national origin.

　　. . .

(b) It shall be an unlawful employment practice for an employment agency to fail or refuse to refer for employment, or otherwise to discriminate against, any individual because of his race, color, religion, sex, or national origin, or to classify or refer for employment any individual on the basis of his race, color, religion, sex, or national origin.

It shall be an unlawful employment practice for a labor organization

(1) to exclude or to expel from its membership, or otherwise to discriminate against, any individual because of his race, color, religion, sex, or national origin;

(2) to limit, segregate, or classify its membership or applicants for membership, or to classify or fail or refuse to refer for employment any individual, in any way which would deprive or tend to deprive any individual of employment opportunities, or would limit such employment opportunities or otherwise adversely affect his status as an employee or as an applicant for employment, because of such individual's race, color, religion, sex, or national origin; or

(3) to cause or attempt to cause an employer to discriminate against an individual in violation of this section.

　　. . .

(d) It shall be an unlawful employment practice for any employer, labor organization, or joint labor-management committee controlling apprenticeship or other training or retraining, including on-the-job training programs, to discriminate against any individual because of his race, color, religion, sex, or national origin in admission to, or employment in, any program established to provide apprenticeship or other training.

　　. . .

(1) it shall not be an unlawful employment practice for an employer to hire and employ employees, for an employment agency to classify, or refer for employment any individual, for a labor organization to classify its membership or to classify or refer for employment any individual, or for an employer, labor organization, or joint labor-management committee controlling apprenticeship

or other training or retraining programs to admit or employ any individual in any such program, on the basis of his religion, sex, or national origin in those certain instances where religion, sex, or national origin is a bona fide occupational qualification reasonably necessary to the normal operation of that particular business or enterprise, and

(2) it shall not be an unlawful employment practice for a school, college, university, or other educational institution or institution of learning to hire and employ employees of a particular religion if such school, college, university, or other educational institution or institution of learning is, in whole or in substantial part, owned, supported, controlled, or managed by a particular religion or by a particular religious corporation, association, or society, or if the curriculum of such school, college, university, or other educational institution or institution of learning is directed toward the propagation of a particular religion.

. . .

(f) As used in this subchapter, the phrase "unlawful employment practice" shall not be deemed to include any action or measure taken by an employer, labor organization, joint labor/management committee, or employment agency with respect to an individual who is a member of the Communist Party of the United States or of any other organization required to register as a Communist-action or Communist-front organization by final order of the Subversive Activities Control Board pursuant to the Subversive Activities Control Act of 1950 [50 U.S.C. 781 et seq.].

(g) Notwithstanding any other provision of this subchapter, it shall not be an unlawful employment practice for an employer to fail or refuse to hire and employ any individual for any position, for an employer to discharge any individual from any position, or for an employment agency to fail or refuse to refer any individual for employment in any position, or for a labor organization to fail or refuse to refer any individual for employment in any position.

(h) Notwithstanding any other provision of this subchapter, it shall not be an unlawful employment practice for an employer to apply different standards of compensation, or different terms, conditions, or privileges of employment pursuant to a bona fide seniority or merit system, or a system which measures earnings by quantity or quality of production or to employees who work in different locations, provided that such differences are not the result of an intention to discriminate because of race, color, religion, sex, or national origin, nor shall it be an unlawful employment practice for an employer to give and to act upon the results of any professionally developed ability test provided that such test, its administration or action upon the results, is not designed, intended or used to discriminate because of race, color, religion, sex, or national origin. It shall not be an unlawful employment practice under this subchapter for any employer to differentiate upon the basis of sex in determining the amount of the wages or compensation paid or to be paid to employees of such employer if such differentiation is authorized by the provisions of section 206(d) of title 29 [section 6(d) of the Fair Labor Standards Act of 1938, as amended].

(i)   Nothing contained in this subchapter shall apply to any business or enterprise on or near an Indian reservation with respect to any publicly announced employment practice of such business or enterprise under which a preferential treatment is given to any individual because he is an Indian living on or near a reservation.

(j)   Nothing contained in this subchapter shall be interpreted to require any employer, employment agency, labor organization, or joint labor-management committee subject to this subchapter to grant preferential treatment to any individual or to any group because of the race, color, religion, sex, or national origin of such individual or group on account of an imbalance which may exist with respect to the total number or percentage of persons of any race, color, religion, sex, or national origin employed by any employer, referred or classified for employment by any employment agency or labor organization, admitted to membership or classified by any labor organization, or admitted to, or employed in, any apprenticeship or other training program, in comparison with the total number or percentage of persons of such race, color, religion, sex, or national origin in any community, State, section, or other area, or in the available work force in any community, State, section, or other area.

...

(l)   It shall be an unlawful employment practice for a respondent, in connection with the selection or referral of applicants or candidates for employment or promotion, to adjust the scores of, use different cutoff scores for, or otherwise alter the results of, employment related tests on the basis of race, color, religion, sex, or national origin.

(m) Except as otherwise provided in this title, an unlawful employment practice is established when the complaining party demonstrates that race, color, religion, sex, or national origin was a motivating factor for any employment practice, even though other factors also motivated the practice.

(n) (1) (A) Notwithstanding any other provision of law, and except as provided in paragraph (2), an employment practice that implements and is within the scope of a litigated or consent judgment or order that resolves a claim of employment discrimination under the Constitution or Federal civil rights laws may not be challenged under the circumstances described in subparagraph (B).

Despite the failure to ratify the ERA, and despite the protections offered by the Civil Rights Act of 1964 (and the later version, the Civil Rights Act of 1991), discussions regarding the treatment of women and racial/ethnic minorities in the workplace have not ceased. Some suggest that a woman or member of a minority group doing the same job as a white, male counterpart is likely to be paid significantly less. Others focus on the lack of advancement possibilities for women and minorities at the highest levels of corporate structure—the so-called glass ceiling. Measuring such inequities, of course, is no small task. Because such claims require all other factors (expertise, education, commitment to a job, performance) to be equal, deciding whether inequities exist (and if so, how large they are) has proven difficult.

Writing to Respond

Considering the many possible perspectives on the ideal of equal pay for equal work, it is a topic that requires a good deal of narrowing and focusing, should you choose to enter this ongoing conversation. Below is a series of documents that are pertinent to the issues surrounding gender, race, and work. As you read each document, use the active reading skills discussed earlier to uncover the topics and approaches to questions of work equity that are possible, considering also how the discourse community and intended audience for each piece change the ways in which the writer proceeds and the types of evidence he or she includes.

You might then choose one of the topics uncovered here as a starting point for further research. Using the skills discussed in Part 3 of this book, inform yourself on this topic as widely as you can in preparation for writing either an informational paper that helps your readers to understand the key issues involved in your topic or a position paper that argues for a more enlightened and informed approach to the issue you are investigating.

The Other Gender Gap

Naomi Barko

Naomi Barko is a freelance journalist who often writes on topics concerning women's rights.

Hazel Dews is slightly embarrassed when you ask about her salary. She pauses and then confesses that after 25 years cleaning the Russell Senate Office Building in Washington five nights a week, she makes barely $22,000 a year. That's not what really bothers her, though. What irks her is that men who do the same job earn $30,000. The men, she explains, are called "laborers." They can progress five grades. The women, however, are called "custodial workers," which means they can only advance two grades. "But," she protests, "they scrub with a mop and bucket. We scrub with a mop and bucket. They vacuum. We vacuum. They push a trash truck. We push a trash truck. The only thing they do that we don't is run a scrub machine. But that's on wheels, so we could do it too."

Thirty-seven years after the Equal Pay Act of 1963, American women working full time still earn an average of 74 cents for each dollar earned by men, according to a new report published jointly by the AFL-CIO and the Institute for Women's Policy Research (IWPR) in Washington. This affects all economic classes, but its impact is strongest on lower-income workers: If men and women were paid equally, more than 50 percent of low-income households across the country—dual-earner as well as single-mother—would rise above the poverty line.

New figures challenge the long-heard arguments that women's lower pay results from fewer years in the work force or time out for childbearing and rearing. The Women's Bureau of the Department of Labor cites a study by the president's Council of Economic Advisers showing that even in light of the vicissitudes of motherhood, 43 percent of the wage gap remains "unexplained," evidently due in large part to discrimination.

The Overview of Salary Surveys, published last year by the National Committee on Pay Equity (NCPE), summarized 23 surveys of specific salary titles conducted by professional associations and trade magazines. It reported that, for instance, among women engineers—where the salary gap averages 26 percent—women with the same qualifications continue to earn less than men even after they've been in the field for many years (20.4 percent less among women with a B.S. degree and 20–24 years of experience; 19.2 percent less among women with an M.S. and 20–24 years experience). Yet another study found that women physicians earned less than men in 44 of 45 specialties, including obstetrics-gynecology (14 percent less) and pediatrics (15.8 percent less), with lower compensation only partly explainable by hours worked or time spent in the field. And a 1999 report by the American Association of University Professors found that though women had grown from 23 to 34 percent of faculty since 1975, the salary gap had actually widened in that time period.

But the biggest reason for the pay gap is not discrimination against individual women but rather discrimination against women's occupations. As the percentage of women in an occupation rises, wages tend to fall. More than 55 percent of employed women work in traditional "women's jobs"—librarians, clerical workers, nurses, teachers, and child care workers. If these women are compared not to male workers, but to women with similar education and experience in more gender-balanced occupations, they would earn about 18 percent—or $3,446—more per year, according to the IWPR. (The 8.5 percent of men in these jobs earn an average of $6,259 less per year than men of comparable backgrounds working in "men's" fields.) Why are "women's jobs" less lucrative? Is a truck driver—who earns an average annual wage of $25,030—really 45 percent more valuable than a child care worker who may have a four-year degree in early childhood education? Is a beginning engineer really worth between 30 and 70 percent more than a beginning teacher? Rarely, in the almost daily reports of teacher shortages, is it mentioned that the market alone cannot account for the striking disparity between teachers' and other professionals' salaries. No one ever suggests that it might have something to do with the fact that 75 percent of elementary and secondary schoolteachers are women.

In response to these disparities, women are beginning to mobilize. Three years ago, for example, Hazel Dews and 300 of her fellow women custodians joined the American Federation of State, County and Municipal Employees (AFSCME), which, after several futile attempts to negotiate, is now suing Dews's employer, the Architect of the Capitol, for equal pay. Since 1997, as women's membership in the labor movement has mushroomed to 40 percent, the AFL-CIO has conducted two surveys to discover the chief concerns of both union and nonunion workingwomen. "And the runaway answer was equal pay," reports Karen Nussbaum, the director of the AFL-CIO's working women's department. Ninety-four percent of women in both surveys said equal pay was a top concern, and one-third—one-half of African-American women—said they did not have equal pay in their own jobs.

Last year, calling pay equity a "family issue," the labor movement helped launch equal-pay bills in both houses of Congress and 27 state legislatures. Also last year, as Dews and her coworkers were demonstrating at the Capitol, the Eastman Kodak Company was agreeing to pay $13 million in present and retroactive wages to employees underpaid on the basis of either race or gender.

The Massachusetts Institute of Technology, after protests by women faculty, made an unprecedented admission that it had discriminated against women "in salaries, space, awards, resources and response to outside offers."

Moreover, since 1997 the Office of Federal Contract Compliance Programs (OFCCP) has collected $10 million in equal-pay settlements from such corporations as Texaco, US Airways, Pepsi-Cola, the computer manufacturer Gateway, and health insurer Highmark, Inc. At the same time, two major national chains, the Home Depot and Publix Supermarkets, agreed to pay more than $80 million each to settle lawsuits based on sex discrimination.

Recently, advocates have arrived at what they believe to be an effective means of generating pay equity—the concept of "comparable worth," which, as the name suggests, requires two people with comparable skills, education, and experience to be paid comparable amounts, even when they're working at two very different jobs. The Xerox Corporation, for example, uses comparable worth analysis, weighing such factors as education, experience, skill, responsibility, decision making, and discomfort or danger in working conditions, to set salary levels within the country. During the 1980s, some 20 state governments studied the comparable worth of their own employees and made adjustments totaling almost $750 million in increased pay to women. Minnesota, the leader in the field, has made pay equity adjustments in 1,544 counties and localities.

Perhaps the most dramatic argument for comparable worth, however, was made by a man. In the class action suit AFSCME v. Washington State in 1982, one of the nine named plaintiffs was Milt Tedrow, a licensed practical nurse at Eastern State Hospital in Spokane. Approaching retirement and realizing that his "woman's" job wouldn't give him much of a pension, Tedrow switched to carpentry at the same hospital. To qualify as an LPN he had needed at least four years of experience, four quarters of schooling, and a license. As a carpenter, he was self-taught, had no paid work experience, and had no need of a license. And yet when he transferred from the top of the LPN wage scale to the bottom of the carpenter's, his salary jumped more than $200 a month—from $1,614 to $1,826. Why, Tedrow wondered at the time, does the state resent "paying people decently who are taking care of people's bodies, when they'd pay a lot for someone fixing cars or plumbing"? Since then, the courts have ruled that evidence of unfair salaries is not enough to prove violation of the Equal Pay Act. Plaintiffs must prove that employers intentionally discriminated by lowering women's wages in comparison to men's. But some unions have prevailed on comparable worth questions by way of negotiations.

Service Employees International Union Local 715, for example, in Santa Clara County, just south of San Francisco, won nearly $30 million for 4,500 county employees, from secretaries to mental-health counselors. A study of some 150 job titles, performed by a consulting firm chosen jointly by the county and the union, showed that underpayment was common in job classes with more than 50 percent minorities, such as licensed vocational nurses and beginning social workers, and that 70 percent of such positions were filled by women. "We worked for at least three years to bring our male members along on this," says Kristy Sermersheim, Local 715's executive secretary. "When the county argued that in order to raise women's wages they'd have to lower men's, we refused to even discuss it. We kept regular pay negotiations completely separate."

Another key to the local's success was the staunch support of allies among local women's groups. "We had 54 women's community groups on our side," reports Sermersheim. "The National Organization for Women, the American Association of University Women, the League of Women Voters, the Silicon Valley women engineers. . . ." On the day the county board of supervisors voted on whether to proceed with the study, the local delivered 1,000 pink balloons—symbolizing the pink-collar ghetto—to workplaces around the city. "We had balloons everywhere," recalls Sermersheim, "We had Unitarian women out there singing 'Union Maid.'"

It is this kind of coalition that pay equity advocates are counting on to push through the equal-pay bills now before state legislatures. Many of the new bills, unlike those passed in the 1980s, would extend comparable worth to private as well as public employees and would specifically extend benefits to minorities. Most are based on the fair pay act designed in consultation with the NCPE—a coalition of 30 women's, labor, civil rights, and religious groups—and introduced in Congress in 1999 by two Democrats, Senator Tom Harkin of Iowa and Representative Eleanor Holmes Norton of the District of Columbia. (A more modest paycheck fairness act, backed by the Clinton administration, would toughen the Equal Pay Act of 1963 by removing present caps on damages and making it easier to bring class action suits.)

So far the new state bills have met with only modest success. The New Jersey and New Mexico legislatures have voted to study pay equity in both public and private employment, and Vermont's legislature voted to study just state employment. In Maine, where the new welfare laws gave rise to a commission to study poverty among working parents, it was discovered that the state already had a 1965 law on the books that mandated equal pay for both public and private employees and that specifically mentioned comparable worth. The state is now studying ways to put the law into effect.

Efforts like these have raised opposition from business and conservative groups. Economist Diana Furchgott-Roth, a resident fellow at the American Enterprise Institute who recently represented business at an NCPE forum, supports "equal pay for equal work" but claims that comparable worth causes labor short-ages because men refuse to take jobs where their wages will be tied to women's. "How can a government bureaucrat calculate if a secretary is worth the same as a truck driver, or a nurse as an oil-driller?"

In Ontario, Canada, Furchgott-Roth says, where the practice of comparable worth is more common, day care centers are actually closing down because par-ents can't afford to pay for the higher salaries. But these charges turn out to be only partially true. Child care centers in Ontario were threatened when a Progressive Conservative government succeeded the liberal New Democrats and slashed fund-ing. But the centers have not closed down. After a court challenge and an enor-mous public outcry, the provincial government is still subsidizing pay equity for child care workers (who, even with subsidies, earn an average of only $16,000 a year).

State employment officials in Minnesota and Wisconsin, two states with comparable worth laws, say that any labor shortages have far more to do with the tight labor market than with comparable worth. "There's a lot of flexibility in the law," says Faith Zwemke, Minnesota's pay equity coordinator. "For informa-tion technology people, for instance, we can give them signing bonuses and let them advance faster within the parameters of the policy."

Some male workers inevitably do resent women getting increases. "But many men can see pay equity as a family issue," says Karen Nussbaum of the AFL-CIO. A recent poll by Democratic pollster Celinda Lake showed that six out of 10 vot-ers, both men and women, said equal pay was good for families. Pay equity advo-cates had better be patient and persistent. The market has been biased against women at least since it was written in the Old Testament that when a vow offer-ing is made to God, it should be based on the value of the person, and "[if] a male, from the age of twenty years up to the age of sixty years, your assessment shall be fifty silver shekels . . . and if it is a female, your assessment shall be thirty shekels." At this rate, winning equal pay may take a long time.

How Equal Is Equal Pay?

Teresa Brady

Teresa Brady is an attorney in private practice in Bucks County, Penn-sylvania. She also is a management consultant and writes frequently on employment law.

Abstract: Women earn 75% of men's median income in 1998. Equal pay structures exist in theory more often than in practice even though the Equal Pay

Act was enacted in 1973. This inequality has an effect on each woman's purchasing power, on the economic well-being of children of single mothers, on general wages and living standards and on the free flow of goods and services. Almost a quarter-century has passed since equal pay became the law. But surprisingly little has changed. Have we come a long way, baby, in receiving the same pay as men for equal or equivalent work? In 1973, when the Equal Pay Act was established, gender-based wage disparities became illegal. Today, 25 years later, equal-pay structures do exist—but more in theory than in practice. The imbalance continues. Why have we come such a short way?

To gain some insight into the matter, I polled college students of both sexes why they believe pay discrimination continues. The quotes listed below are but a few of the responses noted on the survey. Most of these business students are 18 to 22 years old, so they weren't even born when the Equal Pay Act was passed. The fact that they grew up with such legislation in place makes comments such as the following even more disturbing:

- "Stop bitching and do your job like men have been doing for years." (male student)
- "More men are employed in higher-paying positions." (female student)
- "Because God is a man." (male student)
- "When we get a female president, all will change!" (female student)
- "Men are head honchos in companies." (male student)
- "Women don't like to talk about salaries or about their promotions. They would rather talk about children and baby food." (female student)
- "Women are basically talentless compared to men. This is self-explanatory." (male student)

What these students may not realize is that pay disparity for men and women who do the same work has a serious effect on the economy. On the micro level, such inequality directly affects each woman's purchasing power (and it is an established fact that most marketing is directed at the female population). The children of single mothers also suffer as a result.

On the macro level, this imbalance has many repercussions: Wages and living standards become depressed when women receive lower pay than men for equal work, available labor resources aren't fully utilized, labor disputes are instigated and the free flow of goods is hampered. With so many reasons that pay inequality is harmful, why does it continue?

Pay Inequality in the Workplace

Although the Equal Pay Act was passed in 1973, statistics show that the law has not had the intended effect on pay equality. According to the Bureau of Labor

Statistics, in nine instances since 1973 the gap between men's and women's pay actually widened from one year to the next.

Today, women earn approximately 75 percent of men's median income, down from 77 percent just four years ago. Pay equality is most prevalent for those 16 to 24 years old. In that age-group, women earn more than 90 percent of men's wages. But the pay gap widens to roughly 75 percent for those at the height of their careers, in the 25- to 54-year-old-age-group. Differences in pay may occur because women take time off for their full- or part-time childcaring. But other forces may contribute to pay inequality as well:

Welfare reform: Clinton's promise to eliminate public aid as we know it will result in scores of women leaving the welfare rolls. These women will enter the workforce with little or no skills and create a downward pull on median wages.

Economic forces: According to economist Dr. Bette Tokar of Holy Family College Philadelphia, supply-and-demand factors help explain why pay inequity persists. "Traditionally, most women have held very specific occupations, particularly the three S's (schoolteacher, secretary and social worker) as well as nurse, waitress, etc.," says Tokar. "These 'women's jobs' were paid at low rates. Men often did not even consider such jobs because of the lack of prestige in doing 'women's work' and the low rate of pay." Tokar thinks two key factors may change this picture. As men of the 1990s begin to focus more on family needs than on their careers, they will feel more comfortable doing jobs that traditionally have been considered "women's work." Also, as modern women increasingly enter male-dominated fields such as accounting, it is finally being recognized that they, too, need the advanced skills and knowledge their male counterparts have. These simultaneous changes in direction could create more equity all around.

Cultural biases: When the students in my survey were asked why they think pay inequality continues to exist, the most common response cited by male respondents (20 percent) was that "men dominated society." This was the second most common response among women (21 percent). Their most popular response was that "men dominate the workplace" (24 percent). Almost all of these students were born after the Equal Pay Act was passed, so they obviously developed these attitudes at home, at school and at work.

The Equal Pay Act

What does the Equal Pay Act require of companies? Under the 1973 law, covered employers must pay employees of both sexes the same wages for substantially equal work in jobs that require equal skills, effort and responsibility and that are performed under similar working conditions. This requirement applies to all forms of compensation, such as incentives and piece-rate pay, overtime, vacation and holiday pay and employer contributions to fringe-benefit plans.

The Equal Pay Act is part of the Fair Labor Standards Act. Therefore, statutory requirements must be met before the law's coverage takes effect. For example, the employer must be involved in an enterprise engaged in commerce or in the production of goods for commerce, and the plaintiff must be an "employee" as defined by the act. Notably, the term "wages" was defined by the Equal Pay Act or the Fair Labor Standards Act. The EEOC has attempted to define wages very broadly to include all payments made to an employee as remuneration for employment. This definition includes profit sharing, expense accounts, bonuses, use of a company car and fringe benefits. All subcategories of wages, such as "fringe benefits," also are included. As a result, hospital and retirement coverage would be covered. The law applies only to sex discrimination in the form of unequal pay for substantially equal work. In determining the equality of jobs, the courts give some weight to job titles, classifications and descriptions, but the controlling factors are actual job performance and job content. The act defines "equal work" as work that involves equal skills, effort and responsibility and is performed in similar working conditions. Here, a look at each of those factors:

- Equal skill. The courts usually begin their analysis of an Equal Pay Act case by focusing on the equality of skills actually and regularly used in the performance of the jobs in question. Factors such as experience, training, education and ability—as they relate to the performance requirements of the job—are important. The courts do not consider personal or individual skills that a person happens to possess. Nor do they look at an extra skill that is rarely used on the job or is needed for insignificant amounts of time.

- Equal effort. The term equal effort refers to the amount or degree of mental or physical exertion actually and regularly needed for the performance of the jobs being compared. Intermittent or infrequent extra effort will not justify a pay differential if most of the job duties are equal. For instance, in Usery vs. Columbia University, the dispute involved custodial workers who did "light" and "heavy" work. Those in the "light" category were required to do tasks such as dust mopping or vacuuming corridor floors, polishing furniture and emptying ashtrays. Those in the "heavy" category performed duties such as collecting bags of trash, wet mopping floors and cleaning toilets and sinks. Traditionally, female custodians have been light cleaners and male custodians have been heavy cleaners who were paid a differential. The female custodians sued for equal wages, but the court found that the additional lifting, fetching and hauling by the heavy cleaners required greater effort. Therefore, the pay differential was justified.

- Equal responsibility. In determining whether certain jobs involve equal responsibility, the courts also consider such factors as employee accountability. Those who have minor additional responsibilities or occasionally fill in for someone may not justify a pay differential. In the case of Miranda vs. B&B Cash Grocery Store, Inc., Karen Miranda was paid $400 a week as a grocery buyer while her male colleagues received $600. Although the duties were the same, the company explained that the pay differential was based on budgetary constraints. The court disagreed and found the grocery store in violation of the Equal Pay Act.

- Similar working conditions. Working conditions include the physical surroundings of the job and any job hazards that are regularly encountered, such as the presence of toxic chemicals and fumes. A company may pay night-shift differentials if they are based on any factor other than sex. In certain cases, companies may be able to justify unequal pay. For example, a pay disparity may be legal if it is based on a seniority, merit or productivity system, or if a job requires employees to lift or move heavy objects. Unequal pay also may be justified if it is based on any factor "other than" gender. These "other than" factors are numerous: job-evaluation systems, job-classification systems and shift differentials, to name a few. To prove a violation of the Equal Pay Act, an employee must demonstrate that a male and a female worker employed by the same establishment are paid different wages, on the basis of sex, for equal work. The burden then shifts to the employer, who may rebut any of the allegations or prove affirmatively that the unequal pay resulted from a permitted exception to the equal pay requirement.

What HR Needs to Know

No matter what the average person will say, it's illegal to pay women less than men for equal work. Here are some general points you may want to consider:

- Understand the scope of the Equal Pay Act. The law is limited strictly to wage disparities based on gender. It does not apply to any other wage-disparity issue, such as pay differentials for those who work a night shift or work in hazardous conditions.

- Remember that the law is gender-neutral. Nothing in the act would prevent males from using the law to claim pay inequality. However, bear in mind that such instances have been rare.

- Use "red-circle policies" with care. A company must be consistent in its application of red-circle policies, which freeze current wage rates or salary levels for employees who have been demoted or assigned to lower-paying jobs because of a downsizing or an employee's medical situation. If your company has such a policy, it is a good idea not to keep it a secret. Communicate the policy widely and circulate it in your employee handbook and HR manual.

■ Clarify supervisory titles. Make sure these titles accurately reflect the job duties and responsibilities of each position. A company should have a published and consistent pay policy that differentiates between managerial and nonmanagerial positions. For example, the policy might state that all supervisory and management employees are paid 12 percent more than nonsupervisory employees. It is in a company's best interest to stay informed about equal-pay issues. Employees will be less likely to take action against you—and more likely to think you're the one who has come a long way!

To Be Young, Black, and Female: Falling Further Behind in the Shifting Economy

Laura Dresser

Laura Dresser, a member of the Dollars and Sense Collective, which purports to meet the need for "left perspectives on current economic affairs," teaches women's studies at Harvard University.

Abstract: The difficulties that young black women face in the workplace are a result of job shortage and low wages because of national economic problems, and the discrimination harbored against minorities. While white women can claim to be the only demographic group that did not experience wage declines in the recessionary 1980s, their black counterparts suffered most in economic terms. Their fate was especially pitiable in the Midwest states where manufacturing employment plunged. Since the 1970s the average earnings of most workers have been falling consistently. For most young workers the situation has been worse, with job opportunities and wages in sharp decline. The losses have been especially severe for African Americans (see "The Racial Divide Widens," *Dollars & Sense*, Jan/Feb 1995). Among young workers (those who had been in the labor market for less than ten years), white women were the only demographic group whose wages did not fall during the 1980s—and this left African-American women further behind. The degree of losses suffered by black women varied, depending on how much education they had and the area of the country where they lived. Among black women with little education, for example, the declining real value of the minimum wage contributed to relative wage erosion. In the Midwest, the decline in manufacturing jobs disproportionately affected

African-American women. Affirmative action apparently offered no protection to the black community from the downward slide of the 1980s. Remarkably, falling relative wages were most severe among college-educated black workers—the very group that affirmative action programs are thought to have helped the most. Shrinking job markets in education and the public sector, along with declining unionization, were probably responsible for many of the losses to African-American women with college degrees.

What is true for all these groups, however, is that our ability to "explain" the gap between white and black women's wages, based on factors such as those above, has declined. While this gap remains a mystery, one suspects that institutional racism has again surfaced as a source of wage differentials.

A Little History

African-American women occupy the intersection of two major labor market trends—the declining wages of blacks and the increasing wages of women. While black women's wages have fallen, they have not fallen nearly as rapidly as the wages of African-American men. At the same time, they have not experienced any of the gains that made the 1980s the decade of women's economic emergence.

The position of black women in the labor market has always been unique, constrained by race, gender and class oppression. But research on gender and race has tended to ignore the particular experience of African-American women: the title of an anthology about black women, *All the Men Are Black, All the Women are White, but Some of Us Are Brave*, points out the limitations of most mainstream studies of labor markets, especially before the late 1980s. Black women's opportunities have never perfectly reflected the opportunities of either white women or black men. For example, in 1940 more than three-fourths of urban African-American women worked in the personal services industry; mostly they held the "women's" job of maid. At the same time, most rural black women worked as farm laborers—the same jobs that black men held.

In 1959, black women's real hourly wages were 64% of the wages of white women. Migration out of the South and educational and occupational advancement increased African-American women's wages to near parity with white women by 1979.

Since the late 1970s, however, the precarious nature of black women's "success" has been revealed. Like many other workers, black women suffered during the labor market upheaval of the 1980s. Their falling real wages, and growing chances of unemployment and impoverishment, attest to the trials of African-American women. These setbacks have been focused among young workers, as they have been for black men. Young black women (workers who have been out of school for ten years or less) earned 96% of the wages of young white women in 1975, but only 85% in 1991. Since the experience of young workers tends to be a harbinger of things to come, the relative wages of all African-American women are likely to further erode in the future.

Education and Location Matter

Why have white women outpaced black women? The answer varies greatly for different regional and educational groups. The South, for example, has always provided the worst relative wages for black women. But the relative situation there was fairly constant during the 1970s and 1980s—young African-American women with twelve or less years of school consistently earned 10% less than young white women in the same educational group. By contrast, black women in the Midwest fell from parity with whites in 1970 to a 10% disadvantage by 1991, as the manufacturing share of jobs plummeted. In the Northeast, the relative wages of young black women actually improved in the late 1980s.

The relative wages of young African-American high school graduates fell steadily from a 5% disadvantage in 1978 to a 10% disadvantage in 1991. These women had been disproportionately represented by unions and suffered not only from economic restructuring, but also from declining unionization. The declining minimum wage also hurt these black women. Among women without high school degrees wages have fallen rapidly, but the gap between whites and blacks has changed very little.

The relative wages of young college educated African-American women fell dramatically from 1973 to 1991. In 1973, black college graduates earned around 10% more than their white counterparts. By 1991 they were at a 10% wage disadvantage. In inflation-adjusted terms, young white college graduates' hourly wages grew from $12.02 in 1973 to $12.71 in 1991, while those of blacks fell from $13.52 to $11.78. The 1980s were good for most highly educated workers, but African-American women did not reap the same benefits as white women. Why did the wages of young black college graduates fall severely? Job losses in educational and public administration positions, and corresponding declines in unionization of black women, explain part of the trend. In 1973, the education sector employed most college educated women—57% of young whites and 70% of young blacks. Due to declining school enrollments and shrinking budgets, employment opportunities for new entrants to the education labor market declined greatly. In 1989 only 20% of young female college graduates, both black and white, worked in education.

Meanwhile, women college graduates, especially whites, have made inroads into management occupations since the late 1970s. In 1973, 6.8% of white and 7.4% of African-American college graduates were in management occupations. These figures rose to 20.6% and 15.9% in 1989. But black college graduates have been channeled primarily into clerical jobs instead of management. By 1989, 14.5% of young white college graduates and 29.5% of young black college graduates worked in clerical occupations. The obvious wage disparity between management and clerical jobs caused part of the relative losses of black women.

Why the Private Sector Is Worse

While changes in education, residence, industry, occupation, unionization, and the declining minimum wage together explain some of the relative wage losses of African-American women, much of the growth in the racial wage gap cannot be attributed to changes in those statistical factors. What, then, are the causes? One is reduced enforcement of equal opportunity and affirmative action laws, along with the renewed legitimacy of racism within the political mainstream. Labor practices within firms, such as job titles, wage setting, and promotion possibilities, also play a critical role, especially as public service jobs have declined, and black women have looked increasingly to the private sector for employment. Racism and discrimination against black women may have remained imbedded within firms, even as these same firms allowed white women increased access to better jobs.

In private sector management, African-American women face barriers not only to employment but also to advancement within firms. According to Ella Bell and Stella Nkomo, authors of a recent study for the Department of Labor, "The barriers that existed twenty years ago and were believed to be eradicated are alive and well and have grown more complex in a societal climate that is less tolerant of demands for civil rights and in a society where many Whites, and even some African-Americans themselves, believe that racial inequities have been squelched." Bell and Nkomo show that subtle racism pervades the day-to-day experience of most black managers, limiting their access to mentors, information, positive reviews and advancement. Black women's authority is often not accepted by co-workers and their accomplishments are frequently credited to luck rather than skill. Additionally, black female managers within firms are often concentrated in human resource departments and other areas with little hope of significant advancement. Their study suggests that even those black women who do make inroads into managerial positions will not find the same opportunities for advancement that white women will.

As one black manager related, "Joan is okay, but she can never hear anything intelligent from a black person, especially me. I'm in a position where she cannot avoid working with me, but she tries. Joan just refuses to acknowledge the validity of my role. So she'll deal with anyone else around me, but she will not deal with me directly. And I've tried to talk to her about it. . . . I've tried to explain to my boss what I believe the problem to be. Joan refuses to deal with a black woman in authority . . . when I do try to complain, [my boss] thinks I'm being paranoid."

In all regions and at all educational levels, African-American women earn less money than white women. In most cases, these wage differentials are growing. Black women's wage erosion holds special significance both because mothers' incomes are the single source of support for an increasing proportion of all U.S. families, and because on average black women earn a larger share of family incomes than do white women. While debates about welfare reform pervade the political mainstream, the intrinsically related debate about women's labor market opportunities is ignored. In fact, the gains of white women have been used to show the glories of women's participation in the labor market. But for black women, even those with college degrees, the 1980s were a decade to forget.

Resources

Ella Edmondson Bell and Stella Nkomo, "Barriers to Workplace Advancement Experienced by African-Americans," Glass Ceiling Commission, U.S. Department of Labor, March 1994.

"What Stirs below the Surface?" An Exploration of Gender Issues and Family Values

Tracy Hanegraaf

This student essay is by Tracy Hanegraaf, whose proposal for research appears in Reading and Writing Applications 6. Read Hanegraaf's piece in light of the other articles presented above, considering the ways that she uses similar information on the gender-wage gap to develop a different focus for her own study.

Over the past twenty years, my husband and I have struggled with maintaining an adequate income to feed, clothe, shelter, and educate our four children. I am sure that we are not unlike many families today, where parents are forced to make personal decisions that affect their income, careers, and ultimately, their family. Family values are reflected in choices made by these parents, shaping the composition, character, and attitudes of women in the workplace.

While society has been caught up in the fight for women's rights, it has been the rights of working parents that stir the waters below the surface of these issues. In the past forty years, women's rights have focused on the issues of gender discrimination and the wage gap. Alarming figures were released last year from the U.S. Census Bureau, followed by a multitude of reports investigating the continual gender wage battle. These figures claimed that women earn 76.5

cents to every one dollar earned by men ("Closing the Gap," ABC News). Following the release of these new figures, more reports claimed that women continue to be undervalued in the workplace, excluded for promotions, and paid $15,000 a year less than their equally educated male counterparts (Castro; Endicott; Mand; "Salary Disparity"). Are these figures accurate?

Upon examination of this oversimplified figure, one finds that the salaries of all men working thirty-five hours and more are compared to the annual salaries of all women, working thirty-five hours and more. Another method used to create the male versus female ratio uses median weekly pay of full-time workers, and indicates an even larger wage gap (Pine; Sorensen 14–15). These comparisons purposely create alarm, while ignoring the many variables involved in this complicated issue.

In fact, a *Working Women* magazine survey conducted in 1996 compiled extensive data on men and women working in similar positions, in similar fields, and concluded that the wage gap was significantly more narrow (women earn 85 to 95 percent to men) than the media claimed (Lynch and Post). Most importantly, these reports fail to expose evidence that men work more hours per week, and more weeks per year on average than women (Lynch and Post; Sorenson 14–15). A 1984 Census Bureau study found that women spend eight times the number of work years away from work than men.

Time away from work is a direct result of having children. Many studies indicate that the wage gap disappears for women without children. Studies done by June O'Neill suggests that women between the ages of twenty-seven and thirty-three, who never had a child, earned almost 98 percent as much as men in the same occupation (Lynch and Post). The Urban Institute Study found the most significant reason for the remaining gender gap is the fact that only 10 percent of women between the ages of thirty-five and forty-one work continuously. These constantly working women are less likely to marry or have children. They earn 50 percent more than the intermittently working women. In contrast, 93 percent of the intermittently working women marry, and over 86 percent have children (Sorenson 134). This intermittent labor force explains many reasons for women's pay and work issues. All along, economists have argued that women earn less because they work less (Sorenson 134; Pine; Toutkoushion 694; Lynch and Post). So, what is motivating this endless battle of the gender/wage war?

The major catalyst for the gender wage war has its origins in the women's equal rights movement that started at the end of the nineteenth century. Women removed their corsets, but the restrictions that faced them in the workplace at the end of the nineteenth century might as well have replaced them. At this time in history, women were restricted from working by laws. The attitude of the nation controlled views that laws were needed to protect women's maternal role. These laws forbade women from holding certain types of jobs, working night hours, and restricted the number of hours they could work (Conway, Ahern, and Steuernagel 60). However, our changing economy would soon force major changes for working women and increase demands for everyone in the workplace.

In the past twenty years, business in the United States has changed dramatically. Technology leapt by light-years, and employers reduced their work forces to improve efficiency and profits. This compounded workloads for employees, increased work hours, and created a less family-friendly business world. Unfortunately, the eighties society became a me generation that completely overlooked the foundation and conception of family. Parents attempting to balance their work-life with family are finding it increasingly difficult to manage and uphold family values. Statistics show that men and women are working more hours (49.9 hours per week for men and 44 hours per week for women) than ever. However, I question this documented statistic, because it only represents the hours that they work outside of the home. My grandfather worked full-time in a woodworking factory, nights as a ticket seller at a local theatre, was a subsistence farmer, and raised capons to sell at the holidays. He also smoked meats in his smokehouse, made homemade wine, and grew the best crop of sweet corn in southern York County in the middle of this past century. He never owned a car and worked into his eighties. He was also a father of eight children, explaining the amount of work he did. I am certain he worked more than 55 hours a week, but many of those hours were spent at or near his home.

Surprisingly, my grandmother also worked outside of the home during some of the years that she raised her family. How could my grandparents manage this large family while working so much? For one thing, families were larger, but children were spread out many years, as with my grandparents' family. Twenty-four years spanned between my mother, the youngest child, and her eldest sister. This large family looked after one another, with older brothers and sisters caring for younger siblings, sometimes along with their own children.

Until recently, most women who work have done so in the areas of women's work. My aunts, the same ones that cared for my mother at home, took jobs doing women's work, also. Working in sewing factories and paid by piecework, they bided their time until they would marry and start their own families. They undoubtedly had intentions of marrying and bearing children; a career was the last thing on their minds. Even in the 1960s, most women did not expect to be working at age thirty-five (Lynch and Post). As late as the early 1970s, over 60 percent of women felt women belonged at home. In contrast, less than 9 percent of women agree with this stand today (Sorenson 132).

How did attitudes concerning working women change this much in the past thirty years? These attitudes have been slow to change. Men have always been considered the breadwinners for the family. Following the women's rights move-ments of the sixties, women who worked were viewed as being a feminist or doing so out of a desire for extra income. Even today, some people ignore the necessary role that most women's income provides for the family (Endicott). Attitudes have influenced the pay that women receive; a woman working in the same occupation as a man, does not necessarily get paid equally, but laws have improved this situation greatly.

The Equal Pay Act of 1963 was passed to narrow the difference between wages of men and women who perform equal work. Additionally the Civil Rights Act of 1964 and additional orders of this act were intended to increase employment opportunities for women (Conway, Ahern, and Steuernagel 72). These laws made it illegal for employers to refuse to hire someone on the basis of gender (Conway, Ahern, and Steuernagel 72). Women made great strides in equal rights, but at the same time, working families forfeited their family values.

Today, families do not have the benefit of extended family to care for the children. Most parents work outside of the home and mothers are the sole providers and caretakers for their children (1997 National Study). Our society has moved into a completely different style of work era, and our families are suf-fering the consequences of a government and business world that neglects the value of the American family. Too often, the me generation ignores its families.

Attitudes have not always been this way. When I grew up in the 60s and 70s, my divorced mother raised my brother and me. She had a full-time clerical job (a keypunch operator), one that is considered women's work, while her management was primarily male. Her wages were meager, but the benefits were great for a divorced mother. Her male supervisors acknowledged the fact that she was a mother first, and she was excused from work to see to the needs of her children, even with pay. She was fortunate to have such understanding supervisors, although her salary was sacrificed to get the flexibility.

My mother's type of work was not unlike that of many women in my family. A generation ago, women on both sides of my family worked exclusively at women's work. Both of my grandmothers and many aunts worked in sewing factories. Even in my generation, most of my female relatives and friends work at jobs considered predominantly female occupations.

Nearly 60 percent of American women work in predominantly female fields as teachers, office workers, librarians, nurses, and child care providers (Castro). Moreover, these occupations represent the lowest paid professional careers (Castro; England 744). Despite these facts, a long-term study done in the early 1980s to identify reasons for the narrowing gender wage gap suggests one rea-son is the changing occupational characteristics of male and female workers (Sorenson 130). Women have made great strides infiltrating predominantly male professional areas. Female engineers have increased from 1.6 percent in 1970 to 9 percent in 1989 (Conway, Ahern, and Steuernagel 74). Just since 1993, the number of women in full-time executive and management positions has increased 29 percent ("Women Rise"). The percentage of MBAs awarded to women has risen from 3.6 percent in 1970 to 35.6 percent in 1993. The field of science has historically been predominantly male, but the presence of women has increased from 8.4 percent to 37.7 percent in recent years. Even the small percentage (5 percent in 1970) of women obtaining law degrees has multiplied to almost half the degrees awarded (43 percent) in the past twenty years (Lynch and Post). Women given the opportunity to work in predominantly men's fields have done so, leaving the remaining wage disparity to working mothers focused in the fields of women's work.

While women's work contributes partially to the gender wage gap, most of the disparity is related to women's choices regarding motherhood. A study cited in the *New York Times* indicates women lower their lifetime earnings by 13 percent with one child and this increases to 19 percent with the addition of a second child (Hewlett). Regardless of this fact, women are choosing to work fewer hours, take less pay, and remain in possibly less demanding positions, because they are the primary caregivers in their families (Blau and Kahn 626–627). Women enter and leave the job market, work fewer hours, and lose seniority during childbearing years. These are necessary choices that mothers and families are making.

Reasons for the gender wage gap translate into choices and attitudes. Women who desire to surpass the "glass ceiling" can accomplish their goals. The growth of female entrepreneurs shows their businesses employ 35 percent more people than the Fortune 500 companies employ worldwide. A study done in 1994, showed as many as 7.7 million women owned businesses in the United States (Lynch and Post). Women are choosing to be their own bosses. This allows them flexibility to work, to be mothers, and to aspire toward personal growth in their careers.

In our family, my priority was to be the main caregiver and nurturer of my children; these are just as important as feeding and clothing them. Indeed, many parents struggle between their instinctual priorities of family-first and loyalty to employers. Men and women choosing to value the non-monetary work benefits of flexibility, less travel time, and family-oriented careers need to be supported and revered for their decisions.

My children have always been my priority, even after I took a full-time position in a school. One would think that a job in a school would be ideal for a mother, and for the most part the hours were very accommodating. Nevertheless, I had a boss who asked me during my interview what I would do if my children were sick. This should have tipped me off immediately to his masked attitude. I answered him honestly, which should have deterred him from hiring me, since he obviously had a problem with this. He would get furious when I missed work to care for my daughter (who went through a period of repeated strep infections that eventually led to surgery), and he would refuse to communicate with me for several days upon my return. I began to panic whenever my daughter was the least bit nauseous or feverish, not only because of her illness, but the possibility that I would miss work. My dilemma is not uncommon for working mothers, who risk pay, advancement, or attitude issues when missing work to care for sick children.

Many employers display unsupportive attitudes regarding working mothers and fathers. When employers offer paid leave, flexible hours, and affordable child-care, they manifest respect and support for working parents; unfortunately, these are areas that most employers need to improve. A year ago, President Clinton signed an executive order banning discrimination against parents in the federal workplace (Hewlett). It is now illegal to withhold a job position or promotion from government employees because they have children. The rights of parents working for the government have improved, but what about the remaining millions?

Today over 46 percent of workers are parents with children under the age of eighteen at home. Fathers work more hours than men without children; in fact, fathers work an average of more than fifty hours a week. Mothers work more hours than ever, an average of over forty hours a week (1997 National Study). These are hours away from their homes and children. Research shows that most parents want to work less and have flexible job hours, emphasizing the needed support for working parents and a stronger commitment to the value of the family.

America's working women have made tremendous strides toward equality. Yet, the priorities of our nation—a nation troubled with racism, school violence, hate crimes, and teenage suicides—must be refocused on the American family. Family-first priorities should be at the forefront of equal rights for working men and women. "Both man and woman have to confront the conflict between their human needs—for love, for family, for meaning in work and purpose in life" (Friedan 242). Men and women choosing to value the non-monetary work benefits of flexibility, less travel time, and family-oriented careers need to be supported and revered for their decisions. America's children need their parents, and parents need the support and respect of society.

Works Cited

Blau, Francine D. and Lawrence M. Kahn. "Analyzing the Gender Pay Gap." *Quarterly Review of Economics and Finance* 39 (1999): 625–646.

Castro, Ida L. "Worth More Than We Earn: Fair Pay as a Step Toward Gender Equity." *National Forum* 77 (1997): 17. Expanded Academic ASAP. Gale Group. Schmidt Library, York College of PA, York. 20 Feb. 2001 http://web4.infotrac.galegroup.com/.

Conway, M. Margaret, David W. Ahern, and Gertrude A. Steuernagel. "Chapter 4: Equal Employment Opportunity Policy." *Women and Public Policy: A Revolution in Progress.* Washington, D.C.: Congressional Quarterly, 1995.

"Closing the Gap." ABC News.com. New York. 4 July 2000 http.//www.abcnews.go.com.

Endicott, R. Craig. "Gender Gap Always There, 'Exec Laments.'" *Advertising Age* 4 Dec. 2000: S5. Business Index ASAP. Gale Group. Schmidt Library, York College of PA, York. 28 Feb. 2001 http://web4.infotrac.galegroup.com/.

England, Paula. "The Case for Comparable Worth." *Quarterly Review of Economics and Finance* 39 (1999): 743–755.

Friedan, Betty. "The Quiet Movement of American Man." *The Conscious Reader.* Ed. Caroline Shrodes, Harry Finestone, and Michael Shugrue. Needham Heights: Allyn & Bacon, 2001: 242.

Hewlett, Sylvia Ann. "Have a Child, and Experience the Wage Gap." *New York Times* 16 May 2000: A31.

Hinscliff, Gaby. "Meek Women Lose Out in Battle for Pay." *Guardian Unlimited Observer* 10 Dec. 2000, UK. Lexis-Nexis. Schmidt Library, York College of PA, York. 6 Mar. 2001 http://observer.co.uk/uk/.

Lynch, Michael, and Katherine Post. "What Glass Ceiling?" *The Public Interest.* Summer 1996: 27. Expanded Academic Index ASAP. Gale Group. Schmidt Library, York College of PA, York. 16 Mar. 2001 http://web4.infotrac.galegroup.com/.

Mand, Adrienne. "Good News (Sort Of): Male-Female Wage Gap Narrowing (Maybe)." 18 Aug. 2000. Fox News 7 Mar. 2001 http://www.foxnews.com/.

"1997 National Study of the Changing Workforce: Executive Summary." Work-Life Research. Families and Work Institute. 25 Mar. 2001 http://www.familiesandwork.org.

Pine, Art. "Pay Problems." *Los Angeles Business Journal* 4 Dec. 2000: 47. Business Index ASAP. Gale Group. Schmidt Library, York College of PA, York. 28 Feb. 2001 http://web6.infotrac.galegroup.com/.

"Salary Disparity Shrinking But Not Gone." *USA Today* 15 Sept. 2000, natl.: 1A. Lexis-Nexis. Schmidt Library, York College of PA, York. 6 Mar. 2001 http://web.lexis-nexis.com/.

Sorensen, Elaine. *Exploring the Reasons Behind the Narrowing Gender Gap in Earnings.* Washington, D.C.: Urban Institute Press, 1991.

Toutkoushian, Robert K. "The Status of Academic Women in the 1990's: No Longer Outsiders, But Not Yet Equals." *Quarterly Review of Economics and Finance* 39 (1999): 679–698.

"Women Rise in Workplace But Wage Gap Continues." *The Wall Street Journal* 25 April 2000: A16.

Writing Applications

Though gender equality is one topic addressed in all of the above readings, a great number of related issues appear as well, and an almost infinite number of ways to respond with your own writing. With the help of your teacher and classmates, you should limit your area of concern, using the techniques of inquiry and focusing a topic discussed in Chapters 7–9 of this book. Below are just a few possibilities for how and places where you might begin those processes.

1. **Understanding the laws:** Excerpts from government legislation above detail key employment practices that are targeted to attempt to assure "civil rights." The full text of the legislation (which you might examine should you wish to do more in-depth research; it's available online) discusses details of enforcement, including the formation of a commission to oversee that enforcement. But even the excerpt included gives you a good idea of the detail that lawmakers employ in language as well as an understanding of the practices that this legislation is meant to prohibit. There are many possible researched writing projects that you might undertake in conjunction with these pieces of legislation. Here are just a few possibilities:

   - You might write an informational essay, summarizing the legislation and its effects for people who do not know the history and discussing its practical impact.

   - You might write your own version of a civil rights act, first defining what you mean by *civil rights* and then describing necessary measures to implement the measures you legislate.

   - You might interview employers, employees, or people who are old enough to remember how this act changed U.S. culture and its initial reception, your goal being a document that details its actual effects.

   - You might create an electronic text or website with hyperlinks to definitions, examples, other websites, and so on that can help the reader to understand the Civil Rights Act.

   - You might compare the success of the Equal Rights Act with that of the Equal Rights Amendment and consider whether this legislation makes the latter redundant or less necessary. Are rights assured in the Amendment that are not covered in the Act?

   - You might examine this piece as history, discussing the changes in U.S. culture in the last forty years and considering whether this legislation is responsible for some of those changes and whether this law accomplished its purposes. To do so, you might compare the original legislation with the Civil Rights Act of 1991. Enacted 21 November 1991, the more recent legislation was intended "to amend the Civil Rights Act of 1964 to strengthen and improve Federal civil rights laws, to provide for damages in cases of intentional employment discrimination, to clarify provisions regarding disparate impact actions, and for other purposes." The legislation was required because "The Congress finds that (1) additional remedies under Federal law are needed to deter unlawful harassment and intentional discrimination in the workplace; (2) the decision of the Supreme Court in Wards Cove Packing Co. v. Atonio, 490 U.S. 642 (1989) has weakened the scope and effectiveness of Federal civil rights protections; and (3) legislation is necessary to provide additional protections against unlawful discrimination in employment."

2. **Equal rights and the workplace:** After reading the series of positions on race and gender issues above, you might explore the present state of gender or race equity in the workplace. Using the techniques of research that were discussed in Part 3, and beginning from the information supplied through the readings above, write a position paper that explores some facet of this complex topic, weighing in with your own informed opinions on issues including, but certainly not limited to, the following:
   - The role of government in ensuring workplace equity
   - The ways in which specific employers have responded to civil rights/equal pay legislation
   - The relationship between the ethical issues involved in equal rights and the practical implications of fulfilling these ethical obligations
   - The relative potential for job advancement for people of your own race, ethnicity, gender, or religion

3. **Responding to other writers:** Each of the essays above takes a position on the issue of civil rights and equality. But as we have discussed throughout this book, reading actively requires you to examine critically what you read and to respond with your own informed opinions. Choose one of the essays above and, after performing further research, write a carefully planned and detailed response to one of the positions you find there. You might show how one of the articles does not account for all possible perspectives, how it neglects information that you have discovered through further research, or how its perspective is important and valuable (in which case you might extend the writer's argument with additional information you uncover). No matter whether you generally agree or disagree with the position to which you are responding, your job is to present credible evidence and to illustrate your expertise on this topic, developed through mature research processes.

Casebook 3 BOWLING ALONE? WORK, VOLUNTEERISM, AND CIVIC ENGAGEMENT

In his best-selling book *Bowling Alone: The Collapse and Revival of American Community*, Robert D. Putnam discusses the state of civic engagement in the U.S. at the end of the twentieth century. What *civic engagement* means (and how it is measured) is of course a difficult problem of definition. Literally, *civic engagement* refers to the active involvement of citizens in the affairs of their communities (local, state, national). It implies that we as citizens know what is going on both among our elected officials and in our neighborhoods, that we *care* about what is going on, and that we *act on* that knowledge and concern. This, of course, can be demonstrated at many levels: voting (or running for office), going to city council meetings (or running for city council), volunteering our time, writing letters to the editor on issues that concern us, being part of a town watch (or just looking out for the kids on our street).

How well our country is doing in this area is a matter of some debate, and the answers depend at least somewhat on the questions we ask. For example, there is evidence that people are volunteering their time more often—but is volunteering time the same as being engaged in the fate and future of the community? Does it make the volunteer know more? And does knowing more matter? In *What Americans Know about Politics and Why It Matters* (Yale UP, 1996), Scott Keeter and Michael X. Delli Carpini (my brother) argue that it does. They acknowledge that some political scientists suggest that "citizens are able to make reasonably good low-information decisions, and indeed are rational in doing so, because the demands of citizenship in contemporary democracies like the United States are presumed to be few, as are the tangible payoffs for engaging in politics." They, however, "take issue with these perspectives and make the case for the importance of a broadly and equitably informed citizenry."

An informed citizenry depends heavily on the associations we make—our willingness to spend time and share concerns with those with whom we share communities. But like the breakdown in our knowledge base that is reported by Delli Carpini and Keeter, there may also be a breakdown in community relations. In *Bowling Alone*, Putnam notes that

> At the conclusion of the twentieth century, ordinary Americans shared this sense of civic malaise. We were reasonably content about our economic prospects, hardly a surprise after an expansion of unprecedented length, but were not equally convinced that we were on the right track morally or culturally. Of baby boomers interviewed in 1987, 53 percent thought that their parents' generation was better in terms of "being a concerned citizen, involved in helping others in the community,'" as compared with only 21 percent who thought their own generation was better. Fully 77 percent said the nation was worse off because of "less involvement in community activities." In 1992 three-quarters of the U.S. workforce said that "the breakdown of community" and "selfishness" were "serious" or "extremely serious" problems in America. In 1996 only 8 percent of all Americans said that "honesty and integrity of the average American" were improving, as compared with 50 percent of us who thought we were becoming less trustworthy. Those of us who said that people had become less civil over the preceding ten years outnumbered those who thought people had become more civil, 80 percent to 12 percent. In several surveys in 1999 two-thirds of Americans said that America's civic life had weakened in recent years, that social and moral values were higher when they were growing up, and that our society was

focused more on the individual than the community. More than 80 percent said that there should be more emphasis on community, even if that put more demands on individuals.

Studies like those by Putnam and Keeter and Delli Carpini suggest two related but somewhat contradictory observations:

- A type of crisis of actual civic engagement exists.
- The belief that civic engagement is still important remains strong.

Similarly conflicting observations emerge from a study commissioned by the Center for Information and Research on Civic Learning and Engagement and the Center for Democracy and Citizenship:

- "Overall, young adults see politics and elections more as the business of elites, than avenues for democratic participation."
- "Young adults do not see themselves and their generation as particularly significant in the political process."
- "Four times as many young adults see volunteering in the local community as important (49%) as see getting involved in politics and government as important (12%)."
- "Donations to community or church organizations and involvement with a community group or club top the list of volunteer activities in which young adults have participated in the last couple of years. . . . 72 % of young adults say they have donated money, clothes, or food to a community or church organization in the past couple of years. This is the only activity that more than half the young adults have done."
- In comparison, "Fewer than a fifth have participated in an online discussion or visited a politically oriented website (18%). About a tenth have participated in a political march or demonstration (12%), volunteered in a political campaign (13%), joined a political club (13%), or worked for a political party (9%)."

Though increased volunteerism is clearly a positive sign, these statistics also show signs of political detachment. Since, as we've been discussing, so much of our *ethos* is related to the work we do, we might consider ways in which civic engagement can be related to our occupational lives.

Writing to Respond

Robert Putnam suggests in the excerpt from *Bowling Alone* included below that "any solution to the problem of civic disengagement must include better integration between our work lives and our community and social lives." Consider that statement as you read and respond to this piece in your writer's notebook.

Connections in the Workplace

Robert Putnam

Work-related organizations are conventionally seen through two different lenses. Economically, unions and professional societies are sometimes criticized as a form of monopoly cartel, as a modern-day guild, a means by which workers in a particular industry or profession can combine to suppress competition and boost income. Sociologically, however, these organizations are an important locus of social solidarity, a mechanism for mutual assistance and shared expertise. Fundamentally, of course, these two images are mutually reinforcing, since solidarity is a crucial precondition for economic collaboration. Even those who bemoan the economic consequences of teachers' unions or bar associations might acknowledge the social capital they represent.

Work-related organizations, both unions and business and professional organizations, have traditionally been among the most common forms of civic connectedness in America. In our inventory of social capital, this is an important ledger. The figure below summarizes trends in the rate of union membership in the United States over the course of the twentieth century. The details of this historical profile are linked to the specific history of American labor, such as the favorable effects of two world wars and the New Deal on collective bargaining.[1] However, the broad pattern is reminiscent of the pattern we have noted for both community-based and religious organizations: modest growth in the first

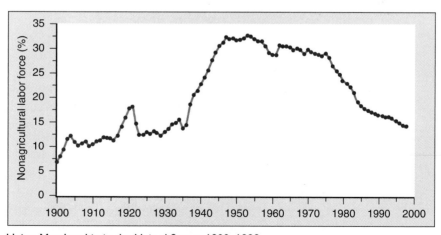

Union Membership in the United States, 1900–1998.

third of the century; rapid growth coming out of the Depression and World War II; a high plateau from the 1950s into the 1960s; and a sharp, sustained decline during the last third of the century.

For many years, labor unions provided one of the most common organizational affiliations among American working men (and less so, working women), and to some extent that has remained true in recent decades.[2] However, the rate of union membership has been falling for more than four decades with the steepest decline occurring since 1975. Since the mid-1950s when union membership peaked the unionized portion of the workforce in America has nose-dived from 32.5 percent to 14.1 percent. By now virtually all of the explosive growth in union membership that was associated with the New Deal has been erased. Moreover, the type of involvement in unions has slackened. Unions are now seen mostly as hired bargaining agents not as a social movement. Although unions, like other voluntary associations have often been plagued by oligarchy, apathy and corruption, historically they both created and depended upon social capital—that is, networks of reciprocity. By the end of the twentieth century, however, this once central element in the social life of working Americans had virtually vanished. The solidarity of union halls is now mostly a fading memory of aging men.

But isn't this decline in unionization simply a natural reflection of the changing structure of the postindustrial American economy? Many people consider collective bargaining "primarily suited for the male, blue-collar, production workers in the goods producing industry—the bastion of unions in the '50s—and of little interest to the female white-collar knowledge worker in the service industries—the vanguard of the new labor force in the post-industrial economy."[3] The decline of manufacturing, the movement of commerce and jobs from the smokestack states of the Northeast to the antiunion Sunbelt, the increase in educational levels, and part-time employment—all those factors that economists refer to as "structural changes"—are plausible explanations for an inevitable decline in union membership.

In fact, however, the strictly economic change from an industrial to a service economy is only about one-quarter of the story and all these structural changes together account for barely half of the total decline in union membership.[4] In other words, even within specific jobs and industries, the fraction of the workforce that is unionized has fallen sharply over the last four decades. Between 1953 and 1997 union membership rates declined by 62 percent within manufacturing, by 79 percent within mining, by 78 percent within construction, by 60 percent within transportation and by 40 percent within the service sector. The only sector to resist this ebbing tide even temporarily was government employment in which unionization increased sharply for a decade and a half between 1962 and 1979 following a legal change in the basis for collective bargaining in the executive branch introduced by the Kennedy administration. However, over the last two decades even in the public sector union membership has been stagnant. Union decline is not mainly a result of the bleaching of blue collars into white collars.[5]

Labor economists have offered a variety of other interpretations of the decline in unionization—adverse changes in public policy, such as the antistrike policy introduced by the Reagan administration during the air traffic controllers strike of 1982, virulent employer resistance, flaccid union strategy, and so on. There is some truth in each of these interpretations, but despite much debate, no consensus yet exists among the experts as to their relative weight, and this is not the place to sort them all out. Interestingly, however, one comprehensive study concluded that "virtually all the decline in unionization between 1977 and 1991 seems to be due to decline in demand for union representation"[6]—fewer union members because fewer workers want to join.

Might this decline in "demand" reflect public disgust at improper union influence, featherbedding, corruption, and the like? At one time that explanation might have been plausible, but public resentment of union power has declined steadily for more than two decades, while membership has continued to plunge. Public resentment may have been a consequence of union power, but it is not a cause of continuing union decline. Perhaps the problem with union membership is not so much skepticism about the idea of "union" as skepticism about the idea of "membership." As labor economist Peter Pestillo presciently observed two decades ago, "The young worker thinks primarily of himself. We are experiencing the cult of the individual, and labor is taking a beating preaching the comfort of coalition."[7]

. . .

The recent history of professional associations seems at first glance entirely different. The percentage of Americans who belong to professional associations and other economic organizations (apart from unions) has doubled over the last four decades. During the 1950s and 1960s most surveys found roughly 8–10 percent membership rates in such organizations, whereas in the 1980s and 1990s virtually all surveys reported equivalent rates of 16–20 percent.[8] The rate of membership in professional and academic societies in the general population rose from 13 percent in 1974 to 18 percent in 1994, an increase of nearly 50 percent in barely two decades.[9]

This impression of rapid growth in professional associations seems confirmed by the membership rolls of the major national professional organizations. Total membership in the American Medical Association rose from 126,042 in 1945 to 201,955 in 1965 and then to a record 296,637 in 1995. The American Institute of Architects is smaller, but its growth has been equally impressive—from 8,500 in 1950 to 23,300 in 1970 and then to a record 47,271 in 1997.

Membership in the American Society of Mechanical Engineers nearly tripled from 19,688 in 1945 to 53,510 in 1968 and then doubled again over the next three decades to 107,383 in 1997. For the Institute of Electrical and Electronic Engineers the equivalent jump was from 111,610 in 1963 to 242,800 in 1997. Growth of the American Bar Association (ABA) was even more breathtaking, as total membership quadrupled from 34,134 in 1945 to 118,916 in 1965 and then tripled again to 357,933 in 1991. And so it goes for most major professional organizations. Here at last, it seems, we find welling up unstaunched in the late twentieth century America's Tocquevillean energies.

Before reaching this conclusion, we must, as always, take into account changes in the size of the relevant constituencies, for these same decades have witnessed massive increases in the numbers of people in professional occupations. The more relevant question for our purposes is not "How big is the ABA?" but "How big is the ABA compared to the number of lawyers in America?" And indeed, the changing rate of membership in professional associations *among* members of a given profession turns out to have followed a surprisingly familiar path.

For roughly the first two-thirds of the century the percentage of practicing physicians, lawyers, architects, accountants, and dentists who belonged to the relevant professional association rose sharply and steadily, except for the familiar slump during the Great Depression. (The figure below displays the average market share of eight major professional associations over much of the twentieth century.)[10] Typically this increase was about tenfold, from roughly 5–10 percent early in the century to 50–90 percent by the 1960s. Strikingly, in virtually every case one can detect the same postwar acceleration in membership growth between the 1940s

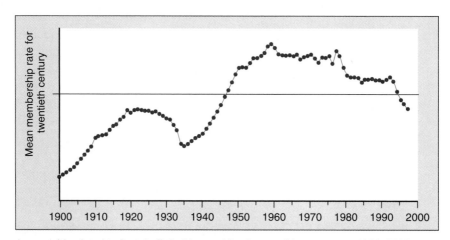

Average Membership Rate in Eight National Professional Associations, 1900–1997.

and the 1960s that we have already seen in community-based and religious organizations. Generally speaking, membership rates in professional associations
roughly doubled between 1945 and 1965, just about the same rate of growth as
we observed earlier in the case of community organizations.

Then in each case the postwar membership boom suddenly slowed,
halted, and in almost all cases reversed. First to reach its peak and begin to
decline was the American Medical Association (AMA) in 1959, followed by
the American Dental Association and the American Institute of Architects
(both in 1970), the American Bar Association (ABA) in 1977, and finally the
American Institute of Certified Public Accountants in 1993. While the number
of registered nurses in America doubled from 1 million in 1977 to 2 million in
1998, membership in the American Nurses Association (ANA) fell from
190,000 to 175,000, so that the ANA's "market share" was cut exactly in half
from 18 percent of all RNs in 1977 to 9 percent in 1998. In the case of the
American Society of Mechanical Engineers (ASME), the postwar boom had
essentially ended by the 1950s, and ASME's market share never regained its
pre-Depression peak. The Institute of Electrical and Electronic Engineers
(IEEE) was formed in 1963 from the merger of two older organizations, both
of which had grown very rapidly in the preceding two decades, but the familiar decline in market share began at the very birth of the IEEE itself.

The downturn in membership rates after 1970 was initially masked by rapid
growth in the national pool of professionals. Even if the rate of catch was declining, the fishing was still very good. For example, membership in the American
Institute of Architects more than doubled between 1970 and 1997, although the
fraction of architects who were members fell from 41 percent to 28 percent
over this period. Membership in the IEEE, drawing on the ebullient electronics
industry, more than doubled from 1963 to 1997, even though its "market share"
was falling from 51 percent to 37 percent.[11]

Gradually the staff and leadership of each association began to notice their
declining membership rates, and eventually in every case relative decline turned
into absolute decline, even though the underlying profession continued to bur-
geon. Thus, just as the leadership of Kiwanis and the League of Women Voters
and the Parent-Teacher Association had begun to fret in the 1960s and 1970s
about how to reverse their membership slowdown, so too the leadership of the
AMA, the ANA, the ABA, and so on now began to discuss what could be causing their slippage.[12]

In each case a broadly similar list of suspects was interrogated—excessive
dues, stale programs, competing local or more specialized associations. One
common theme was the possibility that as the underlying professions were
becoming bigger and more complex, members had shifted their interests and

professional identity from, say, medicine to perinatal anesthesiology or from law in general to, say, the intellectual property bar of New York City. I cannot entirely exclude this interpretation, but some initial probes that we conducted were not consistent with it. For example, even specialized groups like the American College of Surgeons and the American Society of Anesthesiology have experienced stagnating or even declining membership rates in recent decades.[13]

So while the absolute number of Americans who belong to professional associations has grown significantly over the last thirty years—and in that sense, this domain is a singular exception to the general pattern we have seen of declining membership—this is the exception that proves the rule, since even in this area of apparent growth, we see the same pattern of growth in sociability during the first two-thirds of the century, followed by sudden stagnation and then decline during the last third. (I leave aside here the familiar issue of whether membership in unions and professional associations today betokens active membership in local chapters, as it once did.)

    . . .

Thus, social capital in the shape of formal organizations of employees has not increased to offset the declines in political, civic, and religious organizational activity that we noted in earlier chapters. Perhaps, however, a more subtle shift has occurred between residence-based and workplace-based networks, a shift from locational communities to vocational communities. Since more of us are working outside the home today than a generation ago, perhaps we have simply transferred more of our friendships, more of our civic discussions, and more of our community ties from the front porch to the water cooler.[14]

When sociologist Alan Wolfe spoke with several hundred middle-class suburbanites around the country in 1995–96, he encountered a number of people who expressed this thesis. Jeremy Toole of Cobb County, Georgia, estimated that "these days people get about 90 percent of their social connections from the workplace." Diana Hamilton of Sand Springs, Oklahoma, ruminated that "I think people's lives revolve around their work. They make their friends at work, they do their community service through work." And Elizabeth Tyler of Brookline, Massachusetts, added, "I feel very much like I belong to a community of work. . . to a community with my own office, with my own company, within my own industry."[15]

In one sense, such a trend might not be surprising. The Industrial Revolution itself began the process of separating place of work from place of residence, and more and more of our time was spent in factories and offices away from home. By the end of the twentieth century more Americans were in the labor force than ever before—67 percent in 1997, compared with 59 percent in 1950.[16] Professionals and blue-collar workers alike are putting in long hours together, eating lunch and dinner together, traveling together, arriving early, and staying late. What is more, people are divorcing more often, marrying later (if at all), and living alone in unprecedented numbers. Work is where the hearth is, then, for many solitary souls. Even for the minority of Americans who live with spouse and children, argues sociologist Arlie Russell Hochschild, the workplace increasingly serves as a sanctuary from the stresses of marriage, children, and housework.[17] "As more Americans spend more of their time 'at work,'" hypothesizes one thoughtful observer, "work gradually becomes less of a one-dimensional activity and assumes more of the concerns and activities of both private (family) and public (social and political) life."[18]

Changes in the character of work, not just its quantity, might mean that it could account for a greater fraction of our social interaction. After a solitary day's plowing, a farmer might welcome a church social or a Grange meeting, but many of us nowadays work in large, complex organizations, and attending yet another meeting in the evening is the last thing on our minds. Moreover, in the 1980s and 1990s "total quality management," "quality circles," and "team building" became all the rage in management circles. Books with titles like *The Search for Meaning in the Workplace, Creating Community Anywhere*, and *Business as a Calling* urged executives to "establish within the firm a sense of community and respect for the dignity of persons."[19] Many firms put such ideas into practice; by 1992 one survey found that 55 percent of all business establishments had teams (41 percent for a majority of their core workers) and that 41 percent had "quality circles." Architects specializing in office design began to configure the workplace to bolster employees' sense of connectedness, creating spaces with such evocative labels as "watering holes," "conversation pits," and "campfires" where employees come to warm their hands. Sociologist Hochschild concludes that these "new management techniques so pervasive in corporate life have helped transform the workplace into a more appreciative, personal sort of social world."[20]

The modern workplace thus encourages regular collaborative contacts among peers—ideal conditions, one might think, for social capital creation. Many people form rewarding friendships at work, feel a sense of community among co-workers, and enjoy norms of mutual help and reciprocity on the job. According to several surveys in the 1990s by the Families and Work Institute, nine out of ten employees agree that "I look forward to being with the people I work with each day" and that "I feel I'm really part of the group of people I work with." Several studies of friendship and support networks have found that about half of all workers have at least one close personal tie at work. According to a 1997 survey that asked people to enumerate all their conversations on a given day, just over half took place in the workplace. When just working adults were considered, that fraction jumped to more than two-thirds.[21] Clearly many of us have close personal connections at work. From a broader societal perspective, an added benefit of workplace-based connections is that the workplace is much more diverse, racially and even politically, than most other social settings.[22]

Before concluding, however, that the line at the copying machine has replaced the back fence as the locus for social capital in contemporary America, we need to consider three additional factors. First, I know of *no evidence whatever* that socializing in the workplace, however common, has actually *increased* over the last several decades. Indeed of all the domains of social and community connectedness surveyed in this book, systematic long-term evidence on workplace-based connections has proven the most difficult to find. Many of us today have friends at work, but it is unclear whether we are more likely to have friends at work than our parents did. Some indirect evidence discussed later in this section actually suggests a trend in the opposite direction.[23]

Second, social connectedness in the workplace might be described as a glass half-empty, not merely as a glass half-full. Most studies of personal networks find that co-workers account for less than 10 percent of our friends. Workplace ties tend to be casual and enjoyable, but not intimate and deeply supportive. In the most careful study, when people were asked to list their closest friends, less than half of all full-time workers put even one co-worker on the list. On average, neighbors were more likely to appear on the list than co-workers. When people were asked to whom they would turn to discuss "important matters," less than half of all full-time workers listed even a single co-worker. In short, though most of us who work outside the home have acquaintances among our workmates, for only a small minority of us does the workplace account for most of our close personal ties. Americans' most important personal networks are not centered mainly in the workplace.[24]

Third, several important trends in the American workplace over the last decade or two have been quite damaging to social ties there. The nature of the implicit employment contract governing many Americans' work lives was transformed during the 1980s and 1990s by downsizing, "right sizing," "reengineering," and other economic restructuring. During the 1980s layoffs and job uncertainty grew primarily because of the business cycle, but during the 1990s restructuring came to be a regular tool of management, even during prosperous times. In fact, one study found that even in the boom year of 1993–94 nearly half of all firms laid off workers. And these were big cuts, averaging 10 percent of each company's workforce. The old employment contract was not in writing—it didn't have to be—but it was the central organizing principle of employee-management relations and was understood by all. World War II veterans joining IBM were instructed to consult with their wives before taking the job, because "once you came aboard you were a member of the corporate family for life."[25]

A half century later increased competition in the global marketplace, improved information technology, greater focus on short-term financial returns, and new management techniques have combined to make virtually all jobs more "contingent." Perhaps the most telling statistic is this: One of the fastest-growing industries in the 1980s was "outplacement" services. These firms' revenues grew from just $35 million in 1980 to a whopping $350 million in 1989. As management scholar Peter Cappelli sums up more than a decade of research on changing employment practices, particularly among white-collar workers, "The old employment system of secure, lifetime jobs with predictable advancement and stable pay is dead."[26]

One consequence of these changes has been increased employee anxiety, but there have been winners as well as losers. More independence from the firm, flatter hierarchies, less paternalism, and more reward for merit and creativity rather than seniority and loyalty have been good for many firms and their employees. Even when corporate morale and employee commitment have been badly damaged, as they typically are, research often finds that corporate productivity has improved. My purpose here is to evaluate not the economic consequences of these changes, but rather their impact on trust and social connectedness in the workplace.[27] On that score, the balance sheet is negative.

In hundreds of interviews with white-collar workers in firms undergoing restructuring—some ultimately successfully, some not—Charles Heckscher found that the most common reaction to the changed social contract was to "put your head down," focusing more and more narrowly on one's own job. Even workers whose jobs were spared often experienced what is called "survivor shock." While some employees relished the independence and greater opportunity afforded to individuals under the new system, most middle managers even in successful firms agreed with the view expressed by one, "We're all alone out here. It's been very stressful." Said another, "The reorganization disrupted the network of relationships among people at all levels." Relationships with peers became more distant. "Rather than turning on each other, most people drifted apart, becoming more isolated and wanting to be left alone."[28]

In addition to the effects of the changed employment contract on social capital in the workplace, the change is not good for involvement in the broader community. As Peter Cappelli points out,

> Much of contemporary American society has been built on stable employment relationships characterized by predictable career advancement and steady growth in wages. Long-term individual investments such as home ownership and college educations for children, community ties and the stability they bring, and quality of life outside of work have all been enhanced by reducing risk and uncertainty on the job.[29]

All that tends to be undermined by the new deal at work.

The workplace remains a significant recruiting ground for volunteers and an overwhelming majority (92 percent) of corporate executives say they encourage their employees to become involved in community service. On the other hand, according to the most comprehensive national survey of volunteers, the fraction recruited by someone at work slipped from 15 percent in 1991 to 12 percent in 1999.[30] No doubt firms and work-based volunteer recruiters have good intentions, but so far, at least, the workplace remains far less important than churches and other civic organizations as recruitment networks for volunteerism.

Not all employees in America have been affected by these changes in the implicit employment contract. Blue-collar workers have long faced the job insecurity that has recently hit middle management. Nevertheless, over the last three decades job stability at all educational levels in the American workforce has declined. Fewer and fewer of us remain very long in the same job or even in the same company. In fact, although job instability remains higher among blue-collar workers, it has increased much more rapidly among white-collar workers, who account for a growing fraction of the workforce and who have traditionally contributed disproportionately to civic life. This trend toward "job churning" is concentrated among men, who previously had been in more stable jobs, but women continue to have much lower job tenure than men, primarily because they are more likely to move in and out of the labor market. Moreover, what economists call "the returns to tenure" (that is the wage and salary benefits from seniority) have fallen, as more and more of our income depends on what we've done recently and less and less on how long we've been in our job. One consequence of performance-based pay and performance-based job security is to increase, if only implicitly, the degree of competition among peers. Teamwork stops feeling so amicable when you are subtly competing with your teammates for your livelihood.[31]

In addition, a surprisingly large and growing fraction of the American workforce has "contingent" or "nonstandard" jobs—part-time employees, temps, "independent contractors" (consultants), "on-call" workers (such as substitute teachers), and the like. The best recent studies suggest that nearly 30 percent of all U.S. workers fall into this broad category, about one-half of them part-timers and another one-quarter independent contractors. Temping and part-time work both appear to be growing. Many workers—software programmers, for example, or management consultants, or parents who seek to combine work and family obligations—are in these irregular jobs by choice and find them rewarding both personally and financially. Apart from high-status consultants, however, most people in nonstandard jobs say that they would prefer regular, full-time, noncontingent employment.[32]

More important for our purposes, *all* these structural changes in the work-place—shorter job tenure, more part-time and temporary jobs, and even independent consultancy—inhibit workplace-based social ties. Three-quarters of all independent contractors have no regular work colleagues. Part-time workers have only two-thirds as many friends from work as do full-time workers. Friendships at work decrease with job instability, even when the job changes are voluntary. None of these patterns is surprising in the least, since successful investment in social capital takes time and concerted effort. Birds of passage, whether by choice or by necessity, generally don't nest. The implication is clear—nearly one-third of all U.S. workers have jobs that discourage durable social connections, and that fraction is rising.[33]

In short, some features of contemporary American work life—more time at work, more emphasis on teamwork—would seem to foster informal work-place social capital, while other features—downsizing, the fraying of ties to a particular firm, the rise of contingent work—point in the opposite direction. The impact of another potentially important factor—changing office technology, especially e-mail—is harder to evaluate systematically at this point.

As I have noted, hard evidence on long-term trends in the frequency of water-cooler discussions of civic affairs or the incidence of close friendships among co-workers is apparently nonexistent. A weaker form of indirect evidence, however, is available through surveys of job satisfaction. Many studies have shown that social connections with co-workers are a strong predictor—some would say the strongest single predictor—of job satisfaction. People with friends at work are happier at work.[34] If social capital at work has risen significantly in recent decades, presumably that should show up in warmer feelings about work, at least if we control for adverse changes in financial and job security.

In 1955 and again in the 1990s Gallup pollsters asked working Americans, "Which do you enjoy more, the hours when you are on your job, or the hours when you are not on your job?" In 1955, 44 percent of all workers said they preferred the hours on the job, but by 1999 barely one-third as many (16 percent) felt that way. According to Roper polls, the proportion of Americans "completely satisfied" with their job fell from 46 percent in the mid-1970s to 36 percent in 1992. Some of this disaffection is traceable to concerns about job security and personal finances, but even controlling for financial security, the General Social Survey reveals a modest long-term slippage (roughly 10 percent overall) in job satisfaction between 1972 and 1998. Recent surveys suggest that as many as one in four employees are chronically angry on the job, and many researchers believe that incivility and aggression in the workplace are on the rise.[35] Not all survey data point in the same direction, but the balance of evidence appears to be that, quite apart from material insecurity, American workers are certainly no happier in the workplace today than a generation ago and probably are less happy. That evidence is hard to square with the hypothesis that the workplace has become the new locus of Americans' social solidarity and sense of community.

Our judgment must be cautious here. Unlike most other domains of sociability discussed in this volume, in this particular area we lack definitive evidence one way or the other. My own view is that any solution to the problem of civic disengagement in contemporary. America must include better integration between our work lives and our community and social lives. Nevertheless, a final note of skepticism is necessary about the workplace as the new public square for American communities. In the end, "work" entails time and effort destined to serve primarily material, not social, ends. Work-based networks are often used for instrumental purposes, thus somewhat undercutting their value for community and social purposes. As Alan Wolfe observes:

> Because we form such ties to promote the highly secular activities of getting and spending, friendships and connections developed at work are generally assumed to have a more instrumental character: we use people, and they use us, to solicit more business, advance our careers, sell more products, or demonstrate our popularity. . . . If so, it follows that even if the decline of civil ties in the neighborhood is being compensated by new ties formed at work, the instrumental character of the latter cannot be an adequate substitute for the loss of the former.[36]

Moreover, when at work, our time is our employer's, not our own. We are paid to work, not to build social capital, and our employer has the legal right to draw the line between the two. Court decisions have given employers wide latitude to monitor and control communications in the workplace, and monitoring is in fact increasing rapidly, facilitated by the ease of intercepting electronic communications. A private employer may fire workers for what they say, as well as for their political views or activities. According to a 1999 survey by the American Management Association, two-thirds of employers record employee voice mail, e-mail, or phone calls, review computer files, or videotape workers, and such surveillance is becoming more common. Rights of free speech and privacy that are essential to public deliberation and private solidarity are, to put it mildly, insecure in the workplace. Substantial reforms in public law and private practice would be necessary before the water cooler could become the equivalent of the back fence or the town square.[37]

Most of us nowadays are employed, and most of the time most of us work with other people. In that fundamental sense the workplace is a natural site for connecting with others. However, the balance of the evidence speaks against the hopeful hypothesis that American social capital has not disappeared but simply moved into the workplace. Americans at the beginning of the twenty-first century are demonstrably less likely than our parents were to join with our co-workers in formal associations. New forces that might foster socializing in the workplace are counterbalanced by equally new forces that inhibit the types of social ties, durable yet flexible and wide-ranging, that are important to civic life and personal well-being. In addition, for the one American adult in three who is not employed, workplace ties are nonexistent. The workplace is not the salvation for our fraying civil society.

Endnotes

1. War is associated with increases in union membership throughout American history and also in other countries. See Richard B. Freeman, "Spurts in Union Growth: Defining Moments and Social Processes," in *The Defining Moment: The Great Depression and the American Economy in the Twentieth Century*, ed. Michael D. Bordo, Claudia Goldin, and Eugene N. White (Chicago: University of Chicago Press, 1998), 265–295; and Gary N. Chaison and Joseph B. Rose, "The Macrodeterminants of Union Growth and Decline," in *The State of the Unions*, Industrial Relations Research Association Series, ed. George Strauss, Daniel G. Gallagher, and Jack Fiorita (Madison, Wis.: IRRA, 1991), 3–45, esp. 33.

2. A national survey in 1953 found that 23 percent of the respondents belonged to labor unions, the single most common type of membership in voluntary associations. See Charles R. Wright and Herbert H. Hyman, "Voluntary Association Memberships of American Adults: Evidence from National Sample Surveys," *American Sociological Review* 23 (June 1958): 284–294. To be sure, union membership is more likely to be merely nominal than membership in other voluntary associations, in part because union shop rules mean that some union memberships are not voluntary at all. On the other hand, as late as 1987, according to the General Social Survey, nearly half of all union members (46 percent) said that they were actively involved in union affairs.

3. Paul Weiler, "The Representation Gap in the North American Workplace," unpublished lecture, as quoted in Chaison and Rose, "The Macrodeterminants of Union Growth and Decline," 13.

4. For various interpretations of union decline, see William T. Dickens and Jonathan S. Leonard, "Accounting for the Decline in Union Membership, 1950–1980," *Industrial & Labor Relations Review* 38 (April 1985): 323–334; Leo Troy, "The Rise and Fall of American Trade Unions," in *Unions in Transition: Entering the Second Century*, ed. Seymour Martin Lipset (San Francisco: ICS Press, 1986), 75–109; Michael Goldfield, *The Decline of Organized Labor in the United States* (Chicago: University of Chicago Press, 1987); Chaison and Rose, "The Macrodeterminants of Union Growth and Decline"; and Freeman, "Spurts in Union Growth." Henry S. Farber, "Extent of Unionization

in the United States," in *Challenges and Choices Facing American Labor*, ed. Thomas A. Kochan (Cambridge, Mass.: MIT Press, 1985), 15–43, statistic at 38, estimates that structural factors account for 40 percent of the total decline, whereas Richard B. Freeman and James L. Medoff, *What Do Unions Do?* (New York: Basic Books, 1984), put the figure at roughly 55–60 percent. Chaison and Rose, "The Macrodeterminants of Union Growth and Decline," estimate that the change in industrial composition accounts for no more than 25 percent of the total decline.

5. Troy, "The Rise and Fall of American Trade Unions," 87; and *Statistical Abstract of the United States: 1997*, table 691; *Union Data Book 1998* (Washington, D.C.: Bureau of National Affairs, 1998).

6. Henry S. Farber and Alan B. Krueger, "Union Membership in the United States: The Decline Continues," National Bureau of Economic Research working paper no. W4216 (Cambridge, Mass.: National Bureau of Economic Research, 1992), 17–18.

7. Peter J. Pestillo, "Can the Unions Meet the Needs of a 'New' Work Force?" *Monthly Labor Review* 102 (February 1979): 33. In the DDB Needham Life Style surveys, agreement that "unions have too much power in America" dropped from 79 percent in 1977 to 55 percent in 1998.

8. For the 1950s, see Murray Hausknecht, *The Joiners*; and the 1952 National Election Study. For the 1980s and 1990s, see the General Social Survey; Verba, Schlozman, and Brady, *Voice and Equality*; and the 1996 National Election Study.

9. Author's analysis of General Social Survey. On the other hand, the fraction of the population in professional or higher managerial jobs rose by about this same amount. Among those eligible to join professional associations there is a slight downward trend (not statistically significant) in membership rates over time.

10. The second figure is intended as a rough summary of the experiences of eight separate organizations. The standardization technique is used here. Since data are not available for all eight for the entire period, constructing yearly averages involves some arbitrariness. Membership figures were obtained from the national headquarters of the respective associations, numbers of professionals from *Historical Statistics of the United States: Colonial Times to 1970* (Washington, D.C.: U.S. Bureau of the Census, 1975) and unpublished data from the Bureau of Labor Statistics. In each case I divided total membership by the number of people actually employed in that profession nationwide, cross-checking between government and associational statisticians. Figures for employed mechanical engineers for 1930 and 1940 are estimates. Only CPAs may become members of the American Institute of Certified Public Accountants, but consistent historical data are available only for all accountants, not just CPAs. The second figure thus understates membership among CPAs, but the broad trend—rising market share from 1900 to 1980–90 and then slipping—is probably accurate.

11. This pattern applies to a number of other professional associations, such as the National Society of Professional Engineers, but we were unable to construct satisfactory data series to chart the decline in detail.

12. Facing membership decline, many organizations added new categories of "affiliates" for students, apprentices, workers in allied fields, and so on. This practice raised the numerator of the "market share" fraction without any compensating adjustment in

the denominator (people employed in that profession), so the second figure tends, if anything, to understate the post-1970s slump.

13. The fraction of all surgeons who belong to the American College of Surgeons was 62 percent in 1975 and 64 percent in 1996. The fraction of all anesthesiologists in the American Society of Anesthesiology fell from 72 percent in 1970 to 65 percent in 1996.

14. Thanks to Kristin Goss and David Pinto-Duschinsky for exceptional help in preparing this section.

15. Alan Wolfe, "Developing Civil Society: Can the Workplace Replace Bowling?" *The Responsive Community* 8:2 (spring 1998), 41–47, quotations at 44. See also Maria T. Poarch, "Ties That Bind: U.S. Suburban Residents on the Social and Civic Dimensions of Work," *Community, Work & Family* 1 (1998): 125–147.

16. *Statistical Abstract of the United States, 1998*, table 644.

17. Arlie Russell Hochschild, *The Time Bind: When Work Becomes Home and Home Becomes Work* (New York: Henry Holt, 1997).

18. Maria T. Poarch, "Civic Life and Work: A Qualitative Study of Changing Patterns of Sociability and Civic Engagement in Everyday Life." (Ph.D. diss., Boston University, 1997), 166.

19. Michael Novak, *Business as a Calling* (New York: Free Press, 1996), quotation at 146–50; Thomas H. Naylor, William H. Willimon, and Rolf Österberg, *The Search for Meaning in the Workplace* (Nashville, Tenn.: Abingdon Press, 1996); Carolyn R. Shaffer and Kristin Anundsen, *Creating Community Anywhere: Finding Support and Connection in a Fragmented World* (New York: Perigree, 1993).

20. Paul Osterman, "How Common Is Workplace Transformation and How Can We Explain Who Does It?" *Industrial and Labor Relations Review* 47 (January 1994): 173–188; Peter Cappelli, *The New Deal at Work: Managing the Market-Driven Workforce* (Boston: Harvard Business School Press, 1999): 146–147, and the works cited there; Claudia H. Deutsch, "Communication in the Workplace; Companies Using Coffee Bars to Get Ideas Brewing," *New York Times*, November 5, 1995; Arlie Russell Hochschild, "There's No Place Like Work," *New York Times Magazine*, April 20, 1997, p. 53.

21. Ellen Galinsky, James T. Bond, and Dana E. Friedman, *The Changing Workforce* (New York: Families and Work Institute, 1993), 24; James T. Bond, Ellen Galinsky, and Jennifer E. Swanberg, *The 1997 National Study of the Changing Workforce* (New York: Families and Work Institute, 1998), 106, 103, 161. On friendship at work, see sources cited in endnote 24. Author's analysis of a Scripps-Howard/Ohio University national survey of interpersonal communication, June 1997.

22. *Gallup Poll Social Audit on Black/White Relations in the United States*, Executive Summary (Princeton, N.J.: Gallup Organization, June 1997); Peter Marsden, "Core Discussion Networks of Americans," *American Sociological Review* 52 (1987): 122–131; Diana C. Mutz and Jeffrey J. Mondak, "Democracy at Work: Contributions of the Workplace Toward a Public Sphere," unpublished manuscript, April 1998.

23. Evidence will be given later in this chapter.

24. Claude S. Fischer, *To Dwell Among Friends: Personal Networks in Town and City* (Chicago: University of Chicago Press, 1982); Barry Wellman, R. Y. Wong, David

Tindall, and Nancy Naxer, "A Decade of Network Change: Turnover, Persistence and Stability in Personal Communities," *Social Networks* 19 (1997): 27–50; Bruce C. Straits, "Ego-Net Diversity: Same- and Cross-Sex Co-worker Ties," *Social Networks* 18 (1996): 29–45; Gwen Moore, "Structural Determinants of Men's and Women's Personal Networks," *American Sociological Review* 53 (1990): 726–735; Stephen R. Marks, "Intimacy in the Public Realm: The Case of Co-workers," *Social Forces* 72 (1994): 843–858; Peter Marsden, "Core Discussion Networks of Americans."

25. Thomas R. Horton and Peter C. Reid, *Beyond the Trust Gap: Forging a New Partnership Between Managers and Their Employers* (Homewood, Ill.: Business One Irwin, 1991), 3; Cappelli, Bassi, et al., *Change at Work*, 67–69; and more generally, Cappelli, *New Deal at Work*; and Charles Heckscher, *White Collar Blues: Management Loyalties in an Age of Corporate Restructuring* (New York: Basic Books, 1995).

26. Cappelli, *New Deal at Work*, 17; on outplacement, see Horton and Reid, *Beyond the Trust Gap*, 9.

27. In 1989, 63 percent of workers said that employees were less loyal to their companies than ten years earlier, while only 22 percent said employees were more loyal: Horton and Reid, *Beyond the Trust Gap*, 10, citing a survey by Yankelovich Clancy Shulman. While restructuring hurts employee commitment, it often boosts productivity. See Cappelli, *New Deal at Work*, 45–46, 122–136, and Cappelli, Bassi, et al., *Change at Work*, 53–65, 79–84.

28. Heckscher, *White Collar Blues*, quotations at 6, 12, 49, 73. In a few firms Heckscher found a new form of limited community: "I'll do my best for you while I'm here, but neither of us sees this as a long-term relationship." See also Horton and Reid, *Beyond the Trust Gap*, 9–10, 40–43; Cappelli, Bassi, et al., *Change at Work*, 79–84; and Richard Sennett, *The Corrosion of Character: The Personal Consequences of Work in the New Capitalism* (New York: W. W. Norton, 1998).

29. Cappelli, *New Deal at Work*, 14.

30. Points of Light Foundation, *Corporate Volunteer Programs: Benefits to Business*, Report 1029, Fact Sheet (Washington, D.C., n.d.); Hodgkinson and Weitzman, *Giving and Volunteering 1996*, 4–111; *Giving and Volunteering in the United States: Findings from a National Survey, 1999 Executive Summary* (Washington, D.C.: Independent Sector, 1999). The fraction of volunteers who report being asked specifically by their employer is even lower—about 7–8 percent.

31. Lawrence Mishel, Jared Bernstein, and John Schmitt, *The State of Working America: 1998–99*, Economic Policy Institute (Ithaca, N.Y.: Cornell University Press, 1998), esp. 227–235; Cappelli, *New Deal at Work*, 133–135.

32. Mishel, Bernstein, and Schmitt, *State of Working America*, 242–250; Cappelli, *New Deal at Work*, 136–144; Cappelli, Bassi, et al., *Change at Work*, 73–78; Sharon R. Cohany, "Workers in Alternative Employment Arrangements: A Second Look," and Steven Hipple, "Contingent Work: Results from the Second Survey," both in *Monthly Labor Review* (November 1998): 3–35.

33. Ronald S. Burt and Marc Knez, "Trust and Third-Party Gossip," in Roderick M. Kramer and Tom R. Tyler, eds., *Trust in Organizations: Frontiers of Theory and Research* (Thousand Oaks, Calif.: Sage Publications, 1996), 68–89, esp. 77; Katherine J. Klein

and Thomas A. D'Aunno, "Psychological Sense of Community in the Workplace," *Journal of Community Psychology* 14 (October 1986): 365–377, esp. 368; Fischer, *To Dwell Among Friends*. According to 1986 GSS data, the fraction of one's close friends who are co-workers is only two-thirds as great for part-time workers as for full-time workers.

34. Jeanne S. Hurlbert, "Social Networks, Social Circles, and Job Satisfaction," *Work and Occupations* 18 (1991): 415–430; Randy Hodson, "Group Relations at Work: Solidarity, Conflict, and Relations with Management," *Work and Occupations* 24 (1997): 426–452; Ronni Sandroff, "The Power of Office Friendships," *Working Mother* (November 1997): 35–36, and the works cited there.

35. *Gallup Poll Monthly*, no. 332 (May 1993): 21; and http://www.gallup.com (October 1999); respondents with "no opinion" are excluded. Cheryl Russell, *The Master Trend: How the Baby Boom Generation Is Remaking America* (New York: Plenum Press, 1993), 64. Author's analysis of General Social Survey, 1972–98; job satisfaction fell from c. 65 percent to c. 61 percent among workers fully content with their financial situation, from c. 48 percent to c. 43 percent among those more or less content with their finances, and from c. 36 percent to c. 30 percent among those dissatisfied with their finances. Glenn Firebaugh and Brian Harley, "Trends in Job Satisfaction in the United States by Race, Gender, and Type of Occupation," *Research in the Sociology of Work* 5 (1995): 87–104, report no change in job satisfaction through the 1980s, and Bond, Galinsky, and Swanberg, *The 1997 National Study of the Changing Workforce*, ch. 7, found modest growth in job satisfaction between 1977 and 1997. On the other hand, Cappelli, *New Deal at Work*, 122–123, reports that after decades of relative stability, several proprietary survey archives found declining job satisfaction after the early 1980s. I have found no hard evidence on incivility and aggression at work over time, though most Americans believe that it has grown; see John Marks, "The American Uncivil Wars," *U.S. News & World Report*, April 22, 1996; Joel H. Neuman and Robert A. Baron, "Aggression in the Workplace," in *Antisocial Behavior in Organizations*, eds. Robert A. Giacalone and Jerald Greenberg (Thousand Oaks, Calif.: Sage Publications, 1996), 37–67; and Christine M. Pearson, Lynne H. Andersson, and Judith W. Webner, "When Workers Flout Convention: A Study of Workplace Incivility" (unpublished ms., Chapel Hill: University of North Carolina, 1999).

36. Wolfe, "Developing Civil Society," 45.

37. John R. Aiello, "Computer-Based Work Monitoring: Electronic Surveillance and Its Effects," *Journal of Applied Social Psychology* 23 (1993): 499–507; Cynthia L. Estlund, "Free Speech and Due Process in the Workplace," *Indiana Law Journal* 71 (1995): 101–151; David C. Yamada, "Voices from the Cubicle: Protecting and Encouraging Private Employee Speech in the Post-Industrial Workplace," *Berkeley Journal of Employment and Labor Law* 19 (1998): 1–51; "More U.S. Firms Checking E-Mail, Computer Files, and Phone Calls" (New York: American Management Association, April 1999). Thanks to Jason Mazzone for his contribution to this section.

Writing Applications

After reading Putnam's discussion of "Connections in the Workplace," try to imagine how your life's work might in some way involve you and others in the larger work of the community. You might do this in a number of ways:

- Write a personal narrative of discovery, detailing the ways in which the work that most interests you might serve the interests of people around you.

- Interview professionals in a field that interests you, asking specifically about the ways that their work contributes to the community.

- If you have worked as a professional in the past, describe the ways in which your workplace functioned, or failed to function, as a site for political discussion. You might also discuss a particular set of political issues that were important within that profession or workplace.

- Research and write an occupational ethnography (a description of the culture of a workplace) by visiting a job site and observing the types of thinking and community interactions that go on there. What reasoning capabilities are necessary? What interpersonal relations seem most crucial? Do the workers seem personally engaged with one another? Do they share community concerns?

- Analyze and describe the websites of organizations in a field that interests you, focusing especially on the type of community that this organization wants to be, and the role of this organization in the larger social and political community surrounding it. What obligations does this organization seem to feel to its workers? to the community and country?

- Investigate the public *ethos* of a profession and its role in ongoing political issues. Consider how people in that discipline or occupational area are represented in the media and within their communities. What types of roles are they asked to play as expert voices, and what types of language do they contribute to the public discussion on issues?

- Consider the role of volunteer programs and service learning classes with which you have been involved. Did these volunteer activities help you to better understand your community? Did they increase your likelihood to become involved again? Did they increase your desire to learn about political and community interactions? You might write a narrative describing these experiences and what you learned from them, or you might investigate studies of the effects of volunteer programs and service learning on civic engagement, and compare those with your own experiences and/or those of your classmates.

Casebook 4 LIBERAL EDUCATION AND YOUR CAREER

As the previous case illustrates, engagement in one's work is important not only for personal satisfaction. It can help us to find our place within our democracy—a system of government that relies on the work we do as part of a larger community to function well. This was the vision of democratic education and work that John Dewey left us:

> While training for the profession of learning is regarded as a type of culture, or a liberal education, the training of a mechanic, a musician, a lawyer, a doctor, a farmer, a merchant, or a railroad manager is regarded as purely technical and professional. The result is that which we see about us everywhere—the division into "cultured" people and "workers," the separation of theory and practice.

Dewey foresaw danger in separating the world of learning (or "academics") from the worlds of work. This, he believed, would create a division in society between education and the professions, between the "cultured people" and the "workers," who were merely trained to do a job. He suggested that such a situation could create a much weaker democracy, since workers would not really be involved intellectually in the work they did. For Dewey, education should produce informed workers, educated workers—not just trained workers.

This raises questions about the increasing attention that is being paid to careers in many middle and high schools. In Reading and Writing Applications 3, several articles discuss school-to-work initiatives, which encourage career exploration and, in some cases, job training at very young ages. This, of course, has long been the mission of vocational-technical schools. And, although we might question such programs based on Dewey's vision of a democratic education, we must also consider the practical purposes and goals that these initiatives serve—to help people to find lucrative work and so a better lifestyle.

One of the questions that has been raised on this topic regards the role of private organizations and corporations in the development of schools and programs that provide job training. One such program is facilitated by the Marriott Corporation in the Washington, D.C., area, and is described by the company as follows:

> The Marriott Foundation for People with Disabilities founded the Bridges . . . [a] school to work program, in 1989 with the assistance of TransCen. The program was developed to address the traditionally high unemployment rate of youth with all disabilities as they exit high school. We helped design the model, piloted the first implementation and administered the project for the Marriott Foundation until 1998, when the Foundation assumed direct operation of Bridges. Today, TransCen maintains a consultant role with the program and regularly provides training to Bridges staff in all of its national locations, which

include Washington, D.C.; Montgomery County, MD; Chicago; Los Angeles; San Francisco; Philadelphia; and Atlanta.

The purpose of Bridges is to provide critical job experience for youth with disabilities and to help employers meet their human resources needs. Bridges features paid internships for youth with disabilities who are in their last year of high school. These youth receive placement in local companies where the employer pays the intern directly during a specified internship period. Bridges also provides post-school employment support for youth in some of its locations. Over 6,000 youth have benefited from this program to date. The success of the Bridges program underscores the importance of paid work experience as an adjunct to high school curricula for youth, regardless of disability category or severity of disability.

By some accounts, programs like this one have proven successful, and as the last line above suggests, has led some people to wonder whether more direct job training should have a larger role in high school curricula and whether private companies can both serve the needs of the public and their own needs by becoming involved in education. As Marriott notes above, programs like Bridges can "provide critical job experience for youth with disabilities and help employers meet their human resources needs." Other people, however, are concerned that initiatives like the Marriott Hospitality Public Charter School might reduce the importance of education's wider purposes; these concerns echo those of John Dewey above.

Writing to Respond

Read the following essay from *The Common Denominator*, using the techniques for active reading discussed in Chapter 5. After identifying and considering stasis points raised there, use the techniques for focusing a topic that are discussed in Chapters 7 and 8 to develop specific areas for further research on education-corporation partnerships. As you respond, be sure to consider the values of education that are served, or neglected, in such partnerships.

School without Books

John DeVault

Carolina Green was looking for something better when she placed her granddaughter in a brand-new charter school last September. Bright but rambunctious, the 15-year-old was talking back to her teachers at Francis Junior High School and hanging out with friends who were, Green asserted, "brainwashing" her. "The public schools have some students who are very rude," she said disapprovingly. So the new Marriott Hospitality Public Charter High School seemed perfect to Green, who is raising her granddaughter and asked that the girl's name not be used in this story. Marriott Hospitality High, established to "promote hospitality careers for D.C. residents," is funded with millions of dollars from Marriott Corp. and other hotel and restaurant industry leaders. Its brochure promises "a progressive academic curriculum that promotes high levels of student effort and academic achievement." The school is located at 410 Eighth St. NW, near MCI Center.

"They said they are very particular with the students," Green recalled. So she was shocked when she learned that Marriott Hospitality High lacks just one thing: books. On June 9, Green's granddaughter and her schoolmates will complete an entire academic year without a single book in any class—textbooks included. Green now says sending her granddaughter to Marriott Hospitality was "the biggest mistake I ever made. How can the students develop their brains without any books?" she asked.

The school touts high academic goals for its students. The school's full-color, professionally produced brochure says that Marriott Hospitality will prepare students for "management careers" and "academic advancement in a competitive post-secondary institution." "We're not looking at this as a vo-tech," said Principal Flossie Johnson. She said she expects "most" of her students to go on to college. Johnson said the school is setting up partnerships with the Culinary Institute of America and the hospitality programs at Cornell University, Howard University and other colleges. "We're preparing (students) for higher education," she said.

But the only place that books are currently found at Marriott Hospitality is in photos in the promotional brochure: students were given books just for the photo shoot. Green's granddaughter said that when visitors come to the school, administrators tell students to "keep your notebooks open"—to hide the absence of books. Nazanin Samari said a visit to the school late last year aroused her suspicions about its mission. Samari, a research assistant at the American Enterprise Institute who has been a longtime volunteer tutor of a Marriott Hospitality student, said the school's guidance counselor, JoAnne Hurlston, told her that the school was established "because Marriott was having a hard time finding properly prepared employees" in front-line positions like desk clerks, waiters and housekeepers. Samari pointed out that Marriott Hospitality's student body is entirely African-American and Hispanic, and that the school recruited the majority of its 65 students from minority-heavy neighborhoods like Shaw and Columbia Heights. "It seems that way too early, these kids are being put on a track that's much too limited as to their future lives," she said. "My assessment is that they're getting D.C. public education dollars to train Marriott employees."

In an interview last month, guidance counselor Hurlston seemed to confirm that description of the school's goals. Hurlston, who came to her current job from the personnel department at the Bethesda Hyatt Hotel, said Marriott Hospitality was "designed to ensure that we have enough qualified personnel. . . . The hospitality industry needs people with the right personality."

"You need to smile and greet people willingly, not like it's a chore," she said, "It's extremely difficult to find a good server. Nothing is more difficult than to have a server and you can't understand them. So you need to learn English grammar." Hurlston said she sets a monthly career focus for the students, such as, "If you're a door person, how do you stand? You can't stand like you don't care. I have them put their hands behind their back," she said. Other lessons, she said, have included how to prepare for a job interview and on-the-job etiquette. Asked if the school's sponsors, which include at least two hotel chains and Washington's hotel and restaurant associations, had a bigger interest in producing well-mannered waiters and desk clerks for their industry than in preparing students for college, Hurlston replied, "That's probably fair."

Emily Vetter, head of the Hotel Association of Washington, strongly disagreed. "I can't believe somebody at the school told you that," she said. She called Marriott Hospitality "our baby" and insisted, "This (program) isn't about producing happy waiters." Vetter said that every graduate of Marriott Hospitality is guaranteed either a job or a college scholarship. She said that a scholarship fund is currently being developed for the students, who are all in either ninth or 10th grade this year. "They'll get whatever we have in the kitty to give them," she said. "We want to work with Southeastern University in Southwest D.C., which is basically a business school, on a two-year program. For a lot of kids, a two-year program will do it," Vetter said. Green's granddaughter, a ninth grader, said she has a tougher time at Marriott Hospitality High than she did at Francis Junior High because she doesn't have books now. "Some of the things I don't understand, and I can't go back and try to learn it my own self," she said. "I don't feel like I'm ready at all for next year," she added. "I feel like I'm still stuck in the same grade as last year."

Green said she has called the school repeatedly to complain that her granddaughter has no books in any of her classes. She said that when she first visited Marriott Hospitality before it opened, it lacked desks, chairs and books. She said school officials promised they would have all three when the school opened. The school got chairs and worktables, but it never came through with books.

Principal Johnson gave seemingly conflicting explanations for the lack of books in a mid-April interview. At first she said the school lacked books because of a funding hold-up by the D.C. government. "You think you're escaping politics when you get into a charter school, but you're not," she said. Johnson also said she "could easily have selected books, but I wanted our teachers to have a chance to preview materials." Later in the same interview, she said, "We've ordered books." And finally she claimed, "We have them, but we just haven't passed them out yet." Johnson defended the school's failure to provide books to its students by calling them "just supplemental materials." "It's a poor teacher if you have to depend on books to present your lesson," she said. Asked last week to clarify her explanation for the absence of books, Johnson repeated her claim that the school does have books but has chosen not to give them to students. "This is the end of the school year," she said. "Next year we'll pass out the books." "It was decided to see where our students are, where their needs are, before passing out textbooks," she said. "Our teachers are using other materials to meet their objectives. They're using their creativity."

Nelson Smith, executive director of the D.C. Public Charter School Board, said last week that his group was required by law to inspect each charter school before it opened to ensure the school had "the necessary things like teachers' lesson plans on file, classroom furniture and textbooks." "I'm not aware that they have no textbooks," he said of Marriott Hospitality. "I'll have to check on that."

The absence of books seems surprising given the school's heavy-hitting sponsors. The school, one of almost 40 charter schools in the District, is a joint project of the Hotel Association of Washington and the Restaurant Association of Metropolitan Washington—the leading promotional groups for the hospitality industry in the city. The school was established with a $1 million grant from the Marriott Foundation, as well as a $250,000 grant from Hyatt Corp. and $100,000 contributions from Loews Hotels and MeriStar Corp., the largest hotel management firm in the United States.

Some students said the lack of books is a serious roadblock to learning. Victoria Scott, 16, a ninth-grader, said, "I have trouble with math anyway. And then when I get home, my mind is like a blank. If you didn't understand in class, you don't have any references to help you with your homework." Other students said not having books isn't a problem. Kenneth Jackson, 16, a ninth-grader, said that his teachers hand out packets of photocopied material to make up for the lack of books. "The teacher goes over everything we need to know," he said. "And if we don't understand, she goes over it with us (again)." Said Kenneth Butler, 16, a 10th-grader, "It's easier with a book, but the packets are okay. I feel as if we learn." Still, he said that he would return to Gonzaga High School next year. "At least we had old, dilapidated books there," he said.

Green's granddaughter said inexperienced teachers, several with more experience in the hospitality industry than in a school, make things worse. According to Principal Johnson, the school's English teacher is a one-time chef and its Spanish teacher, who has a limited teaching background, is the wife of the general manager of the Omni-Shoreham Hotel. "At Francis, they made us do work," Green's grand-daughter said. But at Marriott Hospitality, she recounted, teachers often give in to student requests for a free period. Her math class, she said, is "just like a play-time period. You can do anything you want—you can curse, you can sleep." She added that when she asked her math teacher for help, "She was like, 'Whoa, girl, you ask so many questions.' I'm like, 'That's my job to ask questions.'"

Green said that after working as a housekeeper at the Washington Hilton for many years, she wants a better future for her granddaughter. "I don't want her to work in a restaurant or a hotel," she said. "I want her to continue with her schooling." Both Green and her granddaughter agree that June 9 will be the teenager's last day at Marriott Hospitality High. "She's not going back to that school," Green said.

Writing Applications

DeVault's article and the articles on school-to-work initiatives in Chapter 4 and Reading and Writing Applications 3 can form the beginnings of a useful researched project. Such a project might begin from the following question:

- How much emphasis should be put on career training and preparedness in the educational system?

  This question, of course, has many implications:

- What is the effect of school-to-work initiatives like the Marriott Corporation's? Do such initiatives just train, or really educate, the students?
- What types of jobs does this type of education prepare people for?
- Is there room for advancement in programs like Marriot's, even though the initial jobs might seem restrictive?
- Is a system of apprenticeship or internship a viable alterative to college for some people? Is there too much focus on formal education and not enough on the work people might want to do?
- What is the place of the liberal arts, subjects that are not tied directly to careers, in the American educational system? What should it be?
- Are children asked to commit to careers too early in life?

In order to write an informed essay, you must use the mature research processes discussed in Part 3 of this book to find the various viewpoints and data that are out there on the topic. Once you are more informed, you will be ready to limit and focus your topic and to make a case for your position.

Casebook 5 WHAT IS A CAREER IN THE TWENTY-FIRST CENTURY?

Many people say that the days where one signs on with a particular company for life are largely gone, making the managing of one's career more of an individual affair. In *Work: Making a Living and Making a Life*, Josh Halberstam chronicles the recent shifts in the way people view careers, noting the change from "having a job" to "doing a job," in response to the current work world: "In the United States today, the average worker will have had ten employers over the course of his work life. For all workers, the average tenure of employment at one company is just four and a half years—and for managers and professionals, just six years." Perhaps, if you are a returning adult student, you might have experienced this desire or need to shift careers yourself.

Halberstam, like many others who have written on the topic of the "new career," advocates responding to this reality by taking charge of one's future and becoming an entrepreneur of one's own career. As you think about your career aspirations—whether you are a traditional student or a returning adult looking for new challenges—exploring this issue can be useful.

Writing Applications

The concept of the so-called new career can be a worthwhile topic to research and write about as you plan for your future. There are many ways that you might gather information about the current state of career fields:

- You might seek out and read some of the many articles on the topic of the new career that you can find in business magazines, journals, and newspapers.

- If you are currently working in a career field, or have done so in the past, you might draw on your own experiences to illustrate changing attitudes toward work.

- You could interview current workers, discussing their commitment to their present job—and their sense of their employer's commitment as well.

- You might read narratives about the ways that current workers are managing their careers and using their mobility to develop personally and professionally.

- You might consider the perspective of employers in the current marketplace and how they are responding to the increasing mobility of workers.

- You might consider how educational institutions (including your own college) are responding to changing definitions of what it means to "have a job."

- You might research the stability of careers in your own field of interest, using paper and electronic sources as well as interviews.

When you have completed your research, write an informative essay or construct a website that illustrates either general principles of the career in the twenty-first century or of the future prospects of a career within a particular field.

Casebook 6   ATTITUDES TOWARD WORK: WRITING AN ETHNOGRAPHY

An ethnography is a type of anthropological study. Until recently, *ethnography* referred largely to studies of primitive societies; but more recently, this method of close observation has been applied to a variety of cultural settings, including the workplace.

One area of interest for many recent ethnographic writers is the attitudes of Americans toward their work. We have already read many such pieces, including the testimony of workers that I interviewed for this book. Josh Halberstam's *Work: Making a Living and Making a Life* discusses at length the relationship between work and other priorities we hold. Barbara Ehrenreich, a widely read columnist, conducted research for her book *Nickled and Dimed* by working in jobs that paid minimum wage to learn first-hand about trying to make a living in such positions. And white-collar workers face important challenges as well, as is chronicled in works like Robert Kegan's 1994 *In Over Our Heads: The Mental Demands of Modern Life.*

Writing to Respond

Perhaps one of the most famous of the writers who has written about work is Studs Terkel. His 1972 book *Working*, which records the words of working-class Americans, is still widely read. As you read the following excerpts from that book, note the way in which Terkel allows the voice of the workers themselves to emerge.

In Charge

Studs Terkel

Ward Quaal

We're at Tribune Square, Chicago. We're in the well-appointed office of the president of WGN-Continental Broadcasting Corporation—"the most powerful broadcast medium in the Midwest." He has been battling a slight sinus condition, but his presence is, nonetheless, felt.

"I'm responsible for all its broadcasting properties. We have radio and television here. We have a travel company here. We have a sales company here. We have the Continental Productions Company here. We have radio and television in Minnesota and translator systems in northern Michigan, Wisconsin, as well as Minnesota. We have cable television in Michigan and California. We have television in Denver. We have sales companies in New York and Tokyo. I operate sixteen different organizations in the United States and Japan."

My day starts between four-thirty and five in the morning, at home in Winnetka. I dictate in my library until about seven-thirty. Then I have breakfast. The driver gets there about eight o'clock and oftentimes I continue dictating in the car on the way to the office. I go to the Broadcast Center in the morning and then to Tribune Square around noon. Of course, I do a lot of reading in the car.

I talk into a dictaphone. I will probably have as many as 150 letters dictated by seven-thirty in the morning. I have five full-time secretaries, who do nothing but work for Ward Quaal. I have seven swing girls, who work for me part-time. This does not include my secretaries in New York, Los Angeles, Washington, and San Francisco. They get dicta-belts from me every day. They also take telephone messages. My personal secretary doesn't do any of that. She handles appointments and my trips. She tries to work out my schedule to fit these other secretaries.

I get home around six-thirty, seven at night. After dinner with the family I spend a minimum of two and a half hours each night going over the mail and dictating. I should have a secretary at home just to handle the mail that comes there. I'm not talking about bills and personal notes, I'm talking about business mail only. Although I don't go to the office on Saturday or Sunday, I do have mail brought out to my home for the weekend. I dictate on Saturday and Sunday. When I do this on holidays, like Christmas, New Year's, and Thanksgiving, I have to sneak a little bit, so the family doesn't know what I'm doing.

Ours is a twenty-four-hour-a-day business. We're not turning out three thousand gross of shoes, beans, or neckties. We're turning out a new product every day, with new problems. It's not unusual for me to get a phone call on a weekend: "What are your thoughts on it, Mr. Quaal? Would you speak out on it?" I'm not going to hide my posture on it. I'm going to answer that. This may mean going into the studio to make a recording. Or I may do tape recording at home. Or maybe I'll just make a statement. I am in a seven-day-a-week job and I love it!

"I grew up in a very poor family. Not only did no one come to us for advice, we went to other people for advice. We wondered what we were going to do for the next dollar. We did manage during the Depression. But I know others who didn't extricate themselves from these difficulties. I won't forget them. A letter from one of those individuals asking for help is just as important to me as a suggestion from the chairman of the board of the Chase Manhattan Bank. They get the same weight.

They get a personal letter from me. He didn't write to my assistant, he didn't write to my secretary. He wants to hear from Ward Quaal."

When I come to the Broadcast Center, I'll probably have about five or six different stacks of mail. One stack urgent and should be acted upon before I make any phone calls. Once I handle that, which usually takes about fifteen, twenty minutes, I start the important phone calls. In-between these phone calls and others of lesser importance. I get into the other mail. On a typical day we'll get thirteen hundred pieces of first-class mail addressed to me personally. Every letter is answered within forty-eight hours—and not a form letter. There are no form letters. If they write to the president of the company, they don't want to hear from the third vice president. They hear from the president. Mail and the telephone, that's the name of the game in this business.

I imagine your phone calls are not long in nature?

No, they're not long in nature. I have this ability—I learned this when I was an announcer years ago, and we were feeding six networks out of here. I could listen to all these channels with earphones and I knew when to say the right cue at the right time. I can still do that.

"In high school I wanted to be a good football player, a good basketball player, a good baseball player. I managed to be captain of every team on which I ever played. At the end of my freshman year my coach said, 'There's a shortage of people to do oratory and declamatory work.' He said, 'We've just simply got to have somebody with your voice. If you would do this, I would excuse you from football practice a couple of nights a week.' I won the oratorical and declamatory championship for the state of Michigan. On the night of the finals in Ishpeming, which were broadcast, the chief engineer of a radio station, a Polish gentleman, called my mother and told her I'd be a network announcer someday.

"I started working during my freshman year in high school as an announcer at WBEO in Marquette. I worked from 10:00 A.M. to 10:00 P.M. and got $17.50 a week. At the same time, I drove a commercial milk truck from four in the morning to eight, and I got $22.50 a week for that. The two jobs gave me money to go to the University of Michigan. I have great pride in my university. I was chairman of the Alumni Fund and its Development Council.

"I won the job as a Detroit radio announcer at thirty-five dollars a week, while still a student. I hitchhiked or took a bus every day from Ann Arbor to Detroit. On the campus I was promotion manager of the yearbook. I was sports and feature writer for the Michigan Daily. I was on the freshman football team, baseball team, and basketball team. And I was president of the fraternity. All at one time. Shows you can do it if you work hard enough.

"When I applied for admission at the university, I was asked what my goal was after graduation. I said, 'The announcing staff of WGN.' I finished my last exam June 8, 1941, and I started at WGN the next day."

I had no desire to be an announcer forever. I wanted to become general manager. I think this is something anybody can do. The number one thing in any business is to go get a background, so you can show your people you can do anything they can do. My people today know I can announce any show they could, I can write a script, I can produce a show, I can handle a camera. If I still had the voice, I would enjoy being back on the air again.

I've had to develop a team effort with all people. I prefer being called Ward rather than Mr. Quaal. Ninety percent of the people do call me by my first name. The young women of the organization do not, although I certainly would not disapprove of them calling me Ward. The last thing I want to be is a stuffed shirt. I'm trying to run this organization on a family basis. I prefer it to be on the informal side.

I've always felt throughout my lifetime that if you have any ability at all, go for first place. That's all I'm interested in. That doesn't mean I'm trying to be an autocrat. Lord knows I'm not a dictator. I try to give all my colleagues total autonomy. But they know there's one guy in charge.

Of course, you have to be number two before you become number one—unless you're born into something. I was born into a poor family. I had to create my own paths. Sure, I've been second vice president, first vice president, and executive vice president. But I had only one goal in life and that was to be president.

A fellow like Ward Quaal, he's one of the old hands now. That doesn't mean I'm going to vegetate. I intend to devote more time to our subsidiaries and to develop young people who come forth with new ideas. I don't look forward to retirement. I feel I have many useful years ahead of me. When the time comes to step aside, I won't regret it at all. I have a lot of writing to do. I'll have so much to do.

You're more of a philosopher-king than a boss . . .

I think that is true. When I came here sixteen years ago, August first, I never had any desire to be a czar. I don't like to say I ruled with an iron hand, but I had to take charge and clean up the place. I am the captain calling the signals and every once in a while I call the right play and we're pretty lucky.

I don't feel any pressure, though my family says I sometimes show it. I'm not under tension. I go to bed at night and I sleep well. The company is doing well. My people are functioning as a team. The success story is not Ward Quaal. It's a great team of people.

Postscript: "On a typical day we get about seven hundred phone calls. We average eighty a day long distance." I estimated that during the time of this conversation, there were about forty phone calls for Ward Quaal.

Dave Bender

It is a newly built, quite modern factory on the outskirts of a large industrial city. Scores of people are at work in the offices. Sounds of typewriters and adding machines; yet an air of informality pervades. He has come into his private office, tie askew; he's in need of a shave. We have a couple of shots of whisky.

"I manufacture coin machine and vending machine parts—components. We also make units for amusement devices. We don't know what they're gonna do with it. We have ideas what they might. I have about two hundred employees. I never counted. They're people. We have tool and die makers, mold makers, sheet metal, screw machine, woodwork, painting, coil winding. You name it, we got it."

I just stay in the background. Myself, I like making things. I make the machinery here. I'm not an engineer, but I have an idea and I kind of develop things and—(with an air of wonder)—they *work*. All night long I think about this place. I love my work. It isn't the money. It's just a way of expressing my feeling.

When we started here we were strictly in the pinball game part business. I kept adding and adding and adding and never stopped. Finally I got into the jukebox end of it. Of course, slot machines came in and then slot machines went out. Never fool with Uncle Sam. When they said no slot machine parts, they meant it and I meant it too. I don't want them checking up on us. You can live without it. We make so many different things. A little of this, a little of that. Not a lot of any one thing.

I made a machine that makes plastic tubes. It becomes like a parasite. It runs through 250 feet a minute, five tubes at a time. I made it with a bunch of crazy ideas and junk I found around the place. I can sell that machine for twenty thousand dollars. If I dress it up and put flowers on it, you can sell it for much, much more.

I was a no-good bum kicked out of high school. I went up to a teacher and I said, "If you don't pass me, I'll blow your brains out." I stole a gun. (Laughs.) I was kicked out. It was my second year. I did some dirty things I can't talk about. (Laughs.) When I was thirteen years old I took a Model T Ford apart and put it together again in the basement. I did some crazy things.

When I talk to people about plastic I take the position *I'm* the plastic and how would I travel through the machine and what would I see. Maybe I'm goofy. In business, I take the position: where would I be if I were the customer? What do I expect of you? Some people are natural born stinkers. I try to find a way to get to them. You can break down anybody with the right method.

I sell all I make. I don't know what to do with 'em. (Laughs.) They use 'em for packaging. I work with wood, plastic, metal, anything. I work with paper. Even at home. Sunday I was taking paper and pasting it together and finding a method of how to drop spoons, a fork, a napkin and a straw into one package. The napkin feeder I got. The straw feeder we made already. That leaves us the spoon and the fork. How do we get it? Do we blow the bag open? Do we push it open? Do we squeeze it down? So I'm shoving things in and pushing with my wife's hair clips and bobby pins and everything I can get my hands on. I even took the cat's litter, the stuff you pick up the crap with (laughs), even that to shove with the bag, to pull it open. This is for schools, inexpensive packaging. It sells for about a penny a package. Plastic. In a bag, the whole darn thing. So what can I tell you?

Everybody is packaging the stuff. Their method is antique. My method is totally automatic. I know what my competitors are doing. I never underestimate 'em, but I'm ten steps ahead of 'em. I can meet them any way they want. But not to cut their heart out. We all have to make a living.

"I started this whole damn thing with forty dollars. In 1940. I borrowed it. In 1938 I was a big dealer. I was the greatest crap shooter in the world. (Laughs.) I was makin' rubber parts and plunger rods for the pin games. Then the war broke out in '41. Where do you get the rods? I took a hacksaw and went to the junkyards. Remember the old rails that went up and down on the beds? I cut that out and made plunger rods. I did some crazy things.

"I started with a couple of people. I made fifteen dollars a week for myself and I didn't even have that. Oh boy, oh boy, oh boy, I tried everything. Making work gloves. I was eighteen. I went into the coal business. I borrowed two hundred dollars from my brother. Suddenly I had four trucks. I got sick and tired of coal and gave my father the keys for the four trucks and I said, 'Pa, it's your business. You owe me zero.' What else did I do? Oh God, making things. Making a factory. I love making.

"Business to me is a method of engineering. Even in advertising. I've always wondered why they don't get people for what they really are. Like this Alka-Seltzer commercial. I operate business the same way—in getting to the people. What are we other than people?"

Even during the war, I never took advantage of a price. I used to sell something for thirty-five cents. During the war I still sold it for thirty-five cents. A customer said, "Dave, I'll never forget you." They're liars. They did forget soon afterward. I never took anybody. I built my business on that. My competitors came and they went and I'm still at it. I'm bigger now than ever.

I hope to be going public. So I have to show an increase. That's the name of the game. I have workers been here twenty-seven, twenty-eight years. I feel I owe them something. I don't know how to compensate them. At least if I go public, I can offer them stock. I'd like to repay people. This is a way of saying thank you.

I was offered all kinds of deals which I turned down—by big vending companies. It would be beautiful for me. I walk away with a million many times over. So what? What about these poor devils? I'll fire 'em all? Huh?

To them, I'm Dave. I know the family. I know their troubles. "Dave, can you give me a dollar?" "Dave, how about some coffee?" I'll go to the model maker and talk about our problem and we'll have a shot of whisky. Ask him how his wife's feeling. "Fine." He wants to put something for his home, can I make it? "Sure." They all call me Dave. When they call me Mr. Bender I don't know who they're talking to. (Laughs.)

I love mechanics. All my fingernails are chopped off. I washed my hands before you came in. Grease. Absolutely. I get into things. You stick a ruler here or a measure here. I want this, I want that. "Frank, you chop this up. Put this in the mill. Out that off." I got three, four things happening at one time.

I'm here at six in the morning. Five-thirty I'll leave. Sometimes I'll come here on Sunday when everybody's gone and I'll putter around with the equipment. There isn't a machine in this place I can't run. There isn't a thing I can't do.

They tell me it don't look nice for the workers for me to work on the machine. I couldn't care less if I swept the floors, which I do. Yesterday some napkins fell on the floor from the napkin feeding machine. I said to the welder. "Pick up the napkins." He says, "No, you pick it up." I said, "If you're tired, I'll pick it up." So I'm pickin' 'em up.

The workers say: "You're the boss, you shouldn't do this. It's not nice. You're supposed to tell us what to do, but not to do it yourself." I tell 'em I love it. They want me more or less in the office. I don't even come in here. If I do it's just to get my shot of booze with my worker and we break bread, that's all. When they call me Mr. Bender, I think they're being sarcastic. I don't feel like a boss to 'em. I feel like a chum-buddy.

I know a lot of people with money and I have very little to do with them. They're a little bit too high falutin' for me. I think they're snobs. They're spoiled rotten, their wealth. I won't mention names. I was born and raised poor. I had zero. I'm a fortunate guy. Whatever I got I'm thankful for. That's my life. I just like plain, ordinary people. I have a doctor friend, but outside of being a doctor, he's my swear-buddy. We swear at each other. A guy who works in the liquor store is my friend. Some of the workers here are my friends.

You're the boss of these people . . .

(Hurt) No, I just work here. They say, "Dave you should give us orders. You shouldn't be pickin' up napkins." Oh, don't misunderstand me. I'm not the easiest guy in the world. I swear at 'em. I'm a stubborn son of a gun. When I finally get my idea straight, I'm rough. I know what I want, give me what I want. But I do have enough sense to know when to leave 'em alone.

Don't you feel you have status in being a boss?

Ooohhh, I hate that word! I tell people I don't want to hear another word about who I am or what I am. I enjoy myself eleven hours a day. When I get home I take my shoes off, get comfortable, pinch my wife's rear end, kiss her, of course, and ask her what she did today. I try not to take my problems home. I have problems, plenty, but I try to avoid it.

Saturdays and Sundays are the worst days of the week. It's a long weekend because I'm not here. I bum around, see movies, go to somebody's house, but I'm always waiting for Monday. I go away on a vacation, it's the worst thing in the world. (Laughs.) My wife got a heart attack in Majorca, Spain. She was in the hospital. I was there six weeks. It was the first real vacation I ever had. I finally went fishing. Here I am drinking wine, eating oranges and cheese, tearing the bread on the boat, had the time of my life. I told my wife it took her heart attack to get me to enjoy a vacation. (Laughs.)

Retire? Hell no. I'd open up another shop and start all over again. What am I gonna do? Go crazy? I told you I love my work. I think it's some form of being insecure. I've always worried about tomorrow. I worried and I fought for tomorrow. I don't have to worry about tomorrow. But I still want to work. I *need* to.

Today I worked all day in the shop with the model maker, two tool makers, and a welder. I don't have neat blueprints. I don't have a damn thing. All I have is this. (Taps at his temple.) I'll take a piece of paper. I can't even make drawings. I'm measuring, taking off three-eights of an inch or put on two inches here. It's the craziest piece of iron you ever saw. I never saw anything like this in my life. But I saw it working the other day.

When I get it fabricated it'll be a packaging machine. You'll see arms going up and down, gears working, things going, reelers and winders, automatic everything. I know it could be patented. There's nothing like it. It's unique. This is all in my mind, yes sir. And I can't tell you my telephone number. (Laughs.)

I never tell people I'm the boss. I get red and flustered. I'm ashamed of it. When they find out—frankly speaking, people are parasites. They treat you like a dirty dog one way, and as soon as they find out who you are it's a different person. (Laughs.) When they come through the front door—"I want you to meet our president, Mr. Bender"—they're really like peacocks. I'd rather receive a man from the back door as a man. From the front door, he's got all the table manners. Oh, all that phony air. He's never down to earth. That's why I don't like to say who I am.

A man comes in and I'm working like a worker, he tells me everything. He talks from the bottom of his heart. You can break bread with him, you can swear. Anything that comes out of your heart. The minute he finds out you're in charge, he looks up to you. Actually he hates you.

My wife's got a friend and her husband's got a job. If only they stopped climbing down my back. I do so many wrong things. Why don't you tell me to go to hell for the things I do? I deliberately see how far I can push them. And they won't tell me to go to hell, because I'm Dave Bender, the president. They look up to me as a man of distinction, a guy with brains. Actually I'm a stupid ass, as stupid as anybody that walks the street.

Yet what the hell did we fight for? A goddamned empty on top of nothing? A sand pile? King of the Hill means you stood there and you fought to get on top of an empty hill. But it did satisfy your ego, didn't it? We do these crazy things. It doesn't have to be a financial reward. Just the satisfaction.

I'm making a machine now. I do hope to have it ready in the next couple months. The machine has nothing to do with helping humanity in any size, shape, or form. It's a personal satisfaction for me to see this piece of iron doing some work. It's like a robot working. This is the reward itself for me, nothing else. My ego, that's it.

Something last night was buggin' me. I took a sleeping pill to get it out of my mind. I was up half the night just bugging and bugging and bugging. I was down here about six o'clock this morning. I said, "Stop everything. We're making a mistake." I pointed out where the mistake was and they said, "Holy hell, we never thought of that." Today we're rebuilding the whole thing. This kind of stuff gets to me. Not only what was wrong, but how the devil do you fix it? I felt better. This problem, that's over with. There's no problem that can't be solved if you use logic and reason the thing out. I don't care what it is. Good horse sense is what it's known as. With that you can do anything you want—determination, you can conquer the world.

Writing Applications

Recalling examples of workplace studies you have read in this book and elsewhere, write your own workplace ethnography. Begin your ethnographic research by observing a professional setting, speaking with workers there about their job satisfaction, their attitudes about the work they do, their relationship with the place they work and their coworkers, the learning they do on the job and that which they did in school. Using both your own observations of the workplace and those you obtain through interviews and other research into the company or field, write a description that helps others to learn about career and job satisfaction, about attitudes toward work, or about the rewards of a particular job. Do your best to make this place, and its people, come to life for your readers by including narrative details and careful characterization.

Casebook 7 ETHICS AND THE WORKPLACE

Though a "business"—a word that could be used to describe most of the places where people work—exists at least partially to make a profit, that need not be its only goal (or its only outcome). The charitable and social contributions of businesses and their owners to the citizens of the country cannot be overlooked. The Carnegie Foundation, the Pew Charitable Trusts (funded with Sun Oil monies), Ronald McDonald Houses, and countless other organizations all illustrate ways that corporate funding can contribute to the advancement of our charitable causes, the arts, culture, and so on.

Some companies also are dedicated to policies in the management of their business that show the highest ethical standards. One such company is Ben and Jerry's Ice Cream. Ben and Jerry's has created a three-part mission for its company, and despite its sale to new owners, has done good work in maintaining high ethical standards for its product, its investors, its employees, and its customers. Here is an excerpt from its company policies:

> Ben & Jerry's is dedicated to the creation and demonstration of a new corporate concept of linked prosperity. Our mission consists of three interrelated parts. Underlying the mission is the determination to seek new and creative ways of addressing all three parts, while holding a deep respect for individuals inside and outside the company, and for the communities of which they are a part.
>
> 1. Product: To make, distribute and sell the finest quality all natural ice cream and related products in a wide variety of innovative flavors made from Vermont dairy products.
>
> 2. Economic: To operate the Company on a sound financial basis of profitable growth, increasing value for our shareholders, and creating career opportunities and financial rewards for our employees.
>
> 3. Social: To operate the Company in a way that actively recognizes the central role that business plays in the structure of society by initiating innovative ways to improve the quality of life of a broad community—local, national, and international.
>
> Underlying the mission of Ben & Jerry's is the determination to seek new & creative ways of addressing all three parts, while holding a deep respect for individuals inside and outside the Company and for the communities of which they are a part.

Ben and Jerry's also supports a charitable foundation, whose mission is as follows:

> The Mission of the Ben & Jerry's Foundation is to make the world a better place by empowering Ben & Jerry's employees to use available resources to support and encourage organizations that are working towards eliminating the underlying causes of environmental and social problems.

Another company which has taken its social mission seriously is Fashion Bug. Dorrit J. Bern, chair and CEO of this women's clothing retailer, has begun to write letters to her customers in a campaign called "Speaking Woman to Woman." She has encouraged women to consider their history and to exercise the relatively new rights afforded to them, including the right to vote. The company has also sponsored an essay contest, inviting writing on women who have advanced the country and community. Using her position as the leader of a company that sells products to women, Bern has been willing to speak out on issues that clearly could be controversial—including the ratification of the ERA: "It might shock you to know," writes Bern in one of her letters, "that the Equal Rights Amendment, which provides for equality of rights under law—regardless of sex—still is not part of the U. S. Constitution. . . . So the right that we take for granted—to be treated equally under the law—isn't necessarily a right at all." Making political statements like this from a purely profit-driven perspective is risky, but this company has been willing to take that chance to increase awareness among women.

Though the previous case suggests that there is certainly room for praise of those companies that do good work, there have been enough scandalous acts in the news to remind us that not all workplaces are centers of ethically sound behavior. Enron, WorldCom, and tobacco companies have greatly lessened public trust in the country's businesses.

Writing to Respond

One ethical decision that many workers face is when to blow the whistle on colleagues who behave in ethically suspect ways, especially when the offending parties are superiors. Following is the story of Trudi Lytle and the problems she faced as she took on her school system over preferential treatment. As you read, consider both the personal sacrifice such actions took and the benefits the community reaps by such behaviors.

Trudi Lytle and the Clark County Public School System

Terence D. Miethe

Parents have long been confronted with the grisly choice between public and private education for their children. The typical advantages of private schools (such as smaller classes, better instruction, higher-quality equipment) are offset by the financial expenses of private schooling. Public schools are clearly cheaper for parents, but the phrase "you get what you pay for" often describes the relative quality of education in these institutions. Clearly, the optimal solution for parents would be to achieve the quality of educational services often thought to characterize good private schools within the context of a public school. Such a situation occurred recently in the Clark County Public School District (CCSD) in Las Vegas, Nevada.

The CCSD is the tenth largest school system in the country. It is also one of the fastest growing, with more than thirteen thousand students added to CCSD each year. Nevada's expenditure for public education of $5,126 per student, however, ranks only thirty-fifth among all states and lags far behind the national average (*Statistical Abstracts of the United States* 1996). When the dramatic population growth in Las Vegas is coupled with the relatively low state support for education, it isn't surprising that the quality of public education is a major social problem in the city.

As is true of other public school systems, several programs are provided for students in CCSD with particular talents or potential. One of these initiatives, the Student Options for Academic Realization (SOAR) program, was a pilot program for gifted students in the Marion Earl Elementary School that was implemented in the 1991–1992 school year. Compared to other programs and classes within this school and throughout the district, SOAR students were given preferential treatment in class size and instructional funds. SOAR classes were capped at twenty students when other classes in the school had far higher student-teacher ratios. Computer equipment and school supplies (such as dictionaries, folders, and workbooks) were widely available to SOAR students but not for other students at Earl.

Although the claim that "regular" students were suffering as a result of the preferential treatment of SOAR students was a severe criticism of the program, the pilot program gained greater notoriety because of the composition of the classroom. Specifically, thirteen of the forty participants in the program's first year were children of school district staff members (*Las Vegas Review Journal* 1994e). Given disproportionate funding for SOAR and the overrepresentation of teachers' and principals' children within this program, critics have charged that district staff were receiving a largely private education for their children at the public's expense.

Trudi Lytle's Whistleblowing Experience

Trudi Lytle is an elementary school teacher with more than twenty years of teaching experience in the CCSD. She was a fourth-grade teacher at Marion Earl Elementary when the SOAR program was implemented. In March 1992, Lytle drafted and submitted a letter to all southern Nevada legislators that exposed the operation of the SOAR program. Parts of the letter were also published in a Las Vegas newspaper. The letter raised questions about the unequal student-faculty ratios across classes, the number of program participants who were children of district staff, and the prevalence of zone variances to allow particular students in other neighborhoods to participate in the SOAR program. Lytle's fourth-grade classroom at the time had thirty-three students and limited school supplies. She called the SOAR program a private school within a public school system (*Las Vegas Review Journal* 1994b).

The direct consequences of Lytle's disclosures are subject to alternative viewpoints. However, several observations can be gleaned from newspaper accounts, court documents, and interviews with this whistleblower:

- Trudi Lytle was transferred from her fourth-grade class at Earl Elementary in January 1993. She claims that the involuntary transfer was due to harassment in retaliation for her letter to state lawmakers and her federal lawsuit against the school district and her former principal. School officials, in contrast, argue that her transfer was not punishment but rather "for the good of the students" and an effort to boost low morale at the elementary school (*Las Vegas Review Journal* 1994b).

- Lytle was reprimanded twice by her principal prior to the transfer. The first reprimand involved her refusal to turn in school keys before summer vacation. The second admonishment cited Lytle for trying to write a letter to parents, criticizing the SOAR program (*Las Vegas Review Journal* 1994c).

- Faculty and staff at Earl Elementary submitted a letter to Dr. Cram (superintendent of CCSD) in October 1992, alleging that Lytle was an argumentative staff member who created an emotional uproar and dissension in the school. Lytle's attorney claimed that these signatures were obtained through coercion and misrepresentation, orchestrated by the principal, SOAR teachers, and specialists who disliked his client.

- Lytle was offered teaching assignments at three other schools after her involuntary transfer. She refused these assignments, saying that she should have the freedom to speak up without facing retaliatory action (*Las Vegas Review Journal* 1994d).

- Lytle was removed from her fourth-grade teaching position during the middle of the school year. Twenty of the twenty-nine parents who were surveyed wanted Lytle to return to continue teaching their children as soon as possible. The superintendent of Clark County schools determined that she should not be returned to Earl Elementary. This decision was made "with the best interest of the students at the school in mind." As a sign of support for Lytle, fewer than half of her students showed up for class for the two days following her transfer (*Las Vegas Review Journal* 1993a).

- Lytle was unable to work after she was notified of her transfer in January 1993. Two physicians testified that Lytle was incapable of returning to work, as she was suffering from stress and high blood pressure. After a period of time and a court injunction, however, she returned to teaching at Earl Elementary.

Legal Action against the School District

After being informed of the transfer, Trudi Lytle had to consider her options. One option was to accept the decision and meekly acquiesce. Alternatively, the teachers' union could have been contacted on behalf of Lytle to determine whether formal rules were violated. Instead of these two alternatives, Lytle consulted an attorney to become more fully aware of her legal protections. Efforts by her attorney to resolve this situation outside of court were unsuccessful.

Lytle filed a civil rights suit in October 1992 against the principal, administrators, and the CCSD for intentionally depriving her of substantive and procedural due process rights. Lytle noted in the formal complaint that she exercised her First Amendment rights by expressing her opinion about the SOAR program but was retaliated against by the principal through harassment, threats and discipline, and transfer for criticizing the program and filing a lawsuit against the defendants. The defendants, however, claimed that Lytle was transferred because she caused dissension and morale problems. Lytle's attorney argued that the retaliation against his client was also designed to send a message to other school district employees that the administration could not be questioned and to "shut up and go along with the program" (*Las Vegas Review Journal* 1994e). As a direct result of the retaliation, Lytle said that she had suffered extreme emotional distress, humiliation, and embarrassment, causing her to be temporarily disabled. In her federal lawsuit, Lytle asked the court for the following relief:

1. An injunction requiring the defendants to place her back at Earl Elementary School
2. Compensatory damages in the amount of $500,000
3. Special damages in the amount of $200,000
4. Punitive damages in the amount of $500,000
5. Other and further relief as the court might wish to entertain

A jury returned a verdict in favor of Trudi Lytle in July 1994. The jury found that "plaintiff's [Lytle's] protected speech regarding the SOAR program was a substantial or motivating factor in the defendants' decisions to take action against the plaintiff." She was awarded damages in the amount of $135,000. The school district filed a motion for a new trial in U.S. District Court, claiming that the jury ignored instructions that required proof "beyond a preponderance of doubt" that school administrators violated her constitutional right to free speech

(*Las Vegas Sun* 1994). Despite strong opposition from the school administration, Lytle's request for injunctive relief to return to Earl Elementary was granted by the federal judge. School officials urged the judge to stop the reinstatement of Lytle, saying the move would bring about a "tense and hostile atmosphere" (*Las Vegas Review Journal* 1994f).

Although the court ordered the school district to reinstate Lytle to Earl Elementary, the judge retained the school's authority to assign teachers to particular classrooms. Upon notification that she was assigned to teach two kindergarten classes, Lytle submitted an emergency motion to the federal court to order the district to place her in her former classroom as a fourth-grade teacher. However, the judge refused this motion.

Lytle's legal disputes with the school district have continued beyond the initial federal case. Her attorney argued in the emergency motion that her placement in the kindergarten class appeared to be intentional harassment because she had never taught kindergarten in her previous twenty years and there was a new, vacant fourth-grade classroom available for that school year (*Las Vegas Sun* 1994). Lytle currently remains in litigation with the school district about continued harassment at Earl Elementary. She has also filed legal action against the school district for not providing coverage of medical and retirement benefits during the bridge time period in which she was unable to work.

Consequences of Whistleblowing

Trudi Lytle's criticism of the SOAR program has dramatically altered her life. The experience of being a whistleblower has affected her physical and psychological well-being, her faith and trust in others, and her feelings of isolation and powerlessness. She has been medically treated for stress and high blood pressure, and the psychological wounds from being removed from her fourth-grade class in the middle of the school year would be felt by anyone in that position. Although most Americans may believe that co-workers would respect and support them for reporting illegal acts by their employer, Lytle feels that she has received little support from co-workers. In fact, she said she was "shocked to find out that many of [my] co-workers had the attitude 'If I close my eyes, it doesn't exist.' " Her continued legal battles with the school district increasingly add to the label of whistleblower as her "master status." In other words, much of who Trudi Lytle is, and what she does, remains intricately tied to her initial allegations of abuse in the public school system.

When I asked how this experience has changed her views about management and work, Lytle made an extremely poignant comment:

> The CCSD knows that very few people have the money or emotional/physical stamina to fight them in a legal battle. Therefore, they blatantly ignore the

Nevada Revised Statutes and/or the U.S. Constitution where a person's only recourse is a legal battle. Although the teacher's union is one of the most powerful in the state, their *only* goal is to elect people to political office and *not* teachers' rights. Hopefully, both organizations will do some rethinking of their goals as a result of my lawsuit.

The Aftermath of Whistleblowing and Its Effectiveness

The effectiveness of Trudi Lytle in changing organizational practices and improving the public school system in Clark County is subject to interpretation and one's perspective. The costs and benefits of her allegations are summarized below.

As a consequence of Lytle's criticism, the SOAR program was disbanded, and there is now a more equal distribution of students across classrooms within each school. Students with the highest academic ability—who would have previously been in SOAR—now attend a regular classroom but are given accelerated training for a short time period each day in another classroom through a program called GATE (Gifted and Talented Education). Parents of these gifted students are probably pleased that their children are receiving some advanced training in public school. However, parents of children in the regular classroom will probably be miffed because their children aren't receiving the same educational advantages. Although the names have changed and the amount of special training has diminished, the continued existence of special classrooms for bright students makes the school district still susceptible to allegations of "elitism" and of running private schools within a public school setting. Under these conditions, Lytle's public exposure of the SOAR program appears to have had little impact on the unequal distribution of educational services in this public school system.

The lasting contribution of Lytle's disclosures on the legal protection of teachers is largely unknown. For example, as a direct consequence of the Lytle litigation, the Clark County School Board developed and approved a whistle-blowing policy to encourage employees to disclose improper school actions (*Las Vegas Review Journal* 1994h). This policy proposed the establishment of channels for reporting misconduct through a hearing officer and mandated that all cases would be reviewed by the School Board. However, it is unclear whether such policies are proactive steps in disclosing misconduct or simply alternative administrative strategies to limit the public disclosures of whistleblowers. Given Trudi Lytle's ordeal and the continued allegations of retaliation against her, it is unlikely that many observers of misconduct in this work setting would speak out even if there were specific protective policies for whistleblowers. Would you?

Finally, the teachers' union, like other unions, would appear to be an ideal outlet for voicing complaints and seeking corrective action for whistleblowers in this context. Union representatives in most organizations provide a buffer to assure that workers' rights are protected. Although Lytle is extremely cynical of the operation of her union, it remains unknown whether her experiences have subsequently altered the responsiveness of the union in protecting teachers' rights.

Writing Application

1. In a time when some corporations have shown a great capacity for greed and a lack of ethical behaviors, you might, in the course of conducting a researched project, seek out and write about companies and organizations that have done outstanding service to their communities, producing an informational report or creating a promotional piece that highlights their good work. This type of report can help restore faith in the work being done by many citizens and can also help people to consider the value of following such ethical standards.

2. As a researched project, you might investigate either through primary research (interviews and case studies) or through secondary research incidents of unethical work behavior or the effects of that behavior on individual citizens, communities, or companies. Do your best to examine the situation from a number of perspectives, studying news reports, press releases, and other statements, and doing whatever is possible to find unbiased accounts. As you write, you might focus on the actions of the individuals involved (using a narrative framework) or on the situation (using a more analytical approach). Consider carefully who the most viable audience for this document might be as well as your purpose in writing (to praise or blame individuals, to cast light on an unethical situation, to bring about change, and so on).

Works Cited

Bern, Dorrit J. *Speaking Woman to Woman.* 2004. Charming Shoppes, Inc. 14 Jan. 2004. http://www.charmingshoppes.com/contact/speakUp.asp.

The Center for Information and Research on Civic Learning and Participation. School of Public Affairs, University of Maryland. 12 Aug. 2003. http://www.civicyouth.org.

The Civil Rights Act of 1964. U.S. Government International Information Programs. 13 Aug. 1996. http://usinfo.state.gov/usa/infousa/laws/majorlaw/civilr19.htm.

The Civil Rights Act of 1991. U.S. Government International Information Programs. 20 Oct. 2003. http://usinfo.state.gov/usa/infousa/laws/majorlaw/civil91.htm

Delli Carpini, Michael X., and Scott Keeter. *What Americans Know about Politics and Why It Matters.* New Haven: Yale UP, 1997.

Delpit, Lisa. "A New Take on Ebonics and Teaching. " *NEA Today* 17.2 (1998): 17.

Dewey, John. *The School and Society.* Chicago: U of Chicago P, 1907. 38, 42, 49, passim.

Eakin, Emily. "Professor Scarry Has a Theory." *New York Times Magazine,* 19 Nov. 2000. 78–81.

The Equal Rights Amendment (proposed). 5 Nov. 2003. Alice Paul Institute. 20 Dec. 2003. http://www.equalrightsamendment.org/.

"Fewer Shark Bites (Really)." *New York Newsday.* 20 Feb. 2002.

Gura, Mark. Rev. of "Amazing Grace: The Lives of Children and the Conscience of a Nation." *Educational Leadership* 54.7 (1997): 9.

Halberstam, Joshua. *Work: Making a Living and Making a Life.* New York: Penguin Putnam, 2000.

The Hartford Web Site. http://www.thehartford.com/.

Job Market. 2004. *New York Times.* 12 Jan. 2004. http://careerexperience.com/explore/aboutmatchme.html/aip=b4832J0EX6T2bxxt4slqn-,NIA_.

Kegan, Robert. *In Over Our Heads: The Mental Demands of Modern Life.* Cambridge: Harvard UP, 1998.

Bridges from School to Work. 2004. Marriott Foundation. 10 Feb. 2004. http://marriottfoundation.org/foundation/default.mi.

Munro, Alice. "Boys and Girls." *Dance of the Happy Shades.* New York: McGraw-Hill Ryerson Ltd., 1968.

National Bioethics Advisory Commission. *Executive Summary.* National Reference Center for Bioethics Literature at Georgetown University. 15 Sept. 2003. http://www.georgetown.edu/research/nrcbl/nbac/pubs/cloning1/executive.htm.

Putnam, Robert D. *Bowling Alone: The Collapse and Revival of American Community.* New York: Simon and Schuster, 2000.

Quintilian. *Quintilian As Educator: Selections from the Institutio Oratoria of Marcus Fabius Quintilianus.* Trans. H. E. Butler. Ed. Frederick M. Wheelock. New York: Twayne, 1974.

Thoreau, Henry David. "Economy." *Walden. The Thoreau Reader: The Works of Henry D. Thoreau, 1817–1862.* http://eserver.org/thoreau/walden00.html.

Todd, Leon W. "Telling It Like It Is about the African-American Students' Plight." *Education* 118.2 (1997): 166–77.

Venezia, Andrea, Michael W. Kirst, and Anthony L. Antonio. "Betraying the College Dream: How Disconnected K-12 and Postsecondary Education Systems Undermine Student Aspirations. " Final Report from the Stanford University Bridge Project. http://www.stanford.edu/group/bridgeproject/.

Williams, Joseph. *Style: Ten Lessons in Clarity and Grace.* 6th ed. New York: Addison Wesley, 1999. 12.

Wordsworth, William. "The World Is Too Much with Us." *The Complete Poetical Works of William Wordsworth. Bartleby.com: Great Books Online.* http://www.bartleby.com/145/.

Credits

permission of Providence Business News in the format Textbook via Copyright Clearance Center. **Page 164:** "Study of School-to-Work Initiatives" from *Studies of Education Reform* by Ivan Charner—www.ed.gov/pubs/SER/SchoolWork/study.html. **Page 175:** "School-to-Work Education Shortchanges Academic Knowledge" by Virginia Miller from *USA Today*, July 2001, v130, i2674. Reprinted by permission of The Heritage Foundation.

CHAPTER 5

Page 192: "Position Statement: Student Assessment and Testing" from Northwest Regional Educational Laboratory—www.nwrel.org/cnorse/booklets/educate/11.html. Reprinted by permission of Northwest Regional Laboratory.

READING AND WRITING APPLICATIONS 4

Page 213: "Management by Stress: The Reorganization of Work Hits Home in the 1990's" from AMERICAN FAMILIES: A MULTICULTURAL READER, edited by Stephanie Coontz, Maya Parson, and Gabrielle Raley, 1999, pages 332–341. Reprinted with permission. Sarah Ryan now teaches labor studies at The Evergreen State College in Olympia, Washington. **Page 223:** "Family-Friendly Workplaces: A Tale of Two Sectors" by Jenny Earle from *Family Matters*, Autumn 2002, page 12(6). "Family-Friendly Workplaces: A Tale of Two Sectors" by Jenny Earle, the Australian Institute of Family Studies research journal, *Family Matters*, No. 61, Autumn 2002, pp. 12–17. Reprinted with permission. **Page 232:** "Company Charged with Ethnic Bias in Hiring" and "SAT Top Quartile Score Declines" from A MATHEMATICIAN READS THE NEWSPAPER by John Allen Paulos, 1995, pages 59–66. From A MATHEMATICIAN READS THE NEWSPAPER by John Allen Paulos. Copyright © 1995 by John Allen Paulos. Reprinted by permission of Basic Books, a member of Perseus Books. L.L.C.

CHAPTER 6

Page 245: "The Narrative Imagination" from CULTIVATING HUMANITY: A CLASSICAL DEFENSE OF REFORM IN LIBERAL EDUCATION by Martha C. Nussbaum, 1997, pages 85–90. Reprinted by permission of the publisher from CULTIVATING HUMANITY: A CLASSICAL DEFENSE OF REFORM IN LIBERAL EDUCATION by Martha C. Nussbaum, pp. 85–90, Cambridge, Mass.: Harvard University Press, Copyright © 1997 by the President and Fellows of Harvard College. **Page 251:** Excerpt from "Science and Hope" from THE DEMON-HAUNTED WORLD: SCIENCE AS A CANDLE IN THE DARK by Carl Sagan, 1996, pages 27–33, 35–39. Copyright © 1996 by Carl Sagan. Reprinted with permission from the Estate of Carl Sagan. **Page 261:** "A Test of Status Consumption: Women's Cosmetics" from THE OVERSPENT AMERICAN: UPSCALING, DOWNSHIFTING, AND THE NEW CONSUMER by Juliet B. Schor, 1998, pages 48–54. From OVERSPENT AMERICAN: WHEN BUYING BECOMES YOU by Juliet B. Schor. Copyright 1998 by Perseus Books Group. Reproduced with permission of Perseus Books Group in the format Textbook via Copyright Clearance Center. **Page 267:** Excerpts from "Building in Creativity and Innovation" by Tom Kelley from THE ART OF INNOVATION: LESSONS IN CREATIVITY FROM IDEO, AMERICA'S LEADING DESIGN FIRM by Tom Kelley, Jonathan Littman, Tom Peters, 2001, pages 19–31. From THE ART OF INNOVATION by Thomas Kelley, copyright © 2001 by Thomas Kelley. Used by permission of Doubleday, a division of Random House, Inc.

READING AND WRITING APPLICATIONS 5

Page 276: Editorial Mission Statement from PMLA—www.mla.org/publications/pmla/pmla_submitting. From www.mla.org/publications/pmla/pmla_submitting. Reprinted by permission of The Modern Language Association. **Page 277:** Editorial Mission Statement from The Academy of Management Review—"Information for Contributors"—www.aom.pace.edu/amr/info.htm. Academy of Management Review by Richard J. Klimoski. Copyright 2003 by Academy of Management. Reproduced with permission of Academy of Management in the format Textbook via Copyright Clearance Center. **Page 278:** "About BioScience" (editorial guidelines for contributors) from http://www.aibs.org/bioscience/index.html. "About BioScience" from www.aibs.org/bioscience/index.html. Copyright, American Institute of Biological Sciences. Reprinted by permission of the publisher. **Page 281:** Abstract of pages 791–799: "Symptom Factors in Early-Onset Psychotic Disorders" by Jon McClellan,

Chris McCurry, Matthew L. Speltz, and Karen Jones from *Journal of the American Academy of Child and Adolescent Psychiatry* 41.7 (July 2002). Reprinted by permission of Lippincott Williams & Wilkins. **Page 282:** Abstract of pages 763–768: "Neurocognitive Enhancement Therapy with Work Therapy" by Morris Bell, Gary Bryson, Tamasine Greig, Cheryl Corcoran, and Bruce E. Wexler from *Archives of General Psychiatry* 58.8 (August 2001). Reprinted by permission of American Medical Association. **Page 286:** Excerpts from "Elaborating on Gender Differences in Environmentalism" by Lynnette C. Zelezny, Poh-Pheng Chua, and Christina Aldrich from *Journal of Social Issues*, Fall 2000, v56, i3, page 443. **Page 291:** "Providing a Regional Context for Local Conservation Action: A Natural Community Conservation Plan for the Southern California Coastal Sage Scrub" by Thomas S. Reid and Dennis D. Murphy from *BioScience*, 45.6 (June 1995), pages 84–91. *BioScience* by Thomas S. Reid and Dennis D. Murphy. Copyright 1995 by The American Institute of Biological Sciences. Reproduced with permission of The American Institute of Biological Sciences in the format Textbook via Copyright Clearance Center. **Page 297:** "The Fish That Will Not Take Our Hooks" by Roger G. Kennedy from *Wilderness*, 58 (Spring 1995), pages 28–31. Originally published in *Wilderness*, the magazine of The Wilderness Society, Spring 1995.

CHAPTER 7

Page 310: "The Contextualization of Affirmative Action: A Historical and Political Analysis" by Fayneese Miller, Xae Alicia Reyes, and Elizabeth Shaffer from *American Behavioral Scientist*, October 1997, v41, n2, page 223(9). Reprinted by permission of Sage Publications, Inc. **Page 325:** Home page from CNN.com. Reprinted by permission.

CHAPTER 8

Page 337: Introduction only to "Putting the Future in Planning" by Dowell Myers from *Journal of the American Planning Association*, Autumn 2001, v67, i4, page 365. Reprinted with permission from *Journal of the American Planning Association*, Suite 1600, 122 South Michigan Avenue, Chicago, IL 60603-6107. **Page 342:** "Network Security: Safeguarding Systems against the Latest Threats" by Eric Moore from *Police Chief*, Feb-

ruary 2003, page 23. From *Police Chief* by Eric Moore. Copyright 2003 by International Association of Chiefs of Police Inc. Reproduced with permission of International Association of Chiefs of Police Inc. in the format Textbook via Copyright Clearance Center. **Page 352:** "How Effective Are Gigabit Intrusion Detection Systems?" by Anthony Adshead from *Computer Weekly*, March 27, 2003, page 48. **Page 356:** Excerpts from "Cybersecurity: Who's Watching the Store?" by Bruce Berkowitz and Robert W. Hahn from *Issues in Science and Technology*, Spring 2003, v19, i3, page 55(8). Reprinted with permission from ISSUES IN SCIENCE AND TECHNOLOGY, Berkowitz and Hahn, "Cybersecurity: Who's Watching the Store?," Spring 2003, pp. 55–62, Copyright 2003 by the University of Texas at Dallas, Richardson, TX. **Page 370:** Abstract of page 6(1): "The Lowdown on Literacy" from *American Demographics*, June 1994, v16, n6. From *American Demographics*, June 1994. Copyright 1994 PRIMEDIA Business Magazines & Media Inc. All rights reserved.

READING AND WRITING APPLICATIONS 6

Page 388: Excerpt from "Jealousy as a Function of Rival Characteristics: An Evolutionary Perspective" by Pieternel Dijkstra and Bram P. Buunk from *Personality & Social Psychology Bulletin*, November 1998, v24, n11, page 1158(9). From *Personality & Social Psychology Bulletin* by Pieternel Dijkstra and Bram P. Buunk. Copyright 1998 by Sage Publications Inc. (J). Reproduced with permission of Sage Publications Inc. (J) in the format Textbook via Copyright Clearance Center. **Page 390:** Excerpt from "The New Genetics and Women" by Mary B. Mahowald, Dana Levinson, and Christine Cassel from *The Milbank Quarterly*, Summer 1996, v74, n2, page 239(45). Reprinted by permission of Blackwell Publishing Ltd. **Page 392:** Excerpt from "Gender and Working Class Identity in Britain During the 1950's" by Stephen Brooke from *Journal of Social History*, Summer 2001, v34, i4, page 773. Reprinted by permission of George Mason University.

CHAPTER 9

Page 409: Abstract from page 36(12): "Coping in Context: Sociocultural Determinants of Responses to Sexual Harassment" by S. Arzu Wasti and Lilia M. Cortina from *Journal of Personality and Social Psychology*, August

2002, v83, i2, page 394(12). Copyright © 2002 by the American Psychological Association. Reprinted with permission. **Page 410:** Excerpt from Introduction to "More than Just Semantics: Court Rulings Clarify Effective Anti-Harassment Policies" by Robert K. Robinson, Neal P. Mero, and Dave L. Nichols from *Human Resource Planning*, December 2001, v24, i4, page 36(12). Reprinted with permission from HUMAN RESOURCE PLANNING, Vol. 24, No. 24 (2001). Copyright 2001 by The Human Resource Planning Society, 317 Madison Avenue, Suite 1509, New York, NY 10017, Phone: (212) 490-6387, Fax: (212) 682-6851. **Page 411:** Abstract from page 3(1): "Sleazy Courtroom Tactics Hit Harassment Cases" from *National NOW Times*, October 1997, v29, i4, page 3(1). Reprinted by permission of National Organization for Women, Inc. **Page 412:** Abstract from page 65(7): "Surveying Sexual Harassment in the Law Enforcement Workplace" by Timothy L. Fuss from *The Police Chief*, June 2000, v67, i6. From *Police Chief* by Timothy L. Fuss. Copyright 2000 by International Association Chiefs of Police Inc. Reproduced with permission of International Association Chiefs of Police Inc. in the format Textbook via Copyright Clearance Center. **Page 412:** Abstract from page 46(4): "A Brief History of Sexual-Harassment Law" by Susan Crawford from *Training*, August 1994, v31, n8, page 46(4). From "A Brief History of Sexual-Harassment Law" by Susan Crawford from *Training: The Human Side of Business*. Copyright 1994 by VNU Business Publications USA. Reproduced by permission of VNU Business Publications USA in the format Textbook via Copyright Clearance Center. **Page 412:** Abstract from page 161(1): "What is a Gender Norm and Why Should We Care? Implementing A New Theory in Sexual Harassment Law" by Linda B. Epstein from *Stanford Law Review*, November 1998, v51, i1. Reprinted by permission of Stanford Law Review.

CHAPTER 10

Page 435: "About APA Style" from APA web site—www.apastyle.org/aboutstyle.html. Copyright © 2004 by the American Psychological Association. Reprinted with permission. **Page 436:** "What Is MLA Style?" from MLA web site—www.mla.org/style. From www.mla.org/style. Reprinted by permission of The Modern Language Association. **Page 437:** Excerpt from

Review of CBE Manual from *Booklist*, December 1, 1994. From *Booklist*, 12/1/94, copyright © American Library Association. Used with permission. **Page 492:** Bypass Grafts figure from CORONARY PROCEDURES: A Patient's Guide by Emmanuel Horovitz, 2002. Illustration © Lynn Larson 2000. Reproduced by permission of the illustrator.

PART IV

Page 496: "The Path to 'Freedom': Alice Kline" and "The Work-and-Spend Cycle in Extremis: Jennifer Lawson" from THE OVERSPENT AMERICAN: UP-SCALING, DOWNSHIFTING, AND THE NEW CONSUMER by Juliet B. Schor, 1998, pages 116–124. From OVERSPENT AMERICAN: WHEN BUYING BECOMES YOU by Juliet B. Schor. Copyright 1998 by Perseus Books Group. Reproduced with permission of Perseus Books Group in the format Textbook via Copyright Clearance Center. **Page 513:** "The Other Gender Gap" from Naomi Barko from *The American Prospect*, June 19, 2000, v11, i15, page 61. Reprinted with permission from *The American Prospect*, Volume 11, Number 15: June 19, 2000–July 3, 2000. The American Prospect, 5 Broad Street, Boston, MA 02109. All rights reserved. **Page 517:** "How Equal is Equal Pay?" by Teresa Brady from *Management Review*, March 1998, v87, n3, page 59(3). *Management Review* by Teresa Brady. Copyright 1998 by American Management Association (J). Reproduced with permission of American Management Association (J) in the format Textbook via Copyright Clearance Center. **Page 522:** "To Be Young, Black, and Female: Falling Further Behind in the Shifting Economy" by Laura Dresser from *Dollars & Sense*, May–June 1995, n199, page 32(3). Reprinted by permission of *Dollars & Sense*, a progressive economics magazine www.dollarsandsense.org. **Page 537:** "Connections in the Workplace" from BOWLING ALONE by Robert D. Putnam, pages 80–92. Reprinted with the permission of Simon & Schuster Adult Publishing Group from BOWLING ALONE by Robert D. Putnam. Copyright © 2000 by Robert D. Putnam. **Page 556:** "School without Books" by John DeVault from www.thecommondenominator.com/052200_news1.html, May 22, 2000. Copyright 2000 The Common Denominator. Reprinted with permission of publisher. **Page 562:** "In Charge: Ward Quaal and Dave Bender" from WORKING: PEOPLE TALK ABOUT WHAT THEY DO ALL DAY AND

Index

as civil right, 505–534
ethics and, 571–578
family, materialism, responsibility and, 494–505
liberal education and, 555–560
readings on meaningful, 41–49
relationship with, 40
in twentieth-first century, 561–562
Work: Making a Living a Life (Halberstam), 561
Working (Terkel), 40–44
Works Cited system, 436
"The World Is Too Much with Us" (Wordsworth), 495–496
World Wide Web. *See* Internet; Websites
Writer's notebook
  characteristics of, 22–23
  as commonplace book, 92–94

electronic, 23–24
explanation of, 21–22
goals of, 24
"Writer/Social Worker" (Bradley), 52
Writing. *See also* Academic writing
  approaches to, 369
  connection between reading and, 204–208
  differences in academic, 13
  as discovery process, 21
  ethos and, 8
  occupational, 183, 273–274
  as product, 424
  rhetorical approach to, 17–19

Z
Zelezny, Lynnette C., 286–290

READINGS AND VISUAL TEXTS IN *COMPOSING A LIFE'S WORK*

Professional Readings

■ Book Excerpts
Studs Terkel, Introduction to *Working*
Richard Feynman, "The Amateur Scientist"
John Allen Paulos, from *A Mathematician Reads the Newspaper*
Martha C. Nussbaum, "The Narrative Imagination"
Carl Sagan, "Science and Hope"
Juliet B. Schor, from *The Overspent American*
Tom Kelley, from *The Art of Innovation*
Henry David Thoreau, from *Walden*
Robert Putnam, "Connections in the Workplace"
Studs Terkel, "Bureaucracy" and "In Charge"

■ Essays
Sarah Ryan, "Management by Stress"
Naomi Barko, "The Other Gender Gap"
Laura Dresser, "To Be Young, Black, and Female"
John DeVault, "School without Books"
Terance D. Miethe, "Trudi Lytle and the Clark County Public School System"

■ Poem
William Wordsworth, "The World Is Too Much with Us"

■ Scholarly Journal Articles
Jenny Earle, "Family-Friendly Workplaces"
Jon McClellan et al., "Symptom Factors in Early-Onset Psychotic Disorders"
Morris Bell et al., "Neurocognitive Enhancement Therapy with Work Therapy"
Lynette C. Zelezny et al., "Elaborating on Gender Differences in Environmentalism"
Thomas S. Reid and Dennis Murphy, "Providing a Regional Context for Local Conservation Action"
Roger G. Kennedy, "The Fish That Will Not Take Our Hooks"

Fayneese Miller et al., "The Contextualization of Affirmative Action"
Dowell Myers, "Putting the Future in Planning"
Teresa Brady, "How Equal Is Equal Pay?"

■ Magazine Articles
Richard Reeves, "The Joy of Work"
Chad Chadwick, "Brave New World"
Eric Moore, "Network Security"
Anthony Adshead, "How Effective Are Gigabit Intrusion Detection Systems?"
Bruce Berkowitz and Robert W. Hahn, "Cybersecurity: Who's Watching the Store?"

■ News Articles
"The Community Pharmacy"

■ Interviews and Letters
Maureen Bradley, Writer/Social Worker
Jodi Heller, High School Teacher
Jane Whittaker, Senior Systems Architect
Robert Colleluori, Owner, Marketing and Advertising Agency
Eric Engle, Geologist

■ Position Statements
Patrick Healy, "School-to-Career Programs Help Students Focus on Future"
Ivan Charter, "Study of School-to-Work Initiatives: Studies of Education Reform"
Virginia Miller, "School-to-Work Education Shortchanges Academic Knowledge"
Northwest Regional Educational Laboratory, "Student Assessment and Testing"
Ben and Jerry's, Inc., Mission Statement

■ Reviews of Literature
Pieternel Dijkstra and Bram P. Buunk, "Jealousy as a Function of Rival Characteristics"
Mary Mahowald et al., "The New Genetics and Women"
Stephen Brooke, "Gender and Working Class Identity in Britain during the 1950s"